Johann Brazda (Ed.)

The Development of the Mutuality Principle in the Insurance Business

Volume II

The Development of the Mutuality Principle in the Insurance Business

An International Comparison

Volume II

edited by

Johann Brazda

LIT

Supported by funds of the Oesterreichische Nationalbank (Austrian Central Bank, Anniversary Fund, project number: 15773).

Bibliographic information published by the Deutsche Nationalbibliothek
The Deutsche Nationalbibliothek lists this publication in the Deutsche Nationalbibliografie; detailed bibliographic data are available in the Internet at http://dnb.dnb.de.

ISBN 978-3-643-90973-2 (pb)
ISBN 978-3-643-95973-7 (PDF)

A catalogue record for this book is available from the British Library.

Flössergasse 10
CH-8001 Zürich
Tel. +41 (0) 76-632 84 35
E-Mail: zuerich@lit-verlag.ch http://www.lit-verlag.ch
Distribution:
In the UK: Global Book Marketing, e-mail: mo@centralbooks.com
In North America: Independent Publishers Group, e-mail: orders@ipgbook.com
In Germany: LIT Verlag Fresnostr. 2, D-48159 Münster
Tel. +49 (0) 2 51-620 32 22, Fax +49 (0) 2 51-922 60 99, e-mail: vertrieb@lit-verlag.de
e-books are available at www.litwebshop.de

Contents

Volume I

Volume II

The Development of Mutuality Principles in Austria – an Analysis of Mutual Insurance Societies

Stefanie Zeman

Abstract

In the current literature, mutual societies are considered to be the revitalized form of organization in times of financial stress for the insurance sector.[1] In contrast to joint stock companies, mutual societies tend to pursue a long-term orientation policy without the pressure to return their capital to shareholders. The supposedly reason is that the customers are members of the insurance company and the main goal is the fulfilment of the demand of risk coverage. Additionally, it is argued that mutuals are more resilient to economic downturns and thus should coexist beside joint stock companies.

This paper focuses on the mutuality principles – equal treatment of members, self-government and self-responsibility – and explores the development of mutualism in the Austrian insurance sectors from a historical point of view. An analysis of the current bylaws of the residual mutual societies shows a clear dilution of the mutualistic principles and contradicts a revitalization of mutual insurance societies. The main purpose of this paper is to show the development of the mutual principles in Austria with its specific forms of mutualism in different times. The last conversion of mutual societies was unique in the international field. The most successful mutual insurance societies restructured their legal form into a capital based legal form while continuing mutuality in a separate company.

A crucial factor for these results was a legal amendment in the early 1990s, which created a worldwide unique legal hybrid form of joint stock and mutual companies – the Mutual Holding Company (MHC). Six out of twelve mutual societies transformed their legal form to MHC and have operated their insurance business since then as joint stock companies while their asset management has been operated in mutual

[1] Cf. Mutual insurance in the 21st century: back to the future? In: Sigma No.4/2016, SwissRe, Zürich.

societies. While the membership of the MHC customers continues, the co-determination rights are restricted to a specified number of members' representatives who are selected by co-optation. The MHCs rank among the leading insurance companies in Austria and represent a market share of 43 percent of the total premium income. Because of the limited opportunities for mutual societies to increase their equity capital, MHCs have chosen to change their legal form and expand their international business in particular in the CEE-countries. After a legal amendment to the Austrian Insurance Supervision Act in 2005, two mutual societies out of one MHC changed the legal form of their asset management from a mutual society to a private foundation. As a result, the members became automatically the beneficiaries of the foundation and the self-government vanished completely.

Six mutual societies are still operating as regular mutual and with their insurance business restricted to region, insurance segment, or policyholders' profession. They have a market share of almost 4 percent, which reflects the minor importance of mutuals in the Austrian insurance landscape. Most of these mutual societies work with a similar self-government system based on co-optation during the general meeting and few co-determination rights for their members. Due to this historical development and to the late introduction of legal foundations for mutual societies, the mutuality principles have been neglected for a long time and the differences between joint stock companies and mutual societies have never made public to their customers. Therefore, according to the authors, neither a renaissance of mutuals in the Austrian insurance sector is to be expected in the near future nor an economic catching-up in times of financial crises can be observed.

1. Introduction

During our research, the question arose how far mutual insurance societies and insurance joint stock companies have been become more and more alike with regard to strategy as well as regarding day-to-day operations. Therefore, it is crucial to analyze where the main differences between mutual insurance societies and joint stock companies are, to find out how mutual insurance societies are able to survive as an alternative to joint stock companies, and to continue their legal form at the same time. Starting with the development of the general insurance business in Austria, the paper investigates the development of mutual insurance societies compared to joint stock companies. The existing statistics, however, do not differentiate between legal forms.

This makes it difficult to derive a general statement concerning our research question. As a result, the paper focuses in particular on legal forms and their economic and structural differences.

The following section presents the general statistics of the Austrian insurance business, in which mutual societies and joint stock companies are not ana lysed separately. It is possible that the small market share of 3.9 percent[2] of the large mutual insurance societies does not encourage the data collectors to differentiate in their statistics between legal forms. Another reason for the standardization is probably the amendment to the Insurance Supervision Act in 1991, which offers mutual insurance societies the option to transfer their day-to-day insurance business completely or in part to a joint stock company. In this case, the mutual society becomes an asset management society and manages the share of the joint stock company. This new legal construction based on several legal forms is called "hybrid form", in which the joint stock companies continue with the operative business covered by one or more asset management societies for each joint stock company. This kind of hybrid form had a market share of 21.66 percent in 2017, based on the premium income. Since the amendment to the Insurance Supervision Act in 2005, mutual insurance societies are able to transform into a private foundation. This possibility was used by two mutual insurance societies of the same joint stock company. This hybrid form (UNIQA) has a current market share of 21.38 percent. This example and the total market share of 43.04 percent of the hybrid form show its important role in the Austrian insurance business.

Figure 1 presents the development of market share differentiating between the legal forms on the Austrian insurance market since 1983. In the 1980s, mutual insurance societies had a market share between 25 and 27 percent. This share was reduced to 4 percent after the amendment to the Insurance Supervision Act in 1991 with its possibility to transfer the operative insurance business to a joint stock company while using the mutual society as an asset management society. The newly created hybrid form had a market share between 21 and 25 percent, while in 2011 it increased to 31 percent and had its peak in 2017 with 43.0 percent. The main reason for such a high share is probably based on several mergers of insurance companies taken up by the UNIQA during the last couple of years.[3] In contrast, the market share of joint stock companies remained at first constant, but dropped in 2011 due to UNIQA's mergers. The market share of mutual insurance societies, however, increased from 2.78 percent in 2010 to 3.72 percent in 2016.

---

[2] Calculation is based on data drawn from the VVO annual report 2017.

[3] Cf. Chapter „Restructuring of the UNIQA group".

Figure 1: Market share based on the total premium income and according to legal forms from 1983 to 2017

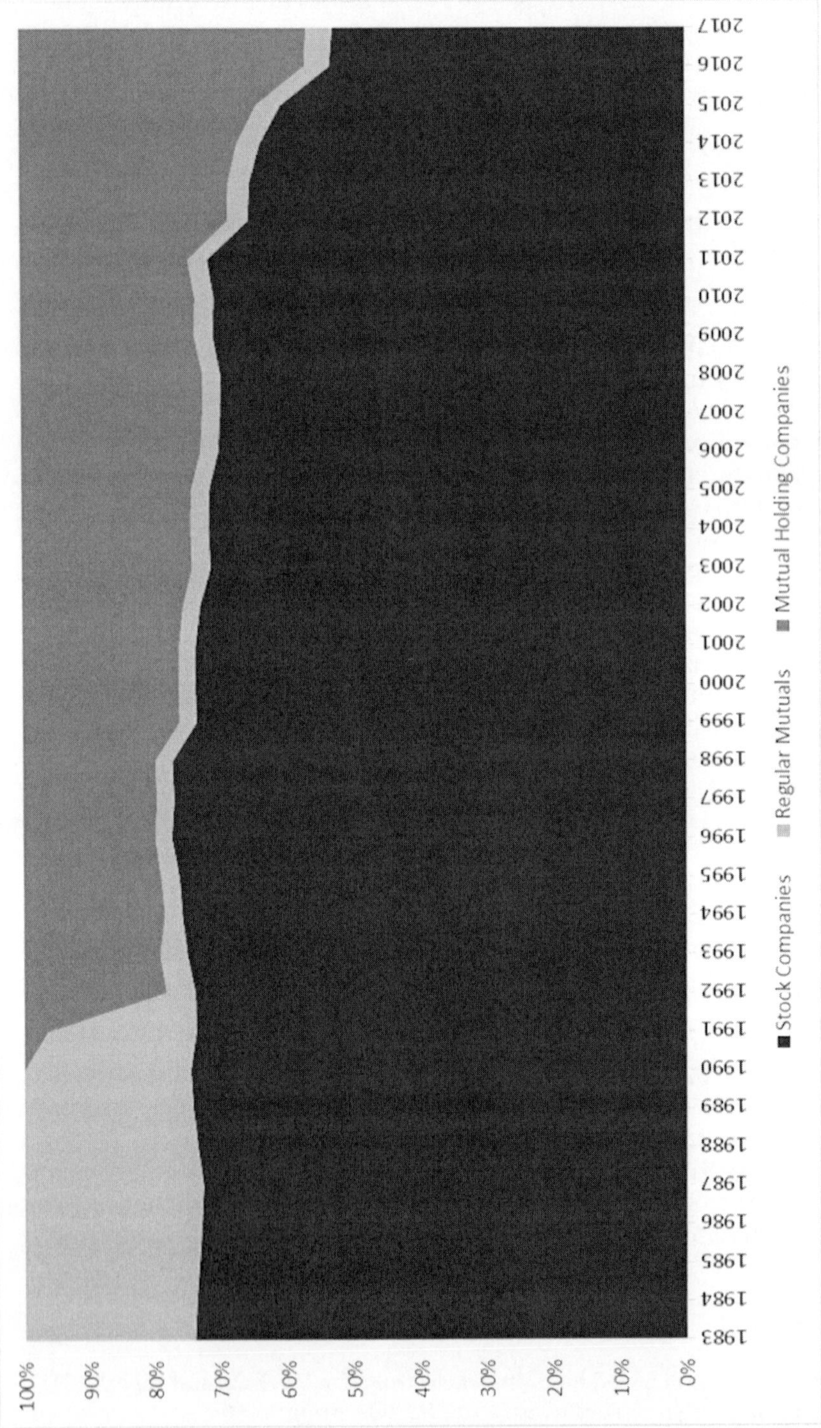

Figure 2: Market share of total premium income according to legal forms in 2017 (without small mutual insurance societies).

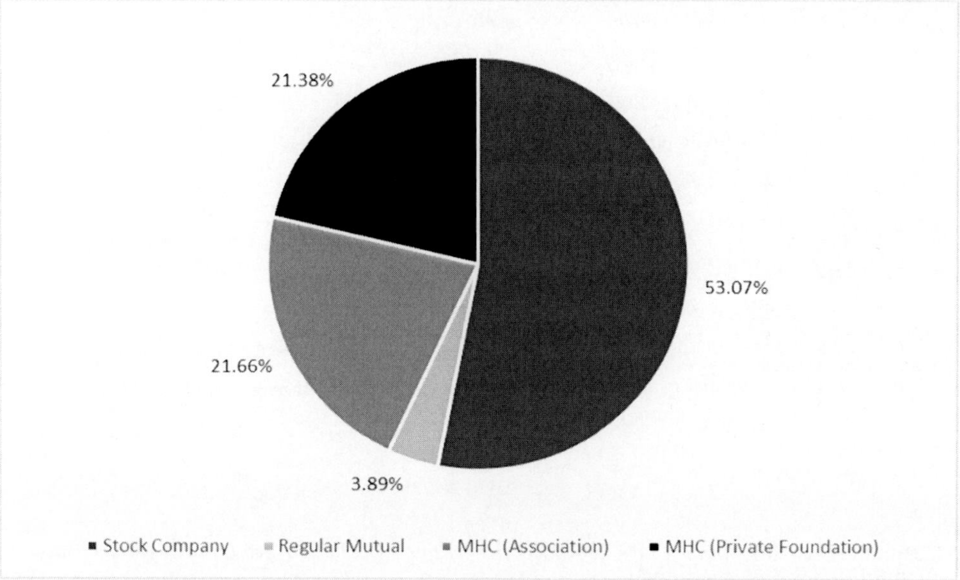

Source: Own presentation based on data drawn from the VVO annual report 2017, p. 112f.

Figure 3 presents the ten largest insurance companies in Austria according to market shares. UNIQA as the market leader increased its market share to 21.23 percent (last year 14.33 percent) due to mergers with *Finance Life Lebensversicherungs AG*, *Salzburger Landes-Versicherung AG* and *Raiffeisen Versicherung AG*. *Wiener Städtische Versicherungs AG*, a former mutual insurance society with 13.65 percent market share, the same as in 2016, is the second largest company. *Wiener Städtische Versicherungs AG* is part of the holding company *Vienna Insurance Group* (VIG), which also comprises the *Sparkassen Versicherung AG* (5.02 percent) and the *Donau Versicherung AG* (4.68 percent). The *Grazer Wechselseitige Versicherungs AG*, as the third former mutual insurance society, is with 2.98 percent the ninth largest company.

In conclusion, the analysis of market shares shows that companies with a hybrid form play a major part on the Austrian insurance market and have strengthened their position over time. In contrast, mutual insurance societies have a small economic impact with a constant market share between 3 and 4 percent.

Figure 3: Market share of the ten largest insurance companies in Austria 2016 (in percent)

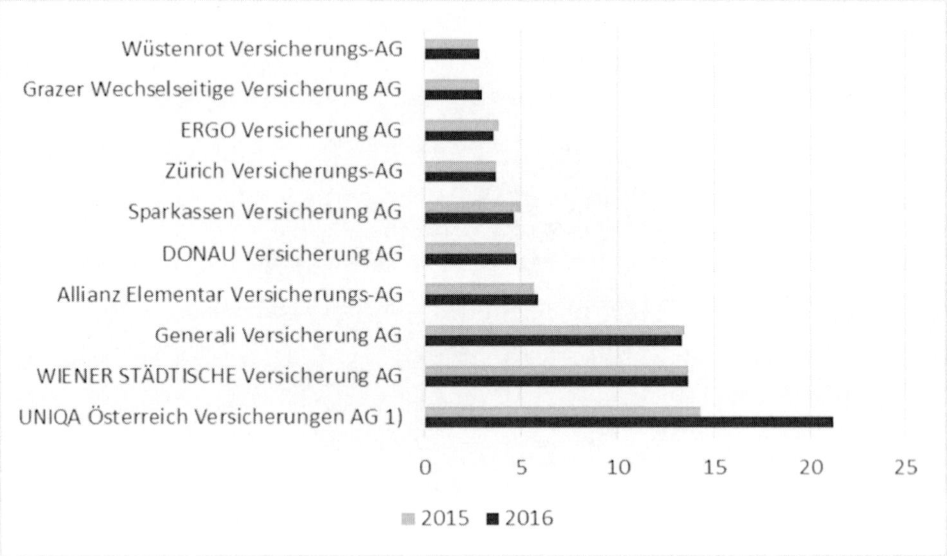

[1] 2016: Merger with *Finance Life Lebensversicherungs AG*, *Salzburger Landes-Versicherung AG* und *Raiffeisen Versicherung AG*.

Source: Own presentation based on data drawn from the VVO annual report 2015, p. 100 and annual report 2016, p. 106.

Figure 4: Market share according to insurance sectors in 2017

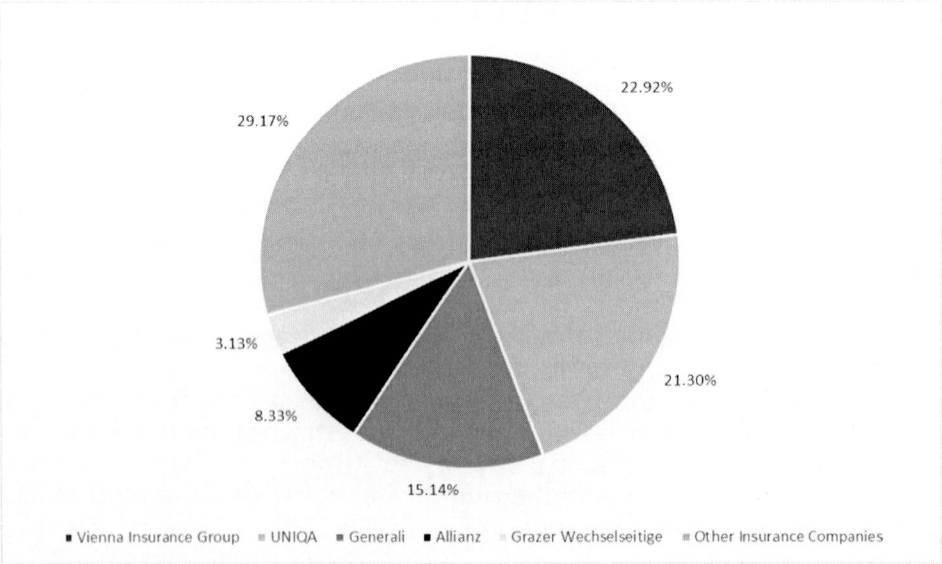

Source: Own presentation based on data drawn from the VVO annual report 2017, p. 114.

2. General economic development of the Austrian insurance business

This chapter presents import key figures of the insurance business and gives a brief overview of the insurance market.

The economic upswing in the 1970s favoured the premium income in the insurance industry (cf. figure 5), which increased continuously, and immensely up to the 2000s in the life insurance sector The liberalization of the Austrian financial markets broadened capital investment opportunities. This had a positive effect on life insurances on the Austrian market since the 1970s. Life insurances developed to attractive long-term capital investments for policyholders. In 1997, however, the growth in premiums stagnated due to increased competition in Austria after joining the EU. The increasing competition in the life insurance sector via alternative investment forms and the withdrawal of taxation support measures for life insurances ended the boom. In 1996, the government executed cost-cutting measures followed by additional financial cutbacks in 1997.[4] The premium income from the insurance business has decreased clearly since 2016 due to long-term cheap money policy by the European Central Bank (ECB) after the finance and economic crisis in 2007. Life insurance lost its appeal as a capital investment form, because the profits from capital investments of the insurance companies decreased, which influenced the guaranteed interest rate negatively. In 2016, the Austrian Financial Market Authority (FMA) reduced the guaranteed interest rate to 1 percent, which led insurance company to sell life insurances without a guaranteed interest rate.[5]

The development of the nominal GDP is connected with the development of insurance premiums. After the economic and finance crisis, the GDP decreased significantly in 2009, while the development of the total premiums was not affected until 2012. The sharp drop was influenced by the decreasing business of life insurances, which had lost its appeal due to low interests and the slow increase of premiums from non-life and accident insurance.[6]

---

[4] Cf. *Gassner-Möstl, E.*; *Kuskardy, I.*: Kennzahlen eines Dezenniums der österreichischen Versicherungswirtschaft 1988-1997, in: Die Versicherungsrundschau, 1999, p. 139.

[5] https://www.trend.at/geld/lebensversicherung-garantiezins-7541522, (28.08.2017).

[6] Cf. *Url, Th.*: Lebensversicherung leidet weiterhin unter niedrigem Zinsniveau, in: WIFO Monatsberichte 9/2013.

Figure 5: Development of premium income and insurance services compared to the nominal GDP in Austria between 1958 and 2017

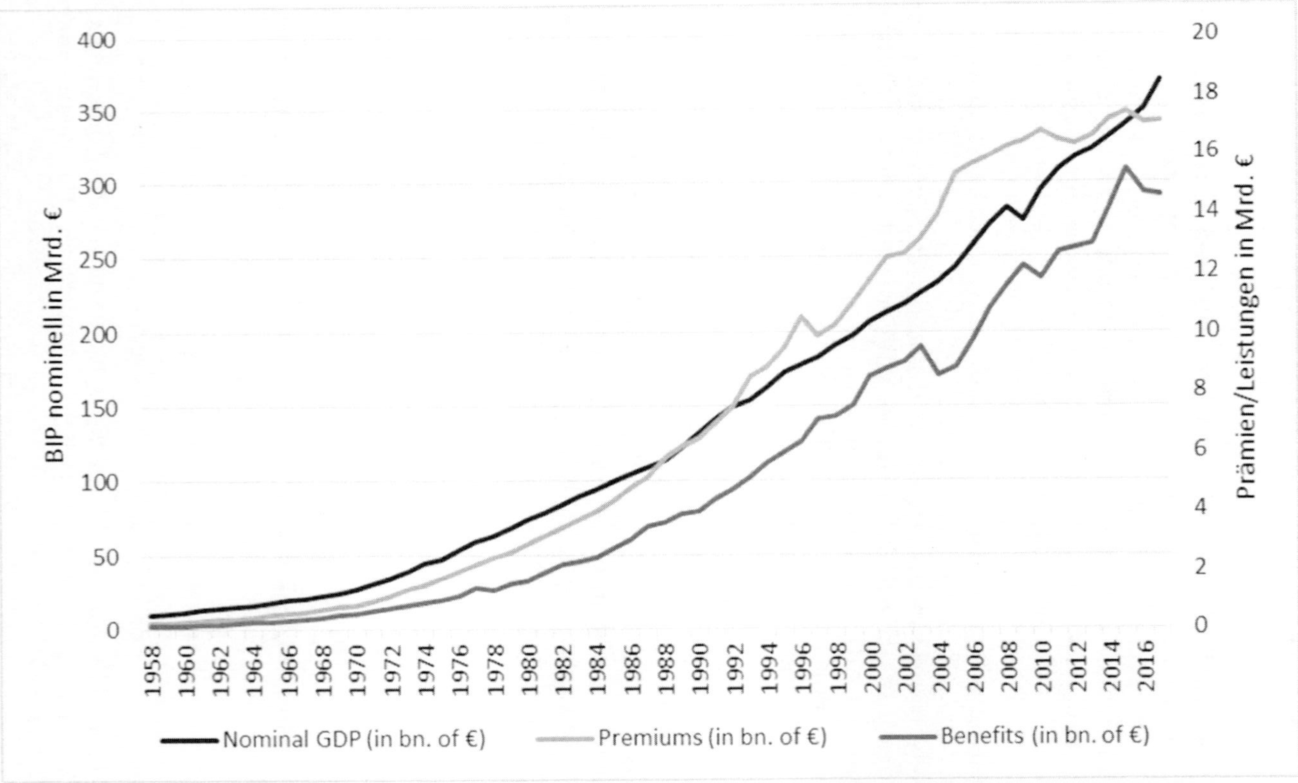

Source: Own presentation, data until 2010 drawn from the VVO annual report 2010, p. 82 f.; from 2011 onwards from the VVO annual report 2016 and 2017, p. 105 and 140f.

3. Development of the number of insurance companies according to their legal form

The following chapter focuses on the development of the number of insurance companies since 1970. Their head office has to be in Austria and their business has to be supervised by authorities, i.e. before 2001 by the federal ministry of finance and from 2001 on by the *Financial Market Authority (FMA)*. At the beginning of the 1970s, the ratio between mutual insurance societies (1971: 19) and insurance joint stock companies (1971: 21) was even, but during the 1980s, the latter developed to become the leading legal form. Small mutual insurance societies, however, are excluded from this analysis, due to their minor regional role and insignificant economic role for the insurance industry. The hybrid form, on the other hand, mirrors the number of asset management societies, which were created due to universal succession since 1991. In this case, the insurance business was transferred from the mutual insurance society to a joint stock company and the society continued as an asset management society. The amendment of the Insurance Supervision Act in 2005 offered asset management societies the possibility to be converted into a private foundation. An option, which was taken up by two insurance societies, namely the *Austria Versicherungsverein auf Gegenseitigkeit* (2005) and the *Collegialität Versicherung auf Gegenseitigkeit* (2012). Today, both private foundations hold shares in the *UNIQA Insurance Group AG*, the successor of the *Austria-Collegialität AG*. To understand figure 6, it is important to note that mutual asset management societies/private foundations do not offer insurances, but hold shares in their joint stock companies and policyholders are members and beneficiaries of the asset management societies/private foundations at the same time. As a result, mutual asset management societies and private foundations have no operative insurance business.

In general, the number of Austrian insurance companies increased until 1996 to 64, five in the legal form of mutual insurance societies and 59 as joint stock companies. Therefore, the period between 1970 until the beginning of the 1990 can be regarded as a phase of growth, followed by a period in which the total number of Austrian insurance companies dropped, caused by joining the EU in 1995. The competition increased between the European insurance companies because of free service transactions in the EU and the newly introduced solvability regulations. Eventually, the Austrian insurance market was confronted with a higher market concentration. As a result, a phase of restructur-

Figure 6: Number of insurance companies according to legal form between 1970 and 2017

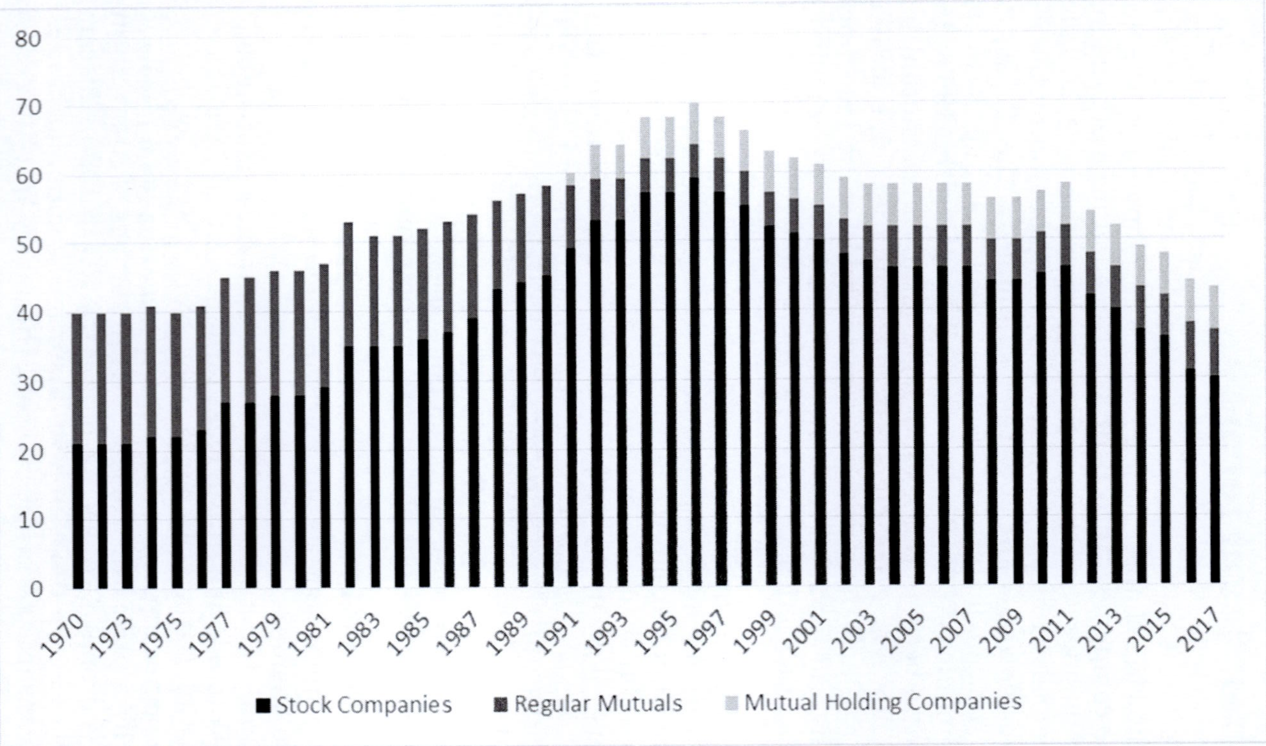

Source: Own presentation based on data drawn from: Statistisches Handbuch für die Republik Österreich (1970 to 1993); from 1993 to 2015 annual reports of the Financial Market Authority (FMA) https://www.fma.gv.at/publikationen/fma-jahresberichte/ numbers regarding the hybrid form between 1991 and 1994 Korinek, S.; Der österreichische Versicherungsverein auf Gegenseitigkeit; in: Rechtliche Rahmenbedingungen für Versicherungen auf Gegenseitigkeit – Festschrift zum 100-jährigen Bestehen der Stuttgarter Lebensversicherung a.G., Hrsg. Bürke, J., Karlsruhe, 2008, p. 169.

ing started in 1991, in which 6 mutual insurance societies transferred their insurance business into joint stock companies, followed by mergers of existing insurance companies and later by developing groups.

4. A renaissance of mutual insurance societies?

The Sigma study[7] regarding insurances in the 21st century presents a positive market development of mutual insurance societies and predicts a renaissance of this legal form. The study points out that new technology such as digitalization holds huge potentials for mutual insurance societies. It seems that using new technology as Smart Analytics, which focuses on winning the needs and preferences of members, are good additions to the member-orientated politics of mutual societies. Another innovation for the future presents the transfer technology "blockchain", in which the insurance company as a mediator or coordinator of insurance service is obsolete. With a "peer-to-peer" system, the policyholders are connected directly and share the risk with each other according the mutuality principle. Real development gives less reason for optimism.

In the 1990s, a wave of demutualization occurred which decreased the market share of mutual insurance societies and predicted the end of the mutuality principle, while joint stock companies enjoyed great popularity due to better capitalization and restructuring possibilities.[8]

The positive trend of mutual insurance societies in current literature is based on successful insurance companies, which have expanded their insurance business to foreign countries, such as the Austrian joint stock companies *UNIQA* and *VIG*.[9] *UNIQA* has two private foundations, which were created from the mutual asset management societies *Austria Versicherungsverein auf Gegenseitigkeit* and *Collegialität Versicherung auf Gegenseitigkeit*. The *Wiener Städtische Wechselseitige Versicherungsanstalt* is the major shareholder for the VIG joint stock company and regards itself as supporter of cultural and social matters of the VIG in Austria as well as in Central- and Eastern European countries in which the company is active. However, it has to be ques-

[7] Cf. Versicherung auf Gegenseitigkeit im 21. Jahrhundert: Zurück in die Zukunft?, In: Sigma Nr.4/2016, Swiss Re.

[8] Cf. Versicherungsvereine bzw. Versicherungsgenossenschaften: Leben Totgesagte länger? In: Sigma Nr.4/1999, Swiss Re, p. 26ff.

[9] Cf. Versicherung auf Gegenseitigkeit im 21. Jahrhundert: Zurück in die Zukunft?, In: Sigma Nr.4/2016, Swiss Re, p. 7f.

tioned critically if both companies were presented as successful mutual insurance societies that herald a renaissance of the mutuality idea. As a result, this paper analyses the development and current situation of the mutuality principle regarding Austrian insurance companies and investigates if a renaissance of mutuality actually happens.

The Insurance Supervision Act is the legal foundation for mutual insurance societies in Austria and from this Act, the characteristics of the mutuality principles can be deduced. The focus of this paper lies on the amendments of this Act and on the effects they have on mutuality of Austrian mutual insurance societies. The analysis shows that mutuality is a transformable principal in Austria, which adjusts to time and different developments.

5. The development from the 1970s

The following large mutual insurance societies (see table 1) were active on the insurance market in 1970 and are part of the analysis:

5.1 The period of growth

The 1970s was a period that was characterized by fast growth in the Austrian insurance landscape. The premium income increased due to a generally prospering economy and a wide group of providers. Between 1970 and 1980, the premium income increased from 812 million to 2,853 billion Euros that is two-and-a-half times within ten years. Foreign insurances were able to get access to the Austrian market via branch offices that led to more competition among insurances.[10]

The legal position of the regional insurance companies was unclear since the end of the Second World War. Before the Austrian Insurance Supervision Act was enacted in 1978, the federal state parliament was the highest body and members' councils were not part of the bylaws. After 1978, the regional insurance companies had to change their bylaws according to the regulations of the Insurance Supervision Act regarding the organizational structures of mutual insurance societies. Upper-Austria, Tyrol, Vorarlberg, and Carinthia followed the rules,

[10] Cf. *Schimetschek, H., Weiser, H.*; Versicherungsverein auf Gegenseitigkeit in Europa: Zukunftsentwicklungen – Österreichisches Modell, in: *Peiner, W.* (ed.), Grundlagen des Versicherungsvereins auf Gegenseitigkeit. Verfasst anlässlich des 175jährigen Bestehens der Gothaer Versicherungsbank VVaG, Köln, 1995, p. 316.

Table 1: Large mutual insurance societies in 1970

Insurance company	**Branches in 1970**
Wiener Städtische Wechselseitige Versicherungsanstalt (WIENER STÄDTISCHE)	Combined insurance
Wiener Verein Lebens- und Bestattungsversicherung a.G. (WIENER VEREIN)	Life insurance
Jupiter Versicherungsverein a. G. (JUPITER)	Life insurance
Österreichische Beamtenversicherung VVaG (BEAMTEN)	Life and accident insurance From 1979 on non-life insurance
Austria Versicherungsverein auf Gegenseitigkeit (AUSTRIA)	Life and health insurance From 1983 on non-life/accident insurance
Collegialität Versicherung auf Gegenseitigkeit (COLLEGIALITÄT)	Combined insurance
Merkur Wechselseitige Versicherungsanstalt (MERKUR)	Combined insurance
Versicherungsverband der Industriellen VVaG (INDUSTRIELLENVERBAND)	Non-life insurance
Gegenseitiger Versicherungsverein für Montanwerke, Maschinen- und Metallfabriken (MONTAN)	Non-life insurance
Versicherungs-Verband für Papier-Industrie a. G. (PAPIERINDUSTRIE)	Non-life insurance
„GLEIMAG" Wechselseitige Haftpflicht- und Sachschaden-Versicherungsanstalt für Gleis- und Magazinanlagen (GLEIMAG)	Non-life insurance
Erste Wiener Spiegelglas-Versicherungsgesellschaft (SPIEGELGLAS)	Non-life insurance
Oberösterreichische Landes-Brandschadenversicherung (OBERÖSTERREICHISCHE)	Non-life insurance from 1977 on life insurance
Salzburger Landes-Brandschadenversicherungsanstalt (SALZBURGER)	Non-life insurance from 1988 on life insurance
Tiroler Landes-Brandschanden-Versicherungs-Anstalt (TIROLER)	Non-life insurance from 1983 on life insurance
Vorarlberger Landes-Feuerversicherungs-Anstalt (VORARLBERGER)	Non-life insurance from 1981 on life insurance
Kärntnerische Landes-Versicherungs-Anstalt (KÄRNTNER)	Non-life insurance from 1985 on life insurance
Wechselseitige Versicherungsanstalt in Graz (GRAWE)	Non-life insurance from 1972 on life insurance

while Salzburg was still a special case.[11] Therefore, it was unclear which legal form the regional insurance company in Salzburg had. Its organizational structure was different from other mutual insurance societies in main points, such as the appointment of members of the management board by the federal state government or parliament as

[11] Cf. *Mayer, L.*: Die Demutualisierung von Versicherungsvereinen auf Gegenseitigkeit (VVaG) in Österreich, in: *Geib, G.* (ed.): Rechnungslegung von Versicherungsunternehmen, Düsseldorf, IDW Verlag, 2001, p. 207ff.

well as the lack of a supreme board.[12] To determine its legal position, the company converted into a joint stock company according to the regulations of the "Strukturverbesserungsgesetz" and with the resolution of the government in Salzburg and the management board. The shares were allocated to the federal state Salzburg and sold to the *Versicherungsanstalt der österreichischen Bundesländer AG* (a regional insurance company) at two occasions.[13] The *UNIQA Austria AG* absorbed the *Bundesländerversicherung*, while the regional insurance company in Salzburg (*SALZBURGER*) (joint stock company) remained until the restructuring of the Group in 2016[14] as a brand and as a subsidiary firm within the *UNIQA Group*.

5.2 Legal development between 1978 and 1991

Before the Austrian Insurance Supervision Act was enacted in 1978, the transition act of the German Insurance Supervision Act was in force in Austria, which did not include regulations regarding the transfer of mutual insurance societies. It only regulated the dissolution of insurance societies and the transfer of the complete or parts of the insurance portfolio to another insurance company. The disadvantage that mutual insurance societies had, in contrast to joint stock companies, was the prohibition to increase their equity capital, this led to the legal amendment of transforming mutual societies into joint stock companies. Between the introduction of the Austrian Insurance Supervision Act in 1978 and the amendment in 1991, (BGBI No. 411) two possible ways were available for the transfer of a mutual insurance society into a joint stock company. Firstly, a modifying conversion (§ 61) which changes the legal form of the mutual insurance society but continues the legal entity. According to § 61 paragraph 11 of the Insurance Supervision Act 2016, members become shareholders from the point of registration. The legal consequence only occurs when the resolution approving the conversion designates that members have a share in the equity capital. However, § 61 paragraph 6 of the same Act allows that the resolution approving the conversion may be different

[12] Cf. *Schira, H.*: Die Geschichte der Salzburger Landes-Versicherung, in: 175 Jahre Salzburger Landesversicherung Eine Dokumentation anlässlich des 175-jährigen Bestehens, 1986: Salzburger Landesversicherung AG.
The legal position of the *Salzburger Landes-Brandschaden-Versicherungsanstalt* has already been discussed at length, because in the bylaws they declared itself as a public Group. However, this legal form does not fit into the Austrian legal system, in which either a mutual insurance society or a joint stock company are allowed to operate insurance business.

[13] Cf. Ibid; Cf. *Mayer, L.*, p. 210.

[14] Cf. Page 634 in this article.

from this paragraph 11. Each member is entitled to raise an objection to the transfer (§ 61 paragraph 2), but the legal consequences are limited.[15] The following mutual insurance societies have used this type of legal transfer: the *Versicherungs-Verband für Papier-Industrie a.G.* (1982), the *Versicherungsverband der Industriellen VVaG* (1987), and the *„GLEIMAG" Wechselseitige Haftpflicht- und Sachschaden-Versicherungsanstalt für Glas- und Magazinanlagen* (1988).

The second type is the transfer conversion that was only used by the *Gegenseitiger Versicherungsverein für Montanwerke, Maschinen- und Metallfabriken* in 1988. In this case, the mutual insurance society establishes a joint stock company and transfers all assets to it, as a result, the mutual insurance society expires as a legal entity and the joint stock company becomes the universal successor. The membership rights expire with the end of the legal entity of the mutual insurance society, because the membership is tied to the insurance relationship. Due to the universal succession, the insurance relationship, in contrast to the membership, is transferred to the joint stock company. In contrast to Germany, the Austrian law does not include legal regulations regarding the fairness of the compensation for the members. Only § 236 paragraph 4 of the company law is applicable to mutual societies and states that the transferred mutual insurance society has to nominate a trustee for receiving a compensation. However, it is required that members have the right of a compensation due to the asset transfer, the individual member has not such right.[16]

Until the amendment of the Insurance Supervision Act in 2016, mutual insurance societies had the possibility to transfer all their assets to an existing joint stock company, which was not established for this purpose. The *Jupiter Versicherungsverein a. G.* became part of the *Volksfürsorge - Jupiter Allgemeine Versicherung AG* in 1983 and the assets of the *Erste Wiener Spiegelglas Versicherungsgesellschaft* were transferred to the *Niederösterreichische (NÖ) Versicherungs-AG* in 1989. This regulation did not become part of the Insurance Supervision Act in 2016, because such an asset transfer has not happened during the last 25 years, probably because the determination of the shares, the allocation of the shares, and the compensation of the members are effortful.[17] Another reason is that the amendment in 1991, i.e. § 62 Insurance Supervision Act 2016, has offered more advantages for mutual insurance societies and was, therefore, used by six societies.

---

15 Cf. *Baran, P.*: Die Fortführung des Betriebes von Versicherungsvereinen durch Aktiengesellschaften, in: Versicherungsrundschau, 1992, pp. 76-83.

16 Cf. Ibid., p. 77f.

17 Cf. *Bartl, K.*, §§ 35-67 VAG 2016, in: *Korinek, S./Saria, G./Saria, S.* (eds.): Versicherungsgesetz VAG, Wien 2016, p. 63.

Members of mutual insurance societies have the right of receiving a share of the annual profit (§ 42 paragraph 1) and in case of dissolution (§ 57 paragraph 5) of the settlement proceeds due to their membership relation. These proprietary claims get lost in case the mutual society is converted into a joint stock company, however, the Insurance Supervision Act states implicitly that members should receive a fair compensation for their membership relations. This can be done when members have a share in the equity capital, which is stated explicitly in case of a modifying conversion, or in case of a transfer conversion. Members can also receive the compensation in cash. The legal position of members to impose their rights is weak, because the legal foundation for any subjective claim towards the acquiring joint stock company is missing. When the members' share in the equity capital does not provide any problems, than the transfer is successful with these legal instruments. Therefore, according to *Baran*, in the amendment in 1991, a new legal instrument was introduced for continuing the business of a mutual insurance society via a joint stock company.[18]

Table 2: Conversions and transfers of mutual insurance societies into a joint stock company in Austria

Year	Insurance	Conversion/transfer
1975	*Salzburger Landes-Brandschaden Versicherungsanstalt*	Conversion into *Salzburger Landes-Brandschaden Versicherungs-AG*
1983	*Jupiter Versicherungsverein a. G.*	Assets conversion into *Volksfürsorge-Jupiter Allgemeine Versicherungs-AG*
1983	*Versicherungs-Verband für Papier-Industrie a. G.*	Modifying conversion in *HAPA AG für Industrie Versicherungen*
1987	*Versicherungsverband der Industriellen VVaG*	Modifying conversion in *Versicherungsverband der Industriellen AG*
1988	*„GLEIMAG" Wechselseitige Haftpflicht- und Sachschaden-Versicherungsanstalt für Gleis- und Magazinanlagen*	Modifying conversion in die *„Gleimag" Haftpflicht- und Sachschaden Versicherungs-AG*
1988	*Gegenseitiger Versicherungsverein für Montanwerke, Maschinen- und Metallfabriken*	Transfer conversion into *Montanversicherung AG*
1989	*Erste Wiener Spiegelglas-Versicherungsgesellschaft*	Assets conversion in die *NÖ Versicherungs-AG*
1991	*Wiener Verein Lebens- und Bestattungsversicherung a.G.*	Merged with *Wiener Städtische Wechselseitige Versicherung*
1991	*Pensionskasse VVaG*	Transfer to Austrian Industries Mitarbeitervorsorge AG[19]

[18] Cf. *Baran, P.*, p. 78f.

[19] The *Pensionskasse VVaG* was established by the *Österreichische Industrie Holding AG (ÖIAG)* in 1989 and was merged, after the outsourcing of the business of the *Pensionskasse* and granting shares to the ÖIAG, with a joint stock company. The foundation fund was transformed into equity capital. Cf. *Mayer, L.*, p. 209.

With the introduction of the Austrian Insurance Supervision Act in 1978, mutual insurance societies were able to convert into joint stock companies to increase their equity capital. With the amendment in 1986, mutual insurance societies had to deal with the solvability regulations, which had to be fulfilled completely for the first time in 1993 after a transition period of seven years. Before this regulation, the Insurance Supervision Authority could only intervene in cases where an insufficient equity capital formation endangered directly or indirectly the policyholders' interests. However, this regulation was unsatisfactory for the Authority, because Austrian insurance companies needed a healthy equity capital basis before joining the EU in the near future. Due to the growth trend of the insurance companies and the aggressive competition on the small Austrian market, the productivity of insurance companies became endangered and, as a result, the policyholders and the insurance industry would be harmed. Consequently, regulations regarding a minimal equity base, connected with the first EC-compensation guideline, and the first EC-life insurance guideline were introduced. The Austrian Insurance Association emphasized the negative position of mutual insurance societies regarding the equity capital procurement and demanded to offer mutual insurance societies the possibility of external financing similar to joint stock companies. In the amendment in 1986 the legislator made it possible for mutual insurance societies to obtain more easily additionally equity capital. Additionally, it became possible to take on additional capital in the form of participation and supplementary capital. The later development shows that no mutual insurance society and only one joint stock company used additional financing, and the latter offered the owners to exchange their participation certificates into shares. The participation capital was neither favoured by mutual insurance societies nor by investors, because the distribution of rights was uncertain, e.g. regarding the reimbursement of premiums of members and owners of the participation capital. The second possibility to take on additional capital (secondary debt capital) included also various uncertainties, which led to the amendment of the Insurance Supervision Act in 1991.[20]

5.3 Demutualization from 1975 to 1991

In 1983, the life insurance company JUPITER transferred its assets to the *Volksfürsorge Jupiter AG*. Before the asset transfer, a co-

[20] Cf. Ibid., p. 210; *Schimetschek, H. / Weiser, H.*; p. 317f; *Gassner, W.*; Die Ausstattung der Versicherungsunternehmen mit Zusatzkapital gemäß VAG Novelle, in: Versicherungsrundschau, 41. Jahrgang, Dezember 1986, Nr. 12, p. 106ff.

operation agreement between the WIENER STÄDTISCHEN and the *Österreichischen Volksfürsorge Allgemeine Versicherungs-AG* had been established. Eventually, the JUPITER was merged with the latter. With more than 40 percent, the JUPITER had the third highest cost quota in this sector, although the cost proportions of the GENERALI and the OBERÖSTERREICHISCHE were proportional to the JUPITER higher. The profit situation became worse and the assets were transferred to the ÖSTERREICHISCHE VOLKSFÜRSORGE. The members received additional insurance claims as high as the contingency reserves and the free reserve funds of the JUPITER.[21] In 2001, the *Volksfürsorge-Jupiter AG* was merged with the *Wüstenrot Versicherungs-AG*, whose owners are the *Bausparkasse Wüstenrot AG* with 94.10 percent and the *Wiener Städtische Versicherung AG Vienna Insurance Group* with 5.90 percent.[22]

Although the PAPIERINDUSTRIE had no problems regarding its direct business, the high losses from reinsurance contracts, in particular from US hail risks, led to its conversion. The members received shares equivalent to the average premiums of the years 1978 to 1982 and the PAPIERINDUSTRIE converted into the joint stock company *HAPA Industrieversicherungen*. After its foundation the share capital was increased twentyfold. The new shares were taken over by the liability association of the German industry mutual insurance societies. The association also bought the shares of the minority shareholders and the *HAPA AG* was merged with the *Hannover International Versicherung*, a 100%-subsidiary of the liability association of the German industry mutual insurance societies.[23] Today this association is known as the *HDI Haftpflichtverband der Deutschen Industrie VVaG* (liability association of the German industry mutual insurance societies). It is the parent company of the *TALANX-group*, which also includes the *HDI Versicherung AG* (joint stock company) and the *HDI life insurance*, both active in Austria.

The reasons for restructuring special non-life insurances are apparent from the ratio analysis of the MONTAN, the INDUSTRIELLENVERBAND and the GLEIMAG. The above average combined ratios of the insurance companies show that they were not able to manage efficiently and, therefore, chose the path of restructuring. In 1987, the INDUSTRIELLENVERBAND was converted into a joint stock company and members who had paid on average at least 200,000 ATS between 1984 and 1986 received shares. All other members received

[21] Cf. Ibid, p. 212.

[22] Cf. https://www.wuestenrot.at/content/dam/wuestenrot.at/dokumente/sfcr/WVAG_SFCR_2017.pdf, p. 4, (05.07 2016).

[23] Cf. *Mayer, L.*, p. 212.; Finanz-Compass Österreich 1983/84, 112. Jahrgang, Compass-Verlag, p. 2179.

their compensations in cash. After the conversion, the equity capital was increased by 133 percent and the new shares were taken over by the joint stock company *ANGLO ELEMENTAR Versicherungs-AG*. The latter became the majority owner of the *Versicherungsverband der Industriellen Aktiengesellschaft* (insurance association of the industrial joint stock company) and merged with the *WIENER ALLIANZ Versicherung-AG*. In 2001, the association was transferred into the joint stock company *Allianz Elementar Versicherungs-Aktiengesellschaft*.[24]

The GLEIMAG and MONTAN were both converted into joint stock companies in 1988. The shares of the GLEIMAG were distributed based on the paid premiums in 1987. The MONTAN allocated payments to members who were part of the society since 1983 based on the premiums paid between 1983 and 1987. Insurances were counted against fixed premiums with a third. The GLEIMAG doubled their share capital and the joint stock company *Interrisk Internationale Versicherungs AG* took over the new shares. When the capital was increased, the WIENER STÄDTISCHE acquired a majority share holding by buying shares from members and by subscribing of shares. At the end of 1995, the GLEIMAG and the MONTAN merged, while the *Interrisk Internationale Versicherungs AG* was at this point in possession of 87.4 percent of the share capital. Nowadays, the *Interrisk Internationale Versicherungs AG* is a 100% subsidiary company of the Vienna Insurance Group and, therefore, part of the group.[25]

The joint stock company *Erste Wiener Spiegelglas Versicherung AG* worked closely with the *NÖ Versicherungs-AG*, even before the asset transfer in 1989. Members got their shares in the contingency reserves and free reserves paid out. The tax-privileged and dormant reserves were credited to the members in form of premium refunds and discounts for the next 15 years.[26] The combined ratios of the *Erste Wiener Spiegelglas Versicherung AG* was with around 75 percent constant until 1987 when the ratio increased to 87 percent and to 93 percent during the restructuring.

The merger of the WIENER VEREIN, as the transferring society, with the WIENER STÄDTISCHEN, as the taking-over society (cf. § 60 paragraph 1, line 1 2016), was done due to problems of the existing sales organization. The company wanted new business because of the decreasing demand of funeral insurances. An expansion of the product range and restructuring of the sales organization would have been expensive, therefore, a merger with the WIENER STÄDTISCHEN was

---

24 Cf. *Mayer, L.*; p. 213.

25 Cf. *Mayer, L.*; p. 213; https://www.interrisk.de/unternehmen_interrisk.html (26.06.2018).

26 Cf. *Mayer, L.*; p. 214.

the best solution in particular due to an already existing cooperation agreement.[27]

5.4 Restructuring phase

Transfer of a mutual insurance society into a joint stock company in connection with the Insurance Supervision Act amendment 1991

As mentioned above, some mutual insurance societies and joint stock companies had problems to fulfil the requirements concerning equity capital within the given time. In particular, mutual insurance societies had disadvantages regarding raising equity capital.[28] The legislator offered mutual societies the universal succession (§ 62 of the Insurance Supervision Act 2016) with the amendment in 1991. Now mutual insurance societies were able to transfer their operative insurance business to a joint stock company and continue the insurance society in the form of an asset management society. Hereby, the number of the involved mutual insurance societies and joint stock companies is not fixed as well as the distribution of the insurance business to several joint stock companies.[29] In Austria, two forms exists, firstly, the transfer of a mutual insurance society into a joint stock company, secondly, a joint transfer of several mutual insurance societies in one joint stock company. However, it is necessary that one or several mutual insurance societies have at least 26 percent of the voting shares of the joint stock company.[30] The membership in the insurance society is tied to the insurance relationships of the joint stock company, in which the insurance business was transferred to. To take out a policy with the transferred joint stock company establishes the membership with the insurance society or in case of several to all societies.[31] As a result, the membership continues after the transfer and the new joint stock company is allowed to take out a policy without establishing a membership with the mutual insurance society if the bylaws state it.[32] The chapter about the analysis of the bylaws investigates the importance of nonmembers business further.

The initiative regarding this holding construction came from experience and, according to *F. Eckert* who worked at the amendment too, from two insurance companies. These societies were successful in the health insurance sector in which they possessed large market shares.

---

[27] Cf. Ibid; Der Finanz Compass Österreich 1992/1993, Geld-, Kredit- und Versicherungswesen/1, Compass Verlag, p. 2186.

[28] Cf. *Schimetschek, H. / Weiser, H.*; p. 318.

[29] Cf. *Bartl, K.*; p. 68f.

[30] Cf. Insurance Supervision Act § 63, paragraph 5 (2016).

[31] Cf. Insurance Supervision Act § 63, paragraph 4 (2016).

[32] Cf. Ibid.

As a result, the synergy potential should be investigated, all possibilities to raise capital in accordance to the company law, and future external participation in a group company should be made possible.[33] These two mutual insurance societies were the *Austria Versicherungsverein auf Gegenseitigkeit* and the *Collegialität Versicherung auf Gegenseitigkeit*. They were the first societies who used this Act and transferred their operative insurance business into a joint stock company, i.e. the *AUSTRIA-COLLEGIALITÄT*, with a ratio of 9:1 (Austria:Collegialität). However, to continue the asset management society they had not to fall below a joint 26 percentage.

The Austrian solution of restructuring a mutual insurance society in a kind of hybrid form with the amendment 1991 was recognized in Germany as "the beginning of the end" of the mutuality idea. It was interpreted that the legislator and the insurance societies introduced a change of the organization structure of insurance societies to joint stock companies to avoid an abrupt replacement from membership rights with shares. *Heinz Schimetschek*, the president of the *AUSTRIA insurance company* at that time, also defended the new amendment and emphasized that the mutuality idea will continue, because even a foreign control of maximal 74 percent will not lead to the dissolution of the society.[34]

Schimetschek regarded the Austrian solution of the universal succession not as a change of structure by the legislator but as a necessity to secure the existence of the mutuality idea and to balance the disadvantages of the mutual insurance society and the joint stock company. In *Schimetschek's* comment, he states that no significant changes in the decision-making are recognizable due to the person identity in the bodies of the society. Additionally, all members' representative were persuaded that no major change concerning the mutuality idea and in particular of the members' rights had occurred.[35] In the amendment of the Insurance Supervision Act 2016 the person identity of societies and joint stock companies were excluded, because the Austrian insurance business had to adjust to the EU-guidelines. The influence of *Schimetschek*, as the president of the first transferred joint stock company, is evident from the reports about the Insurance Supervision Act amendment 1991 and several successful mutual insurance societies followed this path.

---

[33] Cf. *Eckert, F.*; Die Einbringung von Versicherungsbetrieben aus Versicherungsvereinen auf Gegenseitigkeit in Versicherungs-Aktiengesellschaften gem. §§ 61 a bis 61 c österr. VAG – Beitrag zur Erhaltung oder friedliches Ende der Versicherungsvereine auf Gegenseitigkeit? in: Zeitschrift für Versicherungsrecht, 1993, p. 393.

[34] Cf. *Schimetschek, H.*, 1993, Erfahrungen mit der neuen VVaG-Gesetzgebung in Österreich, in: Versicherungswirtschaft, 48. Jg, Heft 11, p. 701ff.

[35] Cf. Ibid.

In 1992, three successful mutual insurance societies, the WIENER STÄDTISCHE, the GRAWE, and the MERKUR, chose the universal succession and transferred their operative insurance business into a joint stock company. The MERKUR and the GRAWE took a share of 100 percent in their transferred joint stock companies and the WIENER STÄDTISCHE had, according to *Mayer* (2001), 81.06 percent of the voting shares.

The *Bank Austria AG* had 8 percent of the preference shares and the minority shareholders had 10.94 percent, which were listed on the Viennese stock exchange, in the *Wiener Städtische Allgemeine Versicherungs AG*.[36] Nowadays, the WIENER STÄDTISCHE mutual insurance society has a share of 70 percent in the *Vienna Insurance Group AG Wiener Versicherung Gruppe* (VIG), which has a share of 99.9 percent in the *Wiener Städtische Allgemeine Versicherungs AG*, and which again has the remaining 0.1 percent in the WIENER STÄDTISCHE VVVaG.[37] In 2009, the *Wiener Städtische Allgemeine Versicherung AG* changed its name to *VIENNA INSURANCE GROUP Wiener Städtische Versicherung AG*. In 2010, the operative domestic insurance business was separated from the international business of the group and the VIG received the international business. The *Wiener Städtische Allgemeine Versicherung AG*, on the other hand, focused on the operative insurance business in Austria. Members of the WIENER STÄDTISCHE Versicherungsvereins (insurance society) are only those policyholders who have a contract with the *Wiener Städtische Allgemeine Versicherung AG*, except contracts that are excluded in the bylaws.[38]

The OBERÖSTERREICHISCHE, as the only regional insurance company, transferred into a joint stock company in 1994, in which the *Raiffeisenlandesbank Oberösterreich* took a share in 1999.[39]

An expansion policy of the Austrian insurance companies in the insurance market of Central and Eastern Europe started in the mid-1990s. This was an important development. The GRAWE started this development in the 1990s, a time in which reconciliation between the central and eastern European economies and the western standards was given. The beginning of a free enterprise system on these markets had the effect that the government did not finance the social security services, but used the help of the private insurance industry. The Eastern and middle European insurance market was profitable for the western insurance companies and from the 1990s onwards western

[36] Cf. Mayer, L., p. 221.

[37] Cf. http://www.vig.com/de/investor-relations/aktie/aktionaersstruktur.html (26.06.2018); https://www.wienerstaedtische.at/fileadmin/user_upload/Dokumentenpool/Unternehmen/Investor_Relations/Wiener_Staedtische_SFCR_2016.pdf, p. 7, (26.06.2018).

[38] Cf. http://www.wst-versicherungsverein.at/profil/ (26.06.2018).

[39] Cf. Ibid.

Table 3: Transfer of mutual insurance societies into a joint stock company in Austria from 1991 onwards

Year	Mutual insurance company	Transfer/Conversion	asset management societies
1991	*Austria Versicherungsverein auf Gegenseitigkeit*	Transfer into the *Austria-Collegialität Österreichische Versicherung AG*	*Austria Versicherungsverein auf Gegenseitigkeit*
1991	*Collegialität Versicherung auf Gegenseitigkeit*		*Collegialität Versicherung auf Gegenseitigkeit*
1992	*Wiener Städtische Wechselseitige Versicherungsanstalt*	Transfer into the *Wiener Städtische Allgemeine Versicherung AG*	*Wiener Städtische Wechselseitiger Versicherungsverein – Vermögensverwaltung – Vienna Insurance Group*
1992	*Grazer Wechselseitige Versicherung*	Transfer into the *Grazer Wechselseitige Versicherung AG*	*GRAWE -Vermögensverwaltung*
1992	*MERKUR Wechselseitige Versicherungsanstalt*	Transfer into the *Merkur Versicherung AG*	*MERKUR Wechselseitige Versicherungsanstalt Vermögensverwaltung*
1994	*Wechselseitige Oberösterreichische Versicherungsanstalt*	Transfer into the *Oberösterreichische Versicherung AG*	*Oberösterreichische Wechselseitige Versicherung Vermögensverwaltung*

primary insurers expanded.[40] The WIENER STÄDTISCHE started its expansion in 1990 in Central and Eastern European countries (CCE) participated in the business start-up of the *"Kooperativa"*, in the former Czechoslovakia, and expanded in Eastern Europe during the next two decades. In 2010, the group was restructured in the way that the *Group Holding Company Vienna Insurance Group* (VIG) incorporated subsidiarity firms with a several-brand strategy in the CEE countries.[41]

5.5 Restructuring of the UNIQA-Group

The *AUSTRIA-COLLEGIALITÄT AG* was incorporated in the *UNIQA-Group* in 1999 and 2000, in which also the former *Bundesländer Versicherung AG* and the *Raiffeisen Versicherung AG* were incorporated. The SALZBURGER, in which the *Bundesländer Versicherung AG* had a share in, became later part of the *UNIQA-Group*, but still acted as a regional insurance company. The *UNIQA Personenversicherung AG* comprised the health insurance business of the *AUSTRIA-COLLEGIALITÄT*, the life insurance business of the *Austria Lebensversicherung AG*, the accident insurance business of the *Austria Schaden- und Unfallversicherung AG*[42] and the life health and accident business of the former *Bundesländer Versicherung AG*. The mutual insurance societies AUSTRIA and COLLEGIALITÄT had a share of 36.6 percent in the *UNIQA Personenversicherung AG* and more than 31.9 percent in the holding company of the *UNIQA-Group*, the *UNIQA Versicherungen AG*. Later several restructuring actions took place.

With the foundation of the *UNIQA-Group*, an important step was taken for the expansion in the new market in Central and Eastern European countries. For this plan, a new subsidiary form of the *UNIQA-Group* was established, the *UNIQA International AG*, which was the head of 18 foreign companies with an existing customer share of 60 percent of the *UNIQA-Group*.[43]

Mutual insurance societies, which have moved their entire insurance business into a joint stock company (asset management societies), have since 2005 the possibility to be converted into a private foundation by a modifying conversion. The members of the mutual insurance society be-

---

[40] Cf. Baumgartner, I.; 175 Jahre Grazer Wechselseitige, Festschrift anlässlich des 175-jährigen Jubiläums der Grazer Wechselseitigen Versicherung, Graz, 2003, p. 105ff.

[41] Cf. 190 Jahre Wiener Städtische, p. 70: https://www.wienerstaedtische.at/fileadmin/user_upload/Dokumentenpool/Unternehmen/Corporate/ONLINE-Ausgabe_Festschrift_190_Jahre_Wiener_Staedtische.pdf (26.06.2018).

[42] Both companies were subsidiaries of the AUSTRIA-COLLEGIALITÄT AG.

[43] http://www.uniqagroup.com/gruppe/versicherung/uniqa-group/uniqa-in-europa/uniqa-international/UNIQA_International.de.html (26.06.2018).

came beneficiaries with an important result: While a mutual insurance society has a three-stage governance system with executive, supervisory board, and the members' assembly respectively members' council as the highest body, a private foundation has assets without owners and is based on the founder's intention. The *AUSTRIA Versicherungsverein auf Gegenseitigkeit* was the first mutual insurance society that used that possibility in September 2005.

However, it is conspicuous that at the same time a parent company (private foundation) with a 100 percent subsidiary company was established and:

- that the direct shares held by the asset management society in the *UNIQA Versicherungen AG* was brought into the *AUSTRIA Versicherungsverein Beteiligungs-Verwaltungs GmbH* (100 percent subsidiary company) via contract.
- that the *AUSTRIA Versicherungsverein auf Gegenseitigkeit Privatstiftung*, now the *UNIQA Versicherungsverein Privatstiftung*, became a private foundation via the conversion of the asset management society.

The reason for such actions was according to Mr. *Schimetschek* that the *AUSTRIA Versicherungsverein Beteiligungs-Verwaltungs GmbH* offered a greater flexibility compared to the *UNIQA Versicherungsverein Privatstiftung*.[44] However, former members of a mutual insurance society have no representatives in a private foundation, in which only an advisory board exists. With regard to the *AUSTRIA Versicherungsverein auf Gegenseitigkeit Privatstiftung*, such board is not established as a regular body according to the laws of a private foundation, but only as a consulting committee.

According to the deed of the foundation (paragraph 8.3), the board of the *Austria Versicherungsverein auf Gegenseitigkeit* private foundation is responsible for the management of the *Austria Versicherungsverein Beteiligungs-Verwaltungs GmbH* by sharing the same board members. However, neither in 1991 as *Austria Collegialität Österreichische Versicherung AG* nor in 2005 as UNIQA Versicherung AG, the joint stock company had the same board members as the *Austria Versicherungsverein auf Gegenseitigkeit* respectively the private foundation. The AUSTRIA has now a portion as a private foundation in the *UNIQA Österreich Versicherungen AG*, apart from the COLLEGIALITÄT VVaG, and both had to have at least 26 percent of the voting shares, according to the Insurance Supervision Act from 2005.

[44] Cf. Record of the 61st Extraordinary General Meeting of the Delegates of the Austria Versicherungsverein auf Gegenseitigkeit, 9/22/2005, p. 5.

Table 4: Conversion of mutual insurance societies into a private foundation from 2005 onwards

Year	Mutual company	Private foundation
2005	*Austria Versicherungsverein auf Gegenseitigkeit*	Conversion into *Austria Versicherungsverein auf Gegenseitigkeit Privatstiftung*
2012	*Collegialität Versicherung auf Gegenseitigkeit*	Conversion into *Collegialität Versicherungsverein Privatstiftung*

In 2012, the COLLEGIALITÄT VVaG converted into a private foundation after the regulation regarding minimum participation threshold of 26 percent was weakened due to the amendment of the Insurance Supervision Act 2011. The regulations regarding dissolution was changed insofar that the dissolution does not happen when the private foundation invests more than half of the total assets in a company which belongs to the group, for example into the joint stock company which was used for the transfer in the first place. Additionally, the companies of the group have to hold together more than 50 percent of the voting shares of the transferred joint stock company. However, when the private foundation has shares in a subsidiary of the group then the assets of this subsidiary is added proportionally.[45] In the plenary meeting of the National Assembly, the regulations regarding the dissolution of private foundations were weakened further. The regulation is not failed to comply when the share of the private foundation in the joint stock company into which the insurance business of the converted society was transferred to is above 26 percent of the voting shares. In case the private foundation has shares in a joint stock company into which several societies have transferred their insurance business, the regulations fail when the total share of the private foundation and the societies in the joint stock company is below 26 percent.[46] The regulations regarding mutual insurance societies remained the same. An influence of the UNIQA in the law-making regarding private foundations can be suspected, because the UNIQA is the only insurance company that chose a former mutual society, now a private foundation, to continue in the form of an asset management society.

A former member of the board of the COLLEGIALITÄT comments in an article in 2015 the disputed modifying conversion of the COLLEGIALITÄT into a private foundation and the connected disempowerment of the members. He states that due to this step the UNIQA-group has left the mutual sector, which he regards critically from the members' point of view. However, the existence of the COLLEGIALITÄT was

---

45 Cf. § 66 paragraph 3 Z 3 Insurance Supervision Act..

46 Cf. § 66 paragraph 4 Insurance Supervision Act.

endangered due to the legal minimum share requirements as well as the integration into the *UNIQA-Group*, which was confronted with structural changes. Until the structural changes the AUSTRIA private foundation and the COLLEGIALITÄT mutual insurance society held a qualified majority in the *UNIQA*. However, the danger of not able to fulfil the required minimum share after the restructuring process was still eminent. The COLLEGIALITÄT chose the way of transforming into a private foundation, because §§ 66 paragraph 3 Z 3 Insurance Supervision Act requires that half of the total assess of the private foundation have to be invested into companies of the group from which the former joint stock company came from.[47]

The total share of both private foundations in the *UNIQA Insurance Group AG* is 51.7 percent, which again has a 99 percent share in the *UNIQA Österreich Versicherungen AG*. Therefore, the private foundations have indirectly a share in the joint stock company, which has taken over the operative insurance business of the *Austria-Collegialität AG*. The *UNIQA Versicherungsverein Privatstiftung* / *(Group)* is composed of the *UNIQA Versicherungsverein private foundation* (7.7 percent share in the *UNIQA Insurance Group*) and the *Austria Versicherungsverein Beteiligungs-Verwaltungs GmbH* (41.3 percent), which is the sole property of the *UNIQA Versicherungsverein Privatstiftung*. Together this group has a share of 49 percent and the COLLEGIALITÄT *Versicherungsverein Privatstiftung* of 2.7 percent in the voting shares of the *UNIQA Insurance Group*. 10.9 percent are in the hand of the *RZB Versicherungsbeteiligung GmbH*. 36.8 percent of the shares are in free float and the company has a share of 0.7 percent.[48]

The UNIQA follows a horizontal concentration policy by merging the *UNIQA Personenversicherung AG*, the *UNIQA Sachversicherung AG*, and the *CALL DIRECT Versicherung AG* in 2012. The three companies were merged into the *UNIQA Österreich Versicherungen AG*, and the policyholders with an insurance contract, with the exception of the contracts regulated in the bylaws, became beneficiaries of both private foundations. In 2016, the restructuring process was continued (UNIQA 2.0) with the strategy to do insurance business in Austria in the form of a primary insurer. For this purpose, the *Raiffeisen Versicherung AG*, the *FINANCE LIFE Lebensversicherung AG*, and the *Salzburger Landes-Versicherung AG* were merged with the *UNIQA Österreich*

---

[47] Cf. *Hauser, P.*, Das Governance-System als Beitrag zur Sicherheit der Versicherungsnehmer und Anspruchsberechtigten. Nach über 20 Jahren der Entwicklung erfolgt die Umsetzung von Solvency II in österreichisches Recht. Eine kritische Betrachtung der fast unendlichen und hoffentlich trotzdem erfolgreichen Geschichte, in: *Rohrbach, W.* (ed.), Versicherungsgeschichte Österreichs, Band XII – Liegst dem erteil du inmitten einem starken Herzen gleich, Beograd – Wien, 2015, p. 249ff.

[48] Cf. http://www.uniqagroup.com/gruppe/versicherung/services/Impressum.de.html (26.06.2018).

Versicherungen AG. The market share was increased to 21 percent. As a result, approximately 2 million policyholders of the UNIQA became beneficiaries of the private foundations and, at the same time, their position as members disappeared unnoticed.

5.6 Foundation of the MuKi mutual insurance society

In 2004, the *MuKi Versicherungsverein auf Gegenseitigkeit* was established after decades of no new foundations and a process of market concentration since the mid-1990s. The number of regular mutual insurance societies increased from 5 to 6 and at first a renaissance of the mutual society can be suspected. However, this foundation was based on the intervention of the Insurance Supervision Authority. The insurance started as a non-profit society *"Mutter und Kind im Krankenhaus"* (mother and child in the hospital), which made an effort that children could be accompanied by a familiar person. The purpose of this society was to pay the in-patient care for a small membership fee and to establish rooms for mothers and children like in some foreign hospitals. It was important to have an affordable membership fee so that all families could use the security of the society.[49]

The society offered a broad range of insurance services and many people became members of the society. As a result, the society reached a size that the Act regulating clubs and associations was no longer applicable to it. In 2004, the society requested a license as an insurance company and chose the form as a mutual insurance society which structure was similar to a regular society.[50] Nowadays, the *MuKi* offers insurance in the sectors health, accident, automobile, legal protection, household & homes, horse keeping, provisions, and trade. From a small society, specialized in families with children, a combined insurance company developed with a market share, according to total premiums, that increased from 0.02 percent in 2004 to 0.47 percent in 2016.

5.7 Conversion of the mutual re-insurance society RVV Rückversicherungsverein auf Gegenseitigkeit

With January 1st, 2016, the number of regular mutual insurance societies increased from six to seven. The reason was the conversion of a small mutual insurance society into a large mutual insurance society. The conversion took place because of the Solvency II regulations

[49] Cf.https://www.muki.com/service/allgemeines/%C3%BCber-uns/geschichte.html (26.06.2018).

[50] Cf. Ibid.

2009/138/EG, which states that sole re-insurance companies are now covered by the Solvency II regulations and that their business are not covered any longer by regulations regarding small mutual insurance societies.[51] This regulation affected the *"Rückversicherungsverein aG der kleinen Versicherungsvereinen aG"*, with head office in Vienna, which operates its business now as a large mutual insurance society under the name *"RVV Rückversicherungsverein auf Gegenseitigkeit"*. Their sphere of business is restricted to re-insurance of small mutual insurance societies in Austria. Within this framework, they support and coordinate members during activities, in particular edp-projects or alliances with insurance companies. The society has the right to establish and manage joint organization and administration institutions.[52] Members of the *RVV* are 22 small mutual insurance societies, from them nine are non-life insurance societies and 13 animal insurance societies.[53]

The gross premium volume of the *RVV* was 2,321,000 Euro in 2016, from that 2,126,000 Euro was paid to other re-insurance companies in form of premiums, and 195,000 Euro was the total net-premiums. From that, the share of insurance services minus the settled services of other insurance companies was 53 percent. The completion and business costs are with 98 percent very high and the combined ratio is, therefore, 151 percent.

5.8 Phase of grouping

The most successful large insurance companies in Austria are those, according to market premiums, which have chosen the path of grouping shortly before the millennium.[54] The *Generali Holding AG*, the *Wiener Städtische Wechselseitige Versicherungsanstalt Vermögensverwaltung*,

---

[51] The system of Solvency II is not applicable to small mutual insurance societies because of their small structure and regional limited business areas. Therefore, the legislator established an exception for small societies, which is based on a volume definition, since the realization of the EU guideline 2009/138/EG in the Insurance Supervision Act 2016. Insurance companies with total premiums of 5 million (without the deduction of the re-insurance) are exempted from the Solvency II regulations. According to an employee of the RVV, the premium income is less than 5 million Euro, but they do only re-insurance business, which forced the Financial Market Authority (FMA) to change their license and to convert them into a large mutual insurance society.

[52] Cf. *Bartl, K.*: §§ 68-81 VAG 2016, in: *Korinek, S. / Saria, G. / Saria, S.* (eds.): Versicherungsgesetz VAG, Wien 2016, p. 6f; Cf. Bylaws of the Rückversicherungsvereins auf Gegenseitigkeit, December 2015.

[53] Source: Information of a RVV employee via phone.

[54] Cf. Figure 4.

and the *UNIQA Versicherungen AG* established the three large group formations that were created in Austria.[55] The GRAWE expanded in 1988 its business area by having stacks in banks, founding an investment trust company, by expanding the estate sector to an important part of the company, and by forming itself in an international company.[56] Today, the groups are the *Generali Holding Vienna AG*, *Vienna Insurance Group*, the *UNIQA Insurance Group*, and the *GRAWE Group*. It is important to note that insurance groups have additional supervision, therefore this papers differentiates between insurance groups and financial conglomerates. The additional supervision comprises all subjects that resulted from the merger of companies and influenced an insurance group or a financial conglomerate. The purpose is to prevent a decrease of the policyholder's security. The affiliation to a company group or a financial conglomerate has also the disadvantage that when one company gets into difficulties the rest of the group may also be effected. An additional supervision can only be performed regarding one company, which as a single company is already under supervision, the so- called solo-plus-supervision. When an unsupervised holding is the top of a Group then the additional supervision is exercised towards the company, which is secondary to the holding company. The proceeding in insurance groups and financial conglomerates are different.[57]

An insurance group is a group of companies, which are connected by a participation relationship with a company at the top which is also an insurance company, or has directly or indirectly shares in an insurance company, or which is the parent company of at least one insurance company. When there is no insurance company at the top, an insurance holding company can be used, which has exclusively or predominately shares in an insurance company. Another possibility is a mixed insurance or financial holding company, in which only the group internal businesses of the insurance group are supervised. However, in an insurance holding company the insurance group is subject to the regulations regarding the consolidation of own funds.[58]

In 2006, the *Vienna Insurance Group* (VIG) was established and in 2010, it was restructured into a company-holding group to separate the operative business in Austria from the international business. While the *Vienna Insurance Group AG Wiener Versicherung Gruppe* is listed

---

55 Cf. *Hauser, P.*; Die Tendenzen zur Konzentration, Ausgliederung und Auslagerung sowie Internationalisierung in der österreichischen Versicherungswirtschaft und ihre Auswirkungen auf die Interne Revision, in: *Rohrbach, W.* (eds); An der Schwelle zum 3. Jahrtausend – Retrospektiven und Perspektiven, Verlag Holzhausen, Wien, 2000, p. 208f.

56 Cf. *Baumgartner, I.;* p. 105ff.

57 Cf. *Baran, P.,* Österreichisches Versicherungsaufsichtsrecht, 2. Auflage, Manz, Wien, 2014, p. 27f.

58 Cf. Ibid., p. 28.

on the stock exchange and works internationally, the *Wiener Städtische Versicherung AG Vienna Insurance Group* focuses on operative insurance business. In addition to international control tasks, the *Vienna Insurance Group AG Wiener Versicherung Group* attends the re-insurance and international company business.[59]

A financial conglomerate is a group of companies, which have a participation relationship with a supervised financing company (e.g. bank, securities firm) or an insurance company at the top, which has a share directly or indirectly in such a company. Another possibly is that the financing company is unsupervised but the parent company of two such companies (cf. mixed financing holding company) is supervised and the group is active in the financing service sector with at least 40 percent. Hereby, each company of a group has to be a bank, a security firm or an insurance company.[60]

The *GRAWE Group* is a financing conglomerate due to their connection between banks and insurance companies. The *GRAWE AG*, which is a 100% property of the *GRAWE asset management society*, is the 100% owner of the *Bank Burgenland*, which again has a share of 54 percent in the bank *Schelhammer & Schattera*. Additionally, the GRAWE is a direct share in the *Capital Bank*, *Sopron Bank Burgenland*, *Brüll Kallmus Bank AG*, and the *Security Kapitalanlage AG*. A media sensation was the previous participation in the economically and financially distressed *Hypo Alpe-Adria Bank AG*, which was nationalized in 2009.[61]

As mentioned above, the UNIQA was restructured in 2016 and became a holding company, the *UNIQA Insurance Group*, which comprises the *UNIQA Österreich*, the *UNIQA International* with regional companies in Central and Eastern Europe, and the *UNIQA Reinsurance*. The UNIQA merged the *UNIQA Österreich* with the *Raiffeisen Versicherung AG*, the *Salzburger Landes-Versicherung AG*, and *Finance Life Lebensversicherungs AG*. As a result, the management was downsized to one level, while the market share was increased.[62] The *Raiffeisen Bank International AG* has now a share of 10.9 percent via its subsidiary *RZB Versicherungsbeteiligung GmbH* in the *UNIQA Insurance Group*. In 2016, the *Raiffeisen Bank International AG* sold

59 Cf. http://www.wst-versicherungsverein.at/profil (26.06.2018); http://www.vig.com/de/presse/pressemeldungen/detail/neue-konzernstruktur-in-kraft-3.html?tx_ttnews%5Byear%5D=2010&tx_ttnews%5Bmonth%5D=07&tx_ttnews%5Bpointer%5D=1 (26.06.2018).

60 Cf. Ibid., p. 30.

61 Cf. Der Grawe-Krimi, in: Format, 1-2, 2015; *Graber, R, Schauder A.*; Akte Hypo Alpe Adria. Von der Geldmaschine zum Milliardengrab. Verantwortliche, Profiteure, Hintergründe, 2nd edition, Linde Verlag, Wien, 2015.

62 Cf. http://www.uniqagroup.com/gruppe/versicherung/uniqa-group/ueber-das-unternehmen/unternehmensstruktur/Unternehmensstruktur.de.html (26.06.2018).

17.64 percent of their shares to the *UNIQA private foundation*. The latter increased its voting share in the *UNIQA Insurance Group* from 31.4 percent to 49 percent.[63] As a result, the UNIQA is still a part of the largest bank group in Austria and is, therefore, a financing conglomerate.

In November 2019, the *UNIQA* announced a merger of the *UNIQA Insurance Group* as well as its two subsidiaries *UNIQA Österreich Versicherungen AG* and *UNIQA International* with *UNIQA Österreich Versicherungen AG* as the parent company, a so-called downstream. *UNIQA Österreich AG* is with 99 percent a subsidiary and *UNIQA International* with 100 percent a subsidiary of the *UNIQA Insurance Group*. However, this merger will not influence the *UNIQA private foundation*, which holds a stock portfolio of the *UNIQA Insurance Group*. This is also true for the owner structure in the event of a downstream merger.[64]

6. Solvability of Austrian insurance companies

The main reason for transferring a mutual insurance society into a joint stock company is the problem of increasing the own funds of a mutual society, which depend on the members' fees and the accumulation of the profits. The introduction of Solvency II, i.e. a standardised guideline regarding the solvability of insurance companies, was a major challenge for regular mutual insurance societies. The European Union needed a standardised and risk-based regulation regarding the capital adequacy requirement of insurance companies due to the events during the economic and financial crisis in 2008. This regulation needed new qualitative requirements concerning management of insurance companies, governance system, and internal processes as well as intensive supervision.

With regard to the governance systems of the developed hypridform of mutual insurance societies and joint stock companies (§ 62 Insurance Supervision Act 2016), the board members of the asset management society and of the joint stock company have to differ, a position which was emphasized by the implementation of Solvency II into the

---

[63] Cf. http://www.uniqagroup.com/gruppe/versicherung/services/Impressum.de.html (26.06.2018);http://www.uniqagroup.com/gruppe/versicherung/media/files/UNIQA_KONZERNBERICHT_2016_DE_2.pdf (26.06.2018), p. 7.

[64] https://www.versicherungsjournal.at/unternehmen-und-personen/uniqa-peilt-fusion-an-19855.php, 21.11.2019; https://www.derstandard.at/story/2000111267232/uniqa-will-dreiheimische-versicherungen-zusammenlegen (21.11.2019).

Insurance Supervision Act 2016 comment. The main point is that it is not justifiable that board members of the society are at the same time board members of the operative joint stock company in which the insurance business was transferred to, because this kind of self-control is not compatible with "good governance".[65]

However, in the management of three of the five hybrid forms[66], the board members of the mutual insurance society, private foundation, or joint stock company are still the same. In the two other companies, former directors are the executive directors of the asset management society and in the position as the major owner's official, they have influence on the operative joint stock company.

An analysis of the reports of 37 Austrian insurance companies, published by the EY (a control and advice organization), regarding solvability and financial situation for the business year 2016 shows that the Austrian insurances possess large capital reserves and high financial stability. The minimum requirement of a 100 percent risk cover by Solvency II has been passed clearly with an average of 257 percent. The combined insurers have an average solvability quota of 218 percent, with the *GRAWE insurance company* at the top (343 percent). The life insurance companies have an average quota of 226 percent, and the non-life insurance of a maximal quota of 314 percent. The Solvency Capital Requirements quota (SCR-quota) is calculated either by a standardised formula or by the insurance company with a Financial Market Authority approved model called partial internal model (PIM).

Table 5: Overview on the solvability quota of mutual insurance societies in 2016 and 2017

Mutual insurance societies	**Insurance sector**	**SCR-Calculation**	**SCR-quota in percent 2016**	**SCR-quota in percent 2017**
HAGEL V.a.G.	Non-life insurance	Standard formula	375%	312%
VORARLBERGER V.a.G.	Combined insurance	Standard formula	262%	235%
ÖBV V.a.G.	Life-insurance	Standard formula	227%	247%
Tiroler Versicherung AG	Combined insurance	Standard formula	224%	244%
Kärntner Landes V.a.G.	Combined insurance	Standard formula	184%	207%
MUKI V.a.G.	Non-life insurance	Standard formula	168%	167%
RVV a.G.	Re-insurance	Standard formula	680%	591%

Source: Report on solvency and financial condition from the respective insurance companies.

[65] Cf. *Bartl, K.*, § 63, p. 75.

[66] The *Collegialität Versicherungsverein Privatstiftung* (insurance society private foundation) is excluded.

The mutual insurance societies have also a Solvency Capital Requirements quota that is higher than the risk based equity base requirement of Solvency II. Table 4 presents the SCR-quota of regular mutual insurance societies, with the HAGEL. (hail insurance) as a non-life insurance at the top (312 percent). The KÄRNTNER and the MUKI have the lowest SCR-quota with 207 percent and 167 percent, which is, nevertheless, above the Solvency II requirements.

The problem of the capital adequacy requirement of mutual insurance societies cannot be explained by the data regarding the solvability of Austrian insurance companies. According to the published data of the companies, the financial stability of all mutual insurance societies is given. As table 5 shows, the insurance joint stock companies, classified as hybrid forms and with mutual asset management societies or private foundations as their main owners, are highly capitalized. According to § 202 Insurance Supervision Act, the asset management societies, as the top level of the holding groups of the GRAWE, MERKUR, and VIENNA INSURANCE GROUP AG, publish the consolidated data concerning solvability and financial situation of the entire holding or group. The reports of the individual insurance and re-insurance societies are published by the respective joint stock companies. The GRAWE as a group (270.42 percent in 2016, figures for 2017 n.a.) and as an individual insurance society (343 percent in 2016 and 328 in 2017) has in particular high solvency ratios, which shows that their own capital assets are threefold higher as the required solvency capital basis. The VIENNA INSURANCE GROUP AG[67] functions as holding company and is obligated to report due to its re-insurance and corporate client business. Additionally, its capital assets are also threefold higher than required. It is interesting that in particular non-life insurances have a major increase regarding the equity capital ratio. Life insurances, on the other hand, have problems on the capital market to build up a high capital basis due to low interests and a low rate of return. However, Austrian life insurance companies present stable figures concerning risk-based equity base.

[67] The VIG Holding with head office in Vienna have stakes in approximately 500 insurance companies in 25 countries, which have more than 24,000 employees. The 230 employees of the VIG Holding work in particular in the branches re-insurance and corporate customer business as well as fields dealing with risk control, which are taken over e.g. by Enterprise Risk Management and Asset Risk Management. Due to its operative position as a holdings company, the VIG has taken over the central coordination within the group. As a result, the VIG has major influence on decision-makings concerning all companies of the group, including finances.

Table 6: Overview on solvability quota (hybrid form) in 2016 and 2017

Insurance joint stock company (hybrid form)	Insurance sector	SCR-Calculation	SCR-Quota in percent 2016	SCR-Quota in percent 2017
UNIQA Group	Combined Insurer - Group	PIM for Non-Life	202%	250%
UNIQA Insurance Group AG	Re-insurance	PIM for Non-Life	370%	377%
UNIQA Österreich Vers. AG	Combined Insurer	PIM for Non-Life	243%	249%
GRAWE Vermögensverwaltung[66]	Combined Insurer - Group	Standard formula	270%	n.a.
GRAWE Versicherung AG	Combined Insurer	Standard formula	343%	328%
MERKUR Wechselseitigen Versicherungsanstalt Vermögensverwaltung (Merkur-Konzern)[67]	Combined Insurer - Group	Standard formula	187%	n.a.
MERKUR Versicherung AG	Combined Insurer	Standard formula	231%	267%
Wiener Städtische Wechselseitiger Versicherungsverein – Vermögensverwaltung – Vienna Insurance Group[68]	Combined Insurer - Group	PIM for Non-Life	173%	n.a.
VIENNA INSURANCE GROUP AG Wiener Versicherung Gruppe	Non-Life	PIM for Non-Life	390%	389%
Wiener Städtische Versicherung AG	Combined Insurer	PIM for Non-Life	209%	245%
OBERÖSTERREICHISCHE Vers. AG	Combined Insurer	Standard formula	183%	207%

Source: Report on solvency and financial situation from the respective insurance companies.

68 The GRAWE asset management society is at the top of the GRAWE Group and publishes the report regarding solvability and financial situation of the entire GRAWE Group (according to §§202-236 Insurance Supervision Act).

69 The Merkur Wechselseitige Versicherungsanstalt-Vermögensverwaltung is on the top level of the group structure, presents the annual group accounts for most of the group companies, and is used as the highest parent company for the calculation of the group solvability.

70 The Wiener Städtische Versicherungsverein publishes the report concerning solvability and financial situation of the entire VIG group (according to §§202-236 Insurance Supervision Act).

7. Analysis of mutuality regarding Austrian insurance companies

According to the *Financial Market Authority (FAM)*, in December 2016 seven mutual insurance societies, six mutual insurance societies used for asset management (from them 2 are carried out as private foundations), and 50 small mutual insurance societies had existed in Austria. Apart from them, 31 insurances operate their business in form of a joint stock company.[71] In the following, the large mutual insurance societies are going to be discussed, including the development of the hybrid form of asset management societies and joint stock companies.

In this paragraph, the question is raised how far the Austrian mutuality principle is still practiced in Austrian mutual insurance societies and hybrid forms that use a mutual society for asset management. By analyzing the principles of mutuality, it can be determined how far this principle still exists in the Austrian insurance companies. As mentioned in the legal part, there is no clear definition of mutuality in the Austrian law, only the characteristics of mutuality or its requirements can be found in various regulations. The mutual insurance society differs from the joint stock company by the unity of policyholder and member of the society and by the dominance of the policyholders' interests. This analysis uses the three mutuality principles self-responsibility, self-government, and equal treatment, which, according to *Nemson*, have to be guaranteed in a mutual society to secure the unity of the member and policyholder's position.[72]

Based on an analysis of the current bylaws of Austrian mutual insurance societies and asset management societies as well as private foundations, the three principles will be discussed. Tables 4 and 5 present the current data of regular insurance societies and hybrid forms. The data concerning the number of member and non-member transactions were collected via E-mail and phone from the operative insurance companies, which, however, were not able to provide exact data regarding the actual numbers.

7.1 Analysis of the bylaws: self-responsibility, self-government, and equal treatment

The principle of equal treatment in Austria is interpreted in such a way that, according to § 44 paragraph 2 2016, fees and the members'

[71] FMA, Jahresbericht 2016, p. 51.
[72] Cf. *Nemson, J.*, p. 159.

The society is allowed to allocate all conditions and expenses to non-members, which are produced by non-member insurance contracts.

All non-member transactions of the *Österreichische Hagelversicherungsanstalt a. G.* are operated in foreign countries. The bylaws state that insurance policies can be taken out without establishing a membership. Such insurances have to be done in a branch of the company or via service transactions and the insurance object has to be outside of Austria.[75] This insurance company has export markets in the Czech Republic, Slovakia, Hungary, Rumania, and Slovenia with approximately 3,500 customers in 2016 and 4,800 customers in 2017, which have strictly non-member contracts. In 2015, the premium share of export markets was 12 percent of the total premiums. The annual report for 2014 shows that the importance of international markets has grown due to the potential of insurable areas and the decreasing availability of insurable areas in Austria, because of more constructions and new agro-political measures such as biodiversity areas. In Rumania, the business activity takes place via service transactions.[76]

The TIROLER insurance presented for 2016 and 2017 exact figures for non-members (29,916 in 2016 and 30,319 in 2017) and customers (114,930 in 2016 and 117,026 in 2017), which corresponds to 26 percent non-members. These policyholders possess e.g. third-party insurances and accident insurances with premiums less than 1,000 Euro or have short-term insurances (e.g. liability insurances for events). The bylaws of the TIROLER regulate that policyholders have to be members of the insurance society, if they have bundle insurance, such as trade, agriculture, private buildings, or an annual premium of more than 1,000 Euro.[77]

The VORARLBERGER had in 2016 96,029 customers while in 2017 the number increased to 97,293; in this case, non-membership transactions are only contracts with re-insurers or few short-term contracts of less than one year. According to the insurance company, these types of contracts are negligible due to their low number. The bylaws state that policyholders are members of the society if the insurance premiums are not fixing. Insurance policies with fix premiums, except re-insurance contracts, are only allowed as long as their total premium is lower than 10 out of one hundred of the total income from fees and premiums of a year.[78]

---

75 Cf. Bylaws of „Österreichische Hagelversicherung Versicherungsverein auf Gegenseitigkeit" (31.03.2010).

76 Cf. Annual report 2014 of the "Hagelversicherung Versicherungsverein auf Gegenseitigkeit", p. 18.

77 Cf. Bylaws of "Tiroler Versicherung Versicherungsverein auf Gegenseitigkeit" (08.05.2014).

78 Cf. Bylaws of "Vorarlberger Landes-Versicherung Verein auf Gegenseitigkeit" (21.05.1997).

obligation to pay further capital and services of the society (based on the membership relationship) have to be determined by the same principles when they meet the same criteria. In this case, both the policyholder and the insurer have to produce the same services. In Austria, only three regular mutual insurance societies (HAGEL, KÄRNTNER, VORARLBERGER) are allowed to demand further payments from their members, all other mutual societies and private foundations have excluded them from their bylaws. When the society is dissolved, the distribution of the assets to the members should also be based on the principle of equal treatment. The law does not regulate the division of assets, because the Insurance Supervision Act assumes that the bylaws include final regulations concerning this topic, however, not all mutual insurance societies have such regulations. In this event, the highest body decides during the last membership relation meeting about the division of assets. The latter is complicated, because it has to be decided if members who left the society during the last business year should be included or not. According to *Bartl*, the division is based on the amount of premiums or the insurance sum and on an average amount of the last years.[73]

An interesting fact is that mutual insurance societies are allowed to operate non-member transactions, which means policyholders are not always members of the society too, when the exceptions are part of the bylaws. The following paragraphs present the results of an evaluation of the number of non-member transactions; the questioning was carried out via E-mail and phone.

7.2 Regular mutual insurance societies

The *MuKi* and *Österreichische Beamtenversicherung VVaG* stated that they have no transactions with non-members. The first explained that, according to the bylaws, a membership is earned when a policy is taken out, and no special regulations exist.[74]

The *Österreichische Beamtenversicherung VVaG*, on the other hand, states that according to the bylaws the society is allowed to take out policies for fixed premiums, which do not establish non-membership rights. However, the number of such transactions has to be less than half of the total number of contracts and less than the total amount of the insurance sum. Policyholders without a membership but with contracts that include profit sharing receive surpluses like members.

---

[73] Cf. *Bartl, K.*, p. 49

[74] Cf. Bylaws of "Österreichischer Beamtenversicherung Versicherungsverein auf Gegenseitigkeit" (28.07.2008); Bylaws of "MuKi Versicherungsverein auf Gegenseitigkeit"(23. 07 2015).

The KÄRNTNER insurance assured that the number of non-member transactions with fix premiums is less than 100. This insurance company had approximately 70,000 customers in 2016 and 84,000 in 2017. The bylaws state that members are policyholders, who have a direct insurance contract with the regional insurance society, with the exception of insurances based on fix premiums. The membership starts after the first or sole payment. All re-insurance contracts are based on fix premiums and establish no membership. Insurance contracts with fix premiums (except re-insurances) are only allowed as long as their total premium is lower than 10 out of one hundred of the total income from fees and premiums of a year.[79]

The RVV, a former small mutual insurance society, had to convert into a large mutual insurance society due to the regulations of Solvency II. The insurance company comprises 22 members, which have re-insurance contracts with the RVV. The members are 9 non-life and 13 animal insurance companies as well as non-members transactions. The business activities of the RVV are not full-time. Additionally, the RVV has a part-time employee and a voluntary employee. So far, no ratios have been published.[80]

7.3 Asset management societies

When a mutual insurance society merged with a joint stock company (cf. § 62 Insurance Supervision Act 2016) a hybrid form develops, in which the society manages the assets while the joint stock company takes over the operative insurance business. In this event, a membership between the policyholder of the joint stock company and the mutual insurance society develops. The policyholders have a share in the annual profit, which, however, only comprises the distributions of dividends of the joint stock company to the society and does not come directly from the insurance business. Non-membership transactions are allowed when stated in the bylaws of the joint stock company and the mutual insurance society. Is the share of non-membership transactions too high, the existence of the society is endangered, as a result, the necessary limits in the bylaws are explained in the next paragraphs.

---

[79] Cf. Bylaws of "Kärntner Landesversicherung auf Gegenseitigkeit".

[80] According to a phone conversation with an employee, the annual premium income is approximately more than EUR 500,000.

Table 7: Overview on the six largest Austrian mutual insurance societies

Mutual insurance society	Customers (2017)	Members (2017)	Non-members (2017)	Total number of employees (2017)	Market share in % (2017)	Combined Ratio (2017)
MUKI	493,717 [79]	493,717	none	141	0.54	104
BEAMTEN	app. 300,000	app. 300.000	none	657 (2016) 628	1.08	87
HAGEL	58,800 (2016) 50,300	app. 55,300[80] (2016) 54,500	3,500 (2016) 4,800	95	0.56	93
TIROLER	114,930 (2016) 117,026	85,014 (2016) 86,707	29,916 (2016) 30,319	293	0.71	91
VORARLBERGER	96,029 (2016) 97,293	96,029 (2016) 97,293	insignificant	198 (2016) 197	0.51	94
KÄRNTNER	app. 70,000 (2016) app. 84,000	app. 70,000 (2016) app. 84.000	<100	192 (2016) 185	0.39	102
RVV	22	22	none	2	n.a.	151

Source: Tiroler Versicherung: http://www.tiroler-versicherung.at/Unternehmen/Daten-Fakten (26.06.2018); ÖBV: Information via Email; Kärntner Landesversicherung: http://www.klv.at/klv-daten-fakten.html (15.06.2015) ; VLV: Information via Email; Hagelversicherung: Information via Email; MuKi: Information via phone; market shares: VVO annual report 2016; RVV: Information via E-mail; https://www.vvo.at/vvo/vvo.nsf/sysPages/jahresbericht.html; Employees according to the annual reports.

81 The Austrian hail insurance has is non-member transactions in the Czech Republic, Slovakia, Hungary, Rumania, and Slovenia with approximately 2,800 customers. In 2015, the premium share of export markets was 12 percent of the total premiums. Membership transactions are limited to Austria.

82 The Muki insurance company had 493 717 insured risks.

The WIENER STÄDTISCHE, with the second highest market share of the Austrian insurance companies, had 1,400,000 customers in 2017 and the WIENER STÄDTISCHE Versicherungsverein had 1,337,203 members. The bylaws of the joint stock company and the mutual insurance society state that a membership is earned when an insurance policy is taken out with the WIENER STÄDTISCHE Versicherung AG VIG. The exceptions are re-insurance and co-insurance contracts and short-time contracts of less than a year. The WIENER STÄDTISCHE Versicherung AG VIG offers also insurances that do not include a membership of the policyholder.[83]

The GRAWE Vermögensverwaltung has at the moment approximately 556,769 members, which corresponds to the number of customers of the GRAWE in Austria. The share of non-member transactions is insignificant. The bylaws of the GRAWE state that members of the GRAWE mutual insurance society are at the same time policyholders of the GRAWE AG.[84] Non-membership transactions include re-insurance contracts, short-time contracts of less than a year, and contracts from another company. The premium from non-membership policies can be at the most a fifth of the total premium income from the direct insurance business of the GRAWE AG.[85]

---

[83] Cf. Bylaws of "Wiener Städtische Versicherungsverein" from July 1st, 2015; Bylaws of "Wiener Städtische Versicherung AG Vienna Insurance Group" from June 2016.

[84] People with services to the Austrian insurance industry can become honorary members by the proposal of the boards of management and supervision and by the decision of the members' representative body. People with special services to the mutual society can become honorary president. There are no additional membership rights or claims connected with the appointment as honorary member or president.

[85] Cf. Bylaws of "Grazer Wechselseitigen Versicherung – Vermögensverwaltung" from May 13, 2014; Bylaws of "Grazer Wechselseitigen Versicherung AG" from May 12, 2015.

Table 8: Overview on asset management societies/private foundations 2016

Asset management societies/private foundations	Members/ Beneficiaries (2016)	Non-members/Non beneficiaries (2016)	Operative joint stock company	Customers of joint stock company (2016)	Employees of joint stock company (2016)	Market share of the joint stock company, all insurance sectors in % (2016)	Combined Ratio of the joint stock company in % (2016)[86]
WIENER STÄDTISCHE Vermögensverwaltung[87]	1,324,870 1,337,203 (2017)	n.a.	Wiener Städtische Versicherung AG	1,400,000 1,450,000 (2017)	3,592 3,657 (2017)	13.65	94
GRAWE Vermögensverwaltung	530,000 556,769 (2017)	insignificant	GRAWE AG	530,000 556,769 (2017)	1,500 1,458 (2017)	2.98	98
OBERÖSTERREICHISCHE Vermögensverwaltung	393,892 402,425 (2017)	8.59 % 8.44 % (2017) of the net premiums	OBERÖSTERREICHISCHE Versicherung AG	448,960 456,851 (2017)	720 698 (2017)	2.38	67
MERKUR Vermögensverwaltung	n.a.	n.a.	Merkur Versicherung AG	n.a.	866	2.56	100
UNIQA Privatstiftung COLLEGIALITÄT Privatstiftung	app. 3.500,000	n.a.	UNIQA Österreich Versicherungen AG	app. 2.300,000	5,980	21.23	97

Source: Information about the number of customers and members received by phone and Email; Number of employees drawn from the annual reports and the homepage of each insurance company; market share: VVO annual report 2016: https://www.vvo.at/vvo/vvo.nsf/sys-Pages/jahresbericht.html(26.06.2018)

86 The combined ratio was calculated with a standardized model.

87 Generally, every policyholders establish a membership in the *Wiener Städtische Versicherungsverein* (mutual society) when taking out an insurance policy with the *Wiener Städtische Versicherung AG*. Exceptions, which do not establish a membership, are co-insurances and re-insurances as well as short-term contracts of less than a year. Cf. http://www.wst-versicherungsverein.at/profil/(26.06.2018)

From all hybrid forms only the OBERÖSTERREICHISCHE insurance company provided exact figures concerning non-member transactions. Now, the company has approximately 456,851 customers with several or long-term contracts, which make them members of the mutual society. The share of non-member transactions is 8.4 percent of the net premiums. According to the bylaws, non-member transactions are short-term insurance polices of less than a year and contracts of other companies. The premiums from direct insurance policies with fix premiums can be at the most a fifth of the total premium income from the direct insurance business of OBERÖSTERREICHISCHEN Versicherung AG.[88] With 8.4 percent, the portion is clearly lower. Reinsurance contracts do not establish a membership in the mutual insurance society.

The MERKUR Versicherung AG did not provide any information concerning their non-member transactions. The bylaws state that a membership is established with taking out an insurance policy with the MERKUR Versicherung AG, except re-insurances and non-member transactions. The company only takes out non-life and accident insurance policies when no membership is established in the society. The premiums from insurances with fix premiums can be at the most a fifth of the total premium income of the MERKUR Versicherung AG.[89]

7.4 Mutual insurance society-private foundation

According to § 66 paragraph 3 line 7 Insurance Supervision Act 2016, the asset of the mutual insurance society presented in the final balance belongs to the mutual insurance society-private foundation. The private foundation has the purpose to preserve and manage the assets as well as the share in the joint stock company. The private foundation has to preserve the mandatory portion of the operative joint stock company and to build up the liquid assets. The annual profit has to be distributed to the shareholders, if not revenue reserves or other laws on foundation state to build up reserves.[90]

The *UNIQA Versicherungsverein Privatstiftung* and the *Collegialität Versicherungsverein Privatstiftung*, which have a joint share of 51.5 percent in the UNIQA Insurance Group, regulate in their foundation charter the surplus sharing as following: the annual profit has to be distributed among the beneficiaries if there is no new bill or used for reserves and provisions. The principles for distributing the an-

---

88 Cf. Bylaws of "Oberösterreichische Wechselseitige Versicherung Vermögensverwaltung" from June 22, 2011; Bylaws of "Oberösterreichische Versicherung AG" from June 6, 2013.

89 Bylaws of "Merkur Wechselseitigen Versicherungsanstalt Vermögensverwaltung" from January 27, 2010; "Bylaws of Merkur Versicherung AG" from June 10, 2013.

90 Cf. Chapter "Legal frameworks for insurance companies in Austria".

nual profit is regulated by the board of trustees after discussed by the advisory board and approved by the supervision board. The board of trustees is allowed to build up the following provisions:[91]

- Reserves and provisions equivalent to the tax benefits.
- A security provision equivalent to 10 percent of the remaining annual profit after setting up reserves and provisions.
- Reserves for provisions concerning the foundation purpose.
- Revenue reserves

Both private foundations have apart from their main purpose, which is regulated mandatorily in § 66 2016, a subsidiary non-profit purpose. As already discussed in the chapter “Legal frameworks for insurance companies in Austria”, a private foundation (§ 66 2016) is not a charitable or non-profit institution. Therefore, the private foundation should only serve its main purpose and to represent the interests of the beneficiaries, i.e. a share of the annual profit and a claim to the assets in the event of a dissolution of the private foundation.
Purpose of the *UNIQA Versicherungsverein Privatstiftung*:

- The direct or indirect support of the beneficiaries in accordance with the legal regulations of private foundations, in particular the Insurance Supervision Act.
- The investment and management of the assets of the private foundation.
- The economic protection of the private foundation.

If the main purpose of the private foundation is not sustainable disturbed, the support of e.g. ecclesiastical organizations with charitable and social purposes, of members of such organizations, and the support of health and welfare institutions, including the support of connected scientific research and technologies, is allowed.[92]
Purpose of the *Collegialität Versicherungsverein Privatstiftung*:

- Direct and indirect support of the beneficiaries in accordance with legal regulations concerning the continuation of the private foundation in particular regarding the Insurance Supervision Act
- Investment and management of the assets of the private foundation
- Economic protection of the continuation of the private foundation

As far as the purpose of the private foundation is not damaged, the following is allowed in a subsidiary way

[91] This regulation is agreed on by both private foundations in sections a), c), and d). The UNIQA Versicherungsverein Privatstiftung states in section b) a more exact wording: a general security provision, which has to be 10 percent of the remaining annual profit, and which is only allowed to be dissolved for balancing a net loss for a year. The supervision board is allowed to decide a minimum or maximum amount of the reserves depending on the business volume.

[92] Cf. Foundation bylaws of “UNIQA Versicherungsverein Privatstiftung” from 02. 06.2014.

- The moderate support of organisations and bodies with social and charitable purposes
- The moderate support of medical, social, economic, and insurance-specific care of former and current policyholders of the UNIQA insurance group
- The moderate support of medical, social, economic, and insurance-specific care of older, sick, and in need of care people including the support of the ideas of life protection and hospice as well as the foundation of rehabilitation, nursing, and hospice institutions
- The moderate support of the existing Collegialität private foundation concerning the realisation of its purpose and securing its existence.

In the event of the dissolution of the *UNIQA Versicherungsverein Privatstiftung*, the remaining assets of the private foundation have to be distributed among the beneficiaries. The management board has to take actions according to an earlier drawn up winding-up plan, approved by the supervision board and the advisory board and the Insurance Supervision Authority.[93]

The UNIQA was not able to provide exact data regarding the number of beneficiaries and non-beneficiaries due to the current restructuring measures, i.e. the merger of the *UNIQA Österreich Versicherungen AG* with its 100 percent subsidiaries the *UNIQA Salzburger Landesversicherung AG*, the *Raiffeisen Versicherung AG*, and the *Finance Life Lebensversicherung AG*. The UNIQA continues the insurance business of the three insurance companies with the name unchanged.[94] As a rough guideline for the number of beneficiaries, the UNIQA stated approximately 2 million beneficiaries before the big fusion in 2015. With 2.4 million customers of the *UNIQA Österreich Versicherungen AG* in 2015, the number of non-beneficiaries has to be around 400,000. Nowadays after the fusion, UNIQA stated approximately 3,500,000 customers but the number of beneficiaries is not available.

According to the bylaws of both private foundations and the *UNIQA Österreich Versicherungen AG*, a designation of a beneficiary is combined with an insurance relationship with the *UNIQA Österreich Versicherungen AG*. The policyholder is the beneficiary, starting with taking effect of the policy and expires with its ending. The beneficiary position is not established by taking out co- and reinsurance contracts and with short-term contracts of less than a year. The *UNIQA Österreich Versicherungen AG* can take over other insurance contracts, which do not make the policyholder to a beneficiary of the private foundation. The bylaws of the *UNIQA Österreich Versicherungen AG* state that those are insurance contracts that cover risks in foreign countries concerning demise risk, equity-linked and index-linked life insurance, and other

93 Cf. Statement of the private foundation of the Collegialität Versicherungsverein Privatstiftung from 07.09.2012.

94 Cf.http://www.uniqagroup.com/gruppe/versicherung/uniqa-group/ueber-das-unternehmen/unternehmensstruktur/Unternehmensstruktur.de.html (26.06.2018).

insurance contracts than stated here if the premium from the domestic business does not exceed a tenth of the domestic premium income.[95]

An essential distinguishing feature of the private foundation compared to the mutual insurance society is that the members' council is not the highest body any longer, but has eliminated itself by converting into a private foundation. The bylaws of the *Collegialität* state that the general meeting of the mutual insurance society becomes, when converted into a private foundation, an advisory board. According to the bylaws, the board is a body, however, according to § 66 of the Insurance Supervision Act 2016, only the supervision board and the board of trustees are bodies of a private foundation. The supervision board elects the board of trustees and appoints succeeding and additional members of the supervision board by itself. In the bylaws of the *Austria Versicherungsverein Privatstiftung*, the advisory board is not regarded as a body, but as a board for the management, established with the approval of the supervision board. As a result, it is not a body as defined in the endowments and private foundations act. The third body in both private foundations is the foundation auditor, who is appointed by the supervision board. However, the Insurance Supervision Act does not require this, because private foundations are audited and supervised by the Financial Market Authority (FMA).

7.5 Overview and summary of the analysis of the bylaws

The following tables give an overview on the three principles of the mutuality principle (personal responsibility, self-government, and equal treatment). The principle of equal treatment of Austrian insurance societies has already been analyzed in a previous chapter. The self-government comprises the members' council as the highest body, which has important participatory rights for all members.

According to § 51 paragraph 2, the composition of the members' representative and the appointment of the representatives have to be regulated by the bylaws. In this case, it is possible that a qualified minority of members can offer a list of candidates. Additionally, the bylaws state in what cases the highest body decides. With regard to management, the highest body can only decide when the board or the supervisory board demand this. The latter is involved in case of a business transaction which needs approval (§ 95 paragraph 5 Companies Act).[96] It is important to note that the highest body of the asset management insurance society has special rights regarding the work of the bodies of the society in the joint stock company (§ 64 paragraph 1

[95] Bylaws of the UNIQA Österreich Versicherungen AG (17.09.2012).

[96] Cf. § 51 paragraph 2, 3 Insurance Supervision Act.

Insurance Supervision Act). Therefore, the director of the society has to demand the decision of the highest body in all matters concerning the competence of the general meeting off the joint stock company. The members' right to demand information includes all matters of the joint stock company which are connected with the topic of the decision. Additionally, with a qualified majority the highest body can appoint examiners for the foundation process or the conduct of business of the joint stock company. The highest body can decide that claims of the joint stock company from the conduct of business can be made against members of the board or the supervisory board.[97] This kind of influence of the members' representative or the members ends with a modifying conversion into a private foundation, because now the members are only beneficiaries of the foundation and the officials of the society are not obliged to the members or policyholders but only to themselves due to self-renewal of the supervisory board. The members have legally no influence on the foundation or the joint stock company.[98]

The examination of the bylaws of the mutual insurance societies will show the individual regulations and present the various differences.

The TIROLER and VORARLBERGER insurance companies involve the regional governments into the highest body by having participatory rights.[99] The KÄRNTNER insurance company states in the bylaws that the tasks of the regional government and the regional parliament result from the Act about the tasks of the federal state regarding the KÄRTNER (Carinthia regional insurance company).[100]

The election of the members' council is important, because it is usually done by co-optation, with the exception of the MUKI, HAGEL, and KÄRTNER insurance companies, in which the members still elect their representatives. As a result, the members' participatory rights are very limited and they are controlled very differently in the bylaws of the insurance societies, as table 6 shows. For example, proposals for the decision-making in the members' council and proposed nominations can be made, when a certain minimum number of members signs them. The minimum number is different in each society and ranges from at least 10 members (e.g. MUKI) to 400 (e.g. MERKUR). In the WIENER STÄDTISCHE (2 percent) and the UNIQA (3 percent), a certain percentage of all members have to sign the proposals.

---

[97] Cf. § 64 paragraph 1 Insurance Supervision Act.

[98] Cf. *Hauser, P.*, p. 253f.

[99] The regional governments have, for example, the following tasks: the appointment and recall of members of the supervision board, determination of the reimbursement to the members of the supervision board, the approval, appointment, and recall of the management board, amendments to the bylaws as well as the dissolution of the society. Cf. Bylaws of the Tiroler Versicherung auf Gegenseitigkeit, § 11. Cf. Bylaws of the Vorarlberger Landesversicherung V.a.G., § 8.

[100] Cf. Bylaws of the Kärntner Landesversicherung auf Gegenseitigkeit, § 7.

The personal responsibility principle comprises asset rights and duties of the members such as the obligation to pay further capital. However, most insurance societies have excluded them from their bylaws. Only the HAGEL, KÄRNTNER, and the VORARLBERGER permit, under certain circumstances, additional payments when all reserves and contingency reserves are exhausted. In asset management societies and private foundations, the obligation to pay further capital is prohibited. Each insurance society regulates the surplus participation differently. In general, the bylaws of insurance societies state the different possibilities to establish the different types of reserves and provisions as well as the distribution of the remaining profit to the members. In the general meeting, the distribution of the remaining profit is decided. The HAGEL defines in its bylaws that the premium reimbursement has to be done in percentage of the mandatory premiums. The reimbursement is distributed proportional to the premiums resulted from the benefits of the federation and states as well as from the members mandatory premiums.[101] The annual reports of the private foundations *COLLEGIALITÄT Versicherungsverein Privatstiftung* (2013) and the *UNIQA Versicherungsverein Privatstiftung* show that the profit was not distributed to the beneficiaries, instead the profit was accumulated and allocated to the reserves. With regard to the COLLEGIALITÄT, the profit was allocated to *COLLEGIALITÄT Privatstiftung*. However, the annual report does not state for what the profit was used.[102]

As mentioned above, the exact members' share of the asset in the event of dissolution is decided in the last assembly of the members' council. The MUKI, the KÄRNTNER, and the VORARLBERGER state in their bylaws that the remaining assets after all debts are settled are distributed among the members according to the shares. The TIROLER states that the remaining assets belong to the state Tirol, when the state takes over the obligations of the pensions and pension contributions of the employees of the TIROLER insurance company.

[101] Cf. Bylaws of the Österreichischen Hagelversicherung.

[102] Cf. Annual statement 2014 of the UNIQA Versicherungsverein Privatstiftung; Annual statement of the Collegialität Versicherungsverein Privatstiftung 2013.

Table 9: Regular mutual insurance societies

Insurance company	equal treatment	self-government	self-responsibility
MuKi	**Non-membership contracts:** no	**Highest body:** members' council **Election of the members' council:** co-optation **Participation rights of members:** Proposals for decision-making by the council have to be signed by at least 10 members. The applicant has the right to send a member to the assembly for the verbally justification.	**Obligation to pay further capital:** no **Surplus participation:** The annual profit has to be distributed among the members if not allocated to a contingency reserve or other types of provisions, as stated in the bylaws, it is not used for the reimbursement of the foundation funds, or for payments, or used for the next business year. **Share in the dissolution assets:** after all debts are paid, the remaining assets are distributed among the current members;
Österreichische Beamtenversicherung	**Non-membership contracts:** yes In total, less than half of the company's total insured sum and less than half of the number of all insurance contracts	**Highest body:** members' council **Election of the members' council:** co-optation **Participation rights of members:** Proposals for decision-making by the council have to be signed by 200 members.	**Obligation to pay further capital:** no **Surplus participation:** After the annual profit is allocated to a contingency reserve or other types of provisions, the remaining profit belongs to the members. With the approval of the members' council, other types of provisions can be established or used for the next business year. **Share in the dissolution assets:** decided during the last members' assembly.
Österreichische Hagelversicherung	**Non-membership contracts:** yes Allowed outside of Austria and the insurance object has to be in a foreign country;	**Highest body:** delegates' assembly **Election of the delegates' assembly:** by members **Participation rights of members:** Proposals for decision-making by the council have to be signed by at least 100 members. The applicant has the right to send a member to the assembly for the verbally justification.	**Obligation to pay further capital:** to the amount of the total annual contribution **Surplus participation**: The reimbursement contribution has to be done in percentage of the mandatory premiums. The reimbursement is distributed proportional to the premiums resulted from the benefits of the federation and states as well as from the members mandatory premiums. **Share in the dissolution assets:** no information available.

Table 10: Regional/federal mutual insurance societies

Insurance company	equal treatment	self-government	self-responsibility
Kärntner Landesversicherung auf Gegenseitigkeit	**Non-membership contracts: yes** For re-insurance contracts and contracts with fixed premiums and when they are lower than 10 out of one hundred of the total income from fees and premiums of a year.	**Highest body:** members' council **Election of the members' council:** The council is elected by the members and via an election suggestion of the supervision board. **Participation rights of members:** Proposals for decision-making by the council have to be signed by at least 200 members. The applicant has the right to send a member to the assembly for the verbally justification.	**Obligation to pay further capital:** up to half of the annual fee if the security reserves are not sufficient to cover the debts. the amount of the total annual contribution **Surplus participation:** The remaining profit have to be used for contribution reimbursements if not used for the next business year or distributed among the members. The provisions are used for fee reimbursements or for paying/granting of members' fee discounts and is proportional to the amount of the fees. **Share in the dissolution assets:** after all debts are paid, the remaining assets are distributed among the current members proportional of their contributions during the last five business years.
RVV Rückversicherungsverein auf Gegenseitigkeit	**Non-membership contracts: no**	**Highest body:** members' council **Election of the supervision board:** by the members' council **Participation rights of members:** each member has at least one but not more than ten votes; the number of votes is based on the relation of the calculated premiums;	**Obligation to pay further capital:** no **Surplus participation**: decided by the general meeting; proportional to the premiums paid by the members; new members participate from the sixth year onwards. **Share in the dissolution assets:** after all debts are paid, the remaining assets are distributed, according to the decision of the general meeting, among the current members who were for at least 5 years members of the RVV during the last five business years.
Tiroler Versicherung Verein auf Gegenseitigkeit	**Non-membership contracts: yes** Members are policyholders with a bundle insurance or with an annual premium of at least 1,000 Euro.	**Highest body:** members' council and regional government **Election of the members' council:** co-optation **Participation rights of members:** Proposals for decision-making by the council have to be signed by at least 200 members or by 5 active members' representative. The applicant has the right to send a member to the assembly for the verbally justification	**Obligation to pay further capital:** no **Surplus participation:** Non-life: The remaining profit have to be used for contribution reimbursements. The profit distribution is taken out of the provisions (according to the decision of the general meeting). Former members do not receive profits. Life: If the remaining profit is not used for reimbursements or the next business year, it is distributed among the members. The surplus has to be paid out in cash or to offset against future fees and distributed among the members proportional of their contributions during the last five business years.

			Share in the dissolution assets: The remaining assets belong to the state Tirol, when the state takes over the obligations of the pensions and pension contributions of the employees of the TIROLER insurance company
Vorarlberger Landesversicherung Verein auf Gegenseitigkeit	**Non-membership contracts:** yes For re-insurance contracts and contracts with fixed premiums and when they are lower than 10 out of one hundred of the total income from fees and premiums of a year.	**Highest body**: members' council and regional government. **Election of the members' council:** co-optation **Participation rights of members:** Proposals for decision-making by the council have to be signed by at least 200 members. The applicant has the right to send a member to the assembly for the verbally justification	**Obligation to pay further capital:** up to half of the annual fee or lowering of the insurance services or both measures if the security reserves are not sufficient to cover the debts. The measures are based on the proposal of the management board and the supervision board and passed by the members' council. **Surplus participation:** Non-life: The remaining profit has to be used for contribution reimbursements. The profit distribution is taken out of the provisions (according to the decision of the general meeting). Former members do not receive profits. Life: After the allocation of the reserves, the amount of the provisions for the reimbursement of fee refunds and the profit participation of the members are based on the business plans. Additional provisions can be made from the remaining surplus and with approval of the supervision board. **Share in the dissolution assets:** after all debts are paid, the remaining assets are distributed among the current members, based on their contributions during the last five business years. The distribution is based on how much the life and non-life department contributed to the company's asset.

Table 11: Asset management-mutual insurance societies

Insurance	equal treatment	self-government	self-responsibility
GRAWE – Vermögensverwaltung **100% share in joint stock company**	**Non-membership contracts:** yes For re-insurance contracts and contracts with fixed premiums and when they are not more than a fifth of the total premium income.	**Highest body:** members' council **Election of the members' council:** co-optation **Participation rights of members:** Proposals for decision-making by the council have to be signed by at least 200 members or by 5 active members' representative. The applicant has the right to send a member to the assembly for the verbally justification	**Obligation to pay further capital:** no **Surplus participation**: The management board submits a proposal for the distribution of the profit to the supervision board. The supervision board's report is submitted to the members' council. The council decides the use of the remaining profit for each year. **Share in the dissolution assets:** the members' council decides during the last assembly
Merkur Wechselseitige Versicherungsanstalt Vermögensverwaltung **100% share in joint stock company**	**Non-membership contracts:** yes For re-insurance contracts and short-term contracts less than a year. In non-life and accident insurance, only insurance policies without membership are taken over and their total premiums have to be not more than a fifth of the total premium income.	**Highest body:** members' council **Election of the members' council:** co-optation **Participation rights of members:** Proposals for decision-making by the council have to be signed by at least 400 members. The applicant has the right to send a member to the assembly for the verbally justification	**Obligation to pay further capital:** no **Surplus participation:** The management board submits a proposal for the distribution of the profit to the supervision board. The supervision board's report is submitted to the members' council. The council decides the use of the remaining profit for each year. **Share in the dissolution assets:** the members' council decides during the last assembly.
Wiener Städtische Wechselseitiger Versicherungsverein – Vermögensverwaltung **70% share in joint stock company**	**Non-membership contracts:** yes For re-insurance contracts and short-term contracts less than a year. Other non-membership activities are also possible;	**Highest body:** members' council **Election of the members' council:** co-optation **Participation rights of members:** Proposals for decision-making by the council have to be signed by at least 2% of the members. The applicant has the right to send a member to the assembly for the verbally justification	**Obligation to pay further capital:** no **Surplus participation:** The reaming annual profit belongs to the members (after creating reserves as well as voluntary and legal provisions). The members' council decides about its use. **Share in the dissolution assets:** no information available.
Oberösterreichische Wechselseitige Versicherung Vermögensverwaltung	**Non-membership contracts:** yes For re-insurance contracts and	**Highest body:** members' council **Election of the members' council:** co-optation	**Obligation to pay further capital:** no **Surplus participation:** The management board submits a proposal for the

90.04% share in joint stock company	short-term contracts less than a year, when the direct premiums are not more than a fifth of the total direct premium income.	**Participation rights of members:** Proposals for decision-making by the council have to be signed by at least 200 members. The applicant has the right to send a member to the assembly for the verbally justification	distribution of the profit to the supervision board. The supervision board's report is submitted to the members' council. **Share in the dissolution assets**: no information available.

Table 12: Private foundations

Insurance	equal treatment	self-government	self-responsibility
UNIQA Versicherungsverein Privatstiftung (former Austria Versicherungsverein auf Gegenseitigkeit) **30.6% share in joint stock company**	**Contracts without beneficiary position[103]:** yes, in case of ... co- and re-insurance contracts, ...short-term contracts less than a year ...risks are in foreign countries, ...contracts concerning demise ... equity-linked and index-linked life insurance ... other insurance contracts when the premiums from the domestic business are not higher than a tenth of the domestic premium income	**Bodies**: board of trustees, supervision board, and auditor for the private foundation; An advisory council, appointed by the supervision board, functions as advisory board. **Election of the supervision board:** co-optation **Participation rights of the beneficiaries:** Submitting a proposal to the management board, which has to be signed by at least 3% of the beneficiaries. The proposal is not binding. If the member recommended by the beneficiaries is not part of the supervision board, the members of the management board need a two-third majority to reject the proposal.	**Obligation to pay further capital:** no **Surplus participation**: The remaining annual profit (after reserves and provisions have been made) has to be distributed among the beneficiaries if not used for new payments. **Share in the dissolution assets**: The remaining assets have to distributed to the ultimate beneficiaries in accordance with the winding up plan, approved by the board of trustees and the Financial Market Authority (FMA). Ultimate beneficiaries are people who were beneficiaries during the dissolution. The remaining assets (after the winding up) have to be distributed among the beneficiaries in accordance with the principles stated by the board of trustees and approved by the supervision board.

1 Beneficiaries are policyholders of the UNIQA Versicherungen AG. Before the conversion of the Austria Versicherungsverein auf Gegenseitigkeit into a private foundation, memberships of the society were converted into a beneficiary position and expired with the termination of the insurance relationship.

Collegialität Versicherungsverein Privatstiftung **2.4% share in joint stock company**	**Contracts without beneficiary position**[102]**:** yes, in case of ... co- and re-insurance contracts, ...short-term contracts less than a year ...risks are in foreign countries, ...contracts concerning demise ... equity-linked and index-linked life insurance ... other insurance contracts when the premiums from the domestic business are not higher than a tenth of the domestic premium income;	**Bodies**: board of trustees, supervision board, and auditor for the private foundation **Election of the supervision board:** co-optation; **Participation rights of the beneficiaries:** Submitting a proposal to the management board, which has to be signed by at least 3% of the beneficiaries. The proposal is not binding. If the member recommended by the beneficiaries is not part of the supervision board, the members of the management board need a two-third majority to reject the proposal.	**Obligation to pay further capital:** no **Surplus participation:** The remaining annual profit (after reserves and provisions have been made) has to be distributed among the beneficiaries if not used for new payments. **Share in the dissolution assets:** The remaining assets have to distributed to the beneficiaries in accordance with the winding up plan, approved by the board of trustees and the Financial Market Authority (FMA).

8. Conclusion

The anchoring of the mutuality principle in today's large mutual insurance societies is hard to recognise, because regular mutual insurance societies as well as hybrid forms do not advertise the mutuality principle and, as a result, the difference between an insurance joint stock company and a mutual insurance society is not identifiable for the customer. Mutual insurance societies have adjusted themselves to joint stock companies on the operative level, in particular since the adjustable contribution procedure was superseded by the fixed premium system and similar legal regulations have been applicable to both legal types. The main characteristic for mutual insurance societies is that they are regionally limited[103], specialised in professions[104], and have chosen this particular legal form due to legal and formal reasons.[105]

The analysis of the current bylaws of regular mutual insurance societies, asset management societies, and private foundations shows that the participation rights of members are annulled due to the use of co-optation when electing the members' representatives (with the exception of two mutual insurance societies[106]). The only possibility of members to participate is to submit a draft resolution to the members' council, which has to be signed by 200 to 400 members of the mutual insurance society. Thus self-government is limited to a small group of people and is used as a power-political instrument, in particular by the holding constructions of asset management societies, an Austrian innovation, and private foundations.

---

[103] *Kärntner Landesversicherung auf Gegenseitigkeit*, *Tiroler Versicherung Verein auf Gegenseitigkeit*, *Vorarlberger Landesversicherung Verein auf Gegenseitigkeit*.

[104] *Österreichische Beamtenversicherung VVaG*, Österreichische Hagelversicherung VVaG.

[105] The *Muki Versicherungsverein auf Gegenseitigkeit* was established as a mutual insurance society in 2004 due to the FMA's intervention. The former non-profit society "mother and child in hospital" had reached a size that was not applicable to the Act regulating clubs and associations. To receive the licence for insurance companies the MuKi chose the legal form of a mutual insurance society, because the structure is similar to a non-profit society. (cf. https://www.muki.com/service/allgemeines/%C3%BCber-uns/geschichte.html (26.06.2018). The RRV Rückversicherungsverein auf Gegenseitigkeit was, before January 1st, 2016, a small mutual insurance society and offered only re-insurance transactions for small mutual insurance societies. With the regulations of Solvency II (EU Richtlinie 2009/138/EG) coming into effect in Austria, the RVV had to convert into a regular mutual insurance society, because sole re-insurance companies could not be small mutual insurance societies anymore.

[106] *Österreichische Hagelversicherung*, *Rückversicherungsverein auf Gegenseitigkeit*, *Kärntner Landesversicherung auf Gegenseitigkeit*.

The several stages of Austrian mutual insurance societies to turn away from the mutuality principle comprise the possibility to convert into a joint stock company (1978), the universal succession (1991), and the conversion of a mutual asset management society into a private foundation. The liberalization of the capital markets influenced the Austrian legislator to focus more on capital orientated joint stock companies and emphasized demutualization, at least regarding the operative insurance business, of Austrian insurance societies as the best way to be successful on the market. The insurance companies, however, wanted to keep their structure and worked out a plan in charge of the former chairperson of the *Austria Versicherungsverein auf Gegenseitigkeit*. The mutual insurance societies continue as the owners of the transferred joint stock company in form of an asset management society and eventually of the private foundation. The mutual insurance society and the co-opted members' council become the highest bodies and, as a result, secure as part or majority owners the influence on the joint stock company. The amendment to the Insurance Supervision Act in 1991 was presented internationally as a success story of mutual insurance societies and as a positive development of the mutuality principle in the Austrian insurance companies.[107] However, the historical development of mutuality shows that this principle was used in particular to preserve power and the wealth of former Austrian mutual societies.

Before the introduction of the universal succession, it was argued that transferring the operative business into a joint stock company would impede business expansion viz merger and cooperation with companies of other legal forms. Another argument was the difficulties to increase the equity capital of mutual insurance societies compared to joint stock companies. The latter cannot be verified empirically, because the operative joint stock companies are completely or in majority part of the mutual asset management societies or of private foundations, which are former mutual insurance societies. The current figures of the solvability quota show that mutual insurance societies have a stable capital basis and hybrid forms have quota and capital reserves above average. This situation results from the high capital reserves of the asset management societies and private foundations.

[107] *Schimetschek, H.*, Erfahrungen mit der neuen VVaG-Gesetzgebung in Österreich, in: Versicherungswirtschaft, Heft 11, 1993, p. 701.

Bibliography

Baran, P., Österreichisches Versicherungsaufsichtsrecht, 2. Auflage, Manz, Wien, 2014.

Baran, P., Die Fortführung des Betriebes von Versicherungsvereinen durch Aktiengesellschaften, in: Versicherungsrundschau, 1992.

Bartl, K., §§ 35-67 VAG 2016, in: *Korinek, S./Saria, G./Saria, S.* (eds.): Versicherungsgesetz VAG, Wien 2016.

Baumgartner, I., 175 Jahre Grazer Wechselseitige, Festschrift anlässlich des 175-jährigen Jubiläums der Grazer Wechselseitigen Versicherung, Graz, 2003.

Der Finanz Compass Österreich 1992/1993, Compass-Verlag.

Der Finanz-Compass Österreich 1983/84, 112. Jahrgang, Compass-Verlag.

Der Grawe-Krimi, in: Format, 1-2, 2015.

Eckert, F., Die Einbringung von Versicherungsbetrieben aus Versicherungsvereinen auf Gegenseitigkeit in Versicherungs-Aktiengesellschaften gem. §§ 61 a bis 61 c österr. VAG – Beitrag zur Erhaltung oder friedliches Ende der Versicherungsvereine auf Gegenseitigkeit? in: Zeitschrift für Versicherungsrecht, 1993.

Gassner, W., Die Ausstattung der Versicherungsunternehmen mit Zusatzkapital gemäß VAG Novelle, in: Versicherungsrundschau, 41. Jahrgang, Dezember 1986, Nr. 12.

Gassner-Möstl, E.; *Kuskardy, I.*, Kennzahlen eines Dezenniums der österreichischen Versicherungswirtschaft 1988-1997, in: Die Versicherungsrundschau, 1999.

Graber, R, Schauder A., Akte Hypo Alpe Adria. Von der Geldmaschine zum Milliardengrab. Verantwortliche, Profiteure, Hintergründe, 2nd edition, Wien, 2015.

Hauser, P., Das Governance-System als Beitrag zur Sicherheit der Versicherungsnehmer und Anspruchsberechtigten. Nach über 20 Jahren der Entwicklung erfolgt die Umsetzung von Solvency II in österreichisches Recht. Eine kritische Betrachtung der fast unendlichen und hoffentlich trotzdem erfolgreichen Geschichte, in: *Rohrbach, W.* (ed.), Versicherungsgeschichte Österreichs, Band XII – Liegst dem erteil du inmitten einem starken Herzen gleich, Beograd – Wien, 2015.

Hauser, P., Die Tendenzen zur Konzentration, Ausgliederung und Auslagerung sowie Internationalisierung in der österreichischen Versicherungswirtschaft und ihre Auswirkungen auf die Interne Revision, in: *Rohrbach, W.* (eds); An der Schwelle zum 3. Jahrtausend – Retrospektiven und Perspektiven, Wien, 2000.

Mayer, L.: Die Demutualisierung von Versicherungsvereinen auf Gegenseitigkeit (VVaG) in Österreich, in: *Geib, G.* (ed.): Rechnungslegung von Versicherungsunternehmen, Düsseldorf, 2001.

Mutual insurance in the 21st century: back to the future? In: Sigma No.4/2016, SwissRe, Zürich.

Nemson, J.: Geschäftsmodell VVaG: Rahmenbedingungen, Herausforderungen und Chancen, Karlsruhe 2014.

Schimetschek, H., Erfahrungen mit der neuen VVaG-Gesetzgebung in Österreich, in: Versicherungswirtschaft, 48. Jg, Heft 11, 1993.

Schimetschek, H., Weiser, H.; Versicherungsverein auf Gegenseitigkeit in Europa: Zukunftsentwicklungen – Österreichisches Modell, in: *Peiner, W.* (ed.), Grundlagen des Versicherungsvereins auf Gegenseitigkeit. Verfasst anlässlich des 175jährigen Bestehens der Gothaer Versicherungsbank VVaG, Köln, 1995.

Schira, H., Die Geschichte der Salzburger Landes-Versicherung, in: 175 Jahre Salzburger Landesversicherung Eine Dokumentation anläßlich des 175-jährigen Bestehens, 1986: Salzburger Landesversicherung AG.

Url, Th., Lebensversicherung leidet weiterhin unter niedrigem Zinsniveau, in: WIFO Monatsberichte 9/2013.

Versicherung auf Gegenseitigkeit im 21. Jahrhundert: Zurück in die Zukunft?, In: Sigma Nr.4/2016, Swiss Re.

Versicherungsvereine bzw. Versicherungsgenossenschaften: Leben Totgesagte länger? In: Sigma Nr.4/1999, Swiss Re, Zürich.

The changing role of mutuals in the American insurance industry

Johann Brazda[1]

1. Introduction

The USA is the largest insurance market in the world due to its size, capacity and impact – accounting for some 38.46 percent of total global insurance premiums comprising life and non-life insurances. USA as the market leader is followed by China (9.48 percent) and Japan (7.39 percent) on the second respectively third rank, while the United Kingdom, as a European country, with 4.96 percent is on the fourth place. Only Germany's and Italy's shares in the global insurance market regarding premiums are with 3.90 respectively 2.72 percent similar to that of the United Kingdom. However, none of these countries comes even close to the 38.46 percent of the USA.[2] The premiums of life/health insurers account for 51.6 percent, while non-life insurers' premiums (property/casualty insurers[3]) account for 48.4 percent (see figure 1).

2. Economic and financial data

The insurance industry in the USA is a constantly growing industry with premiums raised from $1.677 billion in 2008 to $2.321 billion in 2017.

---

[1] This study is based on the master thesis *Gillardin, M.*: Mutuals in the United States in the insurance sector, Vienna 2018 and the master thesis *Kadric, N*: Comparison of demutualization in international context, Vienna 2018.

[2] NAIC Financial Data Repository. Revised Date 8/77.

[3] The property/casualty insurance primarily consists of car, home and commercial insurance, compared to the life/health insurance part, which consists of annuities and life insurance for the most part.

Figure 1: Property/casualty and life/health insurance premiums in 2017 in US $ billions)[4]

Source: NAIC data, sourced from S&P Global Market Intelligence, Insurance Information Institute.

Figure 2: Total US premiums all types of insurance ($ billions)[5]

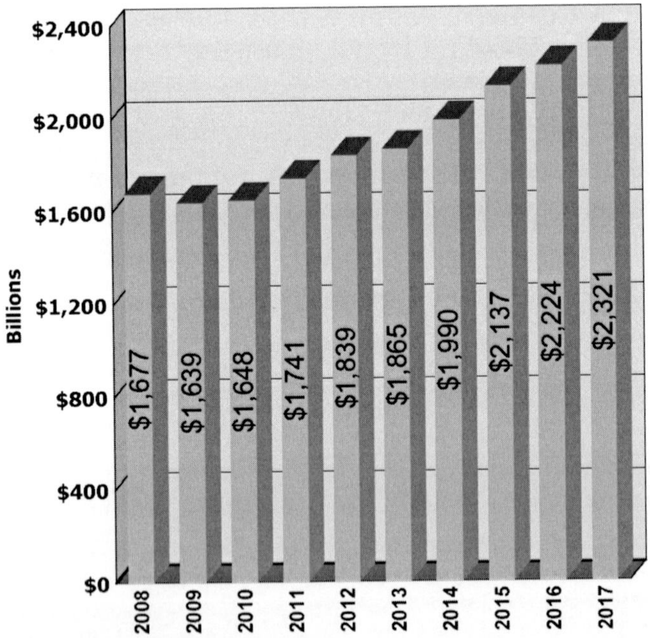

Source: https://www.naic.org/state_report_cards/report_card_wa.pdf accessed on 02.11.2018.

4 Property/casualty: net premiums after reinsurance transactions, excludes state funds; life/health: premiums, annuity considerations (fees for annuity contracts) and deposit-type funds.

5 Premiums from property, life, fraternal, health and title annual statements plus state funds for property and health.

Insurance carriers and related activities contributed $602.7 billion, or 3.1 percent, to the nation's gross domestic product (GDP) in 2017 and in 2016, they contributed roughly 41.7 percent to the US GDP of all the financial institutions.

Figure 3: US gross domestic product shares of financial institutions by component, 2016

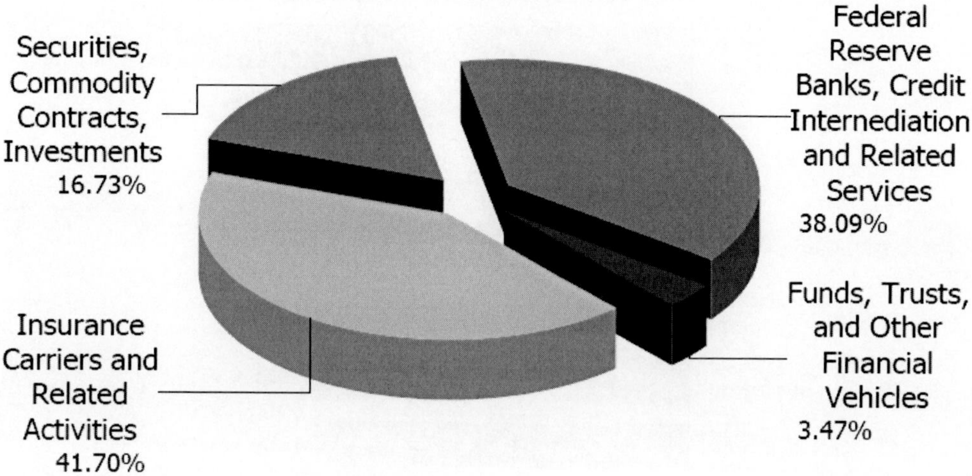

Source: https://www.naic.org/state_report_cards/report_card_wa.pdf accessed on 02.11.2018.

More than half of the 100 largest publicly traded insurance companies in the world are traded on US exchanges and insurance operations from the US generated over 44.6 percent of the worldwide total, which matches the combined market shares in excess of the next five largest countries combined. In 2016, four of the top fifteen global insurance brokerage firms were US companies.

Figure 4: Worldwide largest insurance companies according to the balance sheet total in 2016 (in billion US-Dollars)

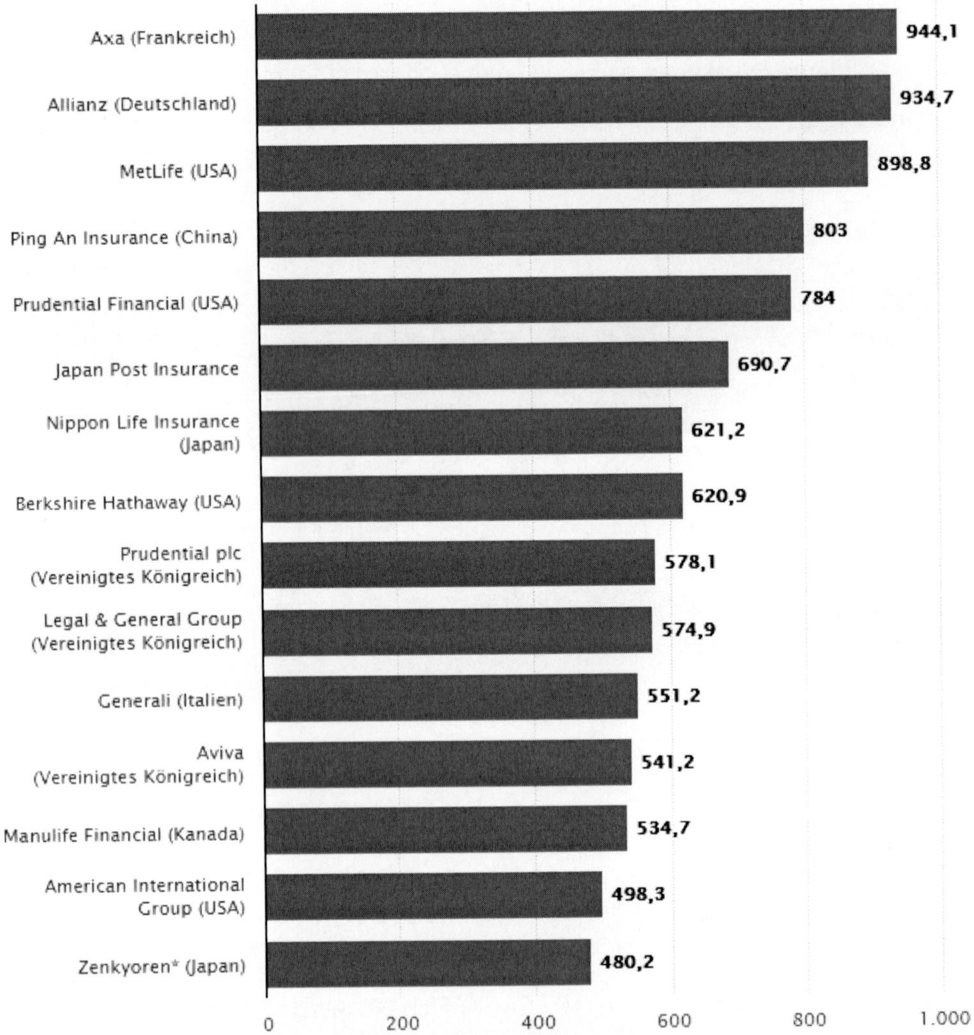

Source: Gesamtverband der Deutschen Versicherungswirtschaft e. V. (ed.): Statistisches Taschenbuch der Versicherungswirtschaft 2018, Berlin 2018, p. 125.

According to the National Association of Insurance Commissioners (NAIC) in 2017, 5,954 domestic insurance companies[6] existed, which includes property/casualty (2,509), life/annuities (852), health (907),

[6] An insurance company resident in the state in which the business is done.

fraternal[7] (82), title[8] (58), risk retention groups[9] (240) and other companies (1,306). All US insurers are subject to regulations in their state of domicile and in the other states where they are licensed to sell insurance. State legislatures are the public policymakers that establish broad policy for the regulation of insurance by enacting legislation providing the regulatory framework under which insurance regulators operate. Each state has its own set of statutes and rules. State insurance departments oversee insurer solvency, review market conduct, rule on requests for rate increases for coverage, among other things.[10]

Additionally, 73,550 licensed foreign insurers[11] were on the market. In 2017, a total of 9.03 million people and entities were licensed and must comply with various state laws and regulations governing their activities to provide insurance services. State insurance departments oversee producer activities in order to protect insurance consumer interests, especially in light of the changes taking place in the financial services marketplace. When insurance producers operate in multiple jurisdictions, states must coordinate their efforts to track producers and prevent violations.

The insurance sector is also a significant source of employment. However, over the last ten years, the insurance industry, as many other industries had to deal with cutbacks and dismissals during the years and the aftermath of the financial crisis. After 2011, however, the insurance industry has seen a rapid and constant growth in employment. In 2018, insurers alone provided employment for almost 2.7 million employees. Of those, 1.5 million worked for insurance companies, including life/health insurers (870,600 employees), property/casualty insurers (621,800 employees) and reinsurers (29,100 employees). The

7 Fraternal benefit societies are non-profit mutual aid organizations that (1) have a fraternal purpose, (2) operate under a lodge system, and (3) insure members and their families against death, disease, disability.

8 Title insurance protects real estate owners and lenders against any property loss or damage they might experience because of liens, encumbrances or defects in the title to the property. Each title insurance policy is subject to specific terms, conditions and exclusions.

9 Liability insurance companies are owned by their policyholders. Membership is limited to people in the same business or activity, which exposes them to similar liability risks. The purpose is to assume and spread liability exposure to group members and to provide an alternative risk financing mechanism for liability. These entities are formed under the Liability Risk Retention Act of 1986.

10 Cf. https://www.iii.org/publications/insurance-handbook/introduction/insurance-industry-at-a-glance accessed on 13.02.2017.

11 Insurance companies that reside in another state in which the company is doing business.

remaining 1.2 million people worked for insurance agencies, brokers and other insurance-related enterprises.[12]

Table 1: US financial sector employment

Insurance Industry Employment in the United States

	Number employed			Average annual percent change	
	2007	2016	2017	2007/2017	2016/2017
Home-office personnel					
Life insurance	352,800	347,800	348,300	-0.1	0.1
Health insurance	434,400	471,100	499,300	1.4	6.0
Other	674,000	668,800	672,300	0.0	0.5
Total	1,461,200	1,487,700	1,519,900	0.4	2.2
Agents, brokers, and service personnel	930,500	1,105,000	1,135,700	2.0	2.8
Aggregate total	2,391,700	2,592,700	2,655,600	1.1	2.4

Source: U.S. Department of Labor, Bureau of Labor Statistics, Current Employment Statistics survey (National).
Note: The Bureau of Labor Statistics adjusts annual employment data in April of the year following its survey.

Source: https://www.naic.org/state_report_cards/report_card_wa.pdf accessed on 02.11.2018.

Property/casualty insurers paid out $101.9 billion in property losses related to catastrophes in 2017, the peak since Property Claims Services (PCS) division of Verisk Analytics began collecting insured loss data in 1949. The $101.9 billion in losses in 2017 was 370 percent higher than $21.7 billion in 2016. There were 46 catastrophes in 2017, compared to 42 in 2016.[13]

3. Legal forms

In the US, insurance companies can take on several legal forms; the three major organization forms are mutuals, joint stock companies, and reciprocals[14]. Material differences exist in their financial situations, balance sheets, ability to raise money and need to disperse profits. While there is no theoretical reason that insurers cannot be owned by an

12 Cf. https://www.iii.org/publications/insurance-handbook/introduction/insurance-industry-at-a-glance accessed on 13.02.2017.

13 Cf. Ibid.

14 Currently, reciprocals only represent a small proportion of companies and operate similarly to mutuals, therefore normally they are combined with mutuals.

individual or partnership, insurance operations require a certain level of stability and financial strength. Perhaps, as a result, US insurers prefer the legal form of a corporation, although both the stocks as well as the mutual are the two prominent organizational forms. Other less common forms are the life/health insurers Lloyd's and fraternal benefit societies. Fraternal organizations, for example, account for only about one percent of the US life/health insurance market. In the property/casualty sector, there are reciprocals[15], and a small proportion of companies take the organizational forms of Lloyd's of London, risk retention group, captive or state insurance funds.

- A mutual company is a private firm formed exclusively for the benefit of the policyholders (or members[16]), and some of them have for years marketed policies on the assertion that the prospective policyholder would become an owner – and sometimes governor – of the company instead of being owned by public or private shareholders. However, this opinion changed during the 1990s. The members have all the same advantages as policyholders of non-mutual insurance companies in the form of policy rights (depending on coverage clauses), protections afforded by state regulation, and access to state guaranty funds in the event of insolvency. Because property/casualty insurance is regulated at the state level in the USA, the regulations that apply to mutual companies respecting members, boards of directors, and by-laws of the company vary from state to state. Additionally directors of mutual insurance companies are generally permitted to develop governance practices appropriate to the regulatory requirements of the states in which they are operating, consistent with their company charter and by-laws, their business environment, and their member needs.[17] Therefore, variations in corporate governance practices exist within the US mutual insurance industry, but are within the parameters established by applicable regulatory requirements.[18]
  Increasing equity capital for mutual companies tends to happen in form

[15] Currently, reciprocals only represent a small proportion of companies and operate similarly to mutuals, therefore normally they are combined with mutuals.

[16] Although the term "membership" more accurately describes the legal and contractual relationship between a mutual insurance company and its policyholders, it is often referred to as the policyholder's "ownership" interest in a mutual insurance company (Cf. https://www.namic.org/policy/futureMutualPolicyRights accessed on 04.11.2019).

[17] There are specific requirements on the form of the proxy, quorum requirements, voting rights, members' right of access to membership lists, members' right to notice of all meetings, how membership meetings are conducted, and qualifications of directors (Cf. https://www.namic.org/policy/futureMutualPolicyRights accessed on 04.11.2019).

[18] Cf.https://www.insuranceandestates.com/mutual-insurance-company-vs-stock-insurance-company/ accessed on 04.11.2019.

of retaining net earnings, because mutual companies do not have common stocks. Because they are not publicly traded, it is more difficult for policyholders to determine how financially solvent a mutual insurance company is, or how it calculates dividends[19] it sends back to its members, also they need to find other ways to raise equity capital. Dividend payments can be used for cash, premium payments, paid up additions[20], earn interest with the insurance company or repay existing loans. Demutualization can occur when a mutual company needs to raise cash for business growth or cover higher than expected claims. Mutual companies may also merge, whereby the resulting entity is typically better off financially because of its expanded market share position.

- Many insurance organizations are formed as joint stock companies, with their respective initial public offering at the stock market and their stockholders and shareholders financing the everyday operations as well as the long-term plans of the company. In joint stock companies, stockholders do not own the company legally they are only customers. The shared ownership gives them a voice in electing a board of directors that oversees company management. Because ownership is vested in stockholders, the stock companies' policyholders have no voting rights regarding board members. In addition to selling shares, stock companies also add capital through operating income, including money earned from assets backing reserve funds. This organizational form is probably the most common and most well-known company form. Note that stock companies may be publicly traded or private. Their biggest advantage is easier access to capital to pay claims or fund business growth among other business purposes. Raising capital is of course much easier for a joint stock company due to the financing of external shareholders, who can buy shares and invest into the company. However, in contrast to mutuals they have no membership status.
- Another possible form of organization for the insurance field is the reciprocal. Although this form seems to be similar to mutuals, due to the customer/policy and owner relationship, there are, however, differences. While mutuals have to have incorporated capital, reciprocals do not. In a reciprocal, one person is selected by the policyholders to lead and direct the company. In a mutual company, however, the policyholders elect a board of directors, which controls the management. A reciprocal is an unincorporated group of individuals, firms or corporations, commonly termed

19 The policyholders may also have the right to participate in the distribution of the company's surplus, but only if permitted by state statute and only if the board of directors and the policyholders approve either a decision to convert to stock ownership form or the company is liquidated. The right to participate in the surplus of the company is conditional, transitory and not guaranteed. No member has a right to "cash out" his individual membership interest (Cf. https://www.namic.org/policy/futureMutualPolicyRights accessed on 04.11.2019).

20 Paid up additions are exclusive to a certain type of dividend paying whole life insurance, also known as participating whole life insurance.

subscribers, who mutually insure one another, each separately assuming his or her share of each risk. Its chief administrator is an attorney-in-fact.[21]

- A captive is an insurance company created and wholly owned by one or more non-insurance companies to insure the risks of its owner (or owners). Captives are a form of self-insurance whereby the insurer is owned wholly by the insured. They are typically established to meet the risk management needs of the owners or members. Captives are formed to cover a wide range of risks; practically every risk underwritten by a commercial insurer can be provided by a captive. The type of entity forming a captive varies from a major multinational corporation — the vast majority of Fortune 500 companies have captive subsidiaries — to a non-profit organization. Once established the captive operates like any commercial insurance company and is subject to state regulatory requirements including reporting, capital and reserve requirements.
- Finally, Lloyds Associations, in which the members are personally liable for their share of risks, constitute another possible form of organization. Since the insurers are the individual underwriters, the manager party and owner party are merged, which obviously allows potential conflicts to be controlled by them. However, potential opportunistic behaviour towards policyholders cannot be excluded, which may result in potential higher costs. [22]

4. Property/casualty insurers

Property insurance includes both pure property coverage such as fire insurance, car physical damage, ocean marine, inland marine, and the property components of multiple peril coverage such as homeowners multiple peril, farm owners multiple peril, commercial multiple peril, and allied lines such as multiple peril crop and federal flood insurance. Casualty insurance includes in particular private passenger car liability, commercial car liability, medical malpractice, product liability, and other forms of liability. Another important property/casualty insurance product in the USA is workers' compensation insurance, which differs from property coverage and liability coverage because it is primarily a no-fault insurance.

[21] Cf. *Mayers, D., Smith, C. W.*, On the choice of organizational form: theory and evidence from the insurance industry, in: *Dionne, G.* (ed.), Handbook of Insurance, second edition. New York 2013, p. 673.

[22] Ibid., p. 674.

Table 2: Top 10 writers of property/casualty insurance by direct premiums in 2017

Rank	Group/company	Direct premiums written (1)	Market share (2)
1	State Farm Mutual Automobile Insurance	$64,892,583	10.1%
2	Berkshire Hathaway Inc.	38,408,251	6.0
3	Liberty Mutual	33,831,726	5.3
4	Allstate Corp.	31,501,664	4.9
5	Progressive Corp.	27,862,882	4.3
6	Travelers Companies Inc.	24,875,076	3.9
7	Chubb Ltd.	21,266,737	3.3
8	USAA Insurance Group	20,151,368	3.1
9	Farmers Insurance Group of Companies (3)	19,855,517	3.1
10	Nationwide Mutual Group	19,218,907	3.0

(1) Before reinsurance transactions, includes state funds.
(2) Based on U.S. total, includes territories.
(3) Data for Farmers Insurance Group of Companies and Zurich Financial Group (which owns Farmers' management company) are reported
Market Intelligence.

Source: https://www.iii.org/fact-statistic/facts-statistics-industry-overview accessed on 02.11.2018.

As for the ranking concerning property/casualty insurance, the "State Farm Mutual Automobile Insurance" is the clear leader with a market share of 10.1 percent followed by the "Berkshire Hathaway Inc." with 6.0 percent, and "Liberty Mutual" with a market share of 5.3 percent. At the eighth place is "USAA Insurance Group", a reciprocal form with 3.1 percent and at the tenth the "Nationwide Mutual Group" with a market share of 3.0 percent.

The property/casualty insurers saw their net income after taxes rise to $60 billion in 2018 from $36.1 billion in 2017, a 66.3 percent increase, helped by double-digit premium growth and a significant decline in catastrophe losses.[23]

23 Cf. http://www.pciaa.net/pciwebsite/Cms/Content/ViewList?cat1Id=9998&stateCode=FED accessed on 13.02.2017.

5. Life/health insurers

The primary purpose of the US life/health insurance industry is to provide a range of different types of insurance contracts that can protect individuals, families, and, to a much lesser extent, corporations against the adverse financial effects of unanticipated mortality and/or morbidity events. The standard insurance lines of life- and health-contingent insurance business for US insurers are as follows: industrial life, individual life, individual annuities, credit life, group life, group annuities, and accident & health. Group insurance coverage is typically obtained by employer-provided benefit plans, while individual (non-group) coverage is not. Credit life is typically sold to protect creditors from losses in the event of borrowers' deaths. Industrial life insurance has been offered historically to low income families and involved weekly or bi-weekly direct collections by insurance company representatives at the residence of the policyholders. This form of life insurance has declined steeply over time as it has been largely replaced by group insurances offered to workers via their employers' benefit plans. Accident and health insurance refer to insurances that pay the additional expenses and lost income associated with impaired health or other losses of capacity to work.

All the various insurance products mentioned above can be divided into four main groups: life insurance, annuities, health insurance and deposit-type contracts. These groups differ significantly regarding the time of disbursements defined by the insurance contracts and, therefore, in the liabilities associated with those payments. For example, life insurance often involves premium build-ups that occur over long periods, while payments are associated with a single event (death). Annuities may or may not involve long build-up periods, but on the other hand, generally do involve long pay-out periods. Health insurance operates for the most part on a year-to-year basis and similar to property/casualty insurance. Deposit-type contracts do not involve mortality or morbidity risks, but may differ in terms of the duration of the disbursements depending on the type of contract.

While insurance companies in the life/health sector often write all four types of business, they tend to differ in the proportion of their businesses associated with each type. As a result and because differences in the nature of contract liabilities have a large impact on the reserves and surplus requirements required by statute, it is difficult to analyse all life/health insurers similarly.

The life insurance industry is integral to the economies of all 50 states and the District of Columbia. Just like the Chinese, Japanese and European markets, life insurance dominated the American market with 52 percent of the total premiums by the end of 2017. Still in the

USA, the life share that was set at 49 percent in 2000 had grown to 57 percent in 2007 before starting a downfall to 52 percent in 2017. At the end of 2017, 781 life insurance companies were in business in the USA with sales and operations across the country. Many of these companies are stand-alone entities, with no life insurer affiliate or subsidiary operating in the USA. Others are organized into groups or fleets of affiliates and subsidiaries. However, the peak of active companies was in 1988, and has fallen since then steadily, mostly due to companies' mergers and consolidations. To increase efficiency, many companies reorganised their structures by reducing operating cost and general overhead. (see table 3).[24]

Most life insurers are organized as joint stock companies or mutuals. While the majority of life insurers are joint stock companies, i.e. 584 respectively 75 percent of the insurance industry, 14 percent are mutuals. Many life insurers are affiliated with other life or non-life insurance companies in groups with a single owner. Besides mergers, two major trends can be recognized in the life insurance industry: demutualization and the formation of mutual holding companies. The latter is a structure that allows easier and less expensive access to capital. To create such a mutual holding company, the mutual insurer has to establish or acquire a joint stock insurance company. It is important to note that, with regard to data, mutual holding companies are included in the totals of pure mutual companies (see table 4).

Joint stock and mutual life insurers together provide most of the insurances and pensions underwritten by US companies. In 2017, mutual insurance companies had \$6.7 trillion (33 percent) of life insurance in force, while joint stock life insurers had even \$13.2 trillion (65 percent). The remaining 2 percent of the US insurance industry is underwritten by fraternal societies and other type companies. In 2017, there were 76 fraternal life insurance companies with \$346 billion of life insurance (2 percent). Additionally, in 2017, 13.7 percent of the life insurers were foreign-owned insurance companies operating in the USA (see table 5).[25]

---

24 Cf. American Council of Life Insurers (ed.): Life Insurers Fact Book 2018, Washington 2018, p. 1.

25 Canada controlled 27 companies; Japan 15; Bermuda 15; Switzerland 14; Cayman Islands 11; France 8; the United Kingdom 5; Germany 5; the Netherlands 4; Spain 2; and Panama. (Cf. Ibid.).

Table 3: USA Life Insurers Organizational Structure

U.S. Life Insurers Organizational Structure, by Year

Year	Stock	Mutual	Fraternals	Other	Total
	In business at year's end				
1950	507	142	NA	NA	649
1955	942	165	NA	NA	1,107
1960	1,286	155	NA	NA	1,441
1965	1,475	154	NA	NA	1,629
1970	1,627	153	NA	NA	1,780
1975	1,603	143	NA	NA	1,746
1980	1,823	135	NA	NA	1,958
1981	1,855	136	NA	NA	1,991
1982	1,926	134	NA	NA	2,060
1983	1,985	132	NA	NA	2,117
1984	2,062	131	NA	NA	2,193
1985	2,133	128	NA	NA	2,261
1986	2,128	126	NA	NA	2,254
1987	2,212	125	NA	NA	2,337
1988	2,225	118	NA	NA	2,343
1989	2,153	117	NA	NA	2,270
1990	2,078	117	NA	NA	2,195
1991	1,947	117	NA	NA	2,064
1992	1,835	109	NA	NA	1,944
1993	1,736	108	NA	NA	1,844
1994	1,565	115	NA	10	1,690
1995*	1,356	259	NA	35	1,650
1996*	1,331	240	NA	36	1,607
1997*	1,193	238	NA	45	1,476
1998*	1,167	248	NA	29	1,444
1999*	1,064	250	NA	33	1,347
2000*	1,018	221	NA	30	1,269
2001*	986	222	117	16	1,341
2002*	956	204	114	10	1,284
2003*	931	180	105	11	1,227
2004*	901	161	108	9	1,179
2005*	857	151	102	9	1,119
2006*	818	142	103	9	1,072
2007*	768	133	99	9	1,009
2008*	741	132	95	8	976
2009*	714	131	93	8	946
2010*	700	121	89	7	917
2011*	687	117	85	6	895
2012*	660	120	82	6	868
2013*	648	113	82	7	850
2014*	636	106	81	7	830
2015*	616	110	81	7	814
2016*	598	113	78	8	797
2017*	584	112	76	9	781

Source: ACLI tabulations of National Association of Insurance Commissioners (NAIC) data, used by permission.

Notes: NAIC does not endorse any analysis or conclusions based on use of its data. After 1993, data include life insurance companies that sell accident and health insurance.

NA: Not available

*Beginning with 1995 data, stock companies that are part of fleets headed by non-stock companies are counted by the parent's ownership type, not as stock companies.

Source: American Council of Life Insurers (ed.): Life Insurers Fact Book 2018, Washington 2018, p. 5.

Table 4: Number of USA Life Insurers, by Organizational Structure

Number of U.S. Life Insurers, by Organizational Structure

	In business at year's end		Average annual percent change
	2016	2017	2016/2017
Stock	598	584	-2.3
Mutual[1]	113	112	-0.9
Fraternal[2]	78	76	-2.6
Other[3]	8	9	12.5
Total	797	781	-2.0

Source: ACLI tabulations of National Association of Insurance Commissioners (NAIC) data, used by permission.
Note: NAIC does not endorse any analysis or conclusions based on use of its data.
[1]Includes stock companies owned by mutual parents (life & PC) and mutual holding companies.
[2]Includes stock companies owned by fraternal benefit societies.
[3]Includes farm bureau, reciprocal, and risk retention groups.

Source: American Council of Life Insurers (ed.): Life Insurers Fact Book 2018, Washington 2018, p. 2.

Table 5: Size of US Life Insurers, by Organizational Structure

Size of U.S. Life Insurers, by Organizational Structure, 2017 (millions)

	Stock	Mutual[1]	Fraternal	Other[2]	Total
Life insurance in force	$13,236,248	$6,653,159	$346,277	$180,008	$20,415,692
Life insurance purchased	1,989,990	1,024,533	38,051	24,925	3,077,499
Assets	5,299,433	1,683,328	171,862	28,749	7,183,372
Benefit payments[3]	479,014	135,048	10,164	1,757	625,982
Premium income[4]	443,044	151,942	10,274	1,892	607,152

Source: ACLI tabulations of National Association of Insurance Commissioners (NAIC) data, used by permission.
Note: NAIC does not endorse any analysis or conclusions based on use of its data.
[1]Includes stock companies owned by mutual holding companies.
[2]Includes farm bureau, reciprocal, and risk retention groups.
[3]Includes payments to beneficiaries, surrender values, policy dividends, annuity payments, matured endowments, and other payments.
[4]Includes life insurance premiums, annuity considerations, and accident and health premiums.

Source: American Council of Life Insurers (ed.): Life Insurers Fact Book 2018, Washington 2018, p. 3.

Table 6 shows the rankings of the 25 largest life insurance groups (stand-alone companies are counted as a group of one) based on premiums.

The life insurer segment gives a different impression, because except "Berkshire Hathaway Inc.", no other insurance companies that dominate the property/casualty sector can be found among the top life

Table 6: The 25 largest life insurance groups, 2017 ($000)

Largest Life Insurers, by Total Net Life Insurance Premiums, 2017 (thousands)	
Northwestern Mutual	$13,425,558
Prudential Financial	12,963,629
New York Life	11,620,571
MetLife, Inc.	9,279,527
Lincoln Financial	5,757,908
State Farm	4,814,990
Guardian	4,601,353
AFLAC	3,804,568
Massachusetts Mutual	3,649,756
Hartford Life, Inc.	3,604,048
Securian Financial Group	3,406,090
Pacific Life	3,266,088
Nationwide	3,079,586
Manulife Financial	2,894,592
AXA Financial	2,739,428
Swiss Re America	2,493,779
Torchmark	2,214,867
Berkshire Hathaway	2,130,096
RGA Group	2,118,631
Zurich Financial	2,055,979
Sammons Financial	1,958,312
CIGNA	1,795,584
Mutual of Omaha	1,665,439
Thrivent Financial For Lutherans	1,641,599
UNUM	1,465,609

Source: ACLI tabulations of National Association of Insurance Commissioners (NAIC) data, used by permission.
Notes: NAIC does not endorse any analysis or conclusions based on use of its data. Group totals represent a collection of life insurers based on organizational structure. Data are as of December 31, 2017. Figures are net of reinsurance.

Source: American Council of Life Insurers (ed.): Life Insurers Fact Book 2018, Washington 2018, p. 103.

insurers. The clear leader is the "Northwestern Mutual"[26] with a market share of 12.38 percent, followed by "Prudential Financial Inc." and the mutual company "New York Life Insurance Group"[27] with market

[26] Founded in 1845 and headquartered in Milwaukee, Wisconsin, "Northwestern Mutual" is the largest mutual life insurance company in the USA and one of the largest life insurers in the world.

[27] "New York Life Insurance" founded in 1845 is the third-largest life insurance company in the US. Headquartered in New York City, New York Life's family of com-

shares of 11.95 percent and 10.71 percent respectively. The "Massachusetts Mutual Life Insurance Co."[28] with 3.37 percent is at the ninth place, followed by the mutual companies "Securian Financial Group" (3.14)[29], "Pacific Life" (3.01)[30] and "Nationwide" (2.84)[31] at the places ten to twelve. The "Mutual of Omaha" (1.54)[32] is at the 23rd place.

6. Mutual insurance company versus joint stock company

The defining difference between mutual insurers and stock insurers is that stock insurers' primary purpose is to provide returns to shareholders, while mutual insurers' purpose is to provide value to policyholders. This difference is the result of distinct organizational forms. Mutual companies do not have shareholders – i.e., they do not have owners in the traditional sense of corporate stock/equity ownership. Instead, in addition to being customers, mutual policyholders possess distinct governance and other control rights in the company.[33]

Since mutual insurers survived and developed through time, it can be concluded that they possess some internal strength which ensures them resilience and flexibility. Otherwise, they would not be present on the market for such a long time. The median age of a mutual insurance company in the USA is 120 years.

---

panies offers life insurance, retirement income, investments and long-term care insurance.

28 Better known as "MassMutual" was founded 1851 as a mutual company and is one of the oldest insurance companies in the USA. From its early beginnings, it has grown to become a financial giant serving over 13 million clients worldwide.

29 Is a mutual holding company and was founded 1880 in St. Paul, Minnesota.

30 "Pacific Mutual Life" was founded in 1868 in Sacramento, California. In 1997, the company dropped mutual from its name, changing it to "Pacific Life Insurance Company". This reflects the company structure's change from a mutual ownership to a mutual holding company structure.

31 Founded 1925 as "Farm Bureau Mutual Automobile Insurance Company" with the goal of providing quality auto insurance at low rates for farmers in Ohio. In 1955, the company changed its name to "Nationwide Insurance". Nowadays, it is a group of large US. insurance and financial services companies based in Columbus, Ohio.

32 Founded in 1909 as "Mutual Benefit Health & Accident Association, Mutual of Omaha", it is now a mutual insurance and financial services company based in Omaha, Nebraska.

33 In a mutual insurer, policyholders, or members, do not have the ability to sell or otherwise transfer individual ownership. The ownership interest arises out of the policy of insurance and does not survive the termination of the policy of insurance (Cf. https://www.namic.org/policy/futureMutualPolicyRights accessed on 04.11.2019).

The mutual form is a unique legal concept and for that reason, mutual insurance companies:

- by definition are owned entirely by their members. But membership is not equivalent to ownership of an equity interest in the mutual insurance company. The member cannot freely sell or pledge as security the mutual insurance policy or his/her rights in it.[34]
- have no need to report good earnings every three months to justify a stock price, so there is no pressure for them to take on extra risk to make a profit.
- have membership rights that are contractual, such as any profits earned by the company must be either kept within the company to build up reserves for good risk provision and future growth or returned to the members in the form of dividend distributions declared by the board of directors or reduced future premiums – a phenomenon called participation.[35]
- have members who have the option to participate in corporate governance, typically by voting for the company's directors, for demutualization, or for a merger; but also the ability to launch legal action against the company's directors and officers if they violate their fiduciary duties. Policy rights are the rights inherent in the actual policy itself: the right to pay the premium, the right to get a death benefit if it's a life company, the right to get an auto claim if it's a property/casualty policy, the right to make a cash value, etc.

---

[34] However, ownership has many meanings. In its most common sense, ownership implies a right of dominion and control over a property interest, including the accompanying right to sell the property. It may be appealing to define the ownership of a mutual insurer in a manner that confers such a right to their policyholders; however, doing so may ignore the essence of the mutual insurer, and the reasons for which it was established. In the extreme case, dissolution of a mutual insurer, it may be no more legitimate to contend that current policyholders have a right to all of the assets of an insurer, than it would be to say they have none. In recognition of this broader concept of ownership, Wisconsin and Minnesota for example, have enacted statutes that recognize beyond a certain limit, assets of a mutual insurer are a public interest, and not the property interest of current policyholders, and other states have provided look-back provisions in their demutualization statutes. In addition, the demutualization laws in Nebraska acknowledge that, in certain circumstances when fair to policyholders, less than the entire value of an insurer may be distributed to its policyholders in the event of a demutualization. (Cf. NAIC (ed.), Mutual Insurance Holding Company Reorganizations, Kansas City 1999, p. 19).

[35] For example, "Lawyers' Mutual Insurance Co.", a California-based company, recently paid a 10 percent dividend to its shareholders. It has paid dividends for 23 consecutive years (Ibid.). https://www.investopedia.com/terms/m/mutualcompany.asp accessed on 13.02.2017). As suggested by the name of that company, mutual companies often are specialized. They were formed by and for a group of professionals who often have common needs.

- have policyholders who are not responsible for losses that exceed the insurance company's resources.[36] However, some mutual companies, known as assessable mutuals, have the right to assess policyholders to obtain additional funds if that becomes necessary for the insurer to meet its obligations. Such assessments typically are limited to not more than one additional annual premium payment.
- have members who receive any outstanding value in case of liquidation or demutualization of the corporation.
- have no need to keep their eyes fixed on shareholder value, on maximizing returns to capital investors, or on the development of the price of their own shares.
- have a board of directors elected by the policyholders. The role of the board of directors is to develop company goals and implement corporate strategy to deliver quality products while assuring the financial solvency of the company. In order to accomplish these objectives, the board of a mutual insurance company must maintain effective control of management and operations, accurately measure company performance, and constantly review the solvency of the company. Meaningful participation by all directors is required to ensure the company's success. Mutual insurance companies may adopt bylaws limiting the number of terms that directors may serve. Term limits ensure that the board remains dynamic and that, over time, no single director dominates the board's activities. However, term limits can also prove harmful to the company if they result in loss of historical knowledge and valuable skills. The board of directors of a mutual insurance company typically includes some members who have experience in the insurance industry. Regardless of the mix, the board must exercise a well-balanced approach to policy decisions. There are certain qualities and attributes which all board members should possess. As a general rule, few state laws or court decisions specifically address the fiduciary duties owed by a mutual board.
- engage strongly with their local communities.[37]

[36] Beware of "Mutual" insurance companies. Policyholders are "owners" of the company and, as such, may benefit from the company's profits. However, on the other hand, in the event of a loss, or much worse yet, a bankruptcy, the policyholders are responsible for the company's debts. Back in the 1960s three related Maryland mutual companies went bankrupt overnight, due to fraudulent mismanagement. Each and every policyholder was sued and required to pay the company's debts, including the lawyers' fees. This amount was established as being six times each of the policyholders' annual premiums, which would be equivalent to thousands of dollars in today's dollars. Of course, this left the policyholders uninsured since the companies were no longer in business, so they then had to buy new policies from another company. It was a disaster (https://www.insurancejournal.com/magazines/mag-partingshots/2001/04/30/18694.htm/?comments accessed on 13.02.2019).

[37] Cf. AMICE. (n.d.). *What is mutual insurance?* Retrieved December 15, 2017, from http://www.amice-eu.org/userfiles/file/AMICE_What is mutuality.pdf, p. 1, accessed on 13.05.2019.

Main weaknesses of mutual insurers can be summarized, according to *Farny*, in the following order:

- the mutual insurance company does not have enough financial income for internal and external growth
- the establishment of mutual insurance companies is legally and practically complicated
- the very nature of the mutual insurance form (legal framework, culture) represents the challenge and potential source of conflict between owners and management
- the mutual insurance company is immune to takeover offers when it comes tonational or international consolidation of the market.[38]

Table 7: Pros and cons of mutual insurers

Advantages	Disadvantages
retention of profit in the company	lack of capital
redistribution of the profit	legal framework in process of establishment
identity principle: owner=policyholder	conflict between owners and management
engagement with local community	immunity to takeover bids

Source: Own representation based on AMICE. (n.d.). *What is mutual insurance?* Retrieved December 15, 2017, from http://www.amice-eu.org/userfiles/file/AMICE_What is mutuality.pdf, p. 1.

Therefore, it is commonly acknowledged that it is more difficult and more costly for mutual companies to raise money from external capital markets than for stock firms. The reasons are lack of channels and instruments to obtain funding as well as a severe information asymmetry between mutual firms and external investors. Additionally, it also takes longer for mutual firms to adjust their capital ratios towards their long-run targets, because mutuals' capital ratios are more sensitive to income than stock firms' are. Consequently, mutual companies tend to

[38] Cf. *Farny, D.*, *Versicherungsbetriebslehre* (5th edition),. Karlsruhe 2006, p. 221f.

keep a higher surplus level within the firm than paying dividends to policyholders/owners.[39]

The two organizational forms of mutuals and joint stock companies dominate the insurance industry in the USA. Each of them has different characteristics, advantages as well as disadvantages. With regard to joint stock companies, they have easier access to additional capital than mutuals because they can take on external capital.

However, mutual and joint stock insurers do not differ regarding premiums. Customers pay a certain amount of money, which gives them the claim to compensation, in the event of damage. While premium is the common denominator between these two organisation forms, their way of operating, ownership structure, etc. differs extensively.[40]

Table 8: Main differences between two organizational forms

Mutual insurance companies	**Joint-stock companies**
Policyholder = owner in a special sense; he/she can be part of decision-making process	Policyholder ≠ owner; in order to get ownership rights, the policyholder should buy company´s stock
Since membership = ownership, policyholder cannot sell his/her part	A stockholder can always sell his/her share in the company
If the business activities are going well, policyholder receives some premium refund	No refund, policyholder can get financial compensation only if a certain event occurs as defined in the policy contract
If the company is going through a hard period, it is possible to ask for financial help by the policyholders	NO such policy, the company cannot ask for support from policyholders in time of crises

Source: Own representation based on *Braun, A., Schmeiser, H., Rymaszewski, P.,* Stock vs. mutual insurers: Who should and who does charge more?, in: European Journal of Operational Research, *242*(3), 2015, p. 875.

Both of these main organizational forms have experienced market-share rises as well as losses due to mutualisation and demutualization waves over the course of years. Having a look at how well they performed, it is evident that the mutuals – mostly formed on the east coast – clearly outlived the stock companies. Of the 30 stock firms cre-

[39] Cf. *Harrington, S.E., Niehaus, G.,* Capital Structure Decisions in the Insurance Industry: Stocks versus Mutuals, in: Journal of Financial Services Research 21/2002, p. 145ff.

[40] Cf. *Braun, A., Schmeiser, H., Rymaszewski, P.,* Stock vs. mutual insurers: Who should and who does charge more?, in: European Journal of Operational Research, 2015 242(3), p. 875-889.

ated until 1848, only one was still in existence 70 years later, while 19 of the 41 mutuals survived during the same time span.[41]

At the end of the 20th century, a huge demutualization wave occurred, when insurance companies were searching for easier ways to raise capital. However, after the financial crises in 2007 and 2008, and due to the people's mistrust in capitalism, another mutualisation wave took place. Suddenly, they started to play a more important role again and to shape business environment. From that very period, the mutual sector in the USA, started to record excellent results in every aspect such as premiums written, total assets held, profits recorded, market growth, etc.

7. US mutual insurance market

For the analysis of the US mutual insurance market, the data is drawn from *Lawrence, S.* (2017): "What It Means to be Mutual, National Association of Mutual Insurance Companies (NAMIC)". Here, mutual insurers are defined as those ultimately owned by and managed for the benefit of policyholders. These include mutual insurers, reciprocal exchanges, and stock companies owned by a mutual or reciprocal. Because they are not managed for the benefit of policyholders, the so-called "county mutual" insurers owned by stock insurance groups in Texas are not counted as mutual insurers. Association-owned stock insurers, such as medical professional casualty insurers owned by a state medical society, are expected to behave similar to mutual insurers. Unfortunately, these data do not identify such insurers; therefore, they are classified as stock insurers.[42]

The US mutual insurance sector is the largest mutual market in the world in terms of premium income by contributing more than a third of the global total. It is also one of the largest global markets in terms of mutual market share.

Mutual insurers range in size from small market companies operating in a single county to large, national carriers operating throughout the country and internationally. Most mutual insurers sell various lines of coverage including those for autos and homes, farms and businesses

---

[41] Cf. *Bainbridge, J.*, Biography of an Idea: The Story of Mutual Fire and Casualty insurance, New York 1952, p 88.

[42] Cf. *Lawrence, S.*, What It Means to be Mutual, National Association of Mutual Insurance Companies (NAMIC), 2017, p. 5.

while others specialize in niche markets such as churches, pharmacists, jewellers, and lumber dealers.

Mutual insurers in the USA held a higher proportion of the total property/casualty market than of the life market. In 2015, 868 mutual insurance companies underwrote $256 billion in property/casualty insurance premiums. This is 38 percent of all active property/casualty insurance companies and 44 percent of all property/casualty premiums in the USA. In some states and lines of insurance, they insure well over half of the total market. In addition, they insure at least 10 percent of each reported line of insurance business and at least 25 percent of premiums earned in each state.

A fairly significant percentage of the property/casualty mutual insurance companies are geographically concentrated, with over 40 percent writing in one state in 2015, while 12 percent wrote only one line of business. While concentration could lead to qualitative competitive advantages such as niche market penetration, enhanced customer service, and greater expertise in their respective markets, this can also pose greater potential risk from extreme weather-related events. Despite these challenges, mutual companies maintain comprehensive reinsurance structures to mitigate catastrophic weather events through smaller retentions, quota shares, and additional unique coverages.

Over the last few decades, the share of total premiums earned by mutual insurance companies has increased. Figure 5 displays the percentage of total premiums earned by mutual insurers from 1984 through 2015. While there is variation from year to year, the overall 32-year trend is increasing from 38 percent in 1984 to 44 percent in 2015. In comparison, the US insurance market grew by 3.6 percent between 2007 and 2015, making the mutual sector the fastest-growing part of the US insurance industry since the crisis.

Figure 6 shows the percentage of premium earned by mutual property/casualty insurers across lines of insurance. The segments in which mutuals have the largest share of earned premium are farm owner's coverage, with 79 percent. Perhaps this represents the mutual insurance industry's roots in farm mutual insurance. In the two largest lines of property/casualty insurance, personal automobile and homeowners, mutual companies earned 57 percent and 64 percent of premiums, respectively. At the other end of the spectrum, mutual insurers write only 12 percent of the financial lines and 10 percent of aircraft coverage.

This categorization of premium by line and organizational form generally follows some of the hypotheses proposed to explain the existence of multiple insurance company forms; however, the alignment is far from perfect, and some of these hypotheses are at odds with each other. Therefore, it is clear that generalizations are insufficient to explain a complex industry. In fact, mutual property/casualty insurers have been

Figure 5: Mutual premium share, 1984-2015

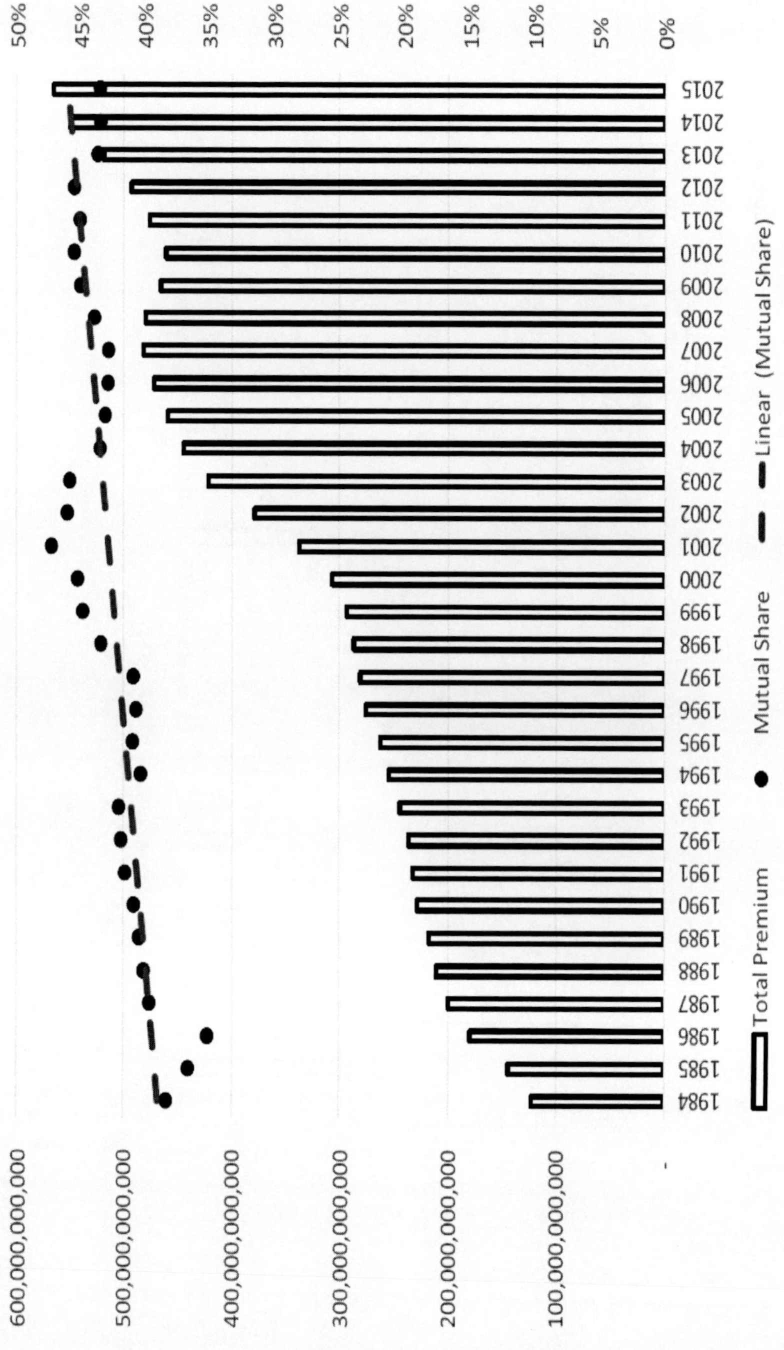

Source: Cf. *Lawrence, S.* (2017): What It Means to be Mutual, National Association of Mutual Insurance Companies (NAMIC), p. 5.

Figure 6: Mutual insurer share of premium earned by line of business, 2015

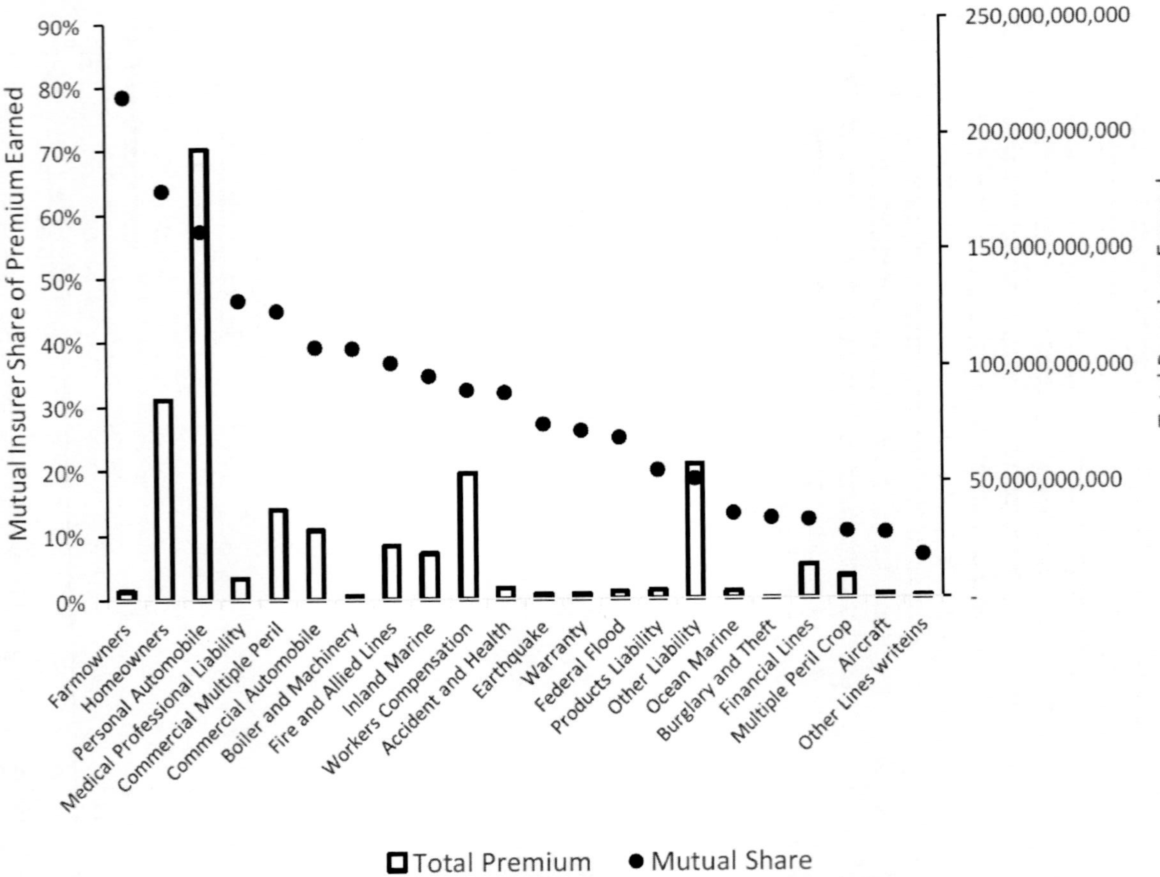

Source: *Lawrence, S.* (2017): What It Means to be Mutual, National Association of Mutual Insurance Companies (NAMIC), p. 6.

trending toward commercial lines underwriting to achieve product diversification and support cautious growth strategies.

Figure 7 presents the share of mutual-company premium across states. Wisconsin leads all states with 62 percent of premium earned by mutual insurers, while Florida brings up the end at 27 percent. There are several explanations for the distribution of mutual insurance across states, none of them mutually exclusive. Mutual insurers could have greater market share where they originally formed, or the distribution across states could represent differences in the industries driving gross state product and earnings by state.

When comparing the mutual property/casualty insurers with each other in 2015 "State Farm Group" dominated in terms of market share with 41 percent, and "Nationwide Group" followed at 13.1 percent. Those two groups were the only ones with a market share greater than 10.0 percent. As in the case with the overall property/casualty market, competition in the mutual space remains high. Many of the mutual carriers expanded into the small commercial market to stay competitive and shift away from personal lines challenges. While it is true that mutuals are customer-focused, there is also heavy emphasis on preserving and steadily increasing surplus levels, which is evidenced by strong pre-tax return measures. Despite some limited financial flexibility, mutuals benefit from surplus notes[43], Federal Home Loan Banks, and other sources to aid liquidity. In addition, mutuals have been actively participating in affiliations over the years, expanding product and geographic diversification efforts. Regardless of the structure, all insurers must have a clearly defined strategic position and solid enterprise risk management capabilities in order to be successful in today's highly competitive and dynamic operating environment. Balance sheet strength, operating performance, business profile and enterprise risk management influence the success of all companies.[44]

An A.M. Best research article[45] argued 2012 that mutual companies lack the pressure for stock price performance. Mutual companies can take a longer view with regard to investment strategy and risk appetite. Consequently, mutual companies have demonstrated a tendency to invest in more common equity than stock companies as they can afford the potential market volatility risk. In addition, because of mutual companies' limited access to the capital markets (as compared to stock companies), NAMIC research regarding investment trends (for property/

[43] Surplus notes are generally allowable pursuant to the domiciliary state's approval requirements as to form and content. States usually prohibit the use of surplus notes as an initial means of capitalization.

[44] Cf.https://www.naic.org/documents/cipr_events_impact_rating_amb_m_report.pdf, September 2016.

[45] Cf. A.M. Best's Special Report: Addressing Structural Differences in the Rating Process, dated Aug. 13, 2012.

Figure 7: Mutual insurer share of premium earned by state, 2015

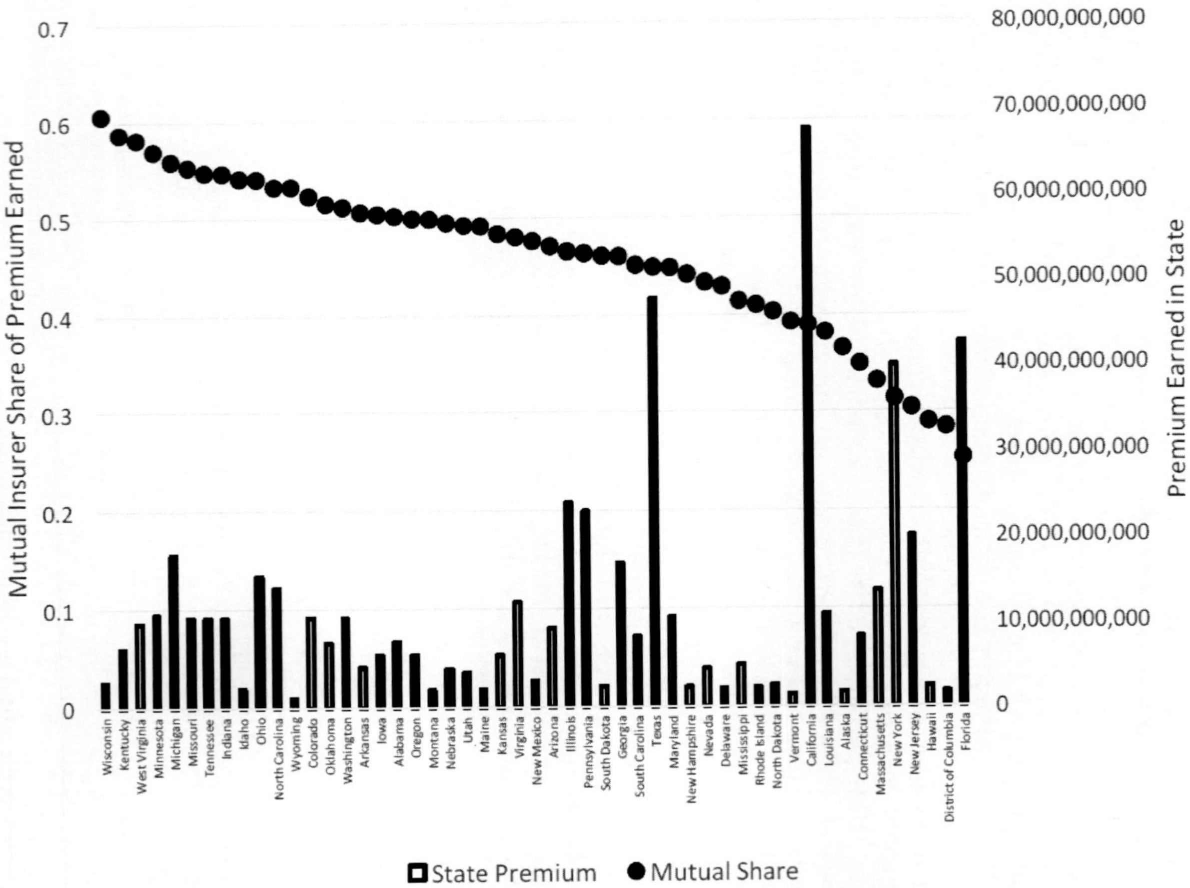

Source: *Lawrence, S.* (2017): What It Means to be Mutual, National Association of Mutual Insurance Companies (NAMIC), p. 7.

casualty mutual companies) noted, "Investment returns generated by mutual companies ... will usually be used for internal company financing to sustain or grow the mutual company, to ensure that the company remains able to meet all of the commitments made to the members."

The A.M. Best study also found that despite a similar trend in direction, property/casualty stock companies demonstrated a higher return on equity than property/casualty mutual companies because of their focus on capital management, though the difference was "immaterial." A.M. Best concluded that the property/casualty mutual companies preferred to focus on maintaining capital for its policyholders/owners rather than seek high returns especially given their long-term investment strategy and "desire to maintain capital for policyholders." Because of limited access to the financial markets, mutual companies also tend to hold more capital on a risk-adjusted basis than stock companies, which also affects returns.

Net premiums throughout the property/casualty mutuals market grew at a moderate pace of 3.1 percent in 2015 and have grown every year since 2010 at a compound average rate of 3.4 percent. Net premiums growth over the last five years can be attributed to rate actions, as dominant players in the mutual space maintain a considerable market share. The ten largest mutual insurers in this population represented over 70 percent of the net premiums written in 2015.[46]

A.M. Best concluded his report: "By focusing on capital preservation coupled with controlled growth, mutual companies exhibit consistent financial stability to benefit policyholders. Despite market challenges and above average expense ratios, steady loss ratios and net investment income in recent years have aided profitability while product diversification has helped to alleviate concentration risk. In today's challenging operating environment, A.M. Best believes well managed companies stand out regardless of organizational structure."[47]

In 2018, A.M. Best rated the mutual property/casualty insurers again and concluded: "Competition remains heightened in this sector amid an insurance industry transformation due to technological advances and economic and demographic changes. Many larger carriers have addressed these market shifts by embracing innovation, but A.M. Best believes some smaller mutuals lag in this area, and that they may invest or secure a partner to keep up with changes. At the same time, although insurtech start-ups have considerable technological expertise, they lack the long-standing experience, market knowledge and relationships of mutuals. Nevertheless, despite the starkly different business models, insurtechs and mutuals are in competition for the same poten-

---

46 Cf.https://www.naic.org/documents/cipr_events_impact_rating_amb_m_report.pdf, September 2016.

47 Ibid.

tial business, and for this reason, adapting to the changing landscape could prove beneficial."[48]

Compared to that the development of mutual life insurance companies was quite different. They are a rare breed nowadays. Most companies that were once mutual have switched to stock insurance companies through "demutualization" or converted to a stock insurance company that is fully owned by a mutual holding company during the 1990s and into the 21st century as a number of large and historically successful life insurers became attracted by the relative advantages of being organized as a stock company. Here the policy owners are typically granted subscription rights in the stock company subsidiary rather than outright shares. As a result, mutual company assets in the life segment fell from 50 percent of assets in the mid-1980s to less than 10 percent by 2006 with the stock form ownership now dominating the industry.[49]

The remaining life mutual companies have focused on their core strength and have not pursued riskier product lines such as variable annuities. The mutuals continue to access capital primarily by issuing surplus notes. As table 9 shows, the mutual life insurance companies were able to maintain their share of 10 percent among the 25 largest life insurance groups based on assets in 2017. When comparing the mutual life insurers with each other, the "Northwestern Mutual" and the "New York Life" had with 23.05 percent respectively 19.50 percent the greatest share.

---

[48] https://www.marketwatch.com/press-release/bests-market-segment-report-us-propertycasualty-mutual-insurers-achieve-moderate-surplus-growth-despite-elevated-losses-2018-09-19.

[49] In 1986, mutual insurers represented 46 percent of the life insurance in force and they issued 38 percent of first year premiums issued in 1986. (Cf. *Erhemjamts, O., Richard D. Phillips,* Form Over Matter: Differences In The Incentives To Convert Using Full Versus Partial Demutualization In The U.S. Life Insurance Industry", in: Journal of Risk and Insurance 2011 79.2, p. 305f.)

Table 9: Largest mutual life insurers, by net life insurance premiums, 2017 (thousands)

Mutual Company	A.M. Best Rating	legal form	premiums	market share in percent
Northwestern Mutual	A++	mutual	13,425	23.05
New York Life	A++	mutual	10,633	19.50
Guardian Life	A++	mutual	8,112	14.18
American United Life	A+	MHC	7,384	12.41
MassMutual	A++	mutual	6,265	10.63
Minnesota Life	A+	MHC	4,588	8.87
Mutual of Omaha	A+	mutual	3,042	5.33
Ohio National	A+	MHC	1,558	3.55
Penn Mutual	A+	mutual	1,280	1.77
Lafayette Life	A+	MHC	402	0.80

Source: Annual reports.

Figure 8 shows the declining of the mutual life insurance company annual dividend interest rates from 1998 to 2017.

Figure 8: Mutual life insurance company annual dividend interest rates from 1998 to 2017

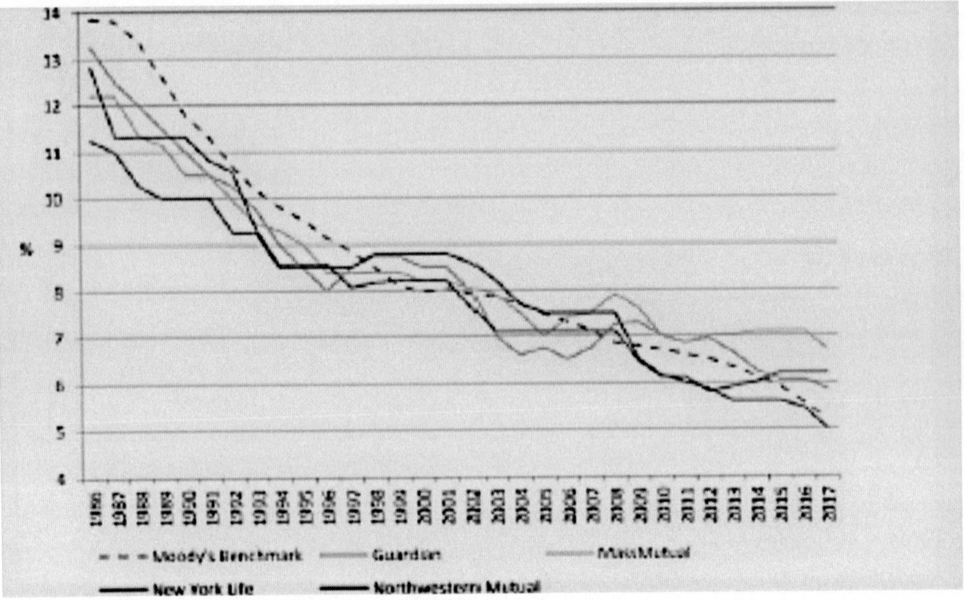

Source: Mutual-Life-Dividend-Rates-2017_0038-2017.pdf

Downward pressures from low new money interest rates have caused dividend interest rates at life insurance companies to decline. As a result, many mutual insurance companies with sizeable blocks of participating whole life insurance liabilities have shifted their portfolios in the direction of riskier, less liquid assets in search of higher yields to support their dividend payments to policyholders.

Below are the declared 2017 dividend interest rates of four major mutual life insurance companies, which are the largest issuers of participating whole life policies:

- "Guardian Life Insurance Co. of America" 5.85 percent (down from 6.05 percent in 2016)
- "Massachusetts Mutual Life Insurance Co." 6.70 percent (down from 7.10 percent)
- "New York Life Insurance Co." 6.20 percent (unchanged)
- "Northwestern Mutual Life Insurance Co." 5.00 percent (down from 5.45 percent).[50]

[50] Cf.https://teekell.com/wp-content/uploads/sites/113/2018/01/Mutual-Life-Dividend-Rates-2017_0038-2017.pdf.

8. History of the insurance market in the USA

The insurance business in the USA mirrors the history of the nation. Insurance has accompanied dramatic population growth, the emergence of commerce, and the elevation of finance. Rapid growth in the new territories also relied on European capital, with investors seeking access to local natural resources. Their aim was to structure the untapped lands in line with European requirements and standards. It is evident that without insurance, businesses cannot be established. The use of underwriting to protect financially property and goods was most prevalent in regions settled by the British. They extended cover to individuals in the form of life and fire insurance. Insurance has helped to increase the nation's prosperity.

Modern fire insurance began in London, England. It was in 1666, when the Great Fire of London took place. 436 acres were completely burnt during a span of 87 hours, amounting to 13,000 destroyed houses. The total property loss was estimated at over 10 million Pounds.[51]

A London speculative builder by the name of *Nicholas Barbon* set up one early form of insurance with his "office for insuring houses and buildings" and started the year after the fire. He operated by himself and therefore had to bear all risks, very different from today's insurance. In 1680, *Barbon* and some other investors created the first stock company insurance against fire located on the Royal Exchange, called "The Fire Office". Moreover, in 1684, the investor *Henry Spelman* created the second fire insurance company. He called it, significantly, "The Friendly Society".[52]

30 years after the "Great Fire of London", in 1696, the first mutual fire insurer was established in England.[53] Originally, it was named "Contributors for Insuring Houses, Chambers or Rooms from Loss by Fire". However, it became known as the "Amicable Contributionship", or "Hand-in-Hand", because of its emblem.[54] This first mutual insurance company against fire was so successful that, by 1732, nearly 46,000 houses were insured by it.[55]

[51] Cf. *Bainbridge, J.*, Biography of an Idea: The Story of Mutual Fire and Casualty insurance, New York 1952, p. 23.

[52] Cf. Ibid., p. 24.

[53] http://www.namic.org/about/mutuals.asp, accessed on 13.02.2017.

[54] Cf. *Bainbridge, J.*, Biography of an Idea: The Story of Mutual Fire and Casualty insurance, New York 1952, p 29.

[55] Cf. Ibid., p. 31.

The modern underwriting system gained only slowly ground from the beginning of the nineteenth century onwards, slowly replacing the old mutual insurance societies during the second half of the century. Many of these societies began to adopt underwriting and thus became insurance companies. Modern insurance also benefited from the rise of the capital markets, which transformed even beneficial and charitable organizations such as the mutual insurance societies into profit-orientated enterprises.[56]

8.1 The beginning

Several colonies had been established through different dispensations of authority under the English crown: Some colonies existed as Royal provinces, while others rather proprietary were owned by wealthy individuals or groups. Each colony had its own government that operated on a basis that was largely independent of the government of the other colonies. Within each individual colony, government institutions mirrored those of their mother country England and were impeded by English mercantilist thinking.

Mutuals rarely exceeded the boundaries of a county. Members knew each other and in particular the secretary, the person responsible for the organization's everyday operations. Membership could be denied to an applicant of reputed bad character (such as a drinker), or bad habits, e.g. someone whose careless farm operations posed too many fire hazards. Immigrants would only allow new members of the same heritage and background, mutuals formed by churchgoers would only accept new members with the same belief and other mutuals formed by professionals, such as craftsmen, would only let the same professionals join the group.[57] The first American insurers modelled themselves after British marine and fire insurers, who were already well-established by the eighteenth century.

8.2 Industrialisation

The arrival of industrialisation and the expansion of world trade brought with it an early and vigorous growth of the insurance industry. However, it became evident that the enormous changes in the economic

56 Cf. *Borscheid, P.*, North America: Overview, in: *Borscheid, P. / Haueter, N.* (ed.): World Insurance The Evolution of a Global Risk Network, Oxford 2012, p. 241.

57 Cf. *Lufkin, J.*, Property Insurance for Iowa Farmers, the Rise of the Mutuals, in: The Annals of Iowa, 1995/1, p. 34.

life in connection with the industrial revolution required a new way in facing risks to life and property. For example, the building of railway bridges, canals and tunnels costed many lives. Work place accidents increased and had to be coped with. One way to face these risks was by increased regulations, but the provision of insurance coverage was also important. Thus, these new risks had to be faced and alleviated by monetary compensation. The developing insurance sector was active in pushing for better and less dangerous work conditions like the National Board of Fire Underwriters (founded in 1866 by over 100 fire insurance companies).[58]

The fragmented US insurance market, with its unique risks, turned out to be an extremely difficult market for all participants. Despite the huge scale and its appeal the supervisory legislation implemented by various US states since the middle of the century made access for foreign companies increasingly difficult. The German fire insurers considered the market as early as 1854, but action was hindered by the outbreak of the American Civil War. The country's rapid economic rise, improvements in transatlantic transport and, compared to Europe, higher premiums meant that increasing numbers of foreign insurers were drawn from the 1870s onwards. Many of them failed.[59]

8.3 Organisational forms

The growth took place in different organisational forms. The organisational tools for new insurance activities were both joint stock companies and mutualism. It has been claimed that the development of the insurance industry is closely connected with the legal framework of a joint stock company. *Robin Pearson* asserts, however, quite correctly that the history of insurance cannot be reduced to the history of the joint stock company.[60]

---

58 Cf. *Pearson. R.*, Organizational Forms in Insurance. A comparison of the USA and Germany during Industrialization, in: *Pearson, R., Yoneyama, T.* (ed.): Corporate Forms and Organizational Choice in International Insurance, Oxford 2015, p. 115.

59 Cf. *Borscheid, P.*, North America: Overview, in: *Borscheid, P. / Haueter, N.* (ed.): World Insurance The Evolution of a Global Risk Network, Oxford 2012, p. 242.

60 Cf. *James, H.*, Introduction: The Insuring Instinct, in: *James, H.* et al. (eds.): The Value of Risks: Swiss Re and the History of Reinsurance, Oxford 2013, p. 8; *Pearson. R.*, Organizational Forms in Insurance. A comparison of the USA and Germany during Industrialization, in: *Pearson, R., Yoneyama, T.* (ed.): Corporate Forms and Organizational Choice in International Insurance, Oxford 2015, p. 114.

The first mutual marine and domestic fire insurers were already well established before the American Revolution[61] and at least ten property companies were created in the two decades following the Declaration of Independence in 1776. More companies would follow and by the mid-1800s most states had a wide variety of enterprises writing insurance contracts. As business and commerce flourished, so did the non-life insurance market. By 1880, per capita insurance spending in the USA equalled that of the United Kingdom.[62]

Joint-stock insurance companies rose to prominence in American fire and marine insurance after the American Revolution. While only a few British insurers were granted the royal charters that allowed them to sell stocks and to claim limited liability, insurers in the young USA found it relatively easy to obtain charters from state legislatures eager to promote a domestic insurance industry. Joint-stock companies started their business originally in the marine sector, where demand and the potential for profits were greater. The reason was that this legal form had not to depend on the financial assets of an individual and provided a higher security than private underwriters did.

8.4 From emerging market to global power

Beginning in the late 1860s, the first formal distribution networks for insurance products started to develop. In 1869, the earliest organization of life insurance agents began in Chicago. Six years later, it saw the emergence of the first agency system for sales in industrial life insurance.[63]

During the boom years of the 1880s, new capital flowed into the insurance sector. The increasing concentration of wealth in cities steadily drove the value of covered property upwards. Between 1880 and 1889, insurance coverage rose by an average rate of 4.6 percent a year, increasing 50 percent overall. By 1890, close to 60 percent of burned down property in the USA was insured, a figure that would not be exceeded until the 1910s, when more than 70 percent of property was insured.[64]

The latter half of the 19th century also witnessed the expansion of US insurance operations into international markets, with most of the

---

61 The American Revolution was a colonial revolt that took place between 1765 and 1783. The American Patriots in the Thirteen Colonies won independence from Great Britain, becoming the United States of America.

62 Cf. Swiss Re Corporate History (ed.), A History of US Insurance, Zurich 2013, p. 7.

63 Cf. *Loftin, G., Xie, X.*, The United States Insurance Market: Characteristics and Trends, in: *Cummins, J.D., Venard, B.* (ed.): Handbook of international insurances. Between Global Dynamics and Local Contingencies, New York 2007, p. 33.

64 Cf. https://eh.net/encyclopedia/fire-insurance-in-the-united-states/, accessed on 13.02.2017.

growth occurring during the period from 1885 to 1905. For example, by 1900, the "Equitable Life Company" had operations in almost 100 different nations and territories.[65]

The outbreak of World War I in Europe in 1914 led to structural changes in the US insurance industry due to the rapid decline of competitors. After the war, German insurers were banned from the US insurance and reinsurance markets, and the Russian Revolution in November 1917 caused a withdrawal of Russian insurers. The US insurance market emerged from the war in relatively good shape, as domestic insurers increased their market shares. From 1910 to 1920, the four top domestic fire insurers collectively increased their premiums by 150 percent.[66]

In addition, US life insurers were confronted with problems, although the demand subsequently increased, as did the prices. By 1905, life premium incomes accounted for about 5 percent of US GDP. As life insurance increased in importance, some of its sectors, such as workers' compensation became compulsory while others became part of America's social security scheme.[67]

After World War I, the USA was undergoing some significant changes. As employment shifted from agricultural to industrial activities, the role of the employer became increasingly important. Increased industrialization and urbanization of the country's workforce stimulated the growth of group insurance arrangements, including employer-provided group health insurance.[68]

World War I had also a devastating impact on international trade and the global currency system, leading to sharp reductions and alterations in the US insurance sector. The exclusion of German reinsurers left a gap that was filled by Swiss and domestic players, but they were also powerless against the many serious and long-lasting economic effects of the war. Inflation, which soon reached excessive levels, had a particularly severe effect on life insurance and was one of the reasons why US life insurers withdrew from other parts of the world to concentrate on their US business. Governmental efforts to rein in the inflationary effects of World War I led to an economic collapse.[69]

The 1920s witnessed the rise of consumer culture and the dawn of mass marketing. Insurance followed the trend as an essential part of

---

[65] Cf. *Murphy, S.* (2005): Life Insurance in the United States through World War I, www.eh.net/enceclopedia/?article Murphy.life.insurance.us.

[66] Cf. Swiss Re Corporate History (ed.), A History of US Insurance, Zurich 2013, p. 17.

[67] Cf. Ibid., p. 19.

[68] Cf. *Loftin, G., Xie, X.* (2007): The United States Insurance Market: Characteristics and Trends, in: *Cummins, J.D., Venard, B.* (ed.): Handbook of international insurances. Between Global Dynamics and Local Contingencies, New York, p. 34.

[69] Cf. *Borscheid, P.*, North America: Overview, in: *Borscheid, P. / Haueter, N.* (ed.): World Insurance The Evolution of a Global Risk Network, Oxford 2012, p. 243.

most households, providing financial cover in the event of a loss of assets or property. US consumers eagerly adopted the latest technology – buying radios, domestic appliances and automobiles. In return, sales of car insurances increased although automobiles proved to be stolen easily, which became a problem for insurers and resulted for a short time in higher premiums that many consumers could not afford. The life insurers thrived during this period. Many companies adopted the mutual form of organization for their enterprises to build confidence[70]. Gradually, low-income families started to buy life insurances. As a percentage of their disposable income, during the 20 years following World War I, Americans increased the amount they spent on life, annuity, and health insurances by 50 percent.[71]

The 1920s ended with the collapse of the US stock market and led to the Great Depression of the 1930s. The optimism of the 1920s was soon replaced by the harsh realities of the Great Depression. Just as insurance was becoming a fundamental motor of the economy, it was impacted by investment losses from unstable investment markets and exchange rates. This situation caused fundamental changes in financial service regulations. As the economy slowed down and unemployment increased, casualty insurance premiums fell by 30 percent. By 1934, fire insurance premiums had fallen to the lowest level in 20 years. The length and severity of the Great Depression triggered the New Deal, with its provisions of welfare and job creation, and reshaped attitudes toward risks and insurance. The leading internationally active companies survived the difficult interwar period by using the phase of rationalization after World War I to expand, mainly through acquisitions and mergers as well as by the growth of insurance needs on national markets.

During the early 1940s, the state of New York enacted the first insurance law regarding the establishment of a state guaranty fund, a sort of state-sponsored reinsurance system with the purpose of limiting the damage for policyholders in the event of insurer insolvency. Such as the common state regulatory initiatives that have been implemented and tested first in large influential states, this development was repeated in other state insurance departments.[72]

---

[70] In response to news reports of corruption among industry executives, in particular, among the executives of the Equitable Life Company, the New York state legislature commissioned the *Armstrong* investigation. This investigation unearthed a host of abuses and paved the way for regulatory reforms that would spill over into the regulatory activities of states across the nation. (Cf. *Ibid.*, p. 31.)

[71] Cf. Swiss Re Corporate History (ed.), A History of US Insurance, Zurich 2013, p. 19.

[72] Cf. *Loftin, G., Xie, X.*, The United States Insurance Market: Characteristics and Trends, in: *Cummins, J.D., Venard, B.* (ed.): Handbook of international insurances. Between Global Dynamics and Local Contingencies, New York 2007, p. 34.

The post-war period was characterised by the decline of the old colonial world and the rise of the two new superpowers, the USA and the USSR. The global engagement of the USA was based on its huge wealth compared to Europe and the possession of nuclear technology. The fundamental catalysts that caused and supported the extraordinary post-war economic increase came from the USA.

The US insurance industry had grown faster than the global economy between 1950 and the 1970s, but began to show negative real growth across all branches in the following decade. During this period, unsustainable economic conditions and increasing regulation drove many foreign insurers out of the USA.

In the uncertain Cold War era, the USA offered an aggressive yet strong and stable market. While large parts of the world slipped behind the Iron Curtain or struggled to emerge from colonial rule, USA maintained new confidence. Health insurance, for example, developed into a key sector, while it remained far less important in other leading industrial nations due to their broad social insurance schemes. Furthermore, product liability legislation made the US considerably riskier for insurers than any other country. Additionally, there were natural disasters such as the danger of hurricanes. Their impacts rose sharply because of increased levels of buildings, wealth, and population in the coastal regions. On the other hand, liberalization, deregulation and globalization brought the markets into closer alignment and made them markedly interdependent.[73]

In addition, the use of automobiles became more prevalent and state laws required car liability insurance. In the 25 years following World War II, property and casualty increased eleven fold; life, health and annuities multiplied eightfold.[74]

To solve their expansion problems, insurance companies in the USA needed to involve themselves from the mid-1980s onwards into new areas of business outside the insurance sector. During this period, they took the first, hesitating steps towards becoming comprehensive financial service providers.[75]

The US life insurance sector grew earlier and more rapid than in most other developed countries, focusing on retirement- and investment-oriented products. By 1990, individual and group annuity products accounted for well over 60 percent of life premium volume in the

---

73 Cf. *Borscheid, P.*, North America: Overview, in: *Borscheid, P. / Haueter, N.* (ed.): World Insurance The Evolution of a Global Risk Network, Oxford 2012, p. 247.

74 Cf. *Loftin, G., Xie, X.*, The United States Insurance Market: Characteristics and Trends, in: *Cummins, J.D., Venard, B.* (ed.): Handbook of international insurances. Between Global Dynamics and Local Contingencies, New York 2007, p. 18.

75 Cf. *Borscheid, P.*, North America: Overview, in: *Borscheid, P. / Haueter, N.* (ed.): World Insurance The Evolution of a Global Risk Network, Oxford 2012, p. 247.

USA. The driving forces behind the life industry's growth were the development in the stock market combined with rising employment and wealth as well as an aging population.[76] However, the expansion of the major equity companies at the end of the century also triggered a wave of demutualization.

8.5 Marine insurance

Marine insurance started in the USA with merchants underwriting each other's ships and cargoes, sometimes in an individual capacity, more often, however, in form of small partnerships or syndicates. Due to its access to the sea, the close distances to the rest of Europe, and easy routes to the USA, London became a huge trading centre and attracted many businessmen to use it as the departing port for their merchandise. It was in *Edward Lloyd's* coffee house where merchants met to conclude their deals. By the middle of the 18th century, *Edward Lloyd's* coffee house, the predecessor of "Lloyd's of London", had become the dominating individual underwriting business. Similar insurance offices where local merchants could underwrite individual voyages began to appear in a number of American port cities.

Before the American Revolution, marine insurance which was traded in Britain and North America was subject to the English legal prohibition favouring the monopoly rights (1720) of two chartered stock corporations, the "Royal Exchange Assurance Corporation" and the "London Assurance Corporation", although the latter sold no insurance in the American colonies. This had a negative effect on the development of the American insurance business, making it impossible for new entrants into the business to compete against the more established London stock insurers. As a result, the mutual concept was the only viable choice available.

The trade centred in Philadelphia, where between 1721 and 1805 at least fifteen different brokerages helped to place insurances in the hands of approximately 150 private underwriters over the course of the 18th century.[77] Only a limited amount of coverage was available. In the middle of the 18th century, Philadelphia was the biggest city of the colonies in America and it continued its rise just to the top. There was not more commerce and trade in Philadelphia than in Boston; it was also the political centre of the country, which would also lead to the signing of the Declaration of Independence in 1776 there. Smaller numbers of brokerages appeared in the southern colonies, and a mutual

[76] Cf. Ibid., p. 19.

[77] Cf. https://eh.net/encyclopedia/fire-insurance-in-the-united-states/, accessed on 13.02.2017.

marine insurance association was launched in Charleston (South Carolina) in 1739. American insurers, however, never replaced the amount of marine insurance from London at any time before the American Revolution.[78]

After the decleration of independence, the USA broke with the British legislative tradition of restricting corporate privileges and introduced liberal incorporation laws. Until the Civil War (1861-1865), the business remained in the hands of American corporations, both mutual and joint stock companies, many of them combined maritime with inland marine and fire insurance. Mutual companies grew particularly rapidly during the 1840s and 1850s.[79]

The Civil War witnessed a sharp decline in American shipping, followed by the re-entry into American insurance market of Lloyd's agents and foreign companies. Consequently, the USA became an important market for English insurers during the mid-1800s. However, the period of reconstruction after the Civil War attracted many insurers from Canada, Germany, Russia and Switzerland to expand their business into the economically flourishing USA.

The growing competition from overseas insurers and the ease, by which the telegraph allowed American risks to be placed at lower rates in London, crushed many American marine insurers, both stock and mutual companies. In 1859, only four American stock and ten mutual marine insurance companies were operating in New York. In the 1890s, domestic marine underwriting became concentrated in two enterprises, the "Atlantic Mutual Marine of New York" and the joint stock company "Insurance Company of North America" (INA). By 1910, foreign companies had captured nearly 60 percent of the US market.[80]

8.6 Fire insurance

8.6.1 The beginning

When fire insurance first appeared in Britain after the Great London Fire of 1666, mutual societies predominated. The earliest American fire insurers followed this model as well. Established in the few urban centres where capital was concentrated, American mutuals were not considered profitable undertakings, but were rather results of volunteer fire fighting organizations. In 1736, Charles town's (South Carolina)

---

[78] Cf. *Crothers, G.*, Commercial Risks and Capital Formation in Early America, in: Business History Review 78/2004, p. 611.

[79] Cf. *Pearson. R.*, Organizational Forms in Insurance. A comparison of the USA and Germany during Industrialization, in: *Pearson, R., Yoneyama, T.* (ed.): Corporate Forms and Organizational Choice in International Insurance, Oxford 2015, p. 118.

[80] Cf. Ibid.

residents formed the first American mutual fire insurance company, the "Friendly Society of Mutual Insuring of Homes against Fire", while the country was still under British colonial rule. It only lasted until 1740, when a major fire destroyed more than 300 houses and put it out of business. The losses sustained by the "Friendly Society" were far too great for its inexperienced operation and the organization eventually failed. In 1752, another company was founded in Philadelphia, this time established by *Benjamin Franklin* and colleagues.

By the 1780s, the growing demand had led to the formation of other fire mutuals in Philadelphia[81], New York[82], Baltimore[83], Norwich (CT), Richmond, Boston and Providence.[84] The first mutual in New York was founded in 1787. The "Mutual Assurance Company of New York" however ceased to operate in the early 19th century. As for Maryland, the "Baltimore Equitable Society", founded in 1794, and the "Mutual Assurance Society of Virginia", founded the same year in Virginia, are still in business until today.[85]

The Embargo Act (1807-1809)[86] and the War of 1812 (1812-1814)[87] interrupted shipping, decreased marine insurers' premiums and forced them to invent additional sources of revenue. These same events also stimulated the development of domestic industries, such as textiles, which created a new demand for fire insurance. Together, these events led many marine insurers into the fire insurance sector, which was previously a sideline for most of them.[88]

---

[81] In 1784, a second mutual fire insurance company was formed in Philadelphia, "The Mutual Assurance Company for Insuring Houses from Loss by Fire".

[82] The "Mutual Assurance Company for Insuring Houses from Loss by Fire in New York" was formed in New York City in 1787, but the company was chartered into a stock insurance company in 1809 and thus ceased operations as a mutual insurance company.

[83] The "Baltimore Equitable Society" was formed in April 1794 in Baltimore, Maryland, and was generally patterned after Franklin's plan of mutual insurance in Philadelphia. The "Baltimore Equitable Society" remains the second oldest mutual fire insurance company still in business in the USA.

[84] Cf. https://eh.net/encyclopedia/fire-insurance-in-the-united-states/, accessed on 13.02.2017.

[85] Cf. Ibid.

[86] The reasons for the trade embargo by Jefferson were the violation of the American neutrality reading the war in Europe and the hindrance to trade between the USA and Europe. In this caste, Britain violated in particular American's maritime law and therefore its neutrality.

[87] In the war of 1812, the tensions of years between the USA and the United Kingdom culminated.

[88] Cf. https://eh.net/encyclopedia/fire-insurance-in-the-united-states/, accessed on 13.02.2017.

Not until 1792, over a decade after the American Revolution, joint stock fire insurance companies were established. While only a few British insurers were granted the royal charters that allowed them to sell stocks and to claim limited liability, insurers in the USA found it relatively easy to obtain charters from state legislatures eager to promote a domestic insurance industry.

The first successful joint-stock company was, as mentioned above, the "Insurance Company of North America" (INA). It was established by *Benjamin Franklin* in 1794 in Philadelphia to sell marine, fire, and life insurances. By 1810, more than seventy companies had been chartered in the USA. Most of the firms incorporated before 1810 operated primarily in marine insurance, although they also underwrote other insurance sectors. Therefore, the US companies started to introduce profit sharing for their clients very early, began to offer loans in 1848, added in 1861 the possibility of surrendering at fixed values, and included the war risks into their insurance coverage. Additionally, the major US life insurers focused on overseas markets.[89]

By the late 1820's, mutual insurance was developing rapidly, especially in the New England area. The mutuality movement started spreading more and more and left its eastern premises. In 1826, the western territory was reached, with the foundation of the "Cincinnati Equitable Insurance Company" in Ohio.[90]

Immigrants were the most important propagators of the insurance system in the USA, carrying it as an integral part of their culture. Economic deprivation and the revolutions in 19th century transport systems persuaded millions to leave Europe and choose the risks and prospects of new territories. Immigration to the USA rose after 1820 in waves, from around 14,000 people per year in the 1820s to around one million in 1911. While in earlier times the British and Irish were the two groups with the highest numbers of immigrants departing to the USA, by the turn of the 20th century, the majority was from Southern Europe. In every decade in the nineteenth century, however, more people emigrated from the United Kingdom than from any other European country. From 1800 to 1835, the US population nearly tripled, rising to nearly 14 million people. This early part of the 19th century was characterised by prosperity for the USA. The opening of the Erie Canal brought new trade possibilities, the first savings banks opened for business and the "Monroe doctrine" of 1823 kept the USA rather safe from external interests of other countries. Moreover, the new middle class

89 Cf. Ibid.

90 Cf. *Bainbridge, J.*, Biography of an Idea: The Story of Mutual Fire and Casualty insurance, New York 1952, p. 76.

could afford to cover their commercial activities far more than farmers and agricultural workers.[91]

A part of the cultural heritage of many immigrants was the concept of insurance, using the same mutual associations and policies that had proven their value in Europe against the financial losses caused by natural hazards and the risks of occupational activities. German[92], Dutch, Norwegian, or Danish immigrants started forming first mutual insurance companies within their ethnic groups in the early 19th century. These mutual insurance societies succeeded mainly because of a localized organizational structure.[93]

In 1835, 13 of the 24 existing states had mutual fire insurance companies. Massachusetts counted 14 mutual companies, while Connecticut had two and Maine, New Hampshire, Vermont, and Rhode Island each had one.[94] It followed the expansion into the Midwest and Plains states with literally hundreds of towns and county farms establishing mutuals through the grass roots efforts of local citizens. It has to be noted that the variations in organisational forms did not always run in a parallel way in the various states of the union.

Since a national US newspaper was still not in existence, the emergence of these newly formed mutual insurance companies was not easy to be documented. Information travelled "word-to-mouth" and people only heard about the existence of a mutual rather late. Intrigued by the idea of creating a mutual company by themselves, founders paid people to travel to Pennsylvania and Massachusetts in order to obtain information about existing mutuals and to model their company around that information. Methods, bylaws and forms were often simply copied from already existing mutuals.[95]

By giving out information on how to establish a mutual and how to do business, the mutuality idea spread much faster. As a result, there was no room for corporate greed.[96]

The founders of these mutuals were mostly well-respected men of the community with a strong belief of togetherness. They were lawyers, scholars, state senators, doctors, bank directors, railroad presidents, etc.. In addition, they usually carried out long terms within the mutu-

91 Cf. Ibid., p. 74.

92 German settlers, in fact, formed Iowa's first farm mutual in 1849, the "Deutsche Brund Gilde". Eventually, they organized twenty-seven other county mutuals with German nationality requirements. (Cf. *Lufkin, J.*, Property Insurance for Iowa Farmers, the Rise of the Mutuals, in: The Annals of Iowa, 1995/1, p. 34).

93 Cf. *Borscheid, P.*, North America: Overview, in: *Borscheid, P. / Haueter, N.* (ed.): World Insurance The Evolution of a Global Risk Network, Oxford 2012, p. 239f.

94 Cf. *Bainbridge, J.*, Biography of an Idea: The Story of Mutual Fire and Casualty insurance, New York 1952, p. 74.

95 Cf. Ibid., p. 77.

96 Cf. Ibid., pp. 77-78.

als, because they were proud of the company's achievements and their own work. Lastly, they were not motivated by financial stipulation. For example, the president of the "Hartford County Mutual Fire Insurance" was paid $30 annually, a large contrast to today's CEOs' income.[97]

In 1852, The Homestead Act, which turned over 270 million acres of public land to private citizens, gave rise to another type of mutual. Following the Civil War, homesteaders settling new farmland were weary of railroad trust monopolies and fire insurers, so they created their own social and political organizations that permitted each state to lobby for laws allowing the formation of farm mutual fire insurers.

The mutuals' main goal was to serve the people in their town or city. Policies were only underwritten for buildings in the restrictions of those areas. The mutual insurers wanted to offer good quality insurances before spreading out. Only after the company had been successful for a few years, it started looking for business outside of its usual territory. The "Worcester Mutual" for example started doing business outside of Massachusetts in 1906, after 83 years of successful operations inside its home state.[98]

This again shows a difference to today's values, where companies no longer made local service their priority but rather expand their operations quickly in order to have access to greater markets with more money.

Just like the "Philadelphia Contributionship" and the "Green Tree Mutual" before, the newly formed mutuals of the early 19th century insured only buildings of good quality and thereby tried to keep their risks very low. Successfully doing so, the losses were extremely low. The "Worcester Mutual" had no loss to report in its first year of business, while the "Pawtucket Mutual" for example had to report no loss for three years straight. The "Hingham Mutual" and the "Mutual Fire of Springfield" even had 10 successful years without any losses.[99]

Instead of working for profits but achieving low losses by offering quality and affordable insurances to its customers at the same time, mutuals often paid out dividends to their policyholders. Later on, although, mutuals decided in favour of lower premiums and therefore paying out lower dividends. In addition, mutuals tried to be prepared for the future by setting up a reserve account, in which they deposit annually certain surplus amounts. How and when a policyholder will receive a participation benefit is a decision made under the direction and control of the board of directors.[100]

---

[97] Cf. Ibid., pp. 78-79.

[98] Cf. Ibid., p. 81.

[99] Cf. Ibid., pp. 84-85.

[100] Cf. Ibid., p. 87.

During the 1830s, a special type of insurance evolved: the so-called class mutual only covered risks for a very special group of professionals such as bakeries, millers, and manufactures. These mutuals had a beneficial impact on the security of the related firms. In 1835, the first mutual fire insurance for mill manufacturers, the "Manufacturer Mutual" was officially established in Providence[101]. Not motivated by high dividends or profits, it expanded slowly but surely. Similar to the first founded fire mutual insurance company, the "Manufacturer Mutual" also opted for an inspection of its insured mills, making sure that no unnecessary risks existed. A second mutual fire insurance for manufacturers, the "Rhode Island Mutual Fire Insurance Company", was founded in 1848 in order to gain new policyholders outside of the mill industry. The founders firmly believed that by increasing the number of mutuals for factories throughout different locations, business would increase. What followed was the foundation of the "Boston Manufacturers Mutual Fire Insurance Company" in 1849. It differed from its predecessors by introducing a full time paid secretary and treasurer and by looking for business on a bigger scale than other mutuals.

Within 50 years, mutuals insuring factories had established themselves as a vital part of the US insurance industry and economy. This movement changed the landscape of the mutual insurance system because it offered now insurances to a completely new sort of demand. However, joint stock fire insurers tried to counter the offensive of mutuals by supporting negative newspaper articles regarding the soundness of mutuals' businesses. The factory insurance association, a syndicate by the joint stock fire insurance, offered discounts on premiums for mill owners who invested in fire protection, such as sprinklers.[102]

Until the late 1830s, most fire insurers concentrated on local markets, with only a few testing new markets through agents in distant cities. Many state legislatures discouraged "foreign" competition by taxing the premiums of out-of-state insurers. This situation prevailed through 1835. A devastating fire destroyed New York City's business district. From this point on, fire insurers regarded the geographic diversification of risks as imperative.[103]

Insurers sought to enter new markets in order to reduce their exposure to large-scale fires. They gradually discovered that contracting with agents allowed them to expand broadly, rapidly, and at relatively

[101] In the 18th century, factory insurance was not a dominant topic, because manufacturing simply did not really exist inside the USA. Goods were mainly imported from England, while no goods at all were produced directly within the country. Agricultural activities were predominant at that time.

[102] Cf. *Bainbridge, J.*, Biography of an Idea: The Story of Mutual Fire and Casualty insurance, New York 1952, p. 92.

[103] Cf. https://eh.net/encyclopedia/fire-insurance-in-the-united-states/, accessed on 13.02.2017.

low costs. Pioneered mainly by companies based in Hartford and Philadelphia, the agency system did not become truly widespread until the 1850s. Once the system began to emerge strongly, it rapidly took off. By 1855, for example, the state of New York had authorized 38 out-of-state companies to sell insurances there. Most were younger than five years old. By 1860, national companies relying on networks of local agents had replaced purely local companies as the backbone of the industry.[104]

As the agency system grew, so too did competition. By the 1860s, national fire insurance firms competed in hundreds of local markets simultaneously. Low capitalization requirements and the widespread adoption of general incorporation laws provided an easy entry into the insurance field. Competition forced insurers to base their premiums on short-term costs. As a result, fire insurance rates were inadequate to cover long-term costs associated with the city-wide conflagrations that might occur unpredictably once or twice in a generation. Therefore, when another large fire occurred, many consumers would be left with worthless policies. Aware of this danger, insurers struggled to raise rates through cooperation. Their most notable effort was the National Board of Fire Underwriters. Formed in 1866 with 75 member companies, it established local boards throughout the country to set uniform rates. Cooperative price setting at the local level became common during the 1870s and 1880s, resulting in a period of relative financial success for insurance firms.[105]

In 1871, a huge fire destroyed the core of Chicago. This fire was burning for a whole day, burning down an area of 4 miles long and 1 mile wide. In this area, 17,500 buildings were destroyed, leaving one third of Chicago's population homeless. Even though fire insurance was available at that time, it was still scarce and many people could not afford home insurance due to money issues or believed that it was not necessary. Therefore, many poorer Chicagoans did not have the funds to buy fireproof materials or skilled masons for rebuilding. Without the means to rebuild or insure their property, thousands of people and small businesses were crowded out of Chicago. As a result, the 'Chicago fire' changed people's opinion drastically regarding insurance.[106]

8.6.2 The pioneer Benjamin Franklin

One of the founding fathers of mutualism in the American Colonies was *Benjamin Franklin*. He was one of the first who believed in insurance and established a fire insurance company in the USA, the

[104] Cf. Ibid.

[105] Cf. Ibid.

[106] Cf. https://www.nationalgeographic.org/news/chicago-fire-1871-and-great-rebuilding/, accessed on 13.05.2019.

"Philadelphia Contributionship".[107] It was, however, better known as the "Amicable Contributionship", or "Hand-in-Hand", because of its emblem.[108]

In 1724, the young man *Benjamin Franklin* left the American colonies to work in England. When he came back to Philadelphia, nearly two years later, he was determined to make a change. Back then, *Franklin* was only 20 years old and Philadelphia was missing a police department as well as a fire department among other crucial elements. *Franklin* once stated "I am humbly of the opinion that the country is ripe for many such friendly societies, whereby every man might help another, without any disservice to himself."[109] Thus, we see that the idea of solidarity or collective self-help is also deeply rooted in the American insurance tradition.

This statement showed his desire and belief that people should help each other. Later in his life, *Franklin* became the editor of the Pennsylvania Gazette, founded the first circulating library in America, created a philosophical society, and formed a society of young men, willing to offer mutual help and work for the benefit of the public.[110]

Benjamin Franklin was always highly interested in the fight against fire. He was pushing homeowners to make their homes safer against fire. At that time, Philadelphia had been spared from any great fires and therefore was still missing a fire department. Only after a fire in 1730, some measures were approved by the city such as fines for smoking in the streets and the purchase of more fire fighting equipment.[111]

Franklin was making his point in his newspaper, the Gazette, by warning people about the dangers of fire and informing them that a fire department would be extremely important. It was after his letter that the first Philadelphian fire fighting association, the "Union Fire Company", was founded by *Franklin* and four other people. Because of the social aspects of this type of association, it precipitated the formation of other fire fighting associations, a development that benefitted all citizens of Philadelphia. Philadelphia, at that time, became suddenly one of the safest cities in America concerning fire. Franklin even invented a new kind of stove that was much safer and did need less fuel.[112]

Obviously, *Franklin* knew that in spite of all of his efforts to make Philadelphia safer that he could never fully eliminate the danger. His

[107] http://www.namic.org/about/mutuals.asp, accessed on 13.02.2017.

[108] Cf. *Bainbridge, J.*, Biography of an Idea: The Story of Mutual Fire and Casualty insurance, New York 1952, p. 29.

[109] Ibid., p. 33.

[110] Ibid., p. 34.

[111] Ibid., pp. 35-36.

[112] Ibid., p. 40.

next step was, therefore, to create a successful insurance company protecting against fire.

In 1750, *Benjamin Franklin* introduced fire insurance to the city. The city counted thousands of buildings and thousands of taxable citizens. He introduced his idea of fire insurance for the first time in a meeting among the members of his “Union Fire Company” on February 26th 1750. By the end of the meeting, all members had contributed equal amounts to set up a fund that would be used in case of a damaged home by fire to one of the members.[113]

On September 7th, 1751, *Benjamin Franklin* along with his “Union Fire Company” met with fellow Philadelphia fire fighters in order to create an insurance company, protecting from possible fires. At that time, six other fire companies existed. It was then decided that an insurance organization should be formed, not only serving the fire companies, but also to serve all citizens of Philadelphia.[114]

Later, in 1752, this first mutual fire insurance company was formed, called the “Philadelphia Contributionship for the Insurance of Houses from Loss by Fire” under the principle “whereby every man might help another without any disservice to himself”.[115]

On February 28th, 1752, the following statement was published:

“All persons inclined to subscribe to the articles of insurance of houses from loss by fire, in or near this city, are desired to appear at the Court-House, where attendance will be given, to take their subscriptions, every seventh day of the week, in the afternoon, until the 13th of April next, being the day appointed by the said articles for electing twelve directors and a treasurer.”[116]

People, who wanted to join, had to sign the “Deed of Settlement” of the “Amicable Contributionship”, very similar to the one from the “Amicable Contributionship” in London. It selected as its fire mark four hands crossed and clasped in a form commonly known as “Jacob’s Chair”.[117] Members of this mutual insurance company agreed to pay equal amounts to the company. These payments would serve to pay for potential losses due to fire that any member would suffer.[118]

On March 25th, 1752, the first meeting among members was held at the courthouse in order to elect twelve directors and the treasurer. The

[113] Ibid., p. 41.

[114] Ibid., p. 42.

[115] http://www.pbs.org/benfranklin/l3_citizen_insurance.html, accessed on 12.04.2017; http://www.namic.org/about/mutuals.asp, accessed on 12.04.2017

[116] Cf. *Bainbridge, J.*, Biography of an Idea: The Story of Mutual Fire and Casualty insurance, New York 1952, p. 42.

[117] Cf. Ibid., p. 43.

[118] Cf.http://www.pbs.org/benfranklin/l3_citizen_insurance.html, accessed on 16.04. 2017.

first directors of the "Philadelphia Contributionship" were *Philip Syng, William Coleman, Joseph Morris, Jonathan Zane, William Griffits, Samuel Rhodes, Joseph Fox, Amos Strettel, John Mifflin, Hugh Roberts, Israel Pemberton*, and, of course, *Benjamin Franklin. John Smith* was the first treasurer, a man with knowledge of marine insurance and underwriting.[119]

The first policy was written out to the same *John Smith* on June 26th, 1752. Ironically, on July 4th, 1752, *Benjamin Franklin* signed two policies for two of his houses in Philadelphia.[120]

This was the foundation process of the very first mutual insurance company in America, initiated by one of the USA founding fathers *Benjamin Franklin*. Until this day, the "Philadelphia Contributionship", as today's oldest mutual insurer in the USA, is still in business and proud about its heritage.

At first, this mutual insurance movement had problems spreading across the country. In fact, the "Philadelphia Contributionship" operated as the only fire insurance company until 32 years later, in 1784. The reason behind this is that during those early years, Americans were still fighting for their independence from England and therefore had little time and interest in the development of insurance business.[121]

Additionally, at this time, the geographical settings of America were unfavourable for spreading the insurance business. Most people were living in rather isolated regions, and only 6 cities had a population of 8,000 or more: Philadelphia, New York, Boston, Charleston, Baltimore, and Salem. The USA as we know them today is not even close to compare to this early period, because most people lived at the east coast of the continent. Nature was still omnipresent and large woods dominated the landscapes. A French traveller once claimed that "compared to France, the entire country is one vast wood."[122]

Communication across the country was very scarce and difficult to transmit as only few roads existed between cities and populations and those roads were closer to paths than actual roads. All of this contributed to the fact that news about the first mutual fire insurance travelled very slowly. This was, however, beneficial to the "Contributionship".[123]

---

[119] Cf. *Bainbridge, J.*, Biography of an idea: the story of mutual fire and casualty insurance, New York 1952 Cf. *Bainbridge, J.*, Biography of an Idea: The Story of Mutual Fire and Casualty insurance, New York 1952, pp. 43-44.

[120] Cf. Ibid., p. 47.

[121] Cf. Ibid., p. 48.

[122] Ibid., p. 49.

[123] Cf. Ibid., pp. 49-50.

Before spreading all across the country, this mutual insurance company could be tested, improved and perfected. The American mutual company added two ideas to its predecessors in England.[124]

- Firstly, the "Contributionship" inspected every building before writing the actual policy. If a house did not satisfy the "inspectors", changes would have to be made, in order to make the house safer and thus eligible for insurance. This was the first ever movement concerning risk classification and with that the principle of selectivity was established. Selectivity brought fewer losses and thereby lower rates for the policyholders.[125]
- Secondly, unlike many English companies, the "Contributionship" did not have fixed rates for either wooden buildings or brick buildings. Every building was inspected considering occupancy (families, type of goods, etc.), construction and other factors to determine the character of the risk at hand. A building storing flammable goods was therefore more expensive to insure than a building for a family.[126]

The first policies lasted for seven years, after which the premium was returned to the policyholder. During the first year of business, there was no single incident caused by fire in the "Philadelphia Contributionship", although 43 policies were issued that year.[127]

After 1750, the progress of the "Philadelphia Contributionship" slowed down due to a drop of the deposits. There was a lack of reserves, threatening the company's existence. In fact, a loss of a few thousand dollars could have put the mutual company out of business. In 1763, the members voted that the deposit fund would no longer be used for the handling of profits and losses of the individual policyholder. They agreed that the interests of the deposit fund should be used to create a common account, handling the losses. Moreover, the deposit money was not allowed to be used until all of the interest money was gone. This decision became the principle of "accumulation of safety reserves", a regulation that is still common in the insurance business.[128]

In 1781, eighteen years after this ground breaking decision, the mutual structure had been tested, improved, and perfected. At this time, the "Contributionship" had approximately 2,000 policies and the mutual movement was ready to spread or to expand, leading to the formation of another mutual fire insurance company in America.[129]

[124] Ibid., p. 50.
[125] Cf. Ibid., p. 50.
[126] Cf. Ibid., pp. 50-51.
[127] Cf. Ibid., pp. 51-52.
[128] Cf. Ibid., p. 54.
[129] Cf. Ibid., pp. 54-55.

Reduction of risk potential was the primary concern of the "Philadelphia Contributionship". In a meeting in 1781, the members of the "Philadelphia Contributionship" decided to no longer insure houses and buildings that were built next to trees or renew such existing policies. The company's opinion was that those buildings had a much higher risk of catching fire with trees standing next to them. Opposing forces tried to counter this decision by offering higher premiums for risky buildings. However, all efforts were unsuccessful, as the "Contributionship" stood firm to its initial decision. The anti-tree decision even became part of the bylaws in April 1784.[130]

In August of that same year, the tree enthusiasts were making initial plans of creating a new insurance company against fire for both buildings near trees and buildings without trees in its surroundings. On September 29th, 1784, the second mutual fire insurance company of America was officially established. The 61 new subscribers had successfully founded the "Mutual Assurance Company for Insuring Houses from Loss by Fire". The company had the nickname the "Green Tree", because of its emblem, a tree in full leaf. It issued its first policy in December of the same year.[131]

It was the "Green Tree" mutual company that ceased to write 7-year policies. Instead, it decided for unlimited policies, called perpetual insurance policies. The "Philadelphia Contributionship" followed this idea 9 years later and until today, perpetual insurance is still in existence.[132]

In 1797, the mutual insurance idea, originally from Philadelphia, had spread to its neighbouring states, to New York, Maryland, and Virginia. In 1823, the "Contributionship" finally dropped its bylaw against buildings near trees and wrote out policies to those houses again. By 1850, both companies had such success that their surpluses had doubled.[133] That same year, the city of Philadelphia experienced its first major fire. On July 9th, a fire and an explosion caused the city to burn. The fire affected 354 buildings and the two mutual insurers suffered a combined loss of approximately $150,000. Fortunately, both insurance companies had operated so successfully in the past, they were able to cover these expenses.[134]

A hundred years after its foundation in 1852, *Horace Binney*, who had been part of the mutual for 41 years, said: "I fervently hope that its operation may never be arrested or impaired, and that the company

130 Cf. Ibid., p. 55.
131 Cf. Ibid., pp. 56-57.
132 Cf. Ibid., p. 58.
133 Cf. Ibid., p. 58.
134 Cf. Ibid., p. 58.

may continue and prosper for centuries to come, a great and perennial public blessing."[135]

Since 1895, the "Contributionship" even allowed dividends to be paid out to policies held for more than ten years. In 1912, the Green Tree mutual followed this idea and started paying out dividends to its members.[136]

8.7 Farm mutual fire insurance

While fire insurance continued to spread throughout New England and down the eastern seaboard over the next several decades in a mix of mutual and stock companies, perhaps the largest catalyst for mutual insurance was the Homestead Act of 1862. It gave 160 acres of western farmland to any citizen willing to claim it. As the population moved west, homesteaders settling new farmland did not trust business and financial entities on the northeast coast. These included the "trust" monopolies for railroad transportation, machinery, and banking as well as the fire insurance industry. This led farmers to create their own social and political organizations, often called "Granges." The "Grange" in each state lobbied for laws allowing formation of farm mutual fire insurance companies, and it often served as an organizational foundation for the state's first farm mutual insurers. This early activity established the farm mutual movement that led to the foundation of approximately 1,100 county farm mutual insurance companies between 1870 and 1900.

From 1900 to 1950, most of the US territory was covered by farm mutual fire insurance. Mutuals have been formed in the states of Kentucky, Tennessee, Alabama, Texas, Oklahoma, Arkansas, Montana, Idaho, Wyoming, Colorado and Utah. The spreading towards the western parts of the country was now definitely in place. Aside from travelling west, new mutuals have been founded in the eastern states, where they were already well established like in New York, Pennsylvania, New Jersey, Ohio, Illinois, Indiana, Michigan, Minnesota, Wisconsin, Iowa, Missouri, North Dakota and South Dakota during this 50 year span.[137]

Even though new farm mutuals were created, fewer mutuals actually operated by 1950 compared to 1900. The reasons behind this development were various. For example, the average farm surface in the USA has gotten bigger and bigger, thus leading to less potential policyholders. In addition, this 50-year time span was characterized by the urbanization of the country, again leading to a smaller farm popu-

[135] Ibid., p. 59.
[136] Cf. Ibid., p. 60.
[137] Cf. Ibid., p. 177.

lation and less farms in general. With fewer farms in business across the country, mutuals were forced to expand their territory, operating in multiple counties. In order to be able to control these larger territories, many mutuals actually consolidated, leading to bigger mutuals and driving smaller mutuals out of business. Even though, there have been less farms and fewer mutuals to cover them, the amount of fire insurance in force for farmers had actually grown. Within approximately 30 years, the number of farm mutuals decreased, while at the same time the insurance value has tripled.[138]

8.8 Further development

By 1860, competition in the fire insurance business had grown fierce. This was because capital requirements were rather low and no regulation laws existed. Therefore, there were many fraudulent insurance companies in the system, leaving policyholders without coverage in case of larger fires. Only 11 out of 41 stock companies survived and one company even brought back the centuries old "tontine" concept in 1868 as a marketing strategy for new established mutual companies to compete against the larger stock companies. This concept worked for both religious institutions and governments. Under tontine policies, premiums were split between ordinary insurance that paid a death benefit and a limited group investment fund that deferred dividend payments for a term of usually 10 to 20 years. At the end of the term, only the surviving participants received the deferred dividend proceeds in form of a lump sum or annuity payment.[139]

Table 10 shows the distribution of fire and marine insurance companies by organizational form during the 1850s in three of America's largest markets and reveals the prominence of mutuals with the introduction of policy dividends. In 1849, a New York State Law passed (prompted by the more established mutuals) that stated an obligatory $100,000 security deposit for all new insurers. This would have been a substantial monetary barrier at that time so the numbers of new mutuals were limited, but, at the same time, it paved the way for new stock company formations. From 1853 to 1865, 41 new stock insurers were organized. Therefore, towards the end of the 1850s, the number of mutuals began to decrease. In New York, their numbers dropped from

[138] Cf. Ibid., p. 178.

[139] Cf. *Obersteadt*, *A.*, The Center for Insurance Policy and Research, State of the Life Insurance Industry: Implications of Industry Trends, A white paper report, August 2013. http://www.naic.org/ accessed on 13.05.2019.

45 in 1854 to 28 by 1859, though they still accounted for nearly one quarter of all fire insurance premiums earned in the state.[140]

Table 10: Distribution of fire and marine insurance companies by organizational form in three American states

	Total	State mutual	State joint-stock	Out-of-state mutual	Out-of-state stock	Foreign stock
New York 1854	145	45	67	2	28	2
New York 1859	187	28	97	-	45	3
Massachusetts 1856	126	70	36	-	17	3
Massachusetts 1860	166	80	35	-	47	4
Pennsylvania 1855	69	33	28	-	-	8

Source: *Pearson. R.*, Organizational Forms in Insurance. A comparison of the USA and Germany during Industrialization, in: *Pearson, R., Yoneyama, T.* (ed.): Corporate Forms and Organizational Choice in International Insurance, Oxford 2015, p. 119.

Pearson indicates a strong growth of fire insurance companies during the latter part of the 19th century. Between 1850 and 1910, the fire insurance sector grew 11 times faster than the population and over three times faster than economy in the whole.[141] In addition, foreign insurers

[140] Cf. *Pearson. R.*, Organizational Forms in Insurance. A comparison of the USA and Germany during Industrialization, in: *Pearson, R., Yoneyama, T.* (ed.): Corporate Forms and Organizational Choice in International Insurance, Oxford 2015, p. 119.

[141] The rapid growth of the industry was also accompanied by an increasing concern over corruption and malfeasance. In 1910, an investigation was commissioned in New York addressing the problem of insolvency in the fire insurance industry. This investigation, instigated by State Senator *Merritt* against a backdrop of insolvencies precipitated by the catastrophic 1906 fire in San Francisco, concluded that a state-regulated rate setting was justified by a need to ensure that reserve levels remained high enough to avoid insolvency. By the early 1920s, within only a decade and a halftel the *Merritt* Committee report, almost thirty states had implemented

were writing significant volumes of business in the USA. By 1881, foreign insurers underwrote around 25 percent of the US fire premiums.[142]

Figure 9 gives the losses due to fire in the USA between 1866 and 1916. The great fires of Chicago and Boston are indicated by an increase in the curve in the late 19th century. Later, during the early 20th century, the Baltimore and especially the San Francisco fire caused huge damages, never before witnessed in the USA (see figure 9).

8.9 The windstorm mutuals

Aside from fire insurance mutuals, windstorm mutuals were among the first to exist in the USA. Iowa is among the leading states in the country suffering from tornadoes. It is no surprise that the first mutual insuring against windstorm was founded in Des Moines, Iowa. The "Iowa Mutual Tornado Insurance Association" was established in 1884. Unlike fire mutuals, which spread westwards, the windstorm mutuals were mainly created in states where actual windstorm hazards were regular. From 1885 to 1900, 41 mutual windstorm companies were founded in 10 different states. They were mostly organized as a separate company from existing farm mutuals. By 1950, there were already 66 farmers' mutual windstorm insurance companies, located in 15 different states, all across the USA.[143]

8.10 Casualty insurance

So far, this paper had mainly introduced fire insurance mutuals and their economic rise as well as their expansion across the country. However, the fire insurance sector is only one of various insurance types but like maritime insurance one of the earliest. Casualty insurance, for example, is a well-known form of insurance these days. A "casualty" loss is a loss suffered from an accident. At the time of its creation, no one could have foreseen its success. Casualty insurance became crucial during the period of the industrial revolution and was originally devised in the UK especially for railway passengers. From 1863 onwards,

some forms of rate regulation. (Cf. *Loftin, G., Xiaoying, X.*, The United States Insurance Market: Characteristics and Trends, in: *Cummins, J.D., Venard, B.* (ed.): Handbook of international insurances. Between Global Dynamics and Local Contingencies, New York 2007, p. 31.)

142 Cf. *Pearson. R.*, Organizational Forms in Insurance. A comparison of the USA and Germany during Industrialization, in: *Pearson, R., Yoneyama, T.* (ed.): Corporate Forms and Organizational Choice in International Insurance, Oxford 2015, p. 121.

143 Cf. *Bainbridge, J.*, Biography of an Idea: The Story of Mutual Fire and Casualty insurance, New York 1952, p. 180.

Figure 9: Annual fire losses in the USA from 1866-1916

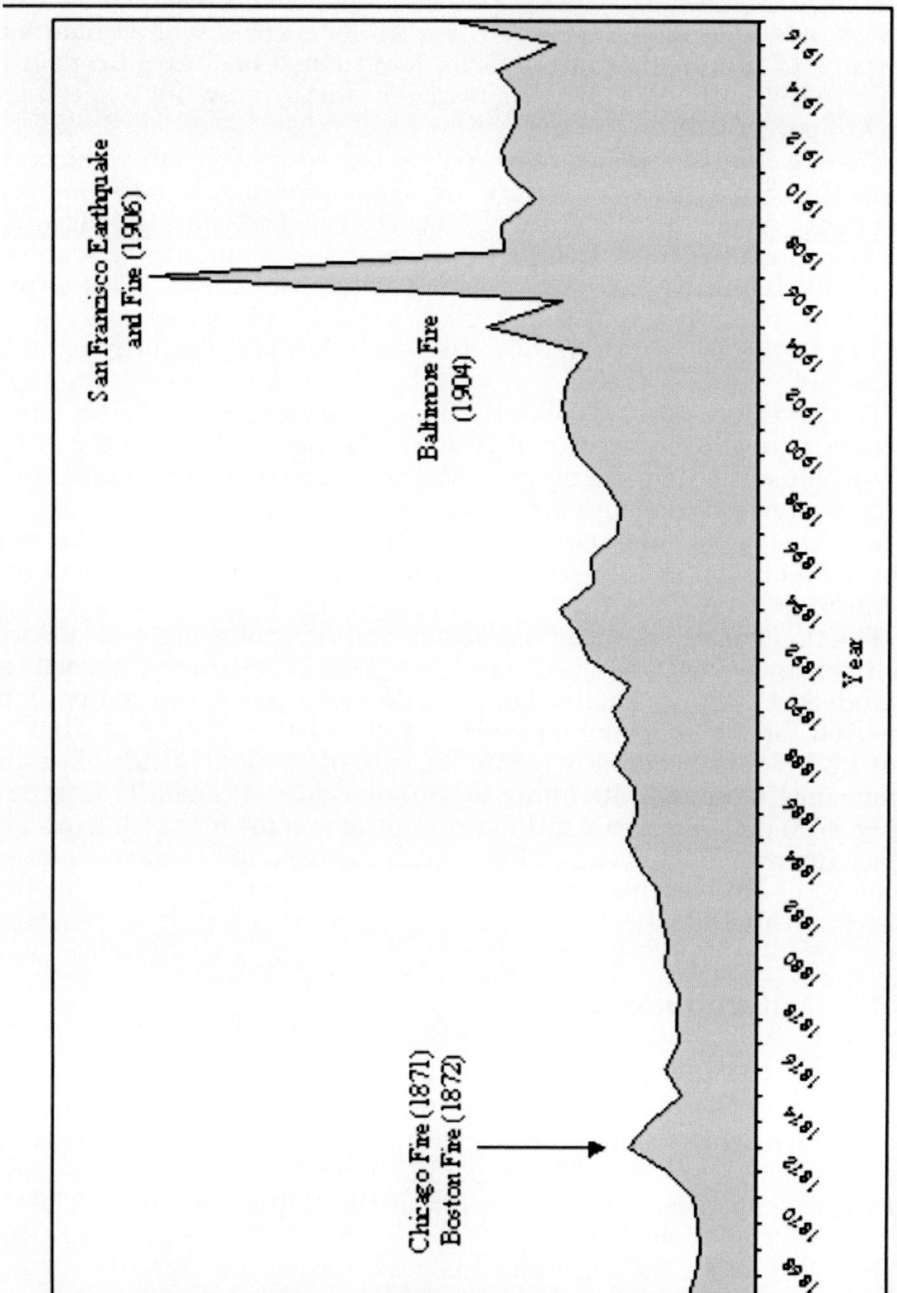

Source: http://eh.net/encyclopedia/fire-insurance-in-the-united-states/.

it was extended in the USA to cover all forms of travel accidents and damage to life. In this latter form, it returned back to Europe. From 1900 to 1950, the casualty insurance industry grew by a spectacular 13,718 percent.[144]

Casualty mutual insurers were rare before 1900. Their predecessors were the "Schaghticoke Society for Apprehending Horse Thieves and Robbers", formed in the state of New York in 1832 and the "Trambauersville Mutual Horse Insurance & Detection Company", established in Pennsylvania in 1868. Their goal was to protect horses, the primary way of transportation at that time. With the coming along of the automobile in the 20th century, these two early forms of casualty insurance vanished.[145]

The first ever mutual casualty insurance company was the "Mutual Boiler Insurance Company of Boston", formed in 1877 in the state of Massachusetts. Its primary goal was to insure boilers and later broadened its horizon to insure air tanks, steam tables, refrigerators, all sorts of machinery, turbines, etc. The company's premiums amounted to just above $6 million in 1950, competing against 203 other mutual casualty insurers at that time.[146]

The first casualty mutual insurance company offering multiple kinds of insurance was the "Mutual Plate Glass Insurance Association", founded in 1880 in Shelby, Ohio. In its early years, the company only insured for its policyholders' glass and focusing purely on that risk, but by 1930, the company expanded into offering all kinds of casualty insurance. Changing its name to "Shelby Mutual Casualty Company", only $700,000 of its $9.2 million premium income was still from plate-glass insurance. This shows how much the casualty insurance line has evolved as well as the development of a huge variety of possible insurances in this industry.[147]

8.11 Automobile insurance

During the 18th and 19th century, the main forms of transportation were trains and horses. The train network in the USA was rather incomplete at that time and therefore people used horses for travelling between cities or when they made business outside of their region. All of this changed with the invention of the automobile in the late 19th century. People had now the choice to travel without any constraints. While the first cars were obviously expensive and far from running

144 Cf. Ibid., p. 257.
145 Cf. Ibid., p. 259.
146 Cf. Ibid., p. 260.
147 Cf. Ibid.

smoothly, the improvements were rather impressive in the following years. In the early years of the 20th century, approximately from 1900 to 1910, the automobile production grew almost one thousand fold. Along with the pouring in of cars into the USA, the insurance companies had to adjust. Starting by offering fire insurance and boiler insurance to the new vehicles, theft insurance was soon introduced. In fact, another 10 years later, around 1920, 30 cars were stolen per month on average. By 1920, 20 years after the earliest automobiles had appeared for the first time, cars had become a common sight due to the introduction of an instalment plan of buying after World War I. As for the automobile insurance, new forms of insurance started flooding the market, which were already customized for automobile owners. In 1907, the first automobile mutual insurance company, the "Automobile Mutual Insurance Company of America" was founded in Providence, Rhode Island. In 1921, the "Factory Mutual Liability Insurance Company of America" was established and both companies were under the same management. By 1950, their combined assets were roughly $31 million, the surplus was approximately $20 million, the total premiums $9.5 million, and the dividends were more than $3 million. At first, fire insurers, workmen's compensation insurers and boiler insurers were among the first to offer automobile insurance. However, more and more specialized automobile insurers started their business in the USA. "State Farm Mutual Automobile Insurance Company", founded in Bloomington, Illinois, is probably the largest automobile insurance mutual ever formed, still dominating the business today. Its founder *George Jacob Mecherle* believed in forming an insurance company that would offer whole life policies that had not been renewed every year. The reasoning behind this was that annual expenses for renewing the policy would cease to exist and that the paying of commissions would vanish. Along with some other new ideas for the insured parties, the insurance company was finally founded on March 29, 1922 and started its business on June 7, 1922. The success story of the "State Farm" was immediate. By 1935, the insurer was operating in 33 US states and by 1950, in 40 states. In the same year, 98.8 percent of the company's total premiums came from the auto insurance sector, showing the insurer's main interest and focus.[148]

[148] Cf. Ibid., p. 317.

8.12 Life, health and accident insurance

It is a well-known fact, that social health care is rather infrequent in the USA. However, other forms of insurances, such as life or property insurance have been part of the American economy for about two hundred years.

8.12.1 Health and accident insurance

In the middle of the 19th century, the pioneers of the companies offering health and accident insurance were established in the USA. The first of such companies was the “Franklin Health Assurance of Massachusetts” founded in 1850. Its goal was to offer insurance for accidents occurring to travellers. However, along with a few insurance companies that followed this model, the “Franklin Health Assurance” was a failure. Only later, policies were improved, health insurance was added and thereby the accident and health insurance industry started to make progress. Another example was the “Commercial Travelers Mutual Accident Association”, established in Utica, New York [149]

In the early 20th century, after great obstacles and struggles, the workmen’s compensation law was finally enacted. The industrial employers were suddenly facing the problem of protecting themselves against possible accidents in their factories. All over the country, mutual casualty insurance companies were founded to protect against possible casualty losses. The mutual movement already incorporated fire, windstorm, and hail insurance. Now mutuals started to underwrite casualty insurances too.[150]

The oldest mutual liability company in the USA is the “American Mutual Liability Insurance Company”, founded in 1887 in Boston, Massachusetts. It was originally established to protect employers against possible lawsuits resulting from machinery accidents. By 1950, along with its associated companies, the “Allied American Mutual Fire Insurance Company” and the “American Policyholders’ Insurance Company” offered nearly all possible forms of insurances, except life insurance. After offering liability insurance for the employers, the “American Mutual Liability Insurance Company” later expanded its business and entered the workmen’s compensation line of business. It provided medical care for injured working people by physicians, doctors, and medical staff available across country to treat their patients. Three clinics in Boston, Newark, and Baltimore were set up for treatment and even rehabilitation centres were established for more severe injuries. Aside from offering direct assistance through medical treatment, the “Ameri-

149 Cf. Ibid., p. 261.
150 Cf. Ibid., p. 269.

can Mutual Liability Insurance Company" also invested in medical research, leading to quicker, better, and more affordable recoveries for the injured workers.[151]

On the other side, there were several mutuals offering purely compensation insurance. The first was founded in Wisconsin, where the first workmen's compensation law was passed in 1911. Industrialists, seeking compensation coverage for their respective companies, founded the "Employers Mutual Liability Insurance Company". The company's founders belonged mainly to the paper and lumber business. They were very familiar with the mutual idea, because mutual fire insurances were already well established. Additionally, the state of Wisconsin advocated for the formation of mutuals to provide compensation insurance. Competing stock firms, spreading negative information about mutual companies and trying to pull policyholders away from such companies, constantly attacked the "Employers Mutual Liability Insurance Company". Despite the fierce competition initiated by the stock firms in 1915 and finally ended two years later by state insurance authorities, the "Employers Mutual Liability Insurance Company" grew at a healthy positive rate during its first fifteen years of operations. The mutual managed to steadily increase its economic figures and compete better and better against other insurance companies, ranking second among all compensation covering insurance companies in the country by 1950.[152]

Like its predecessors, the fire mutuals, the "Employers Mutual Liability Insurance Company" considered preventing losses as the best possible form of insurance. Mutuals have always been the pioneers of this movement. Its slogan was: "Reduction of hazard – to reduce the number of accidents – constitutes one of the chief purposes of this company, we do not want your money, nor do we want to carry your risk, unless you are ready to assist in an earnest effort to carry out the provisions of the Compensation Law, and will lend your aid in every reasonable manner to reduce the hazards and dangers tending to industrial accidents."[153]

Just like the "American Mutual Liability Insurance Company" before the "Employers Mutual Liability Insurance Company" set up workshops to analyse frequently occurring accidents and keep track of the data. By establishing a hygiene division, safety engineers, a physiotherapy squad, and showing educational films, the Employers Mutual was a pioneer and leader in loss prevention in the country at an early stage.

From 1910 until 1920, 42 states and three territories had accepted workmen's compensation laws. During this ten-year span, the US pre-

[151] Cf. Ibid.
[152] Cf. Ibid., p. 276.
[153] Ibid., p. 281.

miums of mutual casualty insurance rose from $1.1 million to $53.1 million.

After 1920, in the state of New York, along with the negative information campaign by stock insurance companies, many people were arguing for an establishment of a monopolistic state fund handling all workmen's compensation insurance. In 1923, the first proposal of such a state fund was turned down. However, several similar proposals followed the next twelve years. The future of quite a few mutual insurance companies was at stake. The solution to the problem was the creation of two funds made up of contributions of insurance companies writing out workmen's compensation in the state of New York. Both mutuals and stock firms were included. As a result, the monopoly state fund could be avoided. All mutuals in business had healthy operations ever since and most of them are still in business until today, although very few new mutuals writing workmen's compensation having entered the state of New York. Comparing Ohio and New York for example between 1924 and 1950, the fatality rate per 100,000 workers has dropped only 30 percent for Ohio, while it has gone down 50 percent for the state of New York.[154]

8.12.2 Life insurance

Of the founding branches of modern insurance, life insurance was the last to develop in the USA. Nevertheless, mortality was the first risk to be insured by this new insurance segment. Several associations were established in the early 1700s to provide care for widows and orphans of their members. In the early 18th century, colonial fraternal societies had to take care of widows and orphans on behalf of their members. The life insurance sector was very small and based on philanthropy. It started in colonial British North America where no restriction or prohibition, like in eighteenth-century Europe, existed, however, it remained a small sector.

In 1759, the synod of the Presbyterian Church provided life insurance on a non-profit basis, financed by donor contributions and later by policy premiums. It was named "Corporation for the Relief of the Poor and Distressed Presbyterian Ministers and for the Poor and the Distressed Widows and Children of Presbyterian Ministers", better known today as "The Presbyterian Ministers' Fund". Another corporation followed in 1769. There were also small fraternal societies that covered their members' funeral expenses.[155]

---

[154] Ibid.

[155] Cf. *Loftin, G., Xie, X* The United States Insurance Market: Characteristics and Trends, in: *Cummins, J.D., Venard, B.* (ed.): Handbook of international insurances. Between Global Dynamics and Local Contingencies, New York 2007, p. 26.

A new wave of insurers developed in the first third of the 19th century, life insurance in form of joint stock companies started to dominate this sector. Two stock companies chartered in Pennsylvania and Massachusetts in 1811 and 1818 respectively sold the first for-profit life insurance. Both provided an income for Philanthropic bodies, namely the "Orphan Society of Philadelphia" and the "Massachusetts Hospital" in Boston. None of the companies sold or tried to sell life insurance on a larger scale, because their policies were expensive due to the use of negative mortality assumptions. Therefore, they offered policies only for a limited period of time (1-7 years).[156] Although it became the largest financial institution in New England, the primary business of the Massachusetts Company managing deposits in trust.[157]

In 1812, the first purely life insurance company was founded in the USA as "The Pennsylvania Company for Insurance on Lives and Granting Annuities". Before the 1830s, a few other companies were chartered to write life insurance, but most of them did not exist very long. Only two joint-stocks, the "New York Life Insurance and Trust" and the "Baltimore Life Insurance", both incorporated in 1830, succeeded in expanding their businesses with more accurate mortality tables, premium rate structures, and with agency networks that extended beyond their home cities. They were rather neutral regarding their mortality assumptions. Thus these companies were neither too expensive nor threatened by bankruptcy. By 1840, the "New York Life Insurance and Trust" accounted for more than half of the life insurance sold in the USA.[158]

It was the reconfiguration of the American life insurance sector following the banking crisis of 1837[159], when mutual companies rose to dominate the industry for the next two decades. They excelled stock insurers primarily due to two competitive advantages: low prices and the duration of insurance policies. Low prices are certainly one of the best and easiest ways to attract customers. However, the second competitive advantage was unique, because mutual insurers offered life insurance policies without a time limit, an innovation stock insurers

156 Cf. *Murphy, S.*, Selecting Risks in an Anonymous World: the Agency System for Life Insurance in Antebellum America, in: Business History Review 82/2008.

157 Cf. *Dalzell, R.*, Enterprising Elite: the Boston Association and the World They Made, New York 1987, p. 81.

158 Cf. *Loftin, G., Xie, X.*, The United States Insurance Market: Characteristics and Trends, in: *Cummins, J.D., Venard, B.* (ed.): Handbook of international insurances. Between Global Dynamics and Local Contingencies, New York 2007, p. 26.

159 The economic crisis of 1837 was one of the biggest in the US history. The reason was a speculative bubble that burst on May 10, 1837 in New York, when every bank stopped the convertibility of the paper currency into gold or silver. (Cf. *Lepler, J.*, The Many Panics of 1837: People, Politics, and the Creation of a Transatlantic Financial Crisis. Cambridge University, New York 2013).

were not able to compete with.[160] As table 11 shows, the initial growth surge occurred during this first peak of mutuals. Whereas the volume of life insurance grew eightfold in the 1830s, it increased by a factor of 21 in the 1840s.[161]

Table 11: The growth of life insurance in the USA, 1840-1910

Year	Number of companies	Life insurance in force ($m)
1820	6	0.1
1840	15	4.7
1850	48	97.1
1860	44	173.0
1870	123	2,006.1
1880	58	1,522.7
1890	60	3,522.2
1900	84	7,573.0
1910	284	14,908.0

Source: *Pearson. R.*, Organizational Forms in Insurance. A comparison of the USA and Germany during Industrialization, in: *Pearson, R., Yoneyama, T.* (ed.): Corporate Forms and Organizational Choice in International Insurance, Oxford 2015 p. 129.

By the end of the 1840s, seventeen new life mutuals had been formed. For example "Mutual of New York" (MONY) sold the first mutual life insurance policy in New York in 1843. Around 1850, mutual insurers covered 85 percent of the US life insurance sector.[162] In 1859, *Henry Hyde* left the Mutual Life Insurance Company of New York to start his own firm, then known as "Equitable Life Assurance Society of

[160] Cf. Swiss Re, Are Mutual Insurers an Endangered Species. Sigma, no. 4/1999, p. 11.

[161] Cf. *Murphy, S.*, Investing in Life: Insurance in Antebellum America, Baltimore 2010, p. 4.

[162] Cf. *Zanjani, G.*, Regulation, Capital, and the Evolution of Organizational Form in U.S. Life Insurance, in: American Economic Review 97/2007, p. 974.

America". In its tenth business year, the "Equitable" wrote more new business than any other company in the world.[163]

One reason for this development was the weak condition of the equity markets, however, *Stalson* suggests that aggressive marketing campaigns using more effective agency networks helped the new mutuals of 1843 to gain ground over the few existing stock companies.[164] *Zelizer*, on the other hand, argues that a more positive religious attitude towards life insurance increased the growth of mutual life insurance in the 1840s, although it was no longer regarded as an industry that undermined people's faith in providence.[165] *Murphy* rejects both explanations. She argues that mutuals constructed their businesses on foundations laid by the early stock companies, while also capturing the optimism of the new urban middle class by marketing life insurance as an investment, rather than simply as a compensation for the death of a wage earner.[166]

Nevertheless, many of the new mutuals had a low financial background and inadequate reserves, consequently, when the growth slowed down during the 1850s, several became insolvent. This increased the concerns about the viability of mutual forms of insurance. Some state legislatures, led by New York in 1849, introduced the requirement that all new life insurance ventures had to raise at least $ 100,000 of equity capital for the protection of their policyholders before commencing business. This resulted in the formation of hybrid companies with financial structures that were part mutual and part stock. The legal stipulation about start-up capital, together with increasing taxation and regulatory restrictions on investments, also explains why the formation process of new companies slowed down during the 1850s. Sales remained weak with the exception of the urban south, where the slave insurance market rapidly grew.[167]

From 1870 to 1895, the life insurances in force increased nearly sixfold as companies introduced industrial and whole life policies. Overall, by the mid-1800s, most states had a wide assortment of enterprises writing insurance contracts.

Coincidentally with the drastic decrease in the influence of fraternal organizations near the turn of the century, life insurance industry as a whole experienced a period of rapid expansion. By 1905, two-thirds of all life insurance in force was Tontine insurance, a combination

[163] Cf. *Murphy, S.*, Investing in Life: Insurance in Antebellum America, Baltimore 2010, p. 6.

[164] Cf. *Stalson, J.O.*, Marketing Life Insurance: History in America, Harvard 1942.

[165] Cf. *Zelizer, G.*, Moral and Markets: The development of Life Insurance in the United States, New Brunswick 1983.

[166] Cf. *Murphy, S.*, Investing in Life: Insurance in Antebellum America, Baltimore 2010, p. 14.

[167] Cf. Ibid., p. 8.

between life insurance and an unusual old-age saving plan. Despite consumer appeal, sales of tontine policies were prohibited in 1906 after the Armstrong Investigation[168] charged the tontine business with corruption and extravagance.[169] The Armstrong Investigation helped spur the mutual movement. During the decade from 1910 to 1920, life insurance (i.e. stock and mutual insurers') in force increased by 158 percent while fraternal insurers' decreased about 9 percent.[170]

We have seen that the mutuals have always performed beyond expectation ever since the first mutual was introduced in the 18th century. Premiums, surpluses, and growths were all solid until the 1950s. However, after 1950, people rarely opted for the mutual form anymore.[171] Nevertheless, prior to the 1960s, mutual insurers were larger than stock insurers and tended to dominate the market for life insurance. In 1965, there were 152 mutual life insurances in the USA. 1998 only 100 of the nation's 1,200 life insurance companies were organized and operated as mutuals, but this handful of companies' controls one-third of the 195 million individual life insurance policies in force.[172]

Zanjani claims that the presence of mutual life insurers in the USA has changed radically in the past two centuries. In 1850, mutual life insurers occupied around 85 percent of the market, whereas that proportion decreased to 15 percent in 2000.[173] Based on this data, it really seems interesting to explore this phenomenon and analyze why this happened. Figure 10 gives us accurate data about the presence of mutual life insurers in the period of previous 150 years (1850-2000). There are two curves in graph, one representing the market share and one representing the number of companies. These numbers and percentages represent the researcher's estimation according to various sources available to him. The upper curve marks the share, whereas the lower curve marks number of companies. Here is a short explanation of these curves.

168 An investigation into abuse and fraud that occurred in the New York State insurance industry. The investigation led to stricter regulation of the industry; for example, insurance companies were required to put their policies' benefits in language a potential policyholder could understand.

169 Cf. *Ransom, R.L. / Sutch, R.*: Tontine Insurance and the Armstrong Investigation: A Case of Stifled Innovation, 1868-1905, in: The Journal of Economic History, Vol. 47, No. 2, 1987, pp. 379.

170 Cf. *Zanjani, G.,* The Rise and Fall of the Fraternal Life Insurer: Law and Finance in U.S. Life Insurance, 1870-1920, New York 2004.

171 *Zanjani, G.*, Regulation, Capital, and the Evolution of Organizational Form in U.S. Life Insurance, American Economic Review 97 2007, p. 973.

172 Cf. *Black, K., Skipper, H.,* Life & Health Insurance, Upper Saddle River, p. 574.

173 Cf. *Zanjani, G.*, Regulation, Capital, and the Evolution of Organizational Form in US Life Insurance, in: The American Economic Revie, 2007 97(3), p. 973-983.

Table 12: Legal reserve formations

Legal reserve formations			
Year	Stock	Mutual	Market share in percent
1900-1909	173	41	19
1910-1919	138	22	14
1920-1929	170	49	22
1930-1939	62	58	48
1940-1949	132	36	21

Source: *Bainbridge, J.*, Biography of an Idea: The Story of Mutual Fire and Casualty insurance, New York 1952, p. 93.

- Market share: In 1850, mutual life insurers were sovereign rulers in the market with a share of 85 percent. In the next 100 years, they successfully kept this position with a lot of ups and downs and even in the most critical period in the beginning of the 20th century, they held around 50 percent of the market. However, from the 1950s onwards mutual life insurers market share declined continuously, ultimately falling below 50 percent during the 1980s. A recovery from this drop of market share was unable to be accomplished by USA mutual insurers. In only 20 years, their market share decreased to 15 percent in 2000.
- Number of companies: The number of companies has steadily increased from 1850 and it reached its peak in the 1960s; around 150 companies. This number was constantly decreasing from that decade until ultimately 70 life insurers were left in the market in 2000. The decade 1939-1949 is omitted since no reliable sources exist.

8.13 Flexibilities of affiliation since the 1990s in the life/health insurance market

The health insurance industry has been in the 1990s subject to rising medical costs, growing demand for healthcare, and an ever-changing and uncertain legislative and regulatory landscape, but health insurers have adapted through strategic partnerships and mergers to ensure diversification and economies of scale. Many mergers arose during a period of consolidation in the mid-1990s in the managed healthcare industry. Amid rising medical costs and sinking profits, larger companies expanded by acquiring smaller, less experienced companies. Size, diversification, market access, economies of scale, and relevance were some of the reasons for the mergers and acquisitions wave. For

Figure 10: Market share and number of mutual insurers (1850-2000)

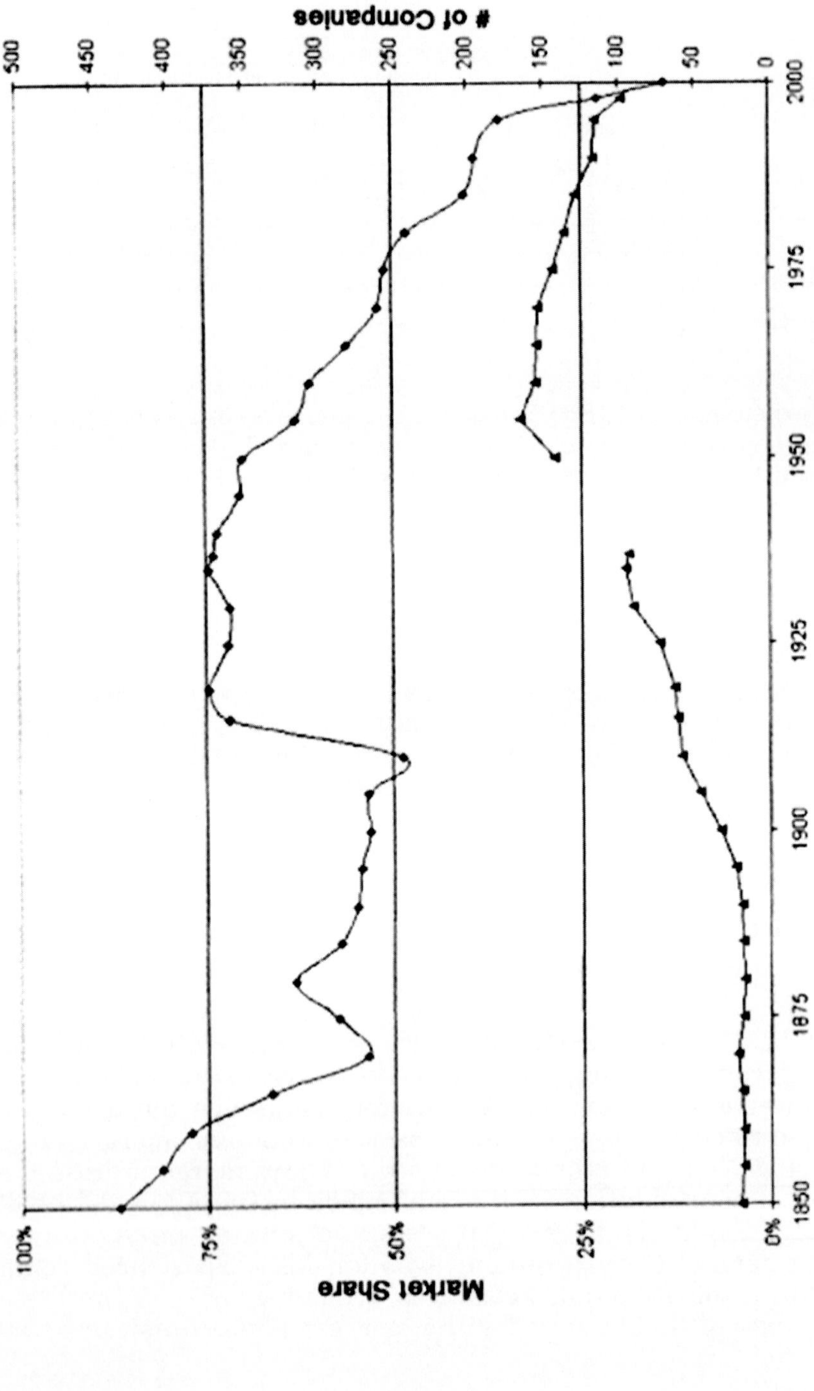

Source: *Zanjani, G.*, Regulation, Capital, and the Evolution of Organizational Form in US Life Insurance, in: The American Economic Revie, 2007 97(3), p. 975.

example, “Anthem” a provider of health insurance acquired or merged between 1997 and 2004 with a series of other healthcare companies. In 2001, “Anthem” underwent demutualization and became a public company via an initial public offering, which made it the fourth largest health care company in the USA. In 2004, “Anthem” merged with “Well Point Health Networks Inc.”, resulting in the largest health benefits company in the USA.[174]

For some life insurers owing to the collapse of the junk bond market, the early 1990s were a turbulent period. One of the main reasons for insurer failure was attributed to improper pricing practices, which led to inadequate reserves and, ultimately, insolvency. Excessive exposure to junk bonds led the California insurance department to seize “Executive Life Insurance Company” in April 1991. Many had assumed that guaranteed investment contracts could not fail. A few months later, the “Mutual Benefit Life Insurance Company” defaulted because of excessive investment in commercial mortgages and real estate, at a time the economy was weakening, prompting the New Jersey Department of Insurance to take over the company. In 1991, life insurers reported 62 insolvencies.[175] It has been through a financial crisis and has been challenged by the low interest rate environment of the past ten years. Life insurers have responded to each of these crises using strategies such as shifting the risk in the guaranteed products to separate accounts (shifting the risk to the policyholder), de-risking a number of variable annuity offerings, and marginally tweaking their portfolios.

Later, with a new environment, new regulations, and facing new competition, demutualization became more and more common. During the 1980s, several demutualization waves occurred, but the most important ones happened in the late 20th and early 21st century.

Everything began with the “Riegle-Neal Interstate Banking and Branching Efficiency Act” of 1994 which removed obstacles to banks opening branches in other states and allowed banks to acquire banks in any state. Further banking deregulation in the late 1990s led to the “Financial Services Modernization Act”, also known as the “Gramm-Leach-Bliley Act” in 1999[176], which removed the barriers between commercial and investment banking, effectively allowing these types of banks to merge.

[174] Cf. The last 25 Years – A Rewiew, in: Best’s Special Report, March 3 2018, p. 1.

[175] Cf. Ibid., p. 2.

[176] It established a comprehensive regulatory framework to permit affiliations among banks, securities firms and insurance companies by repealing the Depression Era Glass-Steagall Act and it affirmed that states should regulate the business of insurance by declaring that the McCarran-Ferguson Act remained in effect. However, Congress also called for state reform to allow insurance companies to compete more effectively in the newly integrated financial service marketplace and to respond with innovation and flexibility to evermore demanding consumer needs.

Banks began developing infrastructure to enter the insurance marketplace directly. The targeted markets were the lower- to middle-income segments as insurers did not maintain efficient cost structures. Life insurers began focusing on cost control to fend off the threat from banks, which were demonstrating their desire to not only distribute annuities, but underwrite them as well. And so banks began developing infrastructure in the mid-1990s to enter the insurance marketplace directly. Favourable court rulings paved the way for banks to sell products like certificates of deposit annuities and, finally, fixed and variable annuities. Despite industry efforts, these products were granted the same tax-exempt status as the products insurers offered. More often banks partnered with insurers as another distribution method. Treasury's rulings would permit banks to conduct insurance and securities underwriting through subsidiaries.[177]

In the 1990s, over 500 mergers and acquisitions activities were recorded. Independent insurance companies were cut by 10 percent, while premiums were up 50 percent. Big companies were looking to purchase the best performing stock companies to get higher outputs.[178] One notable aspect of these transactions was the emergence of international players seeking to be full service global competitors. The enactment of the Gramm-Leach-Bliley Act in 1999 opened the door for extensive financial services consolidation involving banks, insurers, and other financial institutions. European financial institutions were the most active in acquisitions, with banks primarily buying other banks or asset managers.[179]

Insurers have felt pressure to both strengthen their core insurance business and to expand into new financial services markets. In such an environment, access to equity capital was regarded as an increasingly important part of success and even as essential to survive, because competitive forces tend to impose limits on the rate of capital accumulation that is possible through the standard process of retained earnings. As this trend has progressed, the insurance industry as a whole and the life/health industry, in particular, have experienced a clear shift from the mutual to the stock form.[180]

Of the 20 largest mutual life companies in mid-1996, only six decided to remain mutual, with another seven converting to the mutual holding

[177] Cf. The last 25 Years – A Rewiew, in: Best's Special Report, March 3 2018, p. 4.

[178] Cf. *Bonadurer, W.*, Ein tief greifender Wandel – die Entwicklung der Lebensversicherungsbranche in den USA, in: *Spremann, K.* (ed.), Versicherungen im Umbruch, Berlin 2005, p. 502.

[179] Cf. The last 25 Years – A Rewiew, in: Best's Special Report, March 3 2018, p. 4.

[180] Cf. *Loftin, G., Xie, X.*, The United States Insurance Market: Characteristics and Trends, in: *Cummins, J.D., Venard, B.* (ed.): Handbook of international insurances. Between Global Dynamics and Local Contingencies, New York 2007, p. 71.

company form. Being a public company, compared with being a mutual, offered the following prospective advantages:

- Ability to raise capital through public stock offerings;
- Additional flexibility to restructure the company;
- Determination of a market value of the company;
- Creation of a currency - the company's stock - that can be used in transactions;
- Ability to take advantage of market opportunities more quickly;
- Enhanced public scrutiny of company operations and results, increasing the focus on growth and profitability;
- Ability to provide incentives to management and employees with stock and align individual performance with company goals, which has been shown to be a significant enhancer of company performance;
- Ability to use stock as incentives to attract management talent, and
- Accounting comparability with most companies across all industries.

By doing so, "high potentials" of a firm can no longer be easily bought out of the company by some other big economic player.[181]

Clearly, the vast majority of life insurance executives felt that converting to a public company was the way to go. Not all of these benefits have been realized, however. For instance, demutualized companies have not yet materially increased capital and their financial strength. More commonly, capital that was disbursed to participating policyholders as ownership compensation has just been replaced. However, given the potentially advantageous action plans available to a public company, greater financial strength and flexibility could be realized as the plans were executed.

A statistical study in the 2000 life/health edition of A.M. Best's Aggregates and Averages shows that stock-based life/health insurers have performed better than mutuals. From 1990 through 1999, stock companies outperformed mutuals in average annual return on revenue, 3.34 percent to 2.03 percent; return on assets, 0.87 percent to 0.5 percent; and return on equity, 14.13 percent to 9.77 percent.[182] Investors rewarded this performance, particularly for newly demutualized insurers. According to the Credit Suisse report, stock prices of the six insurers that have demutualized since July 1999 collectively rose 127.8 percent through October 6, 2000, compared with a 15.8 percent decline in the Standard & Poor's Life/Health Insurance Index and a 0.8 percent increase in the S&P 500 Index.

---

[181] Cf. *Bonadurer, W.*, Ein tief greifender Wandel – die Entwicklung der Lebensversicherungsbranche in den USA, in: *Spremann, K.* (ed.), Versicherungen im Umbruch, Berlin 2005, p. 502.

[182] Cf. A.M. Best's Aggregates and Averages: Life/Health—2000Edition.

Clearly, demutualization was not the right answer for every company. Another important issue was the relevance of the different structures, and which structure was optimal for supporting a company's vision and business. The answer centred on the particular attributes of the various corporate structures. One reason for conversion had been as mentioned above the ability to access capital. In some insurance businesses, however, there was an overabundance of capital, and competitive returns on equity were difficult to attain. Since there were not enough expansionary opportunities for existing capital – let alone additional capital – to be deployed, the returns in many insurance businesses did not cover the cost of the capital invested in them.[183]

It appeared that either of these organizational forms could have been a positive impact on a company's future prospects, and that one form or the other could have been a better strategic alternative depending on the business characteristics of a given company. However, neither alternative was a panacea to overcome poorly conceived and executed strategies and underperforming operations. Capable management and public company discipline were factors critical to the future success of mutual companies that convert to the stock form of organization. Some of the demutualized companies were challenged to create the dynamic culture and develop the market-focused orientation and financial and actuarial systems necessary to operate successfully in their new competitive arenas.[184]

Due to the stringent initial capital and surplus requirements typical for state insurance regulations, most new insurance companies in this period were founded as stock insurers. In addition, many mutual companies followed the general trend to convert into stock companies. However, demutualization comes along with higher investments in riskier assets and greater profit variability. The mutual companies were facing harsher and more and more competition from all flanks, with companies having great access to public equity markets. By becoming a stock company, the newly formed organization of course becomes eligible for any kind of merger and acquisitions activity. Often times, newly formed stock companies of smaller scale are bought from bigger scale firms, more or less against their will. With this happening, smaller mutuals pass from small operations and knowing their policyholders needs to a great new insurance company, with new ownership and a rather distant communication scheme to its policyholders.

In 1996, the mutual insurance companies started forming mutual holding companies for greater flexibility, but the interests of policyhold-

[183] Cf. A.M. Best Company (ed.), Demutualizations: The State of Conversions in 2002, Special Report, BestWeek, September 30, 2002.

[184] Cf. Ibid.

ers and shareholders become a primary focus, and the cost of capital rises.

Among the companies that opted for a demutualization were some notorious insurance companies like "MetLife Inc.", "John Hancock Life Insurance Co." or "Phoenix Home Life Mutual Insurance Co.".[185] In 1998, "Prudential Insurance Company of America"[186] announced its intent to demutualize[187] – it already became a public company in 2001 –, a further indication that access to the capital markets remained a concern for insurers. While access to capital may be the primary motivation for demutualization, other reasons also existed. These included greater flexibilities of affiliation (i.e. with other financial entities, such as banks) for stock insurers, tax advantages associated with the stock form, and uses of stock that were unrelated to corporate financing. Among these alternatives, the most significant is the greater flexibility of how stock companies can affiliate.[188] By 2001, many large mutual companies had become publicly traded companies. As a result, mutual companies market share in the life segment fell from 50 percent in the mid-1980s to 17 percent by 2001.[189]

Once mutual companies move into the public arena as a result of demutualization, they become subject to increased scrutiny, putting more focus on management's attention to performance measures. Access to the debt market adds to financial flexibility but could pressure the terms of debt offerings if the underlying stock performance is weak. The remaining life mutual companies have focused on their core strengths and have not pursued riskier product lines such as variable annuities. The mutuals continue to access capital primarily by issuing surplus notes.

It is however interesting to note that the stock firms had poor credit-ratings vis-à-vis the existing mutual companies in the USA, given its popularity. One would assume that the stock firms, with its greater capital would have better ratings. However, a study from Moody's in 2003 suggests that the mutual clearly outperform the stock firms in that regard. The mutual did have a far greater solvency rate compared to its fellow competitors.[190]

---

[185] Cf. Ibid., p. 501.

[186] Founded in 1875 as a Friendly Society, "Prudential Insurance Company of America" was the first US company to make life insurance affordable to working-class people.

[187] New Jersey did not have a demutualization statute at the time.

[188] Cf. *Loftin, G., Xie, X.*, The United States Insurance Market: Characteristics and Trends, in: *Cummins, J.D., Venard, B.* (ed.): Handbook of international insurances. Between Global Dynamics and Local Contingencies, New York 2007, p. 71.

[189] Cf. The last 25 Years – A Rewiew, in: Best's Special Report, March 3, 2018, p. 5.

[190] Cf. Moody's: Credit issues and trends for US life insurers, 2003, p. 4.

As table 13 indicates, the mix of stock versus mutual insurers in the US life/health sector has not changed significantly from 1993 to 2003. This is probable, because consolidations among stock insurers have accompanied the wave of demutualisation.[191] However, in terms of premiums written the situation is quite different. The market share of joint stock companies increased continuously from 60.4 percent in 1993 to 82.7 percent in 2003. At the same time, mutuals' share decreased drastically. While they held 37 percent in the US life/health sector in 1993, it shrunk to 14.8 percent in 2003. The reason is that during this period a wave of demutualisation occurred that influenced the market position of the life/health sector significantly. On the other hand, other insurers, which include several medical indemnity plans and insurers with missing or unidentified organizational forms, maintained on the same level (2.7 percent in 1993 to 2.5 percent in 2003) with low points of 1.8 in 1998 and 1999. With regard to net premiums, joint stock companies were able to more than double their net premiums from 1993 ($196,233 million) to 2003 ($416,970 million), while mutuals' net premiums dropped from $120,110 million (1993) to $74,580 million (2003). Again, the group of other insurers slightly increased their net premiums from $8,649 million to $12,395 million during a decade. As this trend has progressed, the life-health industry has experienced a clear shift from the mutual to the stock form.

During the financial crisis of 2008-2009, the stock prices of many insurers fell to dangerously low levels[192], pressuring capital management. Some of the debt or notes issued included unfavourable terms. Publicly held firms like "MetLife Inc.", "Prudential Financial" and "Hartford Financial" have been forced to recognize billions of dollars in losses on mortgage securities, corporate bonds and real estate. With their survival on the line, publicly traded insurers were scrambling for cash by cutting dividends and issuing new shares (weakening existing investors), begging regulators for a relaxation of capital requirements and lobbying Washington for a cut of the $700 billion Wall Street bailout. In contrast, their mutually owned rivals have not asked for any money. Their statutory surpluses (the regulatory counterpart to book value) had held steady or even increased. Stock prices recovered over

---

[191] Cf. *Loftin, G., Xie, X.*, The United States Insurance Market: Characteristics and Trends, in: *Cummins, J.D., Venard, B.* (ed.): Handbook of international insurances. Between Global Dynamics and Local Contingencies, New York 2007, p. 71.

[192] Insurance company stock prices hit bottom in March 2009, declining as much as 75-80 percent from six months earlier. The recovery began in 2010 and by the end of that year, insurance company stock prices had recovered to levels seen before early September 2008.

Table 13: USA Life/Health organisational form counts and net premiums ($ millions), 1993-2003

USA Life/Health organisational form counts and net premiums ($ millions), 1993-2003												
Year	Count	Count in percent	Stock insurers net premiums ($ millions)	Stock insurers' net premiums in percent	Count	Count in percent	Mutual insurers' net premiums ($ millions)	Mutual insurers' net premiums in percent	Count	Count in percent	Other insurers' net premiums ($ millions)	Other insurers' net premiums in percent
1993	1,019	89.4	$196,233	60.4	110	9.6	$120,110	37.0	11	1.0	$8,649	2.7
1994	918	89.0	$212,456	62.1	104	10.1	$122,201	35.7	9	0.9	$7,259	2.1
1995	905	89.4	$239,660	67.0	98	9.7	$109,791	30.7	9	0.9	$7,996	2.2
1996	836	87.7	$241,475	63.3	107	11.2	$131,486	34.5	10	1.0	$8,600	2.3
1997	733	87.5	$287,496	69.6	95	11.3	$116,279	28.2	10	1.2	$9,019	2.2
1998	693	87.3	$334,010	71.5	94	11.8	$124,748	26.7	7	0.9	$8,209	1.8
1999	614	86.2	$356,031	71.8	91	12.8	$130,707	26.4	7	1.0	$9,140	1.8
2000	567	86.0	$444,372	80.7	85	12.9	$95,775	17.4	7	1.1	$10,603	1.9
2001	530	86.5	$395,640	83.0	73	11.9	$70,731	14.8	10	1.6	$10,194	2.1
2002	501	86.7	$426,441	84.2	69	11.9	$69,864	13.8	8	1.4	$9,862	1.9
2003	477	87.0	$416,970	82.7	63	11.5	$74,580	14.8	8	1.5	$12,395	2.5

Source: *Loftin, G., Xie, X.*, The United States Insurance Market: Characteristics and Trends, in: *Cummins, J.D., Venard, B.* (ed.): Handbook of international insurances. Between Global Dynamics and Local Contingencies, New York 2007.

Figure 11: U.S. life/health net premiums in $ millions and percentage, 1993-2003

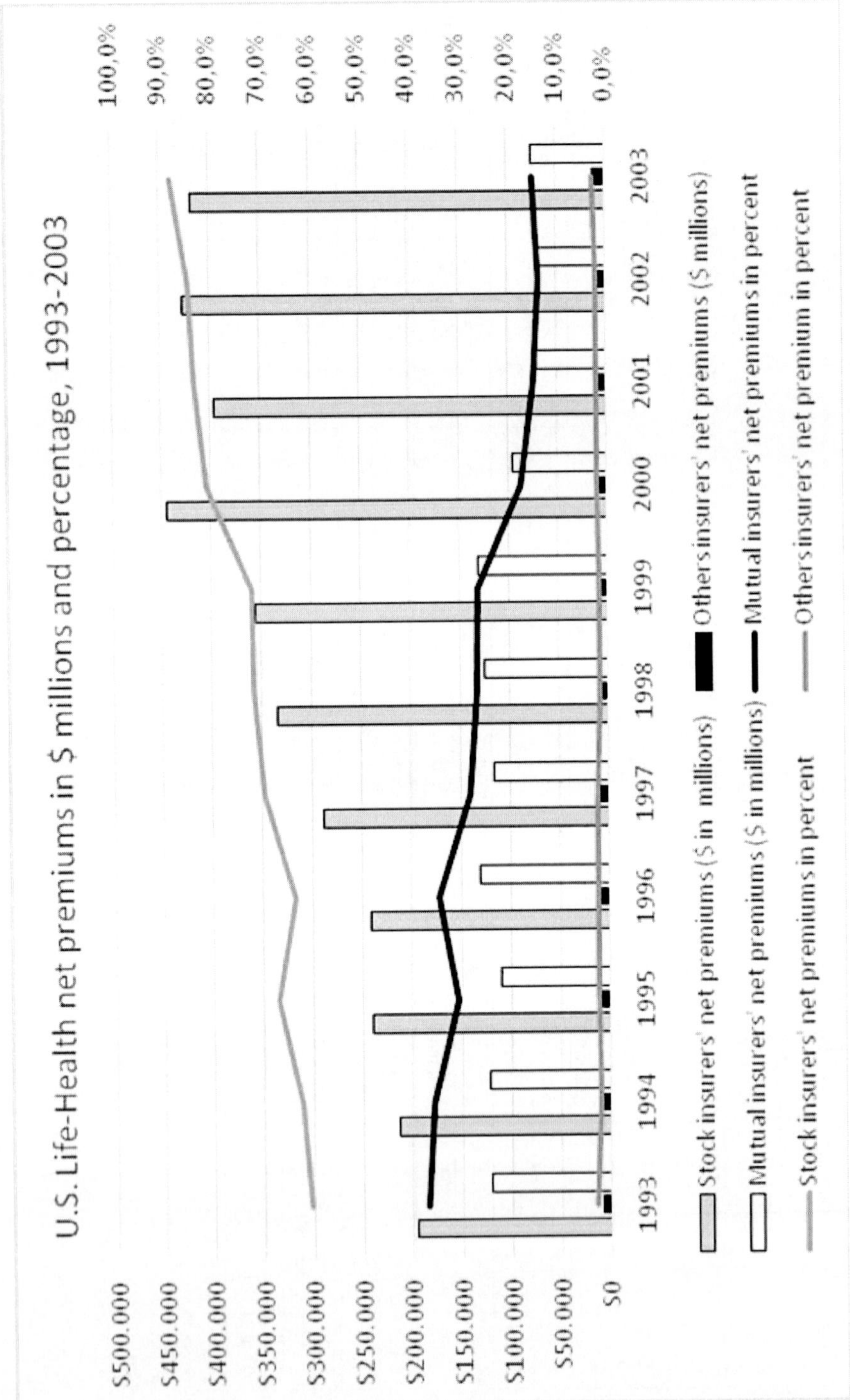

the next several years, but the downturn showed what could happen with publicly traded companies whose stock prices weakened.[193]

In 2008, the near collapse of the "American International Group, Inc.", also known as AIG and the subsequent intervention by the Federal Reserve and Treasury led to increased focus on financial reform measures by congress and regulators. The "AIG Financial Products unit", a non-insurance component of the AIG holding company system, took on huge losses from risky investments. For the life sector as a whole, extraordinary financial losses and elevated risk levels were the primary drivers of rating downgrades.[194]

Given the competitiveness in the insurance industry, both mutual and stock companies have been responsive to changes in the marketplace. A.M. Best closely monitors a number of performance measures of stock and mutual composite groups. Ratings for mutual companies have been more stable than stock companies.[195]

In 2010, the Dodd-Frank Wall Street Reform and Consumer Protection Act was introduced. One of Dodd-Frank's key provisions captured the attention of the insurance industry, particularly the life insurance segment — the creation of the Financial Stability Oversight Council (FSOC), which fell under the jurisdiction of the Treasury Department. Its main focus was to identify risks and emerging threats to financial stability. The FSOC has authority to designate non-bank financial firms for supervision, to minimize the risk that firms considered too big to fail would destabilize the financial system. The FSOC can determine whether any firms pose a grave threat to the financial stability of the USA. It also has the authority to designate firms as systemically important financial institutions (SIFIs), and in 2013 and 2014, it designated three leading insurers — "American International Group, Inc." (AIG), "Prudential Financial", and "MetLife Inc." – as SIFIs on the basis that material financial distress at these companies could pose a threat to the country's financial stability.[196]

8.14 Constant development of mutuals on the property/casualty insurance market

The property/casualty industry has undergone a deep change since the 1990s. It has withstood hurricanes, faced periods of soft pricing and under-reserving, and asbestos and environmental reserve strengthen-

[193] Cf. https://www.forbes.com/forbes/2008/1222/036.html#1b8791551a16 accessed on 13.05.2019.

[194] Cf. The last 25 Years – A Rewiew, in: Best's Special Report, March 3 2018, p. 14.

[195] Cf. Ibid., p. 6.

[196] Cf. Ibid., p. 16.

ing, and been shaken by 9/11, but the property/casualty insurance industry, through enhanced fundamentals as well as innovation and globalization, has emerged stronger.[197]

The development on the property/casualty insurance market was compared to the life insurance sector quite different, because there mutuals still play a very important role. The market share of mutuals regarding the property/casualty insurance market increased at first slightly from 37.9 percent in 1993 to 38.4 in 1994, then dropped, had a peak with 39.3 percent in 1998, dropped down to 32.5 percent in 2001, and increased to 33.1 percent in 2003. Its average market share during this decade was 36.1 percent, which shows a rather constant development in this market segment. A similar development is evident for joint stock companies, because joints held a share of 56.1 percent in 1993, then increased it to 61 percent a year later, had their lowest share in 1998 when mutuals had a peak, and finally increased to 65.3 percent in 2003. With 59.5 percent of average market share, joint stock companies also show a stable development between 1993 and 2003.

Mutuals tend to focus more on personal lines of insurances than on commercial. Mutuals dominate stock firms in farm- (79 percent) and homeowners (64 percent) insurance and represent more than half of the market in private passenger auto physical damage insurance (59 percent) (see table 14). Mutuals have also expanded their business from traditional hazards to new risks insurances, such as medical professional liability. Compared to stock firms, mutuals have a much smaller market share in product liability, workers' compensation, other liability, and financial lines. These segments are more complex, more capital demanding and need more professional services than standard personal insurance and commercial auto insurance. Because of their limited access to capital markets, mutuals have restrictions when raising new capital in the event of unexpected losses. Additionally, mutuals are more susceptible to owner-manager conflicts than stock companies, because policyholders retain minimal control over managers (i.e., they have less access to control mechanisms such as proxy rights, hostile takeovers, and executive stock options compensation). Thus, managers in mutuals may behave more opportunistically. Liability insurance and workers' compensation require more managerial discretion in pricing and underwriting. Consequently, managers must have expert knowledge, ability, or the power to make complex decisions wisely. Subsequently, mutuals are disadvantaged in such segments, because the owners have less control over managers and their decisions. On the

[197] Cf. Ibid., p. 1.

Table 14: USA property/casualty insurance market share, 1993-2003

USA property/casualty insurance market share, 1993-2003												
Year	Number of firms (mutuals)	Number of firms (stock)	Mutual market share in percent	Stock market share in percent	Under-writing expense ratio in percent (mutuals)	Under-writing expense ratio in percent (stock)	Total expense ratio in percent (mutuals)	Total expense ratio in percent (stock)	Loss ratio in percent (mutual)	Loss ratio in percent (stock)	Surplus/ liability ratio in percent (mutual)	Surplus/ liability ratio in percent (stock)
1993	423	620	37.9	56.1	22.7	28.3	35.8	41.7	81.1	78.4	50.8	43.0
1994	488	710	38.4	61.0	23.2	27.8	36.8	41.4	84.8	79.0	49.1	41.8
1995	481	710	37.4	58.2	23.5	27.5	37.7	41.2	80.6	77.7	55.3	48.8
1996	468	696	37.3	57.8	23.8	28.1	37.4	41.1	79.7	76.2	62.3	50.7
1997	455	681	37.5	58.2	24.9	28.5	38.5	41.1	73.7	71.9	76.2	59.8
1998	449	650	39.3	58.3	25.9	29.3	41.1	42.0	79.4	73.9	79.4	63.1
1999	441	610	34.5	58.5	26.2	29.2	42.3	42.0	81.4	76.1	85.0	61.6
2000	431	561	36.3	60.3	25.9	28.8	41.5	41.0	85.0	78.3	79.7	55.7
2001	433	564	32.5	60.1	25.6	27.6	40.0	40.3	89.5	89.4	73.2	45.9
2002	429	561	32.9	60.3	25.3	25.6	38.9	37.6	82.3	79.8	60.7	43.6
2003	396	555	33.1	65.3	24.8	24.9	37.6	37.3	74.7	72.8	68.0	52.0
Average	445	629	36.1	59.5	24.7	27.8	38.9	40.6	81.1	77.6	67.2	51.5

Source: *Loftin, G., Xie, X.*, The United States Insurance Market: Characteristics and Trends, in: *Cummins, J.D., Venard, B.* (ed.): Handbook of international insurances. Between Global Dynamics and Local Contingencies, New York 2007.

Figure 12: U.S. Property/Casualty insurance market share, 1993-2003

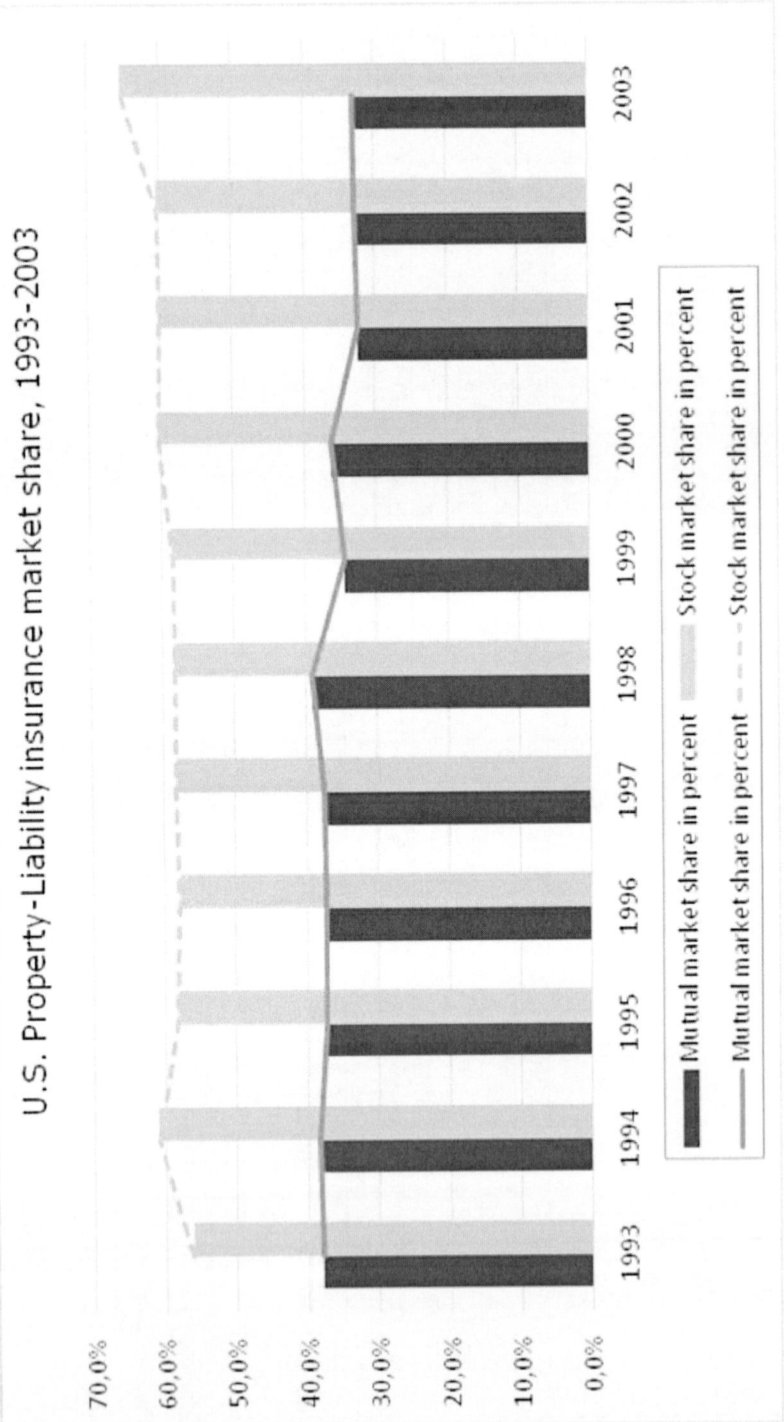

other hand, since policyholders are firm owners, owner-policyholder conflicts are eliminated.[198]

9. Insurance Regulation: an important factor for the development of the different organisational forms

The independent development of the US Insurance industry differentiates it from all other countries, a trend that is also true for its aggressive insurance advertising, insurance regulation, and its life insurance. Unlike Europe, where during the mid-nineteenth century the state controls were restricted allowing company franchises, the USA was swift to establish governmental bodies for the supervision of insurance companies. For most of its history, the US insurance industry has been highly regulated. Unlike other markets, US insurance regulations were and continue to be governed by a complex set of state and federal rules, self-regulations, and international standards.

Regulatory authority for insurance companies developed on a state-by-state basis. The disastrous fire of 1835 in New York City generated concerns about the insurers' solvency to protect consumers. As a result, the states were adopting regulations requiring insurers to be more financially robust to the hazards of large financial losses. Starting with the state New York in 1849, regulations were adopted requiring minimum initial capital amounts for insurance companies' formations. Three years later in 1852, New Hampshire established the first state regulatory body, a state insurance department, charged with oversight of that state's insurance companies. Other states followed shortly thereafter. Due to the initiative of *Elizur Wright*, a state insurance department was established in 1855 in Boston for the state of Massachusetts. In 1860, the state New York followed, which supervision department, regulation and management became the model for many other US union states. Two decades later, insurance departments, led by a commissioner or superintendent, existed in 25 states. In states without

[198] Cf. *Loftin, G., Xie, X.*, The United States Insurance Market: Characteristics and Trends, in: *Cummins, J.D., Venard, B.* (ed.): Handbook of international insurances. Between Global Dynamics and Local Contingencies, New York 2007, p. 101.

formal departments, the state treasurer, comptroller, or secretary of state typically oversaw the insurance regulations.[199]

The Supreme Court affirmed state supervision of insurance in 1869 in the case Paul v. Virginia, which verdict stated that issuing a policy of insurance is not a transaction of commerce. As a result, states were left with responsibility over the taxation and regulation of insurance and would not be subject to any federal regulations over the future decades.[200] The goal of this legislation, which was improved and modified many times, was the establishment of an extensive material state supervision, i.e. a full governmental influence on the business of private insurance companies. This started by granting a licence, continued by a constant supervision of the business activities, and if necessary the intervention into current business transactions.

By the end of the 19th century, most states had insurance regulations that included minimum capital or deposit requirement, investment restrictions, annual financial reporting, and annual liability valuations. But also the laws of each individual state governed the process for a mutual insurance company to demutualize and convert to the stock form of ownership. Full (or traditional) demutualization has been allowed in most US states since the early 1900s. In addition, state insurance regulators typically had the responsibility of conducting company audits and of taking corrective action in the event of insolvency.

State regulations encouraged the creation of state-based local insurance markets, insurance supervisors coordinated their efforts nationally. In 1871, the National Convention of Insurance Commissioners (NCIC) was formed, which after 1935 became known as the National Association of Insurance Commissioners (NAIC). It continues to this day to develop model laws and provide a platform for regulators to discuss changes and communicate with the broader insurance sector. Insurance regulators' responsibilities grew in scope and complexity as the industry evolved. By coordinating the activities of the state bodies, this group exercised even more influence over insurance practice than the states themselves, regarding creating uniform financial statements, standardized reserve requirements, and minimum standards for insurance regulations. By 1900, most states had passed legislation establishing extensive regulations for insurance companies. Although, many states tried to prevent price and other forms of collusion by insurance companies, companies circumvented these measures. It seems that

---

[199] Cf. https://eh.net/encyclopedia/fire-insurance-in-the-united-states/, accessed on 13.02.2017.

[200] Cf. *Ogris, W.* (1988): Zur Entwicklung des Versicherungsaufsichtsrechts und des Versicherungsvertragsrechts in Österreich von der Mitte des 19. Jahrhunderts bis zum Ende der Monarchie, in: Die Ära des klassischen Versicherungswesens, Versicherungsgeschichte Österreichs, vol. II, Vienna, p. 26.

those efforts brought even a necessary order to the insurance market. The existence and activities of the NAIC helps to explain the uniformity of some practices in the US insurance industry, for example, the so-called American system. This system states that companies had to specialise in only one type of insurance. Only a few states, such as New York, actually formally required a separation of activities. As early as 1922, however, the NAIC itself had recommended abolishing the American system, but many companies, especially those in the fire insurance business, preferred to keep out competitors and effectively blocked multiline underwriting until the 1930s. However, even then, some manoeuvres had to be used to get around the restrictions or general trade practice. Finally, after World War II, most restrictions on multiline underwriting were abolished. Today the states maintain at the NAIC the world's largest insurance financial database, which provides a 15-year history of annual and quarterly filings on 5,200 insurance companies.

Another Supreme Court case (United States v. Southeastern Underwriters) led to the overturning of the Paul v. Virginia decision. In the Southeastern Underwriters case the Supreme Court held that insurance was indeed commerce. This caused turmoil as there was a regulatory void that led Congress to enact the McCarran-Ferguson Act in 1945. The McCarran-Ferguson Act clarified that states should continue to regulate and tax the business of insurance and affirmed that the continued regulation of the insurance industry by the states was in the public's best interest.[201]

The Financial Services Modernization Act of 1999, also known as the Gramm-Leach-Bliley Act, established a comprehensive regulatory framework to permit affiliations among banks, security firms and insurance companies by repealing the "Depression Era Glass-Steagall Act". The "Gramm-Leach-Bliley Act" once again acknowledged that states should regulate the business of insurance by declaring that the "McCarran-Ferguson Act" remained in effect. However, Congress also called for state reform to allow insurance companies to compete more effectively in the newly integrated financial service marketplace and to respond with innovation and flexibility to evermore demanding consumer needs. It established the concept of functional regulation where each functional regulator is responsible for regulation of its functional area.[202]

The Wall Street Reform and Consumer Protection Act of 2010, better known as the Dodd-Frank Act[203] once again had an impact on state

---

[201] Cf. Swiss Re Corporate History (ed.), A History of US Insurance, Zurich 2013, p. 13.

[202] Cf. NAIC (Ed.), State Insurance Regulation, Kanses City 2011, p. 1.

[203] The insurance industry was affected by the legislation (a few highlights below) because a large insurer –"American Insurance Group" (AIG) - had a financial product's division that was not regulated by insurance regulators. This led to AIG hav-

insurance regulation. While primarily banking and securities reform legislation, Dodd-Frank did create the Federal Insurance Office as an information gatherer to inform Congress on insurance matters. It also included some reinsurance reform and changed the basis for regulation and taxation of surplus lines insurers. The Federal Insurance Office was granted limited authority to enter into covered agreements with other nations on insurance regulatory matters. However, the primary state insurance regulatory functions remain as they have been since the enactment of McCarran-Ferguson. This allows the States to perform solvency oversight of the US insurance industry and to regulate insurer behaviour in the marketplace.[204]

The question arises how this development of state supervision in the USA influenced mutuals and stock companies. Until the American Revolution and the separation of North America from the British Empire during the 1770s, mutual companies initially had a less privileged position due to the monopoly granted to stock companies loyal to the crown.[205] After the Revolution, none of the various organizational forms had a distinct advantage over the other from a regulatory perspective. Notwithstanding, most of the successful early insurance ventures were stock companies. This situation changed only by the economic crisis of 1837, because in the 1840s it became rather difficult to raise the necessary capital for the foundation of stock companies. However, the result was catastrophic for stock insurers.[206]

Under such circumstances, the mutual company organizational form had a greater appeal than the stock form, especially in the life insurance sector.[207] The mutual insurers primarily thanks to two competitive advantages: low prices and duration of insurance policies. Low prices are certainly one of the best and easiest ways to attract customers. However, the second competitive advantage was unique and something with what stock insurers could not compete. Namely, instead of providing policies for a limited period of time (1-7 years in case of stock insurers), mutual insurers offered life insurance policies without a time limit.

However, this relative advantage did not last long. Starting with New York in 1849, the states began to impose initial capital requirements on

ing obligations to pay out when certain financial instruments, such as collateralized debt obligations, began to sour due to the subprime mortgage lending industry. AIG received federal bailout money (under the Troubled Asset Relief Program), which has since been paid back, plus some, but it was much maligned by the media.

204 Cf. NAIC (ed.), State Insurance Regulation, Kanses City 2011, p. 1.

205 Cf. *Loftin, G., Xie, X.*, The United States Insurance Market: Characteristics and Trends, in: *Cummins, J.D., Venard, B.* (ed.): Handbook of international insurances. Between Global Dynamics and Local Contingencies, New York 2007, p. 29.

206 Cf. Swiss Re, Are Mutual Insurers an Endangered Species. Sigma, no. 4/1999, p. 11.

207 Cf. *Murphy, S.*, Life Insurance in the United States through World War I, 2005, www.eh.net/enceclopedia/?article Murphy.life.insurance.us.

newly forming insurers. Due to the greater difficulty that mutual insurers have in raising capital, this change in the regulatory environment led to a sharp decrease in the number of new mutual insurers founded during the latter half of the 19th century.[208]

Consequently, these measures contributed to the establishment of new joint-stock companies. However, the end result was catastrophic for stock insurers. Although the political-economic climate of that time was good for them, they did not utilize market opportunities. In that manner, around 60 percent of stock insurers established in that time period had dissolved by the beginning of the 20th century.[209]

The New York legislature after the Armstrong Commission Investigation (1905) changed the way people looked at stock companies. The Commission, created by the Legislature and the Governor after a media storm surrounding scandals at several life insurers, was named after its chairman, Senator *William Armstrong* and found evidence of a startling number of abuses within the industry, including illegal loans, massive political contributions, fraudulent financial statements, self-dealing by officers and directors, lavish expenses and improper withholding of dividends to policyholders. Many of the reform recommendations made by the Commission were adopted and are in New York law today. Included in this list is the statute that allows stock companies to convert to the mutual form. This led to the mutualization of "The Equitable Life Assurance Society of the United States", the "Prudential Financial" and the "MetLife Inc." and caused the formation of more mutuals.[210]

At the beginning of the 20th century, the legal regulations were the reasons for the different developments in various insurance sectors. For example, the large fires in Boston and Chicago, Baltimore and San Francisco in the early 1900s triggered the changes decisively. However, by the middle of the first decade of the twentieth century, cooperative price setting in fire insurance business had already ameliorated the worst economic consequences of these disasters.[211]

State governments recognized the value of cooperative price setting and began to abolish anti-compact laws in favour of state involvement in rate setting which took one of two of the following forms: set rates, or state review of industry-set rates. Kansas was the first state to adopt strict rate regulations in 1909, followed by Texas in 1910 and Missouri

[208] Cf. *Loftin, G., Xie, X.*, The United States Insurance Market: Characteristics and Trends, in: *Cummins, J.D., Venard, B.* (ed.): Handbook of international insurances. Between Global Dynamics and Local Contingencies, New York 2007, p. 29.

[209] Cf. Swiss Re, Are Mutual Insurers an Endangered Species. Sigma, no. 4/1999, p. 11.

[210] Cf. https://nyassembly.gov/Reports/Ins/199803/, accessed on 19.09.2019.

[211] Cf.https://eh.net/encyclopedia/fire-insurance-in-the-united-states/, accessed on 13. 02.2017.

in 1911. These laws required insurers to submit their rates for review by the state insurance department, which could overrule them. Contesting the constitutionality of its law, the insurance industry took the State of Kansas to court. In 1914, the Supreme Court of the United States decided German Alliance Insurance Co. v. Ike Lewis, Superintendent of Insurance in favour of Kansas. The Court declared insurance to be a public good and therefore subject to rate regulation.[212]

While the case was pending, New York entered the rating arena in 1911 with a much less restrictive law. New York's law was greatly influenced by a legislative investigation, the Merritt Committee. The Armstrong Committee's investigation of New York's life insurance industry in 1905 leading legislators to call for investigations into the fire insurance industry, where they hoped to discover similar evidence of corruption or profiteering. The Merritt Committee, which met in 1910 and 1911, found instead that most fire insurance companies brought in only modest profits and concluded that the cooperation among firms was often in the public interest, and recommended that insurance boards should continue to set rates. The ensuing law mandated state review of rates to prevent discrimination, requiring companies to charge the same rates for the same types of property. The law also demanded that insurance companies had to submit uniform statistics on premiums and losses for the first time. Other states soon adopted similar requirements. By the early 1920s, nearly thirty states had some form of rate regulation.[213]

New York's data-collection requirement had far-reaching consequences for the entire fire insurance industry. Because every major insurer in the USA did business in New York, any regulatory act passed there had national implications. Moreover, once New York mandated that companies had to submit data, the imperative for a uniform classification system was born. In 1914, the industry responded by creating an Actuarial Bureau within the National Board of Fire Underwriters to collect uniformly organized data and submit it to the states. The regular collection of uniform data enabled the development of modern actuarial science in the fire insurance sector.[214]

The life insurance sector, however, developed completely differently. In this sector, a wave of conversions of the organization forms from a mutual company into a joint stock company (mutualization) as well as the other way around (demutualization) can be observed from the middle of the century onwards.

Mayers and *Smith* analysed 30 life insurance joint stock companies in the USA and Canada that decided for mutualization. With the ex-

212 Cf. Ibid.
213 Cf. Ibid.
214 Cf. Ibid.

ception of two companies, the "National Life Insurance Company" from Vermont (1879) and the "Phoenix Mutual Life Insurance Company" from Hartford (1889) all other 28 companies had converted between 1915 and 1969.[215]

The analysis seems to be thorough, because all firms that started mutualization also completed it. The reasons for mutualisation were collected by personal interviews and reviewing various records such as minutes of the companies' board of directors meetings, legal decisions, and court records.

The rate of mutualization has not been constant over time:

Some of the bunching of dates reflects the enactment of mutualisation laws[216].

- nine firms initiated mutualization within one year of the enactment of the authorizing law[217],
- four firms[218] were mutualized at the time of or following a reorganization,
- other major reasons include estate tax problems (four companies),
- one company, the "Provident Mutual Life Insurance Company" from Philadelphia (1922), stated a change in the tax environment as reason[219].

---

[215] Cf. *Mayers, D., Smith, C.W.*, Ownership Structure and Control The Mutualization of Stock Life Insurance Companies, in: Journal of Financial Economics 1986 16, p. 73ff.

[216] The only potentially motivating legislation were 'remedial' measures in the New York Insurance Laws of 1906.

[217] "Provident Mutual Life Insurance Company" from Philadelphia (1922), "Victory Mutual Life Insurance Company" from Chicago (1933), "Prudential Insurance Company of American" from Newark (1943), "Shenandoah Life Insurance Company" from Roanoke (1955), "Canada Life Insurance Company" from Toronto (1962), "Sun Life Insurance Company" from Montreal (1962), "Manufacturers Life Insurance Company" from Toronto (1963), "Equitable Life Insurance Company" of Canada from Waterloo (1963), and "Confederation Life Association" from Toronto (1968).

[218] "Victory Mutual Life Insurance Company" from Chicago (1933), "Kentucky Home Mutual Life Insurance Company" from Louisville (1935), "General American Life Insurance Company" from St. Louise (1946) and "Pacific Mutual Life Insurance Company" from Los Angeles (1959). It is likely that these four mutualisation were not voluntary. For example, the state insurance commissioners likely had more prominent role in the process for these firms.

[219] Prior to "Provident's" mutualisation, mutual companies were paying a substantial personal property tax based on assets, to which stock companies were not subjected, this law reversed the former regulation. Stock life insurance companies were compelled to pay personal property taxes, and, at the same time, the mutual life insurance companies were relieved from the obligation.

Other motives included such things as

- preventing outside control (eight companies),
- disagreement among stockholders[220],
- a stockholder-manager conflict over the line of business and
- a change of its legal structure and its German name because of the anti-German sentiment following World War II.[221]

A different picture shows when looking at demutualization in the life insurance sector. In three demutualisation waves between 1902 and 1977, 27 mutual life insurers demutualized (see table 15).[222]

The overall goal of legislation concerning demutualization was to establish fairness and equity to policyholders[223]. However, another major reason of demutualization of those life insurers during this period was, according to *Belth*, that demutualization plans allowed a group of investors, including some corporate insiders, to acquire control of a mutual company by giving policyholders only a small amount of compensation for their ownership interest.[224]

---

220 Four families owned 96 percent of the outstanding shares.

221 Cf. *Mayers, D., Smith, C.W.*, Ownership Structure and Control The Mutualization of Stock Life Insurance Companies, in: Journal of Financial Economics 1986 16, p. 79ff.

222 Cf. *Carson, J.M., Forster, M.D., McNamara, M.J.*, Changes in Ownership Structure: Theory and Evidence from Life Insurer Demutualizations, in: Journal of Insurance Issues, 1998 Vol. 21, No. 1, p. 2.

223 Cf. *Hann, L. W.*, New York State of Mind, in: Best's Review (P-C), September 1997, p. 50.

224 Cf. *Belth, J. M.*, The Demutualization of Midland Mutual Life, in: Insurance Forum 1994/21, p. 125ff. It appears that policyholders received little compensation for their ownership interests, leaving considerable amounts for future compensation and possible expropriation. For example, Midland Mutual Life policy owners were compensated only $5.2 million for the termination of their ownership interest of $51.6 million of statutory net worth and $1.2 billion of statutory assets. Stock insurers are subject to greater scrutiny than members of mutuals: stock insurers have two sets of claimholders (policyholders and stockholders) versus only policyholders for mutual insurers.

Table 15: Demutualization in the life insurance sector (1902-1977)

	period	numbers	in percent
1. wave	1902-1918	7[225]	25.93
2. wave	1925-1955	14[226]	51.85
3. wave	1965-1977	6[227]	22.22

Source: *Cole, C.S., McNamara, M.J., Wells, B.P.* (1995), in: Journal of Insurance Issues, Vol. 18, No. 1, p. 44.

In addition, some life insurers, converted numerous times as the following example demonstrates:

In 1896, the "Central Life Assurance Company" was incorporated as a mutual legal reserve life insurance company. Its corporate structure was changed to a non-participating stock life insurance company (demutualization) in 1902. In 1919 the company converted back into a mutual and changed the name into "Central Life Assurance Society of the United States (Mutual)" (mutualisation). The Company merged in 1985 with "Inter-State Assurance Company" and in 1994 with "American Mutual Life Insurance Company", both were domestic mutual life insurance companies, and changed its name to "American Mutual Life Insurance Company". In 1995, the company was reorganized into a mutual insurance holding company structure, the first such structure established in the insurance industry in the USA, formed "American Mutual Holding Company" and became a stock life insurance company and the wholly owned subsidiary of the "American Mutual Holding Company" (semi-demutualization). At the same time, the name of the Company changed into "AmerUs Life Insurance Company". The reorganization separated the contract rights and the membership interests of the owners of the company's policies and annuity contracts. Policyholders' contract rights remained with the company while their

[225] For example, "Central Life Assurance Society" from Des Moines (1902), "Life Insurance Company of Georgia“ from Atlanta (1918), "Peoples Life Insurance Company" from Frankfort (1910).

[226] For example, "American Reserve Life Insurance Company" from Omaha (1925), "St. Louis Mutual Life Insurance Company" from St. Louis (1930), "Washington Life Insurance Company of America" from Lafayette (1953).

[227] For example, "West States Insurance Company" from Los Angeles (1973), "Reliable Life and Casualty Company" from Madison (1965), "Equitable Beneficial Mutual Life Insurance Company" from Philadelphia (1977).

membership rights became membership interests in "American Mutual Holding Company".

In 1996, all of the authorized shares of capital common stock of the company were issued to "American Mutual Holding Company", the company's ultimate parent. Immediately upon reorganization, the ultimate parent contributed all of the shares of capital common stock of the company to "AmerUs Life Holdings, Inc.", the company's immediate parent, in exchange for all of "AmerUs Life Holdings, Inc.'s" initial shares of common stock. Then the ultimate parent contributed all of the initial shares of the company's immediate parent to "AmerUs Group Co." in exchange for all of the initial common shares of "AmerUs Group Co. Under this structure, "AmerUs Group Co." served as an intermediate holding company" between its parent, "American Mutual Holding Company", and its wholly owned subsidiary, "AmerUs Life Holdings, Inc.".

In 2000, the "American Mutual Holding Company" converted into the stock form, changed its name to "AmerUs Group Co.", and acquired the minority interest of "AmerUs Life Holdings, Inc." by issuing "AmerUs Group Co." common stock in exchange for the outstanding shares of "AmerUs Life Holdings, Inc." held by the public (demutualization). "AmerUs Life Holdings, Inc." merged with "AmerUs Group Co." simultaneously with the stock exchange. Prior to the conversion of "AmerUs Group Co." to the stock form, individuals and entities that held insurance policies or annuity contracts issued by "AmerUs" (Members) owned the company. During the conversion phase, "AmerUs Group Co." distributed cash, policy credits and its newly issued common stock to its members in exchange for their membership interests. Following this transaction, the company was a wholly owned stock life insurance company subsidiary of "AmerUs Group Co." Today the company is part of the "Athene USA Corporation".[228]

Mayers and *Smith* also analysed 98 property/casualty mutual insurers that had converted to stock companies between 1920 and 1990. Those conversions were motivated by three main factors:

- firm's ability to grow (growth hypothesis)
- pursue new lines of business (line of business hypothesis)
- potential wealth transfer to executives (private benefits hypothesis)

[228] Cf. https://iid.iowa.gov/documents/examination-reports/life-and-health/athene-annuity-and-life-company-examination-report accessed on 13.05.2019.

So there are significant costs in a mutual company, including opportunity costs and others. Anyone of these cost disadvantages is a reason for a mutual to switch to a stock organizational form.[229]

10. Demutualization

Mutual insurers, as any other type of companies, have always been looking for appropriate ways for growth and expansion. The new economic climate that was created in the 1980s – *Reagan* and *Thatcher* were elected as country leaders of the USA and the United Kingdom – respectively represented a threat, but in the same way an opportunity for them. Endangered/encouraged by new circumstances, many of them started to think about change of their organizational form into joint-stock company. By choosing this transformation process, the company and its insurers were able to gain access to more value and more capital than before, allowing them to grow faster and to expand their offerings as well as markets.[230] In the 1950s under the influence of different professors of Economics who taught at University of Chicago new ideas emerged. They had different approaches in certain matters, but their common denominator was economic liberalism. It meant that they believed in rational behavior of individuals when making decisions and they strongly opposed government interventions. Many believed that greater competition could lead to lower prices and more and better products for the benefit of consumers and the overall economy. It had its peak in the 1980s. Consequently, the USA and the UK started reforms in the 80s reflected in massive tax cuts, deregulation of market and privatization. From this perspective, it is not surprising that these countries were ice-breakers in this process.[231]

---

[229] Cf. *Mayers, D. C., Smith, W.*, Ownership Structure And Control: Property-Casualty Insurer Conversion to Stock Charter", in: Journal of Financial Services Research 2002/2, p. 136.

[230] Cf. http://www.investopedia.com/articles/personal-finance/011916/mutual-vs-publically-traded-insurance-companies.asp, accessed on 24.07.2017.

[231] Cf. *Battilani, P., Schröter, H. G.*, Demutualization and its Problems, in: *Battilani, P., Schröter, H. G.* (eds.): The Cooperative Business Movement, 1950 to the Present, Cambridge 2012, p. 151.

10.1 The challenge of demutualization

It is important to note that demutualization in the USA is not a trend that suddenly emerged in the 1980s, but rather existed for more than 140 years. Demutualization was a usual process but has never been endorsed as in the last few decades of the 20th century. However, one may wonder why it is that the demutualization wave started in the USA and only then spread to other Anglo-Saxon countries and to the rest of the world. The USA was the perfect ground for these activities. The wave of privatization in some way triggered the wave of demutualization. Moreover, after unification of Germany and the fall of the Iron Curtain[232], many recognized these events as a nail in the coffin to communist ideology and the victory of western democratic values and capitalism. People and companies carefully observed the situation in the USA related to organizational forms, financial practices, and government policies and took it as a role model to follow.[233]

In many developed countries, industries are characterized by a mixed structure of mutual (or cooperative) and corporate forms. For example, mutual savings banks, mutual savings and loan associations, agricultural credit cooperatives and credit unions have successfully competed with commercial, for-profit banks in the financial services industry. However, several mutual and cooperative organizations have decided to convert to a corporate form, most notably in Australia, Great Britain, South Africa, the USA, New Zealand and Ireland. The partial conversion of "Credit Agricole" in France and the emergence of 'hybrid' financial structures among agricultural cooperatives suggest that organizational structure changes are more widespread than commonly believed. It does not affect just poor performing mutual insurance companies; traditional well-performing mutual insurance companies are also vulnerable to these trends.[234]

During the past 30 years, the insurance industry has gone through major changes, particularly after 1990s-era legislation removed some of the barriers between insurance companies and banks. As such, the rate of demutualization increased as many mutual companies wanted to diversify their operations beyond insurance and access more capital.

232 Expression used for the border line splitting Europe in two antagonistic political-economic blocs from 1945- 1990; capitalist West and communist East

233 Cf. *Battilani, P., Schröter, H. G.*, Demutualization and its Problems, in: *Battilani, P., Schröter, H. G.* (eds.): The Cooperative Business Movement, 1950 to the Present, Cambridge 2012, p. 152.

234 Cf. *Chaddad, F. R., Cook, M. L.*, The Economics of Organization Structure Changes: A US Perspective on Demutualization, in: Annals of Public and Cooperative Economics, 2004 75 (4), p. 576.

Demutualization has been defined in literature in different ways. In the strictest sense, the process of demutualization refers to "the change in legal status of the exchange from a mutual association with one vote per member (and possibly consensus-based decision making), into a company limited by shares, with one vote per share (with majority-based decision making)"[235].

Chaddad's definition is focusing on the ownership structure. He defines demutualization as a change "in the ownership structure of user owned and controlled organizations from a mutual to a for-profit, proprietary organization. As a result of demutualization, residual claim and control rights are reassigned among stakeholders with implications to firm behaviour and performance. In particular, cooperative membership rights are converted to unrestricted common stock ownership rights in a corporate organization."[236] Individuals involved in demutualization started this process with the best of intentions. The ultimate goal was the improvement of competitiveness, since overall perception was that the mutual form is obsolete.[237]

According to *David Griffiths* demutualization refers to: "the decreased use of mutual organizations to provide services and produce goods and the conversion from mutual to investor ownership [...]"[238]. This definition adds a new element to the discussion – the cooperative identity and values.

Following the literature focusing on the topic of demutualization in the insurance industry, according to *Chugh* and *Meador* demutualization is the "process of converting a mutual life insurance company which is owned by its policyholders into a publicly traded stock company owned by shareholders, pursuant to a plan of conversion approved by policyholders and state regulators."[239] Therefore in the demutualization of an insurance company, the value of the policies is turned into traded stocks and policyholders become stock investors.

---

[235] *Akhtar, S.*, Demutualization of Asian Stock Exchanges in Critical Issues and Challengeses, in: *Akhtar, S.* (ed.), Demutualization of Stock Exchanges. Problems, Solutions and Case Studies, Manila 2002: Asian Development Bank, p. 4.

[236] Cf. *Chaddad, F. R., Cook, M. L.*, The Economics of Organization Structure Changes: A US Perspective on Demutualization, in: Annals of Public and Cooperative Economics, 2004 75 (4), p. 576.

[237] Cf. *Battilani, P. Schröter, H. G.*, Demutualization and its Problems, in: *Battilani, P., Schröter, H. G.* (eds.): The Cooperative Business Movement, 1950 to the Present, Cambridge 2012, p. 151.

[238] *Griffiths, D.*, The Co-op Dictionary. Co-operative Federation of Victoria Ltd. 2004 Second edition, p. 17.

[239] *Chugh, L., Meador, J. W.*. Demutualization in the Life Insurance Industry: A Study of Effectiveness, in: Review of Business, 2006 27(1), p. 13.

The organization change from a mutual to a demutualized structure involves two main features:

- a change in the ownership structure, and
- a change in legal as well as organizational form.[240]

Demutualization is a complex and expensive process of change, which requires a lot of time – it takes 18 to 24 months to be completed[241] – and can very much affect existing and future policyholders.[242] A company which proposes to go through the demutualization process must follow the laws in its state. The plan of demutualization requires prior approval of the policyholders and the state regulators. Of course, demutualization may make sense only in specific circumstances and depends on many factors and potential drivers.

Generally, two basic types of demutualization exist: full and partial demutualization. However, they are subject of different legislation depending on the state. In most of the states, permission of state organs and high approval rate of policyholders is good enough. However, some states require extra conditions, whereas some states do not allow demutualization at all.[243]

10.2 Conversion statutes

The next table gives an overview of the conversion statutes in 2010.

240 Cf. *Akhtar,* Demutualization of Asian Stock Exchanges in Critical Issues and Challengeses, in: *Akhtar, S.* (ed.), Demutualization of Stock Exchanges. Problems, Solutions and Case Studies, Manila 2002: Asian Development Bank, p. 8.

241 For property/casualty companies, the timeframe is usually considerably less, as the process of allocating equity is less complex (i.e., the allocation is usually based on the percentage of premiums paid by each policyholder of record).

242 *Fitzgerald* identified 11 conflicting theories for determining and distributing the surplus of the converting mutual insurer. (Cf. *Fitzgerald, J.*, Demutualizing an Insurance Company: Determining and Distributing Policyholders' Shares, in: Journal of Insurance Regulation, June 1986, p. 103.

243 For example, in 1988, the state of New York lifted the ban on conversion after perennial prohibition. (Cf. *McNamara , M. J., Rhee, G. S.*, Ownership Structure and Performance: The Demutualization of Life Insurers, in: The Journal of Risk and Insurance, 59(2) 1992, p. 223).

Table 16: Conversion statutes by state

Only Full Demutualization Allowed

Alabama	New Jersey	Tennessee
Arizona	New Mexico	Utah
Colorado	New York	Washington
Delaware	North Carolina	West Virginia
Georgia	Oklahoma	Wyoming
Montana	South Dakota	
No Conversion Statutes		
	Connecticut	
Conversion Prohibited		
Alaska	Hawaii	
Full Demutualization and Mutual Holding Company (MHC) Conversion Allowed		
Arkansas (2001)	Maine (2000)	Ohio (1997)
California (1998)	Maryland (2000)	Oregon (1997)
District of Columbia (1996)	Massachusetts (1998)	Pennsylvania (1996)
Florida (1997)	Michigan (2000)	Rhode Island (1996)
Idaho (1998)	Minnesota (1996)	South Carolina (1998)
Illinois (1999)	Mississippi (1998)	Texas (2003)
Indiana (1997)	Missouri (1996)	Vermont (1996)
Iowa (1995)	Nebraska (1997)	Virginia (2001)
Kansas (1997)	Nevada (2001)	Wisconsin (1998)
Kentucky (1998)	New Hampshire (2000)	Louisiana (1997)
North Dakota (1997)		

Source: *Erhemjamts, O., Leverty, T. J.,* The Demise of the Mutual Organizational Form: An Investigation of the Life Insurance Industry, in: Journal of Money, Credit and Banking, 2010 42(6), p. 1032.

Already in the year 1998, 21 states and the District of Columbia had passed legislation allowing their domestic mutual insurance companies to reorganize by forming a mutual holding company (MHC) and converting the mutual insurer into a stock corporation.

The insurance code in Connecticut does not address mutual-stock conversion. Alaska and Hawaii expressly prohibit conversion to stock charter. The methods of full demutualization and mutual holding company conversion are described below. Depending on the state, eligible policyholders may receive compensation for giving up their ownership rights in the form of shares in the newly created stock holding company, cash, and/or policy credits.

The ability of a mutual company to demutualize was further facilitated by Section 312 of the Financial Services Modernization Act of 1999, which allows a mutual insurer that wishes to demutualize but is prohibited from doing so under the laws of its domiciliary state to redomesticate to a state that allows demutualization. Further, Section 313 of the Act pre-empts any state law restricting or penalizing companies or policyholders because of such a redomestication. As a result, passage of the Financial Services Modernization Act meant that any US mutual life insurance company could choose to demutualize regardless of the state of domicile.[244]

10.3 Full demutualization

Simply, in the event of full demutualization, a mutual insurance company[245] will transform into a joint-stock company and all traces of mutuality will be eliminated (distribution rights conversion). "In a full demutualization, the company distributes cash, shares or subscription rights to policyholders in exchange for the membership rights they hold in the mutual association."[246] Stock holding companies as well as a downstream stock insurance subsidiary are created. The holding company wholly owns the stock subsidiary, into which all of the former mutual's insurance obligations are transferred as a result of demutualization. Having an intermediate stock holding company facilitates investment in and acquisition of both insurance and noninsurance subsidiaries.[247] With a full demutualization, passing from a mutual organization to a stock firm organization, the entire company is sold using capital shares. The new shareholders then own their acquired shares,

[244] Cf. *Harman, J, Adney, J., Keene, B.*, The Taxes on Starlight: A Case for the Repeal of Sections 809, 815, and 1503(c) of the Internal Revenue Code, in: Insurance Tax Review 2001 31, p.31.

[245] Full (or traditional) demutualization has been allowed in most US states since the early 1900s. Savings and loan association demutualization was permitted since 1976 (Cf. *Masulis, R. W.*, Changes in Ownership Structure: Conversion of Mutual Savings and Loans to Stock Charter, in: Journal of Financial Economics, 1987 18, p. 29).

[246] Swiss Re, *Are Mutual Insurers an Endangered Species.* Sigma, no.4/1999, p. 26.

[247] Cf. *Viswanathan, K. S., Cummins, D. J.*, Ownership Structure Changes in the Insurance Industry: An Analysis of Demutualization, in: Journal of Risk and Insurance, 70(3) 2003, p. 404.

as well as equity formed before the demutualization process. The demutualized company is then usually publicly listed in the stock exchange to raise new equity capital. One reason for the Initial Public Offering (IPO) is the realization of its true economic value. Demutualization unlocks the economic value of the company. First, the policyholders' surplus (largely retained earnings) under mutual is transformed into marketable shares through creation and distribution of stock to existing policyholders, as well as an IPO; this, stockization liquefies what has been illiquid. Also, stockization of mutual life-insurance companies broadens the set of available securities for investors and completes the market. Figure 13 presents the usual structure of a mutual insurance company after the demutualization process.

Demutualization allows an insurer to raise new capital, creates acquisition currency and facilitates mergers with stock insurance companies.

10.3.1 New York method

Full demutualization also also called the New York method is according to *Chugh* and *Meadow* the most widespread and simplest demutualization method. The state of New York introduced a demutualization statute in the year 1988. It has been used as a blueprint for other several demutualization statutes in the USA in the following years.[248] In this case, the policyholders receive shares in the newly created stock holding company, cash and/or policy credits[249] for their ownership rights in the mutual organization and all principles of mutuality are eliminated. The insurer's aggregate surplus is divided among these eligible policyholders as this amount represents their equity in the firm. The surplus allocation process is the lengthiest and most complex aspect of the demutualization process but it provides a financial and organizational stability. Policyholders will get a full refund for giving up their membership at the former mutual insurance company and in most cases can participate as shareholders in the new demutualized company.[250]

All in all, a very smooth conversion method. The first company in New York was "Portland, ME-based Union Mutual" (later, UNUM),

[248] The New York traditional full demutualization method has been approved by the states of New York obviously (utilized by "Equitable Life Assurance" in 1992), Maine, Nebraska ("Guarantee Mutual Life Insurance Company" demutualized in 1995), Oregon, South Carolina, and several other states (Cf. http://www.insurance-finance.com/files/doc2.html, accessed on 15.08.2017).

[249] Eligibility is determined according to the conversion statute.

[250] Cf. *Chugh, L., Meador, J. W.*, Demutualization in the Life Insurance Industry: A Study of Effectiveness, in: Review of Business, 2006 27(1), p. 14.

Figure 13: Structure of a mutual insurance company after the demutualization process

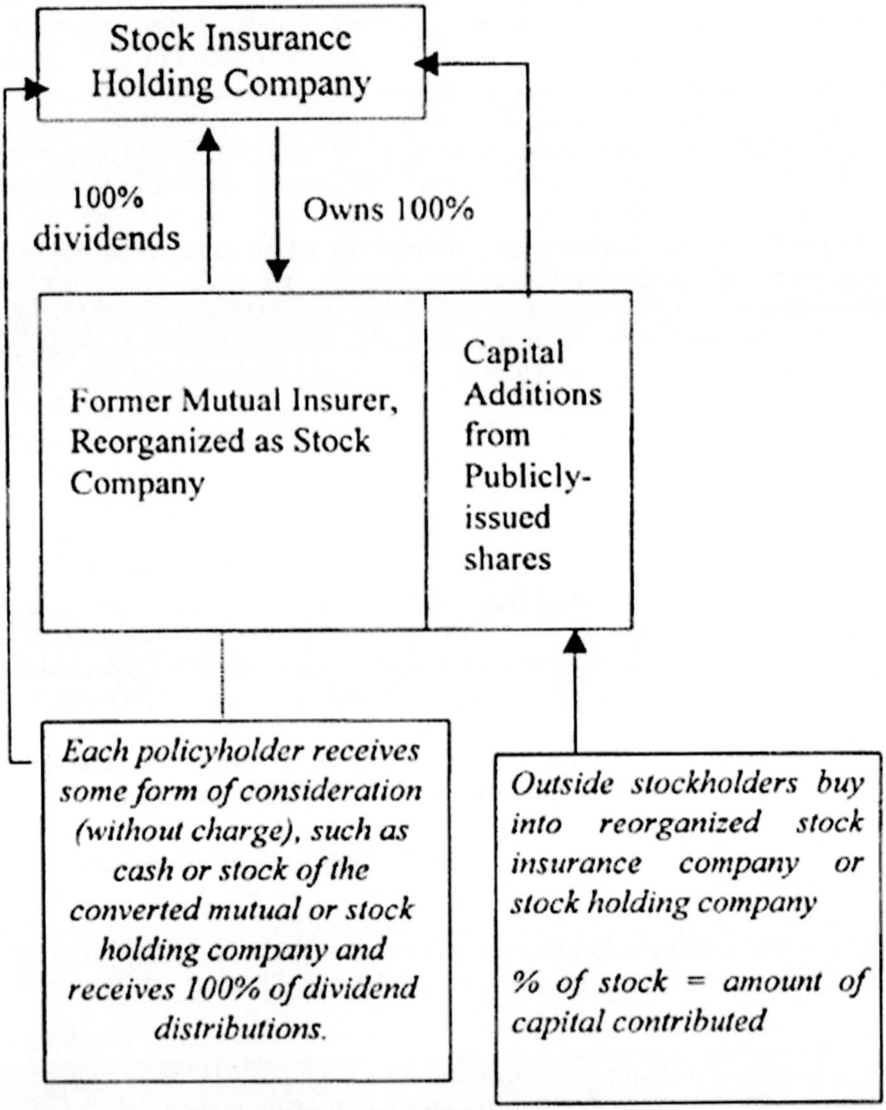

Source: NAIC (ed.): Mutual Insurance Holding Company Reorganizations, 1998, p. 14.

primarily a disability insurance company. Followed by the "Equitable Life Assurance Society of the US" (ELAS) in 1992, "Glenmont, NY-based Farm Family" (FF) in 1996, "Mutual of New York" (MONY; formerly Mutual Life Insurance Company of New York) in 1998, "StanCorp Financial Group" (formerly Standard Insurance Co.) in 1999, Boston-based "John Hancock Life Insurance Co." and "Metropolitan Life Insurance Co." in 2000 (they became "MetLife Inc.") and "Prudential Insurance Company of America" in 2001.[251] [252]

Union Mutual - UNUM - UnumProvident - Maine-based Union Mutual demutualized in November of 1986, and became UNUM Life Insurance Company of America. Eligible Union Mutual policyholders became entitled to receive compensation totaling $650 million. UNUM subsequently merged with The Provident Companies (formerly Provident Life and Accident Insurance Company) on June 30, 1999, becoming UnumProvident Corporation. UNUM shareholders became entitled to receive one share of UnumProvident for every common share owned. UnumProvident stock split several times and currently trades at approximately $29 share.

10.3.2 Illinois/Pennsylvania method

The other option of accomplishing a full demutualization is commonly called the Illinois/Pennsylvania method introduced in 1994. In comparison to the New York method, here the non-transferable subscription rights are given to the former policyholders to buy their own shares in the new stock company, which came into existence after the successful demutualization. This method is known as a controversial one, as the former policyholders do not get any kind of compensation when deciding not to participate in the new form of the company. This conversion is not so popular, because it is the subject of disputes and it often has court epilogues. Only several states approve it. Here the first company was the "Old Guard Mutual Insurance Company" in Pennsylvania. It completed its demutualization in 1995.[253]

[251] Cf. https://nyassembly.gov/Reports/Ins/199803/insureport2.html#t31 accessed on 13.05.2019.

[252] Also three Canadian insurers converted: "Clarica Life Insurance" (formerly "Mutual Life Insurance Company of Canada"), Waterloo, Ont., in July 1999; "Manufacturers Life Insurance Co.", in September 1999; and "Canada Life Assurance Co.", Toronto, in October 1999.

[253] Cf. *Chugh, L., Meador, J. W.*, Demutualization in the Life Insurance Industry: A Study of Effectiveness, in: Review of Business, 2006 27(1), p. 14.

10.3.3 Full demutualization process

Next figure shows in which manner process of full demutualization is executed:

Figure 14: Execution of full demutualization process

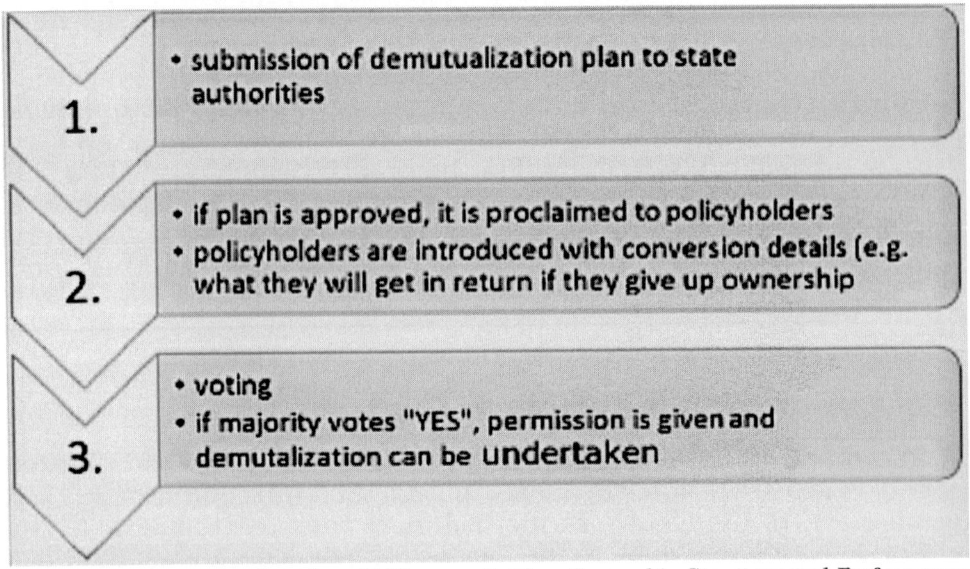

Source: Representation based on *McNamara & Rhee*, Ownership Structure and Performance: The Demutualization of Life Insurers, in: The Journal of Risk and Insurance, 1992 59(2), p. 223.

10.3.4 Full demutualization in the life/health and property/casualty sector

Mutual-to-stock conversions have been occurring for many decades in both the life/health and property/casualty industries. Driving life insurer demutualizations in the early part of the twentieth century was the need for capital and the desire to diversify.[254] These reasons are still considered to be key motivators for undergoing the conversion to stock form. Although life/health demutualizations have occurred

[254] Cf. *Hansmann, H.*, The Organization of Insurance Companies: Mutual Versus Stock, in: Journal of Law, Economics and Organization, 1/1985, p. 125ff.

steadily over time until the 1980s, there have been a sizable number of property/casualty conversions in the 1960s and since.[255] In the decades 1980 and 1990, demutualization activity has been particularly heavy in both the life/health and property/casualty fields. This may signify that the mutual form is increasingly hindering the objectives of certain firms. Mutual firms, given their lack of a tradable currency, are more constrained than stock insurers from participating in the heavy consolidation activity currently underway in the financial services industry. Mutuals must use cash rather than stock in merger and acquisition transactions. By converting to stock form, the converting mutual gains the ability to use its shares for mergers and acquisitions purposes.[256] Stock firms also have tremendous flexibility in raising new capital, having access to both equity and debt markets. Mutuals typically must rely on retained earnings for future growth. What induces certain mutuals to undergo the demutualization process, considering the high accounting, actuarial, and regulatory costs of conversion?

10.3.5 Controversy

Demutualizations have generated substantial controversy, including consumer groups and some regulators. One of the main disadvantages of a full demutualization is its price. As a very expensive and time consuming process, one insurance company can spend lots of money and other resources on the services needed to be done to fully demutualize. It creates the opportunity for the new company with a stock ownership to be taken over. A takeover may or may not benefit policyholders and cause conflicts. The demutualization will likely shorten management's performance time horizon significantly, because a stock company is not being long-term focused as the mutual one was.

In the process of demutualization, normally we saw all the accumulated profits of the mutual company returned to the policy owners. They were returned in the form of cash, stocks or as policy credits. There were cases when some policy owners are unresponsive and, thus, the existence of unclaimed demutualization compensation. "Metropolitan Life" accumulated unclaimed demutualization compensation of 60 million shares worth about $2 billion. "Prudential Life" was unable to locate 1.2 million policyholders entitled to receive 110 million shares

---

[255] Cf. *Carson, J. M., Forster, M. D., McNamara, M. J.*, Changes in Ownership Structure: Theory and Evidence from Life Insurer Demutualizations, Journal of Insurance Issues, 21/1998, p. 1ff.; *Mayers, D., Smith, C.,* Ownership Structure and Control: Property-Casualty Insurer Conversion to Stock Charter, in: Journal of Financial Services Research, 21(1-2) 2002, p. 117ff.

[256] *Tuohy, M.*, Challenges and Issues for Growth in the Life Insurance Industry, in: *Cummins, J. D., Santomero, A. M.* (eds.): Changes in the Life Insurance Industry: Efficiency, Technology, and Risk Management, Norwell 1999.

worth over $3.025 billion. Not every policyholder is entitled to receive compensation, only those who are eligible.[257]

Several of the insurers that have converted have faced some level of backlash from disgruntled policyholders. In addition to the suit filed against "National Life of Vermont", class action suits have also been filed against "MetLife Inc.", "Mutual of New York" (MONY), and "John Hancock Life Insurance Co.", charging either that surplus allocations were inadequate or that management and the board of directors failed in their fiduciary duty to policyholders. Similar to "National Life of Vermont", these particular lawsuits have been dismissed.[258]

10.4 Sponsored demutualization

One more method of full demutualization is particularly interesting. It is called sponsored demutualization. In this case, a so-called sponsor (often another insurance company) overtakes the mutual insurance company. But in this case, there is no initial public offering and the sponsor overtakes the mutual insurance company. In this case: "the investor compensates members with either cash or shares (the consideration) of its stock. In many cases the management of the mutual relinquishes control of the company."[259] For example SBLI USA in New York converted in 2014 from a mutual insurance into a stock insurance company that is owned by the Prosperity Life Insurance Group.[260]

10.5 MHC

The 1987 Competitive Equality Banking Act introduced a new organizational form in the thrift industry known as the mutual holding company (MHC), a hybrid between the "pure" mutual and stock associations (partial demutualization). This legislation addressed the inability of mutual institution – such as a mutual savings and loan institution, or mutual insurance company – to raise external equity by creating MHC and selling minority interest in stock thrift subsidiaries. The MHC structure permits a mutual association to raise incremental amounts of capital while maintaining the mutual ownership base.

---

257 Cf.https://businessmirror.com.ph/2016/07/12/demutualization-in-the-insurance-industry/.

258 Cf. *Viswanathan, K.S., Cummins, J.D.*, Ownership Structure Changes in the Insurance Industry: An Analysis of Demutualization, in: Journal of Risk and Insurance 70/2003, p. 432.

259 Swiss Re, *Are Mutual Insurers an Endangered Species.* Sigma, no.4/1999, p. 26.

260 Cf. https://www.dfs.ny.gov/docs/insurance/exam_rpt/60176c15.pdf, p. 5, accessed on 13.05.2019.

In 1988 the mutual savings institution "People's Bank of Bridgeport, Conn." formed the first mutual holding company in the USA.[261] Eight years later, in 1996, Iowa-domiciled "American Mutual Life" became the first mutual insurer to convert to a MHC, "American Mutual Holding Co.", the parent of "AmerUs Life Holdings Inc." under the State law in 1995.[262] Many states followed this example between 1996 and 1998.[263]

> American Mutual Life - AmerUs - Indianapolis Life Insurance Company - Central Life Assurance - Central Life Assurance merged with American Mutual in 1994. American Mutual Life was renamed AmerUs Life Insurance Company in 1995. On September 20, 2000, it demutualized to become AmerUs Group. In 2001, the company merged with Indianapolis Life, which had also undergone a demutualization. Approximately 300,000 policyholders and heirs became entitled to receive $452 million in AmerUs Group common stock and $340 million in cash and policy credits. Distribution began on July 31, 2001. Eligible policyholders received a fixed component of 20 AmerUS common shares, as well as a variable component based on policy value. Those who elected to receive cash were compensate $26 per share entitlement. In the first year after the initial public offering, the price of an AmerUS common share increased 99%. The current value of AmerUS Group stock is approximately $60 per share.

The "AmerUs Life Holdings Inc." started with the following characteristics:

- The policy rights went to the newly converted stock life insurance company
- The membership rights went to the MHC
- The stock company became responsible for operating in the life insurance business
- The MHC became responsible for managing all subsidiaries including the new stock life insurance company.

---

261 Since 2004, 85 of the 700 mutual savings institutions were organized as "private" mutual holding companies with the primary goal to protect mutuality as a banking option for individuals and business (Cf. https://www.luselaw.com/wp-content/uploads/2017/04/2005_4.pdf accessed on 13.05.2019).

262 This method is also known as the Iowa method because in 1995 Iowa passed legislation authorizing the formation of mutual insurance-holding companies.

263 Cf. *Viswanathan, K. S., Cummins, D. J.,* Ownership Structure Changes in the Insurance Industry: An Analysis of Demutualization, in: Journal of Risk and Insurance, 70(3) 2003, p. 405.

- The MHC was holding all 100 percent of the subsidiaries. If new stocks were issued to raise new capital, the MHC still needed to remain the majority holder.
- After the change, new policyholders became new members of the MHC.[264]

In a MHC conversion process, a new MHC is created as part of a multi-tiered insurance holding company system. Under this conversion method, two new entities are formed:

- a new MHC which is the parent corporation, and
- a new stock intermediate holding company (SHC) which is a subsidiary of the MHC.

Then, the original mutual insurance company is converted into a stock insurance company that becomes a subsidiary of the SHC. Under this arrangement, the insurance policies remain with the converted mutual company which is now a stock company. The ownership rights originally attached to the policy are transferred to the new parent mutual company. To raise capital, the MHC can sell shares of stock in its SHC subsidiary to the public, but typically retains a majority of the voting rights.

It was also in the state of Iowa where the famous 50.1 percent rule[265] was first declared. The mutual holding company must hold at least 50.1 percent of the voting power, and this at all times. The maximum percentage that can be gained with the purchase of Initial Public Offering (IPO) capital shares is 49.9 percent. Nobody can own an MHC and nobody can take you over because you are controlled by the policyholders. The words "voting power" have to be emphasized because that is not necessarily the same as economic control. Voting rights are not the same as economic rights. That means it is potentially possible to sell upwards of 75 percent of the economic value of the stock insurance company while retaining the majority or 50.1 percent of the voting control. You can do that through a series of either super-voting shares or non-voting shares. A big advantage of the Iowa law is that hostile takeovers are theoretically impossible, which allows for a great and sustainable growth of a company, the MHC also gains the opportunity to own banking subsidiaries.[266]

---

[264] Cf. http://www.nli-research.co.jp/en/report/detail/id=51230?site=nli, accessed on 15.08.2017.

[265] In the literature is often mentioned 51 percent.

[266] Cf. *Viswanathan, K. S., Cummins, D. J.,* Ownership Structure Changes in the Insurance Industry: An Analysis of Demutualization, in: Journal of Risk and Insurance, 70 (3) 2003, p. 405.

Figure 15: Mutual insurance Company before and after a MHC reorganization

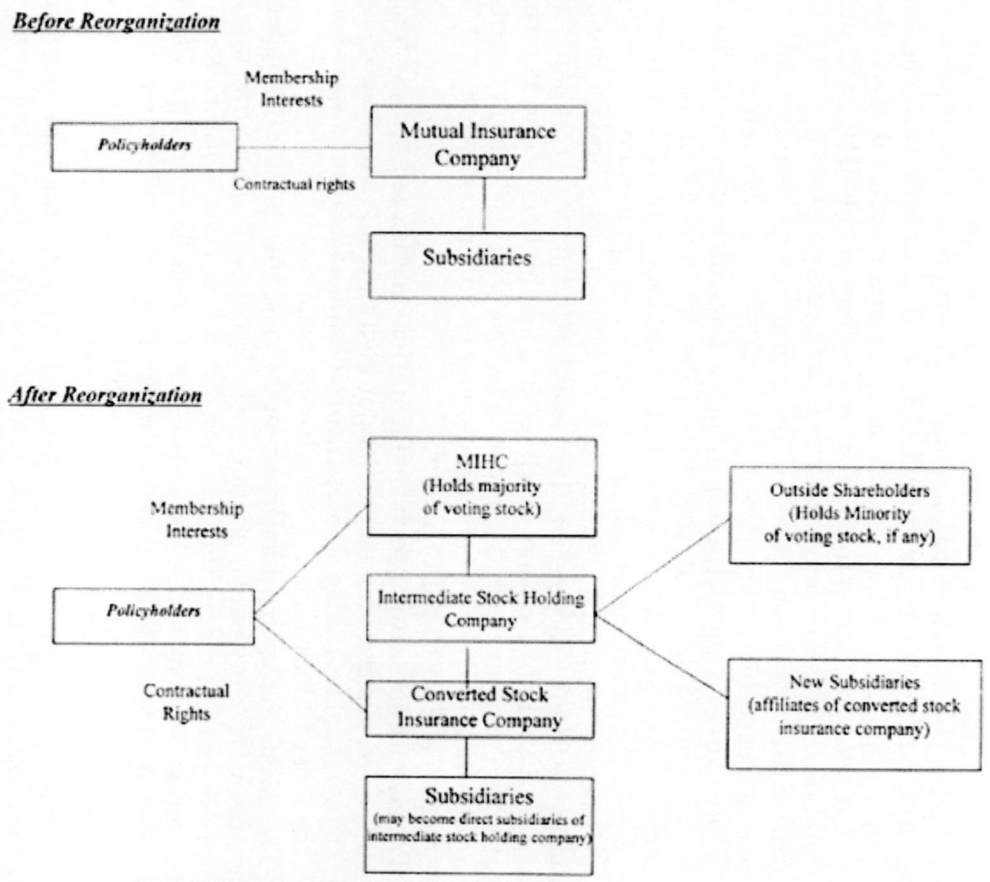

Source: NAIC (ed.): Mutual Insurance Holding Company Reorganizations, 1998, p. 6.

With the establishment of a MHC however, the mutual company can keep its mutual character, while at the same time benefit from external shareholders, pouring in new monetary flows. With the Initial Public Offering (IPO), initial minority shares are being sold to insiders and depositors. Later, a secondary market finalizes the process.[267]

A mutual insurance company contains a couple of different rights for the policyholder: the membership interests and the contractual rights. In a MHC, those two rights are split. The membership interests will end up being resident at the MHC level. The contractual rights will end up going down to the stock insurance company level. Even though you're a policyholder, you are also a member of the MHC, so you will retain both rights and have rights in both companies.

One of the differences between life and property/casualty is the concept of a closed block. The closed block usually refers to life insurance, and generally to participating policies on which a current dividend is being paid. It does not always include 100 percent of the statutory reserves. People don't think about a closed block in relation to a property/casualty company, but if you think of a company like "State Farm", which issues property/casualty insurance but does have a dividend-paying system, it is potentially possible that such a company would have to establish a closed block. It has never been done before, but that doesn't mean it can't happen. The overriding issue is fairness to the policyholder. You will not be allowed to do a transaction that is not deemed to be fair to policyholders.

Policies issued after the transformation are issued out of the stock insurance company. You will no longer be a mutual insurance company. In some respects, it also makes future demutualization easier because all the closed block issues have already been dealt with.

The MHC structure has however heated the debate.[268] Opponents say the MHC may cause agency costs, because insiders are protected from all sorts of discipline methods of the market, potential conflicts of interest may arise and, in case of a future demutualization, costs can be enormous. They argued that mutual insurers have adequate access to capital under current laws. Further they, including consumer groups and some regulators, argue that this method of reorganization is inequitable toward policyholders. They contend that the mutual insurer essentially has reorganized into a stock firm, similar to a full demutualization, but the policyholders are given no compensation for

---

[267] Cf. *Carow, K. A., Cox, S.R., Dianne M. Roden, D.M.,* Demutualization: Determinants and Consequences of the Mutual Holding Company Choice, in: Journal of Banking & Finance 33.8 (2009), p. 1454.

[268] Cf. *Chaddad, F. R., Cook, M. L.,* The Economics of Organization Structure Changes: A US Perspective on Demutualization, in: Annals of Public and Cooperative Economics, 2004 75 (4), p. 578.

the loss of their ownership interest in the firm.[269] Thus, in contrast to a full demutualization, where compensation is distributed to policyholders, policyholders in MHC conversions are being cheated out of such a windfall and it is a scheme for management self-enrichment, especially if management is awarded stock option plans. Directors and officers will profit from the issuance of valuable stock options at the expense of policyholders and such officers' and directors' actions are in breach of the fiduciary duties they owe to policyholders. Further MHC legislation did not provide for adequate disclosure or participation by policyholders, exposed policyholders to considerable risk; and would result in a weakened regulatory regimen. *Schiff* argues that if the newly created stock holding company expands into new insurance and noninsurance activities, value created by these transactions would only accrue to shareholders, not to policyholders. Moreover, MHC conversions are said to create owner-manager incentive conflicts that did not exist prior to the conversion.[270] According to *Chugh* and *Meador*: "Policyholders, regulators and investors generally have not been satisfied with this method of conversion since policyholders lose control of the operating subsidiary without any compensation, and management, as well, is not fully accountable to investors and the capital markets."[271]

Proponents of MHC conversions, on the other hand, consider that it is faster, less controversial and rather interesting, looking at costs. Further is argued that policyholders who were customers at the time of the conversion retain their membership rights through the MHC (the mutual character of the company would not entirely be gone), would benefit from the improved financial strength of the companies and thus may receive increased policyholder dividends resulting from value-enhancing activities undertaken by the firm after conversion.[272] Policyholders would receive enhanced value in the form of subscription rights to purchase stock, and potentially higher dividends and a distribution of stock of greater value than at present in the event of a

[269] Cf. *Adkins, J. B.*, The Policyholder Perspective on Mutual Holding Company Conversions, in: Journal of Insurance Regulation, 1997 16, p. 5.

[270] In any case, "Liberty Mutual" was in the midst of a public relations war with *David Schiff*, editor of *Schiff's* Insurance Observer an occasional 800-pound fly in the industry's ointment. In a edition of his newsletter, *Schiff* labeled "Liberty Mutual's MHC" plan as a "$6-billion ripoff." "Liberty Mutual" policyholders, according to Schiff, would receive on average $6,060 to $9,090 if the company fully demutualized and thereby provided stock or equivalent cash payments to its insureds/"owners" (Cf. *Schiff, D.*, The Big Fix: Mutual Insurance Holding Companies, in: Schiff's Insurance Observer, February 1998, p. 8).

[271] Cf. *Chugh, L., Meador, J. W.*, Demutualization in the Life Insurance Industry: A Study of Effectiveness, in: Review of Business, 2006 27(1), p. 12.

[272] Cf. *Koeppel, J. A.*, Refuting the Myths about Mutual Holding Companies, in: Best's Review-Life/Health, February 1998, p. 52.

full demutualization in the future. Because of the Gramm-Leach-Bliley Act, MHCs may exercise their business in various lines of financial services. Further, proponents argue that MHC conversions provide the firm with the benefits of the stock ownership form at a much lower cost than under a full conversion, while retaining the option to fully demutualize in the future.[273] Initial public offering (IPO) represents also one important advantage. Mutual insurers that opt for full demutualization are expected to do it when initiating conversion (even when situation in the market is unfavourable for the company), whereas in the case of MHC conversion, it can be done anytime.[274] Rather than maximize the value of a firm, managers may wish to maximize own utility.

Table 16: MHC advantages and disadvantages

MHC advantages	MHC disadvantages
quicker than full demutualization	limit to gained capital
less costly than full demutualization	potential conflicts of interest
limited access to capital markets	unnecessary costs if future demutualization

Source: *Carow, K. A., Cox, S.R., Dianne M. Roden, D.M.,* Demutualization: Determinants and Consequences of the Mutual Holding Company Choice, in: Journal of Banking & Finance 33.8 (2009), p. 1454.

The first five life insurance companies nationwide converted to a MHC structure were: “Pacific Mutual”, the largest mutual life insurer in California; “AmerUs Life”, an Iowa insurer; “General American Life of Missouri”; “Acacia Life” in the District of Columbia and “Ameritas Life” in Nebraska.[275]

Finally MHC conversions are also faster. Most of the transactions have been in the six- to nine-month range, whereas, a full demutualization tends to take about 18 months.

[273] In September 2000, American Mutual Holding Co., created in 1996, completed its full demutualization. This was the first demutualization following a MHC conversion.

[274] Cf. *Viswanathan, K. S., Cummins, D. J.,* Ownership Structure Changes in the Insurance Industry: An Analysis of Demutualization, in: Journal of Risk and Insurance, 70 (3) 2003, p. 406.

[275] Cf. https://nyassembly.gov/Reports/Ins/199803/ accessed on 13.05.2019.

10.6 Organizational change

Before we start with the deeper analysis of demutualization, we will shortly refer to this concept from a general perspective. It is a fact that the process of demutualization represents a complete change; transfer from one way of operating to another. It requires a lot of patience, flexibility and caution to be executed perfectly.

Change of the organizational form has always been an actual topic. Even when there is a justified motive for change, there is a fear from failure. Organizations are resistant to change, since every change brings ambiguity and insecurity. What are the possible negative outcomes of the change? How to execute change with minimum consequences on organizational performance? How to manage the organization in a new environment? Will the new form of organization bring desired benefits? Will interests of all involved stakeholders be protected? These are just some questions that should be asked. Reasons for the change of structure are numerous such as fear of competition, improvement of organizational efficiency, better positioning in the market, etc.

Mutual insurance companies are no exception. Being a mutual insurance company is very hard in a competitive environment. In almost every country, mutual insurance companies have been under great pressure in the last 40 years, since macro environment dictated new terms. The mutual form of organization has been considered obsolete and it has lost trust of owners, managers and wider public. According to the evolutionary view of organization, the best organization is the one that fits with its environment. Political-economic developments, technological advancement, etc. are just some factors that shaped the environment of the mutual insurance companies. In the last 150 years, the environment has changed to a great extent. In accordance with this theory, many mutual insurance companies chose the path of demutualization as a strategic option to overcome disadvantages of mutual organizational form.

Both organizational forms, mutual (or cooperative) and corporate forms, have coexisted in the market for decades and each of them has its advantages and disadvantages. In certain periods of time, their presence on the market decreased or increased, because of different factors. Also, a change of organizational form was often practiced and many insurance companies would either demutualize or mutualize if they could not achieve organizational goals with their previous organizational form. However, our subject of interest is one specific time period of this process; the big demutualization wave that started in the 1980s.

At first glance, it is very hard to assess which organizational form is better. Each one has good and bad sides and it is on the player in the market (company in the insurance sector) to choose the right form for itself under the given circumstances.

In order to understand motives behind demutualization, it will be necessary to perform comparative analysis of mutual insurance and joint-stock companies according to various parameters. This comparison will disclose major flaws of mutual insurers and their inferiority towards stock insurers.

In the following lines, the main results from literature that analyze these two organizational forms according to different criteria will be presented.

10.6.1 Efficiency

The very existence of mutual insurers and joint-stock companies in the market is often cited as an argument for their efficiency. *Fama* and *Jensen* propose: "Organizations compete for survival and the form of organization that survives in an activity is the one that can deliver the product demanded by consumers at the lowest price while covering costs."[276] *Smith, C.W.* argues: "The different ownership structures create different incentives for the contracting parties, thus the different costs of controlling the resulting incentive problems lead to the efficiency of the various ownership structures."[277]

According to Swiss Re, when considering efficiency of both organizational forms, a double approach should be used. In order to determine operational efficiency, researchers should not concentrate just on indicators such as turnover, return on equity, etc. It is anticipated that joint stock companies will generate more profit than mutual insurance companies, since profit maximization is not the main objective of mutual insurance companies. Rather, in order to get a clear picture, it should be analyzed which form of organization incurs more cost.[278]

McNamara and *Rhee* analyze 33 life insurance companies before and after performing demutualization process based on two hypotheses: efficiency and expropriation. Their research reveals that improvement of efficiency was the main motive behind decisions to demutualize.[279] This result is identical to the findings of *Mayers* and *Smith*, who suggested

276 *Fama, E. F., Jensen, M. C.*, Agency Problems and Residual Claims, in: The Journal of Law and Economics, 1983 26(2), p. 345.

277 *Smith, C. W.*, On the Convergence of Insurance and Finance Research, in: The Journal of Risk and Insurance, 1986 53(4), 705.

278 Cf. Swiss Re, Are Mutual Insurers an Endangered Species, in: Sigma, no.4/1999, p. 15.

279 Cf. *McNamara , M. J., Rhee, G. S.*, Ownership Structure and Performance: The Demutualization of Life Insurers, in: The Journal of Risk and Insurance, 59(2) 1992, p. 221ff.

these two hypotheses, but they employed them in the case of mutualization of stock insurers. Interestingly, efficiency hypothesis was supported in the case of mutualization and demutualization, while wealth expropriation hypothesis is rejected in both cases.[280]

By definition, efficiency hypothesis stipulates: "Insurers change their organizational structure in an effort to improve financial and operational performance given the costs and benefits inherent in each type of organizational structure."[281] Wealth expropriation hypothesis stipulates that it may come to the wealth transfer during the conversion process at the expense of policyholders.[282]

Cummins et al. use nonparametric frontier efficiency methods to analyze the efficiency of stocks and mutual insurers and argue that mutual insurance companies incur more costs than joint stock companies.[283] Their research confirms expense preference hypothesis of *Mester*.[284] However, a few years later, *Cummins* et al. provided slightly different results. Here, the researchers tested expense preference and efficient structure hypotheses in the Spanish insurance market.[285] This time, they reject the expense preference hypothesis of *Mester*[286] and support the efficient structure hypothesis which proposes coexistence of both organizational forms in the market, since they possess different comparative advantages. Also the results of *Loftin* and *Xie* provide no evidence on this argument for the US insurance.[287] This research

---

280 Cf. *Mayers, D., Smith, C. W.*, Ownership structure and control: The mutualization of stock life insurance companies, in: Journal of Financial Economics, 16(1) 1986, p. 73ff.

281 *Jeng, V., Lai, G. C., McNamara, M. J.*, Efficiency and Demutualization: Evidence from the U.S. Life Insurance Industry in the 1980s and 1990s, in: The Journal of Risk and Insurance, 2007 74(3), p. 684.

282 Cf. *McNamara , M. J., Rhee, G. S.*, Ownership Structure and Performance: The Demutualization of Life Insurers, in: The Journal of Risk and Insurance, 1992 59(2), p. 221ff.

283 Cf. *Cummins, J. D., Weiss, M. A., Zi, H.*, Organizational Form and Efficiency: The Coexistence of Stock and Mutual Property-Liability Insurers, in: Management Science, 1999 45(9), p. 1254ff.

284 The expense preference hypothese includes since owners have weaker control over managers in mutual firms than in stock firms, it is expected that the mutual firm managers are more likely to pursue private bebefits and incur s higher cost. (Cf. *Mester, L. J.*, Testing for Expense Preference Behavior: Mutual versus Stock Savings and Loans, in: The RAND Journal of Economics 20/1989, p. 183ff.)

285 *Cummins, J. D., Rubio-Misas, M., Zi, H.,* The Effect of Organizational Structure on Efficiency: Evidence from the Spanish Insurance Industry, in: Journal of Banking & Finance, 2004 28(12), p. 3113ff.

286 Cf. *Mester, L. J.*, Agency costs among savings and loans, in: Journal of Financial Intermediation, 1991 1(3), p. 257ff.

287 Cf. *Loftin, G., Xie, X.*, The United States Insurance Market: Characteristics and Trends, in: *Cummins, J.D., Venard, B.* (ed.): Handbook of international insurances.

shows vulnerability of big mutual insurance companies since their performance in life insurance sector is very poor. Because of the threat of stock insurers, the efficient structure hypothesis is barely supported in their case. For that reason, they propose them to focus on other products/market segments or to demutualize.

A cross-frontier analysis shows that stock firms and mutuals operate on separate production and cost frontiers, thus suggesting that mutuals and stocks do not operate with the same level of efficiency. Stocks specialize in products that require relatively high level of managerial discretion in pricing and underwriting, while mutuals specialize in products with long payout periods.[288] The study also shows that the stack cost frontier dominates the mutual cost frontier, providing some support for the expense preference hypothesis. However, the cross-frontier analysis neglects the fact that mutuals and stocks compete with each other in the market, and in most of the cases, compete in the same insurance lines. An efficiency analysis pooling together stocks and mutuals shows that stock firms are less cost efficient, but more revenue efficient than mutuals. Big mutual firms are found to be less cost efficient, but have the same revenue efficiency level as big stock firms.[289]

Biener and *Eling* analyze big dataset that has over 20,000 companies from North America and European Union (EU) in the context of the expense preference[290] and efficient structure[291] hypotheses.[292] *Biener* and *Eling* define these hypotheses in the following manner: "The expense preference hypothesis states that mutual insurers are less cost efficient than stock insurers due to unresolved agency conflicts (e.g., higher perquisite consumption by mutual managers). The efficient structure hypothesis claims that the two organizational forms serve different market segments due to differences in managerial discretion and access to capital."[293] Their research brings results identical to *Cummins*

Between Global Dynamics and Local Contingencies, New York 2007, p. 102.

288 Cf. *Cummins, J. D., Weiss, M. A., Zi, H.*, Organizational Form and Efficiency: The Coexistence of Stock and Mutual Property-Liability Insurers, in: Management Science, 45(9) 1999, p. 1254ff.

289 Cf. *Cummins, J. D., Xie, X.*, Economies of Scale and Efficiency Analysis in in the United States Property-Liability Insurance Industry, in: Working Paper, The Wharton School, University of Pennsylvania, 2005.

290 Cf. *Mester, L. J.*, Agency costs among savings and loans, in: Journal of Financial Intermediation, 1(3) 1991, p. 257ff.

291 Cf. *Cummins, J. D, Rubio-Misas, M., Zi, H.*, The Effect of Organizational Structure on Efficiency: Evidence from the Spanish Insurance Industry, in: Journal of Banking & Finance, 28(12) 2004, p. 3113ff.

292 Cf. *Biener, C., Eling, M.*: Organization and Efficiency in the International Insurance Industry: A cross-frontier analysis, in: European Journal of Operational Research, 221(2) 2012, p. 454ff.

293 Ibid., p. 454.

et al.[294]; expense preference hypothesis is not supported and efficient structure hypothesis is supported just in particular regions/sectors. Thus, the conclusion is the same, but findings from this study are more significant since they represent the first cross-country analysis.

10.6.2 Agency conflicts

The emergence of mutual insurers is often explained as a reaction against perceived excessive premiums charged or unacceptable policy conditions imposed by corporate insurance companies.[295] Mutual insurance companies are owned by their customers, the policyholders. Consequently, the major benefit of the mutual organizational form is the elimination of policyholder/stockholder agency conflicts.[296]

In theory, policyholders control the management, but this is true only to a limited extent.[297] The effectiveness of policyholder control in mutual insurance companies is limited because:[298]

- policyholders are numerous and widely scattered geographically;
- they have limited capacity for communication;
- their stake in the company is proportionately minute; and
- many policyholders do not understand the nature of a mutual company or know they have a right to vote.

In other words, the costs of controlling managers in a mutual insurer are very high. Not surprisingly, survey research shows that policyholders do not take full advantage of their voting rights and seldom participate in annual meetings.[299]

---

[294] Cf. *Cummins, J. D., Rubio-Misas, M., Zi, H.,* The Effect of Organizational Structure on Efficiency: Evidence from the Spanish Insurance Industry, in: Journal of Banking & Finance, 28(12) 2004, p. 3113ff.

[295] Cf. *Smith, B.D. Stutzer, M.*, A theory of mutual formation and moral hazard with evidence from the history of the insurance industry, in: Review of Financial Studies, 8/1995, p.545ff.

[296] Cf. *Fama, E. F., Jensen, M. C.*, Separation of ownership and control, in: Journal of Law and Economics, 26/1983, p. 301ff.

[297] Cf. *Pottier, S., Sommer, D.*, Agency theory and life insurer ownership structure, in: Journal of Risk and Insurance, 64/1997, p. 529ff.

[298] Cf. Black, K., Skipper, H.D., Life and Health Insurance (13th ed.). Prentice Hall 2000.

[299] Cf. *Greene, M. R., Johnson, R. E.*, Stocks vs Mutuals: Who Controls?, in: Journal of Risk and Insurance, 47(1) 1980, p. 167ff. A citizen who has the right to vote for elected officials and chooses not to exercise that right does not see that right diminished. Similarly, even if a policyholder chooses not to vote, it reflects an individual choice which rests with the policyholder, but in no event diminishes this right (Cf. https://www.namic.org/policy/futureMutualPolicyRights accessed on 04.11.2019).

For example here are some data from mutual policyholders' voting in annual meetings in 1996 in big New Yorker mutual life insurances.

Table 17: Policyholders' Voting Percentages in their Mutual Insurance Company's Annual Meeting for 1996

	Policyholders(1)	Votes	% Voting
Columbian Mutual Life	275,459	11	.004
The Guardian	633,659	140	.02
MetLife	11,327,000	40,449	.36
Mutual of America	320,440	195	.06
Mutual of New York	1,110,000	6,533	.59
New York Life	3,701,200	1,341	.04
Phoenix	1,508,093	17(2)	.001(2)
Security Mutual Life	138,969	16	.01

(1) Includes individual life, individual annuity, group life, and group annuity.
(2) These figures are for Phoenix Home Life's 1997 annual meeting.

Source: https://nyassembly.gov/Reports/Ins/199803/insureport2.html#t35.

On the other hand with this wave of demutualizations in the 1990s and its heavy press coverage, some consumers (members) may have learned about the difference between a mutual insurer and a stock insurer. The main objective of a mutual insurer has always been to provide long-term value for its policyholder-owners. Those insurers that had chosen to remain mutual had declared that this remains their focus. These firms may be experiencing additional monitoring from their policyholders, particularly those individuals who were newly aware of their ownership rights. In addition, they were faced by increased competition from this growing number of stock insurers. In order for mutual insurance companies to continue to thrive and prosper, they must not be denied the same ability to access the various capital markets as their stock competitors. It is important to recognize and protect the membership interest of mutual policyholders. It is equally important, however, to acknowledge that the ultimate interest of any policyholder is the continued financial viability of the insurance company. Firms that have chosen to demutualize in the years were probably faced by a more informed and vocal ownership group than existed in the past.[300]

[300] Cf. *Viswanathan, K. S., Cummins, D. J.*, Ownership Structure Changes in the Insurance Industry: An Analysis of Demutualization, in: Journal of Risk and Insurance, 2003 70(3), 432.

10.6.3 Manager opinions

Greene and *Johnson* bring statements from managers of mutual and stock insurers regarding pros/cons of these two forms. Managers of mutual insurers argue that the biggest flaw of the mutual form lies in its inability to execute diversification and acquisition processes properly. Consequently, managers in joint stock companies stated above mentioned flaw of mutual insurers as the main source of their competitive advantage.[301] *Mayers* and *Smith* analyze compensation of executives in the life insurance sector. According to them, the compensation of CEOs in mutual insurance companies is lower in comparison with compensation of their counterparts in joint-stock companies.[302]

A very important finding comes from *Wells* et al.. Since managers in joint stock companies are tightly controlled, they do not have so much access to cash. On the contrary, managers in mutual insurance companies have great control over cash and in that context, more space for opportunistic behaviour.[303] That's why, *Carson* et al. argue that there is a great correlation between the amount of free cash flow and the likelihood to change organizational form from a mutual to a stock insurance company.[304]

Zou et al. analyze dividend payments in property/casualty insurance sector. Their finding asserts that mutual insurers distribute lower dividend payments than their counterparts.[305]

10.6.4 Financial constraints

An important reason for mutual firms to demutualize is to abolish the financial constraint. Until introduction of the MHC structure, the alternatives available to a mutual insurer to accomplish the objective of raising new capital consisted of issuing internally generated capital[306],

---

[301] Cf. *Greene, M. R., Johnson, R. E.*, Stocks vs Mutuals: Who Controls?, in: Journal of Risk and Insurance, 47(1) 1980, p. 167ff.

[302] Cf. *Mayers, D., Smith, C. W.*, Executive Compensation in the Life Insurance Industry, in: The Journal of Business, 65(1) 1992, p. 51ff.

[303] Cf. *Wells, B. P., Cox, L. A., Gaver, K. M.*, Free Cash Flow in the Life Insurance Industry, in: The Journal of Risk and Insurance, 62(1) 1995, p. 50ff.

[304] Cf. *Carson, J. M., Forster, M. D., McNamara, M. J.*, Changes in Ownership Structure: Theory and Evidence from Life Insurer Demutualizations, in: Journal of Insurance Issues, 21(1) 1998, p. 1ff.

[305] Cf. *Zou, H., Yang, C., Wang, M., Zhu, M.*, Dividend Decisions in the Property and Liability Insurance Industry: Mutual versus Stock Companies, in: Review of Quantitative Finance and Accounting, 33(2) 2009, p. 113ff.

[306] Increase premiums or reduce costs.

surplus and capital notes[307], engaging in an initial public offering (IPO) of stock in a downstream subsidiary, merger[308] or undertaking the process of converting the mutual insurer to a stock company via demutualization. The mutual insurer's only alternative for gaining the structural flexibility similar to competing stock insurers was to demutualize.

It has been found that converting property/casualty mutuals show significantly lower surplus-to-asset ratios than the non-converting firms, but that this capital constraint eases after demutualization.[309] Some studies compare the pre-conversion performance and post-conversion performance of the demutualized property/casualty firms and find that these firms operate with similar efficiency, before and after the conversion, but incur a capital structure change and a change in business mix.[310]

10.7 What has driven demutualization?

10.7.1 Changes in macro environment

The insurance market is volatile and companies should design strategies and adopt the best practices that will enable them to achieve high performance. If a company is reactive and incapable to anticipate change, there is a great danger for a company's activities. Danger comes from different sides, whether it is an unpredicted economic crisis or a set of legislation enacted by the government. Changes coming from this side represent a threat, but also a chance if a company chooses the right approach. Findings showed internal weaknesses of mutual insurers when it comes to efficiency problems. Reasons for demutualization were mostly grounded on those weaknesses. However, these weaknesses are inherent in the mutual organizational form and very little can be done in order to change that. Although mutual insurers have a great number of weaknesses, they have operated for centuries,

---

307 A capital note is a short-term bond issued by a company to help pay company liabilities.

308 Mutual insurers, however, may not form upstream holding companies because, by definition, they have no stock to contribute or transfer to a holding company. The alternative of forming a downstream holding company for diversification creates regulatory problems arising from limitations on investments in subsidiaries. Further, downstream activities fall within the purview of the domiciliary state insurance regulator.

309 Cf. *Viswanathan, K.S., Cummins, J.D.*, Ownership Structure Changes in the Insurance Industry: An Analysis of Demutualization, in: Journal of Risk and Insurance 70/2003, p. 401ff.

310 Cf. *Cagle, J., Lippert, R., Moore, W.*, Demutualization in the Property-Liability Insurance Industry, in: Journal of Insurance Regulation 14/1996, p. 343ff.

so how come that in the 1980s demutualization became the desired outcome? Namely, great changes happened in the macro environment. The macro environment can be understood as a set of different factors (political, legal, etc.) which create a totally new environment for companies and to a great extent ask from these companies to adapt. These factors are uncontrollable, do not depend on an organization and they drive change. Failure to adapt and react properly to a newly-created environment can cause side effects that can be detrimental for a company's activities. These factors revealed and emphasized weaknesses of mutual insurers in the new environment. For example, access to capital always represented a challenge for mutual insurers, but since the macro environment has changed to a great extent, this weakness was highlighted. Change was necessary and the only way to overcome this weakness was to demutualize in order to raise capital in multiple ways as joint-stock insurer.

Swiss Re describes these factors in the case of mutual insurance companies extensively and considers them as reasons why mutual insurers lost popularity and why stock insurers became more attractive. "Two fundamental, interrelated forces are pressuring mutuals to rethink their ownership structure: competition and consolidation."[311]

10.7.1.1 Dynamic competition

Competition includes change of consumer preferences, technological advancement and tendency towards greater market discipline. The changing dynamics of the US financial services market has heightened competition and caused stock and mutual life insurers to reconsider virtually every aspect of their operations.[312] Financial institutions including banks, security firms and mutual fund companies, in some instances, competed directly with life insurers for consumers' insurance and investment dollars. Consumer preferences have changed from the 1980s. Changing demographics have resulted in consumers demanding more products that provide retirement income and benefits and fewer products providing benefits after death. This change was evident in the relatively low premium and asset growth experienced by life insurers in the 1990s. These years were characterized by high popularity of stock markets. In that sense, consumers saw a chance there and concentrated their activities on investing. Mutual insurers in particular were negatively affected as they depended heavily on internally generated earnings to provide additional capital for growth plans.

---

[311] Swiss Re, Are Mutual Insurers an Endangered Species, in: Sigma, no.4/1999, p. 22.

[312] There were some unexpected insolvencies of some large life insurers in the early 1990s in the USA.

The property/casualty industry was undergoing similarly significant changes, as its marketplace became more global. Corporate insurance buyers were often seeking alternatives to insuring and financing risks, and individual consumers were demanding more products and services from traditional insurers. In addition, soft pricing of certain insurance coverages and overall excess capitalization of insurers have contributed to a need for insurance company management to be flexible in developing long-term strategies. Changing demographics have brought new competitors to the marketplace.

10.7.1.2 Consolidation of industries

Consolidation includes prices of stocks and the deregulation of insurance markets. Numbers of mergers and acquisitions have totally shaken the situation during the end of the 20th century. Smaller players were challenged by this consolidation and started to rethink their business strategies. High prices of stocks facilitated the process of raising capital and thus the acquisition process. Furthermore, high prices of stocks were also attractive to managers since they saw an opportunity to benefit from windfall gains. Low growth prospects resulting from changing market conditions, coupled with a strong bull stock market during the 1990s have led many insurers to consolidate, in order to achieve improved returns on capital.

Given the limitations of mutual organizations, mutual insurers have participated in the consolidation trend on a limited basis. The reasons for this are largely due to a mutual insurer's inability to offer stock as an acquisition currency and their relatively inflexible structure overall. Many competitors of mutual life insurers have been pursuing acquisitions to grow faster, reduce operating expenses relative to their size and to access new distribution channels and financial products.[313]

10.7.1.3 New technologies

In addition to technological advances and innovations, many financial businesses seek new combinations of profit-making opportunities through greater diversification and affiliations. Introduction of new technologies in the past 40 years has completely changed the general pattern of running insurance companies. This can be noticed in almost every insurance sector, from health to vehicle insurance. Internet technology decreased the physical distance, improved communication and provided opportunities for new players to enter easily. Since the technological era requires a different approach to customers, compa-

[313] Cf. Swiss Re, Are Mutual Insurers an Endangered Species, in: Sigma, no.4/1999, p. 22.

nies are forced to invest in electronic services in order to stay competitive. Improvement of market discipline is a strategic step pursued by managers in order to overcome shortcomings of the mutual form. As already explained, the mutual insurance company has a specific legal framework and culture. Since it is very hard to reform a company's culture and implement all desired changes directed to improvement of efficiency, communication, etc., conversion to a joint-stock company becomes a logical option.[314]

In order to have a better picture of changes in the environment, one important model from management science is introduced, the so-called PEST (political, economic, social, technological) analysis.

10.7.2 PEST analysis

The PEST analysis is an analysis of the macro environment and it defines political, economic, social and technological factors that have influence on companies. This model is important for strategic decision-making such as the decision to change the organizational form, since it provides a deeper insight into the environment that impacts a company's performance.

[314] Cf. Ibid., p. 23f.

Figure 16: PEST analysis of demutualization

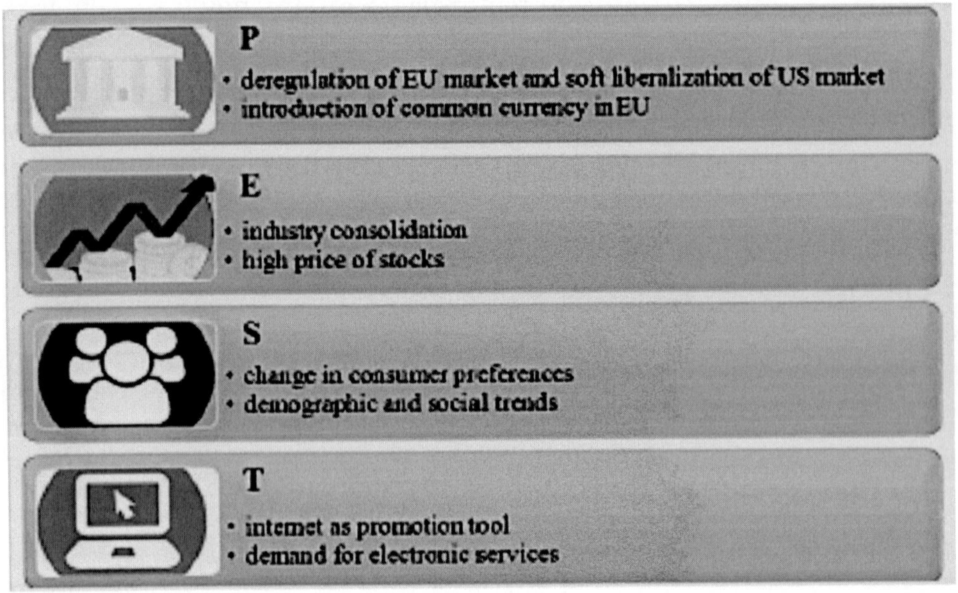

Source: Representation based on Swiss Re, Are Mutual Insurers an Endangered Species. Sigma, no.4/1999, p. 22.

10.8 Demutualization as a process

The primary motivation for conversion is access to capital. Converting life/health mutuals hold a significantly lower proportion of liquid assets; in addition, they have a higher proportion of separate accounts under management. The insurance industry in the USA was experiencing a wave of organizational structure changes since the 1980s as many property/casualty and life/health mutual companies were converting to stock companies, a process known as demutualization. Given that, this is an industry where mutual firms and stock firms have coexisted for more than 100 years, these conversions are receiving much attention from insurance regulators, investors, and consumers. This research focuses on the demutualization process and by examining the business practices of demutualizing insurers in the years surrounding conversion, investigates why they undergo this change. A mutual insurer is collectively owned by its policyholders; these ownership rights are accorded upon policy purchase and end with its termination. In a stock insurer, the customer function and the ownership function are performed by two distinct groups.

A mutual insurance company can only choose to demutualize with the blessing of its board of directors, its policyholders and the state insurance regulator.[315]

The demutualization process begins when a plan is developed by the company and is subsequently approved by its board of directors. Upon board approval, the plan is submitted to the state insurance department for review and consideration.
So a demutualization will require the approval of the

- board of directors of the mutual company. The approval of more than a majority of the members of the board may be required.
- policyholders. The statute, charter and bylaws must be examined to determine the vote needed for policyholder' approval. Most statutes require an affirmative vote ranging from a simple majority to three-fourths of the policyholders who actually vote. The law provides that policyholders must receive a copy or summary of the demutualization plan and other explanatory information to assist the policyholder in reaching an informed decision. A significant part of the plan is the insurer's proposal for valuing and distributing the mutual insurer's equity. Statutes rarely prescribe methods for valuation and distribution, although there are some exceptions.
- insurance regulator. The regulator may impose certain restrictions or conditions with respect to the demutualization. Most demutualization statutes require that the insurance regulator find that the plan of conversion is fair and equitable to the members (policyholders) and not prejudicial to their interests.

  Demutualization statutes generally allow the state insurance regulator discretion in determining an appropriate method of valuation and distribution. Typically, a company will determine its financial position based on generally accepted accounting principles and will include in its demutualization plan a description of the method(s) used to determine the company's value.

  In most states, the regulator is required to hold a hearing to determine whether the terms and conditions of the demutualization are fair and whether the demutualization is detrimental to the public. The regulator may retain, at the expense of the mutual insurer, lawyers, accountants, actuaries and consultants to assist the regulator in determining whether or not a demutualization should be approved.[316]

[315] Cf. https://www.thebalance.com/stock-insurer-versus-mutual-insurer-462504, accessed on 24.07.2017.

[316] Cf. https://www.namic.org/policy/futureMutualAlts accessed on 13.05.2019.

It comes down to a change in the ownership structure of the mutual and its members to a for-profit, proprietary organization. After the demutualization process, residual claim and control rights are reorganized between the stakeholders, impacting the company's performance. Cooperative membership rights are transformed to unrestricted common stock ownership rights.[317]

A key aspect of the process is determining the compensation that the mutual firm's policyholders receive for relinquishing their ownership. Demutualization activity was occurring in insurance markets around the world. The largest life insurer in the USA, "Prudential Life", successfully demutualized in December 2001; the second largest, "MetLife Inc.", also converted in April 2000.[318] Prior demutualization studies suggested that property/casualty conversion was motivated by growth potential, capital needs, and possible management self-interest.[319] The unprecedented wave of mergers and acquisitions in both segments of the insurance industry during the 1990s also differentiates the environment from the prevailing conditions in earlier decades. Given the actuarial, accounting, and regulatory considerations involved, demutualization is a significant endeavour. A converting mutual must follow the demutualization statute of its state of domicile. The demutualization statutes in most states are comprehensive, with extensive rules affecting each phase of the conversion process. As more insurers express interest in conversion, states are updating their regulations. Before any formal plan of reorganization becomes effective, it must receive both regulatory and policyholder approval.

---

317 Cf. *Chaddad, F. R., Cook, M. L.* (2004), The Economics of Organization Structure Changes: A US Perspective on Demutualization, in: Annals of Public and Cooperative Economics, 75 (4), p. 576.

318 Cf. Swiss Re, Are Mutual Insurers an Endangered Species, in: Sigma, no.4/1999, p. 14f..

319 Cf. *Cagle, J. A. B., Lippert, R. L., Moore, W. T.*, Demutualization in the Property- Liability Insurance Industry, in: Journal of Insurance Regulation, 14/1996, p. 343ff.; *Mayers, D., Smith, C.*, Ownership Structure and Control: Property-Casualty Insurer Conversion to Stock Charter, in: Journal of Financial Services Research, 21(1-2) 2002, p. 117ff.

10.9 Demutualization in the life/health and the property/casualty insurance sectors

10.9.1 Property/casualty insurance sector

Viswanathan and *Cummins* analyzed 51 property/casualty conversions between 1981 and 1999.[320] Here, only 3 out of 51 companies opted for MHC conversion.[321] During the 1980s a total of 17 insurance mutuals converted to stock firms, while in the 1990s twice as many mutuals decided to become stock companies. The methodology used for the analysis was the same as in the case of life insurers. The following table gives an overview of these conversions.

Table 18: Conversions of mutual property/casualty insurers (1981-1999)

Year	Number of conversions	Year	Number of conversions
		1990	0
1981	1	1991	5
1982	2	1992	1
1983	1	1993	4
1984	1	1994	3
1985	3	1995	4
1986	4	1996	3
1987	3	1997	5
1988	2	1998	5
1989	0	1999	4
Total	17	Total	34

Source: *Viswanathan, K. S., Cummins, D. J.*, Ownership Structure Changes in the Insurance Industry: An Analysis of Demutualization, in: Journal of Risk and Insurance, 2003 70(3), 419.

[320] Cf. *Viswanathan, K. S., Cummins, D. J.*, Ownership Structure Changes in the Insurance Industry: An Analysis of Demutualization, in: Journal of Risk and Insurance, 2003 70(3), p. 418.Using A.M. Best's Insurance Reports - Property-Liability (1998). There were only conversions included that were motivated primarily for business reasons; conversions imposed by regulators in response to deteriorating financial condition were excluded.

[321] Cf. *Mayers, D., Smith, C.*, Ownership Structure and Control: Property-Casualty Insurer Conversion to Stock Charter, in: Journal of Financial Services Research, 21(1-2) 2002, p. 117.

Further data as asset portfolio composition, liabilities and premiums written in various lines of business, capital and surplus positions, underwriting income, and investment income were collected. These data showed that converting property/casualty mutuals, on average, have significantly lower surplus-to-asset ratios than non converters, as expected. This may have been the accumulated result of poor underwriting performance and/or steady growth in liabilities and despite the possibility of reserve manipulation by management. In addition, converting property/casualty insurers had significantly lower ratios of net cash from operations to assets, lower ratios of underwriting gains to assets, and higher overall operating ratios than non converters.[322]

In the 1990s and early 2000s, while life/health industry experienced a series of notable demutualization cases, the phenomenon was less dramatic in the property/casualty industry. Unlike the giants in life/health industry, the largest property/casualty firm, the "State Farm Group" did not choose to demutualize. One explanation is that the property/casualty market is less sensitive to product changes than the life/health industry market in which firms must maintain flexibility to adapt to the development of new products in the market However, the most significant demutualization in the property/casualty insurance industry during this period is perhaps "Liberty Mutual's" conversion to a MHC in 2001. "Liberty Mutual" is headquartered in Massachusetts and is the largest workers' compensation insurance company in the USA. Before conversion, it had roughly 2.0 million policyholders with $8.9 billion in net premiums written and assets valued $33.3 billion. This case raised a lot of attention because it was the first property/casualty firm that chose the mutual holding company form. The firm's major goal after converting to a MHC was to raise funds for acquisitions and to pursue its global expansion strategy. The demutualized "Liberty MHC" did not launch an initial public offering (IPO), but rather preserved its mutuality.[323]

Before "Liberty Mutual", there were several less influential demutualization cases such as the "Medical Assurance Inc". in 1991, "Farm Family Holdings" 1996, "Summit Holdings and Old Guard Group" in 1997, "MEEMIC Holdings, MIIX Group Inc." and "NCRIC Group Inc." in 1999, and "American Physician's Capital Inc." in 2000. These firms issued demutualization initial public offerings (IPO) and earned a positive IPO return. In the 1980 and 1990s, the demutualization IPOs

322 Cf. *Viswanathan, K. S., Cummins, D. J.*, Ownership Structure Changes in the Insurance Industry: An Analysis of Demutualization, in: Journal of Risk and Insurance, 2003 70(3), p. 419.

323 Cf. *Loftin, G., Xie, X.*, The United States Insurance Market: Characteristics and Trends, in: *Cummins, J.D., Venard, B.* (ed.): Handbook of international insurances. Between Global Dynamics and Local Contingencies, New York 2007, p. 106.

were, in general, found to generate higher IPO returns than the non-demutualization IPOs in the US Insurance market.[324]

10.9.2 Life/health insurance sector

Erhemjamts and *Leverty* bring exact data for the period between 1995-2004. The following table gives an overview about the presence of mutual life insurers and thus the consequences of conversions. In just one decade, the number of mutual life insurance companies radically decreased from 120 in 1995 to 67 in 2004.[325]

Table 19: Mutual life insurers and consequent conversions (1995-2004)

Year	**1995**	**1996**	**1997**	**1998**	**1999**	**2000**	**2001**	**2002**	**2003**	**2004**
No. of insurers	1638	1586	1450	1422	1313	1273	1216	1164	1118	1061
Mutual insurers	**120**	**117**	**108**	**102**	**93**	**89**	**79**	**71**	**71**	**67**
Stock insurers	1498	1459	1335	1315	1210	1176	1126	1080	1027	979
Total conversions	**3**	**2**	**4**	**6**	**7**	**8**	**5**	**3**	**1**	**1**

Source: *Erhemjamts, O., Leverty, T. J.*, The Demise of the Mutual Organizational Form: An Investigation of the Life Insurance Industry, in: Journal of Money, Credit and Banking, 2010 42(6), p. 1013.

Viswanathan and *Cummins* analyze 21 life insurance companies that demutualized in a period of 11 years, namely between 1988-1999[326]. The demutualization process was rather successful during the 1990s, with a total of 21 conversions from 1988 to 1999. Given that at the beginning of this period there were only about 100 life/health mutuals a sizeable percentage had converted during this period. These particular insurers were also among the largest in assets.[327] MHC seemed to be the desired form, so in that way 10 out of 21 underwent only partial demutualization. Companies were analyzed 5 years before their demutualization,

[324] Cf. *Viswanathan, K.S.*, The Pricing of Insurer Demutualization Initial Public Offerings, in: Journal of Risk and Insurance 73/2006, p. 439ff.

[325] Cf. *Erhemjamts, O., Leverty, T. J.*, The Demise of the Mutual Organizational Form: An Investigation of the Life Insurance Industry, in: Journal of Money, Credit and Banking, 2010 42(6), p. 1013.

[326] Using A.M. Best's Insurance Reports - Life-Health (1998).

[327] Cf. *McDonald, L., C. Saucer, C. Winans*, Taking Stock, Best's Review- Property/Liability, December 1997, p. 76.

during the demutualization year and 3 years after demutualization. It can be observed that demutualization intensified in the mid-1990s. The next table gives an overview of these conversions throughout the years.[328]

Table 20: Conversions of mutual life insurers (1988-1999)

Year	Number of conversions	Year	Number of conversions
1988	1	1994	1
1989	3	1995	2
1990	0	1996	1
1991	0	1997	4
1992	1	1998	7
1993	0	1999	1

Source: *Viswanathan, K. S., Cummins, D. J.*, Ownership Structure Changes in the Insurance Industry: An Analysis of Demutualization, in: Journal of Risk and Insurance, 2003 70(3), p. 420.

The life/health mutuals that converted were adequately capitalized but had relatively lower liquidity than non converting life/health firms. The additional capital gained through demutualization eases the liquidity constraint for the converting life/health firms. The data also shows that the converting life/health firms holded a significantly higher percentage of assets in separate accounts and had also higher premium growth rates and percentages of premiums in group lines of insurance than non converters, but these differences were not statistically significant, in part due to the small numbers of life-health firms in the converting and matching categories.[329]

Chugh and *Meador* explore effectiveness of demutualization of life insurers. According to them, the trend of demutualization became tremendously popular several years before the 21st century. Many big players in the life insurance market opted for demutualization as a

[328] Cf. *Viswanathan, K. S., Cummins, D. J.*, Ownership Structure Changes in the Insurance Industry: An Analysis of Demutualization, in: Journal of Risk and Insurance, 2003 70(3), p. 420.

[329] Cf. Ibid.

strategic step. The peak was the demutualization of the "Metropolitan Mutual Life Insurance Co." in 2000, the biggest life insurer of the USA at its time of conversion. Their sample encompasses 11 life insurers that converted between 1997-2001. In order to determine and compare efficiency before and after demutualization, a time interval of 3 years is used, so each company is analyzed 3 years before conversion and 3 years after. These 11 life insurers occupied one fifth of the market and accumulated over $ 100 billion revenue during that time.[330]

These demutualizations have proven to be efficiency-enhancing because: "Management in these companies has successfully implemented a strategy that is based on higher growth, greater profitability, improved cost efficiency, and innovations in product offerings."[331] The conclusion of the study is that demutualization can be assessed as a positive step in case of analyzed life insurers since it brought many positive changes.

Table 21: Conversions of mutual life insurers (1997-2001)

Year	Number of conversions
1997	1
1998	2
1999	3
2000	4
2001	1

Source: *Chugh, L., Meador, J. W.*, Demutualization in the Life Insurance Industry: A Study of Effectiveness, in: Review of Business, 2006 27(1), 13.

Jeng et al. followed a similar approach, but they emploied a different methodology. They also analyze efficiency of the companies in the life insurance market before and after demutualization. Their sample also encompassed 11 life insurers, but in contrast to *Chugh* and *Meador*, the period of demutualization from 1984 to 1995 was considered.

[330] Cf. *Chugh, L., Meador, J. W.*, Demutualization in the Life Insurance Industry: A Study of Effectiveness, in: Review of Business, 2006 27(1), 13.

[331] Cf. Ibid., p. 15.

In order to determine efficiency, a time interval of 5 years was used, so each company is analyzed 5 years before demutualization and 5 years after. They have obtained different results since they showed that these companies did not increase efficiency after the demutualization process.[332]

Table 22: Conversions of mutual life insurers (1984-1995)

Year	Number of conversions	Year	Number of conversions
1984	2	1990	0
1985	2	1991	0
1986	1	1992	1
1987	0	1993	0
1988	1	1994	1
1989	1	1995	2

Source: *Jeng, V., Lai, G. C., McNamara, M. J.*, Efficiency and Demutualization: Evidence from the U.S. Life Insurance Industry in the 1980s and 1990s, in: The Journal of Risk and Insurance, 2007 74(3), p. 709.

Xie, Lu, Reising and *Stohs* tested the efficiency in the case of demutualization of 37 life insurers. Analyzed companies undertook demutualization in the period of 10 years, from 1993 to 2003. In 2003, the total asset share of mutual life insurers was around 15 percent compared to 40 percent in 1993. Out of 37, 24 companies demutualized through a non-initial public offering (IPO) and 13 through an initial public offering (IPO) process. Their findings supported the efficiency[333] rather than the expropriation[334] hypothesis, meaning that the desire towards effi-

332 Cf. *Jeng, V., Lai, G. C., McNamara, M. J.*, Efficiency and Demutualization: Evidence from the U.S. Life Insurance Industry in the 1980s and 1990s, in: The Journal of Risk and Insurance, 2007 74(3), p. 683.

333 The efficiency (value-enhancement) hypothesis says that demutualisation is predominantly driven by the desire for enhanced efficiency and profitability, in addition to a willingness to accept greater contracting costs to manage owner-policyholder agency issues.

334 According to the expropriation hypothesis, the managers of mutual firms (especially top executives such as CEOs) typically can benefit from the demutualisation

ciency was the main driver for demutualization, not managerial private interests and benefits. According to the researchers, no evidence could be found which indicates that policyholders were harmed in any way.[335] These findings are consistent with findings of *McNamara* and *Rhee*[336].

However, effects of demutualization driven by efficiency are slightly different. Companies that underwent demutualization through an initial public offering (IPO) witnessed positive changes in operations, reduction of cost, etc., whereas companies that underwent demutualization through a non-initial public offering were indifferent to these changes. Neither decline nor significant improvement in operations and cost efficiency were recorded in their case. Also, CEOs of companies that converted via IPO were rewarded with higher salaries, whereas remuneration of their counterparts in non-IPO demutualizations stayed unchanged.[337]

Erhemjamts and *Leverty* identifed 40 life insurance companies that demutualized in the period between 1995-2004. According to them, the type of demutualization is heavily influenced with the advantages originating from a partial or full demutualization process. Firms that expressed willingness towards partial demutualization did that because of tax benefits, whereas companies that converted to joint stock companies did that to raise capital and improve operations.[338]

Erhemjamts and *Phillips* analyzed 108 life insurance companies that demutualized in the period of 1986-2004. The period between 1997-2001 is especially interesting since 80 out of 108 analyzed companies underwent demutualization in this period. It means that around 75 percent of all conversions were executed in a period of 5 years; 16 demutualizations per year on average, in the years 1997 and 1998. Applying the method of a multinominal logistic regression, the researchers came to the conclusion that while access to capital was indeed the dominant

---

process through pre-conversion accounting management (of policy-holder surplus) and the arrangement of post-conversion compensation contracts such as increases in salary or incentive compensation (including stock options, stock appreciation rights and restricted stock).

335 Cf. Xie, X., Lu, W., Reising, J., Stohs, M. H., Demutualisation, control and efficiency in the U.S. life insurance industry. Geneva Papers on Risk and Insurance, 2011 36(2), p. 197.

336 Cf. *McNamara , M. J., Rhee, G. S.,* Ownership Structure and Performance: The Demutualization of Life Insurers, in: The Journal of Risk and Insurance, 1992 59(2), p. 221.

337 Cf. *Zou, H., Yang, C., Wang, M., Zhu, M.,* Dividend Decisions in the Property and Liability Insurance Industry: Mutual versus Stock Companies, in: Review of Quantitative Finance and Accounting, 2009 33(2), p. 113.

338 Cf. *Erhemjamts , O., Leverty, T. J.,* The Demise of the Mutual Organizational Form: An Investigation of the Life Insurance Industry, in: Journal of Money, Credit and Banking, 2010 42(6), p. 1011.

reason for mutual life insurance companies choosing to perform full demutualization, the main motivator for the performance of partial demutualizations of USA life insurance companies was tax incentives.[339]

Erhemjamts and *Phillips* explicated that tax incentives stem from the increase of effective surplus taxation following the introduction of the federal Deficit Reduction Act of 1984 Section 809. This section was a compromise in the Deficit Reduction Act of 1984 that sought to create a level playing field between the stock and mutual segments of the industry by limiting the mutual companies' dividend deduction against pre-tax income. Under this act the maximum amount of tax deductibles for policyholder dividends was severely reduced, leading to a substantial increase of effective taxation of mutual insurance companies. Reorganizing themselves under a mutual-holding company structure allowed mutual life insurers to reduce their tax burden without needing to fundamentally alter the organizational structure of the firm and fully demutualize. The reason for not one partial demutualization until 1996 despite mentioned Deficit Reduction Act being passed in 1984 was that from 1995 forward the first states began to pass legislation permitting the possibility of partial demutualization under the mutual holding company structure (see table 23).[340]

Later on, in the early 21st century, the popularity of this rather new organizational form was gone, with a total of only three MHC conversions from 2003 until 2004. It must be added that no full demutualization took place either, so that it can be argued that many life insurers decided to just stick to their organizational form of the time.

However, the financial crisis in 2008, at least temporarily, stopped the demutualization trend first and woke up an interest for a reversal of the process. As it is already known, the USA has been greatly affected during this crisis and the myth about its invulnerability was crushed. Consequently, many demutualized companies suffered in this period and demutualization was after the crises critically questioned.[341]

But even during and after the crisis, the demutualization process has continued steadily. In some cases, the development should be documented as an example (see table 24).

339 Cf. *Erhemjamts, O., Phillips, R. D.*, Form Over Matter: Differences in the Incentives to Convert Using Full Versus Partial Demutualization in the U.S. Life Insurance Industry, in: The Journal of Risk and Insurance, 2012 79(2), p. 305.

340 Until 2006, 33 states passed legislation allowing the method of partial demutualization under a mutual holding company structure. (Cf. Ibid.)

341 Cf. *Battilani, P., Schröter, H. G.*, Demutualization and its Problems, in: *Battilani, P., Schröter, H. G.* (eds.): The Cooperative Business Movement, 1950 to the Present, Cambridge 2012, p. 155.

Table 23: Partial and full demutualization of life insurers (1986-2004)

Year	MHC	Full	Year	MHC	Full
1986	0	2	1996	3	1
1987	0	0	1997	13	1
1988	0	1	1998	13	3
1989	0	3	1999	10	1
1990	0	0	2000	10	11
1991	0	1	2001	1	17
1992	0	3	2002	1	4
1993	0	0	2003	2	0
1994	0	1	2004	1	0
1995	0	5			

Siource: *Erhemjamts, O., Phillips, R. D.,* Form Over Matter: Differences in the Incentives to Convert Using Full Versus Partial Demutualization in the U.S. Life Insurance Industry, in: The Journal of Risk and Insurance, 2012 79(2), p. 305.

Table 24: Recent demutualization examples

Year	Company	Change of organizational form
2005	Westminster American Insurance Company (Maryland)	Full demutualisation
2009	Kingstone Companies, Inc. (New York)	Full demutualisation
2012	Medmarc (Virginia)	Sponsored demutualisation
2013	Florida Blue	MHC
2019	Farm Bureau and Southern Farm Bureau (Colorado)	Sponsored demutualisation

Bibliography

A.M. Best Company (ed.), Demutualizations: The State of Conversions in 2002, Special Report, BestWeek, September 30, 2002.

A.M. Best's Special Report: Addressing Structural Differences in the Rating Process, dated Aug. 13, 2012.

A.M. Best's Aggregates and Averages: Life/Health - 2000 Edition.

A.M. Best's Insurance Reports - Life-Health (1998).

Adkins, J. B., The Policyholder Perspective on Mutual Holding Company Conversions, in: Journal of Insurance Regulation, 1997, 16.

Akhtar, S., Demutualization of Asian Stock Exchanges in Critical Issues and Challengeses, in: *Akhtar, S.* (ed.), Demutualization of Stock Exchanges. Problems, Solutions and Case Studies, Manila 2002: Asian Development Bank.

AMICE. (n.d.). *What is mutual insurance?* Retrieved December 15, 2017, from http://www.amice-eu.org/userfiles/file/AMICE_What is mutuality.pdf, accessed on 13.05.2019.

Bainbridge, J., Biography of an Idea: The Story of Mutual Fire and Casualty insurance, New York 1952.

Battilani, P., Schröter, H. G. (eds.): The Cooperative Business Movement, 1950 to the Present, Cambridge 2012.

Battilani, P., Schröter, H. G., Demutualization and its Problems, in: *Battilani, P., Schröter, H. G.* (eds.): The Cooperative Business Movement, 1950 to the Present, Cambridge 2012.

Belth, J. M., The Demutualization of Midland Mutual Life, in: Insurance Forum 1994/21.

Biener, C., Eling, M.: Organization and Efficiency in the International Insurance Industry: A cross-frontier analysis, in: European Journal of Operational Research, 221(2) 2012.

Black, K., Skipper, H.D., Life and Health Insurance (13th ed.). Prentice Hall 2000.

Bonadurer, W., Ein tief greifender Wandel – die Entwicklung der Lebensversicherungsbranche in den USA, in: *Spremann, K.* (ed.), Versicherungen im Umbruch, Berlin 2005.

Borscheid, P., North America: Overview, in: *Borscheid, P. / Haueter, N.* (ed.): World Insurance The Evolution of a Global Risk Network, Oxford 2012.

Braun, A., Schmeiser, H., Rymaszewski, P., Stock vs. mutual insurers: Who should and who does charge more?, in: European Journal of Operational Research, 2015 242(3).

Cagle, J. A. B., Lippert, R. L., Moore, W. T., Demutualization in the Property-Liability Insurance Industry, in: Journal of Insurance Regulation, 14/1996.

Carow, K. A., Cox, S.R., Dianne M. Roden, D.M., Demutualization: Determinants and Consequences of the Mutual Holding Company Choice, in: Journal of Banking & Finance 33.8 (2009).

Carson, J. M., Forster, M. D., McNamara, M. J., Changes in Ownership Structure: Theory and Evidence from Life Insurer Demutualizations, in: Journal of Insurance Issues, 21/1998.

Chaddad, F. R., Cook, M. L., The Economics of Organization Structure Changes: A US Perspective on Demutualization, in: Annals of Public and Cooperative Economics, 2004 75 (4).

Chugh, L., Meador, J. W., Demutualization in the Life Insurance Industry: A Study of Effectiveness, in: Review of Business, 2006 27(1).

Crothers, G., Commercial Risks and Capital Formation in Early America, in: Business History Review 78/2004.

Cummins, J. D., Rubio-Misas, M., Zi, H., The Effect of Organizational Structure on Efficiency: Evidence from the Spanish Insurance Industry, in: Journal of Banking & Finance, 28(12) 2004.

Cummins, J. D., Weiss, M. A., Zi, H., Organizational Form and Efficiency: The Coexistence of Stock and Mutual Property-Liability Insurers, in: Management Science, 45(9) 1999.

Cummins, J. D., Xie, X., Economies of Scale and Efficiency Analysis in in the United States Property-Liability Insurance Industry, in: Working Paper, The Wharton School, University of Pennsylvania, 2005.

Dalzell, R., Enterprising Elite: the Boston Association and the World They Made, New York 1987.

Erhemjamts, O., Leverty, T. J., The Demise of the Mutual Organizational Form: An Investigation of the Life Insurance Industry, in: Journal of Money, Credit and Banking, 2010 42(6).

Dionne, G. (ed.), Handbook of Insurance, second edition. New York 2013.

Erhemjamts, O., Phillips, R. D., Form Over Matter: Differences in the Incentives to Convert Using Full Versus Partial Demutualization in the U.S. Life Insurance Industry, in: The Journal of Risk and Insurance, 2012 79(2).

Fama, E. F., Jensen, M. C., Agency Problems and Residual Claims, in: The Journal of Law and Economics, 1983 26(2).

Fama, E. F., Jensen, M. C., Separation of ownership and control, in: The Journal of Law and Economics, 26/1983.

Farny, D., *Versicherungsbetriebslehre* (5th edition). Karlsruhe 2006.

Fitzgerald, J., Demutualizing an Insurance Company: Determining and Distributing Policyholders' Shares, in: Journal of Insurance Regulation, June 1986.

Greene, M. R., Johnson, R. E., Stocks vs Mutuals: Who Controls?, in: Journal of Risk and Insurance, 47(1) 1980.

Griffiths, D., The Co-op Dictionary. Co-operative Federation of Victoria Ltd. 2004 Second edition.

Hann, L. W., New York State of Mind, in: Best's Review (P-C), September 1997.

Hansmann, H., The Organization of Insurance Companies: Mutual Versus Stock, in: Journal of Law, Economics and Organization, 1/1985.

Harman, J, Adney, J., Keene, B., The Taxes on Starlight: A Case for the Repeal of Sections 809, 815, and 1503(c) of the Internal Revenue Code, in: Insurance Tax Review 2001 31.

Harrington, S.E., Niehaus, G., Capital Structure Decisions in the Insurance Industry: Stocks versus Mutuals, in: Journal of Financial Services Research 21/2002

http://www.insurance-finance.com/files/doc2.html.

http://www.investopedia.com/articles/personal-finance/011916/mutual-vs-publically-traded-insurance-companies.asp.

http://www.namic.org/about/mutuals.asp.

http://www.nli-research.co.jp/en/report/detail/id=51230?site=nli, accessed.

http://www.pbs.org/benfranklin/l3_citizen_insurance.html.

http://www.pbs.org/benfranklin/l3_citizen_insurance.html.

http://www.pciaa.net/pciwebsite/Cms/Content/ViewList?cat1Id=9998&stateCode=FED.

https://eh.net/encyclopedia/fire-insurance-in-the-united-states/.

https://iid.iowa.gov/documents/examination-reports/life-and-health/athene-annuity-and-life-company-examination-report.

https://nyassembly.gov/Reports/Ins/199803/.

https://teekell.com/wp-content/uploads/sites/113/2018/01/Mutual-Life-Dividend-Rates-2017_0038-2017.pdf.

https://www.dfs.ny.gov/docs/insurance/exam_rpt/60176c15.pdf.

https://www.forbes.com/forbes/2008/1222/036.html#1b8791551a16.

https://www.iii.org/publications/insurance-handbook/introduction/insurance-industry-at-a-glance.

https://www.insuranceandestates.com/mutual-insurance-company-vs-stock-insurance-company/.

https://www.insurancejournal.com/magazines/mag-partingshots/2001/04/30/18694.htm/?comments.

https://www.investopedia.com/terms/m/mutualcompany.asp.

https://www.luselaw.com/wp-content/uploads/2017/04/2005_4.pdf.

https://www.marketwatch.com/press-release/bests-market-segment-report-us-propertycasualty-mutual-insurers-achieve-moderate-surplus-growth-despite-elevated-losses-2018-09-19.

https://www.naic.org/documents/cipr_events_impact_rating_amb_m_report.pdf, September 2016.

https://www.namic.org/policy/futureMutualAlts.

https://www.namic.org/policy/futureMutualPolicyRights.

https://www.nationalgeographic.org/news/chicago-fire-1871-and-great-rebuilding/.

https://www.thebalance.com/stock-insurer-versus-mutual-insurer-462504.

James, H., Introduction: The Insuring Instinct, in: *James, H.* et al. (eds.): The Value of Risks: Swiss Re and the History of Reinsurance, Oxford 2013.

Jeng, V., Lai, G. C., McNamara, M. J., Efficiency and Demutualization: Evidence from the U.S. Life Insurance Industry in the 1980s and 1990s, in: The Journal of Risk and Insurance, 2007 74(3).

Koeppel, J. A., Refuting the Myths about Mutual Holding Companies, in: Best's Review-Life/Health, February 1998.

Lawrence, S., What It Means to be Mutual , National Association of Mutual Insurance Companies (NAMIC), 2017.

Loftin, G., Xie, X., The United States Insurance Market: Characteristics and Trends, in: *Cummins, J. D., Venard, B.* (ed.): Handbook of International Insurances. Between Global Dynamics and Local Contingencies, New York 2007.

Lufkin, J., Property Insurance for Iowa Farmers, the Rise of the Mutuals, in: The Annals of Iowa, 1995/1.

Masulis, R. W., Changes in Ownership Structure: Conversion of Mutual Savings and Loans to Stock Charter, in: Journal of Financial Economics, 1987 18.

Mayers, D. C., Smith, C. W., Ownership Structure And Control: Property-Casualty Insurer Conversion to Stock Charter", in: Journal of Financial Services Research 2002 2.

Mayers, D. C., Smith, C. W., Executive Compensation in the Life Insurance Industry, in: The Journal of Business, 65(1) 1992.

Mayers, D. C., Smith, C. W., On the choice of organizational form: theory and evidence from the insurance industry, in: *Dionne, G.* (ed.), Handbook of Insurance, second edition. New York 2013.

Mayers, D. C., Smith, C. W., Ownership structure and control: The mutualization of stock life insurance companies, in: Journal of Financial Economics, 16(1) 1986.

Mayers, D. C., Smith, C. W., Ownership Structure and Control: Property-Casualty Insurer Conversion to Stock Charter, in: Journal of Financial Services Research, 21(1-2) 2002.

McDonald, L., Saucer, C., Winans, C., Taking Stock, Best's Review - Property/ Liability, December 1997.

McNamara , M. J., Rhee, G. S., Ownership Structure and Performance: The Demutualization of Life Insurers, in: The Journal of Risk and Insurance, 59(2) 1992.

Mester, L. J., Agency costs among savings and loans, in: Journal of Financial Intermediation, 1(3) 1991.

Mester, L. J., Testing for Expense Preference Behavior: Mutual versus Stock Savings and Loans, in: The RAND Journal of Economics 20/1989.

Moody's: Credit issues and trends for US life insurers, 2003.

Murphy, S., Investing in Life: Insurance in Antebellum America, Baltimore 2010.

Murphy, S., Life Insurance in the United States through World War I., 2005, www.eh.net/enceclopedia/?article Murphy.life.insurance.us.

Murphy, S., Selecting Risks in an Anonymous World: the Agency System for Life Insurance in Antebellum America, in: Business History Review 82/2008.

NAIC (ed.), Mutual Insurance Holding Company Reorganizations, Kansas City 1999.

NAIC (ed.), State Insurance Regulation, Kanses City 2011.

Obersteadt , A., The Center for Insurance Policy and Research, State of the Life Insurance Industry: Implications of Industry Trends, A white paper report, August 2013. http://www.naic.org/.

Ogris, W. (1988): Zur Entwicklung des Versicherungsaufsichtsrechts und des Versicherungsvertragsrechts in Österreich von der Mitte des 19. Jahrhunderts bis zum Ende der Monarchie, in: Die Ära des klassischen Versicherungswesens, Versicherungsgeschichte Österreichs, vol. II, Vienna.

Pearson. R., Organizational Forms in Insurance. A comparison of the USA and Germany during Industrialization, in: *Pearson, R., Yoneyama, T.* (ed.): Corporate Forms and Organizational Choice in International Insurance, Oxford 2015.

Pottier, S., Sommer, D., Agency theory and life insurer ownership structure, in: Journal of Risk and Insurance, 64/1997.

Ransom, R.L. / Sutch, R.: Tontine Insurance and the Armstrong Investigation: A Case of Stifled Innovation, 1868-1905, in: The Journal of Economic History, Vol. 47, No. 2, 1987.

Schiff, B.D., The Big Fix: Mutual Insurance Holding Companies, in: Schiff's Insurance Observer, February 1998.

Smith, B.D., Stutzer, M., A theory of mutual formation and moral hazard with evidence from the history of the insurance industry, in: Review of Financial Studies, 8/1995.

Smith, C. W., On the Convergence of Insurance and Finance Research, in: The Journal of Risk and Insurance, 1986 53(4).

Stalson, J.O., Marketing Life Insurance: History in America, Harvard 1942.

Swiss Re Corporate History (ed.), A History of US Insurance, Zurich 2013.

Swiss Re, Are Mutual Insurers an Endangered Species, in: Sigma, no.4/1999.

The last 25 Years – A Rewiew, in: Best's Special Report, March 3, 2018.

Tuohy, M., Challenges and Issues for Growth in the Life Insurance Industry, in: *Cummins, J. D., Santomero, A. M.* (eds.): Changes in the Life Insurance Industry: Efficiency, Technology, and Risk Management, Norwell 1999.

Viswanathan, K. S., Cummins, D. J., Ownership Structure Changes in the Insurance Industry: An Analysis of Demutualization, in: Journal of Risk and Insurance, 2003 70(3), p. 418.Using A.M. Best's Insurance Reports - Property-Liability (1998).

Viswanathan, K.S., The Pricing of Insurer Demutualization Initial Public Offerings, in: Journal of Risk and Insurance 73/2006.

Wells, B. P., Cox, L. A., Gaver, K. M., Free Cash Flow in the Life Insurance Industry, in: The Journal of Risk and Insurance, 62(1) 1995.

Williamson, O. E., Managerial Discretion and Business Behavior, in: American Economic Review, 53/1963.

Xie, X., Lu, W., Reising, J., Stohs, M. H., Demutualisation, control and efficiency in the U.S. life insurance industry. Geneva Papers on Risk and Insurance, 2011 36(2),

Zanjani, G., Regulation, Capital, and the Evolution of Organizational Form in US Life Insurance, in: The American Economic Revie, 2007 97(3).

Zanjani, G., The Rise and Fall of the Fraternal Life Insurer: Law and Finance in U.S. Life Insurance, 1870-1920, New York 2004.

Zelizer, G., Moral and Markets: The development of Life Insurance in the United States, New Brunswick 1983.

Zou, H., Yang, C., Wang, M., Zhu, M., Dividend Decisions in the Property and Liability Insurance Industry: Mutual versus Stock Companies, in: Review of Quantitative Finance and Accounting, 2009 33(2).

Part IV.
“Late Bloomers” of the Insurance Business

Mutuals and Demutualisation in Spain

Robert Schediwy

The idea of mutual self-help and monetary group support against unforeseen hardship came up in Spain at roughly the same time as in the rest of Europe. This idea stood at the origin of modern social security management. The Spanish term is mutualismo, the expression mutualistic movement is used. It has been stressed, however, that mutualistic relationships do not arise via voluntary contractual relationships but rather via the membership in an established social group or liberal profession such as architect or lawyer.

The basic concept is a simple one: The risk of accidents or damages can confront isolated persons or families with unbearable hardship. By spreading these risks (or at least their monetary equivalent) over a larger number of people and objects this danger is made more bearable. This process of risk spreading is usually organized in the way of regular contributions.

The transition from voluntary contribution towards obligation took place in a gradual way, with ups and downs. This transition was depended on political and economic factors, *Hans-Joachim Reinhard* points out correctly that early initiatives to create the initial elements of social security were established in industrial nations (such as Germany) earlier than in less advanced countries. The motives behind this move were quite complex. The conservative German chancellor *Otto von Bismarck* initiated, for example, a social security explicitly for the reason to have a propaganda asset in his fight against the early workers' movement.

Compared to Central and Western Europe, Spain was an economically backward country. The masses of Gold that Spanish colonialism had acquired or rather robbed from its subjects abroad benefitted just a small aristocratic upper crust and the Catholic Church. Lagging behind in industrialization (except for Catalonia and parts of Basque country), Spain was unable to participate in the field of public insurance.[1] In view of a situation where the elements of social security provided by the state were lacking the industrial areas in the North of the Iberian Peninsula developed a stronger mutualismo impulse.

---

1 *Kaufmann, Otto/Hennion, Silvie* (eds.). Steuerung der betrieblichen Altersvorsorge in Europa", Heidelberg-Berlin 2011, p. 136ff.

As time went on, social security offered by institutions of the state reduced in Spain as well as elsewhere the thrust and popularity of the mutualistic impulse. As we see them today, they have survived only as frostings of the cake, i.e. as additional benefits that are regarded as “extras” and not as the basic elements of risk compensation.

1. The Historical Path of Mutuality in Spain

Already during the 11th and 12th century, there was in Spain (as in the rest of Europe) a flourishing of religious brotherhoods (cofradias). These organizations were created in veneration for a particular Saint. Membership in one of these brotherhoods meant that the persons concerned were obliged to help each other in Christian brotherhood. In the course of the development of guilds and fraternities, some of these Cofradias became linked to certain trades and professions and thus contributed to the growth of the guild system (sistema gremial). From the 16th to the 18th century, a system of cofradias and hermandades de socorros mutuos developed with some rather sophisticated features of social provision. During the 18th century, secular authorities tried to take this system out of the hands of clerics. Towards the end of the 18th century there was a foundation wave of hermandades de socorros. These were sometimes based on clerical institutions that were taken over and controlled by the crown. One would not speak of a generalized system, however, and the persons covered by a risk management of this kind could consider themselves to be privileged.[2]

The so-called montepios were a product of the late 18th century. These were Hermandades controlled by the crown via state institutions. They were also just open to certain groups of professions and trades.[3]

The royal decree of January 21, 1921 concerning the workers' pensions was the first mandatory measure with regard to the Spanish system of social security. This was a predecessor of a state system of social security. Over many decades, however, the mutualidades de prevision social linked to certain privileged fields of professional activ-

[2] Cf. *Battaller Grau et al*: El redimensionamiento de las mutualidades de previsión social como instrumento complementario del sistema de seguridad social, Ministerio de Trabajo y Asuntos Sociales, Madrid 2008 p. 30f.

[3] Cf. *Calle Maria, Dolores* de la: Mutualidades Laborales en el régimen de Franco. IX. Congreso de la Asociación Española de Historia Económica 2008; *Molinero, Carme*: La captación de las masas. Política social y propaganda en el régimen franquista, Madrid 2005, Ed. Cátedra.

ity remained important: at first, they were meant as an alternative or substitute to state institutions. Actually, some groups still prefer it today to run their own system of social security. The mutualidades de prevision social were organized by the law of December 6, 1941 at the high point of the "corporatist" orientation of *Franco's* Spain. This law distinguishes between montepios, which offered complementary benefits, and mutualidades, which offered complete coverage.

The dictatorship of *General Francisco Franco*, which existed from 1939 up to the year 1975 when *Franco* died, cannot and should not be seen as a monolithic period. This holds for the positions of the regime with regard to social policy as well as for other matters. At first for example, it seemed that *Franco's* Spain, just like *Mussolini's* Italy and *Hitler's* Germany, would put increased emphasis on state institutions in social as well as economic matters. Later on after the downfall of the fascist powers, private capitalism became stronger. In the field of social security, the dictatorial regime favoured at first mutualism focussing on the welfare of certain key industries represented by "friendly" unions[4]. We can see a parallelism to the ideology of Austrian's corporative state and its interpretation of catholic social doctrine as a post-medieval order, where everyone had his/her well-defined place in society.[5] Employers and employees were supposed to work together harmoniously also in the field of social security. According to this vision of society, mutualidades laboriales for 19 trades were created.

After 1960, the pendulum swung, however, in the direction of the state as the mutualism was best qualified to offer social security.

The sector of insurance was regulated in Spain in 1908 for the first time as a reaction to problems with foreign insurers active on the Spanish market. The Spanish mutuals and montepios were left untouched by this law insofar as they were not orientated towards making profit and if they were ready to deposit their statutes at the office of insurance supervision.

As a consequence of Spain's civil war, there was a slow process of gradually decreasing of the mutualistic instruments of provision.[6] The law on private insurances from December 1954 was part of this tendency. As a consequence, the public servants' mutual society took the cover of the state and turned into a legal entity under public law (personas juridicas publicas).[7] The liberal arts professions, however, kept to their traditional forms.

---

4 Cf. *Reinhard, Hans-Joachim* (ed.): Demographischer Wandel und Alterssicherung. Rentenpolitik in neun europäischen Ländern und den USA im Vergleich. Baden-Baden 2001, p. 137.

5 Ibid.

6 Cf. *Battaller Grau et al.* p. 35.

7 Cf. *Ibid.*, p. 36.

2. A secular Turn towards the Methods and Principles of Private Insurance

The turn towards the methods and principles of private insurance became evident after the end of the *Franco* dictatorship. *Francisco Franco y Bahamonde*, the long-time dictator of Spain died in 1975. Even though he never gave up power, *Franco* understood that his type of government had become an obsolete oddity in modern Europe, and he had destined the crown prince *Juan Carlos* as the person to lead the orderly transition. The newly crowned King of Spain thus was entrusted with the process of bringing Spain back to the model of liberal democracy. This also meant: more liberalism in the realm of the economy.

3. The Law of August 1984 and its Consequences

The law No. 33 of August 2nd 1984 on the subject of private insurances and the Royal Degree of December 4, 1985 have been regarded as milestones of this process of liberalization in the field of the insurance sector. Some have called these provisions a "Copernican Turn". At any rate, they marked an important stage in the process of assimilation that had brought the mutualistic sector nearer to the commercial insurance sector. The mutualidades de prevision social were forced to strengthen their own capital, mathematical methods were now mandatory in the context of their activities as life insurers. The distribution of costs and/or expenses was from now on forbidden. Furthermore, special measures were introduced to control administrative costs. The change of character concerning the mutualidades de prevision social can be seen also in the principles of solvability, which were published by the European Union. On this basis, the International Actuarial Association produced "3 columns of solvability".

4. The three Columns of Solvability

- The necessities to dispose of mechanisms that guarantee a certain amount of own capital.
- The principle of supervision.
- Measures to control the discipline in the market.

Today the largest mutualistic institutions have taken the character of regular enterprises this aspect is in Spain quite similar to the situation in other countries. Some of them actually have turned into multinational or transnational players in the financial markets. In this context, a certain amount of demutualization has proved unavoidable and some of the discussions about the possibility of creating the new legal entity of a European Mutual have been stimulated by these facts. An example of this new type of mutual (that in the end would be demutualized) would the case the case of MAPFRE[8], a car insurer whose case will be treated further down.

The tendency towards assimilation concerning mutualities and for profit insurance enterprises has been noted also in the recent "Study on the current situation and prospects of mutuals in Europe". This study stresses in its final statement that the Solvability II guideline holds for life and non-life insurances regardless whether their business is run in the legal form of a joint stock company (sociedad cooperative), a mutual company, or a co-operative. The fact that the private insurance sector enjoys a somewhat higher ranking is made evident by the fact that the activity of reinsurance can only be exercised by a sociedad anonima.

Mutuals in Spain are non-profit companies. Their officials also have to work without remunerates. Their legal form is defined by the fact that all insured persons are also members of the society (mutualists). They enjoy the same rights regardless of their share in capital.

The private insurance sector has developed the instrument of risk selection, the mutualidades, however, have been hesitant to do so. The fact to be a mutualista often stems, in particular in the life insurance sector, from a membership in a certain well-defined professional group. In that respect, it can be regarded as a social class element that refers back to the history of the mutualidades.

The European Commission has issued a "Manual for drawing up co-operative and mutual society satellite accounts". It contains pertinent statistics for five European countries (Spain, Belgium, Serbia, Bulgaria, and Macedonia). The so-called Third Sector as a whole has, however,

8 Cf. *Caruana de las Caccas, Leonardo*: The Insurance Demutualization Develops in Spain with MAPFRE", in: *Pearson, Robin / Yoneyama, Takai* (eds): Corporate Forms and Organizational Choice in International Insurcance, Oxford University Press, Oxford 2015, p. 284.

only played a modest role in European economic development, neither in a negative sense (stimulating crises) nor as a means of fighting crises.

5. Principles and Juridical Characteristics

Today mutuals are in general characterised by political and religious neutrality (at least formally), further principles are voluntary adherence, democratic organization, contributions equivalent to services, the propagation of education, and professional training and integration for development.

The Spanish mutualistic sector is characterized by the fact that it comprises few big enterprises and a great number of small entities. Globalization and the EU Common market have increased this tendency during the recent decades. In other words: there are few giant mutuals and the rest are mostly small. For the small mutuals the situation can be dramatic. Internationally active private insurers and pension funds compete, one could say, with midgets.

6. Legal Definition

The organization and supervision of insurance and reinsurance companies in Spain is mainly governed by rules originated in the EU and derived from the Solvency II Directive. The laws and regulations are Act 20/2015 of 14 July, for ordination, supervision and solvency of insurance and reinsurance undertakings (LOSSEAR) and Royal Decree 1060/2015 of 20 November, approving the regulations for ordination, supervision and solvency of insurance and reinsurance undertakings (ROSSEAR). Both became effective on 1 January 2016.

Insurance activities can only be carried out by the following types of private company:

- Limited liability company (sociedad anónima).
- European company (sociedad anónima europea).
- Mutual insurance company (mutua de seguros).

- Co-operative company (sociedad cooperativa).
- European co-operative society (sociedad cooperativa europea).
- Mutual provident society (mutualidad de previsión social). (Article 27 of LOSSEAR)

Mutual insurance companies, cooperative companies and mutual provident societies can only operate fixed premium business (Article 27 (1) of LOSSEAR). Operations carried out by entities without legal personality whose purpose is the mutual coverage for their members without giving rise to payment of premiums or constitutions of technical provisions are excluded (Article 4 of LOSSEAR). Mutual insurance companies are defined as non-profit commercial companies whose purpose is to cover their members' risks, whether individual or legal entities, through a fixed premium payable at the beginning of the risk period. They can be active in both life and non-life insurance classes. (Article 41 of LOSSEAR)[9]

In terms of legal status, in 2017 there were 145 public limited liability companies, 31 mutual companies, 49 mutual provident societies (subject to oversight by the Directorate General of Insurance and Pension Funds - DGSFP[10]), and 3 specialized reinsurance companies.[11]

7. The Economic Weight of Mutuals in Spain

The Spanish insurance market continues to be characterized by a high degree of competition. This is the case despite a mid-term trend toward a greater concentration of activity due to inorganic company growth arising from the various commercial transactions that had taken place, due to companies' own organic growth resulting from the rationalization of the banking sector after the crisis of 2012, a process that has led to the disappearance of a large number of financial institutions (mainly savings banks), forcing a renegotiation of the bancassurance agreements that were in force at the time.[12]

---

[9] Cf. ICMIF (2018): Facts and figures – Mutual and cooperative insurance in Europe, AMICE aisbl & ICMIF, Vol 2, p. 72.

[10] Dirección General de Seguros y Fondos de Pensiones.

[11] Cf. Fundación MAPFRE (ed.): The Spanish insurance market in 2017, Madrid, 2018, p. 32.

[12] Ibid. p. 29.

In 2017, there were 464 insurance companies included 228 insurance companies supervised by the Directorate General of Insurance and Pension Funds (DGSFP) present in the Spanish market. This was three fewer than the previous year, thus continuing the trend observed in recent years toward a decline in the number of insurers, particularly led by limited companies.[13] In contrast the number of mutual insurers operating in Spain has maintained stable between 2014 to 2017 (see figure 1).

Figure 1: Number of operating mutual insurance companies in Spain between 2011 and 2017

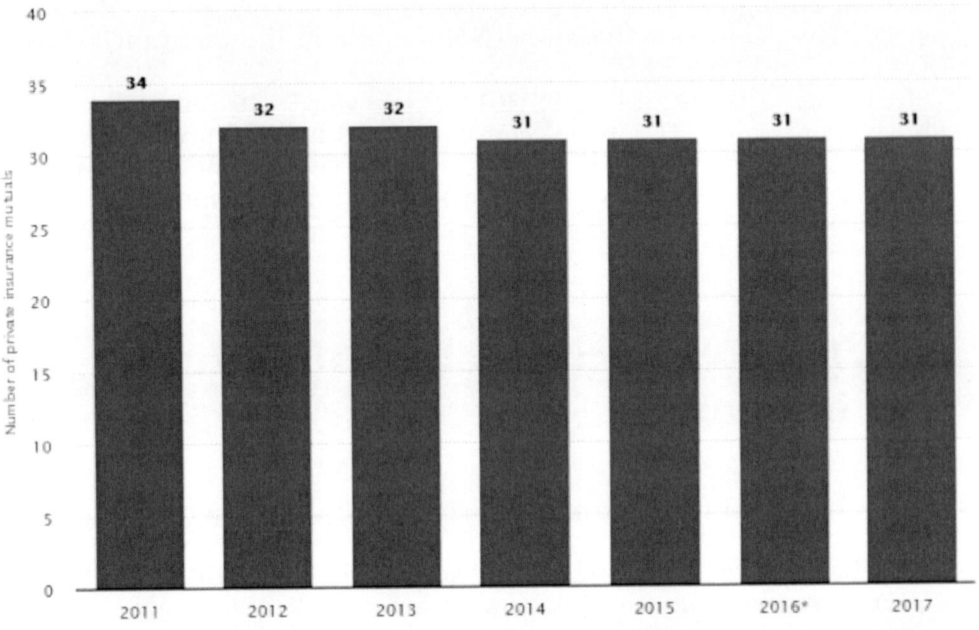

Source: https://www.statista.com/statistics/775525/number-from-mutual-from-insurance-in-spain/

In terms of legal status, in 2017 there were 145 public limited liability companies, 31 mutual companies, 49 mutual provident societies under national supervision, and 3 specialized reinsurance companies. Mutual provident societies are non-profit private insurance companies that offer a voluntary insurance modality, complementary to the com-

---

13 Ibid. p. 32.

pulsory social security system, and can also act as alternatives to the social security regime for self-employed workers. (see figure 2)

Of the 80 mutual insurance companies and mutual provident societies under national supervision, 24 were life insurers, 36 were non-life insurers and 20 were composite insurers.

8. A study done by the University of Valencia

A research group of nine persons has studied recently a possible redimensioning of the insurance mutual of social provision as an instrument of complementary covering of risks. The study was undertaken in view of the looming sight that there are to be enormous problems for the Spanish welfare state in the future.[14] An interesting example could be the following: architects and lawyers already do not participate in general social security. At any rate, the authors of the study have felt compelled to stress the fact that their conclusions are in no way identified with the opinion of the public system social security. There seems to be a certain tension there.

8.1 The economic Situation of the Mutual Sector

The situation of the Spanish mutual sector in this study is described as differentiated. The Valencia study shows a sizeable measure of concentration. The largest five Mutuales der Prevision Social take in about three quarters of the total amount of premium, the largest 15 more than 92 percent.[15]

A large number of small mutualidades can be seen as potentially vulnerable. The big mutualidades, however, do better with regard to efficiency than the private insurers, especially after 2002.[16] The small mutualidades seem to have a considerable problem with administration costs.[17] *Grau* et al recommend the instruments of the formation of Economic Interest groups (Agrupacion de interes economico, i.e. AIE) and the temporary working group (Union temporal de empresas, i.e. UTE). The AIE makes changes in the judicial status easier and so some

[14] Cf. *Battaller Grau* et al. p. 12.

[15] Cf. Ibid., p. 52.

[16] Cf. Ibid., p. 67.

[17] Cf. Ibid., p. 82.

Figure 2: Growth in the number of companies operating in the Spanish insurance industry, by legal structure, 2007-2017

Year	Public limited companies	Mutual companies	Mutual provident societies[1]	Reinsurance companies
2007	206	37	52	2
2008	204	35	55	2
2009	202	34	56	2
2010	195	35	55	2
2011	188	34	55	2
2012	183	32	53	2
2013	178	32	52	2
2014	168	31	53	3
2015	156	31	50	3
2016	147	31	50	3
2017	145	31	49	3

[1] Subject to control by the Directorate General for Insurance and Pension Funds

Source: MAPFRE Economic Research

procedures can be avoided. However, the rights of the members have to be guaranteed. They have to have the possibility to leave its insurance contract. This aspect can create problems when the minimum capital requirements are not met.[18] Extension the continued existence of the mutualistic company but without the actual business is a solution.

The merger of mutualidades is also possible but only within the realm of the same judicial form.[19] Furthermore, it is possible to sell whole blocks of insurance contracts to other insurers.[20]

8.2 A statement by a number of larger Spanish Mutuals

A number of Spanish mutuals, mostly in the field of accidents in the workplace and professional sickness, have commented on an EU document concerning the most recent enlargement of the European Union. The preambula of the document makes it clear that Fremap, Asepeyo, Fraternidad, and Mutua Universal hold the opinion that the European Commission does not know too well their fields of activity.

The MATEPSS (Mutuas de Accidentes de Trabajo y Enfermedades Profesionales) were before 1990 a mutual society of employers (Mutuas Patronales de Accidentes de Trabajo) covering the risks of accidents at work. In 1996, they took over the administration of similar risks for farmers and self-employed persons. The MATEPSS lack, however, the intent to make profit and their financial intakes became obligatory contributions. These contributions, called cuotas, are income by the state. The role of the MATEPSS is just an administrative one. The MATEPSS also do not transfer surpluses back to their owners/members. In the event that such surpluses may arise, they are transferred to a special account within the Spanish Nation and the mutuals can decide upon them. The Ministry of Labour and Social Affairs has to authorise such reimbursements and acts as a general supervisor for these mutuals.

The MATEPSS cannot be regarded as a local phenomenon: They exist in the whole of Spain. Their members are the employers, beneficiaries are their employees. Members are not particularly active. The institution is not furthering the entrepreneurial spirit. The MATEPSS administer public funds and one could almost speak of a certain toleration of the owners inside this public institution.

In the view of these facts, the risks of being a MATEPSS member has to be regarded much less than being a member of a cooperative. Competition between the MATEPSS is not price competition but qual-

18 Cf. Ibid., p. 97.

19 Cf. Ibid., p. 99.

20 Cf. Ibid., p. 156.

ity competition regarding the services rendered to the beneficiaries (hospitals, rehabilitation, and preventive medical check-up).

The characteristics of the MATEPSS make it evident that they feel more uneasy in their interventionist role than necessary. The five big MATEPSS envisage two alternative solutions to this dilemma. The smoother solution would consist in freeing the MATEPSS from their rucksack of bureaucratic formalism and interventionist duties by transforming them into free economic entities. Ex-post controls based on clear principles should take the place of ad hoc authorizations. Instead of monthly reports, there should be yearly ones. An alternative option would consist in taking the risks so far handled by the MATEPSS out of the social security system and privatize the sector with certain guarantees, with yearly balance sheets, and minimum serves.

The risk of accidents in the workplace has been regulated quite differently in different EU-countries. Statal social security is still organized by the state and that creates disparities. Countries with worker-friendly laws such as Spain are faced with an alarming wave of claims. Therefore, a unification on the European level could be highly useful and the MATEPSS could act in the whole area of the European Union.

8.3 Banalization and Demutualization

It is not always easy to obtain detailed information about the development and economic status of mutual societies. This holds for many countries but also for Spain. Also in the case of juridical forms that have a certain ideological connotation, the research done can have a certain ideological slant to studies that are to be considered scientific and which usually keep their distance with regard to articles in the daily press. This seems to be the case in France and Spain too, to some extend understandably, because the echo concerning the important demutualization of recent years was quite critical. The criticism in the Spanish economic press went into three directions.

- The uncommonly active role of government and of the office of insurance supervision (Dirección General de Seguros) was criticised, especially for the time of the PSOE (social democratic government).
- Internal democracy was claimed to be practically inexistence.
- Also, demutualization processes that have taken place were characterized by lack of transparency.

8.4 MAPFRE: A Case of Charismatic Leadership

At this moment, it appears appropriate to mention the MAPFRE case more in detail. MAPFRE was founded in 1933. Originally, it counted under the Mapss as an institution created to benefit agricultural workers in large scale enterprises. It was a Mutua de Accidentes de Trabajo. The reason for its creation by large-scale landowners was the interest of the latifundistas to undercut similar plans by the then ruling leftist government. The Agrupación de Propietarios de Fof initiated the scheme (group of owners of rural). For almost two decades the Mutua was not very successful. In 1944, the institutions struck a deal with the Caja Nacional del Seguro Obligatorio de Enfermedad, but nevertheless it came dangerously close to bankruptcy.

MAPFRE's destiny was dramatically changed after *Ignacio Hernando de Larramendi* (1921-2001) took over its reins. *Don Ignacio* had a charismatic personality. Coming from a traditionalistic deeply catholic background *Larramendi* was once a loyal follower of the Franco regime and a reform-minded modern manager. *Larramendi* never learned how to drive a car himself, but he knew how to read the signs of the time and so he started MAPFRE 1952 in the field of car accident insurance. Mass motorization (1952) was coming and with a policy of expansion, MAPFRE's number of employees grew from about 200 to over 10000 within a short period of time. *Larramendi* engaged in friendly relations with the Basque group of Mondragon cooperatives that took a similar path: also a personal friendship with Mondragon's founding father, the catholic priest *José Maria Arizmendiarrieta* (1915-1976) developed. After *Larramendi* retired in 1990 the successful expansion of MAPFRE continued, but it led eventually to demutualization.

8.5 The Demutualization of MAPFRE and Agrupació Mutual

When demutualization came, MAPFRE had more than 5 million Mutualistas. They had to be reimbursed, so each of them had the choice of getting 73.4 Euro for his/her share or 23 shares in the new joint stock company.

The financial payment was taken only by 1,825 persons that is less than one percent. Media reports of 2006, however, make it evident that this probably was not well explained to the public.[21] The number of share owners fell dramatically during the process of demutualization.

[21] Cf.http://www.economiahoy.mx/empresas-finanzas/noticias/73530/09/06/Mapfre-dificulto-que-sus-mutualistas-optaran-por-dinero-en-lugar-de-titulos.htm.

At the end of 2007, there were only about 565,000 share owners left, approximately one tenth of the number of mutualistas that had been there before. And the number of shareholders continued to decrease. The phenomenon is well known internationally.

Whenever the idea of people's shares has been tried, it has led to a rapid concentration of ownerships. People's capitalism does not work. Sooner or later, the small share owners sell out either by disappointment or to cash in on favorable market conditions.[22] The decision to demutualise MAPFRE, by the way, was taken by a general meeting of 2.000 people that is 0.005 percent of total membership voted. This is not a very impressive show of democracy.[23] On the other hand, the majority of the shares has to be in the hands of the foundation MAPFRE (founded in 1975, a provision that helps against unfriendly takeovers).

Another case of demutualization took place in 2009.[24] It is the case of the Agrupació Mutual[25] when 800 out of 250,000 mutualistas decided. The background was risky speculations of the mutuals that ended in substantial losses. Demutualization was in fact an unfriendly takeover.

8.6 Some conclusion

Demutualization has taken place on a large scale during the recent past. This process has taken place mostly in the Anglo-Saxon world, but Spain shows a similar picture. The legal status of the insurance economy has been changed dramatically during that period. Demutualization concerned flourishing enterprises as well as enterprises, which had run into economic difficulties. The case of MAPFRE is important as one of the biggest insurance companies that have taken actively the road towards demutualization. The reason behind was as usual the wish to get better access to financial markets. The critics have also followed the usual road: they emphasized the lack of transparency and democracy at the crucial points of transition. The better access to capital markets is the classical counter argument.

On a more fundamental level, the question of the kind and intensity of members' contributions and decision-making powers should be discussed (but is discussed only rarely).

---

22 Cf. http://seguros.km77.com/seguros/2011/04/11/mapfre-seguros-base-accionarial.html.

23 El Mundo cf. http://www.elmundo.es/mundodinero/2006/06/15/economia/1150381131.html.

24 Cf. *Caruana de las Caccas*, p. 284.

25 Cf. http://ccaa.elpais.com/ccaa/2012/06/29/catalunya/1340996519_013757.html.

Ownerless assets?

Large cooperatives, saving banks, and mutual societies are sometimes identified as owner less capital. Especially in cases where highly motivated and honest administrators are to be found in top-level positions of such institutions important success stories can be found and economic growth plus self-financed strength are possible.

A strong role of democratic grassroots institutions is however by no means indispensable for the success of such an enterprise. Contrary to the ideas and myths propagated by certain researchers, a strong role of grassroots democracy is neither necessary nor a prerequisite of success. On the contrary: a stronger activity of democratic or pseudo-democratic institutions is often an indication of economic or ideology crises.

The Spanish example of MAPFRE and its charismatic chairman *Ignacio Vicente de Larramendi* can be compared to the role that played *Albin Johansson* who directed during decades the Swedish cooperative Förbundet. The Spanish case supports the thesis that modern mutuals are usually not to be seen as a result of powerful popular movements. It is true that they have developed from pre-industrial cooperatives and religious nuclei of group solidarity. It is, however, a modern phenomenon that highly motivated and honest leader figures wake up these "sleeping beauties" and create large enterprises. This is possible especially in "young" fields of economic activity. After the great charismatic leader has left the realm, normalisation is attractive and often quite unavoidable. These authoritarian figures, who rule on basis of idealism and the hunger for success, are often masters of innovation. If one wants to utilise the term Economie sociale, they are able to accumulate enormous financial reserves during their long stay in office. These reserves are formerly owned by the members or consumers linked to the enterprises. The problem, however, is the following: these owners usually have no idea that they are owners and they usually do not care about "their enterprise". It is easy to denounce a low number of participants who decide during a general meeting on the demutualization of an enterprise. It is easy to denounce those who want to take control over enormous reserves of such an enterprise. The lack of interest of the relevant public is authentic there is no need to accuse evil conspirators. It may well be that some privatisations turn out to be an equivalent of stealing from the public. When thousands of (ex)-members loose part of their ownership rights to the equivalent of some Euros the case is comparable to a situation where 0.2 Eurocent per month are transferred monthly to an unknown beneficiary.

Growth versus Democracy?

The elements of democratic decision-making never have been very strong with Spanish mutuals, but the decision-making structure is often usually dramatically reduced during a process of growth. The cooperative movement has experienced similar processes of growth and banalization. Banalization is a term that comes from French theorists and is generally used in a critically way. It means that enterprises belonging to the "Social Economy" gradually see their differences compared to their private competitors reduced. In this context, one may notice that the democratic impulse that was quite strong during certain "foundation waves" of cooperatives during the 19th century and even later seems to have played a much weaker role in the field of mutual societies from the start on.

The law-giving authorities are not completely foreign to this process of banalization. The regime of *General Franco* cultivated rather interventionist economic policies with rather cumbersome mechanisms of supervision. Since 1978, the year that Spain got its constitution as a modern democratic monarchy, liberalism has been advancing steadily also in the economic field. The law of 1984 is a case in point. The mutualidades de prevision social are treated in that law on an equal footing with private insurance companies. This development has led to considerable restructurings within the sector. The criteria of solvability formulated in that law were so harsh that many smaller mutualities were not able to put them into practise even at the end of a 5 year transitional period (November 1995-November 2000). They had to be liquidated. Even so, the Spanish mutualities are counted among the enterprises of social economy.[26]

In recent years, the misgivings about public systems of social security have risen and the market for additional or substitute benefits has grown in importance. This could offer new chances for mutualities. The entrance of Spain into the Common market gave additional momentum to that tendency.

[26] Cf. *Maria Tereza Sanchez* Univeristy of Granada in einer CIRIEC-Studie. El Mutualismo de Prevision social en En Espana (pp. 225-248).

Bibliography

Armando, Alfredo Moirano: Apuntes para una historia del mutualismo (Las mutuales y el Estado). Centro de Investigaciones de la Economía Social. Found im Internet: Mutualismo Principios del mutualismo in Version HTM.

AISAM/AMICE: Mutual Insurance Companies The regulatory, financial and fiscal arrangements, 2007.

Battaller Grau, Juan (dir) : El redimensionamiento de las mutualidades de previsión social como instrumento complementario del sistema de seguridad social, Ministerio de Trabajo y Asuntos Sociales, Madrid 2008.

Calle Maria, Dolores de la: Mutualidades Laborales en el régimen de Franco. IX. Congreso de la Asociación Española de Historia Económica 2008.

Fundación MAPFRE (ed.): The Spanish insurance market in 2017, Madrid 2018.

ICMIF (ed.): Facts and figures – Mutual and cooperative insurance in Europe, AMICE aisbl & ICMIF, Vol 2 2018.

Godoy, Milton: Mutualismo y educación: Las escuelas nocturnas de artesanos, 1860-1880. Centro de Investigación y Difusión Poblacional de Achupallas. Viña del Mar, Chile 2000.

Kaufmannn, Otto / Hennion, Silvie (eds.): Steuerung der betrieblichen Altersvorsorge in Europa, Heidelberg-Berlin 2011.

Ma de la, Pedro / Torre, San Cristóbal: El mutualismo de previsión social, CIRIEC-España, revista de economía pública, social y cooperativa, Valencia 2003.

Nugent, Ricardo: La seguridad social y sus fuentes. In: Instituciones de derecho del trabajo y de la seguridad social. Universidad Nacional Autónoma de México 1997.

Reinhard, Hans-Joachim (ed.): Demographischer Wandel und Alterssicherung. Rentenpolitik in neun europäischen Ländern und den USA im Vergleich, Baden-Baden 2001.

Sanchez, Maria Tereza: El mutualismo de previsión social en España CIRIEC-España, revista de economía pública, social y cooperativa Univeristy of Granada 2007.

Mutual Insurance and Co-operative Kyosai in Japan

Futoshi Okada, Miho Onzo, Akira Kurimoto

Introduction

The Japanese insurance system was launched in the late 19th century modelling after European and North American examples. *Tokyo Marine Insurance Company* was established in 1879 while *Meiji Life Insurance* was set up in 1881. The Insurance Business Act was created to supervise insurance businesses in 1900. In 1902, *Dai-ichi Life Insurance* was founded as the first mutual company. These insurance companies have evolved to huge enterprises during the 20th century and created the world's second largest insurance market after the one in the United States.

The modern co-operatives were set up under the Industrial Co-operatives Act in 1900. The German Co-operative Act served as an example. They were allowed to conduct multiple businesses of supply, marketing, credit and production (later replaced by service) but they were not allowed to take part in insurance business. They requested to obtain the license for insurance business. Dr. *Toyohiko Kagawa* argued that co-operatives should be allowed to launch insurance business but the project of co-operatives in Japan was in vain due to the strong opposition from existing insurance companies. So they set up Kyoei Fire Insurance Company in 1942 aiming at disseminating insurance in the rural area, which was converted to a mutual company in 1946. After WWII, co-operatives decided to start Kyosai (mutual aid) business for their members. During 1947-1950 Kyosai was incorporated as one of the businesses in the separate co-operative laws for agriculture, fisheries, consumer and SMEs.

The Insurance Business Act allowed only stock companies and mutual companies as legitimate corporate forms. It was amended to the current format in 1995 and further revised in 2005 when Kyosai-like entities without legal recognition were banned. The Insurance Act was enacted in 2008 separating provisions from the Commercial Code and targeting both insurance companies and Kyosai co-operatives.

Since 2000, the insurance sector has faced growing impacts of globalization and demographic shift. Kyoei Fire & Marine Insurance Company was reconverted to a stock company in 2003 as a subsidiary of *Zenkyoren* (National Mutual Insurance Federation of Agricultural Co-ops). Based on the revised Insurance Business Act, Dai-ichi Life was converted to a stock company in 2010. Some mutual companies conducted mergers and acquisitions (M&As) to tap the growth opportunities in other countries but such a move has often been criticized as a deviation from the underlying idea of mutuality.

Today, *Zenkyoren* has grown to the largest co-op in the World Co-operative Monitor (Report 2015), while *Zenrosai* (National Federation of Workers and Consumers Insurance Co-ops), *Kenmin Kyosai* (FJCC: Federation of Japanese Consumer Co-ops), and *CO-OP Kyosai* (JCIF: Japan CO-OP Insurance Consumer Co-op Federation) are also major consumer co-operative insurance federations (ranked at 100th, 107th and 287th). Mutual companies are also ranked high (Nippon Life 7th, Meiji Yasuda Life 13th, Sumitomo Life 20th, Fukoku Life 91^{st,} Asahi Life 126th), but there is very little connection with Kyosai. Their trade associations (LIAJ: Life Insurance Association of Japan and GIAJ: General Insurance Association of Japan) and the American Chamber of Commerce in Japan (ACCJ) often requested the government to offer Kyosai the same competitive conditions regarding regulation and taxation, while the Japan Co-operative Insurance Association (JCIA) argues Kyosai has comparable regulations as insurance companies through the amended legislation and administrative guidelines but should be regulated separately due to historical and institutional reasons. Therefore, the question is whether mutual insurance and co-operative Kyosai are to converge or diverge in Japan.

This paper starts with the description of the origin and evolution of mutual insurance and co-operative Kyosai. The institutional and organizational aspects of mutual companies and Kyosai are explained and a comparison follows. In particular, issues pertaining to the governance, CSR and response to natural disasters are to be analyzed. Then the insurance industry's response to the globalization and demographic shift is described. Finally, the question of conversion or diversion of mutual companies and Kyosai co-operatives is discussed.

1. Origin and evolution of mutual insurance companies

1.1 Mutual organizations before the Insurance Business Act of 1900

A mutual company is an organizational form of insurance business permitted by the Insurance Business Act (IBA). Before the IBA was enacted in 1900, *Kyosai 500 Members*, established in 1880, was well known as the first mutual aid company. Five hundred upper-class people contributed to it for a common financial purpose. It adopted a kind of assessment insurance system under which the surviving members must make a fixed equal contribution, regardless of age, to the next death benefit each time a member died. Its uniqueness was found in an application of *Mujin-Ko*, a mutual-help financial system, which took root in all the farming communities in Japan over a period of time.[1]

A number of small-sized associations followed the Kyosai 500 Members, applying a similar system. But they had troubles with their members and shortly disappeared because their business was not based upon expected mortality rates. Indeed, the failure of the insurance-like business had harmful effects for the emerging industry and caused social problems. However, some of them played a role in providing mutual help for the middle and lower classes. In 1894, Kyosai 500 Members was dissolved and *Kyosai Life* was established as a modern mutual aid company, although it was reorganized into a stock company in 1900.[2]

1.2 Dai-ichi Life as the first mutual life company

Dai-ichi Life was established as the first mutual life insurance company under the IBA in 1902.[3] The founder, *Tsuneta Yano*, advocated the creation of a mutual company in the early 1890s, because he believed it was superior to a stock company as far as life insurance business was concerned. He took up a post of general manager at Kyosai Life in 1894. One year later, he worked at the Gotha Life Insurance[4] in Germany, known as the most advanced mutual company, to study the operation of

1 *Mujin-Ko* or *Tanomoshi-Ko* was a kind of rotating savings and credit association. *Dekle, R.* and *K. Hamada* (2000).

2 *Kyosai Life* was closer to a mutual company than a stock company, because it primarily sold participating insurance and returned more earnings to policyholders.

3 In the general insurance sector, *Toa Fire* was established in 1909 as the first mutual company but dissolved in 1915.

4 The German name was Lebensversicherungsbank für Deutschland zu Gotha.

an actual mutual company. After returning from Germany, he left Kyosai Life and contributed to draft the IBA. Due to his work the articles of a mutual company could be finished. He was appointed as the first director of the insurance regulatory authority in 1900.

1.3 Growth of mutual companies

Chiyoda Life started as the second mutual company in 1904. Following the American style, it was more oriented toward expanded market share. These two mutual companies grew rapidly and ranked in the top five life insurers in the early 1920s. While the number of mutual companies was far smaller than that of stock companies, as Figure 1 shows, they gained over 25 percent of market share since the mid-1930s.[5]

With regard to the popularization of life insurance, insurance companies mainly targeted the upper and middle classes in urban areas or large landowners in rural areas. Some of them sold industrial life insurance for factory workers but did not gain success. In 1916, the Postal Life Insurance was established by the Ministry of Communications and operated the government-managed insurance business for the lower class as a kind of social policy. Co-operative insurance for the socially vulnerable people was not allowed under the IBA.

The rapid growth of Dai-ichi Life and Chiyoda Life was attributable to their strategy of higher premiums and larger dividends, which resulted in the reduction of burden on policyholders.[6] Stock companies followed them and sold participating or dividend-paying insurance.[7] They were called mixed companies with characteristics of both stock company and mutual company. A major part of the business was endowment insurance with dividend (rebate) since the early 1910s, because Japanese households wished to buy saving-type products. Life insurance companies, mutual or stock, returned more of earnings to policyholders for survival.[8] Consequently, mutual companies were

---

5 It is based on premiums received for ordinary life insurance.

6 This is an annually cumulative dividend system. The amount of an annual dividend is easily calculated by multiplying the sum of paid premiums by the dividend rate. Annual dividend is increasing every year. When the dividend rate is five percent, for example, the total sum of dividend in 20 years will be the same as premium which means net premium will be zero. The dividend will be paid in cash after the following year. This system gives policyholders an incentive to keep their contracts going for a long time but damages fairness among policyholders.

7 Nippon Life and Meiji Life as the major stock insurance companies adopted a system of lower dividends for lower premiums to compete with Dai-ichi Life and Chiyoda Life.

8 Especially the stock company Daido Life reduced dividends for share and increased dividends for policyholders than major stock companies.

few in number but established a great presence in the life insurance market.[9]

Figure 1: The number of insurance companies from 1881-2016

* Small Amount and Short Term Insurance Providers and Postal Life Insurance before privatization are excluded.

Source: LIAJ, Historical Transition of Membership Life Insurance Companies of LIAJ in Japan (Japanese).

1.4 Rebirth as mutual companies after World War II

Life insurance companies ran into insolvency on a large scale due to the devastating loss of life during World War II. Most of the stock companies established new mutual companies to recover from fateful crisis and continue business while they were dissolved after transferring new contracts to newly formed companies, as Figure 1 shows. Existing mutual companies, however, continued business as before by increasing the foundation fund. As a result, mutual companies took up 80 % of all the life insurance companies. They had a high market share, which was extremely unusual in the world.

9 Particularly, Fukoku Conscription, the predecessor of Fukoku Life, grew up to take nearly 50 % of the market in terms of premium income. Conscription insurance is a kind of endowment insurance; the insurance proceeds are paid when an insured passes an examination for conscription. A half of them is paid or premium paid is returned when he fails it or dies before it.

The mutualization of insurance companies was regarded as part of the economic democratization promoted by the General Headquarters of the Allied Forces (GHQ). Particularly, it required the zaibatsu-related companies to eliminate the shareholders' control in relation to the dissolution of zaibatsu.

1.5 The modernization of Mutual Insurance Companies

The Japanese life insurance market recovered to its prewar level in the mid-1950s and it grew dramatically to become the world's leading market. This happened in tandem with Japan's rapid economic expansion, as Figure 2 shows, although it is said that policyholders' participation in the governance of mutual companies has largely lost its substance. The Insurance Council, an advisory organization to the Finance Minister, often discussed issues of mutual companies including problems pertaining to corporate governance. In response to discussions, mutual companies introduced a set of improvements in the governance system.

Figure 2: The growth of life insurance business and shares of mutual and stock companies based on premium income

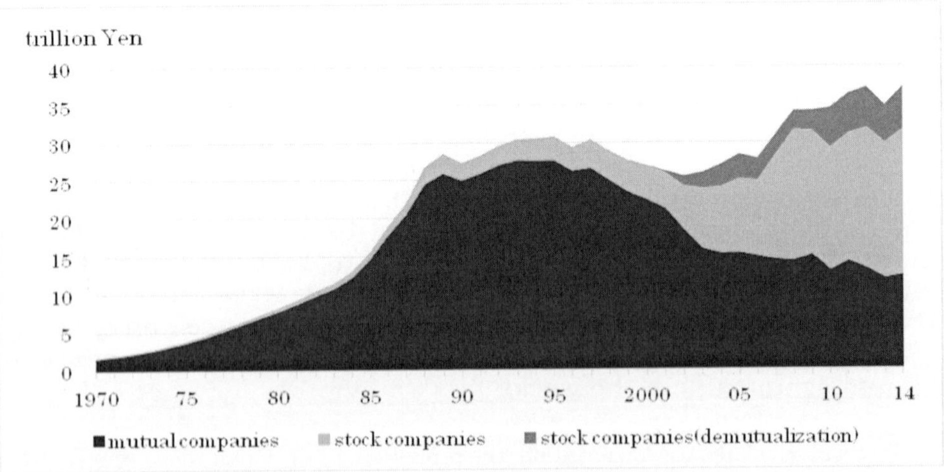

Source: LIAJ, The Summary of Life Insurance Business.

In 1995, the IBA was amended and the provisions for mutual companies were significantly changed toward modernization. Major revisions include (1) strengthening of retained earnings by lowering returns to policyholders, (2) improved governance, and (3) identifying the contractual status of policyholders in mutual or stock companies. Today it seems that little difference between mutual and stock companies in term of the regulation exists. Consequently, the significant question was raised; why mutual companies remained in existence in modern days. Actually, no new mutual companies have been established since 1961.

1.6 Demutualization following failure of mutual companies

Some insurance companies were financially distressed due to the asset deflation after the burst of bubble economy in the early 1990s. Nissan Life went bankrupt in 1997 being the first insolvent life insurance company since the end of World War II. Subsequently, six life insurance companies including Chiyoda Life with nearly a century of history went bankrupt by the end of March 2001.[10] All failed life insurers were medium-sized firms, and many of them sold saving-type products which should yield high-returns, but which actually increased financial burdens. As for some of them, a small group of people managed the companies in an autocratic style while the institutions of corporate governance and internal control did not work properly.

When the IBA introduced the provision to facilitate the transformation from mutual companies to stock companies in 1995, a wave of demutualizations broke loose, mainly for survival. This process took place since the beginning of the 2000s, as Figure 2 shows. Nine mutual companies including three failed companies and two fire insurance companies have been reorganized into stock companies until now. Dai-ichi Life, established as the first mutual life insurance company in 1902, was converted to a stock company in 2010, putting an end to over 100-years history of mutual company. Meiji Life, the first life insurance company, merged with Yasuda Life, the former Kyosai Life, in 2004. This was the first case of a merger between mutual companies. After all, the number of mutual companies decreased significantly to only five companies, accounting for 12.2 % of all the life insurance companies. In

[10] Only two mutual insurance companies existed in general insurance market. Dai-ichi Fire & Marine established in 1949 mainly sold saving-type products for 5-10 years but ran into insolvency in 2000 due to the same reason as failed life insurance companies.

2014, the market share held by mutual companies, based on premium income (37.2 trillion Yen), was 33.2 percent.

As a part of privatization scheme of state-run post-related businesses, Postal Life Insurance (Kanpo) was converted into a stock company in 2006 and Japan Post Insurance started business in the following year. Its presence in the life insurance market is so strong that the question of similar competitive conditions with private life insurers is often raised in Japan and the USA.

1.7 Non-payment scandals by insurance companies

In 2005, Meiji Yasuda Life failed to pay death benefits, while Fuji Fire & Marine did not pay for car insurance correctly. Then, non-payment scandals were found to involve most of the insurance companies, widely criticized by the media and discussed in the Diet. This phenomenon became a social problem and largely damaged the reputation of the industry. The insurance companies were ordered to make investigations and report the results to the Financial Services Agency (FSA). At the end of 2007, the final results revealed that 38 life insurance companies failed to pay 96.4 billion yen for 1.31 million policies during 2001-2006. In 2008, the FSA published business improvement orders for ten life insurance companies including all mutual companies. The insurance companies made substantial efforts to regain consumer confidence by restructuring internal process/policies and making regular contacts with policyholders. Non-payment was also found in Kyosai but on a much smaller scale.

1.8 What modern mutual companies mean?

What is mutuality or mutualism in life insurance? It has been considered that an insurance company provides coverage with low cost and good quality as much as possible. The goal of business is to maximize profits and return them to policyholders as dividends. Recently, mutual companies have accumulated much more retained earnings than the necessary amount for continuing business. The mutuality indeed means customer creed in mutual business, but members of mutual companies seek their own interests rather than common interests, because they consist of many and unspecified customers and do not have a common bond with each other. Therefore, modern-day mutual companies come closer to stock companies. In addition, mutual companies still face a multitude of challenges in ensuring member participation or involvement in the governance.

2. Origin and evolution of Kyosai co-operatives

2.1 Industrial co-operatives longing for insurance business before WWII

Modern co-operation started after the Meiji Restoration in 1868. A number of agricultural and credit co-ops were set up to meet farmers' needs for the joint marketing of products (tea, silk etc.) and finance. The Industrial Co-operatives Act was enacted in 1900 modeled after the German Co-operative Act. The multi-purpose co-operatives were allowed to conduct multiple businesses of supply, marketing, credit and production (later replaced by service), but they were not allowed to undertake insurance business, which was confined to stock or mutual companies under the Insurance Business Act. The Congresses of the Central Union of Industrial Co-operatives resolved to launch life insurance business in 1924, but could not break the strong resistances from the insurance industry while Dr. *Toyohiko Kagawa*, a renowned Christian reformer, insisted on the necessity of co-operative insurance in 1936. When three ailing insurance companies were offered for sale in 1939, the Central Union expressed its intention to buy them. However, these efforts were not successful due to the opposition from the government and existing insurance companies.

However, the insurance industry was obliged to merge into larger companies as part of the war regime in the 1940s and a number of companies were reduced from 40+ to 15 during 1941-1943. The Central Union asked the Tokyo Marine Insurance Company for co-operation in acquiring insurance companies and bought Daihuku Marine and Daito Marine as subsidiary companies of Tokyo Marine. Then *Kyoei Fire Insurance Company* was set up by merging these companies in 1942 aiming at disseminating insurance in the rural area. It was converted to a mutual company in 1946 while other life insurance companies were also mutualized during 1947-1949.

There was an opportunity to include the co-operative insurance as a legitimate form of insurance business in the Insurance Business Act after WWII. Dr. *Kagawa* and Mr. *Tokugawa* (President of Kyoei Fire) advocated for co-operative insurances in the Financial Institutions Council under the Ministry of Finance (MOF) in 1945. Accordingly, the bill for amending the Insurance Business Act was drafted but its contents were diminished under the unstable government and strong resistance of the insurance industry. Finally, it was not submitted to the Diet facing strong opposition by co-operatives since it contained provisions that would restrain co-operative insurances (e.g. prohibition of life insurance). Thereafter, co-operatives abandoned to pursue co-operative insurance under the Insurance Business Act and turned to create co-operative Kyosai under the separate co-operative laws.

2.2 Agricultural and fishery co-operative Kyosai

In the period between the Japanese surrender in 1945 and restored independence in 1952, the US military administration ruled the country. Japan was to be demilitarized and transformed into a democratic state in accordance with the Potsdam Declaration of 1945. In the economic arena, the GHQ introduced the key democratizing measures: legitimating the trade unions by the Trade Union Act of 1945, introducing the agrarian reform to break up landlordism by the Land Reform Act of 1946, and dismantling plutocratic Zaibatsu by the Anti-Monopoly Act of 1947.

The separate co-operative legislation was introduced in line with the industrial policies. The Agricultural Co-operative Act was enacted in 1947 to reinforce the effects of agrarian reform by protecting newly established owner farmers. It was followed by the Consumer Co-operative Act and the Fishery Co-operative Act in 1948 and the Small & Medium Enterprises (SME) Co-operative Act in 1949 to serve the specific needs of co-operatives in each area. Agricultural and fishery co-operatives are regulated by the Ministry of Agriculture, Forestry and Fisheries (MAFF), while consumer co-operatives are regulated by the Ministry of Health, Labor and Welfare (MHLW). The SME co-operatives are subject to the supervision of the Ministry of Economy, Trade and Industry (METI). The separate legislation and different regulating authorities resulted in the different trajectories of co-operatives and diversified co-operative insurance businesses.

Article 10, Section 1 of the Agricultural Co-operative Act originally allowed co-operatives to “make available those facilities relating to mutual relief (Kyosai) of its members against agricultural damage or other disasters”. This clause caused conflicts with the public insurances for damages to crops and livestock which had been launched in 1943.[11] Hokkaido Mutual Insurance Federation of Agricultural Co-ops was set up in 1948 to provide insurances for farmhouse endowment and life, despite the pressure from MOF and insurance companies. In this process, the tying up with Nippon Life to disseminate insurance in rural areas was sought in view of creating co-operative insurance business

11 In 1951, the MAFF’s guidance note indicated that the agricultural disaster indemnity associations (*Nosai*) based on the Agricultural Disaster Indemnity Act of 1947 would deal with compulsory insurance for agricultural products while agricultural co-ops would conduct voluntary insurance for other areas.

but soon abandoned. Zenkyoren was founded by national federations of agricultural co-ops and Hokkaido federation in 1951. It launched the building endowment insurance (Tateko) in 1951 and life insurance in 1952 while setting up prefectural offices to promote Kyosai business among agricultural co-ops. In 1954, the Agricultural Co-operative Act was amended to clarify Kyosai business, for which detailed rules and administrative guidance notes were published. In 1958, federations of agricultural Kyosai were established in all prefectures except for Okinawa. Zenkyoren absorbed all prefectural unions in 2000 to consolidate its financial strength and to offer better services to members. It had 58 million policies for life, Tateko, automobile and others in 2014.

In the fishery co-operative sector, Kyosai business was included in the Fishery Co-operative Act in 1950 and the Zensuikyo (National Association of Fishery Co-ops Kyosai) was set up in 1951 to insure fishermen and processing plant workers. It also made campaigns to establish schemes for the compensation for damages to vessels and the fisheries disaster indemnity (Gyosai) to insure against risks specific to this industry. The special acts were enacted in 1952 and 1964 respectively. In 1983, the amended Fishery Co-operative Act allowed fishery co-ops to undertake Kyosai business and form the national federation. Accordingly, Zensuikyo was reorganized as *Kyosuiren* (National Mutual Insurance Federation of Fishery Co-ops). It comprised 650,000 policies for life, fire and pension in 2014.

2.3 Consumer co-operative Kyosai

The Consumer Co-operative Act has contained several restrictions since its inception; co-operatives have not been allowed to sell to non-members, trade in other prefectures or conduct credit business. Under such institutional constraints, a variety of Kyosai has been founded for communities or workplaces. The former includes FJCC, JCIF, JAFMAC (Japan Federation of Mutual Aid Co-ops) and Kanagawa Kenmin Co-op. The latter is divided into workplace co-ops and industrial union based co-ops (Tansan Kyosai).[12] There are Kyosai co-operatives based on both communities and workplaces (Zenrosai). Herewith the cases of three major consumer co-ops are described to illustrate different origins and evolution processes.

Aiming at creating facilities to protect workers against risks (old age, poverty, diseases, disability, death, accidents etc.), trade unions started to organize Rosai (workers' insurance co-ops) based on the spirit of

---

[12] They include Transport Workers Co-op, JP Group Workers Co-op, Telecommunication Workers Co-op, Forest Workers Co-op, Tabaco Workers Co-op, Water Workers Co-op, Municipal Workers Co-op, Teachers Co-op.

mutual help in the 1950s. The predecessor of the Central Council for Worker's Welfare (Rofukukyo)[13] resolved to establish Rosai in 1951 while the Japanese Consumer Co-operative Union (JCCU) proposed the guidelines of co-operative insurance business in 1952. The first Rosai for fire insurance was founded in Osaka Prefecture in 1954, but it took four years to obtain the approval from the Ministry due to its stringent criteria. In the formative period, Rosai had to overcome difficulties caused by big fires. When Niigata City was hit by a big fire that destroyed nearly 1,000 houses in 1955, Niigata Rosai had not yet accumulated the necessary funds to make payments to the victims since it was founded just five months before. It needed to pay 12.7 million JPY while its assets were approximately 6 million JPY. Facing such a crisis, Niigata Rohukukyo resolved to back up newly established Rosai by an urgent loan from Rokin (Labor Bank) under the guarantee of major trade unions. Although Rosai had a deficit of 3.8 million JPY at the end of fiscal year, such action of solidarity had contributed to enhance its reputation among workers and led to the rapid expansion of insurance business. However, when a big fire hit Uozu in Toyama Prefecture in the next year, the payments only covered the half of the claims. Such events made it apparent that a larger pool of resources against risks was needed which led to the creation of the National Federation of Rosai (Rosairen) as a reinsurance agent in 1957. Rosairen accelerated the formation of Rosai in each prefecture and spread them throughout the country in 1964, except for Okinawa under the US rule.[14] It integrated 40 prefectural Rosai and renamed to Zenrosai in 1976. Zenrosai launched Kokumin Kyosai with the clear intention to compete with rapidly growing Kenmin Kyosai in 1983.[15] It meant that Zenrosai extended its customer groups from trade union workers to involve general households in communities. Around the same time, Zenrosai was joined by industrial trade union based on Tansan Kyosai. It had 30 million policies for life, accidents, fire, automobile, pension etc. in 2014.

The metal workers' union in Saitama Prefecture launched group life insurances for its members and then opened it to all consumers by setting up Saitama Kenmin Kyosai Co-op in 1973. It offered a fixed premium (2,000 JPY per month) to insure persons aged 15-59 for the benefits ranging 4 to 10 million JPY and introduced a simple way of enrolment and premium payment through customer's bank account at the Saitama Bank. Such a business model named Kenmin Kyosai

13 Rofukukyo was set up by trade union centrals and the JCCU to promote labor-oriented co-ops such as *Rosai* and *Rokin*.

14 Okinawa *Rosai* was set up in 1971 to complete the nationwide deployment.

15 *Kokumin* means "nation" while *Kenmin* means "residents in prefectures". There is no difference between these notions that can be equivalent to citizens.

gained quick success and rapidly disseminated among consumers thanks to low premium and simple procedure.[16] The Metropolitan Area Consumer Co-op Federation was set up in 1971 (renamed to FJCC in 1981) and spread this model throughout the country. The FJCC diversified a range of products covering both life and fire insurances, children and elderly. The group had about 38 million policies in 39 prefectures in 2014.

The third stream CO-OP Kyosai was set up by consumer co-ops affiliated with the JCCU. While the JCCU had assisted to establish Rosai since the 1950s and collaborated with Zenrosai as its affiliated member, it felt that the consumer co-op members' needs could not be fully satisfied by the existing products of Rosai. So it decided to launch CO-OP Kyosai for life and fire insurance in collaboration with Zenrosai in 1979 and developed its own comprehensive Kyosai named Tasukeai (mutual help) in 1984. It sought to enroll housewives that had not necessarily been targeted by insurance industry since they constituted a bulk of co-op membership. Then it developed insurance products to cover children's diseases and accidents. Such a strategy proved to be successful as demonstrated by the rapid growth of policyholders. The JCIF had 7.8 million policies for life and fire in 2014.

2.4 SME co-operative Kyosai

The small and medium-sized enterprise co-operatives also had a thorny way in launching Kyosai business. Hokkaido SME Kyosai Co-op (*Hokkyosai*) was set up by SME leaders with a support of the Governor in 1952, but soon faced inquiries of the MOF under the pressure of non-life insurance companies. Aichi Kyosai Co-op was established around the same time. These co-ops founded SME Kyosai Co-op Federation (*Zensairen*) in 1955. MOF drafted a bill to control co-operative Kyosai in the framework of the Insurance Business Act but faced strong resistance from co-operatives. Finally, the SME Co-op Act was amended to include fire Kyosai as one of the businesses that was to be regulated by both METI and MOF in 1957. Accordingly, the existing Kyosai co-ops were reorganized as SME fire Kyosai co-ops and founded the Federation of Fire Kyosai Co-ops (*Nikkaren*) in 1960. Nikkaren took over Zensairen in 2014 and offers now a wide range of Kyosai products through SME co-operatives and trade associations acting as agents.

Rapid motorization is accompanied with a sharp increase of car accidents, while non-life insurance companies raised premiums to

[16] Its policy conditions were approved by the Ministry of Health, Labor and Welfare in 1987. Its impact was so great that Zenrosai started similar products named *Kokumin Kyosai* in 1983 to expand to local communities.

the extent prohibiting drivers from renewing contracts. To meet with their needs, the truck transport Kyosai co-ops were set up in 1971 and formed their federation (*Kokyoren*) in 1972. They tried to reduce traffic accidents in collaboration with transport administration. Likewise, SMEs set up automobile insurance co-ops in 1955 and formed their reinsurance federation (*Zenjikyo*) in 1975. The former public interest corporations conducting Kyosai business for SME set up Kyosai and federated in the SME Welfare Kyosai Co-op Federation (*Chusairen*) in 2012.

3. Institutional and organizational aspects of mutual companies and Kyosai

The Insurance Business Act is a basic legislation for the insurance business, aiming "protect policyholders by ensuring the sound and appropriate business operation of persons conducting insurance business and by ensuring fairness in insurance solicitation, in view of the public nature of this kind of business" (Article 1). Article 2 defines the term "Insurance Business" as the business of underwriting the risks with insurance and exempts some enlisted businesses (those provided in other Acts, those undertaken by local governments or trade unions etc.). Therefore, co-operative Kyosai is exempted from the IBA as it is regulated by co-operative laws. Originally, "many and unspecified" persons were included as a condition of insured, but this part was removed when the Act was amended in 2005. Article 3 provides that (a) no person may conduct insurance business without having first obtained a license from the Prime Minister, (b) the license consists of two types: a life insurance business license and a non-life insurance business license, and (c) the same person may not obtain both a life insurance business license and a non-life insurance business license. Article 5-2 stipulates that Insurance Companies shall either be a stock company or a mutual company. As such, the Insurance Business Act only allows stock companies and mutual companies to conduct insurance business, under the jurisdiction of the Financial Services Agency (FSA). They have no limitation in the operating area while they cannot conduct businesses other than insurance. Shareholders of stock companies have no dividend limit, while policyholders of mutual companies have no share capital and no dividend on shares. The latter pays patronage refund which is similar to co-operatives. Although life and non-life insurance cannot be undertaken by a single company, most of the companies conduct both kinds of businesses through subsidiary companies since 1995. Section 2, Chapter 2 of the Act is dedicated to mutual companies and deals with the act of incorporation, member's rights, governance, accounting, bylaws, and transfer of business regarding incorporations. Section 4, Chapter 10 offers financial assistance provided by Policyholders Protection Corporations, which all licensed insurance companies are obliged to join as a safety net against companies' insolvency. The Insurance Business Act superseded the Act on the Control of Insurance Solicitation (1948) in 1995.

On the other hand, co-operative Kyosai are regulated under separate co-operative laws or special indemnity laws (Table 1). They are allowed to carry out Kyosai business but regulations on it differ from one sector to another. Agricultural Co-operative Act allows co-operatives to conduct multiple businesses including both economic and financial (banking and insurance) but confines operational area within the prefecture. It allows non-members to use Kyosai to the extent of 20% of all contracts. It places a dividend limit to 8% of share capital but allows to pay patronage refund. It allows both life and non-life insurance business. The Consumer Co-operative Act originally allowed co-operatives to conduct multiple businesses including insurance, but prohibited it by the amendment in 2007. Therefore, JCIF was founded separating Kyosai business from the JCCU and its primaries in 2009. The Act also confines operational business to the prefecture and totally prohibits non-members trade. It places a dividend limit to 10% of share capital but allows paying patronage refund. It also allows both life and non-life insurance business. Both of these laws include a wide range of provisions on the Kyosai business (contracts, rules, minimum capital and solvency, transfer of engagements, subsidiaries, accounting, external audit, actuaries, etc.) and extensively apply mutatis mutandis the provisions of the Insurance Business Act or provide for similar regulations in line with the latter. Co-operatives are taxed at the reduced rate of Corporation Income Tax (19%) in comparison with insurance companies (23.4%), while such gap of rates has been reduced from 12% to 4.4% over three decades. They are exempted from application provided by the Anti-Monopoly Act (AMA), provided they abide the Co-operative Principles (to provide mutual support to small-scale enterprises or consumers, voluntarily formed, equal voting rights, limited distribution of profits) and have been formed pursuant to the provisions of the co-operative laws. They are also exempted from the policyholder's protection scheme under the IBA and the government's reinsurance scheme for earthquake insurance.

As mentioned above, the Insurance Business Act is business law that deals with issues pertaining to business practices in relation to the public, other companies and the government. At the same time, it

Table 1: List of Co-operative Insurers According to Applicable Laws

	Applicable Laws	Regu-lators	Major Organizations	
Co-operative Law	Agricultural Co-op Act	MAFF	Zenkyoren (Agricultural co-ops) (*1)	
	Fishery Co-op Act		Kyosuiren (Fisheries co-ops) (*2)	
	Consumer Co-op Act	MHLW	Community	JCIF, FJCC, JAFMAC, Kanagawa Kenmin Co-op (*3)
			Workplace	University Co-op Insurance Fed., Defense Ministry Co-op, Electric Power Workers Co-op, Transport Workers Co-op*, JP Group Workers Co-op*, Telecommunication Workers Co-op*, Forest Workers Co-op*, Tabaco Workers Co-op*, Water Workers Co-op*, Municipal Workers Co-op*, Teachers Co-op*, Postmasters Co-op, Liquor Shops Co-op, Tobacco Sellers Co-op, Salt Workers Co-op, Municipal Employees Co-op, City Workers Co-op, Police officers Co-op, Firefighters Co-op
			Both	Zenrosai, Reinsurance Co-op Fed.
	SME Co-op Act	METI	Fire Kyosai Co-ops, Truck Transport Kyosai Co-ops (*5), Automobile Kyosai Co-ops, Welfare Kyosai Co-ops, Rice Sellers Co-op (*6), Food Business Employees Co-op (*6)	
Special Indemnity Law	Agricultural Disaster Indemnity Act	MAFF	Agricultural Disaster Indemnity Associations (Nosai) (*7)	
	Fisheries Disaster Indemnity Act		Fisheries Disaster Indemnity Associations (Gyosai) (*8)	
	Compensation Act for Damages to Vessels		Hull Damage Indemnity Associations (*9)	

*1, 2, 3, 5, 7, 8, 9: Regulated by Prefectural Levels. *4: Regulated by the Ministry of Land, Infrastructure, Transport and Tourism. *6: Regulated by MAFF.

includes elements of organizational law that deals with the formation and operations of mutual companies while it provides special treatments in applying the Companies Act to stock insurance companies. On the other hand, co-operative laws are basically organizational laws which deal with the issues of incorporation, governance, accounting and administrative supervision but largely involves elements of insurance business law. The contracts of both insurance companies and Kyosai co-operatives are under the jurisdiction of the Insurance Act enacted in 2008 separating it from the Commercial Code.

Table 2: Institutional aspects of mutual companies and Kyosai

	Agricultural co-op	Consumer Co-op	Mutual company	Stock company
Legislation	Agri. Co-op Act	Cons. Co-op Act	Insurance Business Act Companies Act	
Regulator	Min. of Agriculture, Forestry & Fisheries	Min. of Health, Labor & Welfare	Financial Services Agency	
Operational area	Within prefecture	Within prefecture	No limitation	
Non-member trade	Allowed to 20%	Not allowed	Not applicable	
By-business	Allowed	Not allowed	Not allowed	
Dividend cap	8%	10%	Not applicable	No limitation
Patronage refund	Allowed	Allowed	Allowed	Depend on policy
Life + general	Allowed		Not allowed	
Corp. income tax	Reduced rate		Conventional rate	
Competition law	Exempted		Applied	
Policyholders protection scheme	Exempted		Applied	
Govt. reinsurance for earthquake	Not applicable		Applied	
Safety net system	Not applicable		Compulsory	

As a result of the amended co-operative legislations and administrative guidelines published by the appropriate ministries, Kyosai co-operatives have been placed in the regulations comparable with those for insurance companies in the fields of solvency margins, establishment of reserves, assignment of actuaries, accounting standards, solicitation and cooling off. The major differences remain in the regulatory bodies, safety net and taxation.

There exist some noticeable differences in the organizational aspects of mutual companies and co-operative Kyosai. The insurance companies are corporate bodies where hierarchy dominates, while most of Kyosai are characterized by a federative structure where network matters. Under the Agricultural Co-operative Act, both Zenkyoren and primary co-ops are underwriters[17], while the former wholesales Kyosai products to the latter. Zenkyoren has a dual system of supervisory board and management board. On the other hand, only federations are underwriters under the Consumer Co-operative Act. FJCC is a federation of 39 prefectural co-ops, while JCIF is a federation of 151 primary co-ops and five national co-op insurance federations affiliated with the JCCU. Zenrosai has a more complicated structure of a federation, i.e. 47 prefectural co-ops and eight Tansan Kyosai. It is also a corporate body that

[17] Zenkyoren bears 100% of risk, while primary co-ops bear 0%.

operates insurance business on behalf of 47 prefectural co-ops and four Tansan Kyosai. In most of Kyosai co-operatives, qualified field staff acts as sales agents while insurance companies employ qualified salespersons for life insurance, or contract with car dealers/repairers for car insurance or realtors for fire insurance as sales agents. In insurance companies, retail operations are often outsourced to banks or general insurance agents. As far as policyholders are concerned, Kyosai co-operatives in principle solicit membership from a group of people with common bonds in communities, workplaces, occupation or associations (trade unions etc.), while insurance companies sell insurance products to the general public. But this distinction became blurred when we saw Kenmin Kyosai or Kokumin Kyosai soliciting the general public who can easily join and pay premiums through banks, while insurance companies have an increasing number of group contracts which enable employers to provide their employees with insurance coverage at reduced premium. Therefore, the term "many and unspecified" persons was removed from the Insurance Business Act in 2005, as mentioned earlier.

Table 3. Organizational aspects of mutual companies and Kyosai co-operatives

	Agri. co-op	Cons. Co-op	Mutual company	Stock company
Structure	Primary co-ops + federation		Corporate body	
Underwriter	Federation (+primaries)		Company	
Board	Dual board	Unitary board	Unitary board	
Sales agent	Qualified co-op employee		Qualified field staff, car dealer etc.	
Policyholders	Specified		Many and unspecified	

4. Comparison of mutual companies and Kyosai co-operatives

4.1 The Japanese insurance market

Players in the Japanese insurance market mainly consist of insurance companies and Kyosai co-operatives.[18] Insurance companies com-

[18] We do not include specified insurance providers authorized by administrative agencies under the IBA of 2005.

prise 41 life insurance companies (including three foreign insurers), 51 general insurance companies (including 21 foreign insurers), and 84 Small Amount and Short Term Insurance Providers (SASTIP) as of April 2016. Kyosai co-operatives include 13 federations and 21 primary co-operatives[19], according to JCIA.[20] It is difficult, however, for us to know the exact numbers of co-operative Kyosai. Actually, many SME co-operative and consumer co-operative insurers or providers are not included in Kyosai, which the JCIA counts up. Kyosai seems to exceed 200 co-operatives, as Figure 3 shows, although most of them are engaged in small mutual aid business among members.

Figure 3: Market share by number of insurers and premium income in 2014

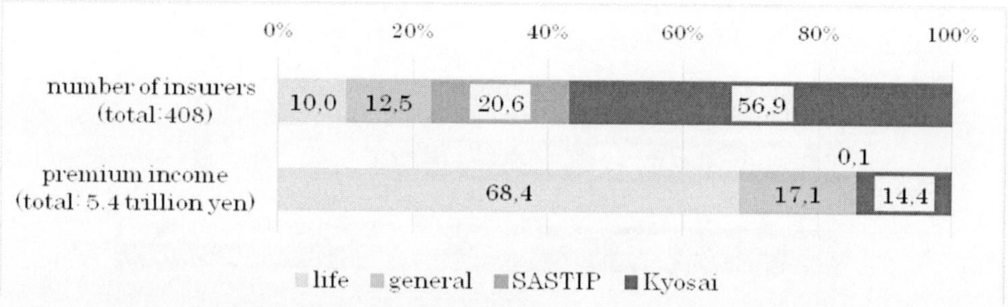

Some non-co-operative Kyosai are included in Kyosai.
Source: LIAJ, GIAJ, FNLIA, SSIAJ, JCIA, MHLW.

Up to date, mutual companies exist only in the life insurance sector. They account for 22.7% of total premium income and if Kyosai co-operatives are included, their market share reaches 37.1%.[21]

Kyosai co-operatives account for 13.1% in the life insurance market and cover 6.1% in annuity market based on premium income[22]. In the last five years, Kyosai's life insurance business decreased by 17.4% and annuity business shrank by 23.1%. Life insurance companies' business

[19] Some SME and consumer co-operatives belong to federations that carry out mutual aid business as insurers, but they are not included.

[20] JCIA (2015), *Kyosai Nenkan*, p.72.

[21] According to ICMIF's global ranking (2016), mutuals in Japan is at 8th place in total premiums, at 9th place in life insurance and at 18th place in non-life insurance in 2014.

[22] Japan Institute of Life Insurance (2015) showed that insurance companies occupied 78.6% of the household's choice of life insurance (including personal pension plan), JA *Kyosai* 8.5% and consumer co-operative *Kyosai* 28.4% respectively.

increased by 36.7%, while their annuity business decreased by 10.0%. Strong sales of single-premium policies for savings were responsible for such a growth. Kyosai's share in the fire insurance market reaches 62.8%. While fire insurance increased by 8.3%, fire Kyosai business increased by 51.1%, because building endowment or savings-type insurance for reconstruction (Tateko) sharply increased. Kyosai also covers 6.4% in personal accident insurance and 11.4% in automobile and compulsory automobile liability insurance. Automobile Kyosai increased by 14.1%, while automobile insurance increased by 16.0%. As Figure 4 shows, life insurance companies have an advantage in annuity or savings-type insurances. On the other hand, Kyosai has an advantage in fire insurances.

Figure 4. Business segments based on premium income in 2014

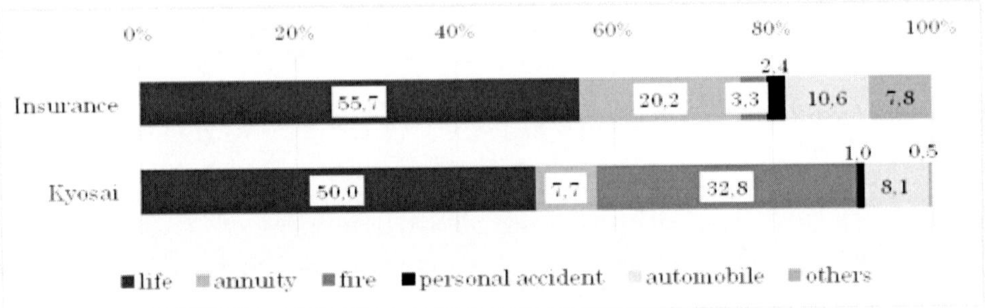

Source: LIAJ, GIAJ, JCIA.

4.2 The current trends of mutual companies

Three major mutual life insurance companies have accelerated overseas operations by M&As in recent years. They seem to be oriented toward steady growth in the global market rather than the mature market of Japan. Each mutual company raised funds (kikin) for that purpose rather than strengthening financial base. Kikin is a kind of debt but usually regarded as a capital base from an accounting viewpoint. When a company redeems kikin with surplus, it must reserve the same amount of the redemption. Kyosai is not allowed to use kikin and is limited to access the outside capital.

A significant part of sales channel was formerly dominated by female sales agents (seiho ladies). In recent years, the increasing number of single-premium policies and annuity products is sold through banks or bank assurance channels. Although the emerging channels of insurance shops and online shops are not used sufficiently, mutual companies nowadays emphasize an optimized mix of multi-products and multi-channels. As regard with Kyosai, banks and financial institutions cannot be used as agents except for Labor Banks (Rokin). Rokin can sell its customers fire Kyosai products as an agent for Zenrosai when it provides a home loan.

Many mutual companies distribute the greater part of their surpluses to policyholders, although they just have to set aside more than 20% of surplus for dividend (rebate) under the IBA of 1995. It is difficult to find a crucial difference between mutual companies and Kyosai on the level of dividend payment, because it depends on dividend/capital policy of each insurer. Kenmin Kyosai distributes nearly 100 % of after-tax net surplus to policyholders in pursuance of actual cost principle or making rebate every year.

In fact, insurance companies adopt a variety of dividend distribution systems including insurance without dividend. Mutual companies sold products at higher premium and paid more dividends in the prewar era. However, modern mutual companies also provide relatively low-priced products for customers who want to save money for insurances in exchange for smaller dividends. Kyosai usually returns surpluses to policyholders in a simple way year after year.

4.3 Outstanding features of Kyosai

A variety of Kyosai is deeply rooted in the communities and workplaces today. Historically speaking, farmers, fishers, workers, consumers, SMEs and the like established co-operatives and started a mutual aid business, because conventional insurance was not available and affordable enough for them to purchase. Kyosai rapidly spread throughout the country. Especially three major consumers co-operative Kyosai developed into businesses comparable to mutual companies in term of individual insurance in force. Kenmin Kyosai was ranked at the 3rd largest, CO-OP Kyosai at the 9th and Zenrosai at the 10th in Japan as of 2014, while Nippon Life at the 2nd, Meiji Yasuda Life at the 6th, Sumitomo Life at the 7th, Asahi Life at the 11th and Fukoku Life at the 19th.

One of the fundamental characteristics of Kyosai is members' homogeneity and the principle of mutual help. In theory, they can help reduce the transaction costs of insurances for marketing products, adjusting claims, and controlling adverse selection and moral hazard.[23]

[23] One of the main reasons that mutual societies dominated the Western insurance markets at the initial stage of growing was often attributed to the greater control

The closer relationships among members are, the more effectively cost reduction is achieved. It is often called the economies of relationship. Insurance companies are likely to spend more costs for carrying out business, because they sell insurance products to many and unspecified persons. Many products of Kyosai are simple and reasonably priced. Some Kyosai offer life insurances at the same rate irrespective of gender or age or fire or earthquake insurances irrespective of residential areas.[24] The average premium system is meant to symbolize the equality among members as Kyosai assumes a role supplementing the social insurance system. However, the weakness inherent in this system is likely to invite adverse selection. The insured with higher risk is willing to purchase more insurance coverage, while the insured with lower risk is willing to purchase less. That results in an imbalance between income and expenditures of insurers and hinders insurance market to work effectively. Therefore, insurance companies classify risks and set a price according to them in principle.

The payment of insurance claims is particularly important for Kyosai, because it directly serves to support damaged members who can see real value in mutuality. Kyosai pays quickly and justly so that policyholders are highly satisfied with the manner of payment.

A scandal over non-payment of insurance claims came to light in 2005. It was particularly problematic that insurance companies did not pay the insurance to beneficiaries in bad faith or negligently despite they essentially should have done so. Consequently, they suffered from a crisis of confidence. Non-payment of claims was also found in Kyosai, but it was considerably smaller in cases and amounts because of its active stance for the payment. In CO-OP Kyosai, for example, field staff often called upon policyholders to see whether or not they had forgotten the application for claims. Nowadays, major life insurance companies visit their policyholders every year and confirm if any unclaimed applications are present.

Kyosai was regarded as maverick outsider in the insurance market but has become a legitimate provider as it gains a growing reputation. For example, a recent survey[25] on customer satisfaction conducted by a public institution revealed that CO-OP Kyosai got a No. 1 ranking for the third year in a row and Kenmin Kyosai took the second place in a row in 2015, while Zenrosai was the third in 2013 and 2015 in the life insurance sector. The survey covered customers who got insurance pay-

---

of adverse selection and moral hazard. Such an advantage decreased after legal rules on insurance contracts were developed.

24 In 2011, the European Court of Justice decided to ban the use of gender in insurance policies from on December 2012 in the light of the principle of equal treatment between men and women.

25 The 5th survey on JCSI (Japanese Customer Satisfaction Index) was conducted in 2015.

ment or benefit or applied for it during the past three years. A member-centered behavior in paying insurance claims led to enhanced customer satisfaction. This can also be attributed to the co-op staff's commitment and their wish to help members.

4.4 The business model of Kyosai

As one of the most standard concepts, "a business model defines how the enterprise creates and delivers value to customers, and then converts payments received to profits."[26] Firstly, the business model of Kyosai is characterized by the way it delivers value to members. As we look back on the history, mutual life insurance companies sold policies at significantly high costs because of high turnover in sales agents. Kyosai promoted to involve co-operative members as policyholders at a lower cost. For example, all the JA staff solicited farmers for contracts for Zenkyoren's products. Half of the members participated in Zenrosai through affinity groups such as trade unions. In Saitama Kenmin Kyosai, Kenmin Kyosai in Saitama prefecture, dedicated staff just handed out leaflets from door to door in a community and promoted a voluntary application rather than soliciting residents in 1973. Thus a unique business model has been developed. In case of CO-OP Kyosai, delivery personnel and staff at store counters in retail co-operatives play a vital role as the first point of contact with members in daily life. These cases unveil the process innovation in marketing or distribution channel of Kyosai products.

Secondly, the business model is concerned with values Kyosai create for members. A product in general contains a value proposition the enterprise delivers to its customers. Zenkyoren launched the Building Endowment Insurance (Tateko) in 1953.[27] It is rooted in property life insurance[28] and covers losses or damage caused by fire, typhoon, earthquake or other natural disasters for five or more years and pays maturity proceeds at an expiry date. In particular, it provided coverage against earthquake much earlier than the earthquake insurance system that was launched by general insurance companies with the government's reinsurance. Maturity proceeds plus rebate will be paid to policyholders at the expiration of the term. Kyoei Fire & Marine Mutual also sold the Building Endowment Insurance as a ground breaker of savings-type insurance in general insurance industry in 1963. They

[26] *Teece* (2010, p. 173).

[27] *Tateko* reached 10,529,000 policies in force and 1,190,420 million yen in amounts insured as of 2014. *Zenkyoren* paid 679,417 claims and 933.5 billion Yen after the Great East Japan Earthquake in 2011.

[28] Hausleben Versicherungs-AG started Sachlebensversicherung in Berlin in 1920.

deliver a value of savings in property insurance to farmers or customers.

Saitama Kenmin Kyosai sold a life insurance plan combined with personal accident protection, targeting low income earners with lower price in 1973. Four out of ten residents in Saitama Prefecture became members in 2015. In fact, its premium was one fifth or sixth as low as that of products sold by life insurance companies at that time. While the operating expense rate was about 10% when the business was started, it is now about 3% of the premium income. Kyosai adopted a flat premium regardless of age or gender at the beginning and established an innovative business model. Insurance companies also developed some product innovations but new products are prone to imitation and it is difficult to sustain competitive advantages.

The word Kyosai literally means mutual aid. Therefore, mutual aid is a significant value. Insurance system is often said to come from a spirit of mutual help or "each for all, all for each", but policyholders of insurance companies may not have a sense of mutuality any longer today. What explains essential nature of Kyosai is that the premium a member paid is used for the damage of other members and the member who has no claim receives the thanks by someone who gets benefits.[29] In short, it means caring for others, which is one of the ethical values of co-operatives. For example, some Kyosai made payments in an extraordinary disaster from retained earnings and not from contracted premium. Especially co-op staff called on suffered policyholders of CO-OP Kyosai. It also provides a special plan by which a member or its family is covered under softer conditions. Even a child with disabilities gets insured if he or she meets some conditions. It puts up a motto "the wider circle of policyholders is, the better an insurance plan is". Members also create a value of mutual aid by participating in Kyosai. Consequently, a mutual aid is the heart of Kyosai or its raison d'etre.

Thirdly, Kyosai returns its surplus to members and local or occupational communities. For example, Zenkyoren initially lent a part of premium income to farming communities. Recently it is engaged in social contribution activities such as accidents prevention and mutual aid after an accident. For example, it assists rehabilitation of traffic accident victims and conducts disaster relief activities.

Finally, an important perspective of the business model of Kyosai is that co-operative members and the staff have a common value and that creates shared value in mutual aid with other stakeholders. JCCU, Zenrosai and other organizations made a considerable contribution in enacting the Act on Support for Reconstructing Livelihoods of Disaster

---

[29] *Tadashi Fukutake*, who was the former president of NFUCA and established *Kyosai* in university co-ops, talked it in 1983.

Victims in 1998 in light of the lessons learned from the Great Hanshin-Awaji Earthquake in 1995.

5. Governance problems

What effect does the difference of ownership structure has on corporate governance? In mutual insurance companies, the characteristics of ownership are that customers own the firm. They have millions of members[30], although the membership is limited to policyholders with participating insurance.[31] Theoretically, owners or shareholders of a stock insurance company may seek their own interests at the expense of customers' interests. But such a conflict between owners and customers does not exist in a mutual company, because members are both customers and owners. This is the advantage of the mutual company. On the other hand, the disadvantage is that monitoring and controlling of management may not be as strong as those in a stock company. Especially, stock market imposes discipline on management in a listed company to act for the owners' interests. Therefore, the challenge is to implement effective corporate governance in a mutual company.

The supreme decision-making body in a mutual company is the policyholders' representative meeting. Meiji Yasuda Life has 221 representatives, Nippon Life has 199, Sumitomo Life has 179, Asahi Life has 149, and Fukoku Life has 117 as of March 31, 2016. Each representative has one vote in the meeting and serves a maximum of two terms for eight years. In a stock company, the highest decision-making body is the shareholders' meeting. For example, Dai-ichi Life has 839,514 shareholders in the same time period and 181,060 shareholders or 20.9% of all the shareholders participated in the meeting in 2015.[32]

The policyholder representative nomination committee selects candidates for policyholder representatives who meet the requirements for selection standards. Next, all the members vote confidently on representatives. Only Meiji Yasuda Life adopts a candidacy system for 22

[30] Nippon Life has 9,432,000, Sumitomo Life has 6,797,000, Meiji Yasuda Life has 6,649,000, Asahi Life has 2,109,000, and Fukoku Life has 1,744,000 members as of March 31, 2016.

[31] Within the specified limit, a mutual insurance company may underwrite non-participating policies whose holders are excluded from its membership under the Insurance Business Act.

[32] They include the shareholders who exercised their voting rights in the Voting Forms or by electromagnetic means.

representatives and a member can apply for a candidate. Policyholder representatives are selected to make a well-balanced mixture regarding age, area, class of insurance, gender, occupation, the time of acquiring membership qualification etc. in order to reflect a variety of members' demands. They should act for all policyholders including non-members and not for the interests of particular members. Some members are permitted to participate in the meeting as observers. In addition, every year mutual companies hold advisory panels with customers in the regions. Each mutual company holds a board of councilors meeting which consists of members or experts from many fields. They discuss important matters of management, opinions from members and the like. Advisory panels and board of councilors are unique systems to complement the formal governance of a mutual company.

Recently, mutual companies react to a series of corporate governance reforms in stock companies. For example, in 2006 Meiji Yasuda Life transformed into a company with several committees. It established nominating, compensation and audit committees separating supervisory and executive functions. Outside directors occupy a majority of these committee members. The main objectives were to enhance supervisory function of the board and transparency in management. Sumitomo Life shifted into a company with a nominating committee in 2015. In this case, executive officers and supervisory board members are separated completely. Sumitomo Life set up outside directors' council, which consists of all outside directors. They discuss diverse opinions among them or with the top floor management regarding major management problems such as mid-and-long term corporate strategy and corporate governance. Nippon Life, Fukoku Life and Asahi life have adopted a conventional company system with board of auditors, although Nippon Life has set up an outside directors committee in 2015. The committee discusses the appointment of directors, executive officers, auditors and an accountant auditor as well as remuneration for directors and executive officers. It also discusses other management matters and submits a report to the board of directors. Outside directors have a chairperson and constitute a majority of board members for increased transparency in the decision-making process. Each mutual company established the basic policy and published report on corporate governance.

Next, we gave a brief overview on the governance of major Kyosai co-operatives, which are organized as a federation. The feature of ownership in a federation is that it is owned by member co-operatives, as Table 4 shows. These primary co-operatives are owned by farmers, workers, consumers and others, while federations provide them with mutual aid insurance. Unlike a mutual insurance company, a Kyosai federation has an indirect governance system for members of primary cooperatives. A federation is controlled in a democratic way according to the co-operative principle.

Table 4: The summary of governance of major Kyosai federation as of March 31, 2015

JCIF	Zenrosai	Zenkyoren
members		
153 members: 148 primary co-ops, 3 national federations (Pal, Seikatsu Club, Green Co-op), JCCU and Zenrosai	58 members: 47 Sociaties (Rosai), 8 Tansan Kyosai, Rreinsurance Fed., JCCU and JCIF	825 members: 777 regular members (686 JAs, 75 prefectural fed., 2 other fed., Zen-noh, Norin Chukin Bank) 48 associate members
delegates		
General Meeting	General Meeting	General & Representative Meeting
292 delegates*: 286 primary co-ops, 3 national federations, 3 other federations	349 delegates** (6 female): 310 Rosai, 30 Tansan Kyosai, 9 National federations	216 delegates: 214 delegates from regular members, 2 delegates from Zen-noh and Norin Chukin Bank
Board of directors		
25 directors: 5 external directors including 2 CEOs, 15 executives of primaries, 5 lay board members of primary co-ops (female)	33 directors: 9 external directors including 4 CEOs, 24 executives of primary co-ops (21 Rosai, 2 Tansan Kyosai, 1 JCCU)	35 directors: 25 supervisory board members, 10 board of directors

* Executives: 70%, Lay members: 30%.
** Delegates are board members of primary co-ops. Most of them are trade union leaders + some executives and community groups. Delegates are elected by primary co-ops (mostly no voting being made since the number of candidates is within a quorum).
Source: Annual reports and interviews.

The supreme decision-making body in a federation is the general meeting or representatives meeting. In the general meeting of JCIF (CO-OP Kyosai) and Zenrosai, the federation assigns the number of votes to delegates of the member co-operative in a well-balanced manner according to the number of members in the primary co-operative. In the representatives meeting of Zenkyoren, representatives are chosen in an election. The range of decision-makings of these bodies in the federation is wider than that in a mutual company. For example, the federation needs to decide on a business report in these bodies. The number of directors in the federation is larger than that in a mutual company in order to reflect diverse demands of primaries.

JCIF and Zenrosai adopt a conventional system with a board of auditors, but Zenkyoren introduced a dual board system in 2002. It is unique in its clear separation between supervisory board and management board. The supervisory board, which comprises farmers and the like, appoints management board directors and entrusts them to conduct business within the range of its decision-making power. The management board of directors mainly makes decisions on the execution of operations. The challenge for the Kyosai federation is to enhance governance in the internal control and compliance in the light of primary co-operatives' members' interests.

6. Social Responsibility

6.1 The importance of Social Responsibility

The importance of SR (Social Responsibility) has been increasingly acknowledged in recent years. In the past, SR activities were recognized as necessary costs of a company. Yet nowadays, SR is being accepted more pro actively, and being discussed from a more strategic standpoint. The strategic implementation of SR is important for enhancing the sustainability of companies. In addition, the concept of strategic SR has developed into the notion of CSV (Creating Shared Value), so that companies need to create new, shared value in their interactions with society[33].

At present, large Japanese insurance companies and Western insurance companies regard their social contribution as having a positive impact on their own companies and regard SR-related activities not as imposed obligations, but as a part of their strategy. Hereafter, SR-related activities at insurance companies and Kyosai co-operatives are examined.

6.2 SR-related activities at insurance companies

Compared with other sectors, the insurance sector is slowly embracing SR, yet insurance companies have taken actions to be aware of their customers' need. A survey by the Financial Services Agency

[33] *Porter, Michael E.* and *Mark R. Kramer* (2010).

(2009)[34] revealed the polarized situation. While some insurance companies are taking positive action on SR, less than 80% of them have not established special dedicated departments.

As for the reasons that insurance companies emphasize SR, almost 50% of the respondents stated that it was due to the public-goods nature of their operations. In recent years, an increasing number of financial institutions has expressed a desire to improve its public image, perhaps as a reaction to various trends among consumers. In case of insurance companies, the proportion of targeting customers and consumers as stakeholders when performing SR-related activities is particularly high. This means that they strongly acknowledge the necessity of SR as a means of enhancing their value as companies.

At present, most insurance companies are implementing SR with reference to guidelines such as the GRI (Global Reporting Initiative) and ISO 26000 series in the fields of their relationship with policyholders and employees, governance, compliance, social contribution, and so on while the enthusiasm regarding this topic varies. They are involved in SR-related activities which are closely linked with their core businesses, including those related to disaster prevention and reduction, environmental protection, and child rearing. One life insurance company, for example, has evaluated SR-related activities for "making a social contribution to the sound rearing of children." By promoting individual SR-related activities such as musical education for children, crime prevention, and cleaning, which had hitherto been performed haphazardly, the company has appealed stakeholders to join and increased the synergies among the activities.

In addition, insurance companies that are proactive about SR, emphasize their relationships with stakeholders. Through stakeholder engagement, which involves a two-way dialog with stakeholders, namely listening to their arguments and suggestions, and incorporating them into its business activities, a company can make itself more sustainable[35]. CSR reports are positioned as tools of stakeholder engagement, and published in paper format or on the company's website. Furthermore, some insurance companies produce videos on activities, which they classify by topics and post on their websites from time to time. Many employees are involved in the preparation of CSR reports; they work with NPOs and engage in dialogs with experts on a one-to-one basis.

[34] The Financial Services Agency has conducted surveys relating to CSR. The latest survey was the "Survey of Specific CSR-Focused Initiatives Being Implemented by Financial Institutions and Follow-up on Initiatives Being Implemented since the Previous Survey (the results of which were published in March 2006)," which was conducted in 2009. The survey targeted 4,652 financial institutions, of which 2,757 responded.

[35] *Kanji Tanimoto* (2006).

6.3 SR-related activities at Kyosai

Kyosai co-operatives also perform various SR-related activities. Some Kyosai co-operatives focus on social contribution to three areas, i.e. disaster prevention and reduction, environmental protection, and child rearing. Others, meanwhile, work with non-profit organizations, providing subsidies to support activities for improving the quality of life in local communities. In addition, some of them participate in the pink ribbon campaign to reduce breast cancers and pursue social responsibility investment. However, these activities are almost similar to the ones performed by insurance companies. They are not necessarily unique to Kyosai.

Kyosai co-operatives are assumed to exhibit solidarity based on the principle of mutual assistance whereby members work together. Their social responsibilities would therefore be expected to be more closely intertwined with their core business than it is the case at ordinary companies, whose top priority is earning profits for shareholders. However, in order to meet their members' needs, Kyosai have transformed more into insurers, offering a wider range of products, and involving a larger number of members. As a result of these developments, their members are less conscious of being members of an association. In addition, insurance companies have endeavored to become more like Kyosai, for example, by reducing the prices of their products. In addition, through strategic SR, they have started to link more closely SR-related activities with their core businesses, thereby making them more beneficial to society at large and more like public goods. As a result, the obvious differences have become smaller between insurance companies and Kyosai cooperatives, which have always emphasized their social role as part of their business philosophy.

SR-related activities only really have value when they are accepted by the beneficiaries, i.e. stakeholders. Therefore, organizations need to articulate how, through their core operations, SR-related activities will serve the society at large. By incorporating the opinions of stakeholders into the management cycle through stakeholder engagement, SR becomes more closely connected with corporate value. In the future, insurance companies that are more conscious of stakeholder engagement can be expected to implement even more strategic SR-related activities. While understanding the ideals of the associations' members is fading, Kyosai will need to strategically incorporate the stakeholder engagement and perform SR-related activities that are befitting of Kyosai.

7. Response to Natural Disasters

7.1 Growing interest in natural disasters insurance

The interest in insurances for natural disasters, especially earthquake insurance, has been growing since the Great East Japan Earthquake in 2011. After this earthquake occurred, both insurance companies and Kyosai moved quickly to make payouts for incurred damages. They established task forces for responding to the disaster victims putting together special teams to investigate damage. The total payout was more than 2.4 trillion Yen (as of FY 2014).[36]

In Japan, government assistance in the case of damage due to natural disasters is currently provided by a scheme for assisting victims in rebuilding their lives. Under the Natural Disaster Victims Relief Act[37], when the building a person is living has been destroyed by an earthquake, he or she can be awarded a maximum of three million Yen. Given the cost of rebuilding homes, this amount is evidently not sufficient. In light of this fact, insurance companies and Kyosai play a significant role in mitigating earthquake risk.

---

[36] Kyosai made payments comparable to those of insurance companies. It might be explained by a number of factors: larger number of contracted policy holders, the special payments beyond contractual liabilities and so on, but evidence-based comparison has not been made.

[37] This law was unanimously enacted as a private bill supported by 25 million signatures collected by Co-op Kobe, JCCU, Zenrosai, and Rengo (Japanese Trade Union Confederation) in 1998 after the Kobe earthquake happened and despite a strong bureaucratic resistance arguing that no official money should be used to compensate private properties.

7.2 Overview of and issues with earthquake insurance

Earthquakes do not only constitute a massive risk, the difficulty in forecasting them makes it hard to assess the insurance risk. So in 1966, the Act on Earthquake Insurance was enacted, giving rise to the household earthquake insurance system. Under this system, the government reinsures large earthquake damages in excess of the earthquake insurance liability borne by private-sector insurance companies. Although earthquake insurance is based on self-help, it is regarded as serving the public good to a high degree.

Under this earthquake insurance, payouts are made to fund the daily living expenses for the time being in case of damage when a residence and/or a person's belongings were burned, crushed, buried, or washed away as a result of an earthquake, volcanic eruption, or a tsunami stemming from such events. Earthquake insurance is automatically included in fire insurance policies and cannot be purchased on its own.

A number of innovations have been employed to ensure that earthquake insurance can be provided at low premiums and in a stable way. Earthquake insurance products are identical from company to company, and the "no loss, no profit" principle is applied to the premiums. Under this principle, premiums do not include a profit for the insurance company. The premium rates are determined by a semi-governmental corporation called the General Insurance Rating Organization of Japan (GIROJ) using stochastic seismic motion prediction maps. In other words, they are applied to each region (prefecture) and each type of structure (wooden or non-wooden) depending on the risk.

The payout amount from earthquake insurance is limited to 30-50% of the fire insurance payout and tops out at 50 million Yen for a house and 10 million Yen for the belongings inside. The payout is based on the degree of damage, and includes three categories: total destruction (in which 100% of the maximum payout is made), semi-destruction (50%), and partial destruction (5%)[38]. The scheme that payouts are not based on the actual loss suffered in an earthquake is designed to ensure that earthquake insurance fulfills its mission of making payouts promptly to a huge number of disaster victims. While the number of people taking out earthquake insurance rises, the system faces problems in terms of its sustainability. According to the GIROJ (FY 2014), 28.8% of the households are enrolled in earthquake insurance, and earthquake insurance is bundled in with 59.3% of fire insurance policies. These figures are more than ten points higher than before the Great East Japan

[38] In 2017 the number of categories was be increased to four.

Earthquake. However, an increase in the number of earthquake insurance policies also leads to a rise in the probable maximum loss (PML).[39]

Under a cabinet order, if the maximum total payout specified for a single earthquake is exceeded, the payout on each policy is reduced in proportion to the value of the policy. When the earthquake insurance was launched, the maximum total payout was 300 billion Yen, but this amount has been revised on several occasions. The 2014 revision increased the maximum total payout to 7 trillion Yen, an amount considered unlikely to result in payout reductions even if a large earthquake will occur. However, if the number and value of policies increase further, and the PML rises, it is possible that the payout received by each policyholder will be reduced.

As a result, in 2014 the premium on new policies was increased by a national average of 15.5%. This was followed by another 19% hike in 2017. On the other hand, to keep the total payout under control, measures to reduce damage in the event of an earthquake are being considered. For example, a discount is applied to the premium if the building meets national standards for earthquake resistance. This should encourage earthquake insurance policyholders to make an effort to reduce potential damage on their own.

7.3 Response of Kyosai to earthquake risk

Some Kyosai also offer coverage of earthquake risks. Coverage differs depending on the Kyosai products, but there is a lot of similarities with earthquake insurance. For example, maximum payouts are set and the amount of each payout is based on the category for the degree of damage. However, Kyosai have a history of meeting the needs of members, so unlike earthquake insurance, there is no uniform product offered in the sector.[40]

The characteristics of Kyosai include the fact that earthquake payouts and premiums are generally set lower than it is the case with earthquake insurance. In addition, while earthquake insurance premiums are set according to different regions, owing to the differences in the degree of risks from one region to another, Kyosai's premiums are identical nationwide, regardless of the location of the property. Furthermore, unlike earthquake insurance, coverage by Kyosai is not

---

[39] PML is an indicator that measures the maximum total payout to all policyholders in the event of a major earthquake.

[40] Some Kyosai co-operatives made special payment for disaster even in the case the damage caused by earthquakes is exempted from liability as an immunity reason while university insurance co-operatives made condolence payments to students' policyholders whose parents were killed by the disaster.

reinsured by the government. Because of this, most Kyosai either go to the reinsurance market to purchase coverage of their entire disaster risk or issue catastrophe bonds. Kyosai also provides assistance to members or policyholders who have suffered from earthquake damage beside the contractual payouts. These schemes, which include special consolation payments, reflect the nature and financial power of the Kyosai as mutual aid organizations.

7.4 Recent development of new products

Despite the coverage offered by earthquake insurance and Kyosai is subject to a maximum payout, it is possible that a policyholder or member will not be able to restore a building etc. to its original condition. In recent years, therefore, several new products and riders have appeared. One of them that has drawn particular attention is a rider offering additional coverage that is added on to the main fire insurance policy. Although the amount of coverage is generous, the coverage provided by the earthquake rider component is provided by the insurance company alone, which makes the premium for the rider relatively high. People who wish, on the other hand, to be insured against earthquakes for comparatively low premiums can take out insurance from small-sum, short-term insurance companies[41], as such companies have launched products that can be purchased by people who have not taken out earthquake insurance. Thus, a wide range of products have developed.

8. How the insurance industry responds to the globalization and demographic shift

8.1 Overseas business expansion by life insurers

The conditions of Japan's insurance market are drastically changing. A wide range of factors including the thorough amendments to the Insurance Business Act in 1996, the nation's low birth rate, aging

---

41 Regarding the companies in the insurance sector, small-sum, short-term insurance companies operate within a certain scale offering a small amount of coverage for a period of one year or less (or two years or less in the case of non-life insurance). And the products they can offer are only indemnity-type.

population, and the attractiveness of overseas markets, prompted the Japanese insurers, both non-life and life, to develop aggressively overseas operations. Since 2010, major life insurers have turned their overseas operations into full-fledged businesses, whereas non-life insurers had been expanding even before that. In this regard, both mutual and stock companies have taken the identical strategy for overseas operations while Kyosai co-operative have focused on the domestic business.

In deploying overseas business expansion, a major issue is how to select future markets, focusing on factors such as insurance penetration rates, market size, and growth potential in addition to population dynamics and the economic/political situation in a given potential market. As growth in the insurance markets of industrialized countries has stagnated in recent years, the growing markets such as those of emerging economies including Asia have attracted greater attention worldwide. However, it is highly possible that it could take some time to earn profits in the insurance markets of these emerging economies.

On the other hand, while acquisition of insurers in developed European and North American markets is costly, it can improve business performance over the short term. It also makes it possible to acquire business expertise from leading firms in developed insurance markets. In other words, overseas operation needs to be advanced with consideration to the business portfolio in addition to the understanding of the insurance market in a target overseas market. Building a portfolio with consideration for these matters can be expected to have the effect of geographically diversifying risks, so that strong performance in overseas markets could make up for slow growth in domestic markets. It can be said that many major life insurers seek to enhance their overseas businesses from the perspectives of securing medium to long-term growth potential and diversifying their business portfolios.

8.2 Overseas business expansion by nonlife insurers

Nonlife insurers had traditionally expanded their overseas operations in tandem with the trading customers and large manufacturers that had been their customers in Japan, but in recent years small and medium enterprises have also begun operating overseas, so the demand for insurance overseas is increasing. In addition, with the encouragement of the FSA, major nonlife insurers are developing their overseas operations through M&A activities.

The three big nonlife insurers[42] have sought to increase the size of and the earnings from overseas insurance operations as the driver

[42] The non-life insurers were forced to integrate and merge in an effort to survive. The end result was the birth of the "three mega non-life insurers" understanding.

for their medium-term growth strategies, and the performance can be said to represent the result of pursuing a growth strategy that offers the balance between advanced-country and emerging-country markets and between nonlife insurance and life insurance. The earnings of the three mega insurers in the fiscal year ended in March 2015 and were the highest ever. Tokio Marine HD, earned almost 30 percent of its premium income and 50 percent of its net income overseas. The mega nonlife insurers also earn large proportions of their net income from life insurance. 12-18 percent of their net income came from life insurance. Their profit structure demonstrates that given weak domestic sales of their mainstay products such as automobile and fire insurances, they have to find new sources of earnings.

8.3 Challenges facing Japanese Insurers in developing overseas operations

Over the past 20 years or longer, the insurance market has undergone rapid changes under the globalization advancing to a considerable degree. It is likely that enjoying economies of scale through expansion activities is the basis of overseas business expansion. Global economies of scale can be linked easily to competitive advantage. However, barriers to the realization of economies of scale include e.g. excessive increases in compliance costs since each nation/region has its own regulations. Therefore, it is conceivable that in order to pursue economies of scale there is a need to standardize the upstream components of the value chain, such as setting insurance premium rates, underwriting, payment of insurance benefits, and investment.

Insurers may try to standardize the upstream portions of the value chain through transfer of knowledge from their home countries, by securing management initiatives in investments. They also absorb knowledge from overseas investments and apply it to their home countries and other investments, aiming to generate group wide synergies. Regarding the Japanese major insurance companies, when nonlife insurers have expanded their business to Asia, a big difference is recognizable between their advances into nonlife and life insurance business. A majority stake is the norm concerning nonlife, whereas almost all the stakes taken are minority concerning life insurances. It is conceivable that it is just the key how the Japanese insurers are able to appreciate global economies of scale through the standardization of upstream portions of a more advanced value chain.

At present, there are 30 non-life insurers (plus 21 foreign insurers and one license specified judicial person) but almost all of them are under the wing of one of three holding companies.

9. Conclusion

This paper investigates the history of mutual companies and Kyosai co-operatives in Japan. They have evolved to world class enterprises in the second largest insurance market. They had not only competed but also often confronted over the institutional framework, in particular regarding regulations concerning insurance businesses. Then, the institutional and organizational aspects of mutual companies and Kyosai have been analyzed and a comparison between mutual companies and Kyosai has been made concerning size and performance, business models and reputation. A more detailed comparison has been made in terms of governance, social responsibility, and response to natural disasters. Finally, challenges of how the insurance industry responds to globalization and demographic shift have been described.

The main question was whether Kyosai co-operatives are heading for conversion with or diversion from dominant insurance companies, will they remain maverick outsiders, or will they become just competitors. The authors share the view of yes and no. The former is converging with the latter in terms of regulations for the insurance business and governance of large enterprises although there are still differences regarding safety net and taxation. But the legal and administrative system has been strongly intertwined with the socioeconomic system and seems to persist for a while since they had been evolved nearly 150 years since the Meiji Restauration.[43] The separate legislation administered by competent ministries in line with industrial policies resulted in the diversified evolution between insurance companies and Kyosai co-operatives. Because of the path dependency, it is not realistic to predict the conversion of legal and administrative system in the near future. In addition, Kyosai co-operatives have challenged the existing insurance companies to fill the gap or satisfy unfulfilled needs of farmers, workers and so on who were not necessarily targeted by insurance companies. They built insurance business based on common bonds and developed unique types of products (tateko, flat-rate Kyosai etc.) and ways of operations (solicitation, communication and education with members). They intend to maintain and strengthen such a "difference" as a marketing tool. In this sense, they seem to retain their uniqueness in the foreseeable future.

[43] Such combination often created a triangle coalition among ministries, politicians and trade associations. It is characterized as "bureau- pluralism" by *Masahiko Aoki*.

References
(English)

Cummins, J. David and *Bertrand Venard* (2008), “Insurance Market Dynamics: between Global Developments and Local Contingencies,” *Risk Management and Insurance Review*, Vol. 11, No. 2, pp. 295-326.

Dekle, R. and *K. Hamada* (2000, “On the Development of Rotating Credit Associations in Japan,” *Economic Development and Cultural Change*, Vol.49, 77-90.

ICMIF (2016), *Global Mutual Market Share 2014*.

Japan CO-OP Insurance Consumer Co-op Federation (2015), *Annual Report 2014*. http://coopkyosai.coop/about/work/pdf/annual_en_2014.pdf

Japan Institute of Life Insurance (2015), *National Survey on Life Insurance* (18th).

Katrishen, Frances A. and *Nicos A. Scordis* (1998), “Economies of Scale in Services: A Study of Multinational Insurers,” *Journal of International Business Studies*, Vol. 29, No. 2, pp. 305-324.

Kotler, Philip and *Nancy Lee* (2004), *Corporate Social Responsibility: Doing the Most Good for Your Company and Your Cause*, John Wiley & Sons, Inc.

Life Insurance Association of Japan, *The Summary of Life Insurance Business* (annuals).

Ministry of Finance, *The Insurance Year Book*.

Pearson, Robbin and *Takau Yoneyama* (eds.) (2015), *Corporate Forms and Organizational Choice in International Insurance*, Oxford University Press.

Porter, Michael E. and *Mark R. Kramer* (2006), “The Link between Competitive Advantage and Corporate Social Responsibility,” *Harvard Business Review* (December), pp. 78-92.

Porter, Michael E. and *Mark R. Kramer* (2011), “Creating Shared Value,” *Harvard Business Review* (January-February), pp. 62-77.

Souma, Toshiyuki and *Tsutsui, Yoshiro* (2005), “Recent Competition in the Japanese Life Insurance Industry”, *ISER Discussion Paper* No. 637, Osaka University.

Swiss Re (2015), “M&A in Insurance: Start of a New Wave?” Sigma, Vol. 3.

Teece, David J. (2010), “Business Models, Business Strategy and Innovation”, *Long Range Planning* 43, pp. 172-194.

Yamori, N. and *Okada, T.* (2007), “The Japanese Insurance Market and Companies: Recent Trends,” in: *Cummins, J. David* and *Venard, Bertrand* (eds.), *Handbook of International Insurance Between Global Dynamics and Local Contingencies*, Springer, pp. 147-204.

Zenkyoren (2015), *Annual Report 2015*.

(Japanese)

Financial Services Agency (2009), *Kinyuu Kikan no CSR Jittaicyousakekka no Gaiyou* (Outline of Survey on CSR-related Activities of Financial Institutions). http://www.fsa.go.jp/news/20/ginkou/20090331-7/01.pdf

Japan Earthquake Reinsurance Co., Ltd. (2016), *Nihon Jishin Saihoken 50nenshi* (50 years of earthquake reinsurance in Japan).

Japanese Customer Satisfaction Index (2015), Dai 5 Kai Kokyaku Manzokudo Shisu Chosa Hokoku (The Results of Fifth Survey on JSCI in 2015). http://activity.jpc-net.jp/detail/srv/activity001457/attached.pdf

Life Insurance Association of Japan, Kaiingaisha no Hensenzu (Historical Transition of Membership Life Insurance Companies of LIAJ in Japan). http://www.seiho.or.jp/member/chart/pdf/chart_01.pdf

Nihon Kyosai Kyokai (eds.) (2012), *Ronbun Koen Shu* (Articles & Lectures Dedicated to the International Co-operative Year).

Nihon Kyosai Kyokai (2015), *Kyosai Nenkan* (Yearbook on Kyosai).

Ogawa, Hiroaki (2008), *Gendai Hokengaku* (Contemporary Insurance Studies), Kyushu University Press.

Onzo, Miho (2015), "Globalization and Economies of Scale of Japanese Life Insurance Company," *Journal of Insurance Science*, No. 630, pp.161-177.

Oshio, Tadayuki (2012), *Gendai Kyosai Ron* (On Modern Kyosai), Nihon Keizai Hyoronsha.

Sakai, Kojiro (2002), *Kyosai Jigyo no Rekishi* (History of Kyosai Business), Nihon Kyosai Kyokai.

Souma, Kenji (2013), *Kyosai Jigyo towa Nanika* (All about Kyosai Business), Nihon Keizai Hyoronsha.

Tanimoto, Kanji (2006), *CSR: Kigyou to Syakai wo Kangaeru* (Considering Enterprises and the Society), NTT Publishing.

Tominaga, Kou (2012), "Kyousai no Tokucyou to Yakuwari (Characteristics and roles of Kyosai)" *2012 Kokusai Kyoudoukumiainen Ronbun / Koensyu*, Japan Co-operative Insurance Association.

The Historic Evolution and Current Status of Different Forms of Organization in the Japanese Insurance Industry

A comparison of the historic development and co-existence of stock companies, mutual companies and mutual-aid cooperatives on the Japanese insurance market

Stefan Preiner

1. Introduction

Looking upon the Japanese insurance market three major forms of organization that actively operate insurance can be identified. These are the stock company, the mutual company and the mutual-aid performing cooperative. Whereas the first of respective organizational forms conducts insurance business with the primary intention of maximizing profits for its shareholders, the latter two differ with respect to this matter, as representatives of both the two latter forms of organization claim to operate insurance based upon the principles of mutuality. Even though legal forms operating insurance upon the principles of mutuality exist in a multitude of various national insurance markets around the globe, the Japanese insurance market can be considered to be special with two such legal forms co-existing alongside stock insurance companies. The peculiarity of this situation is further emphasized by the fact that from a historic point of view mutual insurance companies and mutual-aid operating cooperatives developed separately from each other alongside the stock company form and, as a result, differ with respect to operational characteristics and institutional characteristics. The main intention of this chapter is to investigate, describe and discuss the parallel development and co-existence of various legal forms operating on the Japanese insurance market as well as to examine the current situation and positioning of mentioned various forms of organization in the Japanese insurance industry. Doing so, the chapter focuses first onto the various legal forms' historic emergence and economic development. Here the reasons for the parallel emergence and success of various legal forms in their respective field of operation are being investigated. Second, the chapter examines the various organizational forms' current economic performance and tries to identify operational characteristics similar among or specific to each form. In addition, differences between mutual insurance companies and mutual-aid cooperatives shall be shortly discussed from the standpoint of the principles of mutuality.

2. The historic development of the various forms of organization in the Japanese insurance industry

2.1 The inception and early development of the modern insurance industry in Japan

With the inception and launch of business of the *Tokio Marine Insurance Co., Ltd.* on the 1st of August 1879, the stock company can be classified as the first domestically founded form of organization operating insurance in Japan. Prior to the first domestic insurance company's inception, modern insurance activities had not been performed for long in Japan, as modern insurance practices were for the first time introduced the Japanese nation during the early second half of the 19th century. While it is not entirely clear in which particular year first modern insurance practices were launched within the Japanese economy, it is believed that fire insurance was the first type of modern insurance introduced to Japan, i.e. with the English *Imperial Fire Insurance Company* entering the Japanese market as the first foreign insurance company in January 1861.[1] During the following decade several other foreign insurance companies started insurance operations in Japan. Nevertheless, foreign insurance companies originally refrained from underwriting to Japanese customers until the mid-1870s and were not tremendously successfully in significantly expanding into Japan's domestic market, once extending their business operations to the Japanese populace.[2 3]

1 Cf. Japan Business History Institute (1980), p. 6.

2 Cf. *Yoneyama* (2012), p. 496.

3 Cf. Japan Business History Institute (1980), p. 8.

The first type of business operated by the *Tokio Marine Insurance Co., Ltd.* consisted out of cargo insurance for domestic sea trade. In 1883, the company performed a first extension of business to hull insurance.[4] [5] Despite this rather limited scope of insurance business operated by the *Tokio Marine Insurance Co., Ltd.* during its initial years of existence, the nation's first domestic stock insurance company was able to successfully establish a long-lasting presence. As a key contribution to this successful development of business the stock company's close relationship with the major industrial *zaibatsu* conglomerates *Mitsubishi* and *Mitsui* as well as the *Dai-Ichi National Bank* can be mentioned, representing key clients as well as important supporters for the newly established insurer during its earl years of operation.[6] [7] During the late 1880s and early 1890s, export activities of the Japanese economy increased strongly, causing the demand for marine insurance by domestic customers to increase as well. As a consequence of this development, the *Tokio Marine Insurance Co., Ltd.* lost its initial position as the sole domestic marine insurance company with the inception of three new domestic insurance companies in 1893. These newly founded companies were the *Imperial Marine Insurance Co., Ltd.*, the *Nippon Kairiku Marine Insurance Co., Ltd.* and the *Osaka Insurance Co., Ltd.* all being of the stock company form.[8] With the total number of marine insurance companies having increased to four by the end of 1893, severe price competition soon began to emerge on the nation's recently developed modern marine insurance market.[9] [10]

Whereas mentioned above companies, with the exception of the *Osaka Insurance Co., Ltd.*, all dedicated themselves solely to the operation of marine insurance at the point of their inception, Japan's first modern fire insurance operating company initated its business on the 1st of October 1888 and was named *Tokyo Fire Insurance Co., Ltd.* First domestic competition soon followed with the inception of the *Meiji Fire Insurance Co., Ltd.* in 1891, which also started to underwrite fire insurance product in the Tokyo area. One year later, the *Nippon Fire Insurance Co., Ltd.* began was initiated as the third domestic fire insurer and launched its business operations in Osaka.[11] [12] In general, it can be said that from 1892 onwards the domestic Japanese fire insurance sector experienced a wave of incorporations of new fire insurance companies.

---

4 Cf. Ibid, p. 31.

5 Cf. Ibid, p. 25.

6 Cf. *Yoneyama* (2012), p. 496.

7 Cf. Japan Business History Institute (1980), p. 25.

8 Cf. Yasuda Marine and Fire, (1988), p. 125.

9 Cf. Japan Business History Institute (1993), p. 25-26.

10 Cf. Yasuda Marine and Fire, (1988), p. 125.

11 Cf. Ibid, p. 112.

12 Cf. Japan Business History Institute (1993), p. 21.

Until the end of the year 1894, a total of ten additional domestic fire insurance companies had been established, raising the total number of fire insurance operating companies to thirteen. This surge of fire insurance operating companies occurred despite a rather slow initial development of the nation's domestic fire insurance market, partially caused by the fact that the concept of modern fire insurance was still widely unknown to the general Japanese populace. Moreover, as a consequence of the rapid surge of fire insurance companies, fierce competition soon developed onto the Japan's domestic fire insurance market.[13]

Similar to the situation observable on the Japanese fire insurance market during the last decade of the 19th century, also the nation's marine insurance market experienced an increasing number of participating insurance companies. Adding the number of fire as well as marine insurance operating companies initiated no less than an additional nineteen insurance companies started operations between the years 1895 to 1899. Nevertheless, only a small number of marine and fire insurance companies initiated during the 1890s was able to accomplish a long-lasting presence. In fact, only six out of mentioned nineteen marine and fire insurance companies, being initiated during the second half of the last decade of the 19th century, were still in existence in 1912, whereas only seven out of the sixteen fire and marine insurers existing prior to 1895 survived until the same year. Therefore, the early modern Japanese property and casualty insurance market was characterized by a continuously high fluctuation of actively operating insurance companies. As the major reasons behind this fluctuation factors, weak financial backing of newly established companies, the lack of sound knowledge of insurance practices of companies' management and the omission to utilize adequate statistical methods for calculating premium rates and reserve heights can be named.[14] [15] Additionally, provisions specifically regulating insurance companies and their business operations were still absent within Japanese legislation during respective period of time, which contributed to the emergence of this situation. Moreover, fierce competition resulting from the increasing number of operating fire and marine insurance companies also contributed to the bankruptcy of comparatively inefficient and less competitive insurers.[16]

Parallel to Japan's first domestic marine and fire insurance companies, the nation also experienced the inception of its first domestic life insurance companies. In 1881, the *Meiji Life Insurance Co., Ltd.* was established and started to underwrite life insurance policies as Japan's first domestic life insurance company. Following the *Meiji Life Insur-*

---

13 Japan Business History Institute (1980), p. 35.
14 Cf. Japan Business History Institute (1993), p. 21.
15 Cf. Japan Business History Institute (1980), p. 35.
16 Cf. Japan Business History Institute (1980), p. 35.

ance Co., Ltd., the nation's second and third domestic life insurers were the *Teikoku Life Assurance Co., Ltd.* and the *Nippon Life Insurance Co., Ltd.*, starting their operations in 1888 and 1889 respectively.[17]

Identical to the case of early Japanese marine and fire insurance companies during the 19th century, all of the three mentioned life insurance companies were incepted under the stock company form. Nevertheless, despite being stock companies, the two companies *Meiji Life* and *Nippon Life* claimed to be a hybrid form of a mutual and a stock insurance company during their first decade of existence. Doing so, founders of the two companies emphasised that maximizing profit for shareholders was not the companies' primary objective. Rather the two companies wanted to be seen by policyholders as being organizations that strongly embodied the spirit of mutual insurance within their business philosophy.[18] [19] In order to justify this claim, both, the *Meiji Life Insurance Co.* and the *Nippon Life Insurance Co.*, started to offer policies with dividend participation, which were aimed to be similar to policies sold by a mutual insurance company, from the immediate launch of their insurance operations onwards. Nevertheless, looking upon actual numbers of profit participating policies underwritten in comparison to numbers of policies without profit participation underwritten during the companies' years of operation of the late 19th century, it can be seen that profit participating policies were sold in comparatively insignificant amounts.[20] As a reason for the inconsiderable amount of profit participating policies underwritten the absence of clear terms issued by the two life insurance companies, specifying the calculation method for dividends distributable to policyholders, can be named, making comparatively more expansive profit-participating policies less attractive for potential customers. Furthermore, dividends to policyholders were only issued every four to eight years, depending on the company. Thus, part of literature strongly questions the asserted incorporation of mutuality of the *Meiji Life Insurance Co.* and the *Nippon Life Insurance Co.* during the companies' early years of operation and considers the companies' claim of being hybrid forms of organization as having been marketing strategies by the two mentioned above insurers.[21]

Similar to the case of the Japanese marine and fire insurance market the nation's life insurance market experienced a wave of incorporations, lasting from 1893 to 1900. Between the years 1893 and 1897, a total of thirty-three new domestic life insurance companies were incepted.

---

17 Cf. Japan Business History Institute (1992), p. 18.

18 Cf. Ibid, p. 5-6.

19 Cf. *Yingying* (2015), p. 220.

20 Cf. Ibid, p. 220.

21 Cf. *Yingying* (2015), p. 222-223.

Until 1900, the number of actively operating life insurance companies had further increased to more than forty.[22] Similar to the case of many fire and marine insurance companies, which were newly established within the same period of time, many newly incorporated life insurance companies suffered from an insufficient capitalization, the absence of sound statistical methods used for calculating adequate premium and reserve heights as well as from a lack of knowledge regarding adequate life insurance operations by founders and managers.[23] [24] As a result, several newly established life insurance companies went bankrupt soon after their initial commencement of business.

Due to the number of bankruptcies of both, life and non-life insurance companies, increasing towards the end of the 19th century, causing substantial financial damages to policyholders of respective companies, public criticism of insurance companies' operational practices was soon being voiced. As a reaction to this development, the Japanese government, saw itself forced to act and ordered the *Ministry of Agriculture and Commerce* to draft a first legislation regarding the regulation and supervision of the insurance industry and its activities by the Japanese State.[25] Such legislation was first included in and, therefore, introduced with the enactment of the *Commercial Code* in 1898. Under these first insurance specific laws, insurance companies became required to obtain an insurance license officially issued by responsible Japanese authorities in order to be permitted to conduct insurance business operations. Furthermore, tight regulations regarding insurance companies' annual financial performance and situation were introduced for the first time with the enactment of the *Commercial Code* in 1898. However, regulations regarding insurance operations of the *Commercial Code* had only a short-lived validity, as with the enactment of the *Insurance Business Act* in 1900 a separate body of law with the sole purpose of regulating insurance companies' business activities and financial reporting requirements was introduced by Japanese legislators. The *Insurance Business Act* of 1900 was modelled after the German "Insurance Supervision Act" and contained additional requirements and regulations to the ones already being stipulated in the *Commercial Code*. As important additionally introduced requirements, the necessities to establish "technical reserves", to apply accounting standards and to publish financial results of business operations on an annual basis can be named.[26] [27] Furthermore, the *Insurance Business Act* of 1900 introduced the prohibition for insurance companies to simultaneously

22 Cf. *Tsutsui* et. al. (2004), p. 5.
23 Cf. *Tatsuki* (2003), p. 155.
24 Cf. Japan Business History Institute (1992), p. 19.
25 Cf. Japan Business History Institute (1993), p. 21.
26 Cf. Japan Business History Institute (1980), p. 36.
27 Cf. Japan Business History Institute (1992), p. 22.

conduct or engage into life insurance as well as non-life insurance business operations, leading to a clear separation of Japanese insurers into two groups of companies.[28]

As a reaction to the introduction of insurance specific legislation, the Japanese insurance industry experienced a series of ordered dissolutions of insurance companies, which were unable to fulfill newly stipulated requirements regarding adequate levels of liability reserves, the utilization of appropriate statistical methods and the application of suitable accounting standards.[29] [30] In the case of the nation's life insurance industry, seventeen life insurance companies stopped their operations and were dissolved during the period of 1900 to 1902, significantly reducing the number of domestic insurance companies operating on the Japanese life insurance market.[31]

With the introduction of the first *Insurance Business Act* in 1900, the infant stage of the Japanese modern insurance industry can be considered to have ended. Summarizing the above stated, it can be said that the period between the inception of the first modern domestic insurance company in 1879 and the enactment of the *Insurance Business Act* in 1900 was characterized of being rather chaotic, with the majority of newly established modern insurance companies operating in a highly opaque manner within a highly unregulated, yet competitive, industry. Waves of incorporation as well as bankruptcies of badly operated insurance firms were the result of these circumstances. Nevertheless, with the enactment of the *Insurance Business Act* in 1900, the introduction of regulations regarding reserve building methods, accounting standards and publication of financial results largely changed these characteristics, causing companies that did not comply with these new standards to be liquidated.

Looking upon the period from the point of view of various types of organizational forms, it can be said that, despite the high number of companies entering the insurance business in Japan, none of these companies chose an organizational form different from the stock company form. Thus, all companies that successfully incepted and started their operations between the years 1879 to 1900 were stock insurance companies. As a result, one can also consider respective period of time as a monopoly era for the stock company form. One reason for this development was that no official legal basis for the inception of neither a mutual insurance company nor a cooperative existed under Japanese legislation. Nevertheless, this situation changed with the introduction of the *Insurance Business Act* in 1900, which officially introduced the

---

[28] Cf. Japan Business History Institute (1980), p. 36.

[29] Cf. *Yoneyama* (2012), p. 502.

[30] Cf. *Yingying* (2013), p. 9.

[31] Cf. *Lehrman* (2003), p. 45.

mutual insurance company as the second legal form permitted to operate insurance in Japan and thus allowed to be chosen by insurance companies as their official form of organization.

2.2 The introduction of the mutual insurance company form and its influence upon the Japanese insurance industry's development prior to the Second World War

Following the enactment of the *Insurance Business Act* (IBA) in 1900, the Japanese insurance industry experienced the ordered dissolution of a significant number of insurance companies, which were found to be unable to comply to newly introduced regulations and legal requirements by Japanese authorities. Nevertheless, with the demand for fire, marine and life insurance strongly increasing throughout the first two decades of the 20th century, the number of domestic insurance companies steadily increased during respective period of time. Whereas 26 domestic life insurance companies existed at the end of fiscal year 1905, the number increased to 42 until the end of fiscal year 1920.[32] Moreover, with 26 life insurance companies being initiated and 10 companies being liquidated between fiscal years 1906 to 1920, it can be seen that the nation's life insurance industry was subject to a high fluctuation of market participating insurance companies.[33] In the case of the Japanese domestic non-life insurance industry, the number of domestic insurance companies increased from 17 operating firms in fiscal year 1909 to 47 by the end of fiscal year 1920.[34] [35] In total 35 domestic non-life insurance companies were established within respective period of time, while a total of five companies were liquidated.[36]

In addition to newly financial and operational requirements stipulated in the *Insurance Business Act*, the new legislation also introduced the mutual insurance company as the second type of legal form permitted to operate insurance besides the stock company. In spite of the large number of newly established insurance companies in the non-life insurance industry, only one of these companies was incepted as a mutual company, being the *Toa Mutual Fire Insurance Company* in 1909. Respective mutual fire insurance company was further dissolved in 1915.[37] With no other than the non-life insurance company of the mu-

32 Cf. *Lehmann* (2003), p. 45.

33 Cf. Ibid, p. 45.

34 Cf. Department of Agriculture and Commerce (1912), p. 12-19.

35 Cf. Department of Agriculture and Commerce (1923), p. 12-19.

36 Cf. Department of Agriculture and Commerce (1912) - (1923), v.p.

37 Cf. *Yingying* (2015), p. 217.

tual company form being established until the late 1940s, it can be said that the mutual company form was not able to establish successfully a presence on the Japanese property and casualty insurance market prior to the post-World War II era.

Contrary to the above described development on the nation's property and casualty insurance market, mutual insurance companies were able to enter successfully and establish a lasting presence on the Japanese life insurance market during the first two decades of the 20th century. In fact, the successful entrance of mutual life insurance companies into the Japanese life insurance industry significantly influenced product strategies and business operations of their stock company competitors, leading to an assimilation of stock life insurance companies towards mutual insurance companies with respect to operational characteristics.

In total, seven mutual life insurance companies were incorporated between the years 1902 to 1919. Among these seven mutual life insurance companies special attention has to be given to the *Dai-ichi Mutual Life Insurance Company*, being initiated in 1902, and the *Chiyoda Mutual Life Insurance Company*, being incepted in 1904.[38] Representing the first two mutual insurance companies that were established on the Japanese life insurance market, both companies were able to catch up to the top three market leading stock life insurance companies, namely the *Nippon Life Insurance Co.*, the *Teikoku Life Insurance Co.* and the *Meiji Life Insurance Co.*, in terms of annual premium collected and total amount insured until the mid-1920s. Moreover, these two mutual life insurance companies were predominantly responsible for occurring changes of operational practices of domestic stock life insurance companies during the 1910s and 1920s.

Two major changes caused to the Japanese life insurance industry by the market entrance of the mutual life insurance company form and the success of the *Dai-ichi Mutual Life Insurance Co.* and the *Chiyoda Mutual Life Insurance Co.* can be identified. These changes are the development of profit-participating life and endowment insurance policies into the significantly predominant types of policies underwritten on the Japanese life insurance market and the introduction of predetermined policyholder dividend rates by all major domestic stock life insurance companies.[39] [40]

---

38 The other five mutual life insurance companies, being established during the first two decades of the 20th century, were the *Kokko Mutual Life Insurance Company* in 1908, the *Tokai Mutual Life Insurance Company* in 1910, the *Horai Mutual Life Insurance Company* in 1911, the *Chuo Mutual Life Insurance Company* in 1913 and the *Nihon Ishi Kyosai Mutual Life Insurance Company* in 1919.

39 Cf. *Yingying* (2015), p. 230-234.

40 Cf. *Nishio* (1995), p. 54-55.

After its inception in 1902, the *Dai-ichi Mutual Life Insurance Co.* introduced an annually cumulative dividend distribution system with a predetermined dividend rate of 3 per cent in 1906, being the first life insurer to do so. While policyholder dividend rates were only distributed on a five-year period basis, the system allowed policyholders to easily estimate annually assigned policy dividends by multiplying accomplished premium payments, earned years and the fixed dividend rate with each other.[41] In 1910, the *Chiyoda Mutual Life Insurance Co.* adopted the same policyholder dividend distribution system in the course of launching a new type of endowment insurance, but shortened the dividend distribution period to three years.[42] [43] Two years later, *Chiyoda Life* increased its predetermined policy-dividend rate to 4 per cent.[44] Moreover, it has to be mentioned here that both companies heavily advertised their organizational differences in comparison to stock insurance companies. Doing so the mutual companies argued that while stock companies' primary objective was to maximize profits of their shareholders, the mutual insurance companies' major purpose was to maximize the benefits of their policyholders, who at the same time were owners of mutual companies.[45]

The introduction of respective policyholder dividend system and advertisement efforts proved to be strategically successful and beneficial for both companies. By the end of fiscal year 1919, the *Dai-ichi Mutual Life Insurance Co.* had become the eleventh largest life insurance company out of 37 actively operating companies in terms of total amount insured. At the same time, the *Chiyoda Mutual Life Insurance Co.* had already become the fourth largest operating domestic life insurance company, a position it had reached for the first time during fiscal year 1911.[46] [47]

As a countermeasure to the forthcoming of the mutual insurance company form and as a reaction to the successful entrance of mutual life insurance companies, more and more stock insurance companies began to introduce profit participating insurance products and started to adapt predetermined policyholder dividend schemes during the first two decades of the 20th century.[48] [49] With respect to the three-industry leading stock insurance companies, it can be said that in the case of the *Teikoku Life Insurance Co., Ltd.* management introduced the first

41 Cf. *Tsutsui* et al. (2004), p. 4.
42 Cf. *Yingying* (2015), p. 231.
43 Cf. *Tatsuki* (2003), p. 158.
44 Cf. *Yingying* (2015), p. 231.
45 Cf. Ibid, p. 230.
46 Cf. Department of Agriculture and Commerce (1914), p. 48-49.
47 Cf. Department of Agriculture and Commerce (1921), p. 18-19.
48 Cf. *Yingying* (2015), p. 229-231.
49 Cf. *Nishio* (1995), p. 54-55.

type of profit participating policy in 1902, with the company's president believing in the potential requirement of mutualization in the foreseeable future.[50] In 1912, in the case of the *Meiji Life Insurance Company*, two profit participating insurance product types were lauchned, namely profit participating limited-payment whole life insurance and endowment insurance, in addition to the original profit participating whole life insurance product. Prior to that the company had already introduced predetermined policyholder dividend rates.[51] Contrary to the *Meiji Life* and *Teikoku Life Insurance Co., Ltd*, the *Nippon Life Insurance Co., Ltd.* did not offer profit-participating endowment or whole life insurance products before the year 1915.[52] [53] A fixed policyholder dividend rate of 3 per cent was further introduced as late as 1925.[54] Furthermore, an annual policyholder dividend insurance distribution scheme was introduced as late as in 1929.[55] Therefore, the *Nippon Life Insurance Co., Ltd.*, having been Japan's largest domestic life insurance company during respective period of time, seems to have reacted much slower to the forthcoming of mutual life insurance companies and the trend of profit participating insurance products.

Besides the two industry leaders *Meiji Life* and *Teikoku Life* also the majority of small and medium sized life insurance companies of the stock company form rapidly adopted policyholder dividend schemes and introduced profit-participating policies to their product portfolio during the late 1900s and 1910s. This development can be identified in table 1, which shows the development of in force insurance policies and annual business underwritten with respect to profit-participating and non-participating policy types. With respect to whole life insurance policies, only six small and medium size stock life insurance companies offered profit participating whole life insurance products in 1909, while only 7.8 % of in force policies were of respective product type. In the case of endowment insurance, already 13 small and medium life insurers of the stock company form offered profit-participating policy types. Furthermore, profit participating endowment policies already accounted for 33.5 % of all in force policies of respective type.[56] With regards to the share of profit participating policies of new business underwritten, 24.9 % of new whole life insurance policies underwritten by stock life insurance companies in 1910 were profit participating policies, while

[50] Cf. *Yingying* (2015), p. 230.

[51] Cf. *Yingying* (2015), p. 229-230.

[52] Cf. Department of Agriculture and Commerce (1916), p. 70-75, 78-79, 84-85.

[53] Cf. Department of Agriculture and Commerce (1917), p. 70-73, 78-81.

[54] Cf. *Yingying* (2015), p. 233.

[55] Cf. the Japan Business History Institute (1992), p. 96.

[56] Here it has to be considered nevertheless, that endowment products were the primary products of all then existing mutual life insurance companies, accounting for 97.4% of all in force policies held by mutual insurers at that point in time.

in the case of endowment insurance policies sold by stock life insurance companies, the share of profit-participating policies accounted for approximately 47.3 % in the same year. These figures increased continuously over the following decade. As shown in table 1, the number of stock life insurance companies offering profit participating policies had increased to 18 out of 24 during fiscal year 1917, with 61.5 % of newly underwritten whole life policies being of the profit-participating type. In the case of endowment insurance, all 32 stock life insurance companies offered profit participating products of respective insurance type as of 1917. Moreover, profit participating policies accounted for 88 % of all endowment insurance policies underwritten by domestic stock insurance companies. This trend continued throughout the following years, as can be seen in table 1. In the light of these figures, it can be said that within a rather short period of time, profit participating policies became by far the dominating type of life insurance policy sold by domestic Japanese stock life insurance companies. Finally, the table also shows that endowment insurance became by far the dominating type of life insurance underwritten on the Japanese life insurance market, being a major characteristic of the intensifying competition between mutual and stock life insurance companies during respective period of time.

Considering the above presented development, part of literature concludes that an assimilation of Japanese stock life insurance companies towards the mutual company form took place during the first two decades of the 20th century. Stock life insurance companies unanimously changed and focused onto profit participating policies, while at the same time introducing schemes of predetermined rates of annual policyholder dividends, despite this strategy being in direct competition to stock companies' primary objective of maximizing shareholder revenue. As a possible explanation for this development *Yingying* names the observable high ownership concentration of domestic stock life insurance companies, the avoidance of sudden changes of ownership by inhibiting speculative stock trading as well as the fact that stock life insurance companies were mostly unlisted. In other words, many stock life insurance companies were owned predominantly by a small amount of loyal long-term major shareholders. Sharing profit with policyholders in terms to remain competitive instead of withdrawing from the market can be regarded to have been in the interest of these long-term shareholders, if implying that their major interest was to benefit from the companies' long-term profitability.[57]

Despite the mutual company form under the leadership of the *Dai-Ichi Mutual Life Insurance Co.* and the *Chiyoda Mutual Life Insurance Co.* being able to successfully enter the Japanese life insurance market

57 Cf. *Yingying* (2015), p. 239-240.

Table 1: Development of in force life insurance policies and annual business underwritten with respect to profit-participating and non-participating policy types

	whole life insurance - business in force				endowment insurance - business in force			
fiscal year	profit participating	non - profit participating	❶	❷	profit participating	non - profit participation	❶	❷
1909	25 811	304 620	7,8%	92,2%	227 719	452 001	33,5%	66,5%
1910	35 077	304 832	10,3%	89,7%	280 554	475 081	37,1%	62,9%
1911	46 356	315 579	12,8%	87,2%	359 371	518 390	40,9%	59,1%
1912	60 848	317 322	16,1%	83,9%	465953	567 596	45,1%	54,9%
1913	73 378	317 875	18,8%	81,2%	623 252	613 298	50,4%	49,6%
1914	82 485	312 565	20,9%	79,1%	760 485	617 763	55,2%	44,8%
1915	111 588	261 343	29,9%	70,1%	898 280	461 288	66,1%	33,9%
1916	111 755	251 463	30,8%	69,2%	955 605	445 112	68,2%	31,8%
1917	119 414	246 156	32,7%	67,3%	1 132 067	435 008	72,2%	27,8%
1918	128 363	238 358	35,0%	65,0%	1 532 313	327 668	82,4%	17,6%
1919	139 315	233 158	37,4%	62,6%	1 978 292	327 301	85,8%	14,2%

	whole life insurance - annual new business				endowment insurance - annual new business			
fiscal year	profit participating	non - profit participation	❶	❷	profit participating	non - profit participation	❶	❷
1910	11 034	30 774	26,4%	73,6%	95 075	96 402	49,7%	50,3%
1911	16 455	32 465	33,6%	66,4%	128 418	104 026	55,2%	44,8%
1912	20 272	27 265	42,6%	57,4%	161 774	115 018	58,4%	41,6%
1913	20 260	25 628	44,2%	55,8%	222 855	116 467	65,7%	34,3%
1914	18 588	19 556	48,7%	51,3%	236 053	87 751	72,9%	27,1%
1915	14 917	9 561	60,9%	39,1%	194 297	40 383	82,8%	17,2%
1916	14 326	10 499	57,7%	42,3%	217 381	48 316	81,8%	18,2%
1917	18 366	10 198	64,3%	35,7%	300 990	34 910	89,6%	10,4%
1918	18 188	6 863	72,6%	27,4%	421 131	18 682	95,8%	4,2%
1919	19 106	6 273	75,3%	24,7%	580 466	19 536	96,7%	3,3%

❶ = share of profit participating policies
❷ = share of non - profit participating policies

Sources: The Department of Agriculture and Commerce (1912)-(1921), table established by author.

and conquer a significant amount of market share within the first two decades of mutual insurance companies' existence, stock companies remained the dominant form of organization in terms of number of existing companies and controlled market share. Table 2 presents the development of both organizational forms performance and market share in terms of total amount insured collected between years 1908 to 1931. In view of these figures, stock insurance companies' change towards mostly selling profit-participating types of policies, which were highly similar to those sold by mutual life insurers, appears to have been successful. As a result, there was also no need for mutualization of domestic stock life insurance companies during respective period of time, partially contributing to the explanation why only a limited number of mutual life insurance companies existed throughout the first three decades of the 20th century in Japan. Nevertheless, with 96 % of new life insurance business underwritten being profit-participating insurance products with predetermined dividend rates in 1926, a clear assimilation of domestic stock life insurance companies towards mutual insurance companies in terms of operation characteristics can be recognized.[58] As a result, it appears that the "organizational differences between the stock company and mutual company became ambiguous"[59] during the years of the pre-World War II Japanese life insurance industry. When describing the development of the Japanese life insurance market during the first two decades of the 20th century, it can be said that the Japanese life insurance industry as a whole recorded an almost continuous growth of business between the years 1907 to 1920. Within a respective fourteen years period the Japanese life insurance industry was able to extent its business by about 713 % measured in terms of total amount insured.[60]

From the beginning of the 1920s onwards, Japan experienced a long-lasting economic depression until the early 1930s. Despite the nation's unfavorable economic development, the Japanese life insurance industry continued to expand its business on an annual basis. Yet, annual rates of growth were significantly smaller in comparison to the 1900s and 1910s. In general, competition increased on the Japanese life insurance market. Here two groups of companies became distinguishable based upon their product strategies employed. The first group consisted out of companies which followed a strategy of comparatively high premium rates charged against comparatively high rates of predetermined policyholder dividends promised. The second group of companies employed an opposite strategy, offering policies for low premium rates in comparison to policies offered by companies of the first group. At the

[58] Cf. *Nishio* (1995), p. 55.

[59] *Yingying* (2015), p. 241.

[60] See table 2.

same time, these companies nevertheless offered significantly lower annual policyholder dividend rates. Companies belonging to the first group were the *Dai-Ichi Mutual Insurance Co.*, the *Chiyoda Mutual Insurance Co.* and the *Teikoku Life Insurance Co., Ltd.*, whereas the industry leading *Nippon Life Insurance Co., Ltd.* and the *Meiji Life Insurance Co., Ltd.* belonged to the second group of companies. In total, high premium – high dividend products proved to be the more favorable types of products on the Japanese life insurance market throughout the 1920s, especially among the newly developing urban middle-class population. As a result, also companies of the latter group, including *Nippon* and *Meiji Life*, ultimately shifted to offering "high premium – high dividend" products during the mid-1930s.[61] [62]

Other important developments observable on the Japanese life insurance market from 1927 onwards were a continuous increase of market concentration as well as the governmentally ordered dissolution or merger of several small-scale life insurance companies. The trigger for the former development was the occurrence of a banking crisis in 1927, causing several small-scale banking institutions to go bankrupt. Despite life insurance companies not being directly affected by this crisis, it initiated a trend among policyholders of small and medium scale life insurers to cancel their policy and purchase life insurance policies from market leading large-scale life insurance companies. The major reason behind this behavior was an increasing distrust of the Japanese public against small scale financial institutions' financial soundness, resulting from the occurrence of mentioned above crisis. This trend continued throughout the whole 1930s, resulting that the majority of small and medium scale life insurers experienced a loss of market share.[63] [64] As one of the only exceptions among small and medium size companies, *zaibatsu* affiliated life insurers can be named, being initiated or purchased by respective financial conglomerates during the first two decades of the 20th century. These conglomerate affiliated companies were in fact able to notably expand their business during the late 1920s and early 1930s.

In additio, the second important development, being governmentally enforced dissolutions and mergers of ailing small and medium life insurance companies from 1927 onwards, contributed to the observable increasing market concentration. In the aftermath of the banking crisis in 1927. the *Insurance Business Act* (IBA) was being revised and, including among other changes increased the levels of policy reserves. As a consequence of new regulations introduced, several life insurance companies, not being able to comply with new regulations, were

61 Cf. *Tsutsui* et al. (2004), p. 15.
62 Cf. *Tatsuki* (2003), p. 161-164.
63 Cf. *Tsutsui* et al. (2004), p. 7-8.
64 Cf. *Tatsuki* (2003), p. 166.

Table 2: Business and Market Share development of mutual and stock insurance companies on the Japanese insurance market, FY 1907-1931

Year	Total amount insured by stock insurance companies*	Share of total amount insured by stock companies	Total amount insured by mutual insurance companies*	Share of total amount insured by mutual companies
1907	¥326.617	93,3%	¥23.572	6,7%
1908	¥390.647	92,3%	¥32.450	7,7%
1909	¥437.404	91,1%	¥42.752	8,9%
1910	¥480.144	89,2%	¥58.023	10,8%
1911	¥561.514	86,9%	¥84.654	13,1%
1912	¥670.692	85,1%	¥117.556	14,9%
1913	¥810.431	84,1%	¥152.880	15,9%
1914	¥910.587	83,9%	¥174.451	16,1%
1915	¥899.321	83,9%	¥172.904	16,1%
1916	¥952.225	84,2%	¥179.188	15,8%
1917	¥1.086.328	83,8%	¥209.576	16,2%
1918	¥1.345.140	85,0%	¥238.089	15,0%
1919	¥1.736.042	84,1%	¥327.614	15,9%
1920	¥2.079.460	83,3%	¥418.233	16,7%
1921	¥2.303.187	82,00%	¥505.617	18,00%
1922	¥2.590.538	81,06%	¥605.362	18,94%
1923	¥2.799.582	80,24%	¥689.480	19,76%
1924	¥3.218.529	80,39%	¥784.983	19,61%
1925	¥3.704.406	79,54%	¥952.729	20,46%
1926	¥3.996.448	77,91%	¥1.133.146	22,09%
1927	¥4.216.902	76,36%	¥1.305.481	23,64%
1931	**¥5 467 687**	**71,53%**	**¥2 176 171**	**28,47%**

* in thousand ¥

Sources: Department of Agriculture and Commerce (1912)-(1915), (1917), (1920), (1923), Department of Commerce and Industry (1925)-(1927), (1929), (1933), Yoneyama (2015: 40-41), table established by author.

ordered to either merge or to transfer their active business as a whole to financially stable companies and to dissolve. Here, the merger of the five small-scale mutual life insurance companies, being established in the late 1900s and 1910s, has to be mentioned. After a governmental inspection of the *Kokko Mutual Life Insurance Company* in 1932 resulted in the authorities' conclusion that the company was unable to meet reserve requirements, the merger of small scale mutual life insurers was ordered. Consequentially, the *Showa Mutual Life Insurance Company* was established in 1934 as respective five mutual insurance companies' successor company.[65] Overall, the total number of actively operating life insurance companies was reduced by twelve during the governmentally enforced industry reorganization between the years 1927 to 1934.[66]

With respect to the development of the Japanese property and casualty insurance industry from the viewpoint of different forms of organization, the mutual insurance company form was not able to gain a lasting foothold on the Japanese non-life insurance market. Regarding the economic development of the nation's non-life insurance industry ,it can be said that the first two decades of the 20th century were mostly characterized by continuous and partially outstanding rates of growth. With the outbreak of the Russian-Japanese War, the nation's marine insurance industry experienced a strong increase of business, causing the entrance of several new marine insurance operating domestic companies, elevating the total number of domestic marine insurers to ten by the end of 1908. Furthermore, another period of high growth rates was experienced by Japanese marine insurers between the years 1915 and 1919, caused by the positive impact of the outbreak of World War I onto the nation's exporting activities. In fact, marine insurance companies were able to increase premium income fivefold between the years 1914 and 1918. Resulting from this development the number of marine insurance operating companies had further increased to 34 by 1919.[67] [68]

Whereas growth of business was also recorded on a continuous basis in the case of the Japanese fire insurance industry during the first two decades of the 20th century, the entrance of additional domestic as well as foreign companies into the fire insurance segment resulted in severe price competition. At this point, it has to be mentioned that especially foreign companies were able to establish a significant presence in the fire insurance market, increasing their market share from approximately 14.1 % in 1907 to above 30 % in 1917 in terms of annual premium payments collected. Thus, the Japanese fire insurance market

---

65 Cf. *Nishio* (1995), p. 54-55.

66 Cf. *Lehrman* (2003), p. 45.

67 Cf. Japan Business History Institute (1993), p. 40-41.

68 Cf. Japan Business History Institute (1980), p. 61.

can be regarded as having developed a fairly international character during the first two decades of the 20th century.

Resulting from the situation of severe price competition, attempts to introduce industry wide standardized fire insurance premium rates were being performed as early as 1907. Nevertheless, an industry-wide honored agreement was not being able to be reached before the inception of the *Japan Fire Coalition Insurance Association* in 1917.[69] Only with the inception of mentioned association by eighteen domestic and twenty-four foreign fire insurance companies, originally having emerged out of the earlier founded *Fire Insurance Association*, a first premium tariff rates agreement, which was honoured on an industry wide basis, was able to be agreed upon and introduced. Resulting thereof, competitive behaviour was reduced significantly, and premium rates were raised to an economically reasonable level.

After two decades mostly characterized by substantial economic growth rates, Japan entered into a period of economic depression from the beginning of the 1920s onwards, lasting until the early 1930s. While the nation's fire insurance industry was not strongly affected by this depression and recorded stable rates of growth throughout the 1920s, the nation's marine insurance industry experienced a severe decline in business. The major reason for this development was rapidly declining rates of export experienced by the Japanese economy in the aftermath of World War I. While foreign demand for Japanese commodities had skyrocketed during World War I, demand declined sharply once the former warring European nations' economies returned their focus from producing war-related goods and munitions back to the production of commercial goods and as a consequence re-entered foreign market which were key clients of Japanese products throughout World War I. Resulting in a situation of over-tonnage within the Japanese shipping industry, the nation's marine insurance industry experienced a devastating decline in premium income, dropping from approximately 36,7 million Yen in fiscal year 1920 to 19,6 million Yen in fiscal year 1922. While slowly recovering throughout the late 1920s, the world economic crisis from 1929 onwards did not allow the Japanese marine insurance industry to return to previous heights of premium income until the mid-1930s.[70] [71]

Additionally, in the case of the Japanese fire insurance industry the occurrence of the world economic crisis caused a decline of business. Nevertheless, the industry experiencing growth of business again from

---

69 Cf. *Yoneyama* (2012), p. 505.

70 Department of Agriculture and Commerce (1923), v.p.,

71 Department of Commerce and Industry (1926), (1928), (1930), (1933), (1935), (1937).

1932 onwards.[72] Moreover, the total number of domestic non-life insurance companies had increased to 49 by the end of fiscal year 1935.[73]

In 1937, the Second Sino-Japanese War broke out, marking the beginning of the Second World War in Asia. In the course of the war, extraordinary laws for bundling resources for the war effort were enforced over all types of industry, including the nation's insurance industry. The development of the Japanese insurance industry during the war years 1937 to 1945 will be presented in the next chapter.

Considering once more all the above mentioned, it can be said that the Japanese life insurance industry was characterized by the entrance and successful emergence of the mutual insurance company form. In spite of the fact that the stock company remained the dominant legal form existing on the Japanese life insurance industry during the first four decades of the 20th century, the mutual life insurance companies significantly influenced operational characteristics of the former, as offering profit-participating policies and policyholder dividend schemes with predetermined dividend rates. Being highly similar to those of mutual companies, it became the unified norm for all life insurance operating stock companies. As a result, an assimilation of Japanese stock life insurance companies in terms of operation characteristics towards mutual insurance companies is identifiable, causing stock companies and mutual companies to resemble each other more closely.

2.3 The Japanese Insurance Industry during war-time economic control

The outbreak of the Second Sino-Japanese War marked the beginning of a period of steadily increasing governmental control over the Japanese insurance industry, lasting until the end of World War Two in September 1945. Until then Japanese insurance companies had factually lost all sovereignty regarding their business operations. Moreover, the Japanese insurance industry experienced a successive process of reorganization during the war years, with the Japanese government strongly reducing the number of insurers companies through ordering the several dissolutions and mergers.[74]

Shortly following the outbreak of the Second Sino Japanese War in 1937, the Japanese government introduced several new legislations in order to gain control over the inflow and outflow of monetary funds as well as physical commodities. Among these legislations the Japanese government introduced the so-called *Extraordinary Funds Adjustment*

[72] Cf. Department of Commerce and Industry (1933), (1935), (1937).

[73] Cf. Department of Commerce and Industry (1937), p. 18.

[74] Cf. *Yatsui* (1951), p. 17.

Act in 1937, which heavily restricted Japanese insurance companies in their ability to independently manage their investment activities. Among other the law prohibited insurance companies to issue long-term loans to civilian industries and required insurance companies to apply for approval of the responsible regulatory authority for any kind of future investment activities.[75] [76] [77] Life insurance companies were further required to purchase shares of companies from industries of "national importance", which were mostly corporations engaged in the production of war-related commodities.[78] In addition, newly introduced regulations required Japanese insurance companies to invest into large amounts of governmentally issued war-bonds. In the case of life insurance industry, the twelve industry-leading companies agreed upon increasing the amount of war-bonds up to a minimum level of 7 % in 1937. This level was elevated to 10 % in the following year and applied to the sixteen largest life insurance companies. Moreover, non-life insurance companies became required to hold at a minimum amount of war-bonds equal to 8 % of their working assets in 1937. These requirements were steadily raised throughout the progress of the war, thus also increasing the effective share of government-bonds held by insurance companies. While the average amount of government bonds held by life insurance companies accounting for an approximate 11 % of life insurance companies' assets, these figures had risen to 21 % by 1941 and further increased above an amount equal to 35 % in 1944.[79] Additionally, in the case of Japanese non-life insurance companies the level of war-bonds held increased steadily throughout the war years. However, with only 9 % of total war bonds purchased by insurance companies being held by property and casualty insurers, life insurance companies' significantly higher importance as war-bond subscribers compared to the nation's non-life insurance companies during World War II becomes apparent.[80] [81]

In 1939, the Japanese government introduced a new *Insurance Business Act* and started a process of reorganizing the nation's insurance industry through ordering mergers or dissolutions of several insurance companies. In doing so, the total number of property and casualty insurance operating companies was reduced from a forty-seven companies in 1938 to sixteen in 1945.[82] [83] The number of life insurance com-

75 Cf. *Flath* (2000), p. 63.
76 Cf. Japan Business History Institute (1993), p. 72.
77 Cf. *Flath* (2000), p. 193.
78 Cf. *Tatsuki* (2003), p.174.
79 Cf. Ibid, p. 176.
80 Cf. Japan Business History Institute (1993), p. 72.
81 Cf. Japan Business History Institute (1980), p. 104.
82 Cf. *Yatsui* (1951), p. 26.
83 Cf. Department of Commerce and Industry (1939), p. 20-21.

panies was reduced from thirty-three in 1937 to twenty-one by the end of 1944.[84] In the course of this reorganization, the *Showa Mutual Life Insurance Co.*, having been initiated in 1934 as a successor company for originally existing five small scale mutual life insurers, was ordered to transfer its business to the *Dai-Ichi Mutual Life Co.* and to dissolve.[85] Reasons for this reorganization were emerging ideals of transforming the formerly free market economy into a governmentally controlled economy, as well as the government's objective of shifting labour force of civilian industries to war-related industries.[86]

In May 1942, the governmentally required inception of the *Life Insurance Control Association* (LICA) was performed with the association's major task to execute direct governmental control over Japan's life insurance industry. At around the same time, the prior established *Japan Non-Life Insurance Association* was transformed into the control association for the nation's property and casualty insurance industry.[87] [88] From the perspective of business performance of the Japanese insurance industry, it can be said that during the early war years insurance companies experienced solid rates of business growth. Nevertheless, with the progress of the Pacific War, Japanese insurance companies began to experience increasing economic hardship. From summer 1944 onwards, US air raids were performed on a daily basis, leading to rapidly increasing claims payable by both, life and non-life insurance companies. It was during this time that the demand for war-risk insurance, a type of insurance introduced and directly accepted by the Japanese government, but underwritten by Japanese non-life insurance companies, became heavily demanded by the nation's general public. This kind of insurance was further made mandatory during the last year of the war, if insuring buildings against the risk of fire. Furthermore, a governmentally guaranteed war-risk insurance scheme was also introduced for the nation's life insurance industry in 1942. Under this scheme, the Japanese State directly accepted risks of war-related deaths and injuries, whereas life insurance companies operated as the scheme's underwriting intermediaries.[89]

On September 2nd 1945, the Japanese Empire officially surrendered to the United States of America, which marked the end of World War II. In the aftermath of the war, the Japanese economy underwent a severe process of democratization and re-liberalization under US control, in the course of which large parts of the Japanese insurance industry underwent a sever reorganization.

[84] Cf. *Tatsuki* (2003), p. 159.

[85] Cf. *Nishio* (1995), p. 54-55.

[86] Cf. *Yatsui* (1951), p. 26.

[87] Cf. Japan Business History Institute (1980), p. 108.

[88] Cf. Japan Business History Institute (1992), p. 112-113.

[89] Cf. Japan Business History Institute (1992), p. 115.

2.4 The reorganization of the Japanese insurance industry after the end of World War II

After the end of World War II the Japanese insurance industry found itself in a disastrous situation, which required the industry to be severely restructured throughout the immediate post-war years. In the case of the nation's life insurance industry, this reorganization resulted in a wave of mutualization, making the mutual company the predominant form of organization on the Japanese life insurance market.

To fully comprehend the motives of this development, the immediate situation of life insurance companies following the end of World War II has to be considered. Following the war, life insurance companies faced a devastating financial situation due to several reasons. On the one hand, companies lost all their foreign assets located in formerly occupied areas such as Korea, Taiwan and China, into which life insurers were required to invest during the war years. These foreign assets accounted for approximately twenty percent of total assets held by life insurance companies at the end of the war.[90] Furthermore, life insurance companies experienced high losses of receivables resulting from loans issued to companies, which had been operating in the nation's armament industry, but went insolvent after the war. On the other hand, the indirect stop of governmental *War Indemnification Payments*, originally being promised to war-commodity producing companies during the war, was a major reason for respective companies' failure.[91] Lastly, also shares held by life insurance companies, having been issued by companies of the then insolvent armament industry, became worthless.[92] [93] Resulting from this situation, life insurance companies themselves were highly threatened by bankruptcy, as were many other Japanese financial institutions.

For the purpose of avoiding the imminent collapse of the Japanese financial industry, the Japanese government in compliance with the Allied Force's *General Head Quarter's* (GHQ) issued the *Financial Institution Emergency Accounting Measures Ordinance* in August 1946, which introduced measures for the reorganization and restructuring of Japan's financial industry. Under respective legislation, financial institutions became required to separate their assets and liabilities into two groups, namely old and new accounts. In new accounts, secured assets required for the continuation of their future business were placed,

---

90 Ibid, p. 139.
91 Cf. *Kurogi* (2014), p. 106-107.
92 Cf. Japan Business History Institute (1992), p. 139.
93 Cf. *Kurogi* (2014), p. 106.

while assets whose value were going to extraordinarily depreciate were placed in old accounts.[94] [95]

In the case of life insurance companies, new accounts included among other cash, government and municipal bonds as well as interbank loans, while liabilities transferred to new accounts included policy reserves for insurance contracts with coverage of up to ten-thousand Yen and various public liabilities. The majority of remaining assets and liabilities, including foreign assets seized from insurance companies, shares of insolvent companies, receivables against them as well as policy reserves for contracts above ten-thousand Yen, were placed in old accounts. In addition, legislation ordered to freeze old accounts, prohibiting any further payments for insurance placed under them.

Provisions for handling losses, which resulted from the devaluation of assets in old accounts, were further introduced with the *Financial Institution Rehabilitation Law* in October 1946. Respective legislation enabled insurance companies to write off losses caused by the devaluation of assets held in old accounts, whereas losses had to be amortized through reducing capital as well as using "[…] policy reserves of the insurance contracts in the 'old' accounts"[96]. Moreover, the *Financial Institution Rehabilitation Law* required financial institutions to submit plans for the restructuring of companies, including outlines for a potential continuation, liquidation or merger of respective companies. A further option was also the initiation of successor companies.[97] In the case of life insurance companies, respective legislation stated that in the event of a company being unable to cover losses caused by the devaluation of assets by using the total amount of capital held, respective company would be required to transfer all its remaining in-force insurance policies to another financially stable life insurance company, including a potential successor company.[98] With Japanese life insurance being unable to cover losses of old accounts with capital held, the inevitable choice became to establish successor companies and transfer in-force insurance contracts to them.[99]

In addition, the Japanese life insurance industry was confronted with a situation of low demand for life insurance, strongly increasing operational cost due to a high inflation as well as a decreasing public trust and confidence into Japanese life insurance companies, caused by the utilization of large quantities of policy reserves for the coverage of mentioned extraordinary losses.[100] Resulting from this situation, Japa-

[94] Cf. Institute of Fiscal and Monetary Policy (2010), p. 31-32.

[95] Cf. *Yingying* (2013), p. 185.

[96] Japan Business History Institute (1992), p. 141.

[97] Cf. Institute of Fiscal and Monetary Policy (2010), p. 33.

[98] Cf. Japan Business History Institute (1992), p. 142.

[99] Cf. Ibid, p. 142.

[100] Cf. *Kurogi* (2014), p. 106-107.

nese life insurance companies began to push for the inception of successor companies, fearing of further deterioration of their public image if continuing to operate business under an instable company structure.

Nevertheless, with evaluations of assets under the *Financial Institution Rehabilitation Law* expected to be under process throughout all of 1947, the immediate establishment of successor companies was not possible under the *Financial Institution Rehabilitation Law*. Confronted with this circumstance, the *Nippon Life Insurance Co., Ltd.* seized the initiative and applied for the approval of establishing a successor company of the mutual company form under the regular *Insurance Business Act* (IBA) instead of the *Financial Institution Rehabilitation Law* to the Japanese *Ministry of Finance*. The reason for *Nippon Life* to do so was that by being able to establish a successor company under the IBA, the company would be able to progress with sales activities and business operation under an already newly independent company, even though the settlement of old accounts under the *Financial Institution Rehabilitation Law* was still underway.[101] Under this application, old accounts were proposed to be integrated in the new company, once their final disposition was performed. Approval for the inception was granted to the *Nippon Life Insurance Co.* in May 1947, thus, making the initiation of a successor company under the provisions of the *Financial Institution Rehabilitation Law* obsolete.[102] [103]

With the possibility of establishing a successor company under the IBA prior to the finalization of the settlement of old accounts becoming available to Japanese life insurance companies, thirteen life insurance companies followed the example of the *Nippon Life Insurance Co.* between the years 1947 and 1948. Of these thirteen companies, twelve chose to establish their successor companies under the mutual company form.[104] [105] Table 3 shows respective companies, their successor companies as well as the latter are date of initiation. At this point, it has to be mentioned that all of the total fourteen life insurance companies, which established a successor company, were of the stock company form, as in the case of the *Chiyoda Mutual Life* and *Dai-ichi Mutual Life Insurance Co.* a re-initiation of business under successor companies was not necessary for the companies' financial reorganization. Together with the former mutual conscription insurance company *Fukoku Mutual Conscript Insurance Company*, which after the war changed its business to general life insurance, the number of mutual life insurance companies increased to sixteen in 1948. With only four

[101] Cf. Japan Business History Institute (1992), p. 142-143.
[102] Cf. *Kurogi* (2015a), p. 143.
[103] Cf. Japan Business History Institute (1992), p. 142-143.
[104] Cf. *Kurogi* (2015c), p. 2-5.
[105] Cf. *Kurogi* (2015b), p. 87-93.

stock life insurance companies existing at the end of 1948, the mutual company became the dominant form of organization on the Japanese life insurance market.

Table 3, Overview of life insurance successor companies established between 1947 to 1948

old company name	initiation date of new company	new company name	renaming of new company
Nippon Life Insurance Co, Ltd.	May 1947	**Nippon Mutual Life Insurance Co.**	
Yasuda Life Insurance Co., Ltd.	June 1947	**Hikari Mutual Life Insurance Co.**	***Yasuda Mutual Life Insurance Co.*** *(Jan. 1952)*
Teikoku Life Insurance Co., Ltd.	July 1947	**Imperial Mutual Life Insurance Co.**	***Asahi Mutual Life Insurance Co.*** *(Aug. 1947)*
Meiji Life Insurance Co., Ltd.	July 1947	**Meiji Mutual Life Insurance Co.**	
Nomura Life Insurance Co., Ltd.	July 1947	**Tokyo Mutual Life Insurance Co.**	
Daido Life Insurance CO., Ltd.	July 1947	**Daido Mutual Life Insurance Co.**	
Nissan Life Insurance Co., Ltd.	August 1947	**Nisshin Mutual Life Insurance Co.**	***Nissan Mutual Life Insurance Co.*** *(May 1954)*
Mitsui Life Insurance Co., Ltd.	August 1947	**Central Mutual Life Insurance Co.**	***Mitsui Mutual Life Insurance Co.*** *(June 1954)*
Sumitomo Life Insurance Co., Ltd.	September 1947	**Kokumin Mutual Life Insurance Co.**	***Sumitomo Mutual Life Insurance Co.*** *(June 1952)*
Daihyaku Life Insurance Co., Ltd.	September 1947	**Daihyaku Mutual Life Insurance Co.**	
Yamato Life Insurance Co., Ltd.	September 1947	**Yamato Mutual Life Insurance Co.**	
Itaya Life Insurance Co., Ltd.	October 1947	**Heiwa Life Insurance Co., Ltd.**	
Shin-Nihon Life Insurance Co., Ltd.	November 1947	**Shin-Nihon Mutual Life Insurance Co.**	***Toho Mutual Life Insurance Co.***
Taiyo Life Insurance Co., Ltd.	February 1948	**Taiyo Mutual Life Insurance Co.**	

Source: Kurogi (2014: 105) (2015b: 88) (2015c: 3), table by the author.

While the necessity for the inception of successor companies has been presented earlier, the reasons for former stock insurance companies to predominantly establish their successor companies under the mutual company form have still to be investigated. In doing so, it has to be stated first, that mentioned thirteen companies, which reorganized themselves by establishing mutual successor companies, are separable into two groups, namely zaibatsu conglomerate affiliated companies and non-zaibatsu affiliated companies.

The reasons stated the different pertinent literature for the "mutualization" of representatives of the latter group are largely in compliance with each other, conflicting opinions do exist regarding reasons of *zaibatsu* affiliated life insurers for choosing the mutual company form. Here, disagreeing positions focus upon the issue, whether or not the choice of *zaibatsu* affiliated life insurance companies was politically influenced. Proponents of this assertion argue that the choice of *zaibatsu* affiliated life insurance companies to re-establish them as mutual companies was partially influenced and induced by the *zaibatsu* dismantling policy carried out by the Allied Forces' *General Head Quarter* in the course of the post-war democratization of the Japanese economy. Opponents of this explication deny such a political interference. Instead the shortage of capital, the unattractiveness of life insurance companies for investors, the democratization of the Japanese economy and strategic decisions regarding mutual companies' positive public image are reasons for the inception of mutual successor companies. Nevertheless, this chapter will follow the insights presented in most recent pertinent literature, which provides strong evidence for the existence of political interference executed upon the mutualization of *zaibatsu* affiliated stock life insurance companies.[106]

Recent literature presents evidence supporting the existence of political influence upon the initiation of mutual successor companies of *zaibatsu* affiliated life insurance companies by the Allied Forces' *General Head Quarter* (GHQ). This evidence is identifiable in records of the investigation report by the "*Edwards Zaibatsu Investigation Team*", regarding policy proposals for the *zaibatsu* dismantling. [107] Following the occupation of Japan after the end of World War II, a major policy in the course the *GHQ's* efforts of restructuring and democratizing the nation's economy was the dissolution of the former *zaibatsu* conglomerates. The major reason for the performed break-up of respective industrial conglomerates was that from the Allied Nations' point of view their dissolution would significantly limit Japan's future capabilities of rearmament.[108] In preparation of the break-up of the *zaibatsu* conglomerates, a group of economic experts led by Professor Corwin D. Edwards was given the task to write and file a report with recommendations for

106 Cf. *Kurogi* (2014), (2015a), (2015c).
107 Cf. *Kurogi* (2014), p. 117-118.
108 Cf. Japan Business History Institute (1993), p. 104.

policies regulating respective dismantlement. This report came to be known as the "*Edwards Study Team Report*".[109]

In the finalized version of this report, submitted to the *GHQ* in March 1946, mutualization was described as the most suited and expeditious measure for the reorganization of the insolvent *zaibatsu* life insurance companies and thus recommended by the *zaibatsu* investigation group to be incorporated in policies for the dismantlement of the *zaibatsu* conglomerates. With no adjustments being made by the *GHQ* before sending recommendations for dismantlement policies to official policymakers, it can be assumed that the recommended procedure of re-establishing *zaibatsu* life insurance companies as mutual companies was included in the major guidelines of the *GHQ* for the demolition of Japanese conglomerates.[110] The fact that the *US State Department* further included the policy of mutualization in the preamble of documents regarding suggestions for the official reorganization policy of *zaibatsu* conglomerates represents evidence supporting this assumption.[111] Concluding from there, it appears that the *General Head Quarters* (*GHQ*) indeed pushed former *zaibatsu* affiliated life insurance companies towards initiating their successor companies under the mutual company form. Further evidence for this conclusion is also provided by historic records of several formerly *zaibatsu* affiliated mutual life insurance companies, which indeed name the *GHQ* as a significant driving force behind the choice to reincorporate themselves as mutual life insurance companies.[112] As a result, the "mutualization" of zaibatsu affiliated life insurance companies following the end of World War II can be regarded to have been politically enforced up to a certain degree.

In the case of life insurance companies, which did not belong to one of several Japanese *zaibatsu* conglomerates before and during World War II, no evidence for political interference upon the decision to reestablish themselves as mutual life insurance companies can be identified. It seems that a series of different socio-economic reasons were the motives for the respective companies' decision. Major reasons include the weakening of the shareholder base of Japanese companies after the war, the increasing power of the nation's post-war labor movement as well as the intention of the former majority owners to remain in control of the management of the newly founded successor companies.[113] [114] [115]

In the course of the economic restructuring of the Japanese post-war economy, financial abilities of the life insurance companies' original

---

109 Cf. *Kurogi* (2014), p. 116.

110 Cf. Ibid, p. 117-118.

111 Cf Ibid, p. 119.

112 Cf. Ibid, p. 114.

113 Cf. *Aochi* (2001), p. 38-42.

114 Cf. *Kurogi* (2015b), p. 89-92.

115 Cf. *Kurogi* (2016), questionnaire.

group of major shareholders was severely altered due to the introduction of several polices. Among these policies was the special property tax policy, targeting the group of top wealthy Japanese citizens with high extraordinary tax payments, as well as the stop of war indemnification payments by the Japanese government. Moreover, the attractiveness for and ability of original shareholders to potentially invest into ownership of new successor companies was further limited through the introduction of the *Securities Limit Holding Ordinance*, which prohibited original company shareholders to hold an amount larger than ten percent of total shares issued.[116] The there from resulting weakening of the shareholder base is regarded in literature as one reason for non-zaibatsu affiliated life insurers to choose the mutual form for their successor companies.

Part of the politically initiated democratization efforts of the Japanese economy was the permission and also promotion for esbalishing labor unions. As a result, Japanese labor unions rapidly grew in numbers and size from the immediate post-war years onwards. Moreover, democratization efforts foresaw workforce participation in management and profits of restructured companies. An example of such enforced workforce participation is the *Itaya Life Insurance Co., Ltd.*, representing the only Japanese life insurance company during the immediate post war period that established its successor company under the stock company form. In the case of the *Itaya Life Insurance Co.*, the successor company's shares were evenly distributed among the policyholders, the original company's shareholders and the company employees. As argued by literature, avoiding the direct ownership participation of employees and the there from resulting potential influence of labour unions onto the management of newly established successor companies represented another reason for the former stock life insurance companies to re-establish themselves under the mutual insurance company form.[117] [118] [119]

Another major reason for the mutualization of former stock life insurance companies is the possibility for former majority owners to stay in control of the management, and therefore the company itself, by choosing to establish successor companies under the mutual company form. While this argumentation appears to be somewhat illogical at first, examples for its validity are identifiable when comparing the particular case of the *Itaya Life Insurance Co.*, being the only life insurer to re-establish itself under the stock company form, with the *Daihyaku Life Insurance Co., Ltd.* and *Shin-Nihon Life Insurance Co.,*

116 Cf. *Aochi* (2001), p. 38-39.
117 Cf. *Kurogi* (2015b), p. 91.
118 Cf. *Aochi* (2001), p. 39-41.
119 Cf. *Kurogi* (2016), questionnaire.

Ltd., which both established mutual successor companies. In the case of all three companies, the majority ownership was held by a single family, whose members also occupied top management positions within the companies.

While the *Itaya Life Insurance Company* was permitted to establish a successor company under the stock company form, the new company was required to follow certain provisions, significantly limiting ownership and influence by its former majority owners, namely the *Itaya* family. Under respective provisions, members of the *Itaya* family were prohibited to hold an ownership participation of above ten percent of the total shares issued by the successor company. Moreover, the shareholder dividends were restricted to ten percent of total annual profits earned, while the remaining ninety percent of profits became required to be allocated to policyholder dividends. Finally, family members were prohibited to further occupy any management position within the successor company.

According to literature, the *Daihyaku Life* and *Shin-Nihon Life Insurance Co.* were confronted to be the subject of highly similar provisions, if re-establishing themselves under the stock company form. [120] Contrary to that, no provisions with respect to management participation of original majority owners existed for choosing the mutual company form. As a result, majority ownership holding families of the *Daihyaku Life* and *Shin-Nihon Life Insurance Co.* had the choice to either obtain a minority ownership within a newly established stock insurance successor company or to remain occupying top management positions in newly established mutual companies.[121]

The choice of re-establishing life insurance companies as stock companies became highly unattractive because of severe ownership, dividend and management participation restrictions, therefore the literature concludes that the former majority ownership holding families chose to establish successor companies under the mutual company form. Here it has to be further mentioned that in both of the abovementioned cases, life insurance companies were an important core business of each families' owned company groups. Establishing mutual successor companies allowed the former majority ownership holding families of the *Daihyaku Life* and *Shin-Nihon Life Insurance Co.* to remain holding top management positions and thus to stay in control of life insurance companies.[122]

---

[120] In fact, the *Kiyozo Oda*, president of the *Daihyaku Life Insurance Co., Ltd.* and head of the majority ownership holding *Oda* family, originally intended to establish the *Daihyaku Life's* successor company under the stock company form. (Cf. *Kurogi* (2016, questionnaire))

[121] Cf. *Kurogi* (2016), questionnaire.

[122] Cf. Ibid.

Similar to the situation of life insurance companies, Japanese property and casualty insurance companies were in a desolate financial situation during the immediate post-war years. On the one hand, remaining non-life insurance companies suffered from the confiscation of overseas assets held in formerly occupied areas, representing about 15 percent of companies' total assets held at the end of the war. On the other hand, non-life insurance companies suffered financially from the stop of the War Indemnification Payments by the Japanese Government after the end of the war, as companies had been required to invest into and lend money to military commodity producing industries during World War II. Resulting there from, non-life companies had to reorganize themselves under the *Financial Institutions Reorganization and Readjustment Act*.[123] [124] [125]

Nevertheless, contrary to the mutualization observable among Japanese life insurance companies, no such development occurred within the Japanese property and casualty insurance industry, with only one mutualization having occurred during the immediate post war years. As a potential explanation for this situation, can be seen that all property and casualty insurers were able to cover losses resulting from the devaluation of assets held with internally accumulated reserves and were able to fully finish reorganization by March 1948.[126] [127] As a result, Japanese non-life insurance companies appear to have had no necessity to re-establish themselves through the inception of successor companies. Moreover, despite seven out of fifteen existing Japanese property and casualty insurance companies belonging to one of several *zaibatsu* conglomerates, no mutualization of respective companies has been politically initiated. Instead, the shares of respective seven *zaibatsu* affiliated non-life insurance companies were distributed during the reorganization of companies among a multitude of different shareholders, creating an ownership structure in which no single shareholder held a majority stake in any company.[128] [129] [130]

The sole non-life insurance stock company mutualizing in the course of the post-war reorganization period of the Japanese insurance industry was the *Kyoei Fire and Marine Insurance Co., Ltd.* Nevertheless, its mutualization was not a result of financial reorganization as in the case of many mutualizing life insurance companies. Rather the company' mutualization was voluntarily performed by its majority owner,

123 Cf. Japan Business History Institute (1993), p. 123.
124 Cf. Japan Business History Institute (1980), p. 125-126.
125 Cf. The Non-Life Insurance Institute of Japan (1972), p. 2.
126 Cf. Japan Business History Institute (1980), p. 128.
127 Cf. Japan Business History Institute (1993), p. 123.
128 Cf. *Yoneyama* (2016b), interview.
129 Cf. *Yatsui* (1951), p. 48.
130 Cf. Japan Business History Institute (1980), p. 128-129.

namely the Japanese agricultural cooperative movement. At this point, it has to be mentioned that the *Kyoei Fire and Marine Insurance Co.* represented an early attempt of the Japanese agricultural cooperative movement to enter the nation's insurance industry. In 1942, the Japanese agricultural cooperative movement purchased majority ownership of the *Daito Marine-Fire Insurance Co., Ltd.* and *Daifuku Marine and Fire Insurance Co., Ltd.*, and established *Kyoei Fire and Marine* through the consolidation of respective two companies. In 1946, the Japanese agricultural cooperative movement decided to mutualize the company to be in compliance to the cooperative movement's philosophy of mutuality and reciprocity, thus establishing the *Kyoei Mutual Fire and Marine Insurance Company*.[131] [132]

After the existing non-life insurance company finished the financial restructuring in 1948, another four non-life insurance companies were established between 1949 and 1951. Among them was the *Dai-Ichi Mutual Fire and Marine Insurance Company*, being incepted in 1949. However, the *Kyoei Mutual Fire and Marine Insurance Co.* and *Dai-Ichi Mutual Fire and Marine Insurance Co.* remained the only two mutual non-life insurance companies throughout the second half of the 20th century, as no further domestic non-life insurance companies were established during the following three decades. In total, the number of domestic Japanese property and casualty insurance companies had increased to twenty by the end of 1951.[133] [134]

Summarizing the above, the financial reorganization of the Japanese life insurance industry resulted in a wave of mutualization of life insurance companies during the immediate post-war period. Moreover, despite reasons for the initiation of mutual successor companies varying amongst former stock life insurance companies, ranging from political interference towards financial weakness and retaining power, it can be stated that the mutualization of the nation's life insurance industry was clearly a product of the extraordinary environmental and socio-economic circumstances of the immediate post war era. Concluding there from, it can be said that the emergence of mutual insurance companies' dominance over the nation's life insurance industry was an indirect result of particular extraordinary circumstances of Japan's post-war era. Contrary to the occurrence of mutualization on the Japanese life insurance market, no such development was observable in the case of the nation's non-life insurance industry. Therefore, despite economic democratization efforts being applied to the Japanese property and casualty insurers during the immediate post war period, the stock

131 Cf. Kyoei Fire and Marine (2017), online.

132 Cf. Kyoei Fire and Marine (2005), p. i.

133 Cf. Marine and Fire Insurance Association of Japan (1957), p. 5.

134 Cf. Japan Business History Institute (1980), p. 145.

company remained by the far dominating legal form on the Japanese property and casualty insurance market.

2.5 Domination of the mutual life insurance companies and stock non-life insurance companies on the Japanese insurance market in the post-war era.

From the early 1950s onwards, the Japanese life and non-life insurance industry experienced a steady recovery of business. Being able to increase in-force business approximately 709 % from 1950 onwards, life insurance companies were able to reach and even surpass pre-war levels of life insurance in force in 1958.[135] The nation's life insurance industry further surpassed pre-war levels of total assets held in the fiscal year 1961.[136] [137] [138] A similar positive development was experienced by the Japanese non-life insurance industry, being able to record a growth of about 230 % in terms of annual gross premium payments collected between fiscal years 1950 and 1955. Moreover, domestic non-life insurers recorded a 640 % increase of total assets held between fiscal years 1949 and 1954.[139] From this point forward, the Japanese insurance industry entered a period of almost steady growth, occurring concurrently to Japan's long-lasting economic expansion and lasting for more than three decades until the early 1990s.

During respective period, the Japanese life insurance industry was dominated by life insurers of the mutual company form, being able to conquer and hold a market share of approximately 90 % in terms of total annually collected premium from the mid-1950s until the mid-1990s.[140] Furthermore, Japan's life insurance industry was characterized by severe governmental control and regulations, significantly restricting Japanese life insurers in terms of setting premium rates and introducing new insurance products. Nevertheless, while the wave of mutualization of stock life insurance companies during the immediate post-war years represented the origin of the visible dominance of mutual insurance companies during this period, it was particular regulatory framework that allowed mutual companies to tighten their industry leadership for more than four decades, while at the same time

135 Adjusted by standard wholesale prices.

136 Adjusted by standard wholesale prices.

137 Cf. *Nishio* (1995), p. 57-58.

138 Cf. Japan Business History Institute (1992), p. 255.

139 Cf. Japan Business History Institute (1980), p. 144.

140 Cf. Insurance Research Institute (1955), (1960a), (1971a), (1976a), (1979), (1986a), (1991a), (1996a).

enabling some domestic life insurers to grow into one of the worldwide largest mutual insurance organizations.

From about 1956 onwards, the Japanese government, in form of the *Ministry of Finance* (*MoF*), began to intensify severely governmental control over the nation's life insurance industry through the adoption of new measures of supervision. The major objective of this increase of governmental control was to guarantee maximum policyholder protection. Doing so, the *MoF* adopted the major principle of creating a situation of high stability on the Japanese life insurance market, in which even the least efficient domestic life insurer would be able to operate profitable. Resulting from that characteristic, the *Ministry of Finance'* regulatory procedure of respective period was labeled by literature as the so-called "convoy policy". This kind of policy was to a large extent executed consistently by the *MoF* until the mid-1990s.[141] [142] [143]

In general, the "convoy policy" was executed upon the Japanese life insurance industry through several different channels of control. These included the introduction of mechanisms to standardize products and prices among companies, preferential treatments of small and medium life insurers, and the prohibition of any further market entry of foreign as well as newly incepted domestic life insurance companies.[144] [145] [146] Additionally, Japanese life insurance companies were also subject to regulations regarding their investment activities.[147] [148]

Product and price regulation measures were primarily performed through the *Ministry of Finance'* product approval process. Under respective product approval process the ministry would evaluate and actively set premium rates, including interest rates, for each life insurance product sold on the Japanese life insurance market. Doing so, the *MoF* standardized products sold and premium rates charged by life insurance companies. Consequentially, a situation was created under the Japanese *Ministry of Finance'* "convoy policy" in which all domestic life insurers factually offered the same types of products for the same price.[149] [150] Moreover, with the majority of life insurance companies being of the mutual company form and the overwhelming majority of policies being thus profit participating policies, the *MoF* regulated further companies' payments of dividends to policyholder in order to guarantee

---

[141] Cf. *Soejima* (1986), p. 260.

[142] Cf. *Yoneyama* (1994), p. 184-185.

[143] Cf. Japan Business History Institute (1992), p. 237-238.

[144] Cf. *Yoneyama* (1994), p. 184-185.

[145] Cf. *Yingying* (2013), p. 187-188, 190.

[146] Cf. *Yoneyama* (2008), p. 27-28.

[147] Cf. *Hax* (1961), p. 435.

[148] Cf. Standard & Poor's (1990), p. 7.

[149] Cf. *Yoneyama* (1994), p. 184-185.

[150] Cf. *Yingying* (2013), p. 187-189.

a standardization of prices in the long term.[151] As a result of regulatory authorities' executed control over products sold and premium rates charged, price competition of any kind, was virtually made impossible to be performed among Japanese life insurance companies under the *Ministry of Finance'* "convoy policy".

Additionally, it has to be mentioned that the premium rates set by the *Ministry of Finance* (*MoF*) were always of a height, which allowed even the least efficient life insurers, primarily originating from the ranks of small and medium size insurance companies, to operate profitable. This procedure is further demonstrated by the fact that, in the case of most efficient life insurance companies demanding a cut of applicable premium rates, the MoF did not accede such demands until it was sure that the least efficient insurers would be able to continue to stay profitable when lower rates of premium were applied.[152] [153]

Protection of the profitability of less efficient small and medium life insurers was performed by the Japanese *Ministry of Finance* (*MoF*) through treating them preferentially in the course of the product approval process. Here the *MoF* withheld newly developed products of major industry leading life insurance companies, from the market, until each domestic life insurance company was deemed able to operate respective products profitable.[154] Once issuing approval, newly developed products were consequentially almost simultaneously introduced by all life insurance companies, with small and medium scale life insurance companies being allowed to immediately imitate new products of large scale companies for the purpose of remaining profitable. At the same time, the *MoF* restricted large size industry leading life insurers to imitate immediately new types of products developed and introduced by small and medium life insurance companies. Rather small and medium companies were able to benefit from additional profits, as the *MoF* would not allow industry leading life insurers to introduce products similar to those newly introduced by small scale insures for several years after the launch of the latter. Again, this policy was performed in order to guarantee profitability of less efficient small and medium scale life insurance companies.[155]

Besides the conducted product and premium rate control, another important element of the *Ministry of Finance'* "convoy policy" besides the conducted product and premium rate control was the prohibition of any further market entrances by newly established domestic or foreign life insurance companies. In 1951, the application for the initiation of

---

151 Cf. *Yoneyama* (1994), p. 184-185.
152 Cf. *Ezawa* (2016a), interview.
153 Cf. *Yoneyama* (1994), p. 184-185.
154 Cf. *Ezawa* (2016a), interview.
155 Cf. *Yoneyama* (2008), p. 27-28.

a third mutual property and casualty insurance company, having been submitted by the Tokyo Metropolitan Government, was rejected by the Japanese *Ministry of Finance* (*MoF*).[156] In the following year, provisions regarding the inception of insurance companies were revised, resulting in the situation that the *MoF* would not permit the inception of any new domestic companies.[157] This prohibition of inceptions of further domestic insurance companies was applied upon the Japanese life as well as non-life insurance industry alike.[158]

Moreover, while foreign companies became technically allowed to re-enter the Japanese life insurance market with the enactment of the *Law Concerning Foreign Insurance Companies* in 1949, foreign companies were highly restricted in operating life insurance business, as they were not allowed to operate yen-based insurance policies. Thus, foreign life insurance companies were indirectly excluded from the domestic Japanese life insurance market. This situation did not change until 1972, with the permission of the *American Life Insurance Company* to underwrite certain yen-based life insurance products in accordance to specific provisions of the *MoF*.[159] [160] Nevertheless, with a total number of only five foreign financed companies, having been permitted to start business activities on the Japanese life insurance market between 1972 and 1981, it can be concluded that domestic life insurance companies were still highly shielded from foreign competition and remained to be so until the Japanese financial markets' liberalization from the mid-1990s onwards.[161] [162]

Concluding from the above mentioned, it can be said that Japanese mutual insurance companies were operating in a highly regulated, yet strongly protected market, in which they were guaranteed to be able to operate profitable. Competition on the basis of price or product differentiation was impossible, while at the same time the threat of foreign or further domestic competition was severely limited. At this poin, it has to be mentioned once more, that the intention behind these regulations was to maximize policyholder's protection, whereas the method applied to do so was to create a market framework in which even the

---

156 Cf. Yasuda Fire and Marine Ins. Co. (1968), p. 358.

157 Cf. *Yoneyama* (2012), p. 511.

158 Cf. Japan Business History Institute (1992), p. 238.

159 Cf. *Nishimura* (1975), p. 955-956.

160 Nevertheless, foreign life insurance companies were still restricted in selling the same types of life insurance products as domestic life insurance companies, while being primarily allowed to sell medical insurance products such as cancer insurance, not existent at the point of entrance of these companies in the Japanese life insurance market. (Cf. *Ezawa* (2016), interview)

161 Cf. Insurance Research Institute (1991a), p. 156-168, 276-278.

162 Cf. *Yoneyama* (2012), p. 518.

least efficient life insurance company would be able to stay profitable and thus would not be threatened by failure.[163]

Due to representing the majority of companies within the above-described highly protected industry, Japanese mutual life insurance companies were able to immensely extent their scale of operation and size of business throughout the Japan's period of solid economic growth during the 1960s, 1970s and 1980s. Table 4 shows the development of market share held by mutual life insurance companies and stock life insurance companies in terms of total insurance in force and total annually collected premium payments during respective period. As can be seen in the table, the proportions of market share held by Japanese mutual and stock life insurance companies remained very stable throughout the whole period of time under investigation, with mutual life insurance companies representing the market dominating form of organization. The high degree of governmental control and protection executed upon the nation's life insurance industry can be considered to have highly contributed to mutual life insurance companies' market dominance. Moreover, considering annual figures of total life insurance in force and total annually collected premium payments, the impressively high growth of business accomplished by mutual life insurance companies, and the Japanese life insurance industry in general, during the post-war era of the 1960s, 1970s and 1980s, becomes visible.[164]

Similar to the case of Japan's life insurance industry, the nation's non-life insurance industry was subject to severe governmental control and supervision during the majority of the second half of the 20th century. Almost identical to regulatory measures executed upon life insurance companies, Japan's property and casualty insurance companies were subject to industry wide premium rate standardization, the protection of small scale insurers and the prevention of further domestic competition in the form of new market entrants.[165]

Nevertheless, the procedure of price standardization executed upon Japanese non-life insurance companies differed in comparison to those applied upon the nation's life insurance industry. In 1949, the Japanese National Diet passed the *Law Concerning Non-Life Insurance Rating Organizations*. Following the enactment of respective law, the *Fire and Marine Insurance Rating Association of Japan* was incepted within the same year, with the task to calculate reference premium rates for the

163 Thus the utilization of the synonym "convoy policy", which means a situation in which a shipping convoy can only move as fast as its slowest ship, whereas in this case ships were the Japanese domestic life insurance companies.

164 Cf. Insurance Research Institute (1971a), (1976a), (1979), (1986a), (1991a).

165 Cf. *Yoneyama* (2008), p. 27-28.

market's five major lines of insurance.[166] [167] In 1951, the *Law Concerning Non-Life Insurance Rating Organizations* was revised by the Japanese government and rates calculated by the *Fire and Marine Insurance Rating Association of Japan* became mandatory to be applied by Japanese non-life insurance companies. Resulting there from, prices for property and casualty insurance products became standardized industry wide.[168] Under respective price standardization system, premium rates were calculated by the *Fire and Marine Insurance Rating Association of Japan* and sent to the *Ministry of Finance* (*MoF*) for acceptance. Similar to the case of Japan's life insurance industry, the *MoF* only approved rates, which guaranteed that even the industry's least efficient non-life insurance companies would be able to operate profitable under accepted rates, in order to create a situation of stability within the nation's non-life insurance industry.[169] [170] Doing so, regulatory authorities accepted the fact that consumers had to bear additional costs resulting from respective price regulation, in order to maximize the non-life insurance industry's financial and economic stability.[171]

Moreover, in spite of restricting operational freedom of Japanese non-life insurance companies, it is reported that the price regulation was indeed in the interest of domestic non-life insurance companies, as it allowed them to expand their non-life insurance business rather untroubled.[172]

Following the increasing importance of mandatory as well as voluntary automobile insurance on the Japanese non-life insurance market, the task of calculating rates for automobile insurance was transferred to the newly established Automobile Insurance Rating Organization in 1964.[173]Already two years earlier, the responsibility of calculating hull insurance premium rates was transferred to the newly incepted Hull

---

166 At that time, these were fire, marine, transportation, automobile and personal accident insurance.

167 Cf. Yasuda Fire and Marine Ins. Co., Ltd. (1988), p. 146.

168 Cf. *Kobayashi* et al. (2011), p. 76.

169 Cf. *Yoneyama* (2016b), interview.

170 A minor difference between the price regulation executed on the Japanese life insurance industry and the nation's non-life insurance products, was that not all products were subject to industrywide standardization, with some minor, but rather specific types of products not being subject to rate calculations by rating organizations. Nevertheless, with types of insurance such as fire, automobile, marine, cargo and personal accident insurance, representing major lines of non-life insurance underwritten on the Japanese insurance market, being subject to rate calculations, price competition was for the most part prohibited. Moreover, also insurance companies excluded from rate calculations had to be approved first by the *Ministry of Finance*, before being introduced to the market.

171 Cf. *Yoneyama* (2008), p. 28.

172 Cf. Non-Life Insurance Institute of Japan (1973), p. 17.

173 Cf. *Kobayashi* et al. (2011), p. 76.

Table 4: Development of the business performance of the Japanese life insurance industry, FY 1971-1978

Year	total insurance in force (in mio.	share of insurance in force mutual companies	share of insurance in force stock companies	annual growth rate total insurance in force	total premium collected (in mio. ¥)	share of total premium mutual companies	share of total premium stock companies	annual growth rate total premium collected
1966	¥30 485 575	94,9%	5,1%					
1967	¥38 243 084	94,9%	5,1%	19,9%				
1968	¥47 424 158	94,5%	5,5%	16,5%				
1969	¥60 183 523	94,3%	5,7%	18,3%				
1970	¥78 230 095	94,6%	5,4%	23,1%				
1971	¥98 503 067	94,2%	5,8%	19,6%	¥2 090 968	95,9%	4,1%	
1972	¥122 210 393	94,2%	5,8%	7,0%	¥2 428 619	95,8%	4,2%	0,2%
1973	¥154 008 641	94,2%	5,8%	3,5%	¥2 859 137	95,8%	4,2%	-3,3%
1974	¥205 034 689	93,7%	6,3%	20,6%	¥3 374 569	95,6%	4,4%	6,9%
1975	¥265 410 028	93,6%	6,4%	18,3%	¥3 981 162	95,4%	4,6%	7,9%
1976	¥334 392 561	93,9%	6,1%	18,1%	¥4 716 790	95,3%	4,7%	11,0%
1977	¥400 600 691	93,9%	6,1%	15,7%	¥5 548 704	95,3%	4,7%	13,6%
1978	¥463 558 118	93,8%	6,2%	10,6%	¥6 450 014	95,2%	4,8%	11,1%
1981	¥638 909 795	93,5%	6,5%		¥9 237 476	95,0%	5,0%	
1982	¥700 884 234	93,7%	6,3%	7,7%	¥10 363 849	95,0%	5,0%	10,1%
1983	¥751 975 220	93,6%	6,4%	5,0%	¥11 402 467	94,9%	5,1%	7,7%
1984	¥799 397 043	93,6%	6,4%	4,3%	¥12 995 875	94,8%	5,2%	11,8%
1985	¥871 331 389	94,1%	5,9%	9,4%	¥15 479 793	95,0%	5,0%	19,5%
1986	¥955 765 146	93,5%	6,5%	9,3%	¥18 741 818	94,9%	5,1%	20,7%
1987	¥1 064 292 093	93,7%	6,3%	10,6%	¥21 725 889	94,6%	5,4%	15,2%
1988	¥1 208 710 000	94,0%	6,0%	10,4%	¥26 379 090	93,0%	7,0%	18,0%
1989	¥1 372 734 402	94,1%	5,9%	10,2%	¥28 040 284	92,4%	7,6%	3,1%

Source: Insurance Research Institute (1971a), (1976a), (1979), (1986a), (1991a) table established by author

Insurance Union, for the purpose of being able to determine more flexible rates for this rather specific type of insurance.[174] Notwithstanding these transfers of responsibility, the practice of premium rate standardization was not altered within the Japanese non-life insurance industry. In fact, the standardization of prices on the Japanese non-life insurance market was not abolished until 1998 in the course of the liberalization of the Japanese financial industry.[175] As a result, the procedure of industry wide standardizing premium rates on the Japanese non-life insurance market was conducted during the vast majority of years of the second half of the 20th century.

Second, small and medium property and casualty insurance companies enjoyed preferential treatment with respect to the regulatory approval process for new types of products. Similar to the situation observable in the Japanese life insurance industry during the "convoy policy", small and medium non-life insurance companies were protected from immediate direct competition of major insurance companies in the event of launching newly developed products, as the *Ministry of Finance* would not give permission to the latter to copy immediately new types of products introduced.[176]

Finally, in addition to the standardization of prices and preferential treatment of small and medium size firms, regulatory authorities shielded existent Japanese non-life insurance companies from further domestic market entries from 1952 onwards. This policy of prohibiting further domestic non-life insurance companies to be established was executed by Japan's *Ministry of Finance* until the early 1980s. In 1982, permission was granted for the inception of the *Allstate Automobile & Fire Insurance Co., Ltd.*, representing the first domestic non-life insurance company allowed to be established since 1951.[177] [178]

In conclusion of the above mentioned, it can be said that during most parts of the second half of the 20th century, the Japanese non-life insurance industry was a highly regulated industry, with standardization of chargeable premium rates, protection of small and medium companies

174 Cf. Non-Life Insurance Institute of Japan (1973), p. 17.

175 Cf. *Yoneyama* (2008), p. 35-36.

176 Cf. *Yoneyama* (2008), p. 27-28.

177 Cf. *Yoneyama* (2012), p. 511, 514.

178 Here it has to be mentioned that several foreign non-life insurance companies were permitted to underwrite insurance onto the Japanese non-life insurance market. Nevertheless, these companies only operated through agents appointed within Japan or established branch offices, but did not engage into the Japanese non-life insurance industry in the form of equity participation of domestically established companies or subsidiary companies established under Japanese law. Moreover, their share only accounted for slightly above one percent in terms of market share held and focused onto very specific types of non-life insurance products. (Cf. *Yoneyama* (2012: 514)).

and the prohibition of new domestic market entries being performed by the Ministry of Finance. The major objective of these regulations was to guarantee the highest policyholder's protection possible through maximizing financial soundness and stability of the Japanese non-life insurance industry. Doing so, regulatory authorities accept the fact that consumers bore additional costs resulting from strict regulation of price and competition, as from the point of view of regulators the there from created economic and financial stability of the industry indirectly contributed to policyholders' protection against a loss of their claims due to potential bankruptcy of companies.[179] [180]

Regarding the economic development of the Japanese non-life insurance industry during the 1960s, 1970s and 1980s, it can be stated that also domestic property and casualty insurance companies experienced impressive stable rates of growth during respective period. Table 5 shows the development of market share held by stock and mutual non-life insurance companies in terms of annual premium payments collected by the nation's non-life insurance industry. As can be seen in the table, stock insurance companies were the by far dominating form of organization on the Japanese non-life insurance market during years under observation. With 18 out of 20 companies being of the stock company form and only two mutual non-life insurance companies existing on the Japanese post-war non-life insurance market until the early 1980s, this dominance can be regarded as rather unsurprising.[181] Only throughout the 1960s it appears that mutual-non-life insurance companies were able to extend their market share in terms of net premium collected, increasing from a mere 3.8 % in 1962 to 6.4 % in 1970. Here, mutual companies' increase of market share can be attributed to the development and launch of the so-called "long-term saving insurance policies" by the existing two mutual non-life insurers.[182] In fact, the *Kyoei* and *Dai-Ichi Mutual Fire and Marine Insurance Co.* were the first initiators of long-term saving insurance and the only companies selling this type of insurance for most part of the 1960s. Thus, with respective type of policy quickly gaining popularity among Japanese consumers and with the two companies enjoying a quasi-monopoly on this type of insurance during the early years of its existence, both companies were able to accomplish a successful expansion of their

179 Cf. *Yoneyama* (2016b), interview.

180 Cf. *Yoneyama* (2008), p. 28.

181 Cf. Insurance Research Institute (1986b), 20-21.

182 Long-term saving insurance represents a type of property and casualty insurance that includes a saving element in it. Having a duration ranging from five to ten years, policyholders received a pay-out or refund at the end of their policy's duration, normally being of a height of about 10 % of the originally insured amount. (Cf. The Insurance Research Institute (1986: 17))

Table 5: Development of business operations of domestic non-life insurance companies, FY 1957-1990

Development of net premium received by non-life insurance industry (1957-1990)

year	Non-life industry total net premium (tsd. Yen)	Annual growth rate*	Growth Index (1957=100)	(A-1)	(A-2)	year	Non-life industry total net premium (tsd. Yen)	Annual growth rate*	Growth index (1957=100)	(A-1)	(A-2)
1957	¥67.804.708			96,3%	3,7%	**1974**	¥1.473.340.535	-2,7%	810	94,1%	5,9%
1958	¥71.403.093			96,2%	3,8%	**1975**	¥1.784.486.975	8,4%	878	94,3%	5,7%
1959	¥79.684.416			96,2%	3,8%	**1976**	¥1.967.130.374	0,8%	885	95,0%	5,0%
1960	¥94.561.513			96,1%	3,9%	**1977**	¥2.202.252.359	3,5%	916	95,0%	5,0%
1961	¥112.006.313	12,4%	157	96,2%	3,8%	**1978**	¥2.422.479.896	5,6%	967	95,1%	4,9%
1962	¥127.928.001	7,0%	168	96,0%	4,0%	**1979**	¥2.762.508.292	10,0%	1.063	95,3%	4,7%
1963	¥155.518.424	12,9%	189	95,9%	4,1%	**1980**	¥2.917.231.742	-2,1%	1.041	95,4%	4,6%
1964	¥191.246.631	18,4%	224	95,5%	4,5%	**1981**	¥3.017.868.000	-1,4%	1.027	95,6%	4,4%
1965	¥224.298.435	10,0%	247	95,2%	4,8%	**1982**	¥3.203.497.000	3,3%	1.061	95,7%	4,3%
1966	¥288.109.902	22,2%	302	94,6%	5,4%	**1983**	¥3.425.455.000	5,0%	1.114	95,7%	4,3%
1967	¥362.688.982	21,1%	365	94,2%	5,8%	**1984**	¥3.647.912.000	4,1%	1.159	95,8%	4,2%
1968	¥455.007.996	21,0%	442	93,8%	6,2%	**1985**	¥3.900.411.000	4,8%	1.215	95,7%	4,3%
1969	¥578.247.387	18,9%	525	93,7%	6,3%	**1986**	¥4.085.290.000	4,1%	1.265	95,9%	4,1%
1970	¥788.099.416	26,6%	664	93,6%	6,4%	**1987**	¥4.017.953.000	-1,8%	1.242	95,6%	4,4%
1971	¥908.867.236	8,4%	720	93,5%	6,5%	**1988**	¥4.628.439.000	14,4%	1.422	96,0%	4,0%
1972	¥1.023.897.150	6,6%	768	93,6%	6,4%	**1989**	¥5.100.235.000	7,7%	1.532	96,1%	3,9%
1973	¥1.228.736.642	8,4%	832	93,7%	6,3%	**1990**	¥5.519.385.000	5,0%	1.609	96,2%	3,8%

* inflation adjusted
(A-1) = market share of stock companies in terms of annually collected net premium
(B-1) = market share of mutual companies in terms of annually collected net premium

Source: IRI (1956, 1960b, 1965, 1971b, 1976b, 1981a, 1986b, 1991b), table established by author.

business.[183] Nevertheless, market share of both companies started to decrease slowly and steadily from the early 1970s onwards, coinciding with the entrance of stock insurance companies in the segment of long-term saving type insurance policies.

Whereas the identifiable dominance of mutual companies on the Japanese life insurance market can be described as being partially caused by strict governmental control executed upon the nation's life insurance industry, similar can be argued in the case of the observable dominance of stock insurance companies on the nation's property and casualty insurance market. The immediate post-war reorganization of the Japanese non-life insurance industry did not lead to a wave of mutualization, as was observable in the case of Japanese life insurance companies, existing domestic non-life companies became heavily protected and shielded from increasing inside and outside competition. Furthermore, price competition was mostly inexistent on the Japanese non-life insurance industry due to the performed product and premium rate regulations. As a result, stock non-life insurance companies, having represented the vast majority of existing domestic non-life insurers, were able to capitalize fully from the rapidly increasing demand for insurance during the years of Japan's rapid economic growth of the 1960s, 1970s and 1980s. Moreover, with further market entries being denied from 1952 onwards, following the denial of approval for the inception of a third mutual non-life insurance company sponsored by the Tokyo Metropolitan Government, it became basically impossible for the mutual company form to extent its presence in the Japanese non-life insurance market.

Admittedly, several additional reasons exist for stock companies' dominance over the Japanese non-life insurance market besides the execution of tight governmental control over the nation's non-life insurance industry. For example, both mutual companies can be regarded of having been new entrants to a market that was already dominated by an established group of stock insurance companies. Even though being separated from industrial conglomerates after the war, many non-life stock insurance companies still maintained good relationships to companies once belonging to the same industrial groups during the pre-war era, which became major customers of respective non-life insurance companies. Thus, it appears that many stock non-life insurance companies enjoyed the advantage of an already established customer group.[184] However, besides the admitted existence of several other reasons for the dominance of stock insurance companies over the Japanese non-life insurance market during the second half of the 20th century, it can be concluded that the severe governmental control executed upon

183 Cf. *Yoneyama* (2016b), interview.

184 Cf. Japan Business History Institute (1993), p. 116-117, 140-142.

the nation's non-life insurance industry significantly contributed to the occurrence of the stock company form's industry dominance.

Whereas the mutual company form was only limitedly able to establish a significant presence in the Japanese post-war non-life insurance industry, Japan's second organizational form operating insurance on the principles of mutuality successfully entered the nation's non-life insurance market during the early 1950s and henceforth was able to increase its presence in the market. The historic development, evolution and specifies of respective form of organization, namely the mutual-aid operating cooperative, will be the major subject of the following chapter.

2.6 The emergence of cooperative mutual-aid operations on the Japanese insurance market as an additional form of insurance based on the principles of mutuality

In the course of the democratization of Japan's economy during the early years of the post-war era, Japanese cooperatives became the third form of organization legally permitted to operate insurance. Various cooperative movements already emerged during the early decades of the 20th century, following the enactment of the *Industrial Cooperative Association Act* in 1900. Nevertheless, cooperatives were not allowed to enter the Japanese insurance industry prior to the post-war era, despite engaging in heavy efforts to receive legal permission to do so from the late 1920s onwards.[185] [186] [187] Such effort was also made following the end of World War II, with representatives of the cooperative movement requesting the inclusion of the cooperative as a legal form officially permitted to operate insurance in the Japanese *Insurance Business Act* (*IBA*). Nevertheless, due to various reasons, including insurance companies' strong opposition against the entry of cooperatives into the insurance market, legislation permitting cooperatives to operate insurance under the *IBA* was never introduced. Confronted with this situation, cooperatives engaged into pushing for the introduction of a legal basis separated from the *IBA*, allowing them to operate insurance.

As mentioned above, Japan became subject to extensive reforms during the initial years following the end of World War II, having the purpose of democratizing its economy. In the course of these reforms, a new legal basis for Japanese cooperatives was established. Nevertheless, contrary to the pre-war situation in the case of which different types of cooperatives were established under by the same body of law

185 Cf. *Ashikaga* (1959), p. 11-12.

186 Cf. *Kurimoto* (2009), p. 2.

187 Cf. *Murthy* (1960), p. 94.

cooperative legislation became spilt into four different laws for the purpose of providing adequate regulatory frameworks in accordance to specificities of different types of cooperatives. These laws were the *Agricultural Cooperative Act* (ACA), the *Fishery Cooperative Act* (FCA), the *Consumer Cooperative Act* (CCA) and the *Small and Medium Enterprise Cooperative Act* (SMECA), all of which were enacted between the years 1947 to 1949. Moreover, the enactment of respective new laws also led to the distribution of regulatory supervision on different ministries. In the case of cooperatives established under the ACA and FCA, the *Ministry of Agriculture, Forestry and Fishery* (MAFF) became the official supervising authority. In the case of cooperatives established under the CCA, the *Ministry of Health, Labour and Welfare* (MHLW) became the supervising authority. Additionally, *Ministry of Economy, Trade and Industry* (METI) became the regulatory authority in charge of supervising cooperatives regulated by the SMECA.

These laws provided the regulatory framework for the various cooperatives' different insurance activities. However, laws did not label cooperative insurance activities under with the term "insurance" ("hoken" in Japanese). Rather the insurance business of various cooperatives was summarized under the newly created term "mutual-aid" ("kyōsai" in Japanese) in respective legislation.[188]

Due to the fact that different mutual-aid operating cooperative movements were regulated from the beginning by different regulatory authorities and laws, the different cooperative types' mutual-aid activities developed uniquely and independently from each other, each creating their own specificities. Mutual-aid activities under the *Agricultural Cooperative Act* (ACA) were the earliest being established during the post-war period. After the enactment of the ACA in 1947, the *Hokkaido Agricultural Cooperative Association* became the first Japanese cooperative association to launch mutual-aid operations for its members by establishing the *Hokkaido Mutual Aid Federation of Agricultural Cooperative* in 1948.[189] Following the inception of the mutual-aid federation of agricultural cooperatives in Hokkaido, prefectural agricultural mutual-aid federations were incepted in the prefectures Kanagawa and Nagano in early 1951. Within the same year, forty-one prefectural agricultural cooperative federations joined effort and established the *National Mutual Insurance Federation of Agricultural Cooperatives (Zenkyoren)* as the future national umbrella association for the agricultural cooperative mutual-aid movement. From there on the numbers

188 This, nevertheless, only represents a formal difference, resulting from the fact that cooperative insurance did not become subject to the *Insurance Business Act* (IBA). Nevertheless, despite being labeled differently, mutual-aid clearly represents insurance activities conducted by Japanese cooperatives, being based upon the same actuarial science as "insurance business" under the IBA.

189 Cf. *Yoneyama* (2011), p. 87-88.

of prefectural agricultural mutual-aid federations increased steadily, leading to the situation that by the end of 1958 a federation had been launched in every prefecture, each of which became a member of the former founded national federation *Zenkyoren*. Resulting there from, mutual-aid activities by the Japanese cooperative movement were able to be extended on a nationwide scale during the first ten years of their existence. Under the thereby created organizational structure, primary multi-purpose agricultural cooperatives on the local level became members of their respective prefecture's mutual-aid federations, whereas prefectural federations were unanimously members of *Zenkyoren*, thus creating a three-layer structure. Here it has to be mentioned that all mutual-aid operations conducted under the ACA were operated and therefore unified under the umbrella association of the *National Mutual Insurance Federation of Agricultural Cooperatives (Zenkyoren)*.[190]

However, despite the Japanese agricultural cooperative mutual-aid movement's successful rapid geographic expansion of business during the 1950s, the mutual-aid business also faced several obstacles during the early years of its existence. Although, agricultural cooperatives were technically permitted to operate mutual-aid under the newly introduced Agricultural Cooperative Act (ACA), investigations for the potential violation of the Insurance Business Act (IBA) were launched against the Hokkaido Agricultural Cooperative Association by the Japanese Ministry of Finance (MoF) shortly after the latter's launch of mutual aid activities. The major reason for this investigation was, that the provisions regarding the performance and scope of mutual-aid business of agricultural cooperatives were not yet specified within the newly introduced legislation. Nevertheless, no meaningful result was accomplished by respective investigation.

Representing a further obstacle, the scope of mutual-aid activities performable under the *ACA* were further not clearly separated from those of the *Agricultural Disaster Compensation Act* (ADCA) introduced in 1947. In 1949, the Japanese *Ministry of Agriculture, Forestry and Fishery* (MAFF) extended the scope of mutual-aid business performable by its agricultural disaster mutual-aid organization, established under the ADCA, to cooperative fire insurance for cooperative members. As a consequence, the MAFF strongly opposed the inception of the *National Mutual Insurance Federation of Agricultural Cooperatives (Zenkyoren)*, fearing for cannibalization of business between fire mutual-aid offered by agricultural cooperatives and its agricultural disaster mutual-aid organization. Thus, the MAFF heavily restricted fire insurance conductible by agricultural cooperatives, in order to prevent direct competition between the two mutual-aid schemes. With this situa-

[190] In other words, the mutual-aid movement established under *Zenkyoren* was the only cooperative mutual-aid movement created under the ACA.

tion being unacceptable for the developing agricultural cooperative mutual-aid movement, the issue of overlapping of business operations between agricultural cooperatives and the MAFF's agricultural disaster mutual-aid organization was tried to be resolved with the amendment of the *Agricultural Cooperative Act* (ACA) in 1952. Nevertheless, with only a partial solution being accomplished in the course of respective amendment, an overlap of business continued to exist and was not fully resolved until 1963.[191] In addition, the agricultural cooperative mutual-aid movement under *Zenkyoren* did not officially introduced fire insurance for members until 1955.[192] It was around the same time that the MAFF changed its original policy of opposing the development of the agricultural cooperative mutual-aid movement under *Zenkyoren* and began to actively promote its expansion.[193] [194]

Additionally, the Japanese agricultural cooperative mutual-aid movement was further threatened by the potential introduction of a cooperative insurance bill by the *Ministry of Finance* (*MoF*) during the 1950s, most likely containing restrictive regulations for cooperative insurance activities.[195] As a response to this threat, the agricultural cooperative mutual-aid movement together with other mutual-aid operating cooperatives collectively established the *National Association of Mutual Aid Cooperatives* in early 1954, which began to lobby heavily against the enactment of a cooperative insurance bill. In the end, cooperatives' efforts for the prevention of a bill were successful and no such law was introduced.[196]

The second type of mutual-aid activities established under above mentioned cooperative laws were those under the Fishery Cooperative Act (FCA). During the revision of the act in 1950, the possibility to establish mutual-aid business under the FCA was introduced. Following the amendment, the fishery cooperative movement's National Association of Fishery Cooperatives Mutual-Aid (Zensuikyo) was founded in 1951, with the particular purpose of providing affordable insurance to workers of the fishing industry.[197] [198] [199]

In 1952, the first cooperative being established under the *Small and Medium Enterprise Cooperative Act* launched its operations of cooperative fire insurance in the Hokkaido prefecture. Throughout the following years, several other SME-cooperatives began to operate fire

191 Cf. *Yoneyama* (2011), p. 88, 90-92.
192 Cf. JA-*Kyosai* (2017b), p. 6.
193 Cf. *Yoneyama* (2011), p. 88, 90-92.
194 Cf. *Ashikaga* (1959), p. 68-69.
195 Cf. *Yoneyama* (2011), p. 90-92.
196 Cf. Ibid, p. 90-92.
197 Cf. *Kyosuiren* (2017), online.
198 Cf. *Yoneyama* (2011), p. 114-115.
199 Cf. Kyosuiren Japan (1996), p. 4, 7.

mutual-aid business for small and medium enterprises in prefectures such as Amori, Fukui and Chiba.[200] [201] [202] [203] In 1955, the *National Small and Medium Enterprise Mutual Aid Federation* was established as an umbrella organization for fire mutual-aid operating SME-cooperatives. Similar to the case of the agricultural cooperative mutual-aid movement, the entrance of SME-cooperatives into the fire insurance market was highly opposed by the Japanese private non-life insurance industry, resulting in the launch of an investigation of the *Ministry of Finance* (*MoF*) regarding the legal nature of SME-cooperatives' mutual-aid business.[204] In 1957, the *Small and Medium Enterprise Cooperative Law* (SMECA) was amended. In the course of this revision the responsibility for supervision was equally distributed between the *Ministry of Trade and Industry* and the *MoF*, resolving potential legal conflicts investigated by the latter.[205] Due to the successful and steady growth of business of SME cooperatives' fire mutual-aid business, the necessity for reinsurance emerged. Thus, the *All-Japan Fire Mutual Aid Cooperative Association* (*Nitsukaren*) was initiated by respective cooperatives in 1960 as an umbrella organization providing such reinsurance.[206] [207]

Of the four existing types of cooperatives, consumer cooperatives were the last to successfully initiate mutual-aid operations. On December 1st, 1954, the *All Osaka Workers Mutual Aid Consumer Cooperative (Ōsaka rōdōsha kyōsai seikyō)* was established and began to operate fire mutual-aid. Within the next two years, similar prefecture-wide operating consumer cooperatives were incepted in prefectures such as Niigata, Nagano, Toyama, Hokkaido, Gunma, and Fukushima. By the end of 1958, the number of these prefecture-wide operating mutual-aid consumer cooperatives had increased to 32. Driving force behind the initiation of these cooperatives was Japan's newly emerging labor movement and trade unions, pursuing the objective of being able to offer affordable insurance to Japanese workers.[208] [209] [210]

Besides some regulatory obstacles, respective mutual-aid operating consumer cooperatives also had to overcome financial obstacles during their early years of existence, caused by big fires in cities such as in Niigata an in Uotsu in 1955 and 1956 respectively. Resulting from the

---

200 Cf. *Yoneyama* (2011), p. 131.

201 Cf. Chiba Prefecture Fire Mutual Aid Cooperative Association (2017), online.

202 Cf. Amori Prefecture Fire Mutual Aid Cooperative (2017), online.

203 Cf. Fukui Prefecture Fire Mutual Aid Association (2017), online.

204 Cf. *Yoneyama* (2011), p. 131.

205 Cf. Ibid, p. 131.

206 Cf. *Nikkaren* (2017), online.

207 Cf. *Yoneyama* (2011), p. 89-90.

208 Cf. *Zenrosai* (2017), online.

209 Cf. *Yoneyama* (2011), p. 89.

210 Cf. *Hartmann* (2003), p. 426.

financial strains experienced due to these two fires, the necessity for reinsurance became undeniable. As a result, existing workers' mutual-aid consumer cooperatives established the *Federation of Workers' Mutual Aid Cooperatives Association* as their nationwide reinsurance operating umbrella organization in 1957.[211] [212] [213]

Following the occurrence of big urban fires during the mid-1950s, several fire mutual-aid consumer cooperatives, independent from the workers' mutual-aid cooperative movement, were initiated, such as the *Niigata City Fire Mutual Aid Cooperative Association* in 1955 and the *Himeji Citizen Mutual Aid Cooperative Association* in 1956.[214] [215] Nevertheless, before the occurrence of mentioned fires in urban areas, similar consumer cooperatives were established for the sole purpose of offering cheap cooperative fire insurance to citizens of their respective municipals, including the *Yokohama Citizen Mutual Aid Cooperative Association* in 1953 and the *Nagoya Citizen Fire Mutual Aid Cooperative Association* in 1954.[216] [217] In 1957, municipal based mutual-aid consumer cooperatives initiated their own national umbrella organization for operating reinsurance, the *Japan Federation of Mutual Aid Cooperatives* (JAFMAC).[218] The inception of this national federation separated from the workers' mutual-aid movement, also demonstrates a characteristic specific of cooperative insurance operated under the *Consumer Cooperative Act*. In contrast to other mentioned types of cooperatives, consumer cooperatives are not unified under a single mutual-aid movement. Instead several separate mutual-aid movements developed, originally varying among each other with respect to the targeted segment of population for recruiting their members, which was either limited geographically or based upon members' professions.[219]

In addition to workers' and municipals' mutual-aid movements, various industry and profession-based mutual-aid cooperatives, partially initiated with the support of industries' or professions' trade unions, emerged during the 1950s and 1960s. These were among others the *Tabaco Industry Workers Mutual Aid Cooperative* in 1956, the *Police Officers Cooperative Association* in 1960, the *Defense Ministry Cooperative* and the *National Transportation Worker Mutual Aid Cooperative* in 1963, the *Forestry Industry Workers Mutual Aid Cooperative* and the

211 Cf. Ibid, p. 428.
212 Cf. *Zenrosai* (2017), online.
213 Cf. *Yoneyama* (2011), p. 89.
214 Cf. Himeji Citizen Mutual Aid Cooperative Association (2017), online.
215 Cf. Niigata Citizen Fire Mutual Aid Cooperative Association (2017), online.
216 Cf. Yokohama Citizen Mutual Aid Cooperative Association (2017), online.
217 Cf. Nagoya Citizen Fire Mutual Aid Cooperative Association (2017), online.
218 Cf. JAFMAC (2017), online.
219 Cf. *Hartmann* (2003), p. 434-435.

Teachers Mutual Aid Cooperative in 1965 and the *Telecommunication Workers Mutual Aid Cooperative* in 1967.[220] [221] [222] [223] [224] [225] [226]

From the late 1960s onwards, several of the prefectural workers' mutual-aid consumer cooperatives started perusing the objective of fully integrating their movement's direct insurance operations on a national scale. In 1976 such an integration was being performed by the majority of prefectural workers' mutual-aid consumer cooperatives, which transferred their mutual-aid business to their movement's national federation *Rosairen*. Following this reorganization of the workers' mutual-aid movement, *Rosairen* was renamed into the *National Federation of Workers and Consumers Insurance Cooperatives* (*Zenrosai*).[227]

Regarding operational performance, it can be said that all various mentioned mutual-aid movements were able to expand successfully their scope of business during their early decades of existence. Especially the mutual-aid activities performed by agricultural cooperatives experienced growth rates substantially higher than those of the private insurance industry and other cooperative mutual-aid movements. This development is demonstrated by the fact that the agricultural cooperatives' mutual-aid movement already ranked ninth in terms of total amount insured in the segment of life insurance compared to all other cooperatives and life insurance companies by the end of 1956, being the only cooperative mutual-aid movement among the ten largest life insurance operating organizations. By the end of 1976, the movement had improved this position by having become the third largest life insurance operating organization, which demonstrates the rapid scale of growth experienced during the previous twenty years.[228] [229]

In the case of cooperative insurance conducted under the *Small and Medium Enterprise Cooperative Law* (SMECA), cooperative insurers were able to lobby successful for the extension of their business to the segment of life and injury insurance, introduced with the amendment of the SMECA in 1973. Nevertheless, under the newly introduced regulations fire mutual-aid operations were required to be separated from other types of mutual-aid business. As a result, new SME mutual-aid cooperatives were incepted and separated from those conducting fire mutual-aid operations. Furthermore, newly established mutual-aid co-

---

220 Cf. *Suzuki & Saito* (2010), p. 52.

221 Cf. *Dentsukyosai* (2017), online.

222 Cf. Tabaco Industry Workers Mutual Aid Cooperative (2017), online.

223 Cf. Teachers Mutual Aid Cooperative (2017), p. 3.

224 Cf. Forestry Workers Mutual Aid Cooperative (2017), online.

225 Cf. *Hartmann* (2003), p. 436-437.

226 Cf. National Transportation Worker Mutual Aid Cooperative (2018), online.

227 Cf. *Hartmann* (2003), p. 429.

228 Cf. *Ashikaga* (1959), p. 69.

229 Cf. *Godo* (2001), p. 24.

operatives began to diversify in performing additional types of mutual-aid, such as mutual-aid against the shutdown or suspension of business as well as cooperative automobile insurance.[230] [231] In 1974, the *National Federation of Small and Medium Enterprises Life and Injuries Mutual Aid Association* was incepted as an umbrella organization for respective mutual-aid cooperatives. In 1975, the federation was renamed *National Federation of Small Business Life Injury Mutual Aid Cooperative.*[232] Furthermore, the *National Federation of Motor Insurance Cooperatives* was incepted as an additional umbrella organization within the same year, for the purpose of reinsuring SME cooperatives' automobile insurance operated.[233] [234] Simultaneously to the development of cooperative automobile insurance under the SMECA, several SME cooperatives for the purpose of operating truck transportation mutual-aid were established. A national umbrella organization with the task of offering reinsurance was established by respective cooperatives in 1972, being named the *National Mutual Insurance Federation of Truck Transport Cooperatives*.[235]

In conclusion, it can be said that mutual-aid operations conducted by various types of cooperatives successfully established a presence on the Japanese insurance market between the 1950s and 1970s. Considering this development, the question arises what reasons can be identified explaining cooperatives' attempt to initiate insurance business and their success in doing so.

One important fact important is that cooperatives were not directly supervised by the *Ministry of Finance* (*MoF*), and thus were not subject to the same severe regulatory control executed upon insurance companies under the *Insurance Business Act* (*IBA*). This allowed cooperatives to configurate more freely insurance products as well as to offer certain lines of insurance products for lower premium rates compared to those set for insurance companies by regulatory authorities.[236] [237] Especially in the case of the agricultural cooperative mutual-aid movement, literature reports that cooperatives were allowed to set premium rates of various types of mutual-aid products more freely and thus lower in comparison to those of insurance companies, representing a significant competitive advantage of the former over the latter. This special regulatory treatment was among other reasons granted due to the agricul-

230 Cf. *Yoneyama* (2011), p. 131-132.
231 Cf. Tokyo Kyosai (2017), online.
232 Cf. *Nikkaren* (2017), online.
233 Cf. Kanto Auto Kyosai (2017), online.
234 Cf. Japan Food Hygiene Association (2017), online.
235 Cf. *Kokyoren* (2017), online.
236 Cf. *Takahata* 1997, p. 342-344, 355, cf. *Hartmann* (2003), p. 441.
237 Cf. *Sono* (1962), p. 20.

tural cooperative movement's close ties to the *Ministry of Agriculture, Forestry and Fishery* (MAFF).[238] [239]

Second, it can be concluded from the above mentioned that the majority of mutual-aid cooperative movements were incepted for the primary purpose of offering affordable insurance to certain occupation groups such as teachers, public servants, fishermen, farmers, forestry workers, police officers, and workers of specific industries. In many cases, Japanese citizens belonging to these occupation groups were not particularly targeted by private insurance companies and still were hardly able to afford insurance products offered by private companies. As an example, fire insurance for wooden buildings in urban areas can be mentioned. Here, literature states that fire insurance offered by private insurance companies for wooden buildings was hardly affordable for lower income citizens or in some cases not even offered to them by insurance companies.[240] Moreover, the still existing significant shortcomings of Japan's social security system is another reason for the launch of mutual-aid by various cooperative movements, specifically in lines of life and injury insurance.[241] As a result, it appears that cooperative movements established themselves to focus upon operating insurance in market segments not served by insurance companies or governmental introduced insurance schemes at respective period.

Finally, it has to be considered that mutual-aid cooperatives were able to enter an otherwise highly protected industry, a situation that benefitted mutual-aid cooperatives' ability to establish market presence. As mentioned before, regulatory authorities shielded the Japanese insurance industry from increasing competition in the form of additional market entries of newly established domestic insurance companies during respective period. Moreover, the industry was subject to strict price and product standardization, representing regulations cooperative insurers were exempted from to a certain extend. It can be assumed that this situation lowered competitive pressure experienced by cooperative mutual-aid movements during their early years of operation, thus contributing to the cooperatives' ability to establish successfully a presence on the Japanese insurance market.

---

[238] Cf. *Godo* (2006), p. 7.

[239] Here it has to be mentioned that under the post-war economic development, the Japanese agricultural cooperative movement acted as the key channel through which the Japanese government in the form of the *Ministry of Agriculture, Forestry and Fishery* enforced its agricultural policies. In fact, the Japanese agricultural cooperative movement operated "[...] as a de facto quasi-governmental body" [Godo (2009: 5)] for the MAFF. Resulting from this relationship, preferential regulatory treatment was granted to the agricultural cooperative movement with respect to its financial services during the second half of the 20th century. (Cf. *Godo* (2009: 5))

[240] Cf. *Hartmann* (2003), p. 426-427.

[241] Cf. Ibid, p. 426-427.

From the early 1980s onwards, beforehand mentioned characteristic of cooperatives focusing upon certain segments of population changed in the case of major consumer cooperative mutual-aid movement. In 1981, the *Federation of Japanese Consumer Cooperatives (FJCC)* together with the trade unions of the Saitama prefecture extended the mutual-aid business of the *Saitama Kenmin Kyōsai Cooperative*, originally established by the Saitama metal workers' union for its members, to the whole prefecture's population. These newly introduced mutual-aid movement soon experienced high growth rates of business, with the *FJCC* soon extending *kenmin kyōsai* to the majority of Japanese prefectures.[242] [243] Confronted with the immediate success and expansion of business of the *FJCC's kenmin kyōsai* operations, the *National Federation of Workers and Consumers Insurance Cooperatives* (*Zenrosai*) decided to extend its operations from insuring industrial workers and trade union members to the general public of Japan in 1983 under their newly introduced *kokumin kyōsai* mutual-aid scheme. Resulting from the extension of mutual-aid business to the general Japanese populace, mutual-aid operations under the *FJCC* and *Zenrosai* experienced solid rates of mutual-aid business growth throughout the 1980s, allowing them to extend their scope of business significantly.[244] [245] [246]

In contrast to consumer cooperatives, the agricultural cooperative mutual-aid movement offered cooperative insurance to the general populace from its initiation of activities during the 1950s onwards, by allowing people to become associated members. Here it has to be mentioned that associated members differ from agricultural cooperative general members, as former hold no voting rights in primary cooperatives, but are nevertheless allowed to fully use services offered by agricultural cooperatives. Moreover, while general ownership can only be obtained from people being engaged in farming operations, anybody living within the vicinity of an agricultural primary cooperative is able to become an associated member. With the primary cooperatives having existed throughout the whole of Japan from the reanimation of the agricultural cooperative movement after the end of World War II and the movement's mutual-aid operations having been extended to a nationwide scale by the end of 1958, mutual-aid operated by agricultural cooperatives was offered to the Japanese general public from a much earlier point in time onwards compared to major mutual-aid movements under the *Consumer Cooperative Act*.

242 Cf. Ibid, p. 429.
243 Cf. FJCC (2017b), online.
244 Cf. *Hartmann* (2003), p. 429-433.
245 Cf. *Suzuki & Saito* (2010), p. 94.
246 Cf. Mutual-Aid Insurance Study Group (1988), (1989), (1990), (1991).

Furthermore, high increase of associated members experienced by agricultural cooperatives throughout the 1960s and 1970s represents one reason explaining agricultural cooperative mutual-aid movement's ability of significantly extending its insurance business during respective period, ultimately allowing the movement to become one of the largest insurance operating organization in Japan by the beginning of the 1980s. While the total amount of associated members was approximately 800,000 in 1960, this number had increased to more than 2.24 million by the end of 1980. At the same time, the agricultural cooperative mutual-aid movement had already become the third largest life insurance operator within Japan.[247]

Table 6: Membership development of Japanese agricultural cooperatives, 1955-2002

Fiscal Year	1960	1970	1980	1990	1999	2009
total number of members*	~ 6.600	7.277	7.885	8.609	9.125	9.430
full members*	~ 5.800	5.890	5.641	5.544	5.296	4.890
full members share	~ 88,9%	80,9%	71,5%	64,4%	58,0%	51,9%
associated members*	~ 800	1.387	2.244	3.065	3.829	4.540
associated members share	~ 12,1%	19,1%	28,5%	35,6%	42,0%	48,1%
* in thousand						

Source: *Ishida* (2002: 26), *Kurimoto* (2004: 123), *JA-Kyosai* (2017b: 5) (2009: 49), table by author;

Table 6 depicts the development of membership of the Japanese agricultural cooperative movement from 1960 onwards, showing that the number of associated members also continued to grow during the 1980s and 1990s.

Whereas the *National Association of Fishery Cooperatives Mutual-Aid (Zensuikyo)* experienced solid rates of growth throughout the 1960s and 1970s, mutual-aid activities by the fishery cooperative movement were never able to reach a similar size as mutual-aid operation of the agricultural cooperative mutual aid movement. Following the amendment of the *Fishery Cooperative Act* (FCA) in 1983, the organizational structure of the fishery cooperative mutual-aid movement changed, with primary fishery cooperatives becoming allowed to underwrite directly insurance to cooperative members. Following this revision, the *National Association of Fishery Cooperatives Mutual-Aid (Zensuikyo)*

[247] Cf. *Godo* (2001), p. 24.

was reorganized and transformed into the *National Mutual Insurance Federation of Fishery Cooperatives* (*Kyosuiren*) within the same year, with mutual-aid business being operated from then on directly by primary cooperatives and the movement's new umbrella organization supporting them through providing reinsurance. As a result, the fishery cooperative mutual aid-movement was reorganized into a two-tire structure.[248] [249]

During the late 1970s and early 1980s, further mutual-aid movements emerged under the Japanese *Consumer Cooperative Act* (CCA). In 1979, the *Japanese Consumer Cooperative Union's* (*JCCU*) with the help of the *National Federation of Workers and Consumers Insurance Cooperatives* (*Zenrosai*) established its own mutual-aid operations. Being named *CO-OP Kyōsai*, the *JCCU's* mutual-aid business particularly focused onto providing insurance products targeted at Japanese housewives, representing the main group of participants in the Japanese consumer cooperative movement.[250] [251] In addition to the newly established mutual-aid operations by the *JCCU* the *National Federation of University Consumer Cooperative Associations* (*NFUCA*) also established its own mutual-aid operations in 1981. Here, it can be stated that the *NFUCA's* mutual-aid business especially focused on insurance particularly designed for university students, such as cooperative insurance against the risk of sport injury and hospitalization as well as fire mutual-aid particularly designed for apartment owners.[252] [253]

Table 7 shows the state of operations of various selected major Japanese cooperative mutual-aid movements and its comparison in size against the private insurance industry and among each other during the late 1980s. Comparing operations of different major cooperative mutual-aid movements, the substantially larger size of the agricultural cooperative mutual-aid movement under the leadership of the *National Mutual Insurance Federation of Agricultural Cooperatives* (*Zenkyoren*) comapred to other mutual-aid movements becomes visible. Among consumer cooperative mutual-aid movements the *National Federation of Workers and Consumers Insurance Cooperatives* (*Zenrosai*) clearly represented the largest mutual-aid operating cooperative association during the late 1980s.

Here it has to be pointed out once more that both, agricultural cooperatives belonging to *Zenkyoren* and *Zenrosai*, represented cooperative mutual-aid movements that were offering insurance to the general

248 Cf. *Kyosuiren* (2014), p. 31.

249 Cf. *Kyosuiren* (1996), p. 4, 9.

250 Cf. *Suzuki & Saito* (2010), p. 74.

251 Cf. CO-OP Kyosai (2016), p. 14.

252 Cf. NFUCA (2017), online.

253 Cf. *Suzuki & Saito* (2010), p. 93.

Table 7: State of Operations – Major Cooperative Mutual-Aid Movements, FY 1987-1989

	National Mutual Insurance Federation of Agricultural Cooperatives (*Zenkyoren*)				**National Federation of Workers and Consumers Insurance Cooperatives (*Zenrosai*)**			
fiscal year	mutual aid in-force business*	mutual-aid premium income*	❶	❷	mutual aid in-force business*	mutual-aid premium income*	❶	❷
1988	¥265 724	¥3 328	12.6%	-	¥189 275	¥199.2	0.57%	-
1989	¥283 122	¥3 476	11.1%	-	¥196 477	¥263.3	0.76%	-
1990	¥380 590	¥3 573	12%	5.1%	¥228 814	¥271	0.84%	0.82%

	The Federation of Japanese Consumer Cooperatives (*FJCC*)				**The Japan Consumer Cooperative Union (*JCCU*)**			
fiscal year	mutual aid in-force business*	mutual-aid premium income*	❶	❷	mutual aid in-force business*	mutual-aid premium income*	❶	❷
1988	¥405.9	¥32.4	0.11%	-	-	¥0.2	-	-
1989	¥465	¥39.1	0.12%	-	-	¥0.4	-	-
1990	¥543.6	¥48.4	0.15%	-	-	¥0.7	-	-

	All-Japan Fire Mutual Aid Cooperative Association				**National Mutual Insurance Federation of Fishery Cooperatives**			
fiscal year	mutual aid in-force business*	mutual-aid premium income*	❶	❷	mutual aid in-force business*	mutual-aid premium income*	❶	❷
1987	¥8 975	¥17.9	-	-	¥4 443	¥44.2	0.16%	-
1988	¥9 787	¥18.5	-	-	¥4 902	¥46.2	0.16%	-
1989	¥10 395	¥18.9	-	0.27%	¥5 156	¥48.1	0.17%	-

❶ = comparable size of life mutual aid to private life insurance industry
❷ = comparable size of non-life mutual aid to private non-life insurance industry

* (in billion ¥)

Source: Mutual-Aid Insurance Study Group (1990), IRIJ (1991a) (1991b), table established by author;

Japanese public, whereas other small scale mutual-aid movements remained focusing upon providing insurance to their original target group of potential cooperative members based upon location or occupation. As a result, offering mutual-aid products not only to a specified group of people based upon their profession or residence but to the general Japanese populace appears to have contributed significantly to the agricultural cooperative mutual-aid movement's and major consumer cooperative mutual-aid movements' ability to extent business operations on a faster pace than remaining cooperative mutual-aid movements.

Nevertheless, considering the overall size of mutual-aid business in comparison to operations of private insurance companies established and operated under the *Insurance Business Act* (*IBA*), it can be concluded that combined mutual-aid operating cooperative movements were able to occupy a significant share of the Japanese insurance market. As a result, it can be said that the mutual-aid cooperative movements were able to establish themselves as a highly competitive third form of organization besides the stock and mutual insurance company on the Japanese insurance market.

2.7 The occurrence of company failures and demutualization in the time of financial deregulation and the current development of the Japanese insurance industry

From the mid-1990s onwards, the Japanese insurance industry has experienced a period of transformation that significantly changed the industry's composition and characteristics. This transformation was caused on the one hand by the Japanese insurance market's successive deregulation and on the other hand by the parallel occurrence of the Japanese financial crisis during the second half of the 1990s, in the course of which seven life insurance and one non-life insurance company became bankrupt. Moreover, with five of respective seven life insurance companies being of the mutual company form, and an additional four mutual life insurance companies demutualizing between the years 2002 to 2004, the mutual company form lost its position of dominance in the Japanese life insurance market during respective period.

The gradual deregulation of the Japanese insurance market was commenced with the enactment of the new *Insurance Business Act* (*IBA*) on April 1st, 1996. Under the new *IBA,* life and non-life insurance companies became allowed to enter each other's insurance segment through the inception of subsidiaries, a practice originally being prohibited.[254] The main intention of Japanese legislators behind respective regulatory change was to induce an increase of competition in both, the life and non-life insurance market segment, and thus to countervail

[254] Cf. *Yamori & Okada* (2007), p. 152.

the formerly governmentally precipitated oligopolistic situation of the nation's insurance market.[255] Following the enactment of the new *IBA* on April 1st, 1996, domestic non-life insurance companies incepted a total of eleven life insurance subsidiaries by the 1st of October 1996. Additionally, domestic life insurers established a total of six non-life insurance subsidiaries within the same period of time, leading to an almost instantaneously increase of domestic insurance companies.[256] [257] [258] In conclusion of this development, it can be said that Japanese regulators' former policy of shielding domestic insurance companies from the increase of competition by prohibiting inceptions of new domestic insurance companies had been abandoned the latest with the enactment of the new *IBA* in 1996.

Furthermore, the newly introduced *IBA* also included a first step towards an abolishment of the enforced practice of industry wide standardized prices and products, introducing a notification system for certain types of insurance products.[259] [260] Under respective notification system companies were enabled to simply notify the *Ministry of Finance* (*MoF*) about risk-weighted premium rates set for insurance products, without requiring former to receive additional permission for self-calculated rates by the latter.[261] Nevertheless, only a limited amount of insurance products fell under respective system, while premium rates chargeable for major mainstream products remained under the control of the Japanese *MoF*.

In addition to the new *Insurance Business Act* (IBA) the bilateral conclusion of the *Japan-U.S. Agreement on Insurance Deregulation* contributed to the liberalization of the Japanese insurance market. Generally speaking, the agreement necessitated Japanese regulators to abolish major market entry barriers against foreign insurance companies, and therefore to allow the latter to compete freely with Japanese insurance companies on the nation's insurance market for domestic customers.[262] Here it has to be mentioned once more that prior to regulatory changes introduced, foreign insurance companies were strongly restricted in offering insurance products to the Japanese general public as well as to enter the Japanese insurance industry through direct investment. Following the *Japan-U.S. Agreement on Insurance*

---

255 Cf. *Yoneyama* (2008); p. 36-37.
256 Cf. *Falia* (2015), p. 29.
257 Cf. *Tsuchida* (1998), p. 359.
258 Cf. *Kwon & Skipper* (1997), p. 164.
259 Cf. *Yamori & Okada* (2007), p. 152.
260 Cf. *Yoneyama* (2008), p. 37.
261 Cf. The United States General Accounting Office (1999), p. 43.
262 United States General Accounting Office (1999), p. 43.

Deregulation market entry barriers for foreign insurance companies became incrementally abolished.

In addition, the *Japan-U.S. Agreement on Insurance Deregulation* led to the extension of the list of insurance products falling under the prior introduced notification system. Moreover, Japanese regulatory authorities became obliged to increase transparency of their regulation activities, to improve the approval process for new insurance products, and to reduce the process' duration to a maximum of 90 days.[263] [264]

Nevertheless, the probably largest regulatory change agreed upon in the *Japan-U.S. Agreement on Insurance Deregulation* was the abolishment of industry wide uniform insurance premium rates for major non-life insurance products. In 1998, Japanese legislators conducted a major revision of the *Law Concerning Non-Life Insurance Rating Organizations*. Under the newly revised law companies operating on the Japanese non-life insurance market were no longer required to adopt premium rates calculated by existing non-life insurance rating organizations. Instead companies became allowed to calculate their own rates of premium charged for non-life insurance products offered. Thus, the new legislation stripped the then existing *Property and Casualty Insurance Rating Organization*[265] and the *Automobile Rating Organization* from its original task of calculating industry wide standardized premium rates for major non-life insurance product lines.[266] Despite that, non-life insurance companies were still obligated to obtain approval for self-calculated rates of premium from the *Ministry of Finance* (*MoF*), leaving the ministry some regulatory power over prices for non-life insurance products charged. Nevertheless, the deregulation of prices soon resulted in declining premium rates charged by non-life insurance companies as well as in the development of keen price competition.[267]

Contrary to the nation's non-life insurance industry, measures of product and price standardization were not immediately suspended in the case of the Japanese life insurance industry. It was not until 2005 that these standardization procedures started to be successively loosened, with most regulations having been abolished until today.[268]

Further regulatory changes affecting the Japanese insurance industry were introduced during the late 1990s and early 2000s in the course of Japan's so-called "Big Bang" reforms, being executed upon the nation's financial industry. Two major regulatory changes affecting in-

---

263 Cf. United States General Accounting Office (1999), p. 44.

264 Cf. United States General Accounting Office (1999), p. 43.

265 Respective rating organization originated out of the *Fire and Marine Ins. Rating Association*.

266 Cf. *Yoneyama* (2008), p. 35-36.

267 Cf. Standard & Poor's (2000), p. 21, 24.

268 Cf. *Yoneyama* (2011), p. 517-518.

surance companies can be named, the first introduced of the possibility for banks, securities companies and insurance companies to enter into each other's field of business through subsidiaries. Under respective reform, insurance companies became permitted to enter the banking and securities industry in 1998, whereas banks and securities companies became foreseen to be permitted to enter the nation's insurance market from 2001 onwards.[269] [270] [271] [272] Second, new provisions introduced in the course of Japan's financial "Big Bang" reforms allowed insurance companies to reorganize themselves under a holding company structure.[273] [274] This new possibility of reorganization of company operations was taken advantage of extensively during the transformation of the Japanese life and non-life insurance industry during the past fifteen years.

Congruently to the deregulation of the Japanese insurance market, the nation's life insurance industry experienced the occurrence of the so-called "Heisei Life Insurance Crisis". In the course of this crisis, seven small and medium size life insurance companies went bankrupt. Five of these insurers were of the mutual company form, while two were stock insurance companies. Table 8 delivers an overview of respective life insurance companies.

As the main trigger causing the occurrence of the crisis, the emergence of a "negative spread" situation, which was started to be recorded by Japanese life insurance companies unanimously after the burst of the Japanese asset price at the beginning of the 1990s, can be named.[275] This "negative spread" situation originate out of Japanese life insurance companies' strong focus onto selling saving-type products with long-term fixed interest rates in the course of the development of the Japanese asset price bubble during the second half of the 1980s.[276] [277] [278]

Interest rates guaranteed to customers of these saving type products were as high as 6.25 %, despite the *Bank of Japan's* key interest rate being set at a level of merely 2.5 % in 1987, and were promised in advance for the whole duration of insurance policies sold.[279] Moreover, due to the absence of adequate asset liability management within most

[269] Cf. *Sibbitt* (1998), p. 992.
[270] Cf. *Kwon & Skipper* (1997), p. 162.
[271] Cf. *Yamori & Okada* (2007), p. 155.
[272] Cf. *Toya & Arnyx* (2006), p. 196.
[273] Cf. Ibid, p. 196.
[274] Cf. *Tsuchida* (1998), p. 360.
[275] Here it shall be mentioned that "negative spread" simply speaking describes the situation in which an insurance company is unable to meet interest rates contractually granted to policyholders with the investment income achieved.
[276] Cf. *Sugino* (2013), p. 85.
[277] Cf. *Uemura* (2008), p. 23.
[278] Cf. *Fukao* (2004), p. 9.
[279] Cf. *Yoda* (1993), p. 1, 3.

Table 8: Bankruptcy procedures of failed life insurance companies of the Heisei Life Insurance Crisis

Company	Nissan Mutual Life Insurance Co.	Toho Mutual Life Insurance Co.	Daihyaku Mutual Life Insurance Co.	Taisho Life Insurance Co., Ltd.	Chiyoda Mutual Life Insurance Co.	Kyoei Life Insurance Co., Ltd.	Tokyo Mutual Life Insurance Co.
Date of Bankruptcy	Apr. 1997	Jun. 1999	May 2000	Aug. 2000	Oct. 2000	Oct. 2000	Mar. 2001
Law applied	*Insurance Business Act*	*Insurance Business Act*	*Insurance Business Act*	*Insurance Business Act*	*The Act on Special Treatment of Corporate Reorganization Proceedings and Other Insolvency Proceedings of Financial Institutions*	*The Act on Special Treatment of Corporate Reorganization Proceedings and Other Insolvency Proceedings of Financial Institutions*	*The Act on Special Treatment of Corporate Reorganization Proceedings and Other Insolvency Proceedings of Financial Institutions*
Negative net worth (in bil. ¥)	302.9	650.0	317.7	36.5	595.0	689.5	73.1
Funds from the Policyholder Protection Corporation or other industry safety nets (in billion ¥)	200.0	366.3	145.0	26.7	none	none	none
Subordinated loans and other general liabilities	unknown	unknown	unknown	unknown	all waived	all waived	all waived
Successor or restructuring sponsor company	***Aoba Life Insurance Co., Ltd.***	***GE Edison Life Insurance Co., Ltd.***	***Manulife Life Insurance Co., Ltd.***	***Azami Life Insurance Co., Ltd.***	***AIG Group Inc.***	***Prudential Financial Inc.***	***Taiyo Life Insurance Co., Ltd.*** and ***Daido Life Insurance Co., Ltd.***

Source: *Uemura* (2008: 2), International Monetary Fund (2012: 17).

Japanese life insurers, companies mostly failed to invest in long-term assets matching the long-term interest rate liabilities guaranteed to their policyholders.[280] Rather life insurance companies started to pursue riskier investment strategies focused upon short-term assets in order to meet their high interest rate liabilities. Here, literature reports that while the average duration of companies' liabilities ranged from approximately 15 to 20 years during the late 1980s, the average duration of their asset sides dropped to only 5 years in the case of most life insurance companies.[281] Furthermore, companies strongly increased their investment into domestic shares as well as foreign securities, causing life insurance companies to increase their exposition to risks of share price fluctuation and foreign exchange risk.[282] [283]

During the early years of the 1990s, Japan's economy experienced the burst of the Japanese asset price bubble, resulting in a period of economic depression. From the beginning of 1990 onwards, the *Tokyo Stock Exchange* experienced a rapid decline of its index following the *Bank of Japan's* decision to double its base interest rate. By the end of 1990, the stock exchange had recorded a loss of value of approximately 38.72 %.[284] While remaining stable throughout 1991, another steep decline of value was recorded during 1992, with the *Tokyo Stock Exchange* dropping far below the 20.000 Yen mark. Furthermore, real estate prices started to drop significantly as well from 1991 onwards.[285]

The burst of the asset price bubble in form of the plunge of the *Tokyo Stock Exchange* and the depreciation of value of real estate pushed the Japanese economy into a recession. Moreover, Japan's banking industry entered into a financial crisis. Responding to these developments, the *Bank of Japan* strongly reduced its base interest rate, ultimately adopting a "zero interest rate policy" in 1999.[286] With asset prices sharply decreasing and the base interest rate being gradually lowered in the aftermath of the burst of the asset price bubble, it became practically impossible for domestic life insurers, which due to the absence of adequate asset liability management had not invest in long-term assets matching their long-term interest rate liabilities, to achieve investment yields covering interest rate payments promised to their policyholders. In fact, the average interest yield accomplished by Japanese life insurance companies decreased from approximately 6.8 % in 1989 to 3.88 %

[280] Cf. *Yoda* (1993), p. 6-7.
[281] Cf. *Fukao* (2004), p. 6.
[282] Cf. *Uemura* (2008), p. 27, 39, 75.
[283] Cf. *Sugino* (2013), p. 86.
[284] Cf. *Graham* (2004), p. 9.
[285] Cf. *Ohno* (2006), p. 203.
[286] Cf. *Ohno* (2006), p. 207-208.

in 1993.[287] As a result, life insurance companies one by one started to experience a negative spread situation.

Nevertheless, with all domestic life insurance companies recording negative spreads in the aftermath of the burst of the asset price bubble, the question remains due to what reasons particular seven mentioned small and medium scale life insurance companies became bankrupt, while other life insurance companies were able to survive the industry's crisis.

As the first major reason, differences in profitability existing between various domestic life insurance companies during respective period of time can be mentioned. Despite all life insurance companies experiencing negative spreads from the mid-1990s onwards, several life insurance companies, including major market leaders, were able to cover losses originating from negative spread with recorded mortality profits and expense profits. Nevertheless, in the case of the majority of failed life insurance companies, mortality profits and expense profits recorded were too small to cover negative spread losses throughout the years of the crisis, depicting the generally lower profitability of respective companies' operations.[288] Resulting from this situation, life insurance companies were compelled to start selling assets for the purpose of capitalizing on these assets' unrealized profits. However, large amounts of unrealized capital gains of life insurance companies had been eliminated due to the two-time plunge of the *Tokyo Stock Exchange* and the deterioration of real estate values during the early 1990s, with some companies experiencing latent losses for certain asset classes held.[289] [290] [291] Furthermore, the amount of bad loans held by life insurance companies increased as well in the case of the progressing economic crisis.[292] Selling these assets in order to meet fixed interest payment obligations unavoidably led to a deterioration of above mentioned seven life insurance companies' financial structure. This deterioration of financial structure ultimately led to the bankruptcy of these life insurance companies.

The second major reason was the failure of respective seven companies' management to not identify correctly and adequately react to their companies' worsening financial situation. Contrary to surviving domestic life insurance companies, the management of above depicted seven life insurance companies is reported by literature of having been too slow or even reluctant to set cost-saving or operational re-

287 Cf. *Yoda* (1994), p. 3.

288 Cf. *Uemura* (2008), p. 51, 71, 85, 97-98, 129, 144.

289 Cf. *Sugino* (2013), p. 85.

290 Cf. *Yoda* (1993), p. 5.

291 Cf. *Uemura* (2008), p. 54, 85, 146.

292 Cf. *Uemura* (2008), p. 18, 20-21, 54, 106, 114.

structuring measures necessary for their companies' survival. Moreover, management's disability to implement necessary reforms due to resistance of certain internal interest groups as well as the existence of competency problems among top executives were identified to have contributed to the occurrence of bankruptcy in some of the cases of failing life insurers. As a result, the bankruptcy of above mentioned seven life insurance companies occured to a large extent due to severe management failure.[293] [294] [295]

With five out of seven failing life insurance companies being of the mutual company form, the question arises whether or not form-specific characteristics of mutual insurers' organizational structure contributed to their failure. Nevertheless, with highly similar types of corporate governance problems being identifiable in the case of all seven failing life insurance companies regardless of their form of organization, literature concludes that the mutual company form, if at all, only insignificantly contributed to the occurrence of bankruptcy of mentioned-above five mutual life insurers.[296] [297]

Following dissolution and bankruptcy procedures of the *Insurance Business Act* (*IBA*) as well as the newly introduced *Act on Special Treatment of Corporate Reorganization Proceedings and Other Insolvency Proceedings of Financial Institutions*, bankrupt life insurance companies were either acquired by a so-called "savior company", willing to take over in-force insurance business, or transferred their remaining business to a newly founded successor company. With four out of five "savior companies" being foreign companies, the acquisition of in-force policies of failed life insurers represented an attractive opportunity for foreign companies to enter quickly the previously highly shielded Japanese life insurance market. Savior and successor companies are depicted in the above presented table 8. As shown by the table, all of the successor or savior companies were of the stock company form.

Shortly following the *Heisei Life Insurance Crisis*, Japan's life insurance industry experienced the demutualization of four mutual companies during the years 2002 to 2004. Here it has to be mentioned that the possibility for demutualization did not exist in Japanese legislation until the enactment of the new *Insurance Business Act* (*IBA*) in 1996, whereas detailed provisions regarding the demutualization process itself were introduced in 2000.[298] The four mutual companies performing demutualization were the *Daido Mutual Life Insurance Company*

---

[293] Cf. *Uemura* (2008), p. 75, 114-116, 167-169, 183.

[294] Cf. *Sugino* (2013), p. 91-92.

[295] For a very detailed investigation of internal reasons for failure of life insurance companies during the "Heisei Life Insurance Crisis" see *Uemura* (2008).

[296] Cf. *Sugino* (2013), p. 90-94.

[297] Cf. *Uemura* (2008), p. 44-47.

[298] Cf. *Yamori & Okada* (2007), p. 165.

in 2002, the *Yamato Mutual Life Insurance Company* during the same year, the *Taiyo Mutual Life Insurance Company* in 2003 and the *Mitsui Mutual Life Insurance Company* in 2004.[299]

Reasons for the demutualization differed among the various life insurance companies. In the case of the *Daido* and *Taiyo Mutual Life Insurance Company*, demutualization was performed with the intend of both companies to reorganize themselves under a common holding company and therefore to transform their separate business operations into a single life insurance group. In the 2004, the *T&D Holdings Inc.* was incepted by both companies, with the latter becoming subsidiaries of the former. Moreover, the newly created holding company was listed on the *Tokyo Stock Exchange*. Intending to join the newly created life insurance company group of the *Daido* and *Taiyo Life Insurance Co. Ltd.* was the *Yamato Mutual Life Insurance Company*. Nevertheless, following the Lehmann Shock in 2008 the demutualized *Yamato Life Insurance Co., Ltd.* started to experience financial strain, ultimately causing the company to become bankrupt within the same year.[300] Major reasons behind these three companies' intention to reorganize them under a single holding company structure were the increasing competition on the Japanese life insurance market due to governmentally performed measures of deregulation as well as better access to capital by being able to issue additional shares on the *Tokyo Stock Exchange*. Latter was performed by the *T&D Holdings Inc*. in 2009.[301] [302]

Access to additional funds was a major reason for the *Mitsui Mutual Life Insurance Company* to demutualize. Nevertheless, instead of listing itself on the *Tokyo Stock Exchange*, *Mitsui Mutual Life* demutualized for the purpose to join the *Mitsui Sumitomo Banking Group* as a subsidiary in order to receive the group's financial support. Shortly after demutualizing and joining the banking group, the *Mitsui Life Insurance Co., Ltd.* raised new capital by issuing additional shares to its newly affiliated financial companies.[303] [304] Concluding from the above mentioned, it can be said that despite the strategic intentions behind the demutualization of the four mutual life insurance companies differed, the access to capital, in some form or another, was a key factor contributing to their decision to demutualize.

With a total of five mutual companies having become bankrupt throughout the *Heisei Life Insurance Crisis* and four mutual life insurers performing demutualization between years 2002 and 2004, the

[299] Cf. *Sugino* (2013), p. 86-89.
[300] Cf. *Sugino* (2014), p. 87.
[301] Cf. *Okada* (2016b), questionnaire.
[302] Cf. *Yoneyama* (2016a), interview.
[303] Cf. *Sugino* (2014), p. 92.
[304] Cf. *Yoneyama* (2016a), interview.

total number of mutual life insurance companies was reduced by nine. In addition, the *Meiji Mutual Life* and *Yasuda Mutual Life Insurance Company* performed a merger in 2004, nevertheless, maintaining their mutual company form.[305] As a result, the number of mutual life insurance companies dropped from a total of 16 at the beginning of fiscal year 1997 to 6 by the end of fiscal year 2004. At the same time, the total number of life insurers of the stock company form had already increased to 33 by the end of fiscal year 2004.[306] Notwithstanding this development, remaining mutual life insurance companies maintained holding a majority market share in terms insurance in force, as can be seen in table 9. Moreover, this situation did not change despite the demutualization of the *Dai-Ichi Mutual Life Insurance Co.* in 2009, reducing the total number of Japanese mutual life insurance companies to five.[307] At the end of fiscal year 2014 the remaining five mutual life insurance companies held a market share of 50.49 % in terms of total insurance in force.[308] [309]

Nevertheless, in terms of total annual premium collected, stock insurance companies outperformed mutual life insurance companies from fiscal year 2007 onwards. In fiscal year 2014, stock life insurance companies collected 66.73 % of total premium payments recorded by Japanese life insurance companies.[310] In conclusion, it can be safely stated that mutual life insurance companies lost their dominance over the Japanese life insurance industry during the first decade of the 21st century.

In spite of the burst of the asset price bubble and the following financial crisis experienced in Japan, the vast majority of non-life insurance companies refrained from experiencing similar financial strains, as did domestic life insurance companies. An exception to the majority of companies was the *Dai-ichi Mutual Fire and Marine Insurance Company*. Having focused onto long-term non-life insurance business, *Dai-ichi Mutual* suffered more strongly than other companies from high interest rates promised to policyholder, and thus experienced a lasting negative spread situation in the low interest environment following the burst of Japan's asset price bubble. Resulting from this situation, the mutual insurance company recorded, capital deficit of an estimated 48.8 billion

---

305 Cf. *Meiji Yasuda* (2016), online.

306 Cf. Life Insurance Association of Japan (2015).

307 Here, it shall be mentioned that contrary to demutualization between the years 2002 to 2004, the demutualization of the Dai-Ichi Mutual Life Insurance Co., was of a rather offensive nature, with access to capital for the purpose of extending their oversea business operation being a prime motivation for the company's demutualization. (Cf. *Yoneyama* (2016a, interview.))

308 Cf. Life Insurance Association of Japan (2015).

309 Excluding business of mutual-aid cooperatives.

310 Cf. Life Insurance Association of Japan (2015).

Table 9: Development of Business of Japanese mutual and stock life insurance companies, FY 1996-2013

Year	total insurance in force	total insurance in force mutuals	share of mutuals	total premium collected	total premium collected mutuals	share of mutuals
1996	¥2 087 431 833	¥1 873 525 350	**89,8%**	¥29 353 456	¥25 396 397	**86,5%**
1997	¥1 886 180 521	¥1 690 249 443	**89,6%**	¥30 360 791	¥26 401 195	**87,0%**
1998	¥1 827 638 655	¥1 628 241 308	**89,1%**	¥28 836 841	¥24 709 698	**85,7%**
1999	¥1 782 008 422	¥1 580 912 833	**88,7%**	¥27 607 004	¥23 348 007	**84,6%**
2000	¥1 631 223 109	¥1 480 536 072	**90,8%**	¥25 858 560	¥22 529 502	**87,1%**
2001	¥1 664 618 680	¥1 450 796 399	**87,2%**	¥26 185 887	¥21 280 731	**81,3%**
2002	¥1 606 904 805	¥1 346 541 484	**83,8%**	¥25 511 827	¥18 523 371	**72,6%**
2003	¥1 539 709 137	¥1 253 758 779	**81,4%**	¥25 960 897	¥16 887 530	**65,0%**
2004	¥1 494 552 774	¥1 137 546 088	**76,1%**	¥27 002 768	¥15 338 976	**56,8%**
2005	¥1 451 166 131	¥1 091 296 892	**75,2%**	¥28 332 940	¥15 396 592	**54,3%**
2006	¥1 521 081 143	¥1 121 724 005	**73,7%**	¥27 766 283	¥14 967 746	**53,9%**
2007	¥1 476 614 670	¥1 077 139 200	**72,9%**	¥30 909 689	¥14 490 325	**46,9%**
2008	¥1 430 360 947	¥1 033 345 605	**72,2%**	¥34 063 950	¥14 461 935	**42,5%**
2009	¥1 276 030 035	¥702 954 235	**55,1%**	¥34 116 133	¥12 586 496	**36,9%**
2010	¥1 251 115 539	¥677 964 970	**54,2%**	¥34 454 319	¥13 579 891	**39,4%**
2011	¥1 235 676 992	¥659 811 955	**53,4%**	¥35 978 798	¥14 551 376	**40,4%**
2012	¥1 231 764 039	¥641 606 581	**52,1%**	¥37 140 563	¥13 462 971	**36,2%**
2013	¥1 228 829 607	¥624 946 207	**50,9%**	¥34 738 150	¥12 058 448	**34,7%**
* in million Yen						

Source: IRIJ (1996) (2001) (2006) (2014a), LIAJ (2015), table by author.

Yen in 2000 and was ordered to shut down by regulatory authorities within the same year.[311]

In 2003, the second mutual company existing on the Japanese non-life insurance market, namely the *Kyoei Mutual Fire and Marine Insurance Company*, demutualized.[312] As a result, the mutual company form became inexistent on the Japanese non-life insurance market from respective point in time onwards.[313] Starting with the turn of the 21th century, Japan's non-life insurance industry experienced a period of major reorganization, with several mergers and consolidations being performed among domestic Japanese non-life insurance companies.[314]

Reasons for consolidations and mergers were among others the sharply increasing price competition following the deregulation of the non-life insurance industry during the second half of the 1990s and the early 2000s and the deteriorating business environment caused by low economic growth experienced throughout the first decade of the 21st century.[315] [316] Resulting from this reorganization, Japan's non-life insurance industry became dominated by three large insurance groups as of fiscal year 2010. These three insurance groups were the *Tokio Marine Holdings Inc.*, the *Mitsui-Sumitomo & Aioi-Dowa Holdings Inc.* and the *NKSJ Holdings Inc.* (renamed into *Sompo Holdings Inc.* in October 2016).[317] The dominance of these three insurance company groups over the Japanese non-life insurance market becomes evident, if considering the fact that for fiscal year 2013 recorded market share held by respective three insurance groups in terms of collected net-premium payments was approximately 85 %.[318] This dominance has continued throughout recent fiscal years.

Similar to the nation's non-life insurance industry, Japanese cooperative mutual-aid movements remained financially stable throughout the aftermath of the burst of the asset price bubble at the beginning of the 1990s and the there from following financial crisis. Moreover, cooperative mutual-aid movements offered insurance to the general public, were able to extent significantly business operations during the 1990s and early 2000s. The *National Mutual Insurance Federation of Agricultural Cooperatives (Zenkyoren)* was able to increase its market share held on the nation's life insurance market from 7.5 % in 1989 to 12.4 % in 2000 in terms of total annual premium collected. At the same

311 Cf. Japan Times (2000a), online.

312 Cf. JCRA (2004), p. 1.

313 Cf. FSA (2017), online.

314 Cf. *Yamori & Okada* (2007), p. 159.

315 Cf. *Ezawa* (2010), online.

316 Cf. *Yoneyama* (2012), p. 518.

317 Cf. *Ezawa* (2010), online.

318 Cf. IRI (2015), p. 12-13.

time the agricultural cooperative mutual-aid movement was able to extent significantly its non-life insurance business operations as well.[319]

In the case of the *National Federation of Workers and Consumers Insurance Cooperatives* (*Zenrosai*) life insurance business expanded more than twofold between years 1990 and 2005, whereas the movement recorded a more than 200 % increase of premium received from its non-life insurance operations between the same periods of time, totaling an income of 425.03 billion Yen. At the same time, the life mutual-aid business of the *Federation of Japanese Consumer Cooperatives (FJCC)* was able to catch up in size to cooperative life insurance operations of *Zenrosai*, with recording a total life insurance premium income of 373.44 billion Yen in 2005, representing a 656 % increase of life insurance premium income generated between the years 1990 to 2005.[320] [321] Moreover, the movement successfully established its own non-life mutual-aid business. Special attention has also to be given to the growth of the business of the *Japanese Consumer Cooperative Union's CO-OP Kyosai* movement. While only recording annual premium payments of a height of about 2.01 billion Yen in 1991, this figure increased to 102.77 billion Yen in fiscal year 2005.[322] [323] In total, the market share of life insurance business in terms of premium payments collected by consumer cooperatives increased from a mere 1.11 % in 1990 to 4.3 % in fiscal year 2004, with the main drives behind this development, being the *FJCC*, *Zenrosai* and the *JCCU's CO-OP Kyosai*. Moreover, considering the total number of policies in force as well as the total amount insured, it can be concluded that from this particular perspective both, the *Federation of Japanese Consumer Cooperatives (FJCC)* as well as *National Federation of Workers and Consumers Insurance Cooperatives* (*Zenrosai*), were able to establish themselves as major insurance operators of the Japanese insurance market. With respect to life insurance business in force, the total amount insured by the *National Federation of Workers and Consumers Insurance Cooperatives* (*Zenrosai*) equaled to 110,8 trillion Yen at the end of fiscal year 2005. At the same time, the total amount insured by the *Federation of Japanese Consumer Cooperatives (FJCC)* reached a worth of 61,7 trillion Yen. In comparison, the total sum insured of the largest three life insurance companies at the end of fiscal year 2005, namely the *Nippon Mutual Life Ins. Co.*, the *Meiji Yasuda Mutual Life Ins. Co.* and the *Dai-ichi Mutual Life Ins. Co.*, equaled to 321,1 trillion Yen, 249.9 trillion Yen and 238 trillion

319 Cf. JCIA (1995) - (2015), LIAJ (2015), Godo (2001), p. 24-25.

320 Cf. JCIA (2007), p. 4-9.

321 Cf. Mutual-Aid Insurance Study Group (1993), p. 4-7.

322 Cf. JCIA (2007), p. 4-9.

323 Cf. Mutual-Aid Insurance Study Group (1993), p. 4-7.

Yen respectively.[324] [325] As a factor potentially leading to this increase of business operated, literature mentions social insecurity following the burst of Japan's asset price bubble at the beginning of the 1990s as well as the bankruptcy of several insurance companies, making cooperative life insurance more appealing to costumers.[326]

While mutual-aid cooperatives offering insurance to the general public experienced high rates of growth throughout the 1990s and early 2000s, cooperative movements specializing on certain groups of citizens based upon their profession or residence were exempted from recording similar extensions of business. These movements mostly experienced stable or slightly decreasing levels of annual premium payments received during respective period.[327] [328] Nevertheless, financially stability of these movements was undoubtedly maintained as well, with no bankruptcy experienced among any types of mutual-aid operators.

Besides high rates of growth being experienced by several major cooperative mutual-aid movements throughout the 1990s and early 2000s, several mutual-aid movements experienced a period of restructuring caused by increasing competition as well as regulatory reforms during the first decade of the new millennium. In 2000, the prior three tier structure of the agricultural cooperative mutual-aid movement was reduced to a two-tire structure, representing a cost saving measure of the movement in face of increasing competition on the nation's insurance market.[329] By doing so, existing prefectural federations merged with the movement's national federation *Zenkyoren*, while at the same time, primary cooperatives became direct members of the *National Mutual Insurance Federation of Agricultural Cooperatives (Zenkyoren)*.[330] In addition, the Japanese agricultural cooperative movement experienced a series of mergers among its primary cooperatives, representing general efforts of Japanese agricultural cooperatives to increase efficiency and to reduce costs.[331] [332]

Furthermore, major amendments of existing cooperative acts between the years 2005 to 2008 changed the organizational structure of several cooperative mutual-aid movements. A major revision of the *IBA* and regulations of mutual-aid business within cooperative acts was performed, following the occurrence of scandals involving small-scale insurance like organizations, which operated under the term *Kyōsai*,

324 Cf. JCIA (2007), p. 4-9.
325 Cf. IRIJ (2006), p. 20-23.
326 Cf. *Suzuki* (2001), p. 3.
327 Cf. Mutual-Aid Insurance Study Group (1990) - (1994).
328 Cf. JCIA (1995) - (2007).
329 Cf. *Godo* (2006), p. 7.
330 Cf. *Ishida* (2002), p. 20.
331 Cf. *Ishida* (2002), p. 24.
332 Cf. *Zenkyoren* (2016), p. 5.

but were neither regulated by cooperative acts nor by the *Insurance Business Act* (*IBA*).[333] Here, the assimilation of provisions regarding cooperative insurance business stipulated in the various cooperative acts to provisions of the *IBA* became a main objective.[334] Amendments to mutual-aid provisions under the *Agricultural Cooperative Act* (ACA) were introduced in 2005, whereas mutual-aid amendments in the case of the *Consumer Cooperative Act* (CCA) were introduced respectively in 2007. Mutual-aid amendments to the *Fishery Cooperative Act* (FCA) and the *Small and Medium Entities Cooperative Act* (SMECA) were enacted in 2008.

In the course of these revisions the prohibition for consumer cooperatives to perform mutual-aid business parallel to other types of business was introduced. As a result, consumer cooperative movements that operated mutual-aid business besides other services became required to separate their insurance activities from remaining operations. Resulting from this development, 157 local consumer cooperatives, 3 regional consumer cooperative consortiums and the *Japanese Consumer Cooperative Union* established the *Japanese CO-OP Insurance Consumer Cooperative Federation (JCIF)* in October, 2008, with mutual-aid business transferred to the new federation in the following year. Also, in the case of the university cooperative movement, a new federation for the sole purpose of operating mutual-aid was incepted for the purpose of externalizing the movement's cooperative insurance operations in accordance to the new law.[335]

Besides, consumer cooperatives mutual-aid operations of fishery cooperatives were also reorganized. Following the amendment of the *Fishery Cooperative Act* in 2008, the original task of reinsurance performed by the *National Mutual Insurance Federation of Fishery Cooperatives* (*Kyosuiren*) for its member cooperatives was changed into a relationship of joint underwriting, with insurance risk being able to be distributed among the national federation and its members alike. Nevertheless, in spite of this newly introduced possibility, mutual-aid business of primary cooperatives was fully transferred to *Kyosuiren*, with the latter from thereon acting as the sole bearer of risk and former solely acting as mutual-aid underwriters.[336] A similar reorganization of business was also performed in the case of the *All-Japan Fire Mutual Aid Cooperative Association*, which after the amendment of the *Small and Medium Enterprise Cooperative Act* (SMECA) also became the sole bearer of risk from mutual-aid contracts underwritten by its member

333 Cf. *Kurimoto* (2009), p. 6-7.
334 Cf. *Kurimoto* (2007), p. 7.
335 Cf. UCMAF (2017a), online.
336 Cf. *Yoneyama* (2011), p. 114-115.

Table 10: Overview of major cooperative mutual-aid movements as of March 31st, 2016

Name	*Zenkyoren*	*FJCC*	*JCIF*	*Zenrosai*	*Kyosuiren*	*Nikkaren*
No. of member cooperatives	• 658 primary cooperatives • 32 prefectural credit federations • 33 prefectural welfare federations • 8 prefectural economic federations • 14 other cooperative associations • 2 national federations	43 coop. members: • 39 prefectural mutual-aid federation • Saitama Pref. Workers Coop. • 3 occupation-based cooperatives	148 coop. members: • 146 consumer cooperatives • JCCU • Zenrosai	58 coop. members: • 47 prefectural regional mutual aid worker cooperatives • 8 worker cooperatives based upon occupation, • 3 co-op federations	1052 coop. members	41 cooperative prefectural federations as of March 31st, 2015
No. of policies (ten-thousand)	5815	3908	780	3188	62,2	*85
No. of members (ten-thousand)	1026	1797	1995	1640	*33	*193
Total premium received (billion Yen)	¥5.936,7	¥644,3	¥170,5	¥690,7	¥64,1	*¥154
Main products	Life, fire, automobile, medical, pension, (traffic) accident, injury;	life, pension, annuity, fire, automobile, (traffic) accident;	medical, life, children;	Life, fire, automobile, medical, pension, (traffic) accident, annuity;	life, pension, crew welfare, group credit, fire;	fire, medical, injury, labor accident compensation;

* *as of March 31st, 2015*

Sources: JCIA (2015) (2016), FJCC (2016), CO-OP Kyosai (2016), Zenrosai (2016), JA-Kyosai (2016), table by author.

cooperatives from March 2008 onwards.[337] Moreover, following an additional amendment of the SMECA, the prohibition for fire mutual-aid cooperatives to perform other types of cooperative insurance was abolished. Following this regulatory change, the *All-Japan Fire Mutual Aid Cooperative Association* merged with the *Federation of Small Business Life Injury Mutual Aid Cooperative*, forming the *National Federation of Fire Insurance Cooperatives for Small Business (Nikkaren)* in 2014.[338]

While major cooperative mutual-aid movements during the 1990s and early 2000s experienced a fast expansion of business, growth rates declined in the years that followed. While some major cooperative mutual-aid movements such as those under *Japanese CO-OP Insurance Consumer Cooperative Federation (JCIF)* and the *Federation of Japanese Consumer Cooperatives (FJCC)* continued to experience solid, yet lower rates of growth, other major cooperative insurers such as the *National Mutual Insurance Federation of Agricultural Cooperatives (Zenkyoren)* and the *National Federation of Workers and Consumers Insurance Cooperatives (Zenrosai)* experienced somewhat fluctuating heights of business.

Considering cooperative mutual-aid movements' business operations during the years 2011 to 2014, it can be stated that the combined market share held by mutual-aid operating cooperatives remained rather stable, staying within a range of approximately 14.5 % to 15.5 % in terms of total annual gross premium collected.[339] Table 10 gives and overview of major cooperative mutual-aid movements as of March 31st, 2016.

2.8 Discussion of different organizational forms

As can be concluded from the above described, different insurance operating organizational forms developed separately from each other in Japan at various points in time. The stock insurance company was the first organizational form existing on the Japanese insurance market. First domestic representatives of the stock company form were incepted during the late 1870s and early 1880s, and remained the only type of insurance operating organizations until the beginning of the 20th century. A major reason contributing to this development was that a legal basis for mutual insurance operating organizations was still inexistent in the newly industrializing nation.

---

337 Cf. Ibid, p. 131.

338 Cf. *Nikkaren* (2017), online.

339 Cf. JCIA (2012) - (2015), LIAJ (2015), Insurance Research Institute (2015), ratios calculated by author.

This situation changed with the enactment of the first *Insurance Business Act* in 1900, as respective legislation introduced the mutual insurance company as the second legal form allowed to operate insurance in Japan. Following the introduction of the mutual company form, mutual insurance companies successfully established operations in the nation's life insurance market throughout the first two decades of the new century and had been able to conquer a market share of 18 % by the end of fiscal year 1922.[340] One major reason for the success of mutual insurance companies was the increasing preference of Japan's growing urban population for profit-participating saving-type life insurance products with predetermined fixed dividend rates during respective period. Nevertheless the forthcoming of mutual insurance companies significantly altered the operational practices of life insurers of the stock company form. Partly as a protective measure against and partly as a reaction to the increasing success of newly established mutual life insurance companies, life insurers of the stock company form unanimously changed towards predominantly selling profit participating life insurance products throughout the first two decades of the 20th century. These types of products were highly similar to policies underwritten by mutual companies. In addition, stock insurance companies one by one adopted a policyholder dividend distribution schemes of predetermined fixed dividend rates, identical to those of mutual life insurers. Demonstrating this trend is the fact that the share of profit participating types in the total sum of policies in force within the life insurance industry increased from 28.81 % in 1910 to 84.7 % in 1922.[341]

Concluding from the above stated it can be said that the successful emergence of mutual life insurance companies led to an assimilation of stock life insurance companies towards the former in terms of operational characteristics. Moreover, it can be deduced that by introducing and promoting profit-participating life insurance products, owners of respective stock insurance companies accepted to share profits with their company's policyholders in order to remain competitive against forthcoming mutual insurers in the long term. Resulting from this behavior, Japanese stock insurance companies guaranteed long-term profitability and thus experienced no need to consider mutualization as a need to remain operating successfully.[342] Nevertheless, it can be concluded by the above mentioned that boundaries between mutual life insurance companies and stock life insurance companies on the Japanese insurance market became notably blurred through the assimilation of operational characteristics during the early decades of the 20th century.

340 Market share in terms of total sum insured.

341 Cf. *Yingying* (2015), p. 231.

342 Cf. Ibid, p. 239-240.

Contrary to the development on the Japanese life insurance market, the mutual insurance company form was unsuccessful to establish a lasting presence on the nation's property and casualty insurance market during the first four decades of the 20th century. Resulting from this situation, the Japanese non-life insurance market was solely controlled by insurers of the stock company form for almost the entire first half of the 20th century.

Following the end of World War II, the Japanese life insurance industry underwent a period of significant reorganization. In the course of this reorganization, the majority of existing life insurance companies were forced to restructure their operations through establishing successor companies. Doing so, the vast majority of existing stock life insurance companies established successor companies of the mutual company form, leading to a mutualization of the majority part of the Japanese life insurance industry.

As demonstrated in the above depicted, the life insurance industry's mutualization was partially politically motivated as well as resulted partially from a combination of other factors, originating from poor socio-economic circumstances experienced by the Japanese financial industry during the immediate post-war years of the late 1940s. In the case of *zaibatsu* conglomerate affiliated life insurance companies, the initiation of successor companies of the mutual company form was part of the *zaibatsu* dismantling policies of the Allied Nations' *General Head Quarters*. In the case of life insurance companies not affiliated with *zaibatsu* conglomerates, reasons for choosing the mutual company form were a financially weak post-war shareholder base, worries regarding a potential participation of the emerging Japanese labor movement in companies' management and ownership, as well as obligations that would heavily restrict stock companies' former majority shareholders in ownership and management participation, if choosing to establish successor companies under the stock company form. Therefore, the inception of mutual successor companies in the case of non-zaibatsu affiliated life insurers appears to have been a deliberate decision of respective companies' management and major shareholders, often representing the same persons, in order to remain in control of their companies. Considering all mentioned reasons, it can be concluded that the mutualization of the Japanese life insurance industry during the immediate post-war period was a top-down precipitated process.

Following the mutualization of several life insurance companies' operations during the post-war reorganization of Japan's insurance industry, the mutual company form dominated the nation's life insurance market throughout the second half of the 20th century. Doing so, mutual life insurance companies were able to conquer and hold a market share of above 90 % in terms of total insurance in force and annual premium collected from the mid-1950s until the mid-1990s. Whereas this domination had its origin in the post war industry reorganization, it was severe governmental control executed upon the nation's life insurance industry that strongly contributed to its occurrence and long duration. Under regulatory authorities' so-called "convoy policy" the Japanese life insurance industry became strongly shielded from increasing domestic and foreign competition. At the same time, products sold and prices charged were centrally standardized, with regulators' main objective being to guarantee profitability of even the least efficient domestic life insurers. Under this situation, various domestic life insurers all practically underwrote the same types of products for the same premium rates charged. In conclusion, it can be argued that severe governmental control executed significantly contributed to mutual insurance companies' ability of gaining and maintaining a position of dominance on the Japanese life insurance market during the second half of the 20th century.

Moreover, it can be argued that severe governmental control led to an assimilation of remaining stock life insurance companies' operational characteristics to those of mutual life insurers during respective period. Due to regulatory authorities' industry wide standardization efforts product portfolios of mutual life and stock life insurance companies seems to have been largely identical. Resulting from this situation stock life insurance companies distributed dividends to the vast majority of their policyholders, with policyholders' entitlement to dividend payments thus being the norm in the industry.[343] Moreover, it appears that maximizing shareholder profit was not necessarily stock life insurance companies' prime objective. A reason for this belief is delivered by the fact that in the case of the remaining stock life insurance companies dividends to shareholders had been considerably small in comparison to profits accumulated throughout most parts of the second half of the 20th century.[344] Further evidence can be identified by comparing distributed shareholder and policyholder dividends of stock life insurance companies during respective period of time. Here it can be stated that the comparative size of shareholder dividends in relation to policyholder dividends fluctuated within a range of approximately 0.01 % to 1.1 % between fiscal years 1959 to 1985.[345]

Considering these historic characteristics of the stock life insurance companies during the period of severe governmental control , i.e. during the majority of years of the second half of the 20th century, an assimilation of operational practices of the former with those of mutual life

[343] Here it shall be added, that ratios of annual policyholder dividends paid against total premium income was not significantly different between stock life insurance companies and mutual life insurance companies of the same size, according to data from the Insurance Research Institute of Japan.

[344] Cf. *Yingying* (2013), p. 187-188.

[345] Cf. Insurance Research Institute (1960a), (1971a), (1976a), (1979), (1981a), (1986a).

insurance companies seem undeniable. As a result, boundaries between the two organizational forms were also somewhat opaque during the period of high governmental control of the second half of the 20th century. This conclusion leads to the assumption that domestic companies of the mutual and stock company form always had been notably assimilated in terms of operational characteristics during most parts of the 20th century.

In contrast to the Japanese life insurance industry, non-life insurance companies were not required to restructure their operation through establishing successor companies. Moreover, despite several non-life insurance companies belonging to *zaibatsu* conglomerates, these companies were not required to mutualize them. Rather their ownership was distributed evenly upon the companies' employees, its shareholders and its former shareholders. A wave of mutualization during the immediate post war years was thus not experienced as in the case of the nation's life insurance industry.

Moreover, highly similar to the nation's life insurance industry, existing non-life insurance companies were subject to strict governmental regulations from the mid-1950s onwards, including an industry wide standardization of premium rates for major lines of products. On the other hand, companies enjoyed governmental protection from increasing domestic competition, with the inception of new companies being disapproved by Japanese regulators. In conclusion, the stock companies remained the dominating form of organization on the Japanese non-life insurance market.

During the 1950s, mutual-aid operating cooperatives entered the Japanese insurance industry as the second organizational form operating insurance based upon principles of mutuality. Being subdivided into four different types of cooperatives, namely agricultural, small and medium, fishery and consumer cooperatives, it can be said that early mutual-aid operating cooperatives launched their business for their purpose of offering affordable insurance to particular segments of the Japanese population. Especially in the case of consumer cooperatives mutual-aid became initiated in order to serve insurance needs of specific groups of people based upon their workplace, profession or residence. Major reasons for these cooperative movements to emerge were among other the existence of severe shortcomings of the Japanese social security system as well as the situation that insurance products offered by private companies were still hardly affordable for certain groups of citizens or not offered to them in the first place, as was the case for insurance against the risk of fire of wooden buildings in densely populated urban areas.[346] Providing mutual-aid services to population segments without access to affordable insurance against risks such

[346] Cf. *Hasnmann* (2003), p. 426-427.

as fire, sickness, unemployment, inability to work and death was thus early cooperative insurers' main motivation for launching insurance operations. This particular historic characteristic of early mutual-aid operating cooperatives represents a major difference in comparison to the origin of most mutual-life insurers. Whereas mutual-aid cooperatives were established as a reaction to inadequate social security and market failure during the early post war era with the main purpose of increasing the welfare of their policyholders belonging to particular groups of persons, the majority of mutual life insurance companies originated from political influence and strategic decision of companies' top-management and former owners in order to remain in control of their companies.

Nevertheless, characteristics of some major mutual-aid cooperative movements changed throughout the second half of the 20th century. In the case of the agricultural cooperative mutual-aid movement, profits generated by insurance activities became essential for covering losses resulting from other services and types of business offered and operated by agricultural cooperatives from the 1970s onwards.[347] Extension of business thus became a prime objective of the agricultural cooperative mutual-aid movement during the 1970s and early 1980s, seemingly pushing back the movement's original intent behind its insurance operations. Also, in the case of consumer cooperative mutual-aid operations a change of character was identifiable. From the early 1980s onwards, major consumer cooperative movements began to offer mutual-aid services to the general Japanese population. Among them especially the workers mutual-aid movement under its federation the *National Federation of Workers and Consumers Insurance Cooperatives* (*Zenrosai*) has to be mentioned, which from 1983 onwards began to offer cooperative insurance to the total general population of Japan, thus extending its original operations of insuring industrial workers and trade union members. Prior to that, the newly established *Japan Consumer Cooperative Union* and the *Saitama Kenmin Kyōsai Cooperative* began underwriting mutual-aid targeted to the general Japanese population.

In summary of the historic development and co-existence of various organizational forms on the Japanese insurance market it can be stated that the mutual insurance company form and mutual-aid operating cooperatives developed quite separately from each other alongside the stock company form and differed with respect to historic characteristics. For example, identified differences of incentives and historic reasons for the inception of mutual insurance companies and mutual-aid cooperatives can be named. Moreover, the fact those cooperative insurers were and still are regulated by separate legislation

347 Cf. *Godo* (2009), p. 9.

as mutual and stock insurance companies, contributed to the separate development of cooperative mutual-aid movements from the other two forms of organization of the Japanese insurance industry. Following the historic development and co-existence of various forms of organization operating on the Japanese insurance market, the next chapter will investigate various organizational forms of recent economic performance and current operational characteristics.

3. Economic performance and operational characteristics of various insurance operating forms of organization

As mentioned in the above subchapter, Japan's insurance industry experienced a period of severe restructuring, which lasted from the mid-1990s until the mid-2000s. In the course of this reorganization, the Japanese insurance market was significantly deregulated, with practices of industry wide standardizing premium rates and shielding domestic insurers from additional competition in the form of new domestic and foreign market entries being gradually abandoned. Moreover, due to the failure of five mutual life insurance companies during the years 1997 to 2001 and the demutualization of an additional five mutual life insurers between years 2002 and 2009, the mutual company form gradually lost its position of dominance on the Japanese life insurance market during respective period. Resulting from this development, the stock insurance company form became the most dominant form of organization on both, the Japanese life and non-life insurance market. Table 11 depicts the development of the total annual premium income of different forms of organization between fiscal years 2011 to 2014.

As can be seen in the table, insurance companies of the stock company form recorded a total annual premium income of approximately 78,67 trillion Yen, representing slightly above 56 % of premium payments received by the entire Japanese insurance industry. This market share of stock insurance companies in terms of received premium income increased to a height of approximately 61.9 % throughout the following three fiscal years. Consequentially, mutual insurers' market share decreased during respective period. Especially in the case of remaining mutual life insurance companies the market share held de-

Table 11: Market share and direct premium development of mutual and non-mutual insurers on the Japanese insurance market, FY 2011-2014

Distribution of Total Premium Income Japanese Insurance Industry

	Non-Life Insurance Companies under the IBA			**Life Insurance Companies under the IBA**		
Fiscal Year	Doemstic Non-Life Insurance Companies	Foreign Non-Life Insurance Companies	Mutual Life Insurance Company Subsidiary**	Mutual Life Insurance Companies	Stock Life Insurance Companies	
2014	¥97 222,73	¥6 292,36	¥163,51	¥125 216,09	¥247 007,43	
	17,49%	**1,13%**	**0,03%**	**22,52%**	**44,43%**	
2013	¥93 274,42	¥6 070,82	¥165,43	¥120 584,48	¥226 797,02	
	17,60%	**1,15%**	**0,03%**	**22,75%**	**42,79%**	
2012	¥88 447,21	¥6 363,18	¥157,11	¥134 629,71	¥236 775,92	
	15,04%	**1,08%**	**0,03%**	**22,90%**	**40,27%**	
2011	¥84 953,67	¥6 125,31	¥155,18	¥145 963,76	¥216 927,21	
	15,80%	**1,14%**	**0,03%**	**27,15%**	**40,35%**	

in 100 million ¥

	Mutual Aid Cooperatives under various cooperative laws					**total**
	Zenkyoren*	Zensuiren	Consumer Cooperatives	SME Cooperatives	Others	
2014	¥61 721,24	¥576,00	¥16 226,00	¥851,00	¥695,00	**¥555 971,36**
	11,10%	**0,10%**	**2,92%**	**0,15%**	**0,13%**	
2013	¥64 920,49	¥574,00	¥16 114,00	¥838,00	¥710,00	**¥530 048,66**
	12,25%	**0,11%**	**3,04%**	**0,16%**	**0,13%**	
2012	¥73 253,91	¥757,00	¥16 096,00	¥824,00	¥721,00	**¥558 025,04**
	12,46%	**0,13%**	**2,74%**	**0,14%**	**0,12%**	
2011	¥65 480,56	¥788,00	¥15 691,00	¥816,00	¥744,00	**¥537 644,69**
	12,18%	**0,15%**	**2,92%**	**0,15%**	**0,14%**	

*including ist subsidiary Kyoei Fire Insurance Co. Ldt.

** non life insurance subsidiary of Meiji Yasuda Mutual Life Insurance Co.

Source: JCIA (2012 - 2015), LIAJ (2015), Insurance Research Institute (2015), table established by author.

creased from 27.15 % to 22.52 %, representing a loss of approximately 4.6 % within a three years period.

Also, in the case of the *National Mutual Insurance Federation of Agricultural Cooperatives (Zenkyoren)*, operating the entire insurance business of the Japanese agricultural cooperative mutual-aid movement, a nominal decrease of annual premium rates received was experienced between fiscal years 2011 and 2014, causing a decrease of market share held in terms of total premium payments collected from 12.18 % to 11.1 %. Contrary to this development, insurance premium payments received and market share held by other types of mutual-aid operating cooperatives remained rather stable. Here, the rather small size of market share held by respective mutual-aid cooperatives, accounting only for 3.3 % of total premium payments collected by the entire Japanese insurance industry during fiscal year 2014, leads to the immediate conclusion that mutual-aid operating cooperative movements besides the *National Mutual Insurance Federation of Agricultural Cooperatives* (*Zenkyoren*) are of a significantly smaller scale. Nevertheless, comparing various mutual-aid cooperative movements on the basis of total amount insured, it can be stated that the *National Federation of Workers and Consumers Insurance Cooperatives* (*Zenrosai*) and the *Federation of Japanese Consumer Cooperatives (FJCC)* have developed into major insurance operators of the Japanese insurance industry. While the total sum insured of the *National Mutual Insurance Federation of Agricultural Cooperatives* equaled to a total of 375.3 trillion Yen at the end of fiscal year 2014, the total sum insured by in force policies of the *Zenrosai* and the *FJCC* reached a height of 233.9 trillion Yen and 210,1 trillion Yen respectively.[348] Moreover, in terms of total value of life insurance in force *Zenrosai* and the *FJCC* ranked as the seventh and sixth largest life insurance operators on the Japanese insurance market.[349] [350]

Despite the above observable trend of steadily declining total market share held, major mutual insurance companies still represent some of the largest insurance operating organizations in Japan. Table 12 shows the ranking of the ten largest insurance companies and mutual-aid conducting cooperative groups in terms of premium received for life, non-life and total insurance business operated for fiscal year 2014. As can be seen in the table, three out of the six largest life insurance operating organizations on the Japanese insurance market were of the mutual company form. These companies are the *Nissay Mutual Life Insurance Co.* (former *Nippon Mutual Life*), the *Meiji Yasuda Mutual Life Insurance Co.* and the *Sumitomo Mutual Life Insurance Co.*, occu-

348 Cf. JCIA (2015), p. 9.
349 Cf. LIAJ (2015).
350 Cf. JCIA (2015), p. 9.

pying ranks two, three and six respectively. Moreover, as shown by the table also the *National Mutual Insurance Federation of Agricultural Cooperatives (Zenkyoren)* belonged to the five largest life insurers in terms of premium income received on the Japanese insurance market. In terms of property and casualty insurance operation, *Zenkyoren* even represents the largest single non-life insurance operator within the Japanese insurance industry in fiscal year 2014. Here, it has to be nevertheless mentioned that the *Sompo Japan Nipponkoa Insurance Inc.* and the *Tokio Marine & Nichido Fire Insurance Co., Ltd.* both belong to domestic insurance company groups, whose total premium income recorded by member companies surpassed the one of the *National Mutual Insurance Federation of Agricultural Cooperatives.*[351] In addition to *Zenkyoren* the *National Federation of Workers and Consumers Insurance Cooperatives* (*Zenrosai*) ranks among the ten largest single non-life insurance operators in terms of premium income recorded. Ranking insurance operators of the Japanese insurance industry with respect to total premium income received from both, life and non-life insurance business, the *National Mutual Insurance Federation of Agricultural Cooperatives* (*Zenkyoren)* was even the largest insurance operating organization based on insurance premium income received in fiscal year 2014. Here it has to be mentioned, that *Zenkyoren*, being a mutual-aid cooperative federation, enjoys the privilege of being allowed to underwrite directly and to operate life as well as nonlife insurance business, whereas insurance companies are prohibited to do so under the Japanese *Insurance Business Act* (IBA). On the other hand, *Zenkyoren* only underwrites personal lines of insurance business, being in contrast to major insurance companies, in the case of which commercial lines of insurance represent significant amounts of their business.

In order to investigate operational characteristics of various cooperative insurers besides major cooperative mutual-aid movements such as *Zenkyoren*, *Zenrosai*, and the *FJCC*, table 13 delivers a comparison of annual premiums received and number of lines operated in comparison to average values of medium and small size life and non-life insurance companies, operating on the Japanese insurance industry.[352] Looking upon the table, it can be said that the vast majority of remaining mutual-aid cooperatives represents small-scale insurance operators on the Japanese insurance market. As an exception the *Japanese CO-OP Insurance Consumer Cooperative Federation (JCIF)*, the *Cooperative*

[351] Cf. Insurance Research Institute (2015).

[352] Here it has to be mentioned that small scale cooperatives included in the table are those listed in the Japan Cooperative Insurance Association's annual report of performance of mutual-aid cooperatives. Nevertheless, a multitude of additional mutual-aid cooperatives do exist in Japan, which are of a comparatively insignificant size and are thus not included in statistics issued by the Japan Cooperative Insurance Association.

Table 12: List of the ten largest insurance companies and mutual aid operating cooperative groups, FY 2014

Ten largest Insurance Companies and Mutual Aid conducting Cooperative Groups based upon Total Amount of Premium Income recorded for FY 2014						
Rank	Life Insurance & Life Mutual Aid	premium income	Non-Life Insurance and Non-Life Mutual Aid	premium income	Total Insurance	premium income
1.	Japan Post Insurance Co., Ltd.	¥5 954	JA-Kyosai (Zenkyoren)	¥2 971	JA-Kyosai (Zenkyoren)	¥5 972
2.	Nissay Mutual Life Insurance Co.	¥5 336	Sompo Japan Nipponkoa Insurance Inc	¥2 627	Japan Post Insurance Co., Ltd.	¥5 954
3.	Meiji Yasuda Mutual Life Ins. Co.	¥3 407	Tokio Marine & Nichido Fire Insurance Co., Ltd.	¥2 512	Nissay Mutual Life Insurance Co.	¥5 336
4.	Dai-Ichi Life Insurance Co. Ltd.	¥3 266	Mitsui Sumitomo Insurance Co., Ltd.	¥1 782	Meiji Yasuda Mutual Life Ins. Co.	¥3 407
5.	JA-Kyosai (Zenkyoren)	¥3 201	Aioi Nissay Dowa Insurance Co., Ltd.	¥1 449	Dai-Ichi Life Insurance Co. Ltd.	¥3 266
6.	Sumitomo Mutual Life Ins. Co.	¥2 575	Fuji Fire and Marine Insurance Co., Ltd.	¥325	Sompo Japan Nipponkoa Insurance Inc	¥2 627
7.	Dai-Ichi Frontier Life Ins. Co., Ltd.	¥1 716	AIU Insurance Co., Ltd.	¥262	Sumitomo Mutual Life Ins. Co.	¥2 575
8.	American Family Life Assurance Co. Ltd.	¥1 495	Zenrosai	¥203	Tokio Marine & Nichido Fire Insurance Co., Ltd.	¥2 512
9.	MetLife Life Insurance Co., Ltd.	¥1 445	The Kyoei Fire & Marine Insurance Co.,Ltd.	¥200	Mitsui Sumitomo Insurance Co., Ltd.	¥1 782
10.	Gibraltar Life Insurance Co., Ltd.	¥1 335	The Nisshin Fire & Marine Insurance Co., Ltd.	¥166	Dai-Ichi Frontier Life Ins. Co., Ltd.	¥1 716

mutual insurance company	in billion ¥
stock insurance company	
cooperative	

Source: JCIA (2015), LIAJ (2015), IRIJ (2015), table by author.

Table 13: Comparison of annual premium payments received and lines of business operated of cooperative mutual-aid movements and insurance companies

Name	National Mutual Ins. Federation of Fishery Coop.	COOP-Insurance/JCIF	Kanagawa Prefecture Mutual Aid Coop. Society	Japan Post Group Workers Mutual Aid Coop. Ass.	Japan Teachers' Mutual Aid Coop. Society
❶	576.19 ¥	1704.74 ¥	151.62 ¥	26.05 ¥	758.23 ¥
❷	7	4	4	2	8
Name	**Nat. Transportation Worker Mutual Aid Coop. Society**	**All-Japan Municipal Workers Mutual Aid Coop. Ass.**	**Telecom. Industry Workers Mutual Aid Cooperative Society**	**Police Officers Mutual Aid Cooperative Ass.**	**University Coop Mutual Aid Federation**
❶	35.73 ¥	45.06 ¥	121.88 ¥	688.26 ¥	85.31 ¥
❷	4	2	4	5	2
Name	**National Federation of Electric Power Cooperatives**	**Nationwide Liquor Sales Industry Coop.**	**Nationwide Tobacco Sales Coop. Ass.**	**Japan Salt Industry Coop. Ass.**	**Nationwide Cities' Employees' Mutual Aid Coop. Society**
❶	24.24 ¥	4.26 ¥	7.30 ¥	1.63 ¥	40.43 ¥
❷	1	2	3	2	2
Name	**National Towns' and Villages' Employees Coop. Ass.**	**All-Japan Firefighter Mutual-Aid Coop. Ass.**	**Coop. Ass. of the Ministry of Defense**	**National Federation of Small Business Fire Insurance Coop.**	**National Rice Selling Business Mutual Aid Coop. Ass.**
❶	67.72 ¥	4.33 ¥	99.57 ¥	193.9 ¥	4.85 ¥
❷	2	1	2	5	5
Group	Mid non-life insurance companies	Bottom non-life insurance companies		Mid-third life insurance companies	Bottom-third non-life insurance companies
❶	**Ø 739.01 ¥ (846.77 ¥ – 217.33 ¥)**	**Ø 127.81 ¥ (213.75 ¥ - 37.36 ¥)**		**Ø 3526.67 ¥ (5445.81 ¥ - 984.97 ¥)**	**Ø 178.89 ¥ (910.36 ¥ - 0.11 ¥)**
❷	**Ø 10.22 (22 – 1)**	**Ø 7.6 (22 – 1)**		-	-

❶ = premium income (FY 2014), ❷ = insurance lines operated, (FY 2014);

Sources: JCIA (2015), LIAJ (2015), IRIJ (2015), table established by author.

Association of Police Officials and the *Mutual Aid Cooperative Association of Teaching Staff* can be named, which rather rank among the group of medium size insurance operators on the Japanese insurance market. Furthermore, it can be identified that the majority of cooperative mutual-aid movements only operate a very limited number of lines of business, ranging from five to one. Considering this fact, it can be said that the majority of mutual-aid cooperative movements represent rather specialized insurance operators within the Japanese insurance industry.

Identifiable reasons for the comparatively smaller size and high specialization of the majority of mutual-aid cooperative movements are the following.

On the one hand, small scale cooperative insurers represent mutual-aid movements, which only offer mutual-aid services to particular groups of people, either based upon their profession, the industry they work in or their place of residence. Here, it has to be considered that several of respective industry- or profession-based mutual aid cooperative movements were established with the support of trade unions of respective industries in order to make affordable insurance particularly accessible to their members. Considering respective profession, industry or residence based cooperative insurers, it appears that intentions for the extension of business beyond offering insurance services to the initial target groups of policyholders have not emerged or existed within respective movements throughout their historic development. As a result, the majority of small scale cooperative insurers seem to have maintained their originally intended scope of operation. With only a specific group of people out of the Japanese population targeted as potential policyholders, the comparatively small size of industry-, profession- and residence-based cooperative mutual-aid movements appears to be a logical consequence.

On the other hand, various cooperative acts legally restrict cooperative movements in their insurance activities. In the case of agricultural, fishery and consumer cooperatives, only natural persons are allowed to become members of respective types of cooperatives on the primary level. As a result, mutual-aid movements under the *Agricultural Cooperative Act*, *Fishery Cooperative Act* and *Consumer Cooperative Act* are restricted to the operation of personal lines of insurance and are prohibited from operating commercial lines of insurance. By contrast, mutual-aid operating small and medium enterprise cooperatives are only permitted to grant membership to entrepreneurs and small and medium sized companies specified under the *Small and Medium Enterprise Cooperative Act* (SMECA). Therefore, mutual-aid operating cooperatives under the SMECA are prohibited from selling insurance to natural persons and thus the general Japanese public, therfore they are only allowed to underwrite insurance to small and medium enterprises.[353] [354] With no such regulations existing under the *Insurance Business Act* (IBA), the comparatively higher diversification of business of large to medium scale insurance companies becomes plausible.

As was already depicted in the above, three out of the five existing mutual insurance companies within the Japanese insurance industry rank among the six largest life insurance operators on the Japanese insurance market. At the same time, the remaining two mutual life insurance companies, namely the *Fukoku Mutual Life Ins. Co.* and the *Asahi Mutual Life Ins. Co.* can be regarded as medium size life insurance companies in terms of total sum insured and annual premium payments received during the fiscal year 2014. Furthermore, if comparing the diversification of product portfolios of mutual life insurance companies to those of stock life insurance companies of similar size, no significant difference between representatives of the two different organizational forms in terms of the total number of various insurance products underwritten can be identified. Especially the three large-size mutual life insurance companies offer a large variety of insurance products of different lines of business, being significantly larger than those of medium and small-scale life insurers. As a result, mutual life insurance companies appear not to differ with respect to the diversity of types of insurance underwritten in comparison to competitors of similar size of the stock company form.

Nevertheless, when looking upon the share of total in-force business represented by different lines of insurance operated, it appears that in the case of the majority of mutual life insurance company's group life and group annuity insurance represents a larger share of total business operated than in the case of stock life insurance companies. Table 14 provides a comparison between mutual life insurance companies and stock life insurance companies regarding the share of business represented by group life insurance and group annuity products in terms of total amount insured and premium income received.

As can be seen in table 14, with the share of group insurance and group annuities operated by stock life insurance companies ranging on average between 9 % to 15.6 % of total business operated, the focus of most mutual life insurance companies on group life and group annuity insurance lines is higher in comparisons to the majority of stock life insurance companies. As a result, it can be concluded that mutual life insurance companies represent the Japanese insurance industry's major operators of group life and group annuity insurance lines. The only exception among mutual insurers is the *Asahi Mutual Life Ins. Co.* in which group life and group annuity insurance only represents a small portion of the company's overall business.

353 Cf. article 7, paragraph 1, SMECA (1949).

354 Cf. article 8, paragraph 1-3, SMECA (1949).

Table 14: Comparison of group life insurance business operated by mutual and tock life insurance companies, FY 2014

Name	Nissay Mutual Life	Meiji-Yasuda Mutual Life	Sumitomo Mutual Life	Fukoku Mutual Life
❶	38.2%	57.3%	25.1%	40.6%
❷	32.5%	33.7%	19.9%	43.2%
❸	5.336 ¥	3.407 ¥	2.575 ¥	643 ¥
Name	Asahi Mutual Life	Stock insurance companies top-third	Stock insurance companies mid-third	Stock insurance companies bottom- third
❶	5.3%	Ø 9.4%	Ø 9%	Ø 15.6%
❷	1.8%	Ø 5.4%	Ø 3.4%	Ø 8.5%
❸	406 ¥	Ø 1.688 ¥	Ø 353 ¥	Ø 18 ¥

❶ = share of group life insurance in terms of total insurance in-force
❷ = share of group insurance in terms of annual premium collected
❸ = annual premium collected, FY 2014 (in billion ¥)

Source: LIAJ (2015), table established by author.

Nevertheless, besides respective exception, the comparatively high share of group life and group annuity insurance among the total business of mutual life insurance companies can be considered an operational characteristic that distinguishes mutual life insurers from the majority of life insurance operating stock companies. This identifiable operational characteristic can be considered as somewhat unexpected, as, according to agency cost-based hypotheses regarding the coexistence of mutual and stock companies on insurance markets, product lines of group insurance and group annuities are expected to be more common and thus to a larger extent operated by insurers of the stock company form.[355]

Nevertheless, besides the comparatively higher focus of mutual life insurance companies onto group life insurance and group annuity product lines, mutual companies operating on the Japanese life insurance market seem to resemble largely their stock company competitors of similar size with respect to identifiable operational characteristics. Types of life insurance products operated by mutual and stock life insurance companies are highly similar to each other, while the amount of different lines of insurance operated by mutual and stock insurance companies of similar size does not differ significantly between repre-

355 See *Pottier & Sommer* (1997), p. 532-533, *Viswanathan & Cummins* (2003), p. 425.

sentatives of the two forms of organization. Moreover, with three out of five mutual insurers representing major insurance operators on the Japanese life insurance market and two remaining mutual life insurance companies ranking among the group of medium scale life insurance companies, no significant difference in size between mutual life insurers and stock life insurance companies is identifiable. As a result, it can be concluded that from the perspective of discussed operational characteristics, mutual and stock insurance companies operating on the Japanese life insurance market seem to have remained quite assimilated to each other, as was the case for most part of their historic coexistence. At the same time, it can be inferred that the majority of mutual insurance companies and mutual-aid operating cooperative movements differ from each other in terms of operational characteristics such as size, scope and business concentration, despite both forms of organization claiming to operate insurance based upon the principles of mutuality.

4. Conclusion

The main intention of this chapter was to examine, describe and discuss the congruent historic development and co-existence of the various forms of organization operating on the Japanese insurance market. Moreover, the chapter attempted to investigate respective organizational forms' current situation and positioning on the Japanese insurance market as well as to identify operational similarities and differences between them.

Doing so, the initial emergence of insurance companies of the stock and mutual company form was observed at first. Here, it was shown that the emergence of the mutual insurance company form on the nation's life insurance market at the beginning of the 20th century caused life insurers of the stock company form to change their operational practices. Resulting from these changes an assimilation of stock companies towards their mutual competitors in terms of operational characteristics was identifiable, despite stock companies remaining to be the more dominant form of organization on the nation's life insurance market for most part of the first half of the 20th century.

Following that, reasons for the mutualization of the Japanese life insurance industry in the course of its post-war reorganization during the late 1940s were investigated. Here it was shown that former stock life insurance companies' practice of reinitiating their business under successor companies of the mutual form were in some cases politically stimulated, while in other cases a reaction to the socio-economic environment and to legal restrictions imposed upon life insurance companies, remaining under the stock company form. Moreover, reasons for the inexistence of a similar mutualization process in the case of Japanese non-life insurance companies were discussed as well.

Next, the development of the Japanese insurance industry during the period of high governmental control, lasting throughout the second half of the 20th century, was examined. Here, high similarities of operational practices and characteristics between mutual and stock life insurance companies were identified. In fact, it appeared that throughout the period of tight governmental control, during which mutual life insurance companies represented the prevailing form of organization on the Japanese life insurance market, the practice of issuing dividends to the vast majority of policyholders represented the predominant standard among remaining stock life insurance companies. At the same time, annual dividends issued to shareholders of respective stock companies were only of a fractional amount in comparison to dividend payments assigned to the companies' policyholders, if being issued at all. Considering these characteristics, it was argued that during the period of severe governmental control an assimilation of operational practice of mutual and stock life insurance companies can also be identified.

The chapter focused further upon the emergence of mutual-aid operating cooperative movements, representing the third insurance operating organizational form on the Japanese insurance market, as well as their following historic development. Doing so, reasons for the initiation of cooperative insurers and their successful entrance into the Japanese insurance market from the early 1950s onwards were tried to be identified. The reasons for the inception of mutual-aid cooperative movements were among others the shortcomings of Japan's social security system during the early post-war era as well as the fact that insurance of personal property against risks such as fire were still hardly affordable for large parts of the Japanese population. As reasons contributing to cooperative insurers' ability to establish successfully a lasting presence on the Japanese insurance market was on the other hand the fact that cooperatives entered a highly regulated, yet strictly shielded industry, while at the same time being exempted from certain regulations applied to insurance companies. In fact, cooperative insurers did not become subject to provisions under the Japanese *Insurance Business Act*, and were furthermore able to set premium rates and policy contents more freely than their insurance company competitors.

Moreover, historic characteristics of mutual-aid operating cooperative movements were described. Here especially the fact that the majority of cooperative insurance operators were initiated for the purpose of providing affordable insurance to certain groups of people, defined either upon the latter's profession, residence or industry they work in, was argued to represent a characteristic, distinguishing mutual aid cooperative movements from their insurance company competitors.[356] This characteristic nevertheless changed in the course of the historic development of certain types of cooperative movements. In the case of the *National Federation of Workers and Consumers Insurance Cooperatives (Zenrosai)*, business was extended from insuring industrial workers and trade union members to the total general public of Japan in 1983. Prior to that the *Federation of Japanese Consumer Cooperatives (FJCC)* together with the trade unions of the Saitama prefecture extended the mutual-aid business of the *Saitama Kenmin Kyōsai Cooperative* to the general population of the entire prefecture in 1981 and soon expanded its operation to other regions of Japan. Furthermore, in the case of the agricultural cooperative mutual-aid movement, the general public was targeted from a very early moment of the movement's operations onwards, with people not being engaged in agricultural activities able to join agricultural cooperatives as so-called associated members. Those movements, nowadays offering cooperative insurance to the general Japanese public and, represent today's major cooperative mutual-aid movements.

After investigating the historic development of various insurance conducting cooperative movements, the chapter focuses onto the Japanese insurance industry's recent development during the last three decades. Doing so, measures for deregulating the Japanese insurance industry, started to be implemented gradually from the mid-1990s onwards, were described. Moreover, reasons for the occurrence of the failure of several life insurance companies, following the Japanese financial crisis during the early 1990s, and the demutualization of four mutual life insurers during the years 2002 and 2004 were investigated in more detail. In addition, the financial crisis' effects upon the operations of non-life insurance companies and mutual-aid operating cooperative movements were shortly examined. Here, it was shown that, while the mutual company form lost its position of dominance on the Japanese life insurance market, caused by the failure and the demutualization of several mutual insurance companies, mutual-aid operating cooperative movements were rather unaffected by the occurrence of the Japanese financial crisis of the early 1990s. In fact, cooperatives were able to extend their size of business and market share held throughout the 1990s and early 2000s significantly. Furthermore, the occurrence

[356] As an exception mutual-aid operating small and medium enterprise cooperatives can be named, which were established by SME cooperatives for the purpose of offering cheap insurance to small and medium enterprises. Nevertheless, being not allowed to underwrite insurance to private customers and to insure only enterprises of a certain scale, it is undeniable that also mutual-aid operating small and medium enterprise cooperative movements focused upon a particular group of potential policyholders.

of major consolidations among Japanese non-life insurance industries was shortly examined.

Lastly, the chapter investigates the current situation and positioning on the Japanese insurance market as well as tidentifies operational similarities and differences between the different organizational forms. Here it was shown that, despite the total number of mutual companies having decreased to five, the total market share held by remaining mutual companies is still of a significant size. Moreover, it was demonstrated that mutual-aid operating cooperatives had indeed been able to conquer a notable share of the Japanese insurance market, which remained largely stable throughout recent years observed. Combining business of mutual insurance companies and cooperative insurers, it could be presented that almost 37 % of total premium recorded by the Japanese insurance industry was collected by organizations claiming to operate insurance based upon principles of mutuality.

Regarding operational similarities and differences of various organizational forms, it was shown that besides major cooperative insurers in the form of the *National Mutual Insurance Federation of Agricultural Cooperatives* (*Zenkyoren*), the *National Federation of Workers and Consumers Insurance Cooperatives* (*Zenrosai*) and the *Federation of Japanese Consumer Cooperatives (FJCC)*, the vast majority of mutual-aid operating cooperatives represent small scale insurance operators on the Japanese insurance market, focusing upon a comparatively limited amount of lines of business. As a major reason for these characteristics can be mentioned the fact that respective small scale cooperative insurers adhered to their initial practice of only offering mutual-aid services to particular groups of potential policyholders, based upon the latter's profession, residence or other characteristics.

With respect to operational characteristics of the remaining mutual life insurance companies it can be said that, besides a comparatively higher share of group life and group annuity insurance operated, no significant differences in terms of the number of products operated and diversification of business in comparison to life insurers of the stock company form could be identified. In fact, three out of the remaining five mutual life insurance companies belonged to the group of the ten largest insurance operating organizations in terms of total annual premium collected in fiscal year 2014, while the remaining mutual companies rank among medium size insurers on the Japanese life insurance market. Thus, whereas institutional characteristics do differ between mutual and stock insurance companies, no significant differences in size or in the kind of insurance business operated could be identified.

Here, it has to be further mentioned that signs of assimilation of remaining mutual companies towards nowadays existing stock life insurance companies can be identified in the former's recent development. For example, mutual insurance companies became allowed in the course of the liberalization of the Japanese insurance market to conduct 20 % of their total business with non-member customers.[357] As a result, not all policyholders of today's mutual insurance companies are company owners or hold profit-participation rights. Moreover, whereas mutual companies used to be required to allocate 80 % of their annual profits to policyholder dividends prior to regulatory changes of the last two decades, this threshold were lowered to 20 % in 2002.[358] Finally, major Japanese mutual life insurance companies have engaged into notable foreign expansion efforts throughout the last two decades. Doing so, mutual companies have acquired substantial equity stakes in several life insurance corporations and have entered in joint venture agreements in foreign markets such as the United States, Australia, India, China, Indonesia, Thailand, and Vietnam. Doing so, mutual life insurers engaged into similar strategies of internationally diversifying their operations as did Japanese stock insurance companies. It is questionable how these efforts of expansion comply with interests of mutual insurance companies' policyholders and thus principles of mutuality. Nevertheless, considering these developments it can be argued that strategic behavior and operational practices of remaining mutual insurance companies have steadily resembled more closely to those of stock insurance companies throughout recent decades.

Considering the recent development of mutual insurance companies, the current as well as historic differences between mutual-aid operating cooperative movements and the former shall be shortly discussed from the standpoint of principles of mutuality.

With respect to the historic differences it can be stated that ideas of mutuality were more strongly present in the initiation process of cooperative mutual-aid movements, than they were during the establishment of today's existing Japanese mutual insurance companies. As was described in the course of this chapter, cooperative mutual-aid movements' emergence was among others a reaction to the existence of severe shortcomings of the Japanese social security system as well as the situation that insurance products offered by private companies were still hardly affordable for certain groups of citizens. Thus, cooperative insurance emerged for the purpose of offering affordable insurance to particular segments of the Japanese society based upon principles of mutuality and reciprocity. In other word, cooperative insurance movements were established for the purpose of providing targeted groups of people with the possibility to perform mutual self-help against common risks and shared problems, and thus can also be described as mutual

[357] Cf. *Kobayashi* et al. (2011), p. 213-214.

[358] Cf. *Yoneyama* (2002), p. 38.

self-help organizations with the objective of maximizing the total welfare of their members.[359]

In comparison to cooperative mutual-aid movements, the reasons why today's existing mutual life insurance companies emerge differed from the immediate post war era of the late 1940s.[360] As depicted in the above, the majority of mutual life insurance companies, existing throughout the second half of the 20th century, were initiated as successor companies of former stock life insurance companies during the post-war reorganization of the Japanese financial industry. The decision of stock life insurance companies to re-establish themselves under the mutual company form was in some cases caused by political interference. In other cases, the re-organization under the mutual company form represented a deliberate decision of respective companies' top executives, often being majority owners of their respective company, in the face of the socio-economic environment and legal restrictions imposed upon remaining stock life insurance companies. As a result, ideals of reciprocity and mutual self-help against common risks shared were not on the forefront of reasons for today's existing Japanese mutual life insurance companies to be established.

The characteristic of representing mutual self-help organizations, through which members of a particular group of people, either based upon their profession or residence, are able to insure themselves on principles of reciprocity, was largely maintained in the case of the majority of cooperative mutual-aid movements throughout their historic development during the second half of the 20th and early 21st century. Contrary to this development, mutual life insurance companies became large scale insurance operates, which insure several millions of people today. Here, literature argues that mutual awareness has been largely absent among the policyholders of mutual insurance companies.[361] Moreover, recent developments such as the above-mentioned introduction of the permission for mutual insurance companies to operate a certain amount of non-member business as well as the increasing foreign expansion of mutual insurance companies can be regarded as being in conflict with key elements of mutual insurance such as policyholders' collective ownership of mutual insurance operating organizations as well as the collective distribution or coverage of profits and losses. At the same time, the expansion into foreign markets through the acquisition of equity stakes in foreign stock insurance companies represents an indication that profitability is a more pronounced element within

[359] Cf. *Okada* (2012), p. 173-175.

[360] As an exception the Fukoku Mutual Life Insurance Company has to be named, which had originally been a mutual conscription insurance prior to the end of World War II.

[361] Cf. *Okada* (2012), p. 172.

remaining mutual insurance companies compared to mutual-aid operating cooperatives.

Nevertheless, also some cooperative mutual-aid movements have become major insurance operating organizations with several millions of members insured, due to starting promoting mutual-aid to the general Japanese public. With policyholders of these cooperative movements not belonging to a group of people that share similar traits such as profession or residence it is hard to neglect that mutual awareness should have decreased among them as well. Moreover, the Japanese agricultural cooperative mutual-aid movement is allowed to conduct up to 20 % of its insurance business with non-member policyholders.[362] Therefore, in contrast to small-scale cooperative insurers, also major cooperative movements' deviation from the principles of mutual insurance might have increased in the course of their ongoing development and expansion of business. Nevertheless, further investigations of current institutional and operational characteristics of cooperative mutual-aid movements are needed in order to compare mutual-aid cooperative movements and mutual insurance companies from the standpoint of principles of mutuality in more detail.

The main intention of the presented chapters is to deliver an investigation of the historic development and co-existence of various forms of organization, existing on the Japanese insurance market. Doing so, it was shown that stock companies, mutual companies and mutual-aid operating cooperatives have competed and coexisted successful with each other for almost seven decades. Moreover, major insurance operators of today's Japanese insurance industry have developed under the organizational framework of the three different legal forms. In addition, representatives of each organizational form have been able to conquer and remain in control of notable shares of the Japanese insurance market throughout their long historical development. As a result, insurers of all three forms of organization will most likely remain on the Japanese insurance market throughout the foreseeable future.

[362] Acc. to the ACCJ (2017), p. 3.

References

American Chamber of Commerce in Japan, Insurance Committee (2017): "Ensure a Level Playing Field between Kyosai and FSA-Regulated Insurance Companies", *ACCJ viewpoint*, 8 p.

Amori Prefecture Fire Mutual Aid Cooperative (2017): "Association Summary", original Japanese title: "組合概要", Japanese only, http://www.kyosai-aomori.jp/contents/aboutus.html, retrieval: 29.03.2017

Aochi, M. (2001): "The Mutualization of Japanese Life Insurance Companies in 1947--From the Viewpoint of Corporate Governance Structure", original Japanese title: "論文>戦後日本における生命保険会社の相互会社化：コーポレート・ガバナンス構造の視点から", Japanese only, *Japan business history review*, Vol. (36(1), pp. 27-47.

Ashikaga, T. (1959): "Agricultural cooperative associations in Japan", Agricultural cooperative associations in Japan, Tokyo, 76 p.

Bureau of Insurance, Department of Commerce and Industry (1925): "The Assurance Year Book – Home Company. 1922 and 1923", The Life Insurance Companies Association, Tokyo, n. p.

Bureau of Insurance, Department of Commerce and Industry (1926): "The Assurance Year Book – Home Company 1924", The Life Insurance Companies Association, Tokyo, 160 p.

Bureau of Insurance, Department of Commerce and Industry (1927): "The Assurance Year Book – Home Company 1925", The Life Insurance Companies Association, Tokyo, 168 p.

Bureau of Insurance, Department of Commerce and Industry (1929): "The Insurance Year Book – Home Company 1927", The Life Insurance Companies Association, Tokyo, 176 p.

Bureau of Insurance, Department of Commerce and Industry (1933): "The Insurance Year Book 1931 – Part A. Home Companies. (I)", The Life Insurance Companies Association, Tokyo, 62 p.

Chiba Prefectural Government (2016): "Enterprise Tax of corporation", https://www.pref.chiba.lg.jp/zeimu/aramashi/shurui/houjin-jigyou/, retrieval: 01.05.2016.

CO-OP Kyosai (2016): "Annual Report 2016", Japanese only, Japan Co-op mutual aid Consumers' Cooperative Federation, Tokyo, 94 p.

Dentsukyosai (2017): "Outline of Dentsu Mutual Aid Association", original Japanese title: "電通共済生協概要", Japanese only, https://www.dentsu-kyosai.or.jp/outline/index.html, retrieval: 27.03.2017.

The Department of Agriculture and Commerce (1923): "The Assurance Year Book – Part A. Home Companies. 1921-1922", original Japanese title: "保険年鑑. 大正10年度 甲", Japanese only, The Association of Life Insurance Companies, Tokyo, n. p.

The Department of Agriculture and Commerce (1920): "The Assurance Year Book – Part A. Home Companies. 1918", original Japanese title: " 険年鑑. 大正7年度　甲(内国会社", Japanese only, The Association of Life Insurance Companies, Tokyo, 138 p.

The Department of Agriculture and Commerce (1917): "The Insurance Year Book – Part A. Home Companies. 1915", original Japanese title: " 保険年鑑. 大正4年度 甲", Japanese only, The Association of Life Insurance Companies, Tokyo, 317 p.

The Department of Agriculture and Commerce (1915): "The Insurance Year Book 1913", original Japanese title: "保険年鑑. 大正2年度", Japanese only, The Association of Life Insurance Companies, Tokyo, 319 p.

The Department of Agriculture and Commerce (1914): "The Insurance Year Book 1912", original Japanese title: "保険年鑑. 明治45年度", Japanese only, The Association of Life Insurance Companies, Tokyo, 289 p.

The Department of Agriculture and Commerce (1913): "The Insurance Year Book 1911", original Japanese title: "保険年鑑. 明治44年度", Japanese only, The Association of Life Insurance Companies, Tokyo, 233 p.

The Department of Agriculture and Commerce (1912): "The Insurance Year Book 1910", original Japanese title: "保険年鑑. 明治43年度", Japanese only, The Association of Life Insurance Companies, Tokyo, 289 p.

The Department of Agriculture and Commerce (1916): "The Insurance Year Book – Part A. Home Companies. 1914", original Japanese title: " 保険年鑑. 大正3年度 甲", Japanese only, The Association of Life Insurance Companies, Tokyo, 319 p.

The Department of Agriculture and Commerce (1918): "The Insurance Year Book – Part A. Home Companies. 1916", original Japanese title: " 保険年鑑. 大正5年度 甲", Japanese only, The Association of Life Insurance Companies, Tokyo, 150 p.

The Department of Agriculture and Commerce (1919): "The Insurance Year Book – Part A. Home Companies. 1917", original Japanese title: " 保険年鑑. 大正6年度 甲", Japanese only, The Association of Life Insurance Companies, Tokyo, 132 p.

The Department of Agriculture and Commerce (1921): "The Insurance Year Book – Part A. Home Companies. 1919", original Japanese title: " 保険年鑑. 大正8年度 甲", Japanese only, The Association of Life Insurance Companies, Tokyo, 138 p.

The Department of Commerce and Industry (1926): "The Assurance Year Book – Home Companies 1924", original Japanese title: "保険年鑑. 大正13年度", Japanese only, *The Association of Life Insurance Companies*, Tokyo, n.p.

The Department of Commerce and Industry (1928): "The Assurance Year Book – Home Companies 1926", original Japanese title: "保険年鑑. 大正15年度 甲、内國会社", Japanese only, *The Association of Life Insurance Companies*, Tokyo, n.p.

The Department of Commerce and Industry (1930): "The Insurance Year Book – Part A. Home Companies 1928", original Japanese title: "保険年鑑. 昭和3年度　甲、内國会社", Japanese only, *The Association of Life Insurance Companies*, Tokyo, n.p.

The Department of Commerce and Industry (1933): "The Insurance Year Book – Part A. Home Companies 1931 (1)", original Japanese title: "保険年鑑. 昭和6年度　甲、内國会社（前編）", Japanese only, *The Association of Life Insurance Companies*, Tokyo, 62 p.

The Department of Commerce and Industry (1935): "The Insurance Year Book – Part A. Home Companies 1933 (1)", original Japanese title: "保険年鑑. 昭和8年度　甲、内國会社（前編）", Japanese only, *The Association of Life Insurance Companies*, Tokyo, 62 p.

The Department of Commerce and Industry (1937): "The Insurance Year Book – Part A. Home Companies 1935 (1)", original Japanese title: "保険年鑑. 昭和12年度 甲（内国会社）前編", Japanese only, *The Association of Life Insurance Companies*, Tokyo, n.p.

The Department of Commerce and Industry (1939): "The Insurance Year Book – Part A. Home Companies 1937 (1)", original Japanese title: "保険年鑑. 昭和１４年度　甲（内国会社）　前編", Japanese only, *The Association of Life Insurance Companies*, p. 63.

Ezawa, M. (2016a): "Expert-Interview regarding the History of the Insurance Market in Japan", Professor at the Faculty of Commerce of the Waseda University, Tokyo, 6th of May.

Ezawa, M. (2010): "The New Era of Three Mega Casualty Insurers: Their Aims and Benefits for Policyholders", *The Japan News - Waseda Online*, http://www.yomiuri.co.jp/adv/wol/dy/opinion/gover-eco_090427.html, retrieval: 21.03.2017.

FJCC (2017b): "History", original Japanese title: "沿革", in Japanese only, http://www.kyosai-cc.or.jp/aboutus/outline/history.html, retrieval: 12.03.2017.

Flath, D. (2000): "The Japanese Economy", *Oxford University Press*, New York, 368 p.

Financial Service Agency (FSA) (2017): "List of non-life insurance companies (domestic companies) (as of January 4, 2017) - List of foreign non-life insurance companies (Branch Offices) (as of April 3, 2017)", http://www.fsa.go.jp/en/regulated/licensed/ins_nonlife.pdf, retrieval: 05.03.2017.

Forestry Workers Mutual Aid Cooperative (2017): "Introduction of Mutual Aid Forestry Federation Headquarters", original Japanese title: "森林労連共済本部のご紹介", Japanese only, https://www.zenrosai.coop/zenkoku/shinrin/shinrin0.php, retrieval: 27.03.2017.

The Foundation for the Advancement of Life & Insurance Around the world (FALIA) (2015): "Overview of Life Insurance Industry in Japan", presentation at FALIA Seminar July 29th of 2015, 91 p.

Fukao, M. (2004): "Fixing Japanese Life-Insurance Companies", *US-Japan Conference on the "Solutions for Japanese Economy"*,

Fukui Prefecture Fire Mutual Aid Association (2017): "Association Summary", original Japanese title: "組合概要", Japanese only, http://www.ken-kyosai.jp/Company/, retrieval: 29.03.2017.

Godo, Y. (2001): "The Changing Economic Performance and Political Significance of Japan's Agricultural Cooperatives", Asian Pacific Economic Papers, No. 318, 31 p.

Godo, Y. (2006): "Financial Liberalization and Japan's Agricultural Cooperatives", *International Association of Agricultural Economists Conference*, Queensland, Australia, 10 p.

Godo, Y. (2009): "The changing political dynamics of Japanese agricultural cooperatives", *In International Association of Agricultural Economists Conference Proceedings*, Beijing, China, 22 p.

Graham, F. (2004): "Japanese Company in Crisis – Ideology, strategy and narrative", *Routledge*, Abington, 255 p.

Hartmann, P. (2003): "Konsumgenossenschaften in Japan: Alternative oder Spiegelbild der Gesellschaft?", *Monographien aus dem Deutschen Institut für Japanstudien*, Vol. 29, *Iudicum Verlag*, München, 628 p.

Hax, K. (1961): "Japan – Wirtschaftsmacht des fernen Ostens", *Westdeutscher Verlag*, Köln - Opladen, 637 p.

Himeji Citizen Mutual Aid Cooperative Association (2017): "About the Himeji Citizen Mutual Aid Cooperative Association", original Japanese title: "ひめじ市民共済について ", Japanese only, http://www.himeji-siminkyosai.or.jp/about/index.html, retrieval: 29.09.2017.

The Institute of Fiscal and Monetary Policy (2010): "Fiscal and Monetary Policies of Japan in Reconstruction and High-Growth - 1945 to 1971", *Ministry of Finance*, 250 p.

International Cooperative and Mutual Insurance Federation (ICMIF) (2014): "Global Mutual Market Share 2012", *ICMIF*, 37 p.

Insurance Research Institute (hoken kenkyujo) (1955): "Insurance - The Statistics of Japanese Life Insurance -1954", original Japanese title: "インシュアランス. 生命保険統計号 - 昭和30年版", Japanese only, Insurance Research Institute, n. p.

Insurance Research Institute (hoken kenkyujo) (1986a): "Insurance - The Statistics of Japanese Life Insurance -1985", original Japanese title: "インシュアランス. 生命保険統計号 - 昭和61年版", Japanese only, Insurance Research Institute, n. p.

Insurance Research Institute (*hoken kenkyujo*) (1971a): "Insurance - The Statistics of Japanese Life Insurance -1970", original Japanese title: "インシュアランス. 生命保険統計号 - 昭和46年版", Japanese only, *Insurance Research Institute*, 207 p.

Insurance Research Institute (hoken kenkyujo) (1960a): "Insurance - The Statistics of Japanese Life Insurance -1959", original Japanese title: "インシュアランス. 生命保険統計号 - 昭和35年版", Japanese only, Insurance Research Institute, n. p.

Insurance Research Institute (*hoken kenkyujo*) (1976a): "Insurance - The Statistics of Japanese Life Insurance -1970", original Japanese title: "インシュアランス. 生命保険統計号 - 昭和51年版", Japanese only, *Insurance Research Institute*, 207 p.

Insurance Research Institute (*hoken kenkyujo*) (1979): "Insurance - The Statistics of Japanese Life Insurance -1978", original Japanese title: "インシュアランス. 生命保険統計号 - 昭和54年版", Japanese only, *Insurance Research Institute*, 219 p.

Insurance Research Institute (*hoken kenkyujo*) (1981a): Insurance – The Statistics of Japanese Non-life insurance -1980", original Japanese title: インシュアランス. 損害保険特別統計号 - 昭和56年版, Japanese only, *Insurance Research Institute*, n. p.

Insurance Research Institute (*hoken kenkyujo*) (1991a): "Insurance - The Statistics of Japanese Life Insurance -1990", original Japanese title: "インシュアランス. 生命保険統計号 - 平成3年版", Japanese only, *Insurance Research Institute*, 281 p.

Insurance Research Institute (*hoken kenkyujo*) (1986b): Insurance - The Statistics of Japanese Non-life insurance -1985", original Japanese title: インシュアランス. 損害保険特別統計号 - 昭和61年版, Japanese only, *Insurance Research Institute*, n. p.

Insurance Research Institute (*hoken kenkyujo*) (1956): Insurance - The Statistics of Japanese Non-life insurance -1955", original Japanese title: インシュアランス. 損害保険特別統計号 - 昭和31年版, Japanese only, *Insurance Research Institute*, 92 p.

Insurance Research Institute (*hoken kenkyujo*) (1960b): Insurance - The Statistics of Japanese Non-life insurance -1959", original Japanese title: インシュアランス. 損害保険特別統計号-昭和35年版, Japanese only, *Insurance Research Institute*, n. p.

Insurance Research Institute (*hoken kenkyujo*) (1965): Insurance - The Statistics of Japanese Non-life insurance -1964", original Japanese title: インシュアランス. 損害保険特別統計号 - 昭和40年版, Japanese only, *Insurance Research Institute*, 140 p.

Insurance Research Institute (*hoken kenkyujo*) (1971b): Insurance - The Statistics of Japanese Non-life insurance -1970", original Japanese title: インシュアランス. 損害保険特別統計号 - 昭和46年版, Japanese only, *Insurance Research Institute*, 211 p.

Insurance Research Institute (*hoken kenkyujo*) (1976b): Insurance - The Statistics of Japanese Non-life insurance -1975", original Japanese title: インシュアランス. 損害保険特別統計号 - 昭和51年版, Japanese only, *Insurance Research Institute*, n. p.

Insurance Research Institute (*hoken kenkyujo*) (1981b): Insurance - The Statistics of Japanese Non-life insurance -1980", original Japanese title: インシュアランス. 損害保険特別統計号 - 昭和61年版, Japanese only, *Insurance Research Institute*, n. p.

Insurance Research Institute (*hoken kenkyujo*) (1991b): Insurance - The Statistics of Japanese Non-life insurance -1990", original Japanese title: インシュアランス. 損害保険特別統計号 - 平成3年版, Japanese only, *Insurance Research Institute*, n. p.

Insurance Research Institute (*hoken kenkyujo*) (1996): "Insurance - The Statistics of Japanese Life Insurance -1995", original Japanese title: "インシュアランス. 生命保険統計号 - 平成8年版", Japanese only, *Insurance Research Institute*, n. p.

Insurance Research Institute (*hoken kenkyujo*) (2001): "Insurance - The Statistics of Japanese Life Insurance -2000", original Japanese title: "インシュアランス. 生命保険統計号 - 平成13年版", Japanese only, *Insurance Research Institute*, 316 p.

Insurance Research Institute (*hoken kenkyujo*) (2006): "Insurance - The Statistics of Japanese Life Insurance -2005", original Japanese title: "インシュアランス. 生命保険統計号 - 平成18年版", Japanese only, *Insurance Research Institute*, n. p.

Insurance Research Institute (*hoken kenkyujo*) (2014): "Insurance - The Statistics of Japanese Life Insurance -2013", original Japanese title: "インシュアランス. 生命保険統計号 - 平成26年版", Japanese only, *Insurance Research Institute*, n. p.

Insurance Research Institute (*hoken kenkyujo*) (2015): Insurance - The Statistics of Japanese Non-life insurance -2014", original Japanese title: インシュアランス. 損害保険特別統計号 - 平成27年版, Japanese only, *Insurance Research Institute*, 224 p.

International Monetary Fund (2012): "Japan: Insurance Core Principles—Detailed Assessment of Observance", *IMF Country Report*, No. 12. (228), 76 p.

Ishida, M. (2002): "Development of Agricultural Co-operatives in Japan (III), Historical Perspective of Co-operative Development", Bull. Fac. Bioresources, Mie University, No. 29, pp. 47-61.

JAFMAC (2017): "History and Business overview", original Japanese title: "沿革・事業概要", Japanese only, http://www.zenkyoren.or.jp/index.html, retrieval: 16.09.2017; JA-Kyosai (2017b): "Current Status of JA-Kyosai", original Japanese title: "ＪＡ共済連の現状, Japanese only, *National Mutual Insurance Federation of Agricultural Cooperatives*, Toyko, 161 p.

JA-Kyosai (2017b): "Current Status of JA-Kyosai", original Japanese title: "ＪＡ共済連の現状, Japanese only, *National Mutual Insurance Federation of Agricultural Cooperatives*, Toyko, 161 p.

JA-Kyosai (2009): "Current Status of JA-Kyosai 2009", original Japanese title: "ＪＡ共済連の現状 2009, Japanese only, *National Mutual Insurance Federation of Agricultural Cooperatives*, Toyko, 122 p.

Japanese Business History Institute (1980): "The Tokio Marine & Fire Insurance: The First Century 1879-1979", *Tokio Marine & Fire Insurance Company*, 209 p.

Japan Business History Institute (1992): "The 100-year history of Nippon Life: its growth and socioeconomic setting, 1889-1989", *Nippon Life Insurance Company*, 389 p.
The Japan Business History Institute (1993): "Sumitomo Marine & Fire Insurance: The First Century, 1893-1993", Sumitomo Marine & Fire Insurance Company, 250 p.
Japan Cooperative Insurance Association (1995): "Mutual Aid Yearbook", original Japanese title: "共済年鑑", Japanese only, Vol. 30, 72 p.
Japan Cooperative Insurance Association (1996): "Mutual Aid Yearbook", original Japanese title: "共済年鑑", Japanese only, Vol. 31, 77 p.
Japan Cooperative Insurance Association (1997): "Mutual Aid Yearbook", original Japanese title: "共済年鑑", Japanese only, Vol. 32, 80 p.
Japan Cooperative Insurance Association (1998): "Mutual Aid Yearbook", original Japanese title: "共済年鑑", Japanese only, Vol. 33, n. p.
Japan Cooperative Insurance Association (1999): "Mutual Aid Yearbook", original Japanese title: "共済年鑑", Japanese only, Vol. 34, n. p.
Japan Cooperative Insurance Association (2000): "Mutual Aid Yearbook", original Japanese title: "共済年鑑", Japanese only, Vol. 35, 81 p.
Japan Cooperative Insurance Association (2001): "Mutual Aid Yearbook", original Japanese title: "共済年鑑", Japanese only, Vol. 36, 81 p.
Japan Cooperative Insurance Association (2002): "Mutual Aid Yearbook", original Japanese title: "共済年鑑", Japanese only, Vol. 37, 81 p.
Japan Cooperative Insurance Association (2003): "Mutual Aid Yearbook", original Japanese title: "共済年鑑", Japanese only, Vol. 38, 81 p.
Japan Cooperative Insurance Association (2004): "Mutual Aid Yearbook", original Japanese title: "共済年鑑", Japanese only, Vol. 39, 81 p.
Japan Cooperative Insurance Association (2005): "Mutual Aid Yearbook", original Japanese title: "共済年鑑", Japanese only, Vol. 40, 113 p.
Japan Cooperative Insurance Association (2006): "Mutual Aid Yearbook", original Japanese title: "共済年鑑", Japanese only, Vol. 41, 117 p.
Japan Cooperative Insurance Association (2007): "Mutual Aid Yearbook", original Japanese title: "共済年鑑", Japanese only, Vol. 42, 118 p.
Japan Cooperative Insurance Association (2008): "Mutual Aid Yearbook", original Japanese title: "共済年鑑", Japanese only, Vol. 43, 73 p.
Japan Cooperative Insurance Association (2009): "Mutual Aid Yearbook", original Japanese title: "共済年鑑", Japanese only, Vol. 44, 73 p.
Japan Cooperative Insurance Association (2010): "Mutual Aid Yearbook", original Japanese title: "共済年鑑", Japanese only, Vol. 45, 73 p.
Japan Cooperative Insurance Association (2011): "Mutual Aid Yearbook", original Japanese title: "共済年鑑", Japanese only, Vol. 46, 68 p.
Japan Cooperative Insurance Association (2012): "Mutual Aid Yearbook", original Japanese title: "共済年鑑", Japanese only, Vol. 47, 70 p.
Japan Cooperative Insurance Association (2013): "Mutual Aid Yearbook", original Japanese title: "共済年鑑", Japanese only, Vol. 48, 71 p.

Japan Cooperative Insurance Association (2014): “Mutual Aid Yearbook”, original Japanese title: “共済年鑑”, Japanese only, Vol. 49, 72 p.

Japan Cooperative Insurance Association (2015): “Mutual Aid Yearbook”, original Japanese title: “共済年鑑”, Japanese only, Vol. 50, 72 p.

Japan Credit Rating Agency (JCRA) (2004): “Ratings on Foundation Funds of Mutual Life Insurance Companies”, *Japan Credit Rating Agency Ltd.*, 3 p.

Japan Food Hygiene Association (2017): “Association Overview (History)”, Japanese only, original Japanese title: “協会概要（沿革）”, http://www.n-shokuei.jp/outline/history.html, retrieval: 17.03.2017.

Japan Times (2000a): “First bankruptcy of nonlife insurer, Daiichi Mutual ordered to shut down”, https://www.japantimes.co.jp/news/2000/05/02/national/daiichi-mutual-ordered-to-shut-down/#.WZhH31FJaUk, retrieval: 19.08.2017.

Kanto Auto Kyosai (2017): “The history of the union”, original Japanese title: “組合の歩み“, http://www.kanjikyo.or.jp/web/guide/history.html, retrieval 17.03.2017.

Kobayashi, N., Mikami, T., Umekawa, Y. (2011): “Insurance Law in Japan“, *Kluwer Law International*, Netherlands, 260 p.

Kokyoren (2017): “Overview and History”, original Japanese title: “概要と沿革”, Japanese only, http://www.kokyoren.or.jp/3enkaku.htm, retrieval: 27.09.2017.

Kurimoto, A. (2009): “Separation of Insurance and Retail Functions in Cooperatives”, *Consumer Co-Operative Institute of Japan News*, No. 58, pp. 1-8.

Kurimoto, A. (2007): “Consumer Cooperative Law Amended after 50 Years since its Enactment”, *Consumer Co-Operative Institute of Japan News*, No. 53, pp. 1-15.

Kurimoto, A. (2004): “Agricultural Cooperatives in Japan: An Institutional Approach”, Journal of Rural Cooperation, Vol. 32, No. 2, pp. 111-128.

Kurogi, T. (2014): “Postwar Mutualization of Zaibatsu Life Insurers: Verification of the GHQ Instruction Hypothesis”, original Japanese title: “財閥系生保の戦後の相互会社化: GHQ指導説の検証”, Japanese only, Journal of insurance Science, No. 624, pp. 103-122.

Kurogi, T. (2015a): “Nippon Life’s Postwar Mutualization, based primarily on Oral History Analysis of Fujimoto’s Dialogue”, Japanese only, original Japanese title: “日本生命の戦後の相互会社化:藤本談話のオーラルヒストリー分析を中心に”, Journal of insurance Science, No. 628, pp. 139-157.

Kurogi, T. (2015b): “Separation of Ownership and Management in the Postwar Rehabilitation of Japanese Life Insurers”, Japanese only, original Japanese title: “終戦後の生保会社再建における所有と経営の分離“, NUCB Journal of Economics and Information Science, Vol. 60, No.1, pp. 85-94.

Kurogi, T. (2016): "Expert Questionnaire: The mutualization of Japanese life insurance companies in the immediate after war period, Professor at the Department of Commerce of the Nagoya University of Commerce & Business, Nagoya, 23.08.2016.

Kwon, W., Skipper, H. (1997): "Regulatory changes in the Japanese insurance market", *Journal of Insurance Regulation*, Vol. 16 (2), pp. 151-169.

Kyoei Fire and Marine Insurance Company Ltd. (2017): "The Formation of Kyoei Fire", original Japanese titel: "共栄火災の成り立ち", Japanese only, https://www.kyoeikasai.co.jp/about/company/history.html, retrieval: 2.3.2017.

Kyoei Fire & Marine Insurance Co., Ltd. (2005): "Annual Report 2005", *Kyoei Fire & Marine Insurance Co., Ltd.*, 33 p.

Kyosuiren (2017): "Business Activity of JF Mutual Aid", in Japanese, http://www.kyosuiren.or.jp/html/contents1-1.html, retrieval: 4.3.2017.

Kyosuiren (2014) "Current Status of JF-Ky suiren", original Japanese title: "「JF共水連」の現況", Japanese only, *National Fishery Mutual-Aid Cooperative Federation*, 74 p.

Kyosuiren (1996): "An Outline of Fishery Cooperative Insurance in Japan", Zengyoren regional conference on insurance and credit for sustainable fisheries development in Asia, pp. 1-11.

Lehrman, W. (2003): "Organizational Ecology in Japan: The Case of The Life Insurance Industry, 1881 to 1994", Chiba University of Commerce Review Papers, original Japanese title: **千葉商大論叢**, Vol. 39, No. 4, p. 37-61.

The Life Insurance Association of Japan (LIAJ) (2015): "Life insurance business overview (Heisei era 27th year version) CD-ROM", Tokyo, CD-Rom.

Marine & Fire Insurance Association of Japan (1957): "Development of non-life insurance business in Japan and its activites", *Marine & Fire Insurance Association of Japan*, Tokyo, 31 p.

Murthy, N. (1960): "Agricultural Credit and Insurance in Japan", International Studies, Vol. 2, No. 1, pp. 92-96.

Nagoya Citizen Fire Mutual Aid Cooperative Association (2017): "Overview of the Nagoya Fire Mutual Aid", original Japanese title: "**市民火災共済の概要**", Japanese only, http://www.nagoya-kyosai.or.jp/outline/, retrieval: 27.09.2017.

Meiji Yasuda (2016): "History of Meiji Yasuda Life Insurance Company", http://www.meijiyasuda.co.jp/english/about-us/history.html, retrieval: 02.11.2016.

Mutual-Aid Insurance Study Group (1989): "Mutual Aid Yearbook", original Japanese title: "共済年鑑", Japanese only, Vol. 24, 46 p.

Mutual-Aid Insurance Study Group (1990): "Mutual Aid Yearbook", original Japanese title: "共済年鑑", Japanese only, Vol. 25, 46 p.

Mutual-Aid Insurance Study Group (1991): "Mutual Aid Yearbook", original Japanese title: "共済年鑑", Japanese only, Vol. 26, 46 p.

Mutual-Aid Insurance Study Group (1992): "Mutual Aid Yearbook", original Japanese title: "共済年鑑", Japanese only, Vol. 27, 50 p.

Mutual-Aid Insurance Study Group (1993): "Mutual Aid Yearbook", original Japanese title: "共済年鑑", Japanese only, Vol. 28, 50 p.

Mutual-Aid Insurance Study Group (1994): "Mutual Aid Yearbook", original Japanese title: "共済年鑑", Japanese only, Vol. 29, 58 p.

National Transportation Worker Mutual Aid Cooperative (2018): "Information on the Transportation Mutual Aid", original Japanese title: "交運共済のご案内", Japanese only, http://www.kouun.or.jp/info/index.html, retrieval: 28.02.2018.

NFUCA (2017): "History of the University Cooperative Mutual Aid", original title in Japanese:" 学生総合共済のあゆみ", in Japanese only, http://kyosai.univcoop.or.jp/group/history.html, retrieval:12.03.2017.

Niigata Citizen Fire Mutual Aid Cooperative Association (2017): "association summary", original Japanese title: "組合概要", Japanese only, https://www.niigata-kasaikyosai.jp/gaiyo.html, retrieval: 26.9.2017.

Nikkaren (2017): "History of Nikkaren", Japanese title: "日火連について > 沿革", Japanese only, http://www.nikkaren.or.jp/about/history/index.html, retrieval: 17.03.2017.

Nishimura, T. (1975): "The Japanese Life Insurnace Market – opening to foreign insurers – a Japanese view", *The Forum (Section of Insurance, Negligence and Compensation Law, American Bar Association)*, Vol. 10 (3), pp. 952-976

Nishio, S. (1995): "The "Modern" Mutual Insurance Company in Japan", in: Peiner, W. (ed.) (1995): "Grundlagen des Versicherungsvereins auf Gegenseitigkeit", *Verlag Versicherungswirtschaft e. V.* , Karlsruhe, pp. 50-64.

The Non-Life Insurance Institute of Japan (1972): "Fire Insurance and Automobile Insurance in Japan", *The Non-Life Insurance Institute of Japan*, Tokyo, n. p.

The Non-Life Insurance Institute of Japan (1973): "Marine Insurance and Inland Transit Insurance in Japan", *The Non-Life Insurance Institute of Japan*, Tokyo, 306 p.

Ohno, K. (2006): "The Economic Development of Japan - The Path Traveled by Japan as a Developing Country", *GRIPS Development Forum*, National Graduate Institute for Policy Studies, Tokyo, 243 p.

Okada, F. (2016b): "Expert-questionnaire regarding mutual insurance companies' members' representative election system and reasons for the demutualization of medium size Japanese life insurance companies during the early years of the 21st century", Professor at the College of Commerce of the Nihon University, Tokyo, 6th of September.

Okada, F. (2012): "Mutual Aid and Insurance Its Homogeneity and Heterogeneity - From the viewpoint of strategic management", original

Japanese title: "共済と保険 その同質性と異質性 - 戦略的経営の観点から", Japanese only, 20th Anniversary of the Japan Mutual Aid Association – International Cooperative Year Papers and Lecture Collections 2012, original Japanese title: "日本共済協会　結成20周年・2012国際協同組合年　論文・講演集", Japanese only, JCIA, Tokyo, pp. 169-186.

Pottier, S., Sommer, D. (1997): "Agency Theory and Life Insurer Ownership Structure", *The Journal of Risk and Insurance*, Vol. 64 (3), pp. 529-543.

Sibbitt, E. (1998): "A brave new world for M&A of financial institutions in Japan: big bang financial deregulation and the new evironment for corporate combinations of financial institutions", *University of Pennsylvania Journal of International Economic Law*, Vol. 19, pp. 965-1027.

Small and Medium-Sized Enterprise Cooperatives Act (1949), Version: Act No. 109 of 2006, Translation Date: 01.04.2009. http://www.japaneselawtranslation.go.jp/law/detail/?al%5B%5D=S&re=02&ky=%E6%A0%AA%E5%BC%8F&page=2, retrieval: 16.03.2016.

Soejima, A: (1986): "Postwar Development of the Insurance Industry in Japan and Its Future Role in World Economy", in: Wasow, B., Hill, R. (ed.) (1986): "The Insurance Industry in Economic Development", *New York University Press*, New York, n.p.

Sono, K. (1962): "The Co-operative Insurance in Japan", *Keio Business Review*, No. 1, pp. 17-22.

Standard & Poor's (2000): "Japan Insurance Digest 2000", p. 32.

Sugino, F. (2013): "Corporate Governance and Mutual versus Stock Ownership: A Case Study of Heisei Life Insurance Crisis", *Commercial Review of Senshu University*, Vol. 96, pp. 81-95.

Sugino, F. (2014): "A Case Study on Demutualized Life Insurers in Japan: From Viewpoint of Comparison between Mutual versus Stock Ownership", 専修商学論集, Vol. 98, pp. 75-94.

Suzuki, T. (2001): "Co-operative Insurance and Consumer Co-operation in Japan" , CCIJ News, No30, Consumer Co-operative Institute of Japan, p. 1-5.

Suzuki, T., Saito, Y. (2010): "A Brief Chronicle of the Modern Japanese Consumer Cooperative Movement" , the *Japanese Consumers' Co-operative Union (JCCU)*, 149 p.

Tabaco Industry Workers Mutual Aid Cooperative (2017): "Introduction of Tobacco Mutual Aid Headquarters", original Japanese titile: "たばこ共済本部のご紹介" , Japanese only, https://www.zenrosai.coop/zenkoku/tabako/tabako0.php, retrieval: 27.03.2017.

Tatsuki, M. (2003): "A Historical Account of Japan's Life Insurance Companies in the 1920s and 1930s", in. Kasuya, M. (ed.) (2003): "Coping with Crisis: International Financial Institutions in the Interwar Period", *Oxford University Press*, New York, pp. 155-177.

Teachers Mutual Aid Cooperative (2017): "Information 2017 – Guide to the Teachers Mutual Aid Cooperative ", original Japanese title: "Information 2017 – 教職員共済のご案内", Japanese only, *Japan Teachers Mutual Aid Co-Operative Society*, 8 p.

Tokyo Kyosai (2017): "History – 50 Years of History" , original Japanese title: "沿革 -50年のあゆみ-", http://www.tokyo-kyosai.or.jp/tokyo_kyosai/history.html, retrieval: 17.03.2017.

Tsuchida, T. (1998): "An Outlook on the Private Life Insurance Business in Japan", *The Geneva Papers on Risk and Insurance*, No. 88 (23), pp. 356-363.

Toya, T., & Amyx, J. A. (2006): "The political economy of the Japanese financial Big Bang: institutional change in finance and public policymaking.", *Oxford University Press*, 328 p.

Tsutsui, Y., Sekiguchi, M., Chano, T. (2004): "Japanese Life Insurance Industry in the Interwar Period", *Osaka Economic Papers*, Vol. 54 (1), pp. 1-24.

UCMAF (2017a): "The History of University Cooperative Mutual Aid" , Japanese title: "学生総合共済のあゆみ ", Japanese only, http://kyosai.univcoop.or.jp/group/history.html, retrieval: 16.03.2017.

Uemura, N. (2008): "The failure without management Truths behind the Seiho crisis in the Heisei era" , *Nikkei Publishing Inc.*, 227 p.

United States General Accounting Office (1999): "U.S. Japan trade: the Japanese insurance market: report to the chairman, Subcommittee on Trade, Committee on Ways and Means, House of Representatives" , *DIANE Publishing*, 50 p.

Viswanathan, K., Cummins, D. (2003): "Ownership Structure Changes in the Insurance Industry: An Analysis of Demutualization", *The Journal of Risk and Insurance*, Vol. 70 (3), pp. 401-437.

Yamori, N., Okada, T. (2007): "The Japanese Insurance Market and Companies: Recent Trends", in: Cummins, J., Venard, B. (ed.) (2007): "Handbook of international insurance: between global dynamics and local contingencies", *Springer Science & Business Media*, Vol. 26, pp. 147-204.

Yasuda Fire and Marine Insurance Co., Ltd. (1988): "The Yasuda Fire and Marine Insurance, 1888-1988: A Century of Achievement", *Yasuda Fire and Marine Insurance Company*, 203 p.

Yatsui, I. (1951): "Property insurance in Japan: past and present", *The Insurance Institute of Japan*, Tokyo, 58 p.

Yingying, J. (2013): "Organizational Forms in the Postwar Japanese Life Insurance Business: An Application of Corporate Ownership Theory", original Japanese title: "戦後日本の生命保険業における企業形態 - 所有権理論による分析", Japanese only, *Journal of Insurance Science*, No. 620, pp. 179-198.

Yingying, J. (2015): "The Development of the Mutual Form and Its Influence on the Life Insurance Industry – Evidence from Japan during the Period 1881 to 1935", In: *Person, R., Yoneyama, T.* (ed.): "Corporate Forms and Organizational Choice in International Insurance", *Oxford University Press*, pp. 217-242.

Yoda, G. (1993): "The Japanese Insurance Industry: Update Learning a Lesson in Survival", *Economic Research*, Credit Suisse Japan, 17 p.

Yoda, G. (1994): "Japan's Insurance Industry: Adversity Continues", *Credit Suisse Japan - Economic Research*, 14 p.

Yokohama Citizen Mutual Aid Cooperative Association (2017): "Overview of the association", original Japanese title: "組合の概要", Japanese only, http://www.yokohamashimin-kyosai.or.jp/about/index.html, retrieval: 27.9.2017.

Yoneyama, T. (2012): "The Role of Insurance in the Rapid Modernization of Japan", in: Borscheid, P., Haueter, N. (ed. by): "World Insurance: The Evolution of the Global Risk Network", *Oxford University Press*, p. 495-521.

Yoneyama T. (1994): "The industrial organization of Japanese life insurance: historical aspects", in: Yuzawa, T. (ed.) (1994): "Japanese Business Success: the Evolution of a Strategy", *Routledge*, pp. 167-189.

Yoneyama, T. (2008). "Conversion of the postwar insurance system", Japanese only, original Japanese title: "戦後型保険システムの転換 ", *2008 Japan Insurance Society: Symposium "verification of liberalization after 10 years*, pp. 25-44.

Yoneyama, T. (2011): "Historical role and significant existence of cooperative mutual aid in Japan – A Framework of Ownership theory", original Japanese title: "日本における協同組合共済の歴史的役割と存在意義 所有権理論の枠組み ", Japanese only, 20th Anniversary of the Japan Mutual Aid Association – International Cooperative Year Papers and Lecture Collections 2012, original Japanese title: "日本共済協会　結成20周年・2012国際協同組合年　論文・講演集", Japanese only, JCIA, Tokyo, pp. 87-146.

Yoneyama, T. (2016b): "Expert-Interview regarding the History of the Insurance Market in Japan", Professor at the Graduate School of Commerce and Management of the Hitotsubashi University, Tokyo, 27th of June.

Zenrosai (2017): "History of Zenrosai", original Japanese title: "全労済のあゆみ", Japanese only, https://www.zenrosai.coop/zenrosai/profile/about/ayumi.html, retrieval: 10.3.2017.

Part V.
Global Insurance Business

Mutual Insurers from an International Point Of View

Gabriela Csulich

1. Introduction

The focus of this paper is to examine the available data concerning mutuals in an international respectively global context and to address the problems that arise from the different points of view when defining mutuals as legal organizational form. The question is what type of enterprise can be considered as a mutual company respectively what legal framework and key characteristics are necessary to understand companies as mutuals. This query is important when the performance of companies with different organizational structures, i.e. mutuals, joint stock companies, public institutions, are compared. The economic success of such companies can be measured for example by their global market share, their market share in a specific country, or their premium income. Part of the data for the analyses is taken from global sources, some originate from European sources. For a global overview of the insurance business, the publication Sigma Re "World insurance: the great pivot east continues"[1] (2019) edited by the Swiss Re Institute provides the most up to date figures from 2018. However, this publication does not distinguish between the various legal forms such as mutuals, joint stock companies etc.. Therefore, only a broad overview on market shares and premium incomes can be analyzed regarding life and non-life sectors in different regions and the global market share of various countries. However, Swiss Re investigated the mutual insurance business globally in 2016, which can be used to compare with the results of ICMIF, the International Cooperative and Mutual Insurance Federation, that investigated the same topic using data from 2017.[2]

In addition to these two data sources, a study on behalf of the European Union was published in 2012 focusing on the situation of the mutual insurance industry in states of the European Union. In general, the European Union favours the ideas of entrepreneurship and the

---

[1] Sigma 03/2019, World insurance: the great pivot east continues.

[2] Cf. *Telfer, B.,* (2019). Global Mutual Market Share 10. Bowdon: ICMIF.

idea of social economy. According to the latter concept, the legal forms of companies are crucial, i.e. with regard to insurances, enterprises in the organizational structures of mutuals, non-profits, and co-operatives. The latter also considered the idea of a European co-operative, a concept that, however, did not function well. Although the notion of social economy is today practically obsolete, the definition of what type of mutual companies exist respectively what can be regarded as such led to the wide definitions of Swiss Re respectively ICMIF. According to their view, mutual companies or societies that do not fit under the three mentioned legal forms are usually excluded from the data. This holds in particular for the Spanish insurance market in which three forms of insurers exist: companies, societies as well as Mutualidades de Prevision Social. The latter provides additional social security and service.[3]

Using the data as a starting point, the main task was to compare the results of the different sources and to analyze if the outcomes were similar or different. In the event of any divergences between the results, we tried to investigate the reasons for any kinds of inconsistencies. Although the data of all three studies was based in general on the data pool provided by Swiss Re, the results differed for example regarding the market shares of mutuals enormously. This became even more evident when the findings were compared with the research provided in the various chapters in this book. Consequently, it became crucial to investigate the reasons for the different outcomes. While the wide or narrow definitions of mutuals were one possibility, the data source was another. The comparison of the sources used by Swiss Re, ICMIF, and the European study on the one hand, and the data basis for the various country studies in this book on the other hand, became so the central point of investigation. As a result, this study presents the insurance business globally using data by Swiss Re and ICMIF for the global mutual market and compares the results to the findings of the country studies in this book. Additionally, if necessary, the outcomes of the European study were used.

As mentioned before, during this study it became evident that apart from various data sources the definition "what a mutual is" and what Swiss Re, ICMIF and the authors of the various country studies include under the term "mutuals" varied enormously. Therefore, it is useful to start by investigating the historical development of mutuality and then examining the various definitions of mutuality. Moreover, it is of interest to survey if the original roots of mutuality can still be found in today's definitions of mutuality.

---

3 Cf. *Schediwy, R.* Mutuals and Demutualisation in Spain. (chapter about Spain in this book).

2. Historical development

When looking at the historical development of mutuality, four sources can be identified. Firstly, the Teutonic law and *Gierke's* concept of mutual help that was important for the development in Germany and in Austria. Secondly, the Great Fire of London (1666) and the development of Friendly Societies respectively mutual insurance companies as opposed organizational structures to joint stock companies in the British insurance business. Thirdly, the development of social security in France that is closely connected with the events of the French Revolution in 1789. It led eventually to the development of the solidarity principle, the concept of social economy, and to the development of a broad definition of mutuality in the European Union.[4] Finally, the prominence of P & I (Protection and Indemnity) clubs, a type of mutual transport insurance companies that maintained until today the adjustable contribution principle, which is one of the historical core elements of mutuality.

2.1 Gierke's concept of mutual help

An important starting point for the mutuality principle, is the Teutonic law with its focus on the Germanic family and the concept of mutual help among extended family members respectively clan members in the event of catastrophes or fires. The Germanic risk community was based on family and clan connections. The Politian and legal historian *Otto von Gierke* regarded cooperative law as the central point of the German law from which eventually the concept of mutual insurance derived. According to this view, an insurance contract was the best option to eliminate or reduce existing risks.[5] *Gierke* developed a historical legal framework with the concept of a corporate body in its core by using the principle of mutual help. He distinguished between cooperative associations (clan, family, in the Middle Ages cooperate body) and the associations of power (fief associations, later public institutions)[6] regarding the individual always as part of a group. He developed the

[4] Cf. *Brazda, J., Csulich, G., Zeman, St.* (2018). Das Gegenseitigkeitsprinzip im Versicherungswesen aus historisch-analytischer Sicht, in: *Brazda / Blisse* (eds.): Beiträge zur kritischen Genossenschaftsforschung, Wien, pp. 47-74.

[5] Cf. *Koch, P.* (1998). Geschichte der Versicherungswissenschaft in Deutschland, Karlsruhe, p. 101.

[6] Cf. *Gierke, O. v.* (1999). Das Wesen der menschlichen Verbände. Darmstadt 1902 (1954); *Song, Ho-Young* (1999). Die Verselbständigung der juristischen Person im deutschen und koreanischen Recht,. Osnabrück, p. 35.

idea of a corporate body as a legal entity and distinguished between an association with an organism developed out of itself and an institution receiving a legal entity from the outside replacing mutual help.[7] Perceiving humans as social beings, *Gierke* became an early critic of individualism. His concept led to the development of public institutions based on the mutuality principle in Germany and to regional insurance institutions (Landesanstalten) in Austria.

Applying *Gierke's* concept to the insurance business, each individual was now connected with a legal entity based on mutuality, i.e. a mutual insurance company, by a contract, while any connections among each other ceased. This concept can be found in Germany, when during the 17th century, the fire contracts in Hamburg, which based on mutual help, were replaced with a fire insurance fund and the first insurance company (1676) was introduced. While the accession to this institution was voluntarily at first, it became compulsory and a monopoly in 1817. In Bavarian, the public Bavarian country fire insurance company (Bayerische Landesbrandversicherungsanstalt) was established in 1811 and had the monopoly regarding building insurances. In today's insurance business, the insurance contract has replaced mutual help in general[8], with the exceptions of small local insurance societies in Austria.

In contrast, *Ernst Wilhelm Arnoldi* was concerned with the introduction of British life insurance companies on the German market and their potential dominance. As a reaction, he developed a concept for mutuals to overcome their business restriction to regional insurance markets, adopting the marketing ideas of joint stock companies, e.g. of the very successful companies in Trieste, for mutuals. His goal was to break the foreign monopoly of the English joint stock companies and to offer members low-priced insurances. By shifting the mutuality principle from small local insurance societies with social background to large nationwide mutual insurers with increasing economic orientation, he combined the idea of a mutual insurance society with a joint stock company.[9] Nowadays, profit-orientated companies in the organizational structure of joint stock companies dominate the insurance industry, while mutuals represent the other end of the scale. They have found a successful business function in small and highly specialised segments of the insurance industry. They only exception to this trend are mutuals on the US[10] insurance market.

7 Cf. *Gierke, O v.* (1999). Das Wesen der menschlichen Verbände, p. 37.

8 Cf. the chapter about Germany in this book: *Lorenz, R.* Historical development, structural change and perspectives of mutual insurance societies in Germany.

9 Cf. Ibid.

10 On the US insurance market, mutual insurance companies can be found in the car, life insurance, and agriculture industry. Cf. *Brazda, J.* The changing role of mutuals in the American insurance industry (chapter about the US insurance market in this publication).

In Germany, nowadays, public insurance institutions work on a much smaller scale and were replaced by new forms of insurers. Due to the demutualization wave during the 20th century, the complex organizational forms of mutual insurance groups with a holding structure dominate today's German insurance business. This framework of a VVAG group is also an essential reason for the different findings when investigating the performance of mutuals. While official statistics in Germany (BaFin) regarded each company as mutual, joint stock, or a public institution, depending on its legal form, other data sources, e.g. KIVI institute in Cologne, take a different view. According to this standpoint, all subsidiary companies within a group are considered as mutuals, despite their own legal form, when the parent company is mutual. This view will be explored further when ICMIF and Swiss Re's data sources and their definition of mutuality are compared to the findings of this study.

2.2 Concept of mutuality in Great Britain

In the Anglo-American region in general, and in the United Kingdom in particular, mutuality developed differently. The Great Fire of London (1666) tested the existing form of mutuality, i.e. the concept of charity briefs. This license was granted by the crown to receive charity for losses that were too high for small societies and villages to cover by their own. Such a brief, approved by the King's Seal, was printed and distributed to every parish in Britain where it was read during the holy mass. Later the congregation donated money that would then be remitted back to the royal patent office, which distributed the funds to the people or to the groups in need. The charity brief was, therefore, an early invention of redistributing social risks among a larger group of people. However, this scheme was also open to fraudulent behavior, which eventually led to the end of this fund-raising system.[11] Due to the catastrophic events in London in 1666, it became evident that the system of charity briefs was not sufficient to cover the enormous losses in London. Consequently, the idea of establishing insurance companies started to develop in various organizational forms, i.e. mutuals, friendly societies, joint stock companies, and public institutions.

While the idea of establishing a public institution by the City of London (1680) in form of a municipal insurance failed very quickly, people preferred the concepts of mutuals, friendly societies, and joint stock companies to insure their buildings. The idea of establishing an

[11] Cf. *Ismay, P.* (2018). Trust among strangers. Friendly Societies in Modern Britain, p. 36f.; *Ismay, P.* (2010), Trust among strangers: Securing British Modernity `by way of friendly society,' 1780s-1870s; unpublished Dissertation University of California, Berkeley, p. 17.

insurance business for buildings was originally generated by *Nicholas Barbon* when he offered insurances against losses by fire for buildings as an individual underwriter. During the Great Fire in London, whole areas were destroyed and became uninhabitable. Many people had to stay in provisional dwellings with no prospect of new homes in the near future. During this time, *Barbon* discovered the potential of fire insurances and became a pioneer with his idea of building brick houses instead of timber buildings. Although his own insurance business faced massive financial losses, others took up his concept of providing fire insurance. While *Barbon* was forced to establish a company in form of a partnership with joint stock capital in 1681 ("Insurance Office for Houses"), avoiding any interference with the Act of Monopolies[12] (1610) that prohibited all foundations of insurance companies, his competitors chose either the legal form of mutuals or friendly societies for establishing fire insurance business.[13]

In 1684, the "Mutual friendly Society for Securing Houses from losses by Fire" (known as the "Friendly Society") was established by *Henry Spelman* and *William Hale*. In Great Britain, friendly societies are based on the mutuality principle and the concept of helping each other in the event of fire. The philosophy was rooted in the Christian value of neighborliness stressing cooperation and mutual aid. As part of the local credit networks, friendly societies based on the trusts of the borrower and the lender in small communities, usually parishes.[14] *Henry Spelman* and *William Hale*, however, used this notion in a capitalized way for their enterprise. The reason was their caution towards neighborly help and the fulfilling of social obligations of each policyholder, naming the different financial situations (poor and rich) of their members. Therefore, *Spelman and Hale* decided that people had to pay up front an amount of money indicating their commitment to contribute for rebuilding any members' house. Moreover, they also had to sign a contract binding them to do so.[15] Despite their capitalised concept, *Spelman* and *Hales'* Friendly Society worked quite successfully around a century. With establishing the first mutual insurance company in 1696, the "Amicable Contributors for Insuring from Loss by Fire", renamed "Hand-in-Hand" in 1706, and existing until 1905, a rival mutual enterprise developed that distributed, in contrast to the friendly society, the

[12] This was a proclamation by King James I. against Grants and Monopolies (confirmed by Act 21 James I, cap 3, 1623) and prohibited the foundation of Speculative Associations or the raise of transferable stocks with the exception of "Charters to Corporations, Municipal or Trading". Cf. *Relton, F. B.* (1893), An account of the fire insurance companies, p. 10f.

[13] Cf. *Relton, F. B.* (1893), An account of the fire insurance companies, p. 80.

[14] Cf. *Ismay, P.* (2018), Trust among strangers. Friendly Societies in Modern Britain, pp. 25-30; Cf. *Csulich, G; Preiner, S.* The development of the insurance system in Great Britain (chapter about the development in the United Kingdom in this book).

[15] Cf. *Ismay, P.* (2018), Trust among strangers. Friendly Societies in Modern Britain, p. 40.

profits among its members. While large friendly societies in cities were the exception, the concept of mutual insurance companies flourished in the urban environment, in particular during the 18th century, and has influenced the British insurance business until today.

2.3 Social solidarity in France

The third root of the mutuality principle comprises the concept of social solidarity that developed out of the events during the French Revolution in 1789. In his book about social economy (1898), *René Worms* perceives the concept of social economy as a new development and extension of the political economy. He states that this idea is a transition between the science of the material interests of the family and the global economy that comprises the whole society.[16] Social economy is therefore a principle that was created to rethink the relation between the individual and the society. Adopting this notion to the insurance business, a technique developed to neutralise social risks by establishing provision and insurance societies as well as producers' cooperatives based on mutuality.[17] The "associative impulse" from which mutual societies had originated and flourished as part of the 'response of the most vulnerable and defenceless social groups [...] to the new conditions of life [...] in the 18th and 19th centuries'[18] generated the development of mutual-type organizational that can be found in the concept of social economy within Europe.

Additionally, social economy can also be regarded as a program respectively a political model. According to this view, a society should be organized in form of an extensive insurance, being a useful instrument for conducting a negotiation with itself in the future. With the development of social legislation, which is a new type of law with its own changeability and connection to the political economy, a new political and social organization, the "association", was established. Finally, the society transforms into a large "association mutuelle" or mutual society. Insurance proceedings used within the concept of solidarity, however, did not derive from solidarity as a principle or from its main assumption. Instead, when solidarity gives an insurance such crucial position than the theory of solidarity is only possible within the rationality of an insurance. In particular within the way of thinking between its entire-

[16] Cf. *Papilloud, C.; Rol, C.* (2019). Moral – Recht – Nation. Die Soziologie der Solidarität Gaston Richards (1860-1945), p. 43f.

[17] Cf. *Fiegle, Th.* (2003). Von der Solidarité zur Solidarität: ein französisch-deutscher Begriffstransfer, Münster, p. 99; *Jeantet, T.* (2010): Economie Sociale. Eine Alternative zum Kapitalismus. Neu-Ulm, p. 43.

[18] Centre international de recherches et d'information sur l'économie publique, sociale et coopérative (CIRIEC), The Social Economy in the European Union, 2007.

ness and its parts. According to *Renouvier*, insurance has several functions within the solidarity belief. The model of rationality provides the framework for analyzing social problems. From the principle of moral solidarity, legal demands such as requests for a progressive income tax or the foundation of a general system of social fundamental rights derive. The latter should also include the right of work, education, social welfare as well as a general insurance against social risks in the industrial society. *Renouvier* regards the concept of insurance to be examined within the insurance model. He concluded that the insurance of social risks is something that should be based on mutuality (mutualite) and as the solution for the social question. Consequently, the state and the society as a whole should be organized like a huge insurance company with the function to enable solidarity. With the state connecting each individual, the concept of social economy developed.[19]

The Charta of social economy itself states that enterprises based on this concept have to be connected in solidarity (Article 1) and cooperatives, non-profits, and mutual companies as its forms of organization (Article 2).[20] Legal forms that can also be found in ICMIF and AMICE's definitions of mutuals. The European Union originally supported the concept of social economy comprising mutuals, cooperatives, non-profits, co-operatives, private foundations, and social enterprises as its organizational forms. This concept, however, did not work out as well as the idea of a European co-operative. Although social economy did not develop to a sector of its own, it is crucial for securing employment.[21] Moreover, it is the reason for the development of a very wide definition of mutuals that can be found regarding ICMIF and Swiss Re's notion of mutuals.

2.4 Transport insurances

Transport insurances and respectively the so-called P & I (Protection and Indemnity) clubs can be regarded as the fourth root of mutuality. P & I clubs provide risk pooling, information and representation for their members. In contrast to a marine insurance company, which reports to its shareholders, these mutual insurance associations report exclusively to their members. Originally, P & I Club members were typically ship-owners, ship operators or demise charterers, but more

19 Cf. *Fiegle, Th.* (2003). Von der Solidarité zur Solidarität: ein französisch-deutscher Begriffstransfer, Münster, p. 99, 137.

20 Cf. Charta of Economie Sociale.

21 Cf. *Monzón, J. L. / Chaves, R.* (2018). Public Policies towards the Social Economy in Europe at the National and Regional Level in the Recent Period (2010-16), in: *Brazda, J. / Blisse*, H. (2018). Beiträge zur kritischen Genossenschaftsforschung. Festschrift für Robert Schediwy zum 70. Geburtstag, pp.143-155.

recently, freight forwarders and warehouse operators have been able to join. With regard to the legal status, the European Union Directive 2009/20/EC was implemented in all member states by January 1, 2012 and requires compulsory P & I to cover for EU and foreign ships in EU waters and ports. If foreign vessels do not comply with the EU Directive they may be expelled or refused to enter into any EU port. This legal regulation is crucial, because P & I clubs provide cover for a carrier's third-party risks for damage caused to cargo during carriage, war risks, and risks of environmental damage such as oil spills and pollution. Consequently, P & I clubs provide most of the global insurance for oil tankers based on a pay-to-be-paid-policy. This means that P & I clubs refund the costs after the member had already been drawn on but not in advance. P & I clubs are therefore the last large mutual organization form that uses adjustable contribution procedure, a concept that is a historical main root of the mutuality principle and originally an essential feature of mutuals. This notion also suggested that all members should prevent damage in their own financial interest. Another characteristic of P & I clubs is the calculation of insurance premiums based on general information such as the size and age of the vessel and not individually for each member.[22] The success of the mutual P & I clubs is evident when the British P & I clubs turned international and established the "International Group of P & I clubs". Nowadays, ship-owners still favour the mutuality principle as a very good option for transport insurance.[23] In the following section, mutuality as a characteristic of insurance companies will be discussed.

3. Definition of the mutuality principle

The mutuality principle is a principle that can be regarded from two different points of view: firstly, from a descriptive angle, and secondly, from a legal perspective. The descriptive approach focuses on the human behavior of mutual help to establish and secure civilizations. At the same time, mutuality was a crucial starting point for the development of market economy, which needed a way dealing with uncertainties and asymmetric distribution of information. The mutuality principle is an early form of covering and distributing risks within a group

---

[22] Cf. *Altfuldisch, R.* (2007). Haftung und Entschädigung nach Tankerunfällen auf See. Bestandsaufnahme, Rechtsvergleich und Überlegungen de lege ferenda, p. 174, 110.

[23] Cf. *Pearson, R.; Doe, H.* (2015), Organizational choice in UK marine insurance, p. 64f.; https://tindallriley.co.uk/company-profile/ (02.08.2019).

of people. For example, people across clans joined by oath helped each other in the events of fire, illness, poverty, or death.[24] Later the impulse to cover and mitigate risks by mutual help led to organized societies such as brotherhoods, mutual benefit societies, and with regard to Great Britain, to friendly societies.

From a legal point of view, a crucial requirement for the mutuality principle is the foundation of risk balance communities. This community is based on the members as the responsible body of a mutual and results from the connection between the membership and the insurer. However, a mutual company is a legal entity of the civil law and therefore, an economic and legal connection exists between the individual member/policyholder and the insurer. It is important to note that any legal links between members are impossible, because all members form an independent legal society that is the insurer.[25]

Mutuality regarded as a philosophical problem describing how we live with others is concerned with situations in which an individual has to join others to "secure together what one cannot secure alone". For this goal, values, principle, and practices are necessary and have to be specified. The mutual relationship and therefore mutuality are based on normative characteristics such as mutual respect, mutual esteem, dignity, equality, fairness, and care. When looking at the organizational level, a mutual company can be defined as a member-owned business, i.e. members (consumers and producer) own and control the business, with benefits allocated to the members. It is important to note that both benefits as well as problems (risks) have to be distributed equally among members. The legitimacy of a mutual company is a process developing over time when members evaluate and concluded that the proceedings and results responsible for the distribution are fair and mutually profitable.[26] Therefore, the mutualization of risks, i.e. the spreading of the risk over a homogeneous group of people, can be regarded as the most elementary and simple form of insurance in general. This form of bearing risks mutually has a long history and it has proven to be an effective way of insuring people.

However, according to *Farny*, the mutuality principle has not only changed over time, it is not clearly defined and can be interpreted differently. The core principle refers to the relation of each member/policyholder and the mutual insurance society, which is based on corporate and contractual components. A wider definition states that corporate

---

24 Cf. *Brazda, J., Csulich, G., Zeman, St.* (2018). Das Gegenseitigkeitsprinzip im Versicherungswesen aus historisch-analytischer Sicht, in: *Brazda, J. / Blisse, H.* (eds.): Beiträge zur kritischen Genossenschaftsforschung, Wien, p. 47.

25 Cf. Ibid., p. 48.

26 Cf. *Yeoman, R.* From traditional to innovative multi-stakeholder mutuals. The case of Rochdale boroughwide housing, In: *Michi, J., Blasi, J.; Borzaga, C.* (eds.) (2017). The Oxford handbook of Mutual, co-operative, and co-owned business, p. 481.

action of all members are important, i.e. establishment of one's objectives, financing the insurance services. However, the equitation of the mutuality principle and the insurance principle is obsolete, because today the policyholder and the insurance company are not a necessary criterion of an insurance.[27] This more recent definition can also be found in a current version of an insurance dictionary, which states that nowadays the mutuality principle can only be lived in small local mutual societies (Bauernassekuranzen). With abolishing the obligation to make further contributions in the bylaws of large mutual insurance companies, the insurance risk is only connected to the legal entity of the mutual and not any more to each member in the sense of a mutual insurance company.[28]

4. Various definitions of mutuality

The core element when investigating the economic performance of mutual companies in general and in the insurance sector in particular is the statistical information regarding market share, premium income, and global mutual market share. Therefore, one of the first steps is to define what a mutual insurance company is and to what degree an organization meets the criteria of being a mutual insurance company. This alone is difficult when examining the legal structure of mutual companies in one country, and even more challenging when comparing such companies in various countries respectively on a global scale. One possible way to look at are the core elements of mutuality such as the rights and obligations of members or the considerations of their interests within a mutual company. The legal framework deciding if a company is mutual should mirror these core elements. Consequently, the question rises if only pure mutuals should be considered or if companies that are part of VVaG groups (e.g. Germany) or within a MIHC system (e.g. USA) should also be regarded as mutuals. Another approach is the consideration of the historical roots of mutual insurance companies in the various countries and their existence in today's insurance business.

---

[27] Cf. *Farny, D.* (2006). Versicherungsbetriebslehre, 4th edition, p. 207f.

[28] Cf. https://www.versicherungsmagazin.de/lexikon/gegenseitigkeit-1945348.html (12.06. 2019).

4.1 Legal framework

When looking at the legal framework of mutuals within the European Union, the Panteia study from 2012 provides an overview what legal entity is considered as a mutual insurance company in the EU.

Table 1: Overview of legal entities and legal framework

Country	Legal entity	Legal framework applicable to mutual companies
Austria	**Insurance mutual** (Versicherungsverein auf Gegenseitigkeit)	• Insurance Supervision Act 2016
	Small insurance mutual association (Kleine Versicherungsvereine auf Gegenseitigkeit)	
Finland	**Mutual insurance companies** (Keskinäinen vakuutusyhtiö/ömsesidigt försäkringsbolag)	• Insurance Companies Act (amended in 2015)
	Insurance association (Vakuutusyhdistys/försäkringsförening)	• Act on Insurance Associations 2008
	Pension Insurance Companies (Työeläkevakuutusyhtiöistä / arbetspensionsförsäkringsbolag)	• Act on Pension Insurance Companies 1997
Germany	**Mutual insurance association** (Versicherungsvereine auf Gegenseitigkeit)	• Insurance Supervision Act 2015
	Small insurance mutual (Kleine Versicherungsvereine auf Gegenseitigkeit)	
Norway	**Mutual insurance company** (Gjensidige forsikringsselskaper)	• Law on insurance companies, pension companies and their business activity
Spain	**Mutuas de seguros** (mutual insurance company)	• Act 20/2015 (ordination, supervision and solvency of insurance and reinsurance undertakings, LOSSEAR) • Royal Decree 1060/2015 (approving the regulations for ordination, supervision and solvency of insurance and reinsurance undertakings ROSSEAR).
	Mutualidades de previsión social (mutual provident societies)	
United Kingdom	In United Kingdom, mutual-type organisations are defined broader than in other countries and the legal framework largely leaves open which form one chooses for being a mutual.	• registered societies established under the Friendly Societies Acts 1992 • the legal form of an unlimited company under the Companies Act of 2006. • a registered society under the Co-operative and Community Benefit Societies Act 2014 or a credit union • the legal form of a private company, which is either limited by shares of by guarantee and which falls under the regulations of the Companies Act of 2006. • a building society • an EEA mutual society

Source: *Broek, S., Buiskool, B., Vennekens, A., & Van der Horst, R.* (2012). Study on the current situation and prospects of mutuals in Europe. Zoetermeer: Panteia – EIM, pp. 59-62; cf. the country studies of Austria, Finland, Germany, Norway, Spain, and the United Kingdom.

The table shows clearly, how diverse the various countries in the European Union interpreted mutuality. This means that what can be considered as a mutual insurance company, based on the legal regulations in each country, is a question difficult to answer. Moreover, the overview stresses the diversity of legal frameworks applying to mutuals in each country. Therefore, using a legal framework as a guideline when considering if a company is mutual or not is a possible way but probably not sufficient to establish a general rule.

4.2 Current situation

Another criterion when establishing the organizational form of a company is the historical root that influenced this type of enterprise in a specific country or region. When looking at the four historical roots of mutuality, public insurance institutions, mutual companies, social solidarity, and mutual transport insurance (e.g. P & I clubs), it becomes evident that not all of these four roots are used in the same way as originally. Although in today's insurance industry, the dominance of joint stock companies is evident, mutuals have not become obsolete, they just have changed and adapted to the necessities of today's business. Such adaptation can be found in Austria, where legal regulations during the 1990s made it possible to establish hybrid forms in the event of demutualization. These new companies are closely connected with asset management societies and private foundations. This complex construction of mutual companies generates the question if such companies can still be considered as mutuals or not. The answer has a huge impact regarding the results of statistics and will be discussed further in this study. While, for example, ICMIF uses a wide definition of mutuality, the author of this study prefers a much narrower. For example, in Austria exist so-called Landesanstalten, insurance companies based on the mutuality principle without compulsorily legal membership but financially supported by the regional government. This type of insurers has a long tradition since the 1830s and still exist in Tyrol, Vorarlberg, and Carinthia.[29]

When looking at the Anglo-American region, the concept of a legal entity, as introduced by *Gierke* ("juristische Person"), connecting a member of a mutual company with the insurer is unknown. With regard to the USA, the state as the supervisor of insurers decides about the significance of the concept of membership in a mutual company. A state insurance holding company regulation was first introduced in the 1970s, while the U.S. system of state-based insurance regulation has

---

[29] Cf. the chapter about Austria in this book: *Brazda, J.* Mutual insurance society in Austria. Developments of a principle.

included a review of the holding company system for decades focussing on each insurance legal entity. At the same time, the National Association of Insurance Commissioners (NAIC)[30] adopted its Insurance Holding Company System Regulatory Act, the so-called Holding Company Act, and Insurance Holding Company System Model Regulation to supervise insurance companies for each state individually. Originally, most state insurance laws had limited the investments of an insurance company into its subsidiaries, which, on the other hand, were not allowed to do insurance business. The NAIC Insurance Holding Company System Regulatory Act, the so-called Holding Company Act, restricted the investments into subsidiaries to less than 10 percent of the insurer's assets respectively 50 percent of the insurer's surplus.[31] This regulation concerning mutual insurance companies, however, was not very attractive, because it limited the freedom to support subsidiaries with capital.[32]

Due to the demutualization wave during the 1980s and 1990s, the position and rights of members in mutual companies became important. In 1997/1998, a debate about the question if policyholders were owners of their mutual company was generated in the USA. In the event of a demutualization, the question if members of a mutual company were owners of the company or not had a huge impact on any financial transactions regarding the assets of the company. When a mutual company demutualizes, members exchange all equity and surplus rights for shares in the new joint stock company respectively holding company. However, this process is very expensive and time-consuming in particular for life insurance companies, because it is crucial to determine and guarantee the policyholders' financial claims supervised by the regulatory authorities. As a reaction, the special legal form of the MIHC was created, allowing a mutual insurance company converting into a stock corporation, which becomes a wholly owned subsidiary of the MIHC or a new intermediate holding stock holding company.[33] The construction of the MIHC had the goal to strengthen the members' rights. In the

[30] NAIC is an organization of state insurance regulators from the 50 states, the District of Columbia and the four U.S. territories. NAIC functions as a regulatory support organization and serves the public interest by promoting uniformity of legislation and regulation, facilitating the fair and equitable treatment of insurance consumers, promoting the reliability, solvency and financial solidity of insurance institutions, and supporting and improving state regulation of insurance.

[31] Cf. National Association of Insurance Commissioners (1999). Mutual Insurance Holding Company Reorganizations, December 7, 1998, p. 12.

[32] Cf. *Brazda, J.* The changing role of mutuals in the American insurance industry (chapter about the US insurance market in this publication); National Association of Insurance Commissioners (1999). Mutual Insurance Holding Company Reorganizations, December 7, 1998.

[33] Cf. National Association of Insurance Commissioners (1999). Mutual Insurance Holding Company Reorganizations, December 7, 1998, p. 4f.; *Brazda, J.* The changing role of mutuals

organizational structure of a MIHC, policyholders have membership rights in the MIHC that holds the majority of the voting stocks as well as contractual rights in the converted stock insurance company. With the Holding Company Act, a supervisory authority supervises the transactions and relationships between the MIHC, the converted insurance joint stock company, the intermediate stock holding companies as well as affiliated companies.[34] The idea behind this concept is that the state is the only one able to supervise an insurance company in the long term. On the other hand, it also means that the mutuality principle is not practiced anymore. This is evident when considering the regulation that when a member does not attend a general meeting his/her approval of all decisions made during the session is assumed.[35]

When the organizational form of the MIHC was created, the question arises if this new type of company is still mutual or not. The answer to this query can be found in the statistical data. Without official statistics, the NAIC (National Association of Insurance Commissioners) provides the data for non-life companies considering holding companies as mutuals when their parent company has this specific organization structure. NAIC also includes joint stock companies, despite their lines of business, as mutuals when a mutual company owns them. With regard to life insurers, the American Council of Life Insurers offers data for this segment published in "Life insurers fact book 2018"[36].The following table is drawn from this publication and shows the number of US life insurers by organizational structure for 2016 and 2017. Table 2 is published by the American Council of Life Insurers, which draws its data from the National Association of Insurance Commissioners (NAIC). The table shows clearly that the category of mutuals is used in a wider sense. According to the publication, the group "mutuals" comprises stock companies owned by mutual parents (life and non-life) as well as mutual holding companies. A similar point of view can be regarded for the group of insurance companies owned by fraternal benefit societies. According to the American Council of Life Insurers, stock companies that were owned by such institutions are also considered as fraternal, while the category "other" comprises farm bureau, reciprocal, and risk retention groups.

---

in the American insurance industry (chapter about the US insurance market in this publication).

[34] Cf. National Association of Insurance Commissioners (1999). Mutual Insurance Holding Company Reorganizations, December 7, 1998, p. 6; 37.

[35] Cf. *Brazda, J.* The changing role of mutuals in the American insurance industry (chapter about the US insurance market in this publication).

[36] American Council of Life Insurers (2018). Life insurers fact book 2018, p. 2.

Table 2: Number of life insurer by organizational form 2016 and 2017

Number of U.S. Life Insurers, by Organizational Structure	In business at year's end		Average annual percent change
	2016	2017	2016/2017
Stock	598	584	-2.3
Mutual[1]	113	112	-0.9
Fraternal[2]	78	76	-2.6
Other[3]	8	9	12.5
Total	797	781	-2.0

Source: American Council of Life Insurers (2018). Life insurers fact book 2018, p. 2.

Based on this information, it seems that the American Council of Life Insurers respectively the National Association of Insurance Commissioners (NAIC) regard mutuals in a wider sense, which means that both have the same point of view as Swiss Re and ICMIF. Both institutions also draw their data from the NAIC respectively the NAMIC for their analyses of the US insurance market.

With the four historical roots, the different legal frameworks in the various countries, the special construction of MIHC in the USA, VVAG groups in Germany, and the Austrian hybrid forms in mind the complexity of creating a statistical framework of mutuals is evident. The starting point for expanding the original narrow definition of mutuals can be located in two events: firstly, in establishing the social economy concept in Europe comprising various forms of enterprises, and secondly, in the demutualization waves during the 1990s. Both events were not regional limited but concerned the insurance industry globally.

The problem of how the interpretation of data influences the findings was also addressed in a report regarding statistical data of cooperatives.[37] In this paper, the problem of considering what criteria are necessary respectively sufficient when creating statistics for cooperatives on a global scale is discussed at length. The study analyzed the different legal frameworks of cooperatives (pure or hybrid forms), a classification system of cooperatives for statistical purposes, and key characteristics of cooperatives as guidelines to answer the question how statistics can be created to mirror the current situation of cooperatives in the most accurate way. A second study[38] investigated the

[37] Cf. Conceptual Framework for the Purpose of Measurement of Cooperatives and its Operationalization. Report discussed at the COPAC Technical Working Group on Cooperative Statistics Meeting, Geneva, May 2017.

[38] Cf. International Labour Office (2017). Use of statistics on cooperatives in national policy making, Geneva.

same problem and concluded that firstly, official statistical institutions should provide accurate up to date statistics, that secondly, international standards are crucial for the comparison of data and that thirdly, the highest quality criteria for statistics in general are necessary.[39] However, it is difficult to achieve such goals when official statistics are not available. Consequently, the historical roots of mutuality have to be regarded when analyzing the data and creating statistics. The following concepts for mutuals, with the exception of any type of hybrid forms, should be considered today: firstly, for the German-speaking area, *Gierke's* concept of a legal entity ("juristische Person"), secondly, P & I clubs for mutuals working in the transport insurance segment. Thirdly, the concept of the state as supervisory authority to strengthen and guard the rights of members in a MIHC over generations (cf. the situation in the USA).

With confronting by the problem of how to present a most precise situation of the performance of mutuals based on the available data, the authors of this publication chose a narrow point of view regarding mutuals. ICMIF and Swiss Re have published data for Europe on a global scale, however, it is difficult to verify their results. In the following sections, the attempt is made to give better insights how these two institutions define mutuals and consequently analyze the performance of mutual companies in general. Moreover, it is the intention of this book to present an alternative point of view how the available data can be evaluated.

4.3 The concept of mutuality based on Swiss Re and ICMIF's definition of mutuality in the insurance business

The purpose of this study is to present and compare the results of the various country studies in this book with data from ICMIF and Swiss Re's publications, starting with the wide definitions of mutuals by Swiss Re and ICMIF. By showing the problems when defining mutual insurance companies on a global scale respectively in different countries or regions, the diverse points of views what kind of the available data should be used become evident. Moreover, by comparing ICMIF and Swiss Re's perspectives with the narrower approach used in this publication, the intentions of both institutions as organizations protecting the interests of their members become apparent.

Moreover, in June 2019, Swiss Re announced that it has become a Supporting Member of the International Cooperative and Mutual Insurance Federation (ICMIF), which functions as the main umbrella

---

[39] Cf. Ibid. pp. 57-60.

body for the cooperative and mutual insurance industry on a global scale. Swiss Re's aim is to provide ICMIF's members with the opportunity to use their knowledge, expertise and support to anticipate and manage risks.[40] While Swiss Re provides reinsurance, insurance and other forms of insurance-based risk transfer, ICMIF focuses on its members and on the mutual and cooperative sector. This cooperation has started earlier when ICMIF has contributed to Swiss Re's research into the cooperative and mutual insurance sector in its Sigma publication. Moreover, ICMIF has already based the global insurance figures quoted in the Global Mutual Market Share report[41] on the research of Swiss Re.[42] One can only speculate about the aim behind this collaboration, however, the trend towards demutualization in the insurance sector was and still is evident[43], therefore, it may be ICMIF's attempt to counteract this development. Additionally, as mentioned by *Robert Glasser* from the Munich Re, the mutual insurance schemes could be a solution for covering insurance requirements in underdeveloped countries. In particular, because in those countries the risks of natural disasters are much higher and therefore the risks for insurance companies are much higher too. *Glasser* claims that mutual insurance companies are more accomplished to develop suitable products to cover particular groups of the population against such risks, implying that risks faced in such countries can be covered through domestic self-organization of the developing nations' population.[44] Maybe with this statement in mind Swiss Re's second issue of Sigma[45] in 2019 about natural catastrophes as well as ICMIF's announcement to develop new types of insurances can be seen.

4.3.1 Swiss Re

When looking at Swiss Re's definition of a mutual company, it is defined as "an autonomous association/organization of legal entities or persons operating in (and sometimes across) different sectors, including healthcare, banking, insurance and many others. The primary purpose of a mutual is to satisfy its members' common needs, rather than to make profits or provide a return on capital. Mutual organizations are run for the benefit of its member-owners, as opposed to being owned

---

40 Cf. https://www.swissre.com/media/news-releases/nr-20190626-swiss-re-joins-icmif.html (23.07.2019).

41 Cf. *Telfer, B.*, (2019). Global Mutual Market Share 10. Bowdon: ICMIF.

42 Cf. https://www.icmif.org/news/icmif-welcomes-swiss-re-new-supporting-member (22.07.2019).

43 Cf. The development on the US life insurance market: Demutualizations: The state of conversions in 2000, in: A.M. Best, Special Report September 30, 2002.

44 Cf. Munich Re (ed.). Corporate Responsibility Report 2017/2018, p. 89.

45 Cf. Sigma 2/2019: Secondary natural catastrophe risks on the front line.

and controlled by outside investors."[46] Swiss Re addresses here the interests of the members of mutuals, but does not explain this core element further. Therefore, it is unclear how important Swiss Re considers the rights and interests of members for its definition. For example, in Austria the co-optation system makes it practically impossible for members to be involved actively in mutual insurance companies, with the exception of small regional insurance companies. This is even more evident regarding hybrid forms and the so-called Landesanstalten. On the other hand, in the USA the state has the task to protect the members' interests in a MIHC, which however is usually considered as mutual. Therefore, Swiss Re's definition of mutual insurers addressing the common needs of members is vague and does not give further information about this feature.

To show the diversity of what Swiss Re considers as a mutual insurer, the following figure presents an overview. According to it, mutuals insurance companies include privately run entities that are owned by their members, underwriting non-life and life insurance risks that are governed by insurance principles and laws, and regulated accordingly. It comprises the various business lines of financial mutuals and cooperatives based on core activity (insurance and healthcare) as well as on legal form.[47] Swiss Re, however, excluded mutual-type organizations that are part of the public or quasi-public welfare system such as the sickness funds in Germany or private non-profit health insurers (Consumer Operated and Oriented Plan, or "CO-OPs") in the United States that are funded by low-cost state loans. On the other hand, it includes French mutual benefit societies such as mutuelles 45 and institutions de prevoyance (see Figure 1).

Swiss Re focuses on registered insurers in various legal forms and includes mutuals, mutual holding companies, including the subsidiaries of mutuals despite their legal forms, friendly and fraternal societies. This group refers clearly to the categorisation that can be found by NAIC and AMBest in the United States and therefore also to the legal construction of a MIHC. Additionally, Swiss Re also includes risk retention groups, reciprocal insurers, and discretional mutuals. The latter can be found in the United Kingdom offering members the opportunity to apply for a funding of support to cover losses arising from a qualifying risk or incident. This application for assistance can be accepted or refused by the board of the mutual completely or to a degree. It is interesting that Swiss Re excludes P & I clubs (Protection & Indemnity) as well as Takaful providers (Shari'a-compliant). While the latter are exclude due to the missing self-government, P & I clubs are unquestionably mutuals. As mentioned above, P & I clubs developed from small

[46] Swiss Re Sigma No 4/2016, p. 2.

[47] Cf. Swiss Re Sigma No 4/2016, p. 3.

regional transport insurers to international mutual insurers focusing in particular on the insurance of oil tankers[48], therefore, it is difficult to understand Swiss Re's decision excluding such an important group of mutuals, while ICMIF categorises these clubs as mutual companies.

Figure 1: In-scope and out-of-scope of mutuals regarding Swiss Re's definition[49]

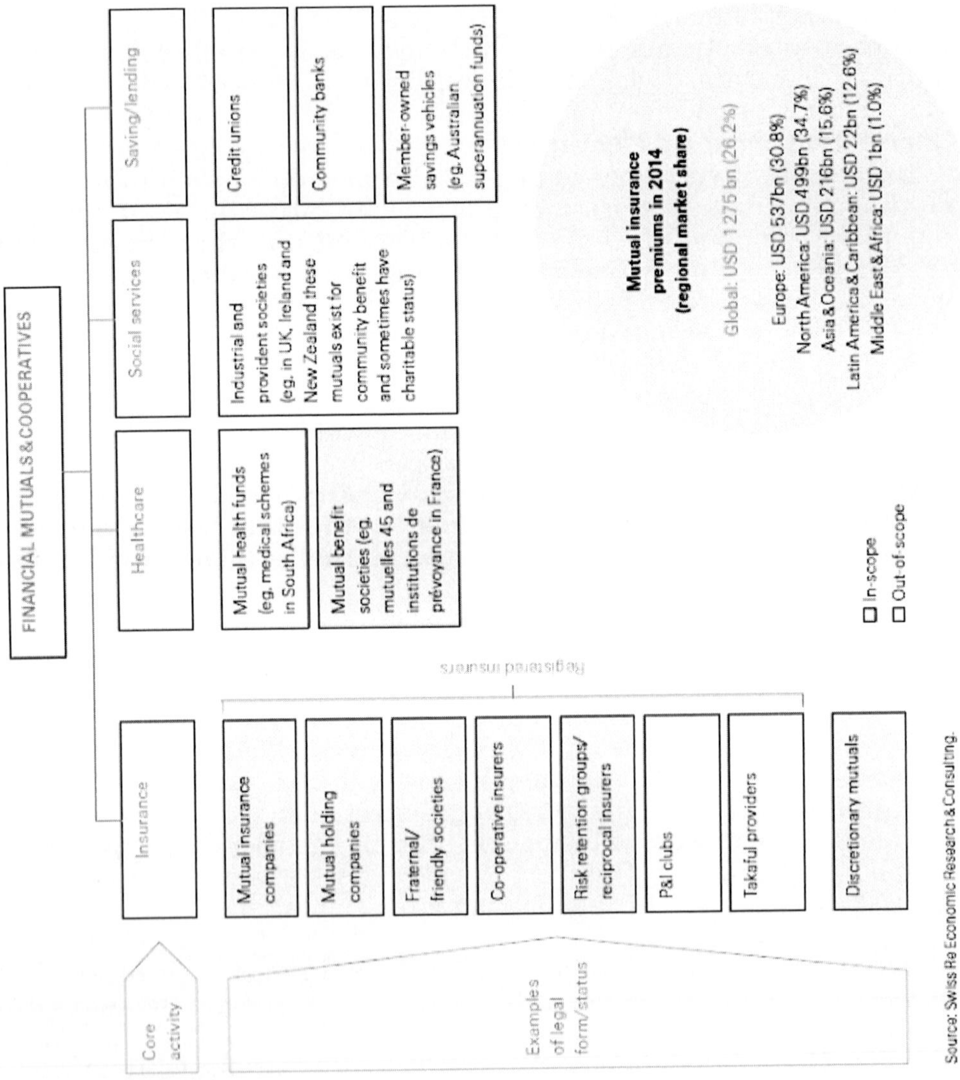

[48] Cf. Swiss Re Sigma No 4/2016, p. 3.
[49] Swiss Re Sigma No 4/2016, p. 4.

Swiss Re's classification of what a mutual company is or is not, is closely connected with the general problem of verifying the sources that this organization uses for its analyses. In the methodology section of its latest Sigma publication (2019), Swiss Re states that the insurance data "originate primarily from national supervisory authorities and, in some cases, from insurance associations. Macroeconomic data was sourced from the International Financial Statistics of the IMF, Oxford Economics and IHS Markit."[50] This explanation can only be considered in the best way as vague.

A similar wide definition of mutuals is presented by ICMIF, an institution that has recently announced to join Swiss Re. In contrast to Swiss Re, ICMIF investigates the performance of mutual insurance companies from a global[51] as well as from a European[52] point of view. The latter publication is made with AMICE[53] (Association of Mutual Insurers and Insurance Cooperatives in Europe). The organization describes itself as "the voice of the mutual and cooperative insurance sector in Europe" with the aim "that the interests of its members are taken into account in securing a level playing field for all insurers in Europe regardless of their legal form"[54]. While today both organizations publish their results in one report, previously separated reports with different results can be found. For example, in 2008 AMICE stated that more than half of all insurers in Europe were mutuals or cooperatives. Moreover, subsidiaries of mutuals and cooperatives or insurance companies acting like mutuals or cooperatives represented an additional 10 percent.[55] As a result, the market share of mutual and cooperative insurers and their subsidiaries was 18.3 percent in 2008 and even 26.1 percent when including insurers that are controlled by mutuals or cooperatives. This comprised also insurers that were influenced by the mutual idea and/or they are not "influenced by outside capital interests".[56] When comparing the results with ICMIF's data from that time, the 27.7 percent European mutual market share is similar to AMICE's results when using the broad definition. This wide definition can also be found nowadays in their joint publication as well as in ICMIF's global report.

In the global report "Global Mutual Market Share 10", the organization states the following: "ICMIF's definition of "mutual" and "coopera-

[50] Swiss Re Sigma No 3/2019: World insurance: the great pivot east continues, p. 32.

[51] Cf. *Telfer, B.*, (2019). ICMIF Global Mutual Market Share 10.

[52] Cf. AMICE and ICMIF Facts and figures. Mutual and cooperative insurance in Europe Vol 2, 2018.

[53] Cf. https://www.amice-eu.org/ (25.07.2019)

[54] Ibid.

[55] Cf. AMICE. (2012). Facts and figures: Mutual and cooperative insurance in Europe. Brussels: AMICE.

[56] AMICE. (2012). Facts and figures: Mutual and cooperative insurance in Europe. Brussels: AMICE, p. 7.

tive" in this report includes organizations whose legal status may not be classified as such in their national law, but whose structure and values reflect the mutual/cooperative form, i.e. companies which are owned by, governed by and operated in the interests of their member policyholders." This classification includes limited companies owned by people-based organizations, fraternal benefit societies (fraternals), friendly societies, Takaful providers, reciprocals, non-profits, exchanges, discretionary mutuals, protection and indemnity (P & I) clubs, community organizations and foundations. According to ICMIF, extending the definition in this way has enabled the organization to include all organizations that operate on mutual/cooperative principles, in line with the "research objectives, without being restricted by legal definitions of which there is a wide variety across the globe and of which some are particular to one country or organization alone."[57] It is important to note that ICMIF, in contrast to Swiss Re, includes Takaful providers as well as P & I clubs. ICMIF justifies its wide definition with the aim to analyze all organizations based on mutual and/or cooperative principles without the restriction of legal definitions that can be found, for example, in one particular country or organization.[58] However, it has to be kept in mind that ICMIF is an organization representing the cooperative and mutual insurance sector and therefore its members. The latter own, govern and guide the organization actively, therefore, ICMIF respond to "their members' needs and expectations". According to ICMIF's concept, the purpose is to promote and work with the cooperative and mutual insurance sector in order to provide unique, valuable and up-to-date market information to their members. However, as mentioned before, the transparency of what kind of data is used for the analyses and how the data is obtained is blurry. According to the references listed in the publication Global Mutual market Share 10, ICMIF gains its data from the following member associations:[59]

- AAM (Association des Assureurs Mutualistes), France
- A.M. Best
- AFA (American Fraternal Alliance), USA
- AFM (Association of Financial Mutuals), UK
- L'Argus de l'Assurance, France
- BaFin (Federal Financial Supervisory Authority), Germany
- CAMIC (Canadian Association of Mutual Insurance Companies), Canada
- CNEPS (Confederación Española de Mutualidades), Spain
- Danish Insurance Association, Denmark
- FFA (Fédération Française de l'Assurance), France
- FNMF (Fédération nationale de la mutualité française), France

57 Email conversation wih *Ben Telfer* (25.06.2019).

58 *Telfer, B.*, (2019). ICMIF Global Mutual Market Share 10, p. 19.

59 Cf. *Telfer, B.*, (2019). Global Mutual Market Share 10. Bowdon: ICMIF, p. 20.

- JCIA (Japanese Cooperative Insurance Association), Japan
- NAIC (National Association of Insurance Commissioners), USA
- NAMIC (National Association of Mutual Insurance Companies), USA
- OECD (Organisation for Economic Co-operation and Development)
- ROAM (Réunion des Organismes d'assurance mutuelle), France
- Swiss Re

With respect to Germany, ICMIF refers to the official statistical institution BaFin, which, however, does not distinguish between legal forms. For the US insurance market, ICMIF uses data from NAIC (National Association of Insurance Commissioners) and NAMIC (National Association of Mutual Insurance Companies), institutions that consider stock companies owned by mutual parents (life and non-life) as well as mutual holding companies as mutuals.

In 2018, ICMIF introduced a classification system with three definitions relating to the legal structure and ownership of a mutual company or cooperative. According to this system, the first category comprises mutual or cooperative insurers in the legal form, the second, their subsidiaries, and the third, mutual or cooperative-type insurers. In addition, the first category also includes both insurance undertakings with a similar legal structure to the mutual or cooperative model and insurance companies with a legal structure different to a joint-stock (limited) company. These undertakings include friendly societies, community benefit societies as well as P & I clubs. As mentioned before, the latter is a mutual insurance association that provides risk pooling, information and representation for its members. In contrast to a marine insurance company, P & I clubs report only to its members who were typically ship owners, ship operators or demise charterers, but more recently, freight forwarders and warehouse operators. Therefore, ICMIF recognizes P & I clubs as companies with a mutual legal form, which contrasts Swiss Re's point of view.

With regard to the subsidiaries of mutual companies and cooperatives (second definition), ICMIF considers them as mutuals when the parent company is actively engaged in insurance activities, even if only to a limited extent. These subsidiaries usually operate in the legal form of a joint stock or limited company. According to ICMIF and AMICE's wide definition, insurance companies within this category include both domestic and foreign-based (including non-European markets) subsidiaries.[60]

The third definition focuses on mutual and cooperative-type insurers that are neither included in the first or second group. These insurers

[60] Cf. AMICE and ICMIF Facts and figures. Mutual and cooperative insurance in Europe Vol 2, 2018, p. 10f.

are companies owned by, governed by and operated in the interests of their members or policyholders. They are characterized by mutualist and/or cooperative ideas and/or organized in such a way that outside capital interests do not control them in majority. As a result, ICMIF and AMICE's definition comprises companies with different organizational structures, including limited insurance companies[61] that are majority owned by a non-insurance mutual or cooperative organization or group (including banks). Moreover, this category also includes insurance undertakings that are owned by or governed by a membership or community organization, charitable trust, foundation, union or other non-profit organization. By including the latter, ICMIF refers here to the concept of social economy, a notion with a wide definition of mutuality.

Figure 2[62] applies the three definitions to the European mutual insurance market. According to ICMIF's point of view, the Austrian market seems to be dominated by mutual insurers that are based on the mutual or cooperative idea, only a few exist in the legal form, and none as subsidiaries in the legal form. Consequently, ICMIF and AMICE concluded a market share of 60.5 percent for Austria in 2015.

Figure 3[63] shows a more detailed picture of the development of the Austrian mutual market share by applying the three definitions to the companies. While until 2011, subsidiaries of mutuals in the legal form of mutuals existed (1.1 percent), they vanished completely and only companies categorized into the first and third definition can be found on the Austrian market nowadays.

As mentioned before, the definition of what is considered as a mutual insurance company varies and differs between ICMIF, the Panteia study, and the authors of this publication. This is evident when comparing the results of the market shares that are based on various sources and on definitions, wide or narrow, regarding what can and cannot be regarded as a mutual insurance (cf. table 3).

---

61 In certain markets where insurance companies cannot take the legal form of a mutual or cooperative (or have restrictions on the line of business which they can offer), figures may nevertheless be indicated for the mutual/cooperative insurance market due to the presence of definition 2 and definition 3 insurers. These insurers hold a significant share of the national market in some of the smaller such as Slovakia, Czech Republic, Latvia, Estonia and Croatia. AMICE and ICMIF Facts and figures. Mutual and cooperative insurance in Europe Vol 2, 2018, p. 11.

62 AMICE and ICMIF Facts and figures. Mutual and cooperative insurance in Europe Vol 2, 2018, p. 6.

63 AMICE and ICMIF Facts and figures. Mutual and cooperative insurance in Europe Vol 2, 2018, p. 17.

Figure 2: European Market Share by definition (2015)

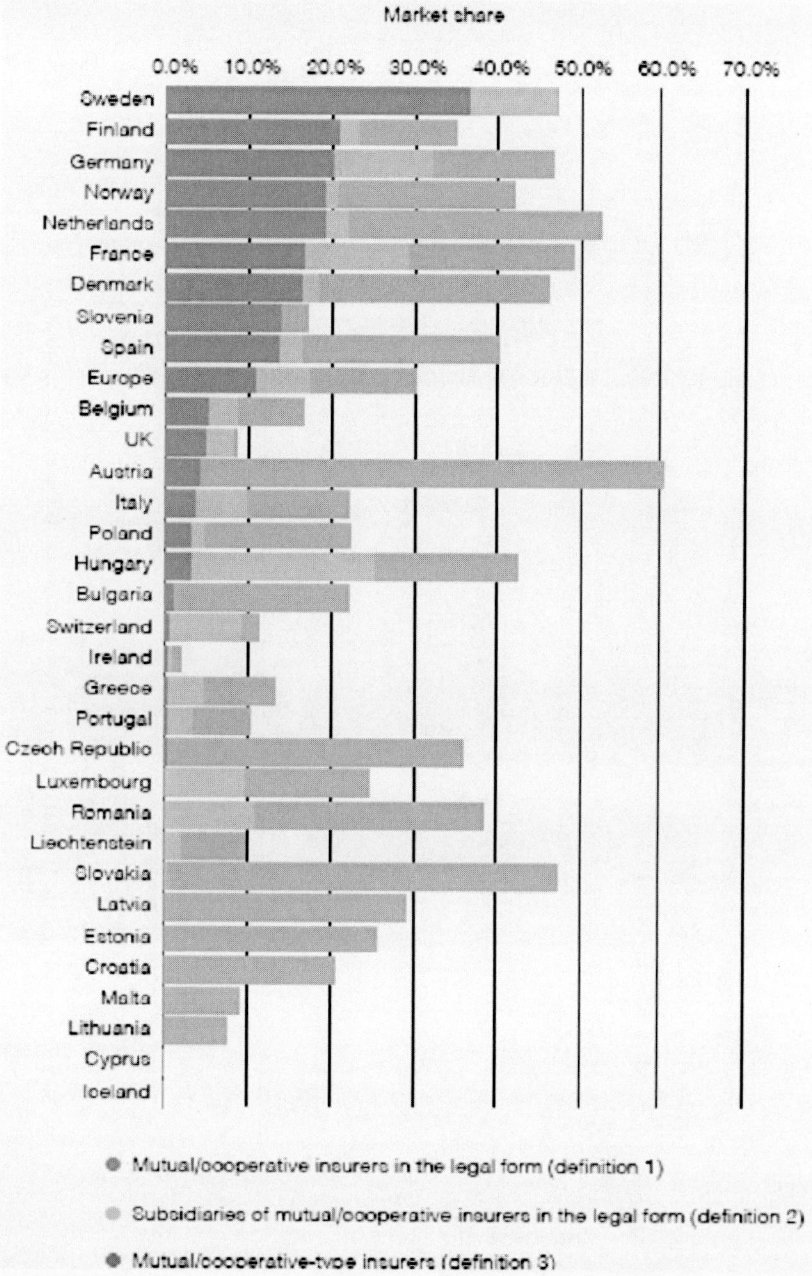

Source: AMICE and ICMIF Facts and figures. Mutual and cooperative insurance in Europe Vol 2, 2018, p. 6.

Figure 3: Market share of the mutual/cooperative insurance sector (2007-2015)

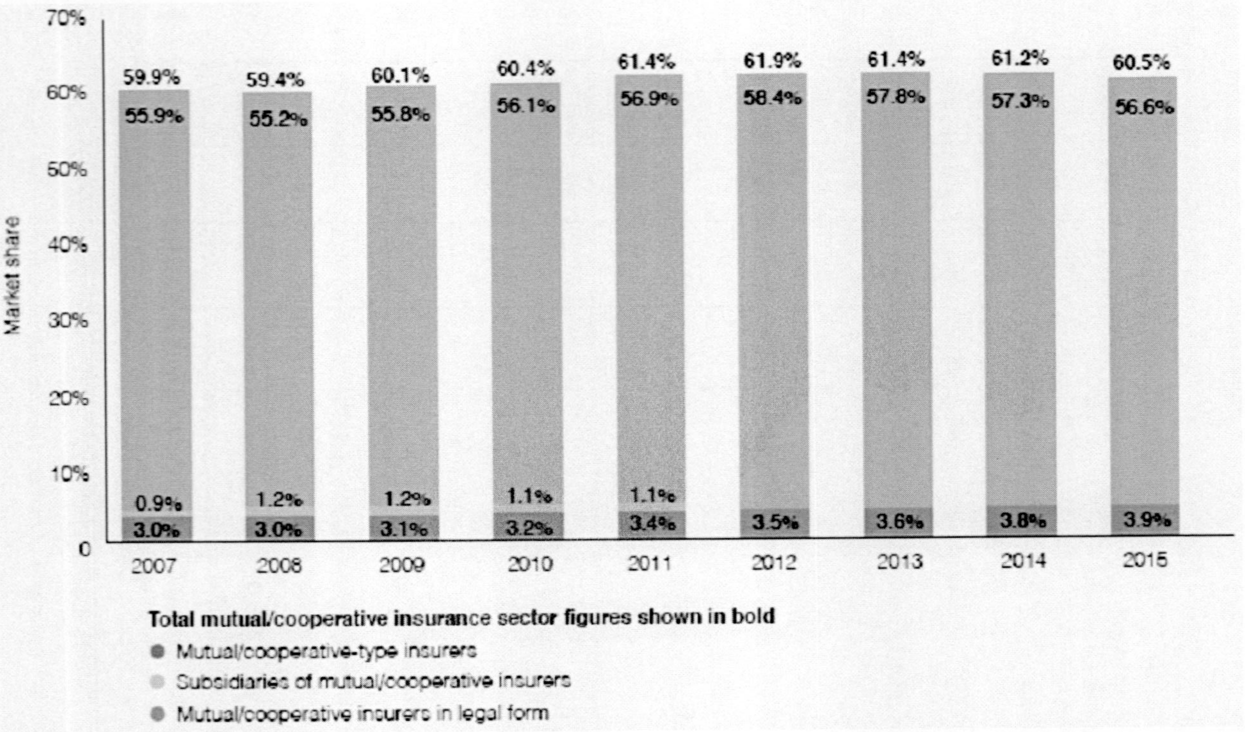

Source: AMICE and ICMIF Facts and figures. Mutual and cooperative insurance in Europe Vol 2, 2018, p. 17. It is important to note that ICMIF and AMICE adapted in later publications the figures.

Table 3: Mutual market share from 2008 to 2017 by various sources

Country	Mutual market share in percent (2008)[64] ICMIF	Mutual market share in percent (2010) European Study[65]	Mutual market share in percent (2015) ICMIF[66]	Mutual market share in percent (2017) ICMIF[67]	2017[68]
Austria	59.8	8	60.5	59.9	3.89
Germany	43.9	31	47.0	47.3	34.78 (2016)
Norway	40.4	18	42.3	44.4	46.7 (2015)
Finland	73.6	23	35.1	56.2	37.5 (2014)
Spain	28.8	14	40.4	-	-
United Kingdom	5.3	7	8.5	10.6	-

Source: *Lenton, D., Yokomizo, D., Tarbuck, S., Lageu, F., & McGee, M.* (2010). Mutual Market Share & Global 500 for 2007-2008. Bowdon: ICMIF, pp. 8; 18ff; *Broek, S., Buiskool, B., Vennekens, A., & Van der Horst, R.* (2012). Study on the current situation and prospects of mutuals in Europe. Zoetermeer: Panteia – EIM; AMICE and ICMIF Facts and figures. Mutual and cooperative insurance in Europe Vol 2, 2018; *Telfer, B.*, (2019). Global Mutual Market Share 10. Bowdon: ICMIF; Market shares are drawn from the various country studies in this book.

Table 3 shows clearly the different results of the market shares when using various data sources. The most intriguing variation can be observed regarding the Austrian insurance market. ICMIF and AMICE calculated a mutual market share of 59.9 percent for 2017, while the calculations of the author of the Austrian study[69] show a share of 3.89 percent. According to ICMIF and AMICE, Austria was ranked as the market with the highest mutual market share (59.9 percent) in 2017, followed by Finland (56.2 percent). With the knowledge of the situation in Austria, it was the aim to clarify the difference of 56.01 percentage points between ICMIF's and our results. Therefore, we contacted *Ben Telfer*, Vice-President, Business Intelligence, ICMIF and lead researcher of ICMIF's Global Mutual Market Share publication. According to *Ben Telfer*[70], the reason for the differences in the results is

64 *Lenton, D., Yokomizo, D., Tarbuck, S., Lageu, F., & McGee, M.* (2010). Mutual Market Share & Global 500 for 2007-2008. Bowdon: ICMIF, pp. 8; 18ff.

65 *Broek, S., Buiskool, B., Vennekens, A., & Van der Horst, R.* (2012). Study on the current situation and prospects of mutuals in Europe. Zoetermeer: Panteia – EIM.

66 AMICE and ICMIF Facts and figures. Mutual and cooperative insurance in Europe Vol 2, 2018.

67 *Telfer, B.*, (2019). Global Mutual Market Share 10. Bowdon: ICMIF.

68 Market shares are drawn from the various country studies in this book.

69 Cf. The chapter about Austria's current situation in this book: *Zeman, S.* The Development of Mutuality Principles in Austria – an analysis of Mutual Insurance Societies.

70 The information is based on an email conversation with *Ben Telfer* from June 25, 2019.

the definition of mutual companies. ICMIF and AMICE use a "wider definition that extends beyond the legislation definition of "mutual", in order to provide a more consistent and accurate representation of the impact of mutual, cooperative, member-owned and nonprofit (i.e. the majority of profits not being distributed to external shareholders) on the Austria insurance market". In contrast, the definition in this publication on which the calculations are based on is much narrower. As mentioned before, the author of this study, and in particular of the Austrian chapter, used only pure mutual insurance companies for their analyses, which include the following seven mutuals:

- Österreichische Beamtenversicherung
- Österreichische Hagelversicherung
- Kärtner Landesversicherung auf Gegenseitigkeit
- MUKI
- Tiroler Versicherung Verein auf Gegenseitigkeit
- RVV Rückversicherung auf Gegenseitigkeit
- Vorarlberger Landesversicherung auf Gegenseitigkeit

ICMIF and AMICE, on the other hand, include also former mutual companies that transformed into holding companies (so-called hybrid forms) into the analyses. These hybrid forms use asset management societies (Vermögensverwaltungsvereine) that have already excluded any kind of insurance business. To decide if hybrids are mutuals or not, it is important to remember that one core element of mutuality is membership. The special status of members in a mutual company has to be considered and is evident in general meetings or when distributing profits. However, those features are not used anymore in hybrid forms and with regard to private foundations, no members exist at all. Moreover, in the hybrid form the operational part lies in the joint stock company, while the mutual company performs the asset management. According to our point of view, hybrids should rather be regarded as joint stock companies instead of mutual organizations, because their premium income is used to cover the insurance benefits and thus costs experience.[71]

Table 4 displays the special situation regarding the interplay between mutual holding companies and private foundations, showing the conversion of two former mutual companies into private foundations.

[71] Cf. *Brazda, J.* (2017). Entwicklung, Strukturwandel und Perspektiven der Wechselseitigkeitsversicherungen. Wien: Universität Wien, Fachbereich für Genossenschaftswesen, 161-167.

Table 4: Conversion of mutual insurance societies into a private foundation from 2005 onwards[72]

Year	Mutual company	Private foundation
2005	*Austria Versicherungsverein auf Gegenseitigkeit*	Conversion into *Austria Versicherungsverein auf Gegenseitigkeit Privatstiftung*
2012	*Collegialität Versicherung auf Gegenseitigkeit*	Conversion into *Collegialität Versicherungsverein Privatstiftung*

Source: *Zeman, S.* The Development of Mutuality Principles in Austria – an analysis of Mutual Insurance Societies.

Both private foundations hold shares in the UNIQA Insurance Group AG, the successor of the Austria-Collegialität. With regard to the UNIQA, the company has a private foundation, which means there are no members or members' representative and all policyholders are beneficiaries. In general, mutual asset management societies/private foundations do not offer insurances, but hold shares in their joint stock companies and policyholders are members and beneficiaries of the asset management societies/private foundations at the same time. As a result, mutual asset management societies and private foundations have no operative insurance business. This is situation is displayed in table 5.

Table 5: Overview on asset management societies/private foundations 2016[73]

Asset management societies/private foundations	Operative joint stock company
WIENER STÄDTISCHE Vermögensverwaltung	Wiener Städtische Versicherung AG
GRAWE Vermögensverwaltung	GRAWE AG
OBERÖSTERREICHISCHE Vermögensverwaltung	OBERÖSTERREICHISCHE Versicherung AG
MERKUR Vermögensverwaltung	Merkur Versicherung AG
UNIQA Privatstiftung	UNIQA Österreich Versicherungen AG
COLLEGIALITÄT Privatstiftung	

Source: *Zeman, S.* The Development of Mutuality Principles in Austria – an analysis of Mutual Insurance Societies.

[72] Cf. The chapter about Austria's current situation in this book: *Zeman, S.* The Development of Mutuality Principles in Austria – an analysis of Mutual Insurance Societies.

[73] Cf. The chapter about Austria's current situation in this book: *Zeman, S.* The Development of Mutuality Principles inAustria – an analysis of Mutual Insurance Societies.

Overall, it can be said that ICMIF's definition, which includes two forms of insurance companies (non-profit organizations and insurance cooperatives) that do not exist in Austria, is fuzzy and cannot be related in this way to the Austrian market. In particular, when looking at the three definitions[74] ICMIF uses for European countries, and which can also be found in the global report[75], the Austrian mutual companies should be categorized under the first definition. However, ICMIF comprises most of Austrian mutuals under the third definition. With that in mind, we calculated 3.89 percent as Austria's mutual market share. According to *Ben Telfer*, our calculations are correct when using our narrow definition of mutuals Therefore, the question arises, how a reader is able to verify the data and the results of the analyses at all. *Ben Telfer* confirmed that ICMIF uses in addition to annual reports data from the supervisory authority of the various countries, i.e. in Austria from the FMA. However, the latter does not differentiate between legal forms in the analyses. Therefore, it is still unclear how ICMIF and AMICE calculate a mutual market share of 59.9 percent for Austria, because even when adding the 21.66 percent market share of MHC associations, the 21.23 percent of MHC private foundations, and the 3.89 percent of mutual companies, the result is with 46.78 percent still lower than ICMIF's calculation.

The problem of different calculations is also evident when the German market share is analyzed. Germany, like Austria, has large and small insurance mutuals. Small insurance mutuals, however, are organized locally and insure a specific group of people. These mutuals are defined as associations pursuing activities limited to a specific geographic area, insurance lines, and circles of customers. Whether a mutual is considered as a large or small insurance company is classified by the German Supervision Authority BaFin (Federal Financial Supervisory Authority). This supervisory authority controls large mutual companies while small mutual insurers fall under the supervision of the federal states. ICMIF and AMICE calculate a mutual market share of 47.3 percent for Germany using annual reports as well as data from the BaFin. However, the BaFin distinguishes between the different legal forms without considering group and holding structures. The Register of Companies does not take into account the legal form of the group or enterprise; consequently, a joint stock company that is a 100 percent subsidiary company of a mutual insurance society is regarded as a joint stock company. Therefore, it is not useful to distinguish the companies regarding their legal forms like in official statistics (e.g. BaFin), in which each company has the same legal form that can be

[74] Cf. AMICE and ICMIF Facts and figures. Mutual and cooperative insurance in Europe Vol 2, 2018, p. 10f.

[75] Cf. Global Mutual Market Share 10, p. 19.

found in the Register of Companies (cf. the section about Germany in this book).

Our own calculations are based on data from the KIVI[76] institute in Cologne that takes the group and holding structures into account. Based on our assumptions, in Germany in 2016 mutual insurance societies comprised 128 insurance companies and from them 80 had the legal form of a joint stock company respectively 48 of a mutual company. The total market share of these insurance companies was 34.78 percent. However, it is important to note that in Germany the group structure allows insurance mutuals as the parent company to establish subsidiaries. These subsidiaries can offer any kind of insurance segment independently from the insurance type of the parent company. With that legal construction, German subsidiaries can circumvent the EU regulation that insurance companies cannot be composite insurers.

In the Anglo-American region, in contrast, the concept of a legal entity ("juristische Person") that connects the member of a mutual company with the insurer is unknown. With regard to the USA, the state decides about what the concept of membership in a mutual company means. State insurance holding company regulation was first introduced in the 1970s. The US system of state-based insurance regulation has included a review of the holding company system for decades emphasizing on each insurance legal entity. While changes have been made in the model laws over time, the approach to group supervision has been primarily a segmented approach without full clarity of the potential risks a holding company system could face. Approximately, at the same time, the NAIC adopted its Insurance Holding Company System Regulatory Act, the so-called Holding Company Act, and Insurance Holding Company System Model Regulation. As mentioned before, NAIC as well as AMBest consider a MIHC as mutual. With this knowledge in mind the perspective of ICMIF respectively Swiss Re appears to be the norm rather the exception when analyzing and classifying companies into mutuals and other legal forms. However, the question arises if this point of view shows a true picture of the current situation of mutuals when the definition of mutuals is extremely wide. Although it is understandable for a global comparison of mutuals to apply a broader definition, nonetheless, in particular for the European region this concept is problematic. Consequently, when comparing the results of ICMIF's statistics with our own studies the differences are evident. With regard to the European region, Austria and Germany's market shares differed enormously due to reasons explained above. The results regarding Finland are drawn from the official statistics, Finland Insurance (Finance Finland). However, in the latest publications only

[76] Cf. KIVI: Die Marktanteile der Anbieter auf dem deutschen Versicherungsmarkt 2016, the data was made available by *Michael Thiemermann*.

the market shares for various life and non-life companies are calculated but not the total market share. ICMIF presents a market share of 46.2 percent for Finland for 2017. When comparing that figure with the figure from 2014 provided by the official statistics an increase of 8.7 percentages is evident, this could be considered as a huge rise for three years. Therefore, it can be concluded that ICMIF's calculated a higher market share for Finland in general, similar to other countries. The result of Norway's market share is based on various sources[77] and was calculated by the author, it differs only slightly.

Table 6: Mutual market shares of various countries and data sources

Country	Mutual Market share ICMIF (2017)	Mutual Market share in percent (calculations by authors of this book)	World Market Share Swiss Re 2018[78]	World Market Share NAIC 2017
Austria	59.9	3.89 (2017)	0.39	0.34
Germany	47.3	34.78 (2016)	4.65	3.90
Finland	46.2	37.5 (2014)	0.52	0.46
USA	39.9	10 (life segment in 2017)[79] 44 (non-life segment in 2015)[80]	28.29	38.46
United Kingdom	10.6	-	6.48	4.96
Norway	44.4	46.7 (2015)	0.41	0.35

Source: Sigma 03/2019 World insurance: the great pivot east continues, p. 37; ACLI tabulations of NACI data; *Broek, S., Buiskool, B., Vennekens, A., & Van der Horst, R.* (2012). Study on the current situation and prospects of mutuals in Europe. Zoetermeer: Panteia – EIM, p. 49.; calculations by authors of this book; Global Mutual Market Share 10.

With regard to the USA, unfortunately, a total mutual market share is not available, however, the market shares for the life (2017) and non-life segments (2015) are accessible. The results show the dominance of the latter insurance line, while the mutual life insurance sector is with 10 percent much smaller. ICMIF and AMICE calculated a US total market share of 39.9 percent in 2017. It is important to note that the

77 Cf. Chapter about the insurance business in Norway: *Lovescher, B.* Mutual Insurance and limited companies in the Norwegian insurance industry, Table 5.

78 Sigma 03/2019 World insurance: the great pivot east continues, p. 37.

79 ACLI tabulations of NACI data.

80 National Association of Mutual Insurance Companies (NAMIC)..

US world market share presented by Swiss Re and NAIC differs more than 10 percentage points, which is a huge discrepancy.

5. Global data

In the following sections, the global mutual insurance market will be presented focusing on geographical regions as well as on the various lines of insurance business. The first subchapter looks at the development of the mutual life and non-life insurance sectors in Europe, while the next concentrates and compares the five global regions North America, Europe, Asia and Oceania, Latin America and Africa. The data for both sections is drawn from the ICMIF publication "Global Mutual Market Share 10" providing statistics for the mutual insurance sector for the year 2017. However, it is important to keep in mind that ICMIF's wide definition of mutuality also applies to these statistical results and therefore probably provide a more positive picture of the mutual insurance market. This is evident when comparing ICMIF's market share results with the previous mentioned study by the European Union (2012)[81]. In the latter study, the market shares are lower than the figures provided by ICMIF, probably because ICMIF includes cooperatives in its reports, while the Panteia study focused solely on mutual-type organizations excluding cooperatives (see table 7).

With regard to Austria, it has already been proven that ICMIF's point of view differs in various ways from the authors' interpretation presented in this publication. As far as possible, the findings of the various authors in this book are used to present the differences regarding the data, however, for the global analysis of the mutual sector only ICMIF's data is available for the mutual sector. This fact alone shows the general problem when investigating the mutual insurance sector and makes the availability and transparency of data in this sector to a crucial question when asking what can be regarded as mutual company and what not.

[81] Cf. *Broek, S., Buiskool, B., Vennekens, A., & Van der Horst, R.* (2012). Study on the current situation and prospects of mutuals in Europe. Zoetermeer: Panteia – EIM, p. 49.

Table 7: Mutual market shares of various countries by ICMIF and Panteia

Country	Mutual market share ICMIF (2008)	Mutual market share Panteia (2008)
Germany	43.9	31.0
France	38.7	26.0
Netherlands	33.1	28.0
Italy	15.1	4.0
UK	5.3	5.0

Source: *Vennekens, A., & Van der Horst, R.* (2012). Study on the current situation and prospects of mutuals in Europe. Zoetermeer: Panteia – EIM; Mutual Market Share 2007-2008 & Global 500.

5.1 Global mutual market (Europe)

In the latest edition of Global Mutual Market Share[82] published by ICMIF and AMICE in 2019, a European mutual market share of 32.7 percent was reported. Compared to the calculated market share of 24.1 percent in 2007, the European mutual market share increased by 8.6 percent until 2017. Between 2007 and 2017, a steady growth was noted, with the exception of 2015, when the market share dropped by 0.7 percent, but increased again by 2017 (32.7 percent). According to the publication, the ten largest European mutual insurance markets can be found in Austria (59.9 percent), Finland (56.2 percent), the Netherlands (55.9 percent), Slovakia (53.4 percent), France (51.8 percent), Denmark (48.1 percent), Germany (47.3 percent), Sweden (45.3 percent), Norway (44.4 percent), and Hungary (43.6 percent).[83] However, as mentioned before, Austria's mutual dominance in the European insurance industry has to be questioned as well as the calculation for other European countries. Moreover, the question if mutual companies have a renaissance is hard to be answered. In Austria, the question has to be denied in particular when considering, in addition to use only pure mutuals for the statistics, that the concept of co-optation, which means instead of member's representatives decide about the company in their meeting, is the norm. In the Northern countries, the answer is yes respectively no. While in Norway and Finland, the development of mutuals is positive, for example due to re-mutualization, the rights of members in mutuals have not been strengthened.

82 Cf. *Telfer, B.*, (2019). Global Mutual Market Share 10. Bowdon: ICMIF.

83 Cf. *Telfer, B.*, (2019). Global Mutual Market Share 10. Bowdon: ICMIF, p. III (3).

Figure 4: European mutual market share

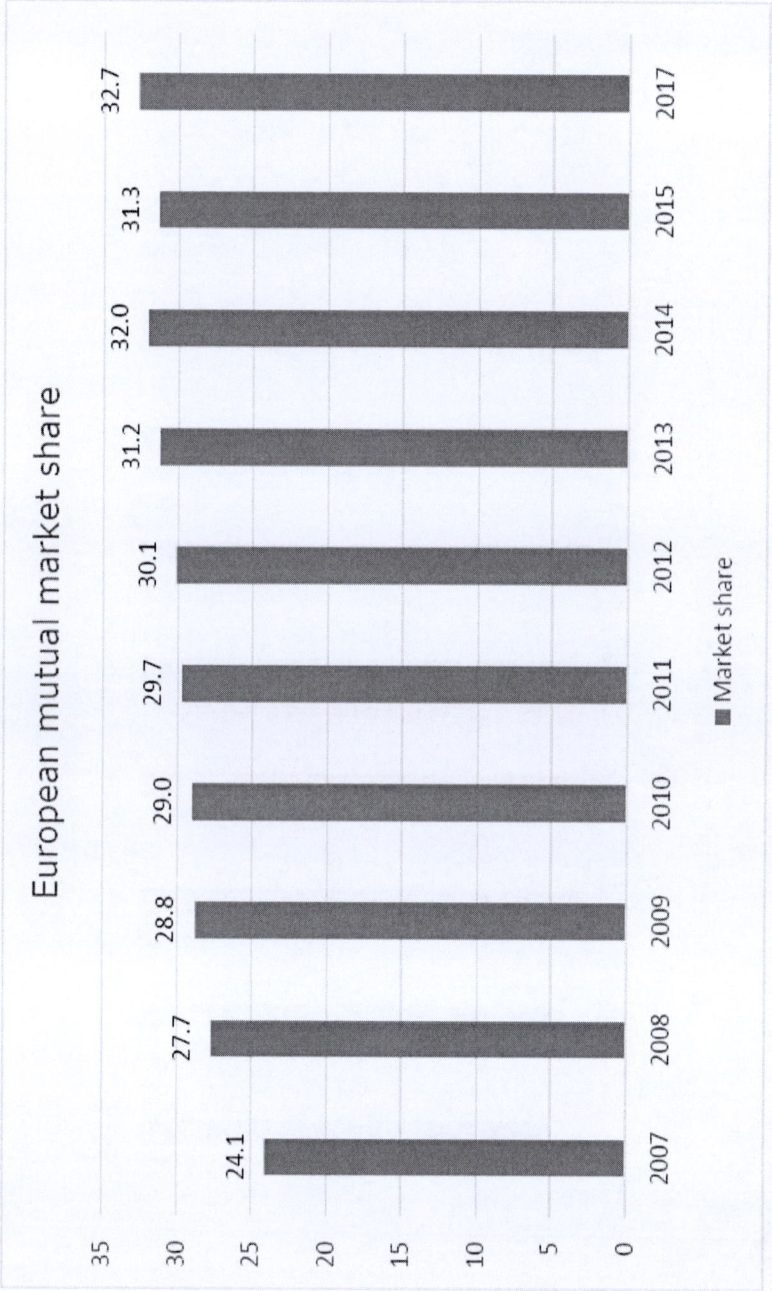

Source: *Telfer, B.*, (2019). Global Mutual Market Share 10. Bowdon: ICMIF, p. 8

Figure 5: European life and non-life market share

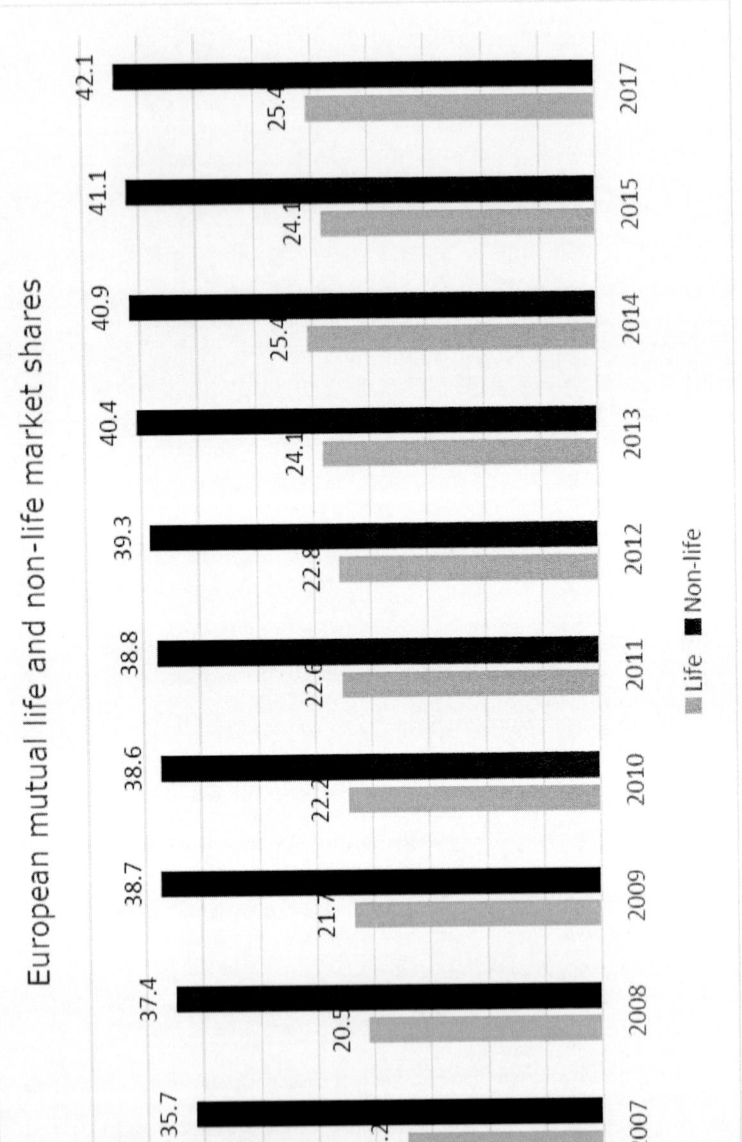

Source: Global Mutual Market Share 10. Bowdon: ICMIF, p. 8.

With regard to ICMIF's data, the European mutual life and non-life insurance market shares increased as well. In 2007, the life insurance market had a share of 17.2 percent, while it increased to 24.4 percent in 2017, the same number as in 2014, after an increase in 2015 (24.1 percent). In the non-life insurance line, mutuals' market shares grew in contrast steadily over the years without exceptions. In 2017, the market shares accounted for 42.1 percent, which highlights an increase of 6.4 percent since 2007.[84]

The figure 5 presents the European life and non-life market shares from 2007 to 2017.

In addition to the European mutual market share, ICMIF and AMICE published in their latest report from 2019 the development of the global mutual market shares between 2007 and 2017. The ten-year overview shows a constant increase of the mutual market shares, although they always stayed over 24 percent. With 24 percent in 2007, the lowest share can be found, while it grew to 26.7 percent in 2017. The highest global mutual market shares were recorded in 2011 and 2013 with a peak of 27.6 percent. In both years after the peak, 2012 and 2014, the share decreased slightly to 27.5 percent, and dropped in 2015 to 26.4 percent, before it increased to 26.8 percent in 2016 and to 26.7 percent in 2017.

Figure 6: Mutual market share and annual premium growth between 2007 and 2017

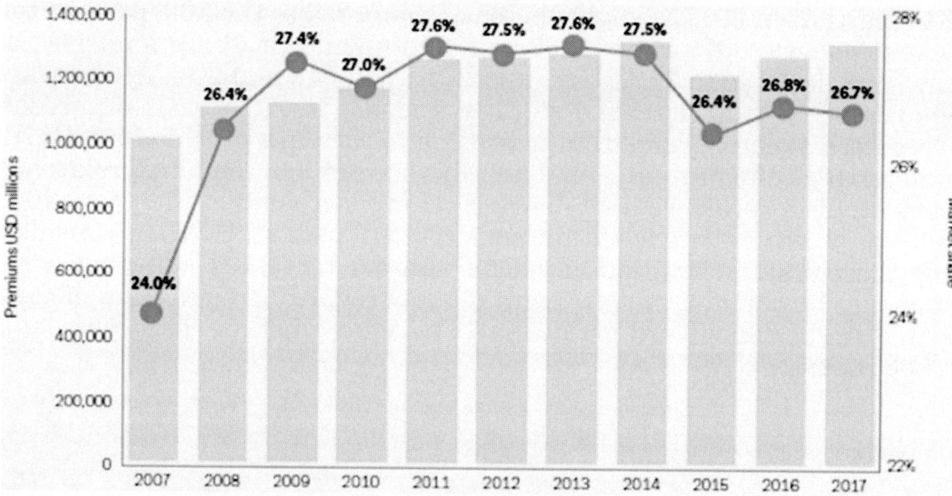

Source: Global Mutual Market Share 10. Bowdon: ICMIF, p. 3.

[84] Cf. *Telfer, B.*, (2019). Global Mutual Market Share 10. Bowdon: ICMIF, p. 8.

The global mutual insurance sector wrote USD 1,310 billion in insurance premiums in 2017, and reached so the second-highest level of premium volumes ever written by the mutual sector. It was only slightly behind the USD 1,320 billion of premiums recorded in 2014. With regard to annual premium growth, the global mutual market increased by 3.0 percent in 2017 compared to 2016 (USD 1,272 billion), which represented the ninth year of positive premium growth since 2007 with the exception of 2015. In this year, the premium volume decreased. The annual growth of the mutual sector exceeded the global market's average growth in five of the previous 10 years, and is most notably in the years 2008 and 2009, the earliest two years of the financial crisis. In 2008, the mutual sector grew extraordinarily by 9.8 percent compared to the premium stagnation in the total market (0.0 percent). In 2009, the mutual sector again grew by 1.2 percent, while the global market reduced about 2.4 percent. Between 2007 and 2017, the mutual sector reported a compound annual growth rate of 2.6 percent overtaking the total market by 1.6 percentages. As a result, mutual insurers' global market share grew from 24 percent in 2007 to 26.7 percent 2017.[85]

When looking at the life and non-life insurance sector, the results for these both lines of businesses differ evidently (see figure 7).

According to ICMIF and AMICE, the mutual life insurance sector was able to increase of three percentage points of the global market since 2007, and its market share rose from 19.5 percent to 22.5 percent in 2017. However, the mutual share had fallen from a peak of 24.5 percent in the years 2011 and 2012 and had its lowest point in 2015 with 22.4 percent. In the non-life sector, global mutual market share was 31.6 percent in 2017, a slight increase compared to the 30.8 percent ten years earlier (2007). From 2007 to 2009, the market share increased at first and declined to 31.4 percent in 2012. In 2013 and 2014, the market share once again increased slightly and fell in 2015 to 31.4 percent. Therefore, it can be said, that according to the data provided by ICMIF and AMICE, the mutual global non-life market has remained relatively consistent in recent years, following strong increases in the years 2008 and 2009, when it reached its peak of 32.7 percent.[86] When considering these results, it would be crucial comparing ICMIF's findings with analyses based on a narrow point of view regarding what kind of company can be considered as mutual. Therefore, further research seems to be necessary.

85 *Telfer, B.,* (2019). Global Mutual Market Share 10. Bowdon: ICMIF, p. 3.

86 Cf. *Telfer, B.,* (2019). Global Mutual Market Share 10. Bowdon: ICMIF, p. 5.

Figure 7: Mutual market share and premiums in the life and non-life sector

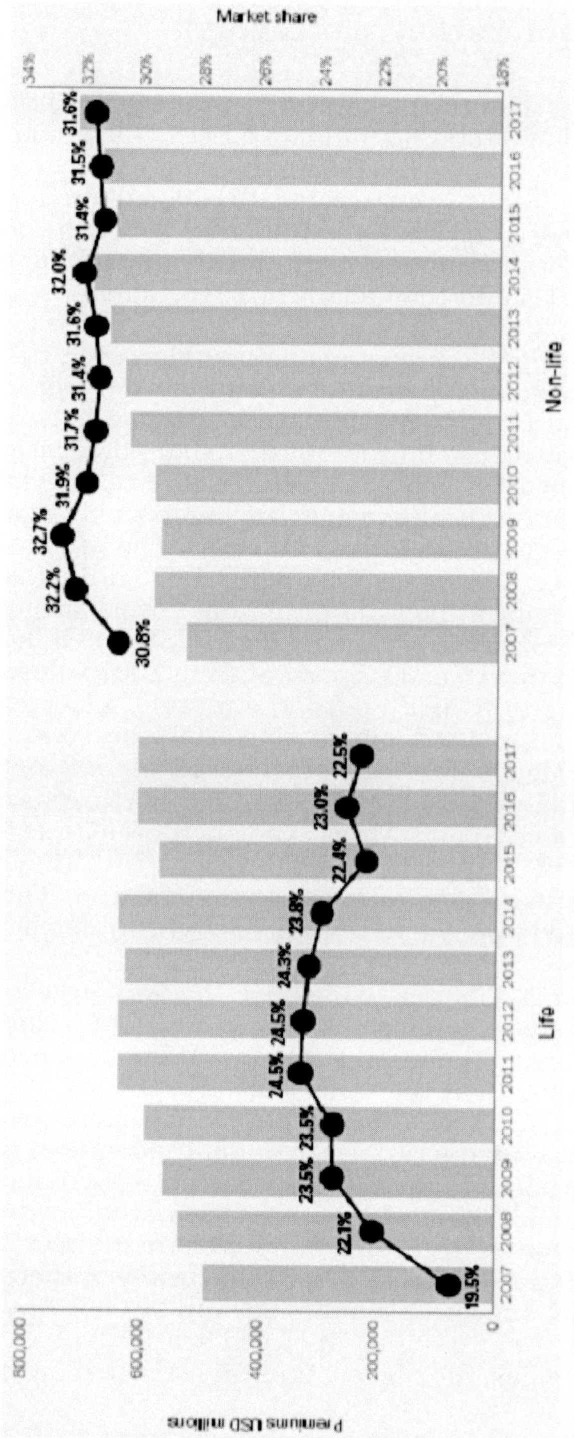

Source: Global Mutual Market Share 10. Bowdon: ICMIF, p. 5.

5.2 Global mutual market (per region)

Since 2007, the growth of the global life insurance market has been unstable and resulted in a total premium of USD 2,669 billion in 2017, which was compared to 2007 (USD 2,505 billion) only 6.6 percent higher. The mutual life insurance sector wrote USD 602 billion in premium income in 2017, compared to USD 488 billion in 2007. In contrast to the total market, with an annual growth in the mutual life business between 2007 and 2011, and then again in 2016, added to an overall premium increase of 23.4 percent since 2007, the total market growth was surpassed by nearly 17 percentage points. Moreover, the mutual sector gained a further three percentage points of the global market since 2007, and its market share rose from 19.5 percent in 2007 to 22.5 percent in 2017. However, the mutual market share decreased from a peak of 24.5 percent in 2011 and 2012. With regard to the global non-life industry, this sector has been stronger and more stable than the life sector since the beginning of the financial crisis. The premium levels increased by 32.1 percent between 2007 (USD 1,695 billion) and 2017 (USD 2,239 billion). Mutual non-life premiums levels surpassed the USD 700 billion level for the first time in 2017 (USD 708 billion), demonstrating an overall growth of 35.7 percent from 2007 volumes (USD 522 billion). According to ICMIF's data, the mutual sector had seven positive years of premium development since 2007, and outperformed the total market average in six of the previous 10 years.[87]

When looking at the various regions, Europe, North America, Asia & Oceania, Latin America, and Africa, and the development of their mutual market shares, it appears that all regions with the exception of Asia and Oceania were able to increase their shares. The mutual market share increased from 24 percent in 2007 to 26.7 percent in 2017 (see figure 8).

In Europe and North America, which are the two largest regional markets, the market share developed stronger until 2017. North America had the highest regional mutual share in 2017 of 38.3 percent and with 9.5 percentage points at the same time also the largest increase regarding mutual market share since 2007 (28.8 percent). In Europe, the mutual sector accounted for 32.7 percent of the regional market in 2017 and improved therefore more than 8 percentage points between 2007 (24.3 percent) and 2017 (32.7 percent). The mutual insurance sector in Latin American grew regarding market share between 2007 and 2017, rising from 9.9 percent to 11.2 percent. However, their regional market share in 2017 was lower than its peak in 2014 of 13.0 percent. Although in Africa, the mutual insurance penetration was much lower compared to other regions, the highest mutual market share until now

[87] Cf. Ibid.

Figure 8: Regional mutual market share between 2007 and 2017

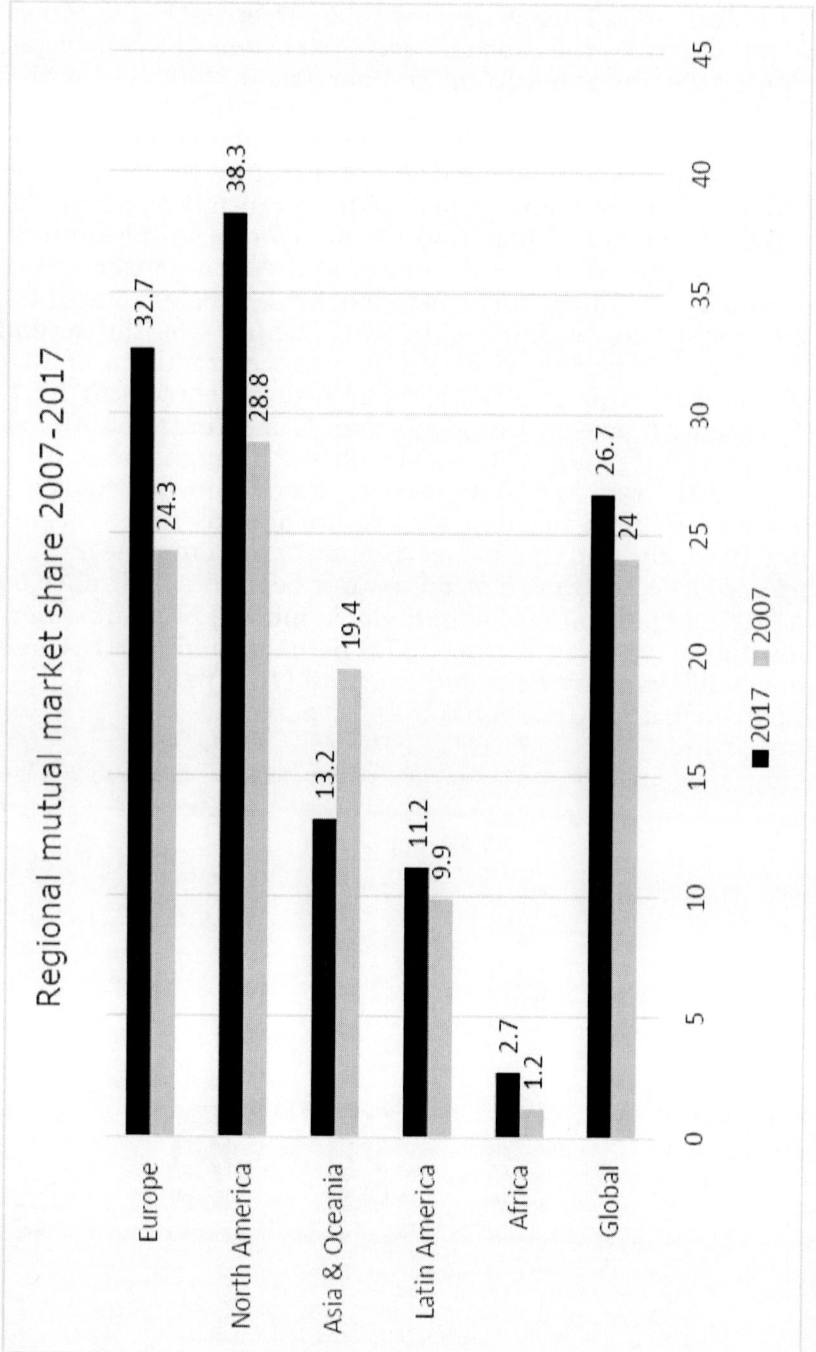

Source: Global Mutual Market Share 10. Bowdon: ICMIF, p. 7.

was achieved (2.7 percent in 2017), which was more than double compared to ten years earlier in 2007 (1.2 percent). On the other hand, in Asia and Oceania, the mutual sector experienced a loss regarding the market share, dropping from 19.4 percent in 2007 and with a former peak of 22.6 percent in 2011 to 13.2 percent in 2017. According to ICMIF, the reason for such a decrease can be found in the decline of the Japanese Yen, which impacted the regional mutual figures negatively due to a larger contribution of Japanese mutual business. Japan contributed 84 percent of Asia and Oceania's mutual premiums in 2017, compared to only 26 percent regarding the total market. Additionally, the rise of the Chinese insurance markets, which is one of the largest in the world, had an impact. In 2017, China was the second largest total insurance market with total insurance premiums of 32.4 percent in Asia and Oceania in 2017, compared to 9.8 percent in 2007. Japan's involvement, however, dropped from 47 percent in 2007. Currently, Japan's mutual penetration is very low. Although the mutual market share in 2017 was low (0.2 percent), a new mutual insurance law in China has enabled licences for mutual insurers to be issued by the China Banking and Insurance Regulatory Commission (CBIRC). In February 2017, the first mutual insurer began its insurance business.[88]

In 2017, 82 percent of the total global mutual premiums were written by mutual insurers in Europe (37.9 percent) and North America (43.8 percent), followed by Asia and Oceania (16.8 percent), Latin America (1.4 percent), and Africa with only 0.1 percent.

Figure 9: Regional split of global mutual premiums in 2017

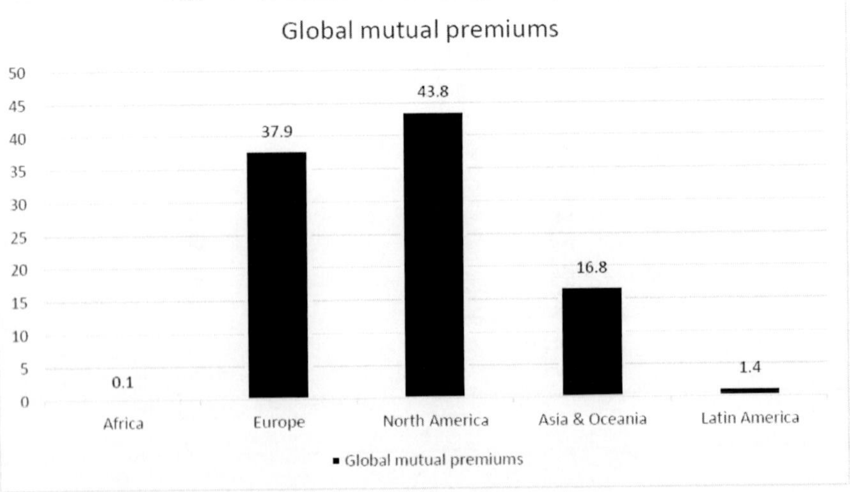

Source: Global Mutual Market Share 10. Bowdon: ICMIF, p. 6.

---

[88] Cf. *Telfer, B.*, (2019). Global Mutual Market Share 10. Bowdon: ICMIF, p. 7.

With 43.8 percent of the global total mutual premiums, respectively USD 573 billion in premiums, North American was the strongest mutual region in 2017. European mutuals contributed 37.9 percent (USD 496 billion) of the total mutual business. The reasons for the success of the North America region are the strong growth combined with the negative currency effects of the Euro compared to the US dollar. As a result, North America surpassed Europe as the largest region in terms of mutual insurance business. In 2007, the contribution to the global mutual market shares of North America and Europe was 38.2 percent respectively 42.8 percent. Mutuals in Asia and Oceania generated 16.8 percent and USD 221 billion of the total global business in 2017, a slight decrease compared to 2007 (18.1 percent). As mentioned above, the recent weakness of the Japanese Yen led to a decrease in the proportion of global business written in the region, from a peak of 24.2 percent in 2012. In Latin America, on the other hand, mutual insurers only wrote 1.4 percent (USD 18 billion) of global mutual premiums in 2017, while in Africa the figures are even smaller, 0.1 percent and USD 1.5 billion.[89]

With regard to the growth of each region between 2007 and 2017, four of the five regions exceeded the total market growth rate (see figure 10).

According to these figures, Europe was the only region with a negative growth of 14.8 percent in premiums for the total insurance industry, while the mutual insurance sector grew of 14.8 percent. Mutuals in the North American region also recorded a stronger growth in premiums (+48.6 percent), higher than the total industry's regional premium growth (+11.7 percent). Although Africa was the smallest region in terms of total mutual premiums written in 2017, it recorded the strongest regional growth for mutuals since 2007. Its increase regarding premiums was of 170 percent, and outperformed significantly the total industry average of 18.8 percent. The Latin American mutual sector also doubled in size between 2007 and 2017. Its growth was faster (+113 percent) than the rest of the market (+88 percent). Asia and Oceania, on the other hand, was the only region where mutual growth was lower compared to that of the total market since 2007. When looking at the joint growth rate of mutual insurers, the rate was 21.0 percent between 2007 and 2017, which was much lower compared to the total market expansion of 77 percent.[90]

With regard to the regional mutual market sector, it can be said that in the life insurance business, mutual insurers in North America held with 35.7 percent the highest share of their regional market in 2017,

[89] Cf. *Telfer, B.,* (2019). Global Mutual Market Share 10. Bowdon: ICMIF, p. 6.

[90] Cf. Ibid.

Figure 10: Compound annual growth rates per region between 2007 and 2017.

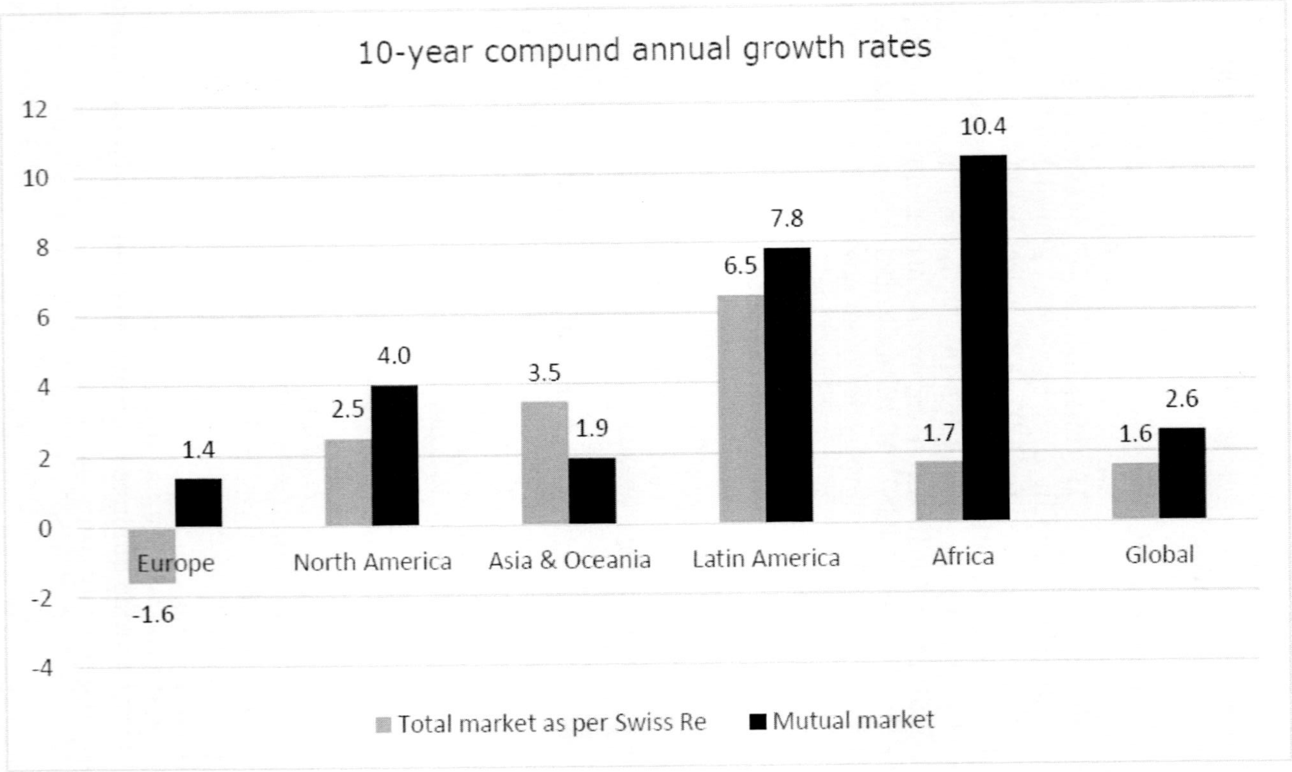

Source: Global Mutual Market Share 10. Bowdon: ICMIF, p. 9.

followed by Europe (25.4 percent). Both regions had a considerable rise in their market share compared to 2007.[91]

Figure 11: Mutual market share in the life insurance business 2017

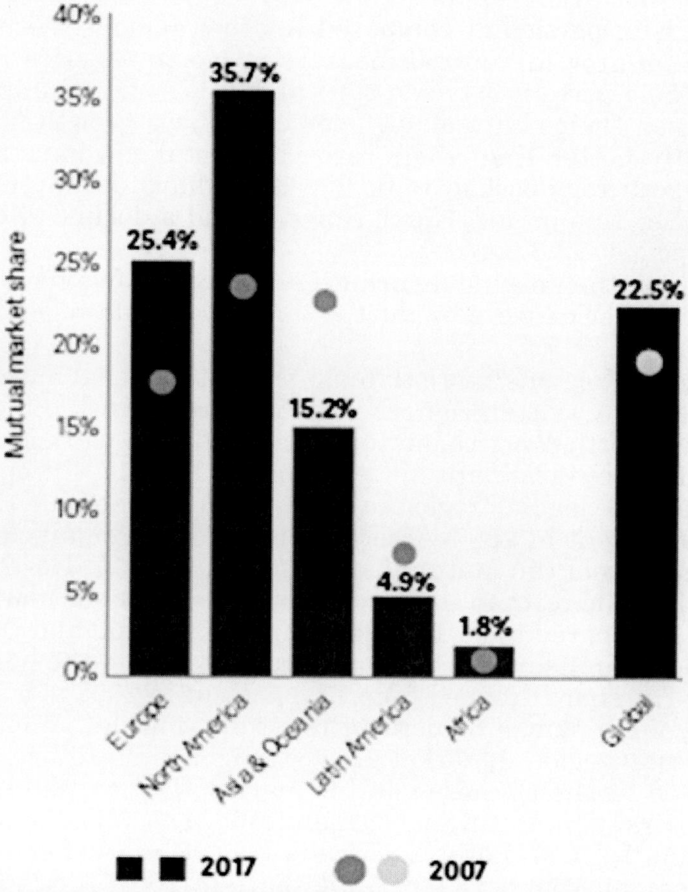

Source: *Telfer, B.,* (2019). Global Mutual Market Share 10. Bowdon: ICMIF, p. 8.

In the life insurance segment, North American mutuals increased 13 percentage points from 22.7 percent in 2007 to a market share of 35.7 percent in 2017. European mutual insurers also improved their share of the market by more than 8 percentage points over the 10-year

[91] Cf. Ibid., p. 8.

period, from 17.2 percent in 2007 to 25.4 percent in 2017. The region Asia and Oceania was the only one where mutual market share was better in the life sector than in the non-life sector. Mutual insurers held a share of 15.2 percent of the regional life market in 2017, compared to 9.5 percent in the nonlife business. However, the market share in the life insurance business reduced from 21.8 percent in 2007 (26.8 percent in 2011). In the life insurance segment in Latin America and Africa, mutuals' penetration remained low with 4.9 percent respectively with 1.8 percent, in particular compared to other regions. With regard to life premium growth, mutual insurers in North America had a total growth of 50.4 percent between 2007 and 2017, while European mutuals increased their share of 14.1 percent. These growth figures were significantly better than their respective total life industry results, which in both regions had to deal with a sharp decline in premium volumes over this period, North America had a decline of 4.2 percent and Europe lost 22.8 percent.

Concerning the non-life insurance sector of the five regions, Europe and North America were by far the largest non-life regional markets for mutuals in 2017.[92]

In these two regions, more than 90 percent of global mutual non-life premiums were written compared to 72 percent in the life sector. In Europe and North America, mutuals achieved high market share levels in 2017 and grew gradually since the crisis. In 2017, Europe was with 42.1 percent the leading region in terms of mutual non-life share, rising from 35.9 percent in 2007. According to ICMIF, a significant share of it originated from the mutual health sector. In 2017, North American mutuals held more than 40 percent of their regional market for the first time, compared to 34.1 percent in 2007. In Asia and Oceania, the mutual non-life insurance business declined like in the life insurance business. The share dropped from 12.3 percent in 2007 to 9.5 percent in 2017. Despite a plus of 82 percent regarding mutual premium expansion, the total regional market grew stronger (plus 137 percent), basically driven by the Chinese non-life market. The mutual share of the non-life markets in Latin America and Africa was higher compared to life markets. In 2017, Latin American's non-life market share extended to 16.9 percent from a 12.4 percent share in 2007. Africa was able to double almost its regional share from 2.6 percent in 2007 to 5.0 percent in 2017.[93]

[92] Cf. Ibid.

[93] Cf. Ibid.

Figure 12: Mutual market share in the non-life insurance business 2017

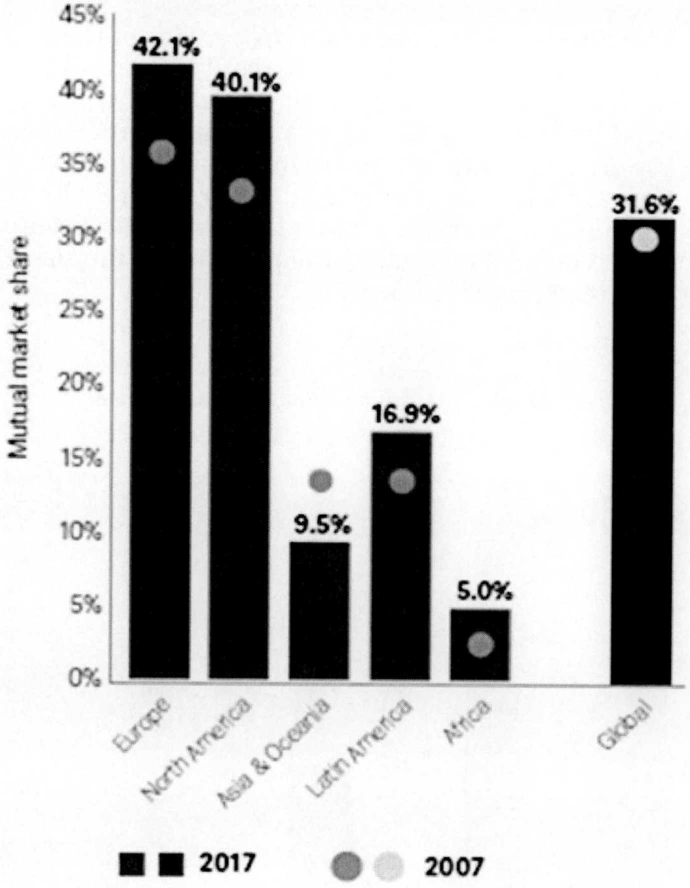

Source: *Telfer, B.*, (2019). Global Mutual Market Share 10. Bowdon: ICMIF, p. 8.

5.3 Global market share by lines of business and per region

In 2017, life insurance accounted for 45 percent of the global mutual life business written. Additionally, 36 percent of mutual life premiums in 2017 came from pension and annuity products, while 11.5 percent were generated by investment and retirement savings policies of mutual life premiums. It is important to note that the majority of over 98 percent came from European mutual insurers, while the remaining 7 percent of mutual life premiums came from long-term health and disability insurance as well as miscellaneous lines of life insurance, such as creditor and income protection.

Figure 13: Mutual life premiums by line of business 2017[94]

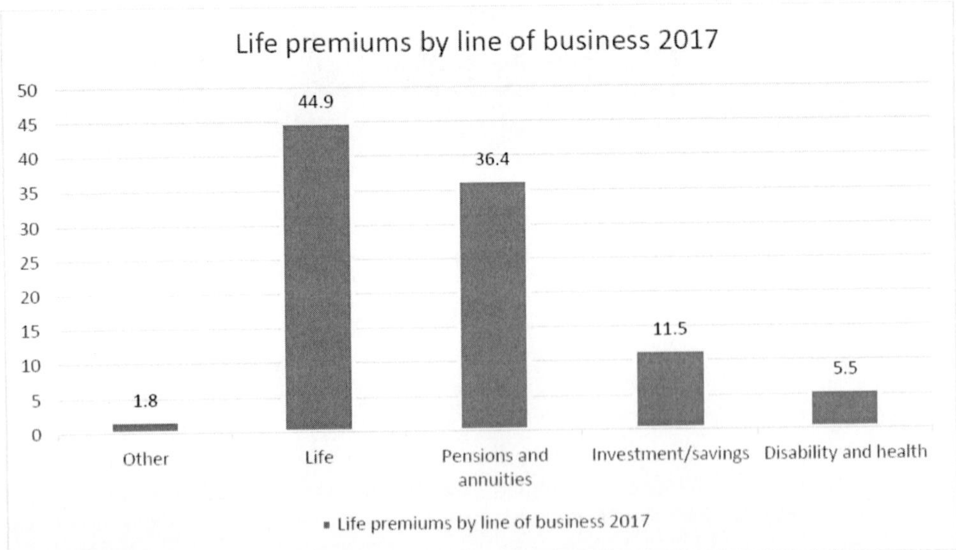

Source: *Telfer, B.,* (2019). Global Mutual Market Share 10. Bowdon: ICMIF, p. 11.

[94] Ibid., p. 11.

Concerning the regional level, the main contributor of the mutual life business was still the life protection policies in most of the regions in 2017 (see figure 14).

In Africa and Latin America, life insurance was with 90 percent respectively 70 percent the predominant line of mutual life business. In Latin America, disability and health insurance had a share of approximately 20 percent, which is the large proportion compared to other regions. In African, on the other hand, pensions and annuities appeared in 2015 for the first time. In 2017, these lines of business comprised almost 10 percent of the life insurance business. In Asia and Oceania, two-thirds of mutual life business in 2017 derived from life insurance products, followed by pensions and annuities. Disability and health insurance as well as other lines of business covered rather a low share. In North America (41 percent) and Europe (34 percent), life insurance was lower concentrated. Pension and annuities were the largest lines of the life insurance sector for mutual insurers in North America, underwriting 48 percent of mutual life premiums in 2017. It is important to note that more than a quarter of the mutual business in Asia and Oceania (29 percent) as well as Europe (28 percent) derived from pension products.[95]

[95] Cf. Ibid.

Figure 14: Lines of mutual life business by region 2017[96]

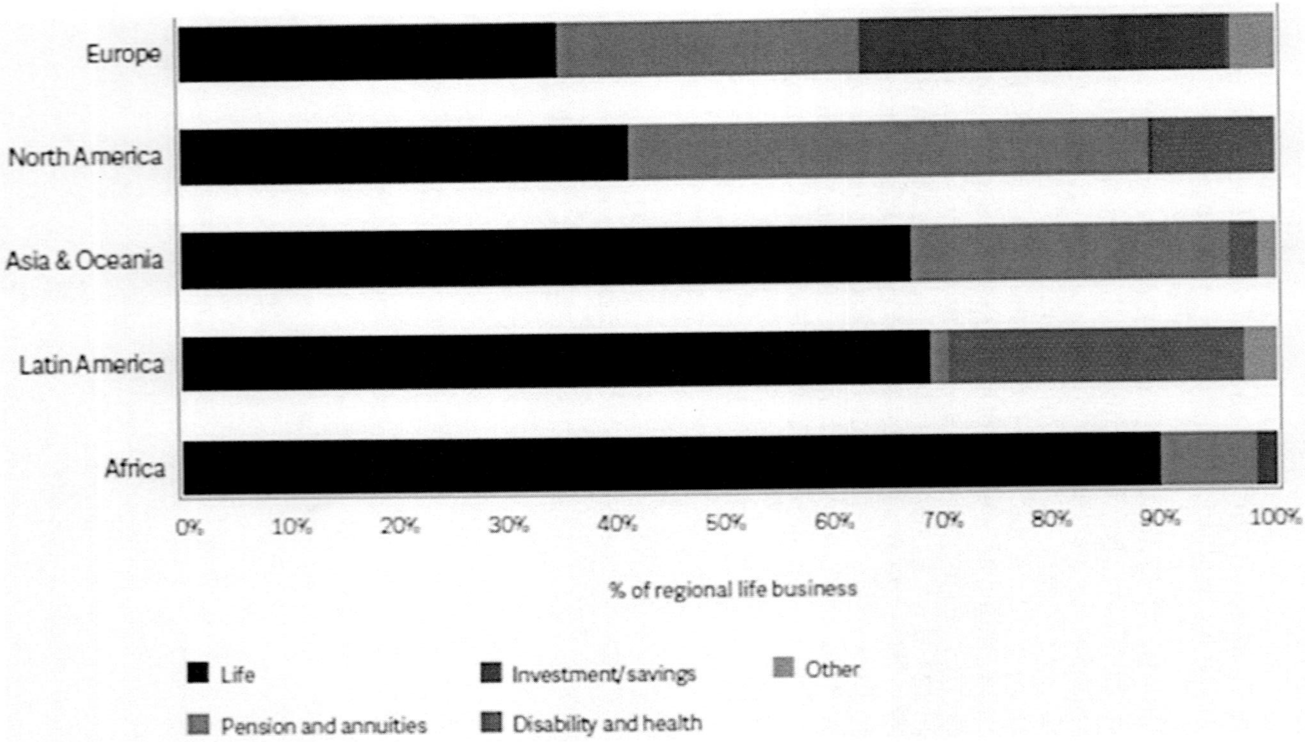

Source: *Telfer, B.,* (2019). Global Mutual Market Share 10. Bowdon: ICMIF, p. 11.

[96] Ibid.

6. Conclusion

When looking at the findings and in particular analyzing the results presented in chapter five, the dominance of Swiss Re and ICMIF's data is significant. By providing global data about the performance and development of mutuals in their various publications, both organizations show a very positive picture of mutual companies in Europe as well as in many regions of the world. However, the questions about the definition of mutuals and the interpretation of statistics, if they are even accessible respectively available, are a crucial problem and points of discussion. Using a wide definition of what can be considered as mutuals, deriving from the concept of social economy and the demutualization waves during the 1980s and 1990s, leads to the impression of a renaissance of mutuality in Europe as well as worldwide. However, as several authors of this publication have already proven the results and figures regarding market shares of mutuals differ enormously when applying a narrow point of view defining a mutual company. Therefore, it is most crucial to reconsider the current available data by investigating the statistics of individual countries and comparing the findings with results deriving from large institutions such as Swiss Re and ICMIF. This appears to be the best option to gain better insights at the current performance and development of mutual insurance companies in various insurance segments respectively on a global scale.

Bibliography

Altfuldisch, R. (2007). Haftung und Entschädigung nach Tankerunfällen auf See. Bestandsaufnahme, Rechtsvergleich und Überlegungen de lege ferenda

American Council of Life Insurers (2018). Life insurers fact book 2018

AMICE (2012). Facts and figures: Mutual and cooperative insurance in Europe. Brussels: AMICE

AMICE and ICMIF (2018). Facts and figures. Mutual and cooperative insurance in Europe Vol 2

Brazda, J. (2017). Entwicklung, Strukturwandel und Perspektiven der Wechselseitigkeitsversicherungen. Wien: Universität Wien, Fachbereich für Genossenschaftswesen

Brazda, J., Csulich, G., Zeman, St. (2018). Das Gegenseitigkeitsprinzip im Versicherungswesen aus historisch-analytischer Sicht, in: *Brazda / Blisse* (eds.): Beiträge zur kritischen Genossenschaftsforschung, Wien

Broek, S., Buiskool, B., Vennekens, A., & Van der Horst, R. (2012). Study on the current situation and prospects of mutuals in Europe. Zoetermeer: Panteia – EIM.

Centre international de recherches et d'information sur l'économie publique, sociale et coopérative (CIRIEC). The Social Economy in the European Union, 2007

Charta of Economie Sociale

Conceptual Framework for the Purpose of Measurement of Cooperatives and its Operationalization. Report discussed at the COPAC Technical Working Group on Cooperative Statistics Meeting, Geneva, May 2017

Farny, D. (2006). Versicherungsbetriebslehre, 4th edition

Fiegle, Th. (2003). Von der Solidarité zur Solidarität: ein französisch-deutscher Begriffstransfer, Münster

Gierke, O. v. (1999). Das Wesen der menschlichen Verbände. Darmstadt 1902 (1954)

https://tindallriley.co.uk/company-profile/ (02.08.2019)

https://www.amice-eu.org/ (25.07.2019)

https://www.icmif.org/news/icmif-welcomes-swiss-re-new-supporting-member (22.07.2019)

https://www.swissre.com/media/news-releases/nr-20190626-swiss-re-joins-icmif.html (23.07.2019)

https://www.versicherungsmagazin.de/lexikon/gegenseitigkeit-1945348.html (12.06.2019)

International Labour Office (2017). Use of statistics on cooperatives in national policy making, Geneva.

Ismay, P. (2010). Trust among strangers: Securing British Modernity `by way of friendly society 1780s-1870s; unpublished Dissertation University of California, Berkeley

Jeantet, T. (2010). Economie Sociale. Eine Alternative zum Kapitalismus. Neu-Ulm

KIVI: Die Marktanteile der Anbieter auf dem deutschen Versicherungsmarkt 2016

Koch, P. (1998). Geschichte der Versicherungswissenschaft in Deutschland. Karlsruhe

Lenton, D., Yokomizo, D., Tarbuck, S., Lageu, F., & McGee, M. (2010). Mutual Market Share & Global 500 for 2007-2008. Bowdon: ICMIF

Monzón, J. L. / Chaves, R. (2018). Public Policies towards the Social Economy in Europe at the National and Regional Level in the Recent Period (2010-16), in: *Brazda, J. / Blisse*, H. (2018). Beiträge zur kritischen Genossenschaftsforschung. Festschrift für Robert Schediwy zum 70. Geburtstag

Munich Re (ed.). Corporate Responsibility Report 2017/2018

National Association of Insurance Commissioners (1999). Mutual Insurance Holding Company Reorganizations, December 7, 1998

National Association of Insurance Commissioners (1999). Mutual Insurance Holding Company Reorganizations, December 7, 1998

Papilloud, C.; Cécile Rol, C. (2019). Moral – Recht – Nation. Die Soziologie der Solidarität Gaston Richards (1860-1945)

Pearson, R.; Doe, H. (2015). Organizational choice in UK marine insurance

Relton, F. B. (1893). An account of the fire insurance companies

Song, Ho-Young (1999). Die Verselbständigung der juristischen Person im deutschen und koreanischen Recht. Osnabrück

Swiss Re Sigma No 3/2019, World insurance: the great pivot east continues

Swiss Re Sigma No 4/2016.

Swiss Re Sigma 2/2019, Secondary natural catastrophe risks on the front line

Swiss Re Sigma 3/2019, World insurance: the great pivot east continues

Telfer, B., (2019). Global Mutual Market Share 10. Bowdon: ICMIF

The development on the US life insurance market: Demutualizations: The state of conversions in 2000, in: A.M. Best, Special Report September 30, 2002

Yeoman, R. (2017). From traditional to innovative multi-stakeholder mutuals. The case of Rochdale boroughwide housing, In: *Michi, J., Blasi, J.; Borzaga, C.* (eds.). The Oxford Handbook of Mutual, co-operative, and co-owned business

Keywords

B

C

D

J

K

L

M

N

O

P

R

S

T

U

V

W

Z

Names

Insurance companies

A

B

C

D

J

K

L

Johann Brazda; Markus Dellinger; Dietmar Rößl (Hg.)
Genossenschaften im Fokus einer neuen Wirtschaftspolitik
Bericht der XVII. Internationalen Genossenschaftswissenschaftlichen Tagung (IGT) 2012 in Wien. Im Auftrag der Arbeitsgemeinschaft Genossenschaftswissenschaftlicher Institute (AGI). Teilbände: 1 – Hauptvorträge und Podiumsdiskussionen; 2 – Bestandsaufnahme und Ausgangssituation; 3 – Zukunftsperrspektiven; 4 – Länderstudien (als E-Book)
Als Folge der Finanzkrise stehen die Genossenschaften weltweit „im Fokus einer neuen Wirtschaftspolitik". Sie stehen vor den Aufgaben, ihre Position neu zu bestimmen und Herausforderungen zu bewältigen. Der Tagungsband zur XVII. Internationalen Genossenschaftswissenschaftlichen Tagung (IGT) 2012 in Wien enthält zur Krisenbewältigung viele originelle Antworten und Anregungen aus rechtlicher und wirtschaftlicher Perspektive wie z. B. zum Reformbedarf im europäischen Genossenschaftsrecht, zur Verbundproblematik bei Kreditgenossenschaften, zu erfolgsbasierten Managementvergütungssystemen, der sozialen Funktion der Genossenschaften, zu Neugründungen in Deutschland, Österreich, Italien oder Schweden, zu Member Value und Corporate Social Responsibility bei kooperativen Finanzinstitutionen, zu neuen Aufgaben von Energie-, Umwelt- und Erzeugergenossenschaften oder zu Wohnbaugenossenschaften und Energiegewinnung. Er ist damit eine Fundgrube für viele offene Fragen.
Austria: Forschung und Wissenschaft – Wirtschaft, Bd. 6, 2013, 1224 S., 99,90 €, br., ISBN 978-3-643-50515-6

Sebastian Brun
(Neu-) Bewertung von Integrated Assessment Modellen im Kontext des Klimawandels
Der zehnte Band der vorliegenden Schriftenreihe untersucht die Themenbereiche der Risikobewertung und der intergenerationellen Verteilung der Lasten im Bereich der Ökonomie des Klimawandels. Nach einer Einführung in die Thematik des Klimawandels und der Ökonomie des Klimawandels wird das gängige Modell erweitert um eine tiefere Analyse in den beiden genannten Bereichen zu erlauben. Intensiv werden die Möglichkeit permanenter Schäden und die damit verbundenen Probleme der Pfadabhängigkeit untersucht. Zu diesem Zweck werden Monte Carlo Simulationen eingesetzt und die hier ermittelten Strategien dann in einer Kreuzanalyse unter den jeweils anderen Bedingungen getestet.
Schriften zur internationalen Wirtschaftspolitik, Bd. 11, 2019, 104 S., 39,90 €, br., ISBN 978-3-643-14203-0

Arne Heise
The Socioeconomics of Economics
Essays on the Construction of the Economic Discipline and its Critique
The economic discipline has always been an object of investigation. But unlike in former times, when methodological and epistemological developments had been the object of historians of economic thought, recently the focus of inquiry shifted towards the constitution, organisation and performativity of the economic discipline. It is the intention of the book to contribute to a better understanding of the working and failures of the 'market for economic ideas'.
Studien zur Staatswissenschaft, vol. 9, 2019, 266 pp., 39,90 €, pb., ISBN 978-3-643-91127-8

Przemysław Rotengruber
Dialogical Foundations of Business Ethics
Wirtschaft: Forschung und Wissenschaft, vol. 40, 2019, 318 pp., 49,90 €, hc., ISBN 978-3-643-91060-8

Christian Keuschnigg; Michael Kogler
Finanzplatz Österreich
Eine Strategie für Wachstum und Stabilität
Wirtschaftspolitische Schriften des WPZ, Bd. 1, 2018, 102 S., 19,90 €, br., ISBN 978-3-643-80271-2

Konstantin Barrmeyer
Negotiations with Interim Contracts
Integrative and Distributive Focus under Time Pressure
Betriebswirtschaftliche Schriftenreihe, vol. 90, 2017, 218 pp., 44,90 €, pb., ISBN 978-3-643-90884-1

LIT Verlag Berlin – Münster – Wien – Zürich – London
Auslieferung Deutschland / Österreich / Schweiz: siehe Impressumsseite